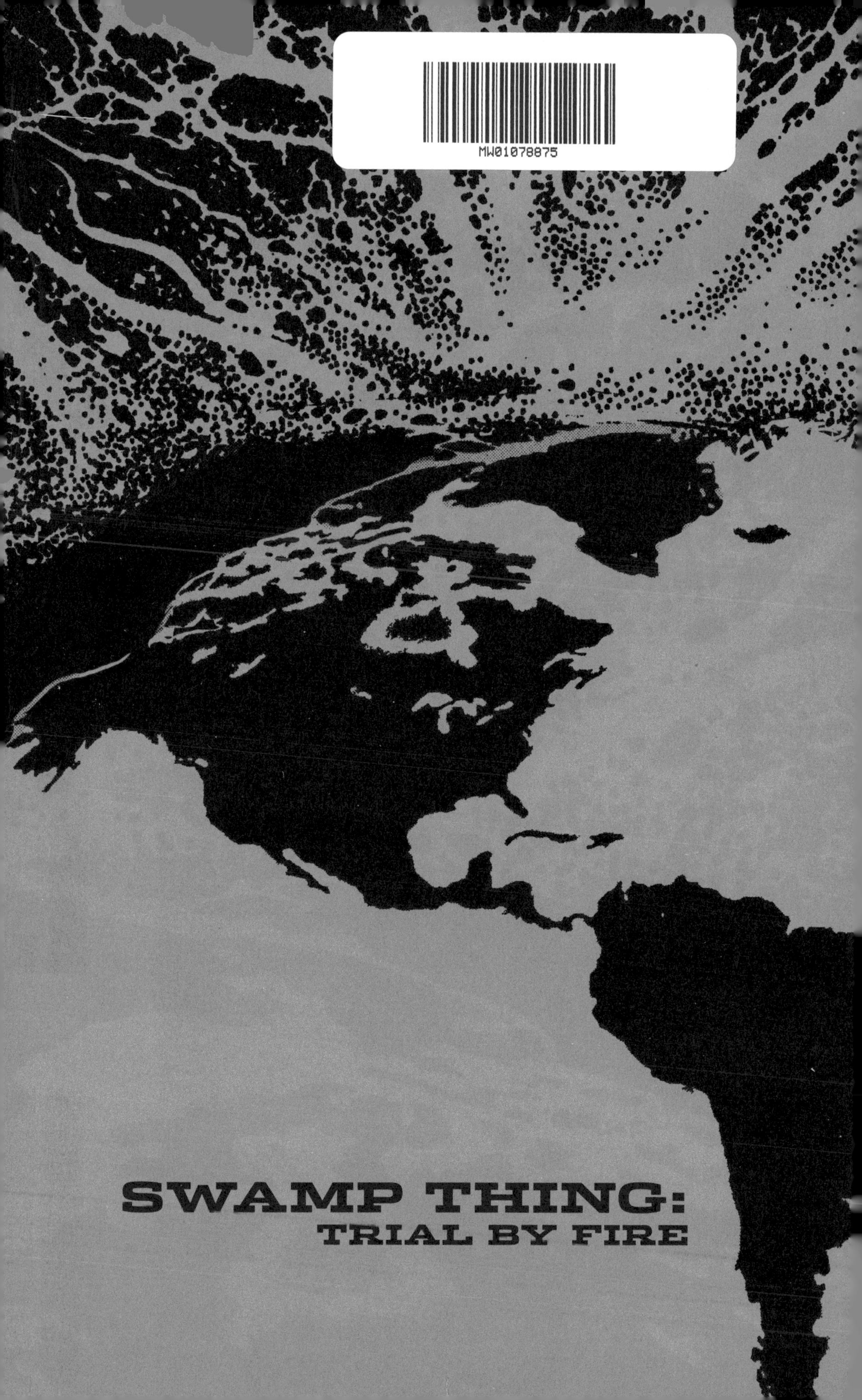

SWAMP THING:
TRIAL BY FIRE

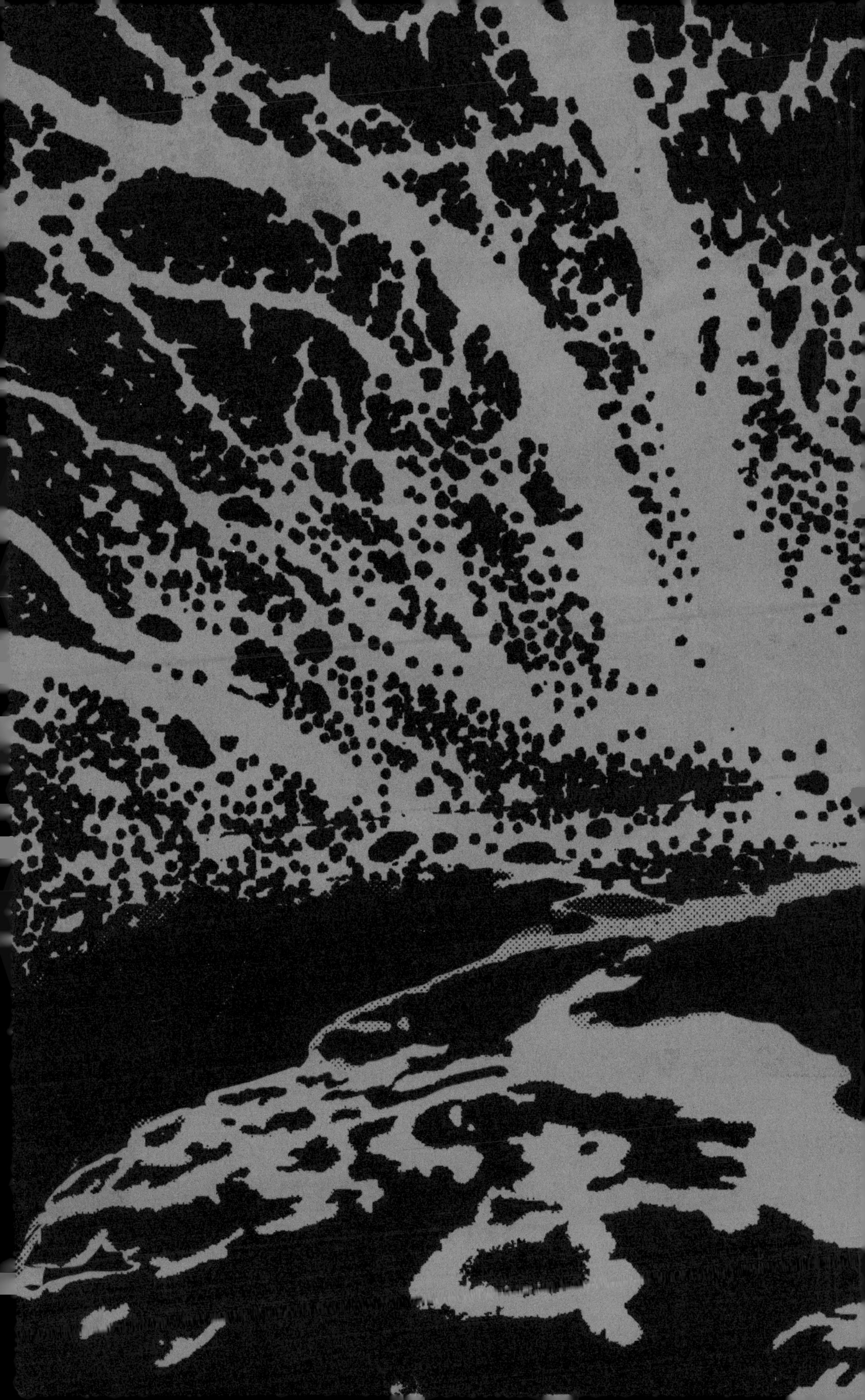

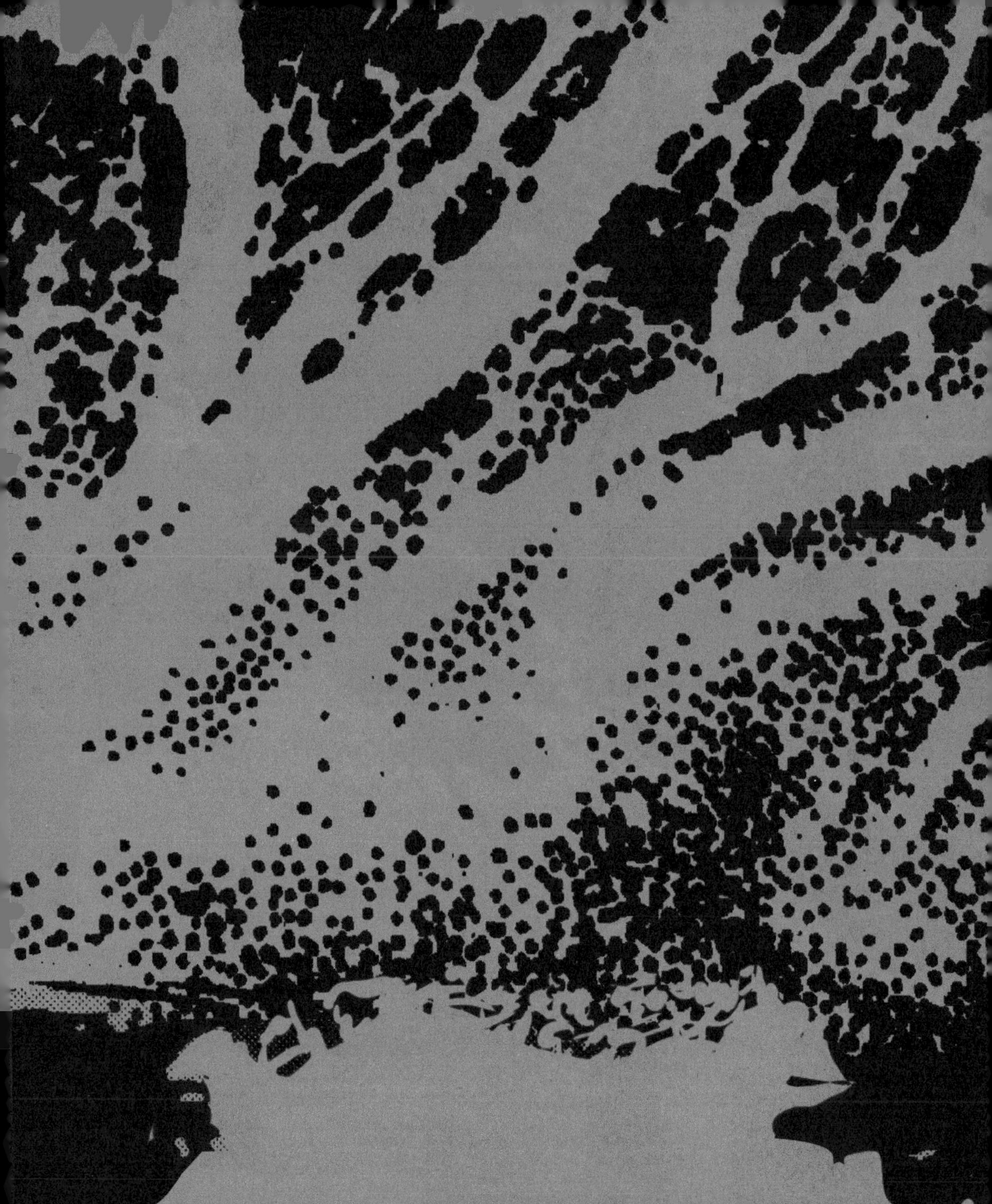

SWAMP THING:
TRIAL BY FIRE

Mark Millar Writer
Phil Hester Kim DeMulder Curt Swan Artists
Tatjana Wood Colorist
Richard Starkings/Comicraft Letterer
John Totleben Cover Art
John Totleben and Curt Swan Original Series Covers
Swamp Thing created by Len Wein and Bernie Wrightson

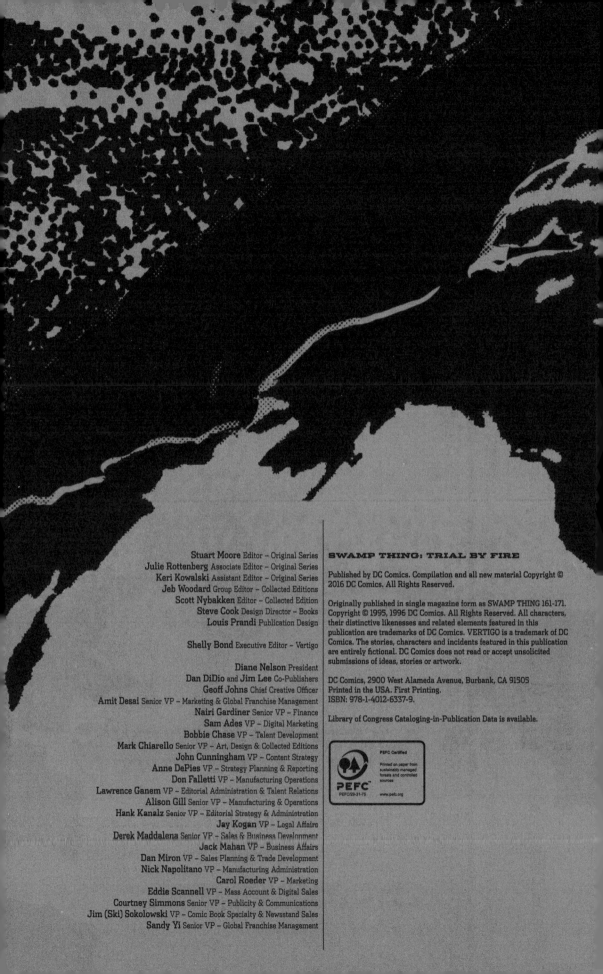

Stuart Moore Editor – Original Series
Julie Rottenberg Associate Editor – Original Series
Keri Kowalski Assistant Editor – Original Series
Jeb Woodard Group Editor – Collected Editions
Scott Nybakken Editor – Collected Edition
Steve Cook Design Director – Books
Louis Prandi Publication Design

Shelly Bond Executive Editor – Vertigo

Diane Nelson President
Dan DiDio and Jim Lee Co-Publishers
Geoff Johns Chief Creative Officer
Amit Desai Senior VP – Marketing & Global Franchise Management
Nairi Gardiner Senior VP – Finance
Sam Ades VP – Digital Marketing
Bobbie Chase VP – Talent Development
Mark Chiarello Senior VP – Art, Design & Collected Editions
John Cunningham VP – Content Strategy
Anne DePies VP – Strategy Planning & Reporting
Don Falletti VP – Manufacturing Operations
Lawrence Ganem VP – Editorial Administration & Talent Relations
Alison Gill Senior VP – Manufacturing & Operations
Hank Kanalz Senior VP – Editorial Strategy & Administration
Jay Kogan VP – Legal Affairs
Derek Maddalena Senior VP – Sales & Business Development
Jack Mahan VP – Business Affairs
Dan Miron VP – Sales Planning & Trade Development
Nick Napolitano VP – Manufacturing Administration
Carol Roeder VP – Marketing
Eddie Scannell VP – Mass Account & Digital Sales
Courtney Simmons Senior VP – Publicity & Communications
Jim (Ski) Sokolowski VP – Comic Book Specialty & Newsstand Sales
Sandy Yi Senior VP – Global Franchise Management

SWAMP THING: TRIAL BY FIRE

DC Comics, 2900 West Alameda Avenue, Burbank, CA 91505
Printed in the USA. First Printing.
ISBN: 978-1-4012-6337-9.

Library of Congress Cataloging-in-Publication Data is available.

PEFC Certified

Printed on paper from
sustainably managed
forests and controlled
sources

PEFC/29-31-75   www.pefc.org

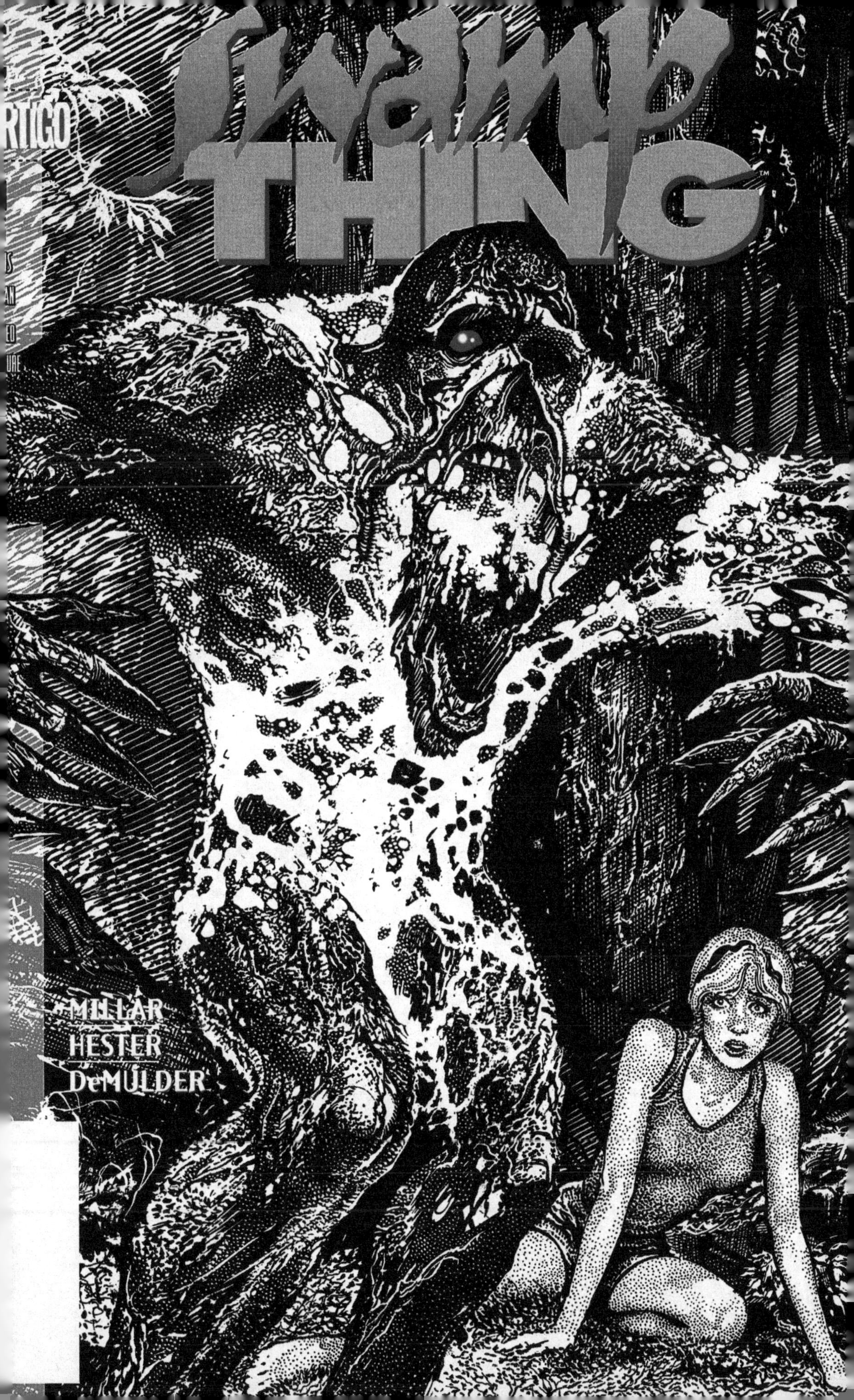
RTIGO
Swamp
THING™
MILLAR
HESTER
DeMULDER

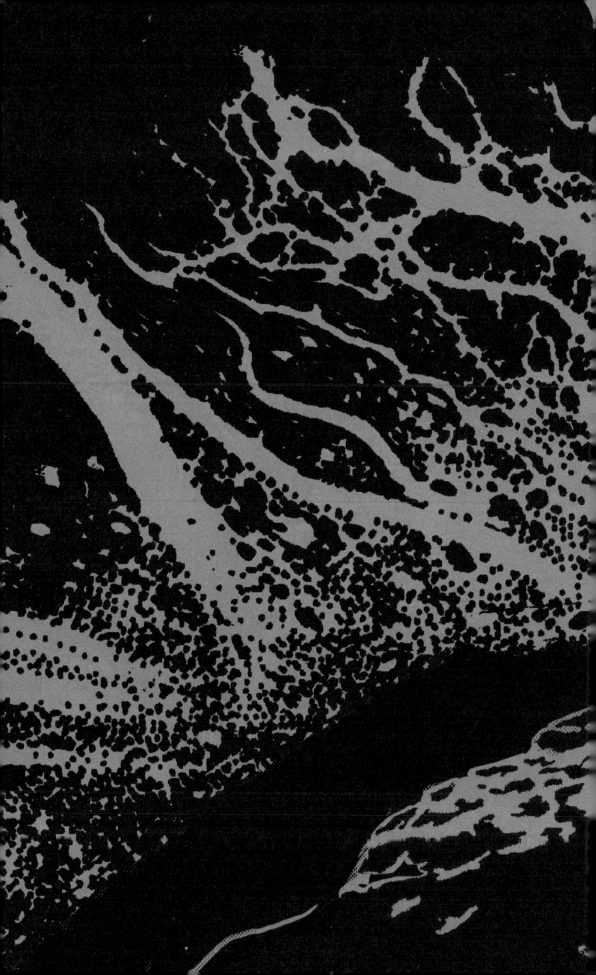

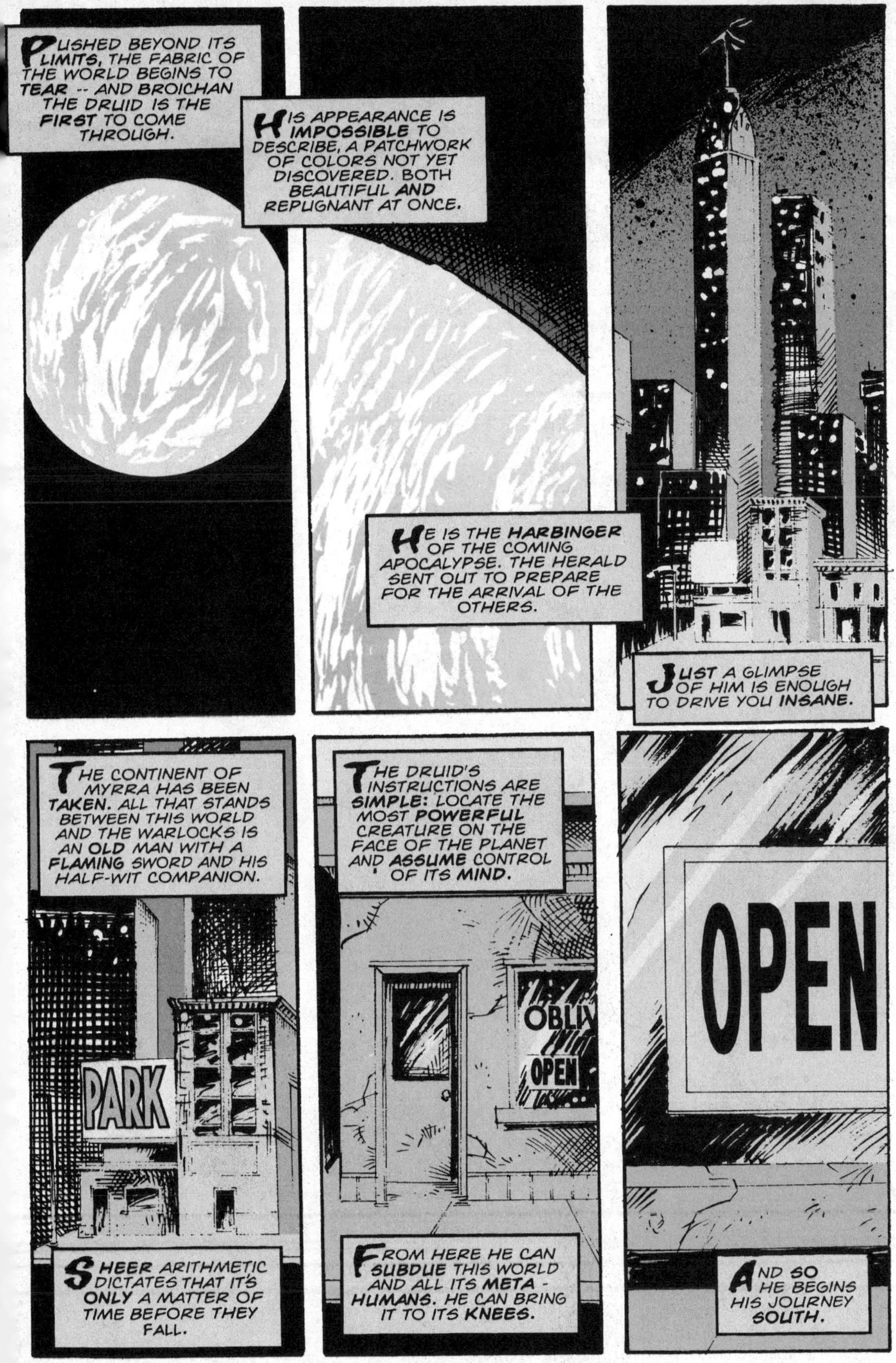
PUSHED BEYOND ITS LIMITS, THE FABRIC OF THE WORLD BEGINS TO TEAR -- AND BROICHAN THE DRUID IS THE FIRST TO COME THROUGH.
HIS APPEARANCE IS IMPOSSIBLE TO DESCRIBE, A PATCHWORK OF COLORS NOT YET DISCOVERED. BOTH BEAUTIFUL AND REPUGNANT AT ONCE.
HE IS THE HARBINGER OF THE COMING APOCALYPSE. THE HERALD SENT OUT TO PREPARE FOR THE ARRIVAL OF THE OTHERS.
JUST A GLIMPSE OF HIM IS ENOUGH TO DRIVE YOU INSANE.
THE CONTINENT OF MYRRA HAS BEEN TAKEN. ALL THAT STANDS BETWEEN THIS WORLD AND THE WARLOCKS IS AN OLD MAN WITH A FLAMING SWORD AND HIS HALF-WIT COMPANION.
PARK
SHEER ARITHMETIC DICTATES THAT IT'S ONLY A MATTER OF TIME BEFORE THEY FALL.
THE DRUID'S INSTRUCTIONS ARE SIMPLE: LOCATE THE MOST POWERFUL CREATURE ON THE FACE OF THE PLANET AND ASSUME CONTROL OF ITS MIND.
OBLIV
OPEN
FROM HERE HE CAN SUBDUE THIS WORLD AND ALL ITS META-HUMANS. HE CAN BRING IT TO ITS KNEES.
OPEN
AND SO HE BEGINS HIS JOURNEY SOUTH.

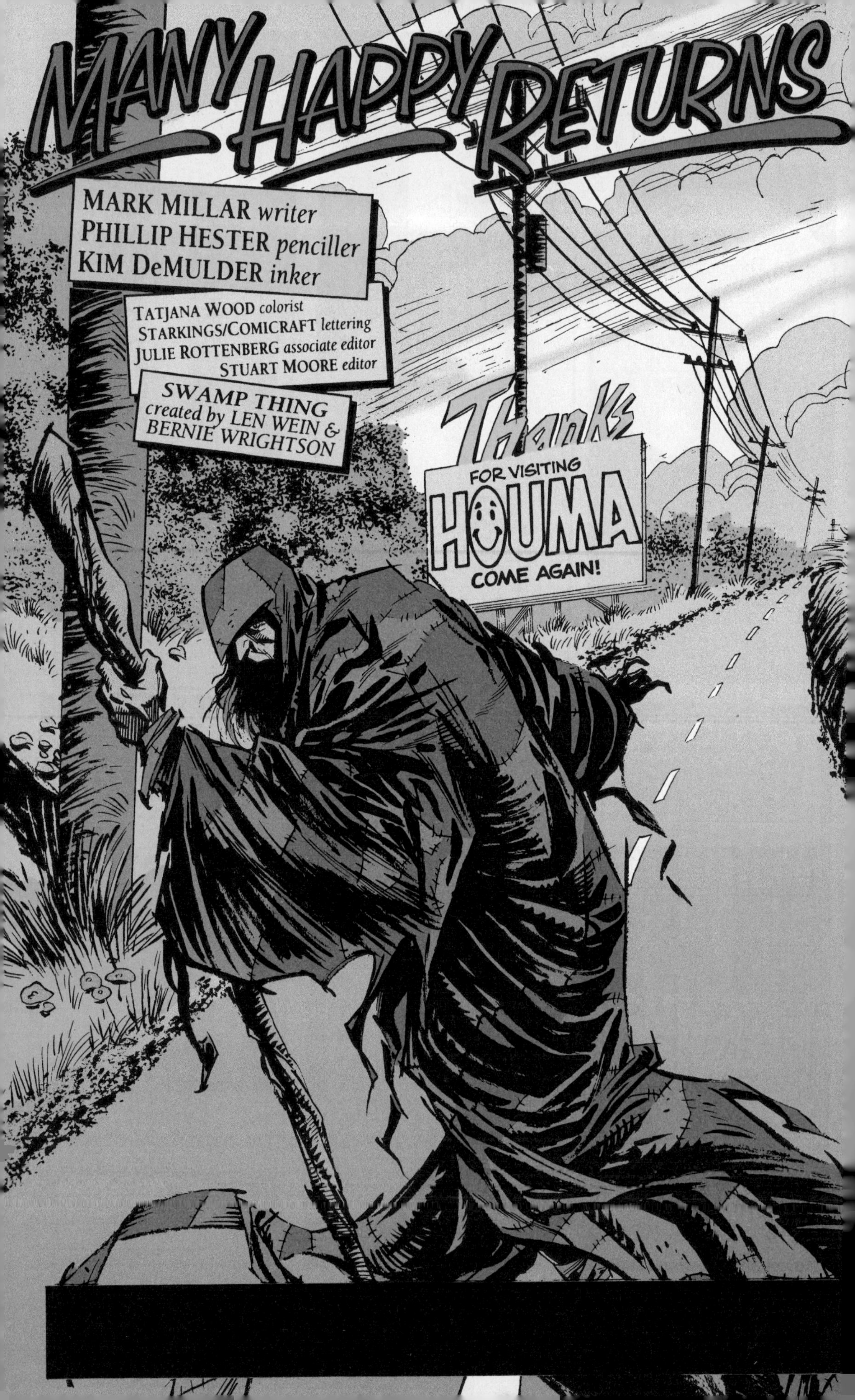
MANY HAPPY RETURNS
MARK MILLAR writer
PHILLIP HESTER penciller
KIM DeMULDER inker
TATJANA WOOD colorist
STARKINGS/COMICRAFT lettering
JULIE ROTTENBERG associate editor
STUART MOORE editor
SWAMP THING
created by LEN WEIN &
BERNIE WRIGHTSON
Thanks
FOR VISITING
HOUMA
COME AGAIN!
[redacted]

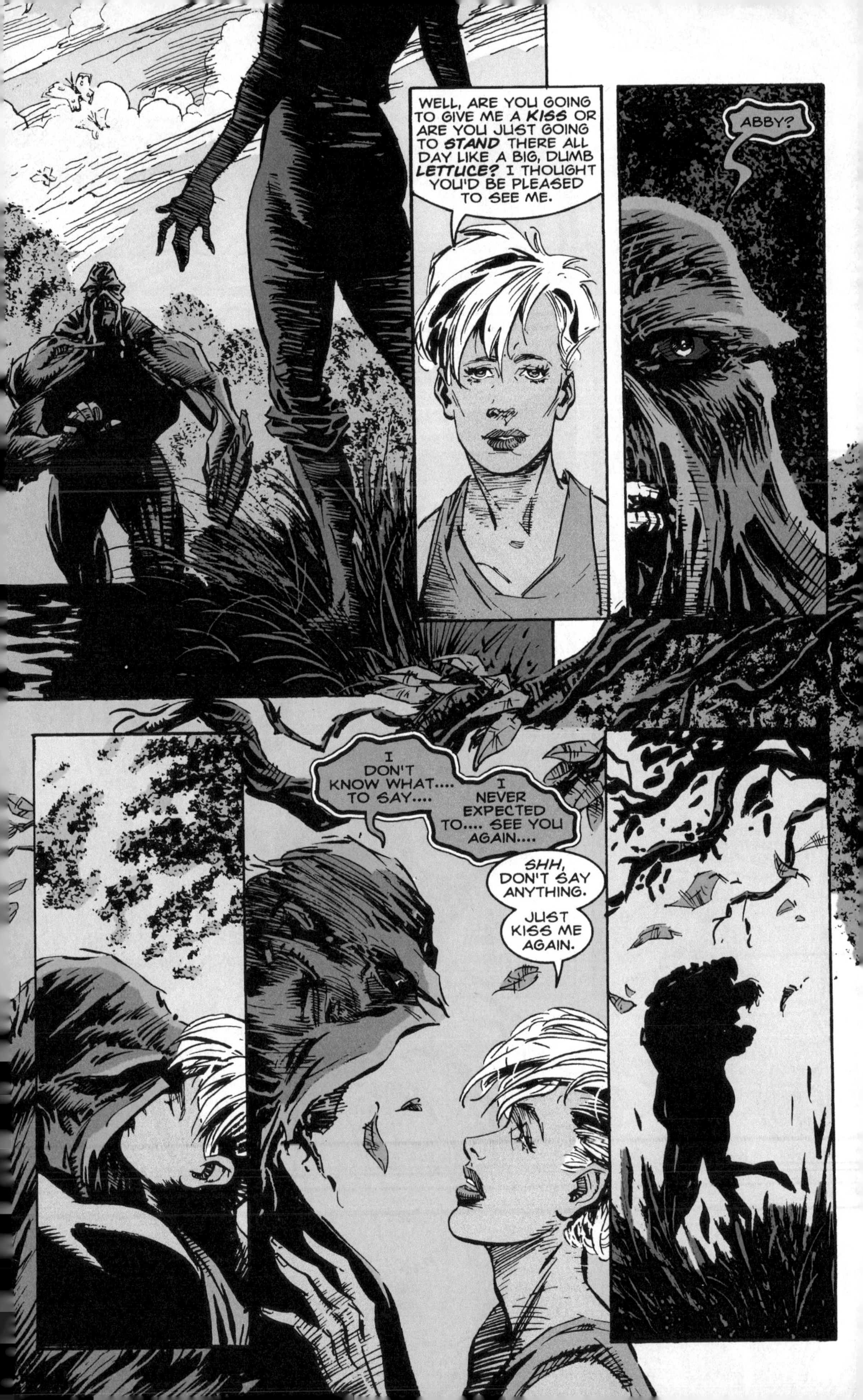
WELL, ARE YOU GOING TO GIVE ME A KISS OR ARE YOU JUST GOING TO STAND THERE ALL DAY LIKE A BIG, DUMB LETTUCE? I THOUGHT YOU'D BE PLEASED TO SEE ME.
ABBY?
I DON'T KNOW WHAT.... TO SAY.... I NEVER EXPECTED TO.... SEE YOU AGAIN....
SHH, DON'T SAY ANYTHING.
JUST KISS ME AGAIN.

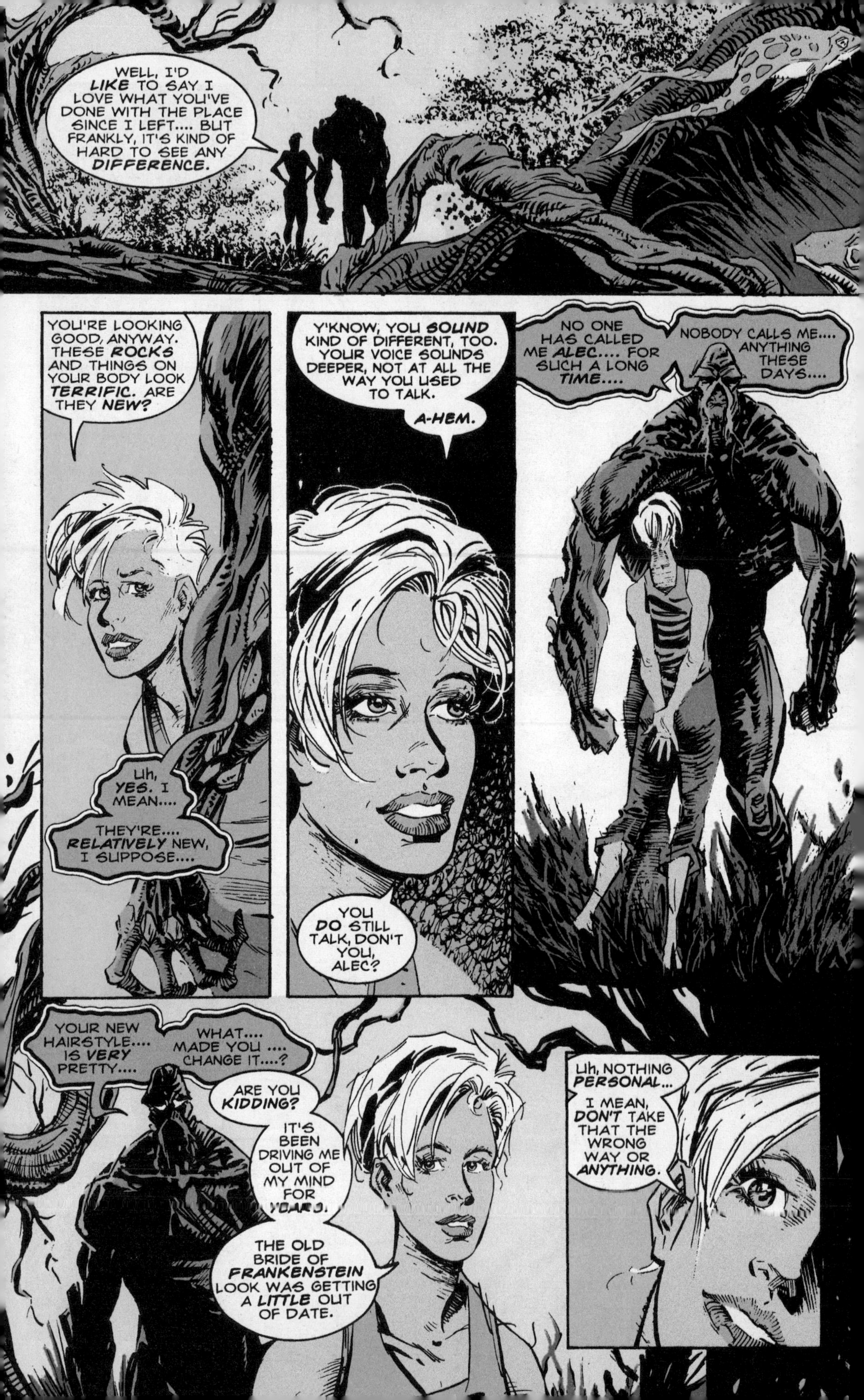
WELL, I'D LIKE TO SAY I LOVE WHAT YOU'VE DONE WITH THE PLACE SINCE I LEFT.... BUT FRANKLY, IT'S KIND OF HARD TO SEE ANY DIFFERENCE.
YOU'RE LOOKING GOOD, ANYWAY. THESE ROCKS AND THINGS ON YOUR BODY LOOK TERRIFIC. ARE THEY NEW?
UH, YES. I MEAN....
THEY'RE.... RELATIVELY NEW, I SUPPOSE....
Y'KNOW, YOU SOUND KIND OF DIFFERENT, TOO. YOUR VOICE SOUNDS DEEPER, NOT AT ALL THE WAY YOU USED TO TALK.
A-HEM.
YOU DO STILL TALK, DON'T YOU, ALEC?
NO ONE HAS CALLED ME ALEC.... FOR SUCH A LONG TIME....
NOBODY CALLS ME.... ANYTHING THESE DAYS....
YOUR NEW HAIRSTYLE.... IS VERY PRETTY....
WHAT.... MADE YOU .... CHANGE IT....?
ARE YOU KIDDING?
IT'S BEEN DRIVING ME OUT OF MY MIND FOR YEARS.
THE OLD BRIDE OF FRANKENSTEIN LOOK WAS GETTING A LITTLE OUT OF DATE.
UH, NOTHING PERSONAL...
I MEAN, DON'T TAKE THAT THE WRONG WAY OR ANYTHING.

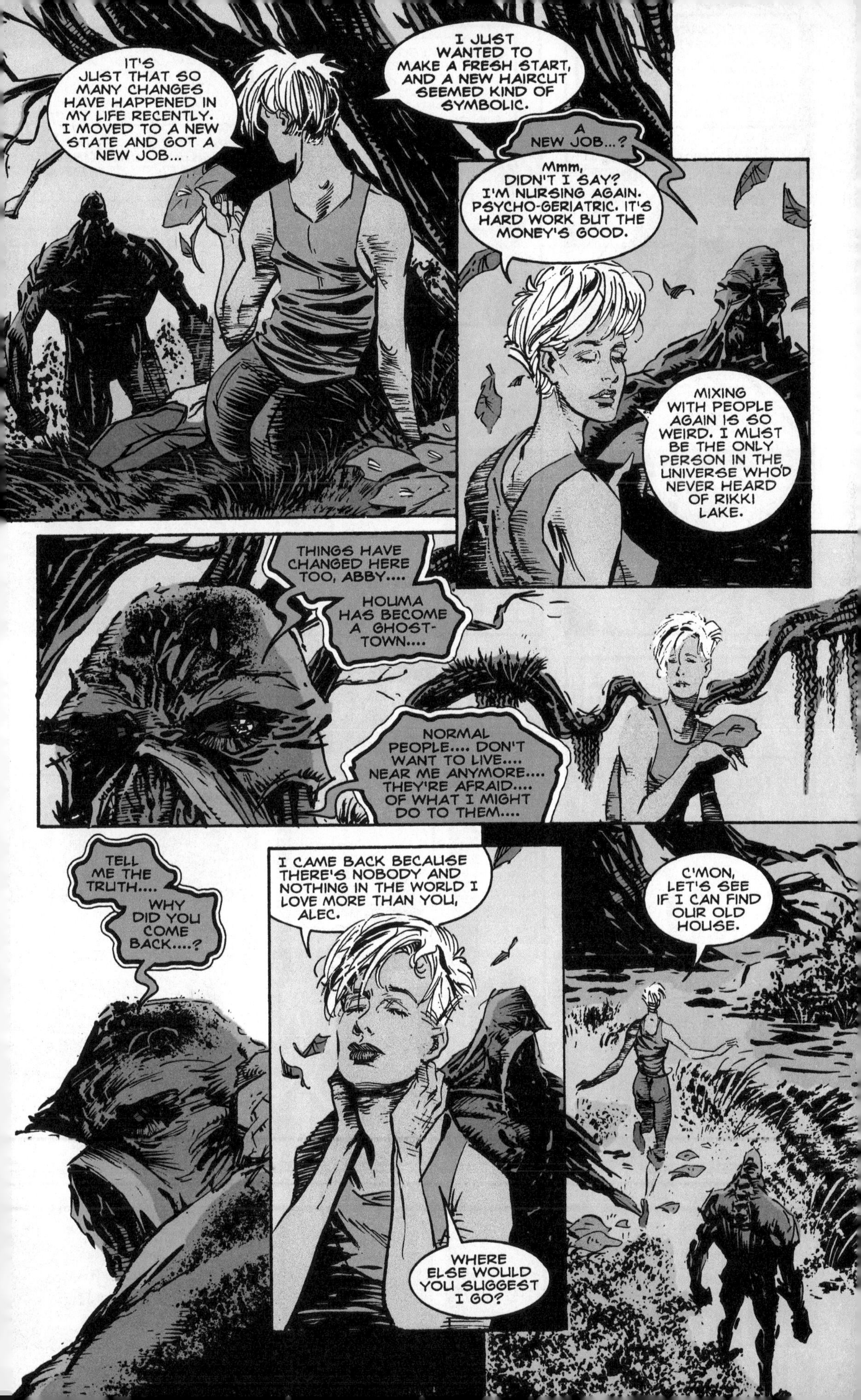
IT'S JUST THAT SO MANY CHANGES HAVE HAPPENED IN MY LIFE RECENTLY. I MOVED TO A NEW STATE AND GOT A NEW JOB...
I JUST WANTED TO MAKE A FRESH START, AND A NEW HAIRCUT SEEMED KIND OF SYMBOLIC.
A NEW JOB...?
Mmm, DIDN'T I SAY? I'M NURSING AGAIN. PSYCHO-GERIATRIC. IT'S HARD WORK BUT THE MONEY'S GOOD.
MIXING WITH PEOPLE AGAIN IS SO WEIRD. I MUST BE THE ONLY PERSON IN THE UNIVERSE WHO'D NEVER HEARD OF RIKKI LAKE.
THINGS HAVE CHANGED HERE TOO, ABBY....
HOUMA HAS BECOME A GHOST-TOWN....
NORMAL PEOPLE.... DON'T WANT TO LIVE.... NEAR ME ANYMORE.... THEY'RE AFRAID.... OF WHAT I MIGHT DO TO THEM....
TELL ME THE TRUTH....
WHY DID YOU COME BACK....?
I CAME BACK BECAUSE THERE'S NOBODY AND NOTHING IN THE WORLD I LOVE MORE THAN YOU, ALEC.
WHERE ELSE WOULD YOU SUGGEST I GO?
C'MON, LET'S SEE IF I CAN FIND OUR OLD HOUSE.

BRETT HARRIS YAWNS AND WAITS FOR HIS BODY TO WAKE UP, BLISSFULLY UNAWARE THAT HE'LL NEVER OPEN HIS EYES IN THIS BED AGAIN.

HE SHAVES FOR THE LAST TIME, THINKING ABOUT HIS WIFE AND HIS UNBORN SON AND ALL THEIR SOON-TO-BE REDUNDANT PLANS FOR THE FUTURE.

POTENTIAL BABY NAMES DRIFT IN AND OUT OF HIS MIND, BUT NOTHING REALLY HITS THE MARK.

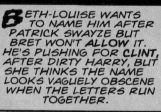

BETH-LOUISE WANTS TO NAME HIM AFTER PATRICK SWAYZE BUT BRET WON'T ALLOW IT. HE'S PUSHING FOR CLINT, AFTER DIRTY HARRY, BUT SHE THINKS THE NAME LOOKS VAGUELY OBSCENE WHEN THE LETTERS RUN TOGETHER.

DOWNSTAIRS, HE SMOKES HIS LAST NICOTINE BREAKFAST AND CATCHES A COUPLE OF CHEAP CARTOONS ON NICKELODEON.

BRIEFLY HE CONSIDERS THE NAME LEE, AS IN LEE VAN CLEEF AND, OF COURSE, LEE MAJORS, THE SIX MILLION DOLLAR BIONIC MAN.

NAH, HE DECIDES.

IT'S GOT TO BE CLINT.

WASHED, DRESSED AND REMAINING HAIRS COMBED, HE CLIMBS INTO HIS POLICE CAR AND BEGINS THE LAST DAY OF HIS LIFE.

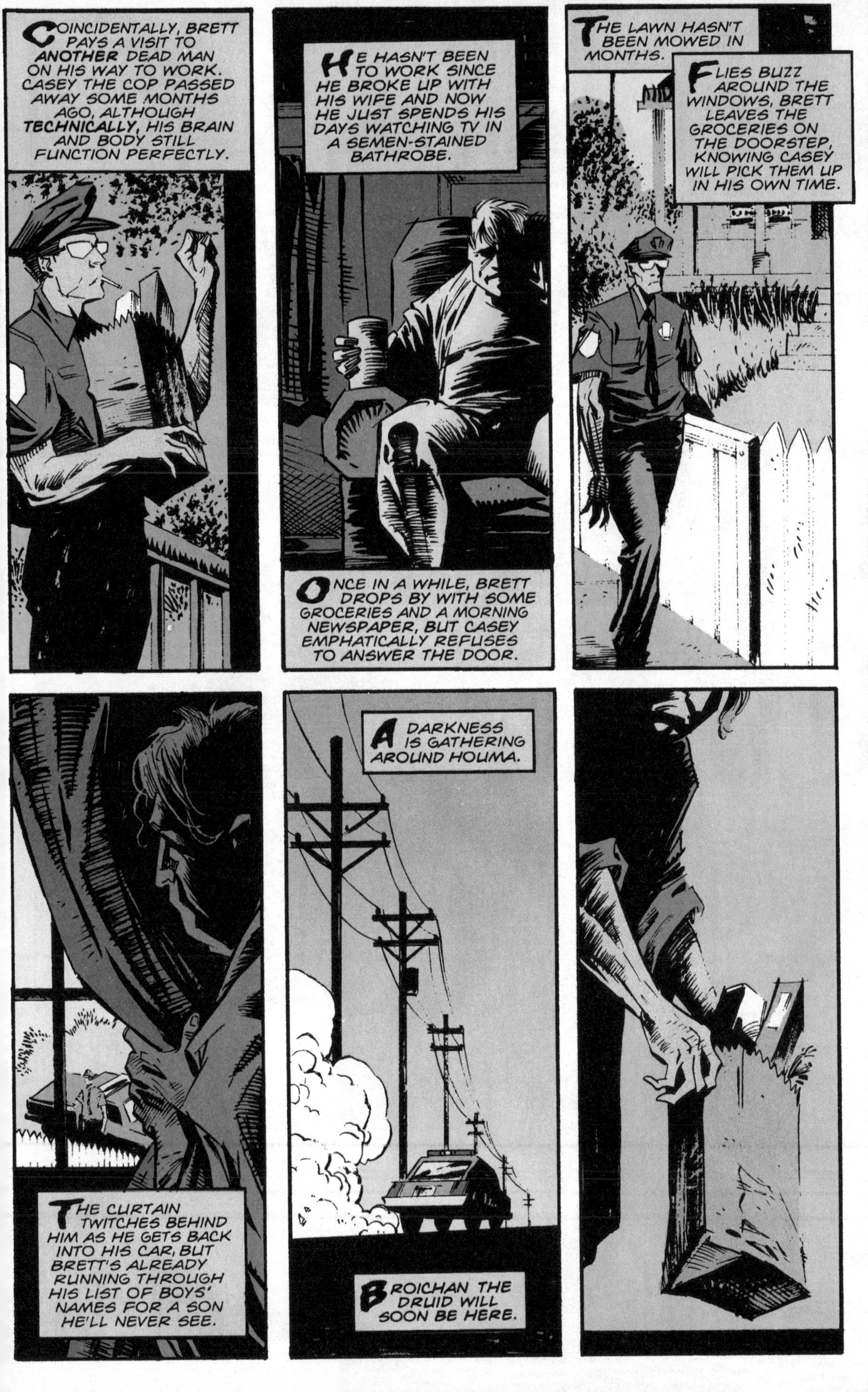
COINCIDENTALLY, BRETT PAYS A VISIT TO ANOTHER DEAD MAN ON HIS WAY TO WORK. CASEY THE COP PASSED AWAY SOME MONTHS AGO, ALTHOUGH TECHNICALLY, HIS BRAIN AND BODY STILL FUNCTION PERFECTLY.
HE HASN'T BEEN TO WORK SINCE HE BROKE UP WITH HIS WIFE AND NOW HE JUST SPENDS HIS DAYS WATCHING TV IN A SEMEN-STAINED BATHROBE.
ONCE IN A WHILE, BRETT DROPS BY WITH SOME GROCERIES AND A MORNING NEWSPAPER, BUT CASEY EMPHATICALLY REFUSES TO ANSWER THE DOOR.
THE LAWN HASN'T BEEN MOWED IN MONTHS.
FLIES BUZZ AROUND THE WINDOWS, BRETT LEAVES THE GROCERIES ON THE DOORSTEP, KNOWING CASEY WILL PICK THEM UP IN HIS OWN TIME.
THE CURTAIN TWITCHES BEHIND HIM AS HE GETS BACK INTO HIS CAR, BUT BRETT'S ALREADY RUNNING THROUGH HIS LIST OF BOYS' NAMES FOR A SON HE'LL NEVER SEE.
A DARKNESS IS GATHERING AROUND HOUMA.
BROICHAN THE DRUID WILL SOON BE HERE.

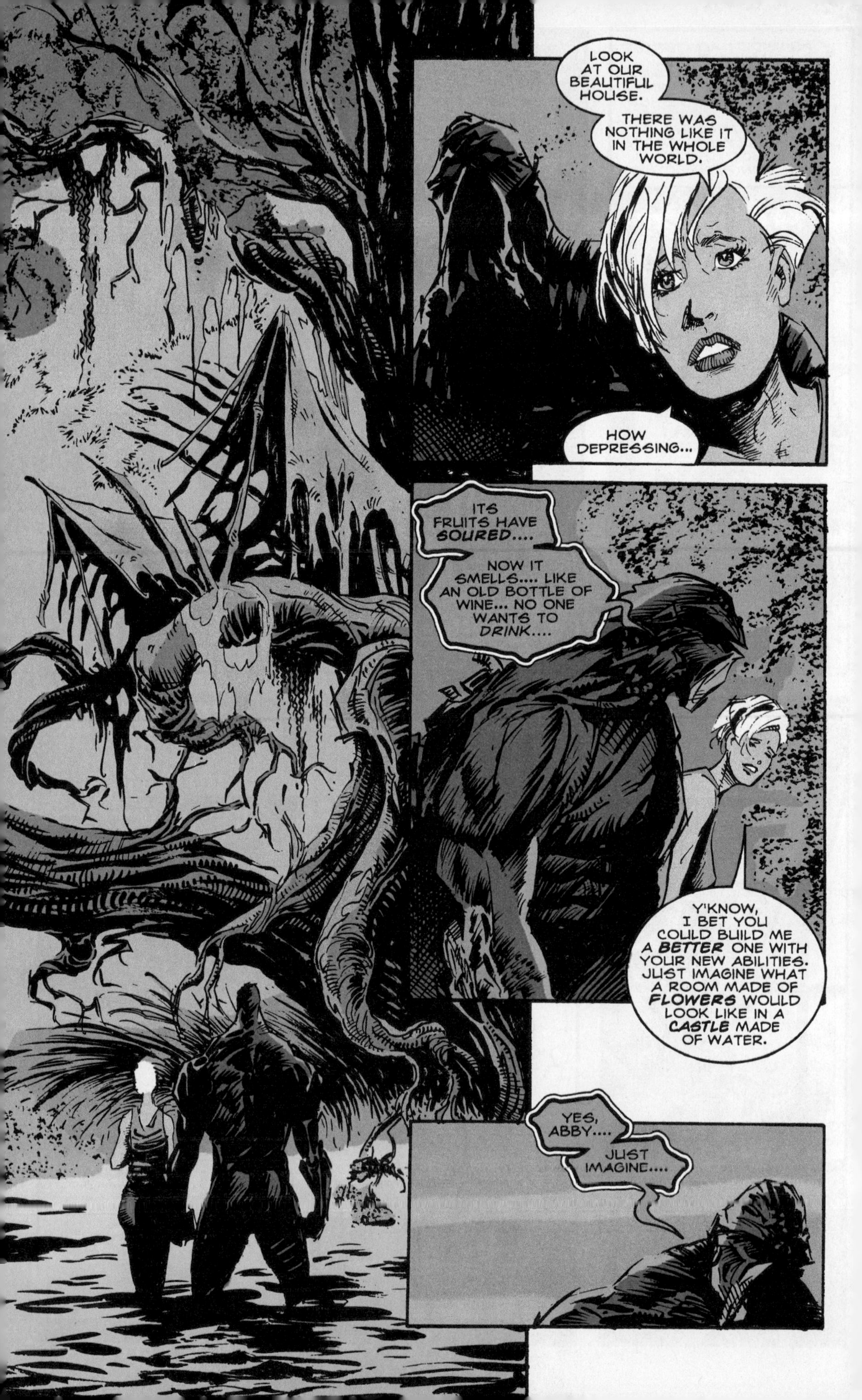

LOOK AT OUR BEAUTIFUL HOUSE.
THERE WAS NOTHING LIKE IT IN THE WHOLE WORLD.
HOW DEPRESSING...
ITS FRUITS HAVE **SOURED**....
NOW IT SMELLS.... LIKE AN OLD BOTTLE OF WINE... NO ONE WANTS TO *DRINK*....
Y'KNOW, I BET YOU COULD BUILD ME A **BETTER** ONE WITH YOUR NEW ABILITIES. JUST IMAGINE WHAT A ROOM MADE OF **FLOWERS** WOULD LOOK LIKE IN A **CASTLE** MADE OF WATER.
YES, ABBY....
JUST IMAGINE....

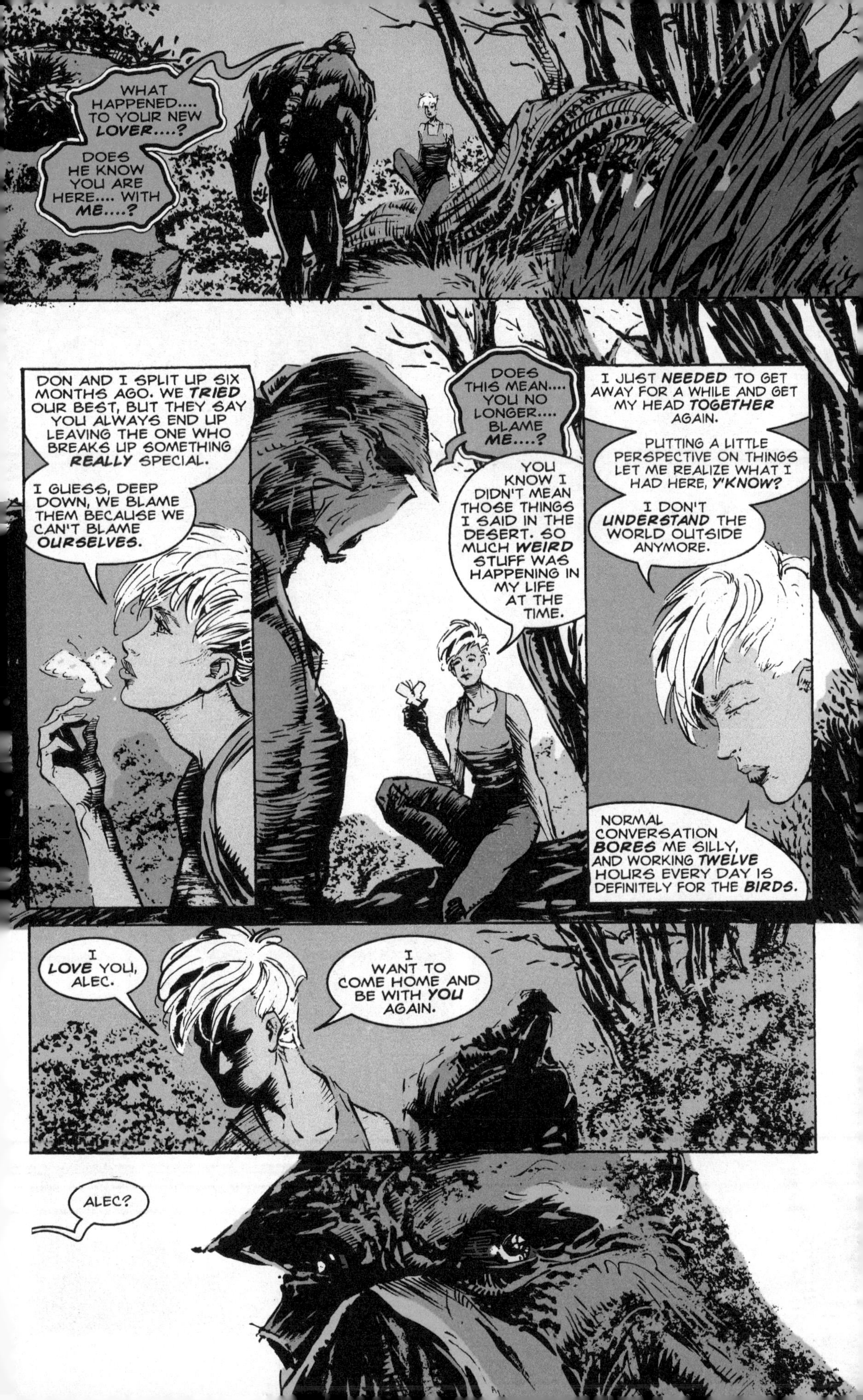
WHAT HAPPENED.... TO YOUR NEW LOVER....?
DOES HE KNOW YOU ARE HERE.... WITH ME....?
DON AND I SPLIT UP SIX MONTHS AGO. WE TRIED OUR BEST, BUT THEY SAY YOU ALWAYS END UP LEAVING THE ONE WHO BREAKS UP SOMETHING REALLY SPECIAL.
I GUESS, DEEP DOWN, WE BLAME THEM BECAUSE WE CAN'T BLAME OURSELVES.
DOES THIS MEAN.... YOU NO LONGER.... BLAME ME....?
YOU KNOW I DIDN'T MEAN THOSE THINGS I SAID IN THE DESERT. SO MUCH WEIRD STUFF WAS HAPPENING IN MY LIFE AT THE TIME.
I JUST NEEDED TO GET AWAY FOR A WHILE AND GET MY HEAD TOGETHER AGAIN.
PUTTING A LITTLE PERSPECTIVE ON THINGS LET ME REALIZE WHAT I HAD HERE, Y'KNOW?
I DON'T UNDERSTAND THE WORLD OUTSIDE ANYMORE.
NORMAL CONVERSATION BORES ME SILLY, AND WORKING TWELVE HOURS EVERY DAY IS DEFINITELY FOR THE BIRDS.
I LOVE YOU, ALEC.
I WANT TO COME HOME AND BE WITH YOU AGAIN.
ALEC?

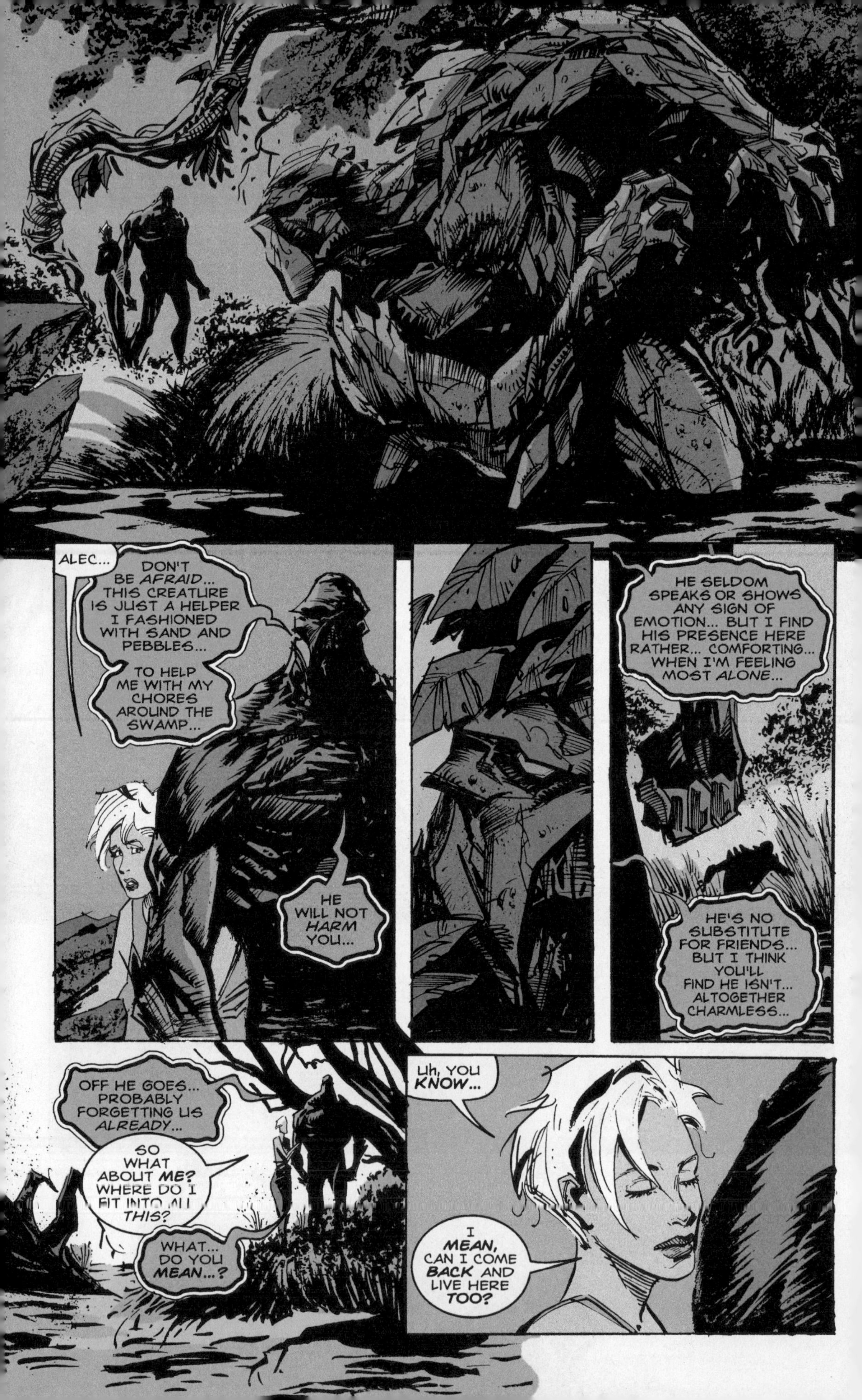
ALEC...
DON'T BE AFRAID... THIS CREATURE IS JUST A HELPER I FASHIONED WITH SAND AND PEBBLES...
TO HELP ME WITH MY CHORES AROUND THE SWAMP...
HE WILL NOT HARM YOU...
HE SELDOM SPEAKS OR SHOWS ANY SIGN OF EMOTION... BUT I FIND HIS PRESENCE HERE RATHER... COMFORTING... WHEN I'M FEELING MOST ALONE...
HE'S NO SUBSTITUTE FOR FRIENDS... BUT I THINK YOU'LL FIND HE ISN'T... ALTOGETHER CHARMLESS...
OFF HE GOES... PROBABLY FORGETTING US ALREADY...
SO WHAT ABOUT ME? WHERE DO I FIT INTO ALL THIS?
WHAT... DO YOU MEAN...?
UH, YOU KNOW...
I MEAN, CAN I COME BACK AND LIVE HERE TOO?

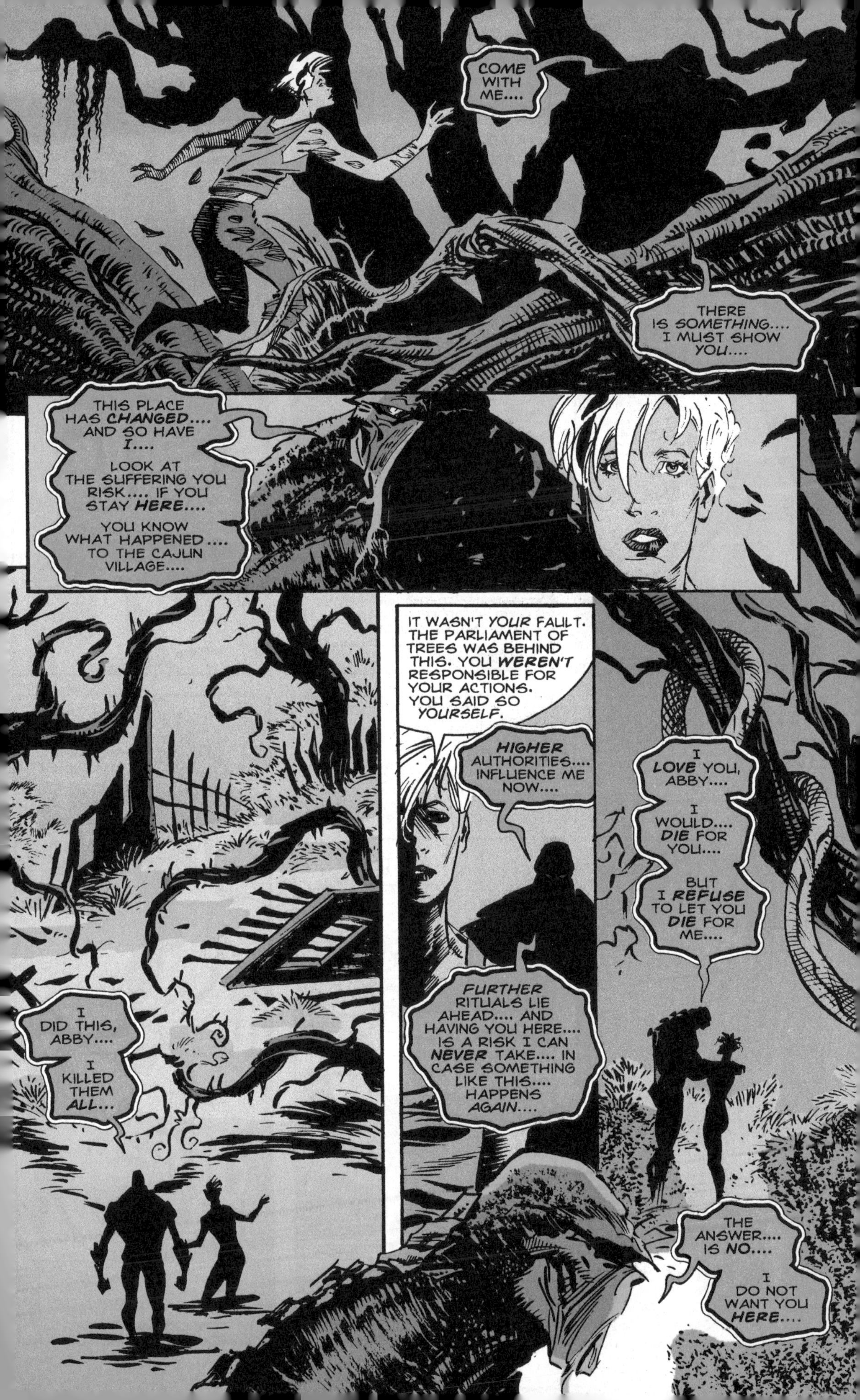
COME WITH ME....
THERE IS SOMETHING.... I MUST SHOW YOU....
THIS PLACE HAS CHANGED.... AND SO HAVE I....
LOOK AT THE SUFFERING YOU RISK.... IF YOU STAY HERE....
YOU KNOW WHAT HAPPENED.... TO THE CAJUN VILLAGE....
I DID THIS, ABBY....
I KILLED THEM ALL...
IT WASN'T YOUR FAULT. THE PARLIAMENT OF TREES WAS BEHIND THIS. YOU WEREN'T RESPONSIBLE FOR YOUR ACTIONS. YOU SAID SO YOURSELF.
HIGHER AUTHORITIES.... INFLUENCE ME NOW....
FURTHER RITUALS LIE AHEAD.... AND HAVING YOU HERE.... IS A RISK I CAN NEVER TAKE.... IN CASE SOMETHING LIKE THIS.... HAPPENS AGAIN....
I LOVE YOU, ABBY....
I WOULD.... DIE FOR YOU....
BUT I REFUSE TO LET YOU DIE FOR ME....
THE ANSWER.... IS NO....
I DO NOT WANT YOU HERE....

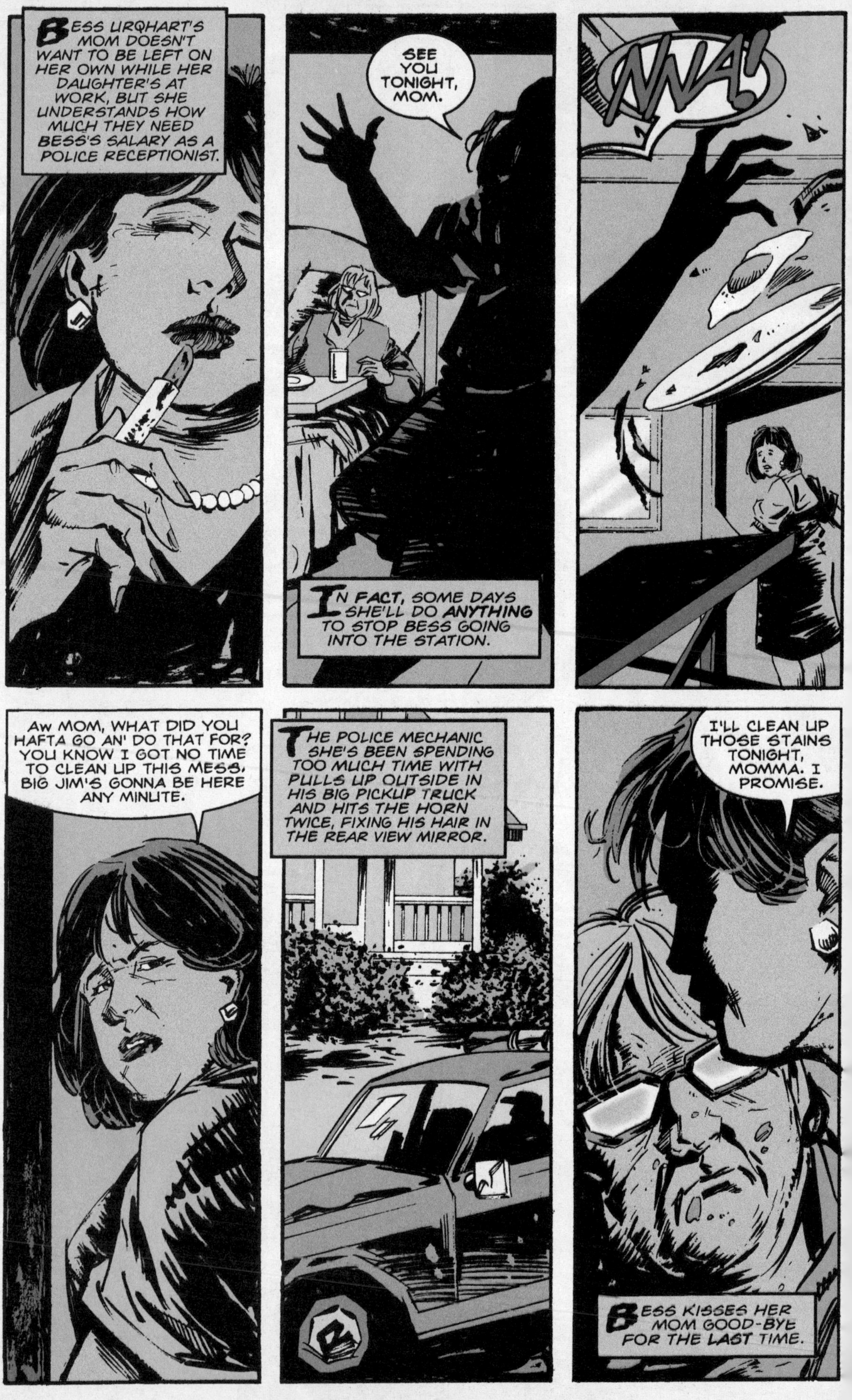
BESS URQHART'S MOM DOESN'T WANT TO BE LEFT ON HER OWN WHILE HER DAUGHTER'S AT WORK, BUT SHE UNDERSTANDS HOW MUCH THEY NEED BESS'S SALARY AS A POLICE RECEPTIONIST.
SEE YOU TONIGHT, MOM.
IN FACT, SOME DAYS SHE'LL DO ANYTHING TO STOP BESS GOING INTO THE STATION.
NNA!
Aw MOM, WHAT DID YOU HAFTA GO AN' DO THAT FOR? YOU KNOW I GOT NO TIME TO CLEAN UP THIS MESS. BIG JIM'S GONNA BE HERE ANY MINUTE.
THE POLICE MECHANIC SHE'S BEEN SPENDING TOO MUCH TIME WITH PULLS UP OUTSIDE IN HIS BIG PICKUP TRUCK AND HITS THE HORN TWICE, FIXING HIS HAIR IN THE REAR VIEW MIRROR.
I'LL CLEAN UP THOSE STAINS TONIGHT, MOMMA. I PROMISE.
BESS KISSES HER MOM GOOD-BYE FOR THE LAST TIME.

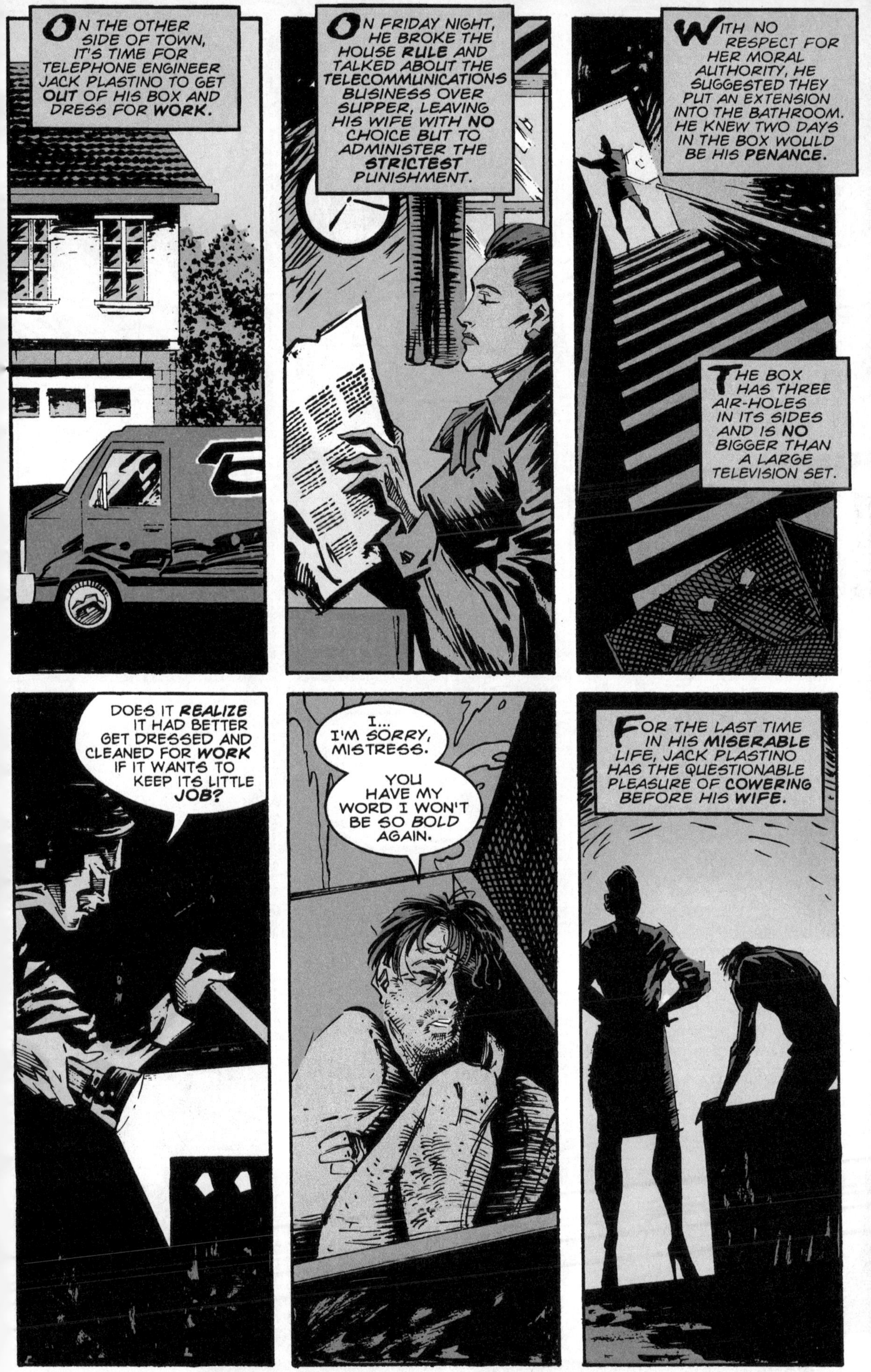
ON THE OTHER SIDE OF TOWN, IT'S TIME FOR TELEPHONE ENGINEER JACK PLASTINO TO GET OUT OF HIS BOX AND DRESS FOR WORK.
ON FRIDAY NIGHT, HE BROKE THE HOUSE RULE AND TALKED ABOUT THE TELECOMMUNICATIONS BUSINESS OVER SUPPER, LEAVING HIS WIFE WITH NO CHOICE BUT TO ADMINISTER THE STRICTEST PUNISHMENT.
WITH NO RESPECT FOR HER MORAL AUTHORITY, HE SUGGESTED THEY PUT AN EXTENSION INTO THE BATHROOM. HE KNEW TWO DAYS IN THE BOX WOULD BE HIS PENANCE.
THE BOX HAS THREE AIR-HOLES IN ITS SIDES AND IS NO BIGGER THAN A LARGE TELEVISION SET.
DOES IT REALIZE IT HAD BETTER GET DRESSED AND CLEANED FOR WORK IF IT WANTS TO KEEP ITS LITTLE JOB?
I... I'M SORRY, MISTRESS.
YOU HAVE MY WORD I WON'T BE SO BOLD AGAIN.
FOR THE LAST TIME IN HIS MISERABLE LIFE, JACK PLASTINO HAS THE QUESTIONABLE PLEASURE OF COWERING BEFORE HIS WIFE.

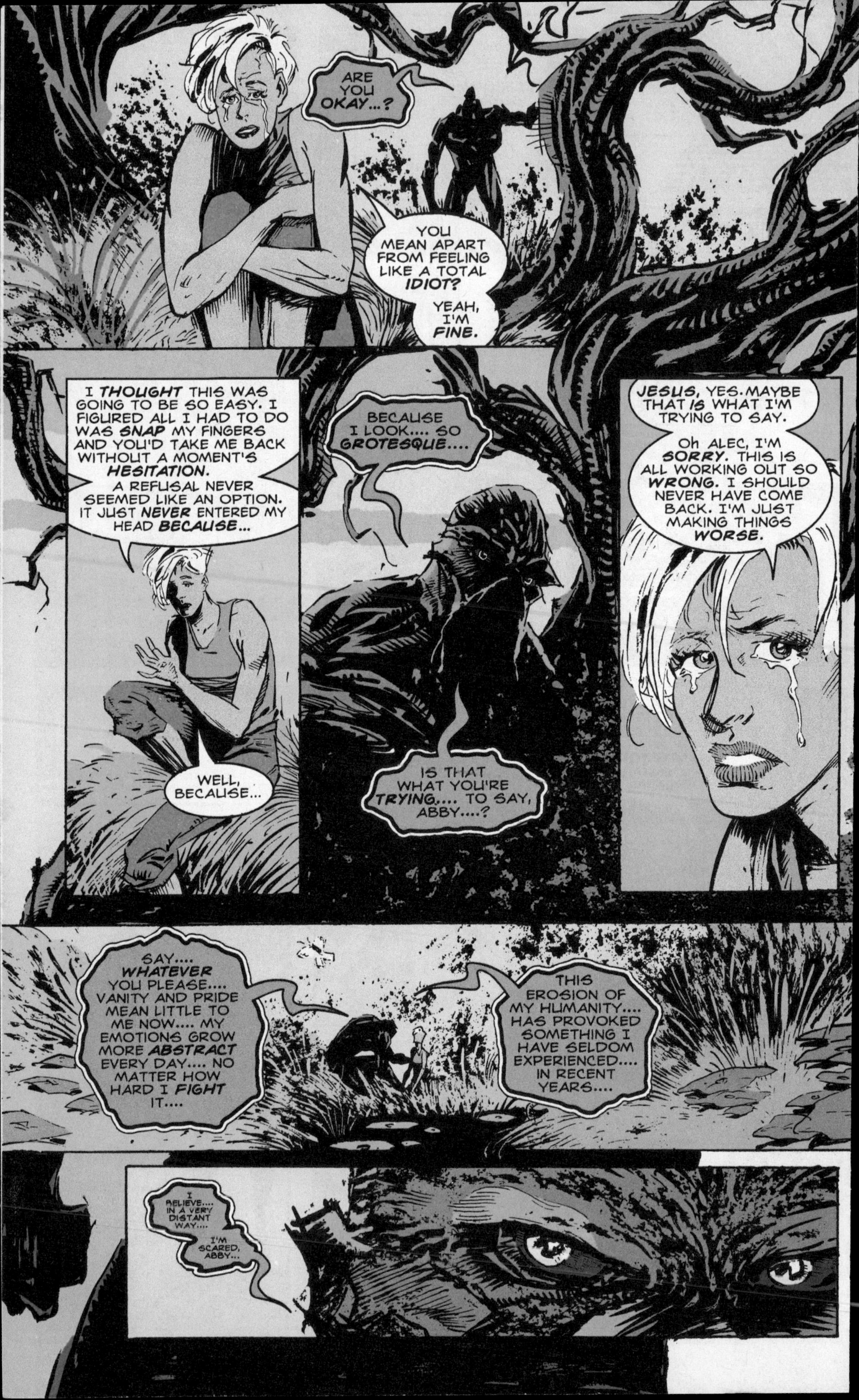

ARE YOU OKAY...?
YOU MEAN APART FROM FEELING LIKE A TOTAL IDIOT?
YEAH, I'M FINE.
I THOUGHT THIS WAS GOING TO BE SO EASY. I FIGURED ALL I HAD TO DO WAS SNAP MY FINGERS AND YOU'D TAKE ME BACK WITHOUT A MOMENT'S HESITATION.
A REFUSAL NEVER SEEMED LIKE AN OPTION. IT JUST NEVER ENTERED MY HEAD BECAUSE...
WELL, BECAUSE...
BECAUSE I LOOK.... SO GROTESQUE....
IS THAT WHAT YOU'RE TRYING.... TO SAY, ABBY....?
JESUS, YES. MAYBE THAT IS WHAT I'M TRYING TO SAY.
Oh ALEC, I'M SORRY. THIS IS ALL WORKING OUT SO WRONG. I SHOULD NEVER HAVE COME BACK. I'M JUST MAKING THINGS WORSE.
SAY.... WHATEVER YOU PLEASE.... VANITY AND PRIDE MEAN LITTLE TO ME NOW.... MY EMOTIONS GROW MORE ABSTRACT EVERY DAY.... NO MATTER HOW HARD I FIGHT IT....
THIS EROSION OF MY HUMANITY.... HAS PROVOKED SOMETHING I HAVE SELDOM EXPERIENCED.... IN RECENT YEARS....
I BELIEVE.... IN A VERY DISTANT WAY....
I'M SCARED, ABBY...

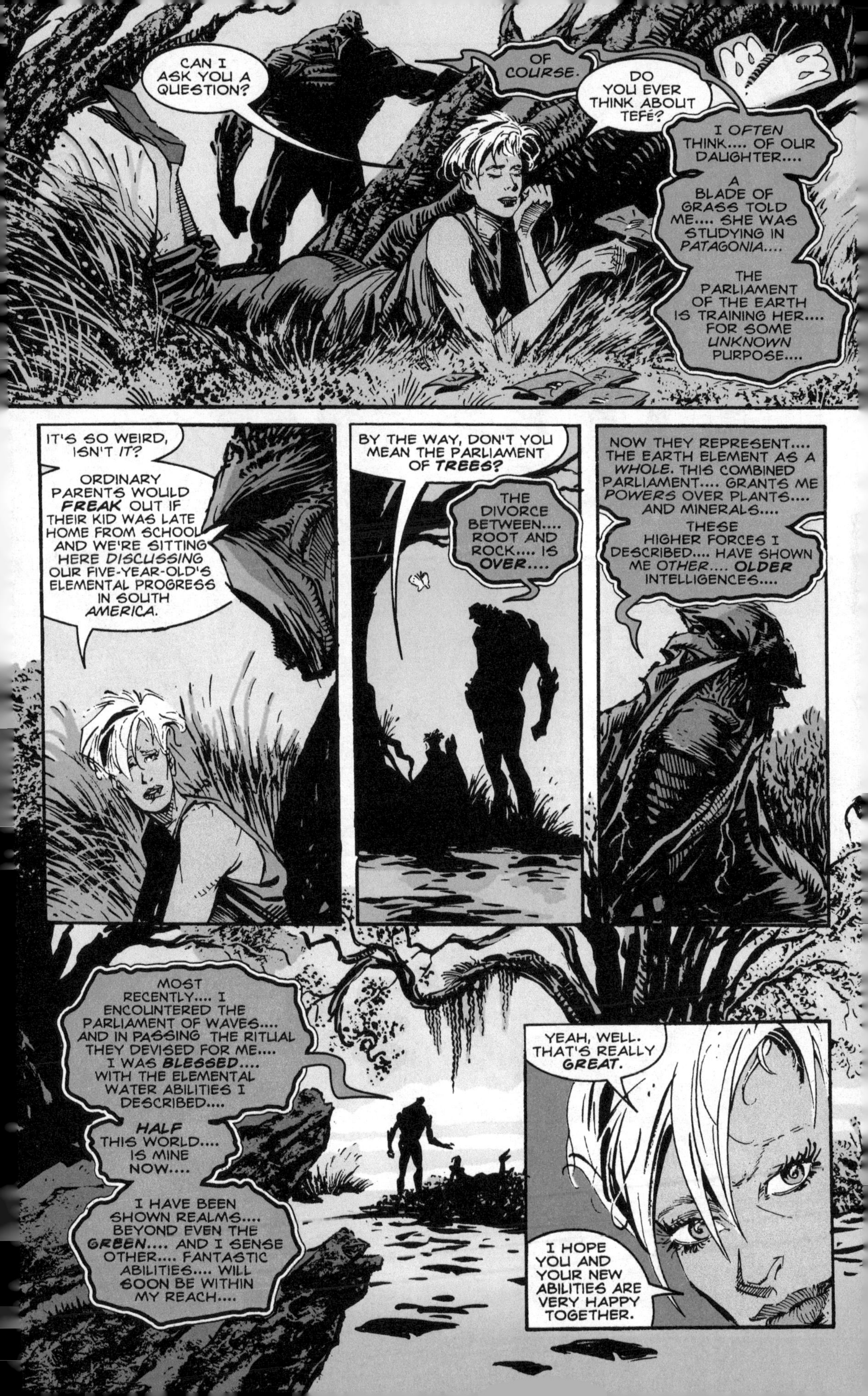

CAN I ASK YOU A QUESTION?
OF COURSE.
DO YOU EVER THINK ABOUT TEFÉ?
I OFTEN THINK.... OF OUR DAUGHTER.... A BLADE OF GRASS TOLD ME.... SHE WAS STUDYING IN PATAGONIA.... THE PARLIAMENT OF THE EARTH IS TRAINING HER.... FOR SOME UNKNOWN PURPOSE....
IT'S SO WEIRD, ISN'T IT? ORDINARY PARENTS WOULD FREAK OUT IF THEIR KID WAS LATE HOME FROM SCHOOL AND WE'RE SITTING HERE DISCUSSING OUR FIVE-YEAR-OLD'S ELEMENTAL PROGRESS IN SOUTH AMERICA.
BY THE WAY, DON'T YOU MEAN THE PARLIAMENT OF TREES?
THE DIVORCE BETWEEN.... ROOT AND ROCK.... IS OVER....
NOW THEY REPRESENT.... THE EARTH ELEMENT AS A WHOLE. THIS COMBINED PARLIAMENT.... GRANTS ME POWERS OVER PLANTS.... AND MINERALS.... THESE HIGHER FORCES I DESCRIBED.... HAVE SHOWN ME OTHER.... OLDER INTELLIGENCES....
MOST RECENTLY.... I ENCOUNTERED THE PARLIAMENT OF WAVES.... AND IN PASSING THE RITUAL THEY DEVISED FOR ME.... I WAS BLESSED.... WITH THE ELEMENTAL WATER ABILITIES I DESCRIBED.... HALF THIS WORLD.... IS MINE NOW.... I HAVE BEEN SHOWN REALMS.... BEYOND EVEN THE GREEN.... AND I SENSE OTHER.... FANTASTIC ABILITIES.... WILL SOON BE WITHIN MY REACH....
YEAH, WELL. THAT'S REALLY GREAT.
I HOPE YOU AND YOUR NEW ABILITIES ARE VERY HAPPY TOGETHER.

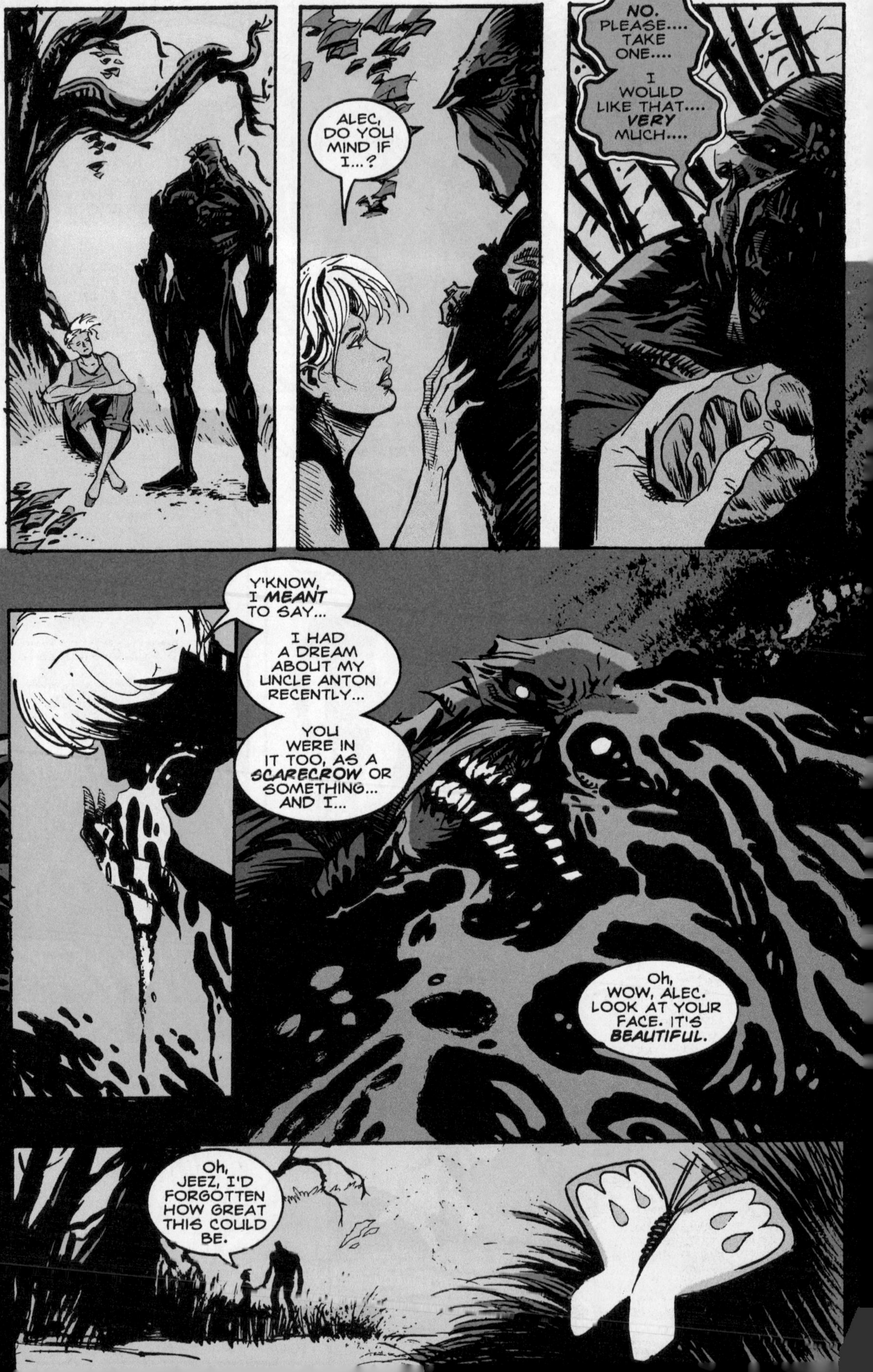
ALEC, DO YOU MIND IF I...?
NO. PLEASE.... TAKE ONE....
I WOULD LIKE THAT.... *VERY* MUCH....
Y'KNOW, I *MEANT* TO SAY...
I HAD A DREAM ABOUT MY UNCLE ANTON RECENTLY...
YOU WERE IN IT TOO, AS A *SCARECROW* OR SOMETHING... AND I...
Oh, WOW, ALEC. LOOK AT YOUR FACE. IT'S *BEAUTIFUL*.
Oh, JEEZ, I'D FORGOTTEN HOW GREAT THIS COULD BE.

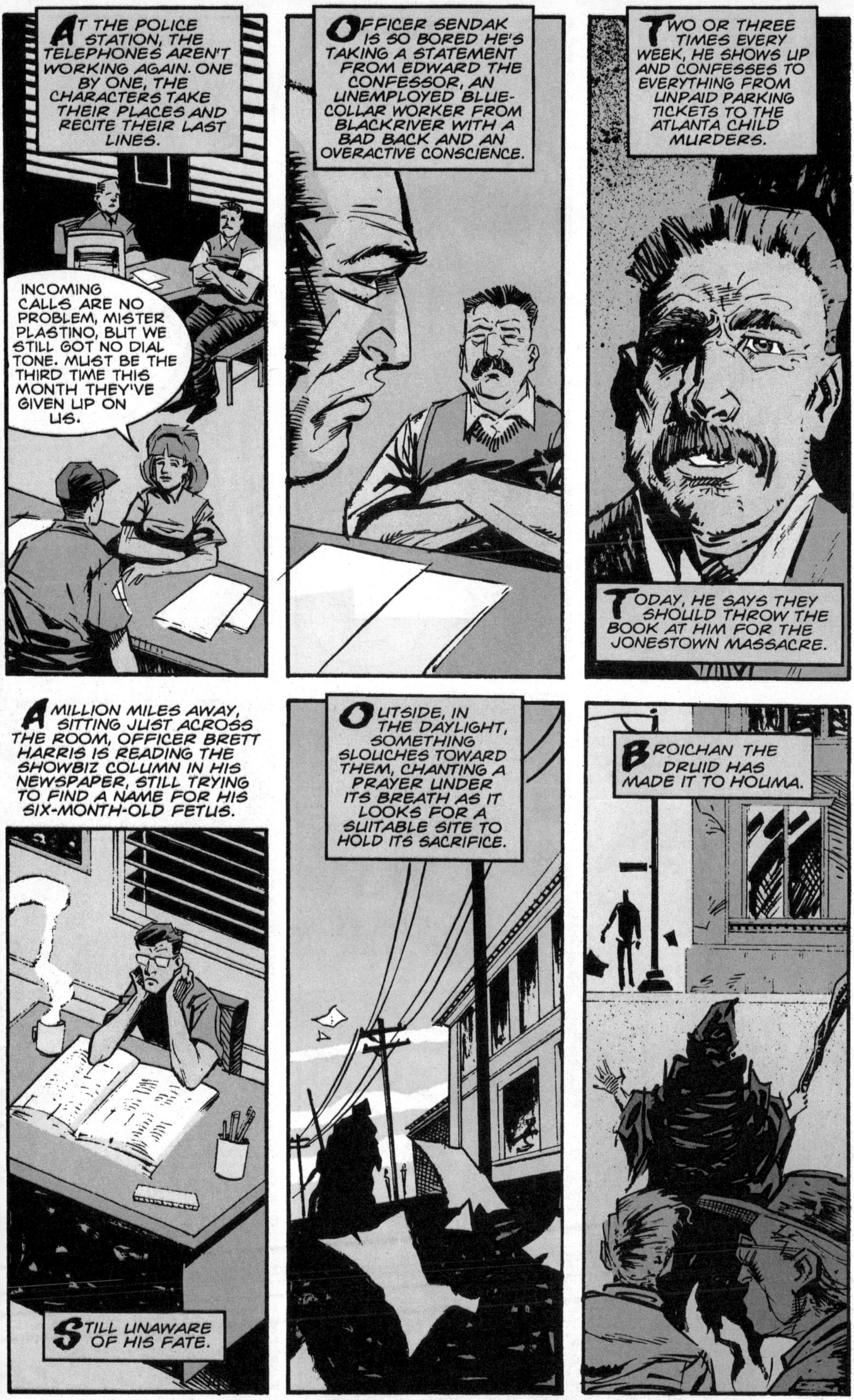
AT THE POLICE STATION, THE TELEPHONES AREN'T WORKING AGAIN. ONE BY ONE, THE CHARACTERS TAKE THEIR PLACES AND RECITE THEIR LAST LINES.
INCOMING CALLS ARE NO PROBLEM, MISTER PLASTINO, BUT WE STILL GOT NO DIAL TONE. MUST BE THE THIRD TIME THIS MONTH THEY'VE GIVEN UP ON US.
OFFICER SENDAK IS SO BORED HE'S TAKING A STATEMENT FROM EDWARD THE CONFESSOR, AN UNEMPLOYED BLUE-COLLAR WORKER FROM BLACKRIVER WITH A BAD BACK AND AN OVERACTIVE CONSCIENCE.
TWO OR THREE TIMES EVERY WEEK, HE SHOWS UP AND CONFESSES TO EVERYTHING FROM UNPAID PARKING TICKETS TO THE ATLANTA CHILD MURDERS.
TODAY, HE SAYS THEY SHOULD THROW THE BOOK AT HIM FOR THE JONESTOWN MASSACRE.
A MILLION MILES AWAY, SITTING JUST ACROSS THE ROOM, OFFICER BRETT HARRIS IS READING THE SHOWBIZ COLUMN IN HIS NEWSPAPER, STILL TRYING TO FIND A NAME FOR HIS SIX-MONTH-OLD FETUS.
STILL UNAWARE OF HIS FATE.
OUTSIDE, IN THE DAYLIGHT, SOMETHING SLOUCHES TOWARD THEM, CHANTING A PRAYER UNDER ITS BREATH AS IT LOOKS FOR A SUITABLE SITE TO HOLD ITS SACRIFICE.
BROICHAN THE DRUID HAS MADE IT TO HOUMA.

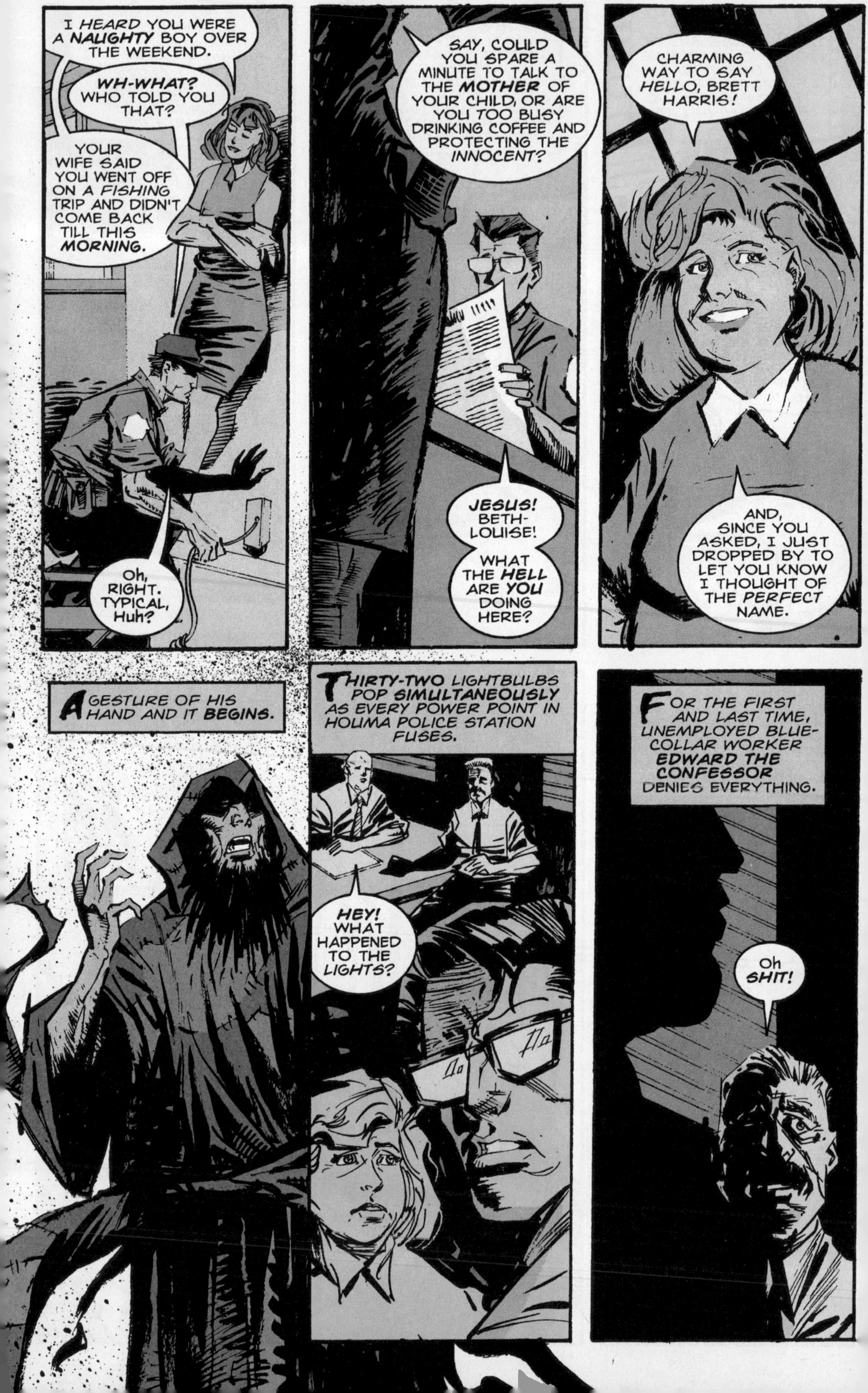
I HEARD YOU WERE A NAUGHTY BOY OVER THE WEEKEND.
WH-WHAT? WHO TOLD YOU THAT?
YOUR WIFE SAID YOU WENT OFF ON A FISHING TRIP AND DIDN'T COME BACK TILL THIS MORNING.
Oh, RIGHT. TYPICAL, Huh?
SAY, COULD YOU SPARE A MINUTE TO TALK TO THE MOTHER OF YOUR CHILD, OR ARE YOU TOO BUSY DRINKING COFFEE AND PROTECTING THE INNOCENT?
JESUS! BETH-LOUISE!
WHAT THE HELL ARE YOU DOING HERE?
CHARMING WAY TO SAY HELLO, BRETT HARRIS!
AND, SINCE YOU ASKED, I JUST DROPPED BY TO LET YOU KNOW I THOUGHT OF THE PERFECT NAME.
A GESTURE OF HIS HAND AND IT BEGINS.
THIRTY-TWO LIGHTBULBS POP SIMULTANEOUSLY AS EVERY POWER POINT IN HOUMA POLICE STATION FUSES.
HEY! WHAT HAPPENED TO THE LIGHTS?
FOR THE FIRST AND LAST TIME, UNEMPLOYED BLUE-COLLAR WORKER EDWARD THE CONFESSOR DENIES EVERYTHING.
Oh SHIT!

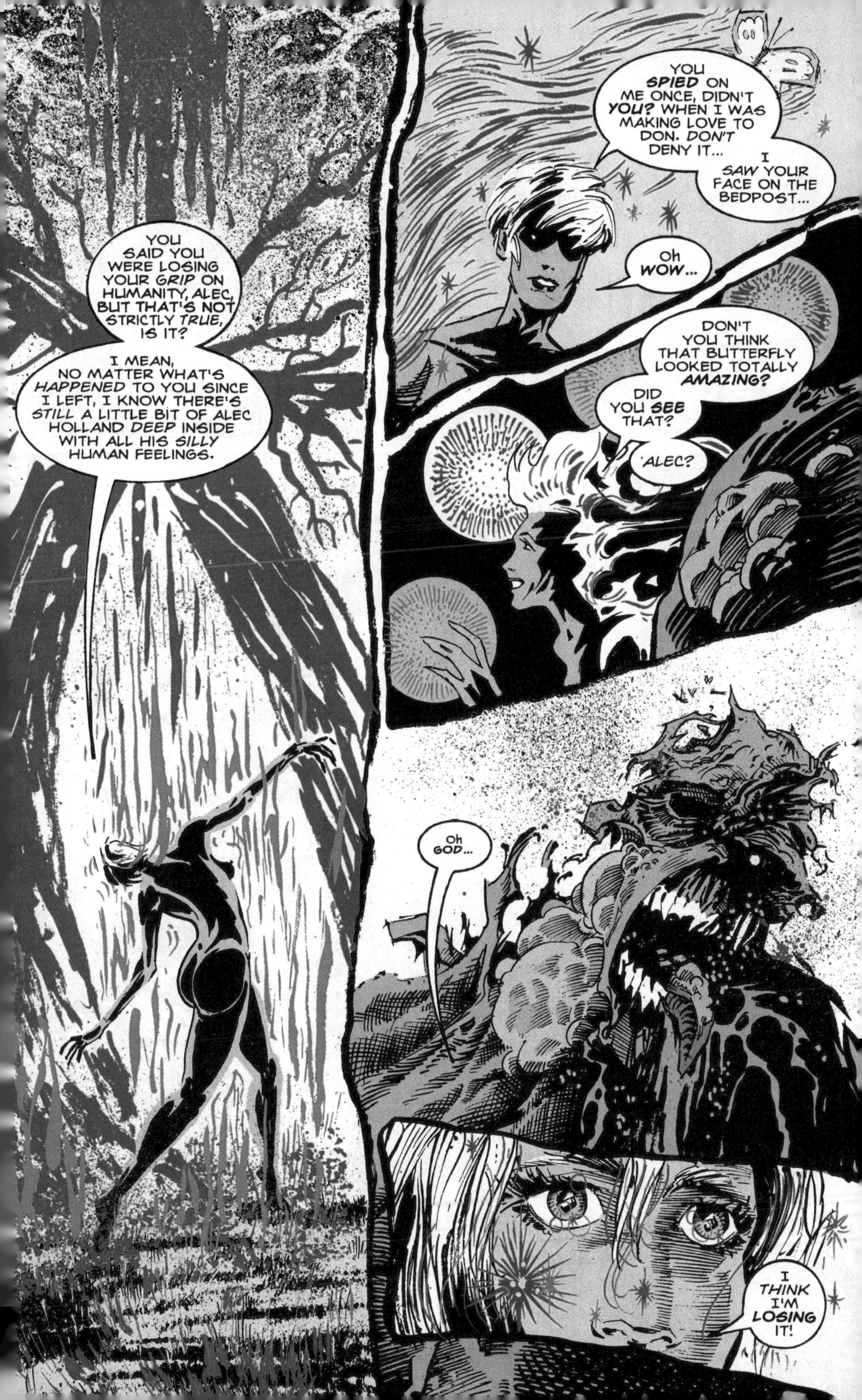
YOU SAID YOU WERE LOSING YOUR GRIP ON HUMANITY, ALEC, BUT THAT'S NOT STRICTLY TRUE, IS IT?
I MEAN, NO MATTER WHAT'S HAPPENED TO YOU SINCE I LEFT, I KNOW THERE'S STILL A LITTLE BIT OF ALEC HOLLAND DEEP INSIDE WITH ALL HIS SILLY HUMAN FEELINGS.
YOU SPIED ON ME ONCE, DIDN'T YOU? WHEN I WAS MAKING LOVE TO DON. DON'T DENY IT...
I SAW YOUR FACE ON THE BEDPOST...
Oh WOW...
DON'T YOU THINK THAT BUTTERFLY LOOKED TOTALLY AMAZING?
DID YOU SEE THAT?
ALEC?
Oh GOD...
I THINK I'M LOSING IT!

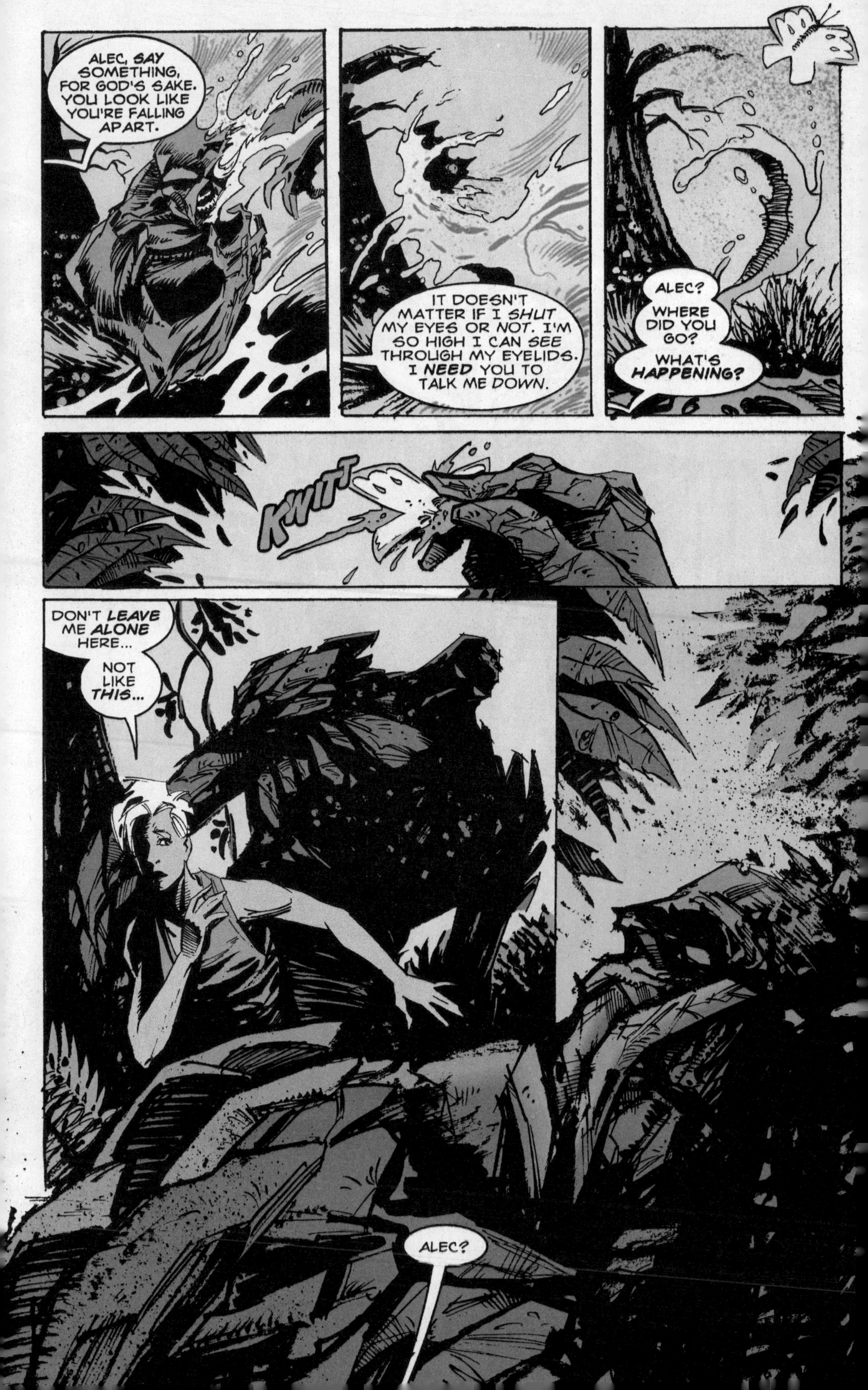
ALEC, SAY SOMETHING, FOR GOD'S SAKE. YOU LOOK LIKE YOU'RE FALLING APART.
IT DOESN'T MATTER IF I SHUT MY EYES OR NOT. I'M SO HIGH I CAN SEE THROUGH MY EYELIDS. I NEED YOU TO TALK ME DOWN.
ALEC?
WHERE DID YOU GO?
WHAT'S HAPPENING?
KWITT
DON'T LEAVE ME ALONE HERE...
NOT LIKE THIS...
ALEC?

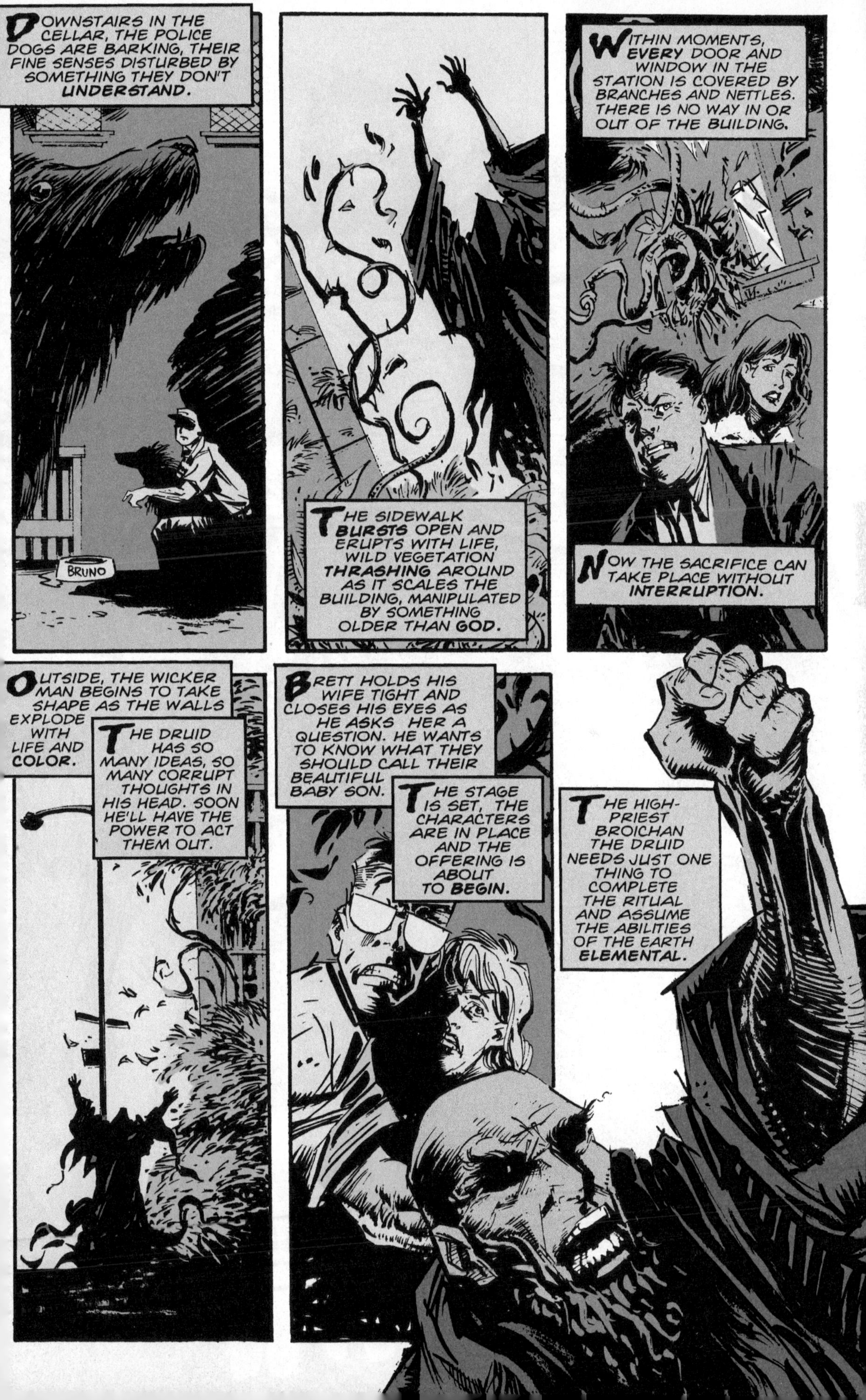
DOWNSTAIRS IN THE CELLAR, THE POLICE DOGS ARE BARKING, THEIR FINE SENSES DISTURBED BY SOMETHING THEY DON'T UNDERSTAND.
BRUNO
THE SIDEWALK BURSTS OPEN AND ERUPTS WITH LIFE, WILD VEGETATION THRASHING AROUND AS IT SCALES THE BUILDING, MANIPULATED BY SOMETHING OLDER THAN GOD.
WITHIN MOMENTS, EVERY DOOR AND WINDOW IN THE STATION IS COVERED BY BRANCHES AND NETTLES. THERE IS NO WAY IN OR OUT OF THE BUILDING.
NOW THE SACRIFICE CAN TAKE PLACE WITHOUT INTERRUPTION.
OUTSIDE, THE WICKER MAN BEGINS TO TAKE SHAPE AS THE WALLS EXPLODE WITH LIFE AND COLOR.
THE DRUID HAS SO MANY IDEAS, SO MANY CORRUPT THOUGHTS IN HIS HEAD. SOON HE'LL HAVE THE POWER TO ACT THEM OUT.
BRETT HOLDS HIS WIFE TIGHT AND CLOSES HIS EYES AS HE ASKS HER A QUESTION. HE WANTS TO KNOW WHAT THEY SHOULD CALL THEIR BEAUTIFUL BABY SON.
THE STAGE IS SET, THE CHARACTERS ARE IN PLACE AND THE OFFERING IS ABOUT TO BEGIN.
THE HIGH-PRIEST BROICHAN THE DRUID NEEDS JUST ONE THING TO COMPLETE THE RITUAL AND ASSUME THE ABILITIES OF THE EARTH ELEMENTAL.

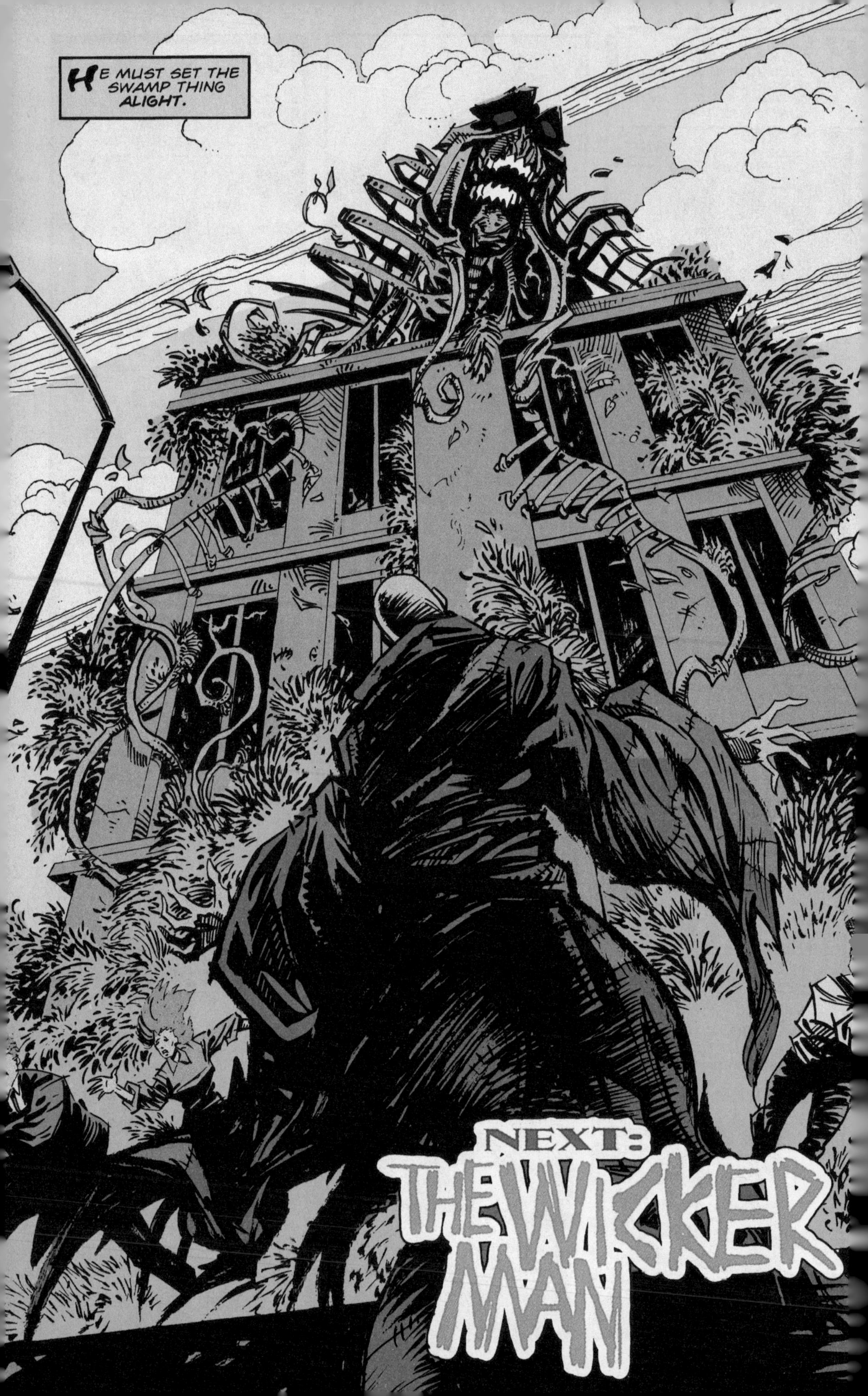
HE MUST SET THE SWAMP THING ALIGHT.
NEXT:
THE WICKER MAN

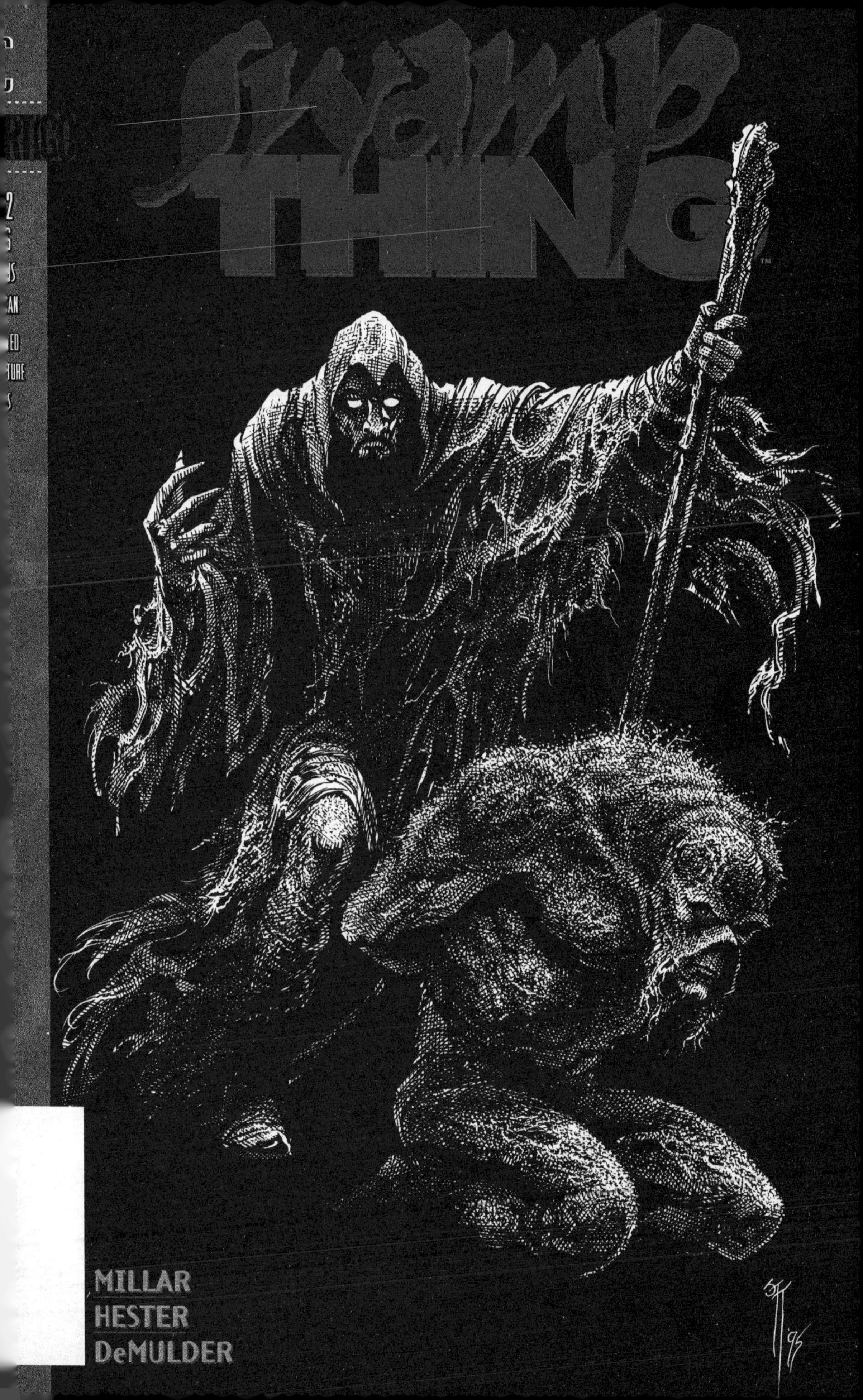
SWAMP
THING™
MILLAR
HESTER
DeMULDER

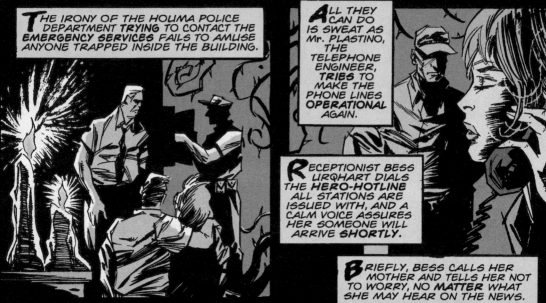

THE IRONY OF THE HOUMA POLICE DEPARTMENT **TRYING** TO CONTACT THE EMERGENCY SERVICES FAILS TO AMUSE ANYONE TRAPPED INSIDE THE BUILDING.

ALL THEY CAN DO IS SWEAT AS Mr. PLASTINO, THE TELEPHONE ENGINEER, **TRIES** TO MAKE THE PHONE LINES **OPERATIONAL** AGAIN.

RECEPTIONIST BESS URQHART DIALS THE **HERO-HOTLINE** ALL STATIONS ARE ISSUED WITH, AND A CALM VOICE ASSURES HER SOMEONE WILL ARRIVE **SHORTLY.**

BRIEFLY, BESS CALLS HER MOTHER AND TELLS HER NOT TO WORRY, NO **MATTER** WHAT SHE MAY HEAR ON THE NEWS.

WAITING PATIENTLY, OFFICER BRETT HARRIS WONDERS HOW HE CAN **POSSIBLY** EXPLAIN THIS SITUATION TO HIS ELDER HALF BROTHER, TRYING HARD NOT TO EAVESDROP ON Mr. PLASTINO'S **WHIMPERING** CALL HOME.

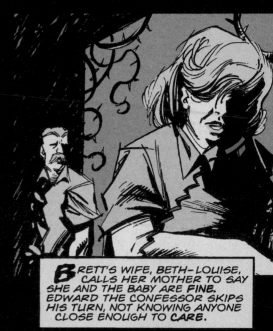

BRETT'S WIFE, BETH-LOUISE, CALLS HER MOTHER TO SAY SHE AND THE BABY ARE **FINE.** EDWARD THE CONFESSOR SKIPS HIS TURN, NOT KNOWING ANYONE CLOSE ENOUGH TO **CARE.**

OFFICER SENDAK IS THE **LAST** TO CALL HOME, UNABLE TO THINK OF A CLEVER WAY TO BEGIN WHAT MIGHT **CONCEIVABLY** BE THE LAST TELEPHONE CALL OF HIS **LIFE.**

UNDER THE CIRCUMSTANCES, IT'S HARDLY SURPRISING.

Ahh, HILARY, SWEETHEART...

...YOU REMEMBER I WAS COMPLAINING THAT NOTHING EXCITING EVER HAPPENED AT THE STATION?

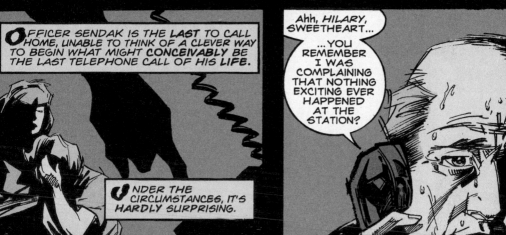

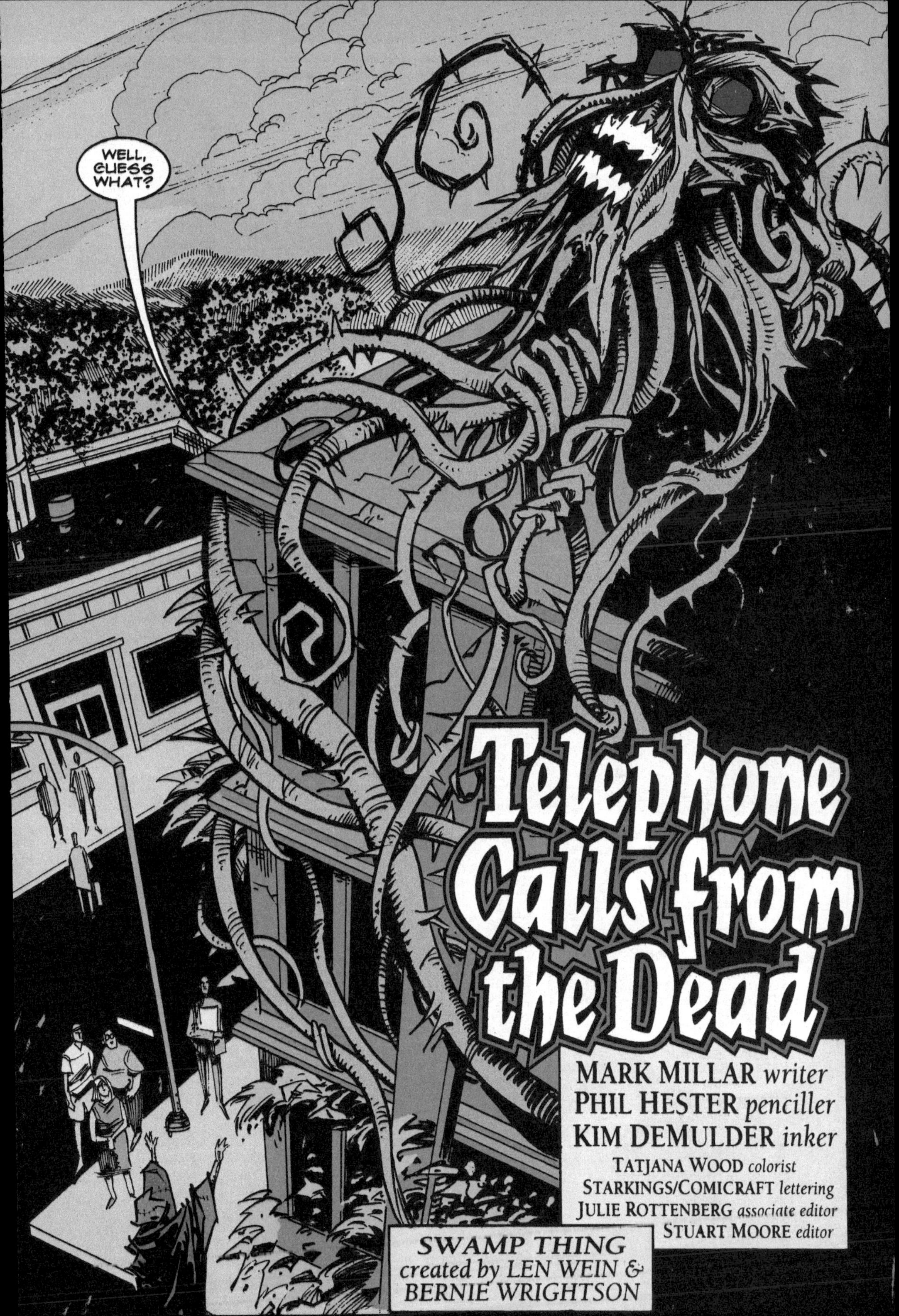
WELL, GUESS WHAT?
Telephone Calls from the Dead
MARK MILLAR writer
PHIL HESTER penciller
KIM DEMULDER inker
TATJANA WOOD colorist
STARKINGS/COMICRAFT lettering
JULIE ROTTENBERG associate editor
STUART MOORE editor
SWAMP THING created by LEN WEIN & BERNIE WRIGHTSON

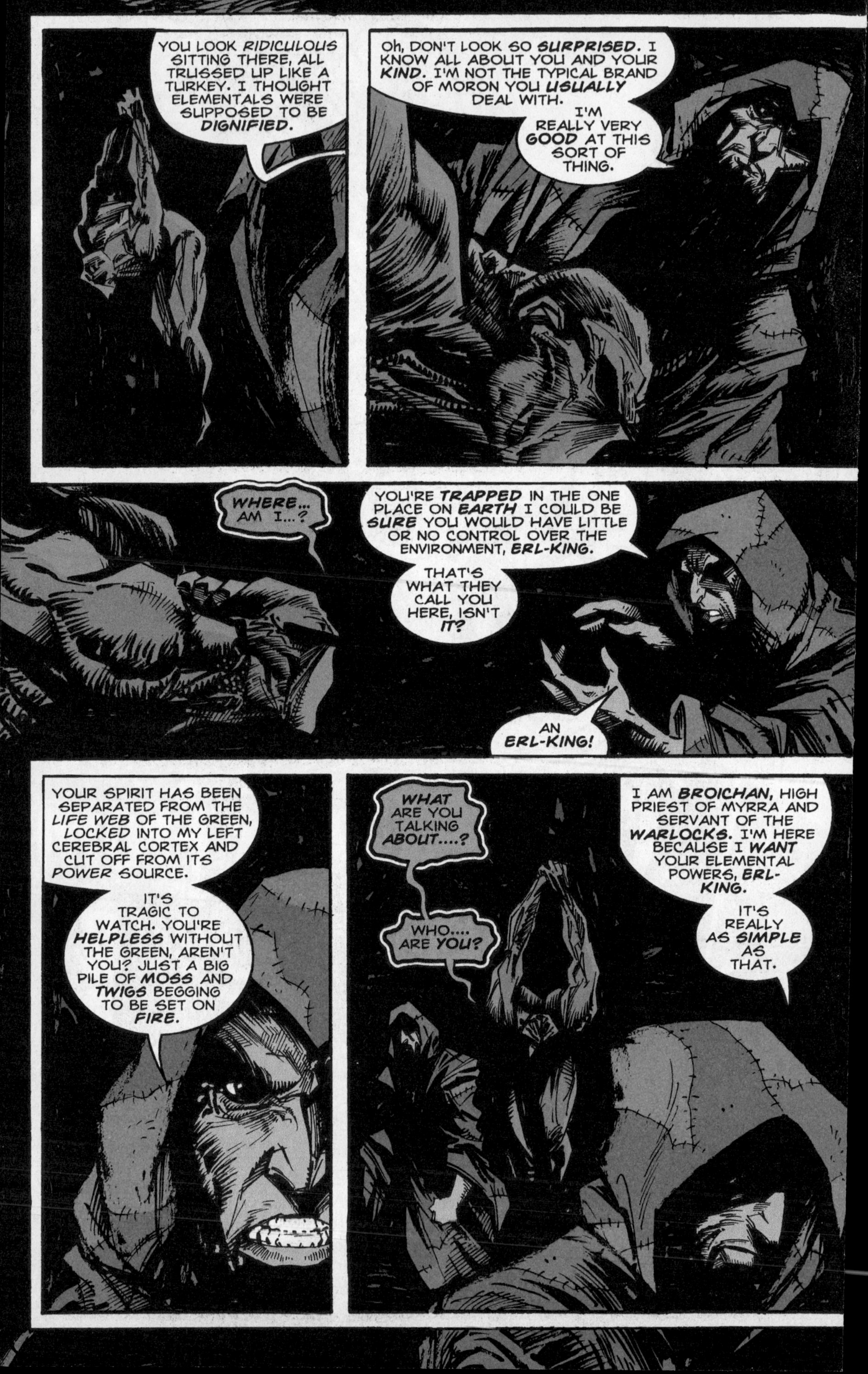

YOU LOOK RIDICULOUS SITTING THERE, ALL TRUSSED UP LIKE A TURKEY. I THOUGHT ELEMENTALS WERE SUPPOSED TO BE DIGNIFIED.
Oh, DON'T LOOK SO SURPRISED. I KNOW ALL ABOUT YOU AND YOUR KIND. I'M NOT THE TYPICAL BRAND OF MORON YOU USUALLY DEAL WITH.
I'M REALLY VERY GOOD AT THIS SORT OF THING.
WHERE... AM I...?
YOU'RE TRAPPED IN THE ONE PLACE ON EARTH I COULD BE SURE YOU WOULD HAVE LITTLE OR NO CONTROL OVER THE ENVIRONMENT, ERL-KING.
THAT'S WHAT THEY CALL YOU HERE, ISN'T IT?
AN ERL-KING!
YOUR SPIRIT HAS BEEN SEPARATED FROM THE LIFE WEB OF THE GREEN, LOCKED INTO MY LEFT CEREBRAL CORTEX AND CUT OFF FROM ITS POWER SOURCE.
IT'S TRAGIC TO WATCH. YOU'RE HELPLESS WITHOUT THE GREEN, AREN'T YOU? JUST A BIG PILE OF MOSS AND TWIGS BEGGING TO BE SET ON FIRE.
WHAT ARE YOU TALKING ABOUT....?
WHO.... ARE YOU?
I AM BROICHAN, HIGH PRIEST OF MYRRA AND SERVANT OF THE WARLOCKS. I'M HERE BECAUSE I WANT YOUR ELEMENTAL POWERS, ERL-KING.
IT'S REALLY AS SIMPLE AS THAT.

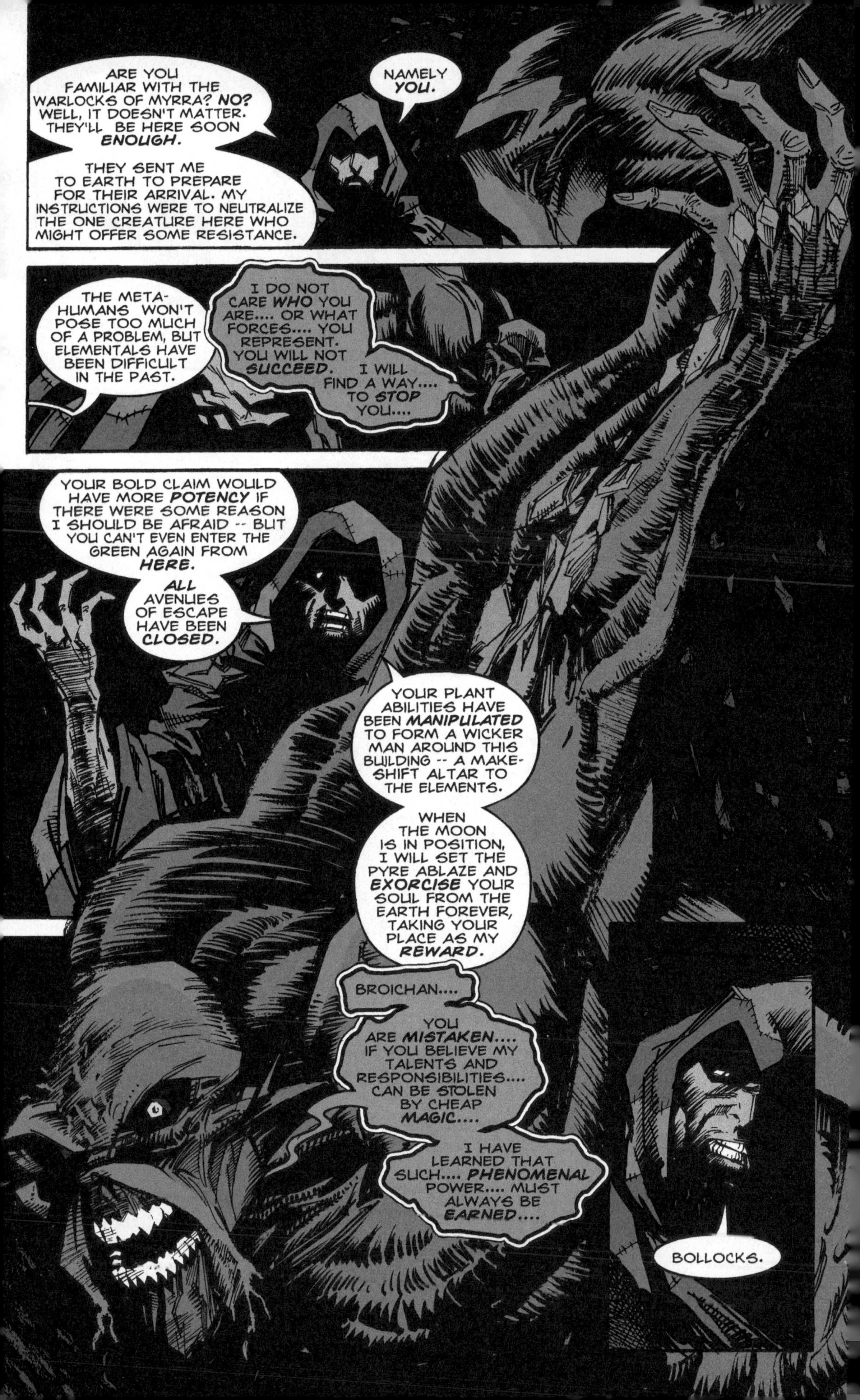

ARE YOU FAMILIAR WITH THE WARLOCKS OF MYRRA? NO? WELL, IT DOESN'T MATTER. THEY'LL BE HERE SOON ENOUGH.
THEY SENT ME TO EARTH TO PREPARE FOR THEIR ARRIVAL. MY INSTRUCTIONS WERE TO NEUTRALIZE THE ONE CREATURE HERE WHO MIGHT OFFER SOME RESISTANCE.
NAMELY YOU.
THE META-HUMANS WON'T POSE TOO MUCH OF A PROBLEM, BUT ELEMENTALS HAVE BEEN DIFFICULT IN THE PAST.
I DO NOT CARE WHO YOU ARE.... OR WHAT FORCES.... YOU REPRESENT. YOU WILL NOT SUCCEED.
I WILL FIND A WAY.... TO STOP YOU....
YOUR BOLD CLAIM WOULD HAVE MORE POTENCY IF THERE WERE SOME REASON I SHOULD BE AFRAID -- BUT YOU CAN'T EVEN ENTER THE GREEN AGAIN FROM HERE.
ALL AVENUES OF ESCAPE HAVE BEEN CLOSED.
YOUR PLANT ABILITIES HAVE BEEN MANIPULATED TO FORM A WICKER MAN AROUND THIS BUILDING -- A MAKE-SHIFT ALTAR TO THE ELEMENTS.
WHEN THE MOON IS IN POSITION, I WILL SET THE PYRE ABLAZE AND EXORCISE YOUR SOUL FROM THE EARTH FOREVER, TAKING YOUR PLACE AS MY REWARD.
BROICHAN....
YOU ARE MISTAKEN.... IF YOU BELIEVE MY TALENTS AND RESPONSIBILITIES.... CAN BE STOLEN BY CHEAP MAGIC....
I HAVE LEARNED THAT SUCH.... PHENOMENAL POWER.... MUST ALWAYS BE EARNED....
BOLLOCKS.

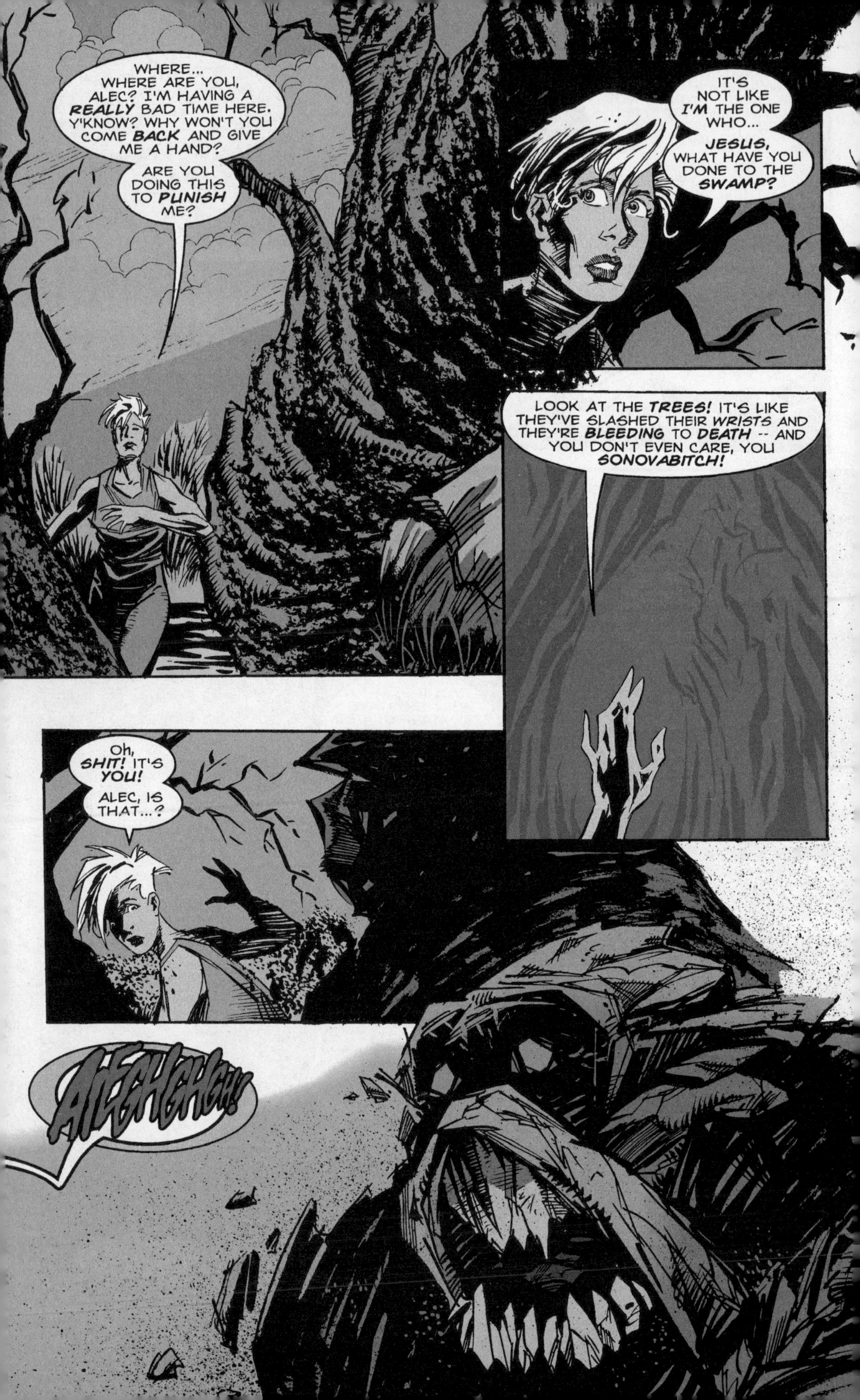
WHERE... WHERE ARE YOU, ALEC? I'M HAVING A REALLY BAD TIME HERE. Y'KNOW? WHY WON'T YOU COME BACK AND GIVE ME A HAND?
ARE YOU DOING THIS TO PUNISH ME?
IT'S NOT LIKE I'M THE ONE WHO...
JESUS, WHAT HAVE YOU DONE TO THE SWAMP?
LOOK AT THE TREES! IT'S LIKE THEY'VE SLASHED THEIR WRISTS AND THEY'RE BLEEDING TO DEATH -- AND YOU DON'T EVEN CARE, YOU SONOVABITCH!
Oh, SHIT! IT'S YOU!
ALEC, IS THAT...?
AIEGHGHGH!!

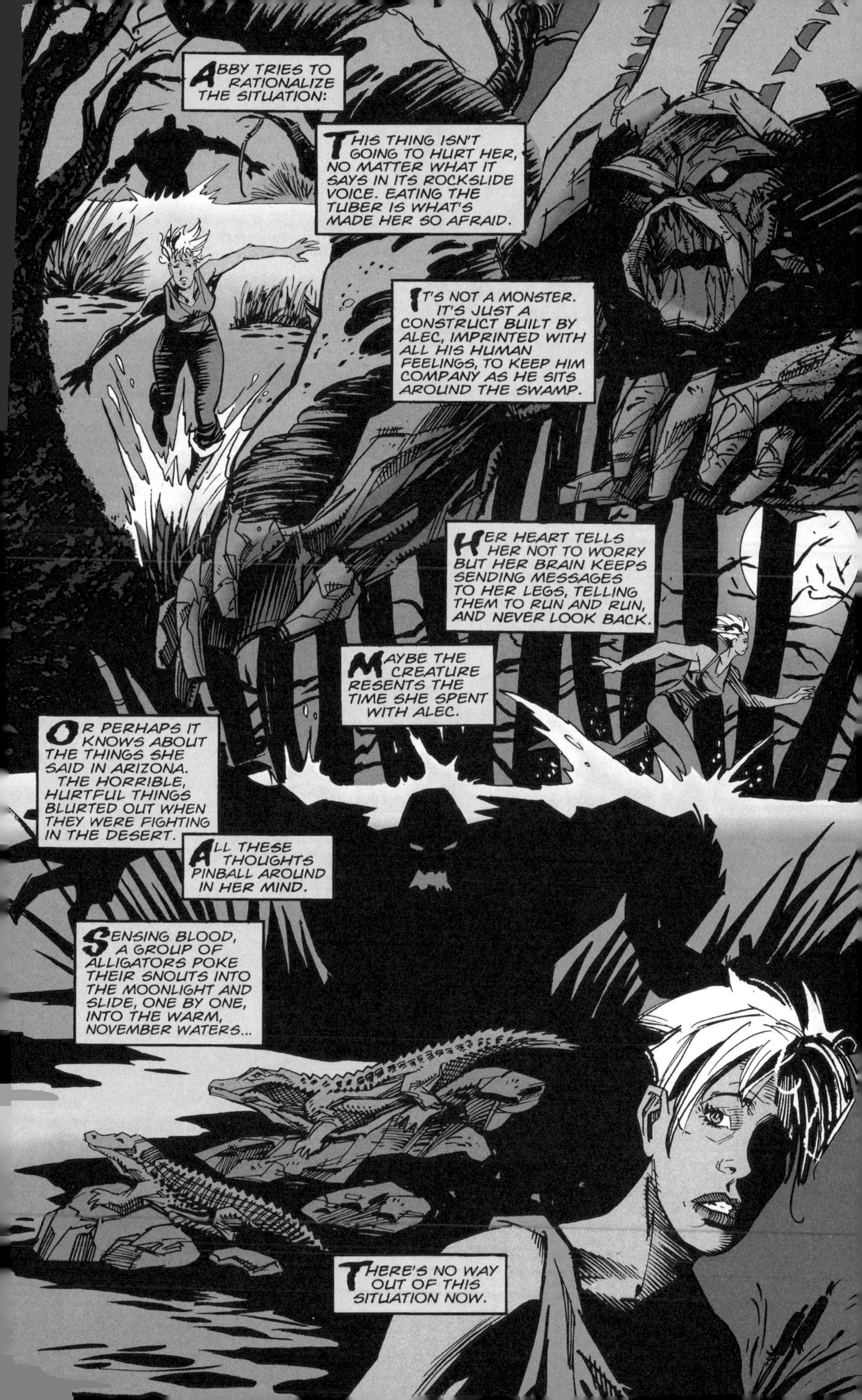
ABBY TRIES TO RATIONALIZE THE SITUATION:
THIS THING ISN'T GOING TO HURT HER, NO MATTER WHAT IT SAYS IN ITS ROCKSLIDE VOICE. EATING THE TUBER IS WHAT'S MADE HER SO AFRAID.
IT'S NOT A MONSTER. IT'S JUST A CONSTRUCT BUILT BY ALEC, IMPRINTED WITH ALL HIS HUMAN FEELINGS, TO KEEP HIM COMPANY AS HE SITS AROUND THE SWAMP.
HER HEART TELLS HER NOT TO WORRY BUT HER BRAIN KEEPS SENDING MESSAGES TO HER LEGS, TELLING THEM TO RUN AND RUN, AND NEVER LOOK BACK.
MAYBE THE CREATURE RESENTS THE TIME SHE SPENT WITH ALEC.
OR PERHAPS IT KNOWS ABOUT THE THINGS SHE SAID IN ARIZONA. THE HORRIBLE, HURTFUL THINGS BLURTED OUT WHEN THEY WERE FIGHTING IN THE DESERT.
ALL THESE THOUGHTS PINBALL AROUND IN HER MIND.
SENSING BLOOD, A GROUP OF ALLIGATORS POKE THEIR SNOUTS INTO THE MOONLIGHT AND SLIDE, ONE BY ONE, INTO THE WARM, NOVEMBER WATERS...
THERE'S NO WAY OUT OF THIS SITUATION NOW.

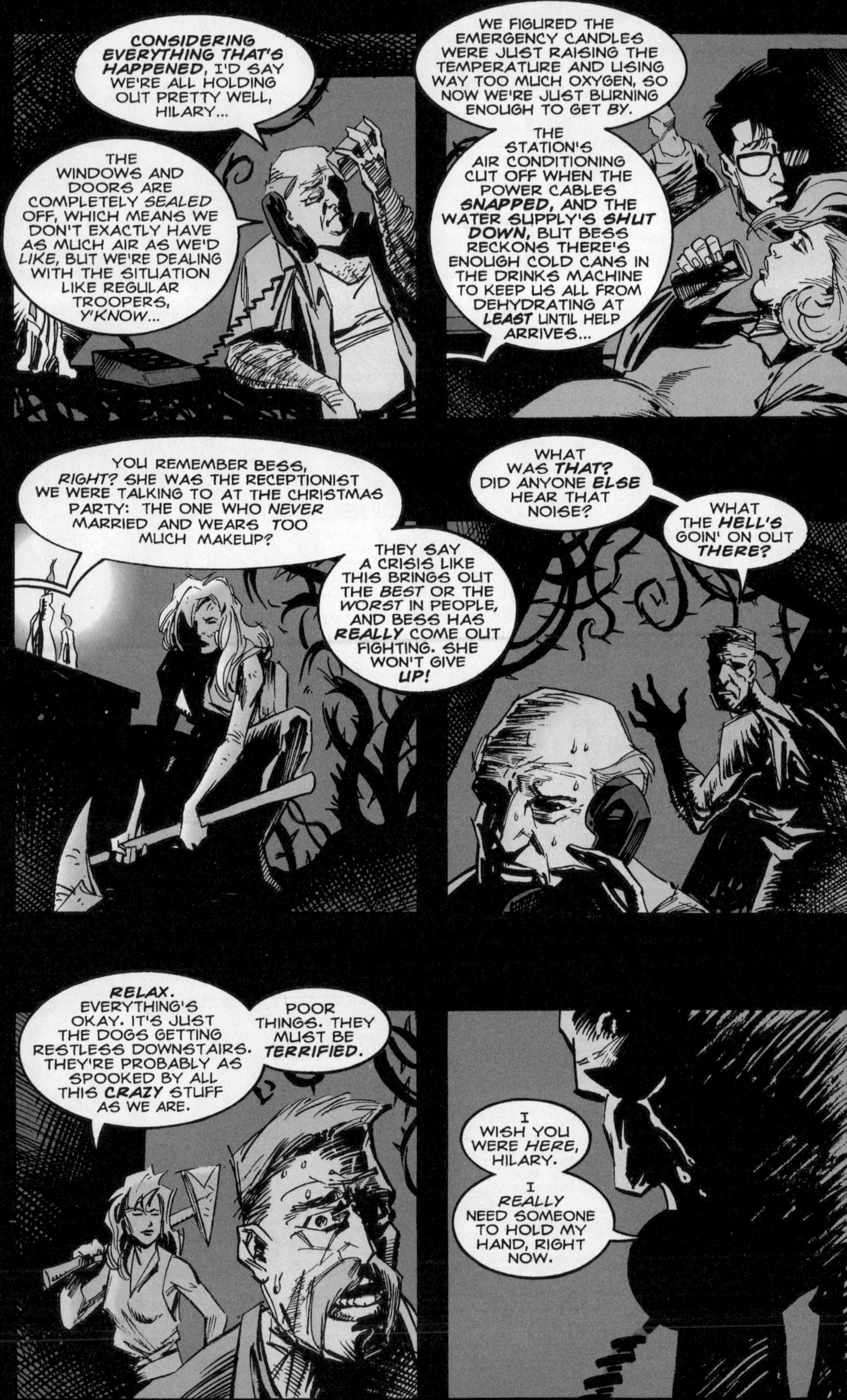
CONSIDERING EVERYTHING THAT'S HAPPENED, I'D SAY WE'RE ALL HOLDING OUT PRETTY WELL, HILARY...
THE WINDOWS AND DOORS ARE COMPLETELY SEALED OFF, WHICH MEANS WE DON'T EXACTLY HAVE AS MUCH AIR AS WE'D LIKE, BUT WE'RE DEALING WITH THE SITUATION LIKE REGULAR TROOPERS, Y'KNOW...
WE FIGURED THE EMERGENCY CANDLES WERE JUST RAISING THE TEMPERATURE AND USING WAY TOO MUCH OXYGEN, SO NOW WE'RE JUST BURNING ENOUGH TO GET BY.
THE STATION'S AIR CONDITIONING CUT OFF WHEN THE POWER CABLES SNAPPED, AND THE WATER SUPPLY'S SHUT DOWN, BUT BESS RECKONS THERE'S ENOUGH COLD CANS IN THE DRINKS MACHINE TO KEEP US ALL FROM DEHYDRATING AT LEAST UNTIL HELP ARRIVES...
YOU REMEMBER BESS, RIGHT? SHE WAS THE RECEPTIONIST WE WERE TALKING TO AT THE CHRISTMAS PARTY: THE ONE WHO NEVER MARRIED AND WEARS TOO MUCH MAKEUP?
THEY SAY A CRISIS LIKE THIS BRINGS OUT THE BEST OR THE WORST IN PEOPLE, AND BESS HAS REALLY COME OUT FIGHTING. SHE WON'T GIVE UP!
WHAT WAS THAT? DID ANYONE ELSE HEAR THAT NOISE?
WHAT THE HELL'S GOIN' ON OUT THERE?
RELAX. EVERYTHING'S OKAY. IT'S JUST THE DOGS GETTING RESTLESS DOWNSTAIRS. THEY'RE PROBABLY AS SPOOKED BY ALL THIS CRAZY STUFF AS WE ARE.
POOR THINGS. THEY MUST BE TERRIFIED.
I WISH YOU WERE HERE, HILARY.
I REALLY NEED SOMEONE TO HOLD MY HAND, RIGHT NOW.

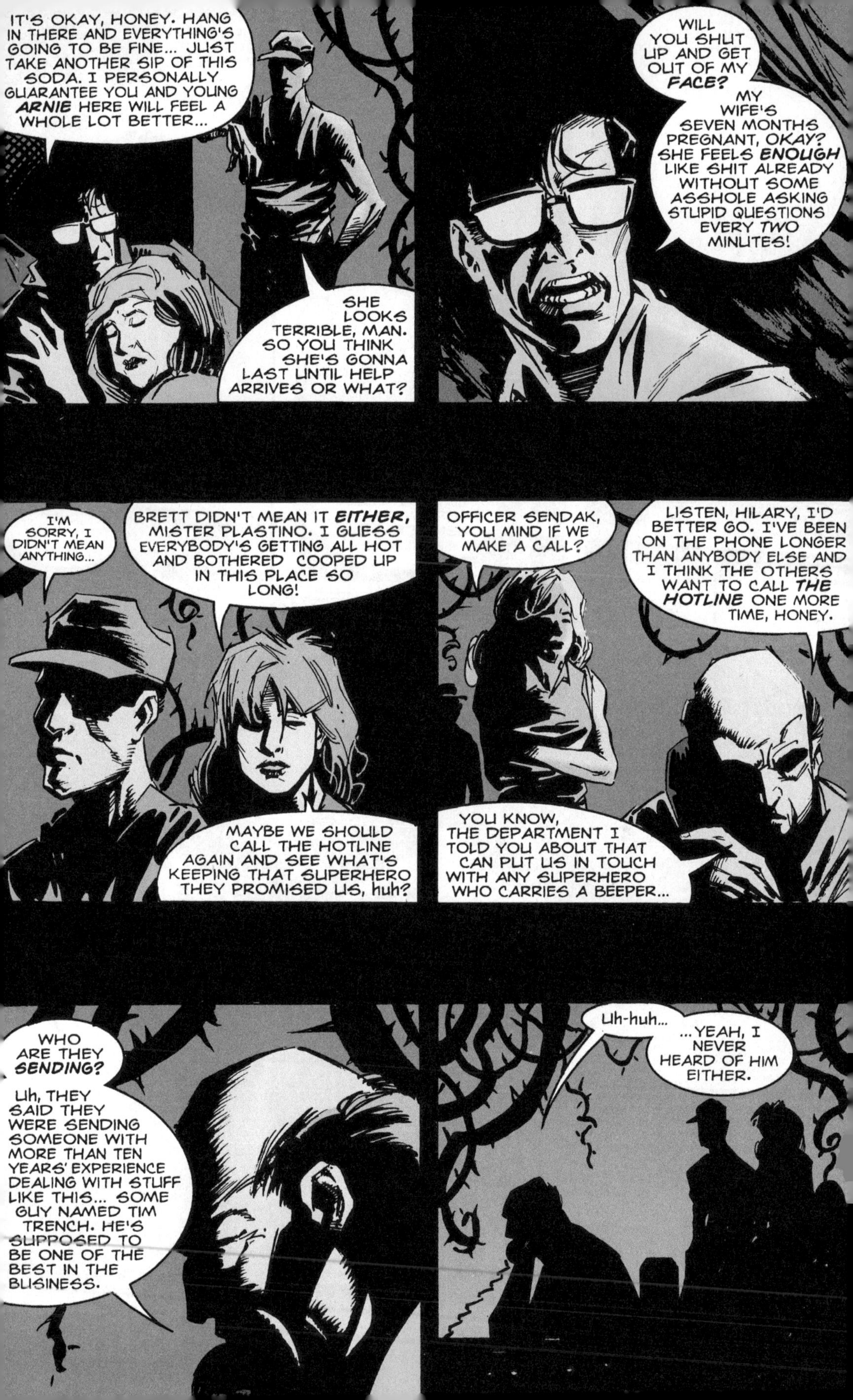
IT'S OKAY, HONEY. HANG IN THERE AND EVERYTHING'S GOING TO BE FINE... JUST TAKE ANOTHER SIP OF THIS SODA. I PERSONALLY GUARANTEE YOU AND YOUNG ARNIE HERE WILL FEEL A WHOLE LOT BETTER...
SHE LOOKS TERRIBLE, MAN. SO YOU THINK SHE'S GONNA LAST UNTIL HELP ARRIVES OR WHAT?
WILL YOU SHUT UP AND GET OUT OF MY FACE?
MY WIFE'S SEVEN MONTHS PREGNANT, OKAY? SHE FEELS ENOUGH LIKE SHIT ALREADY WITHOUT SOME ASSHOLE ASKING STUPID QUESTIONS EVERY TWO MINUTES!
I'M SORRY, I DIDN'T MEAN ANYTHING...
BRETT DIDN'T MEAN IT EITHER, MISTER PLASTINO. I GUESS EVERYBODY'S GETTING ALL HOT AND BOTHERED COOPED UP IN THIS PLACE SO LONG!
MAYBE WE SHOULD CALL THE HOTLINE AGAIN AND SEE WHAT'S KEEPING THAT SUPERHERO THEY PROMISED US, huh?
OFFICER SENDAK, YOU MIND IF WE MAKE A CALL?
LISTEN, HILARY, I'D BETTER GO. I'VE BEEN ON THE PHONE LONGER THAN ANYBODY ELSE AND I THINK THE OTHERS WANT TO CALL THE HOTLINE ONE MORE TIME, HONEY.
YOU KNOW, THE DEPARTMENT I TOLD YOU ABOUT THAT CAN PUT US IN TOUCH WITH ANY SUPERHERO WHO CARRIES A BEEPER...
WHO ARE THEY SENDING?
Uh, THEY SAID THEY WERE SENDING SOMEONE WITH MORE THAN TEN YEARS' EXPERIENCE DEALING WITH STUFF LIKE THIS... SOME GUY NAMED TIM TRENCH. HE'S SUPPOSED TO BE ONE OF THE BEST IN THE BUSINESS.
Uh-huh...
...YEAH, I NEVER HEARD OF HIM EITHER.

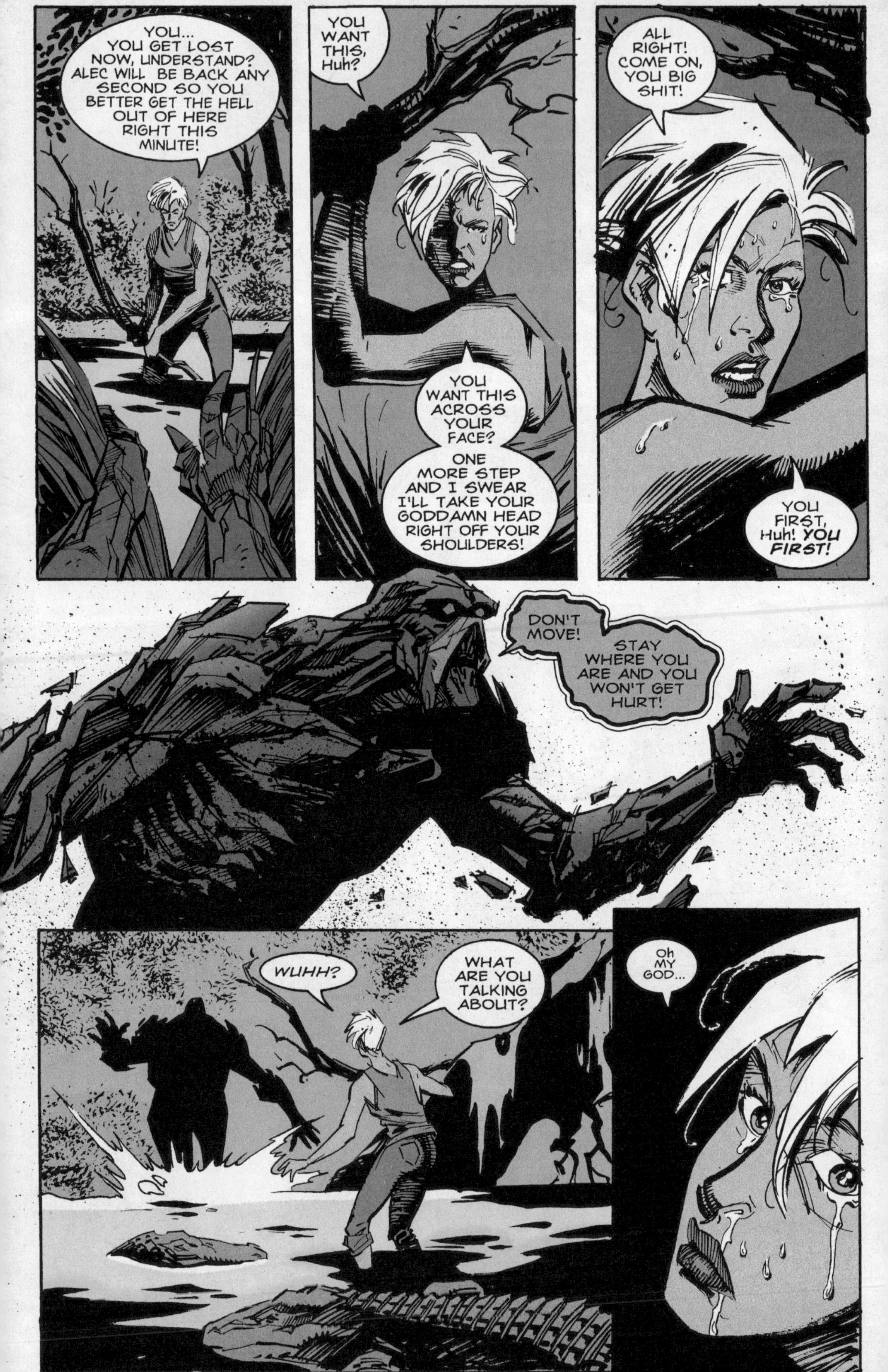
YOU... YOU GET LOST NOW, UNDERSTAND? ALEC WILL BE BACK ANY SECOND SO YOU BETTER GET THE HELL OUT OF HERE RIGHT THIS MINUTE!
YOU WANT THIS, Huh?
YOU WANT THIS ACROSS YOUR FACE?
ONE MORE STEP AND I SWEAR I'LL TAKE YOUR GODDAMN HEAD RIGHT OFF YOUR SHOULDERS!
ALL RIGHT! COME ON, YOU BIG SHIT!
YOU FIRST, Huh! YOU FIRST!
DON'T MOVE!
STAY WHERE YOU ARE AND YOU WON'T GET HURT!
WUHH?
WHAT ARE YOU TALKING ABOUT?
Oh MY GOD...

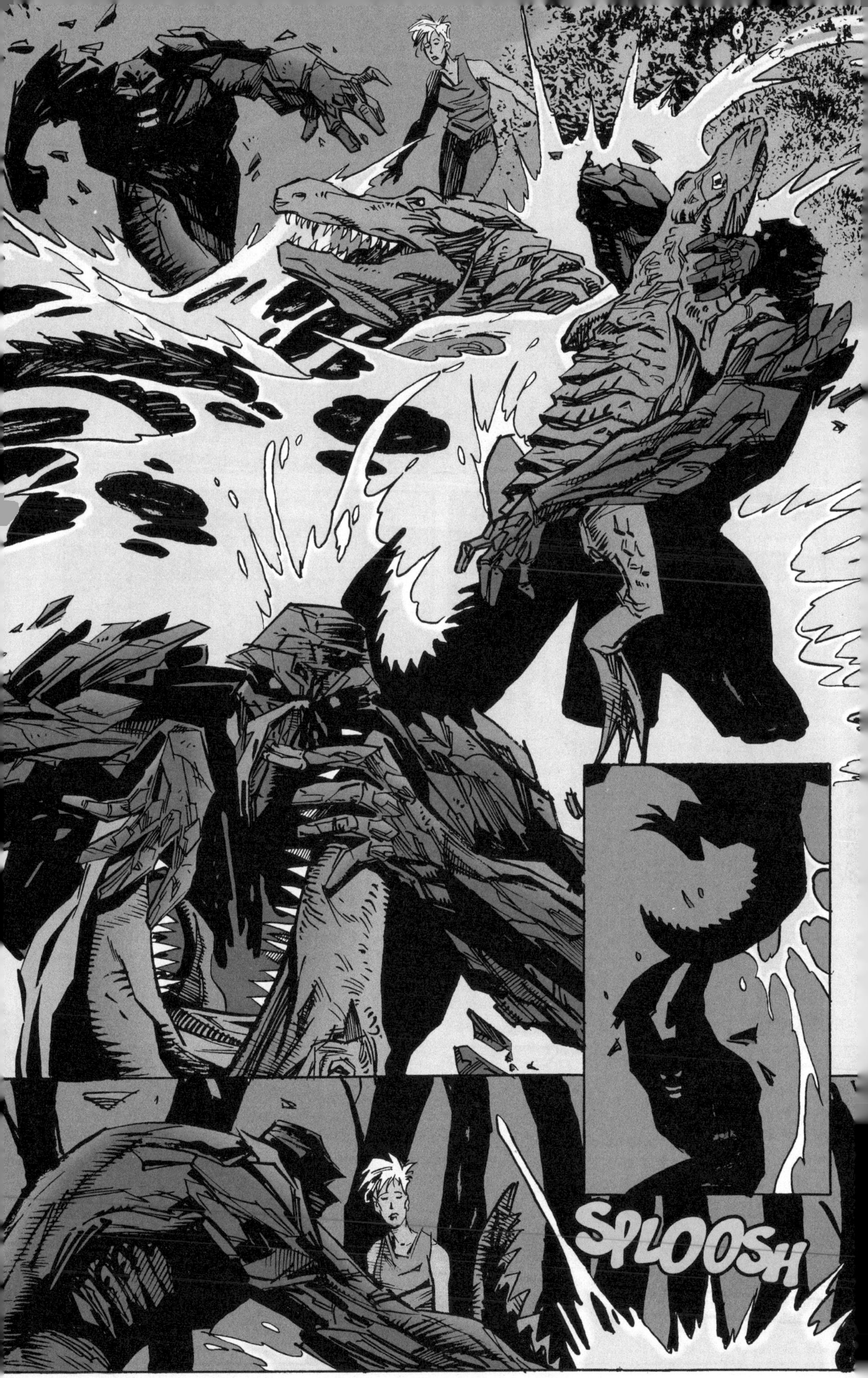
SPLOOSH

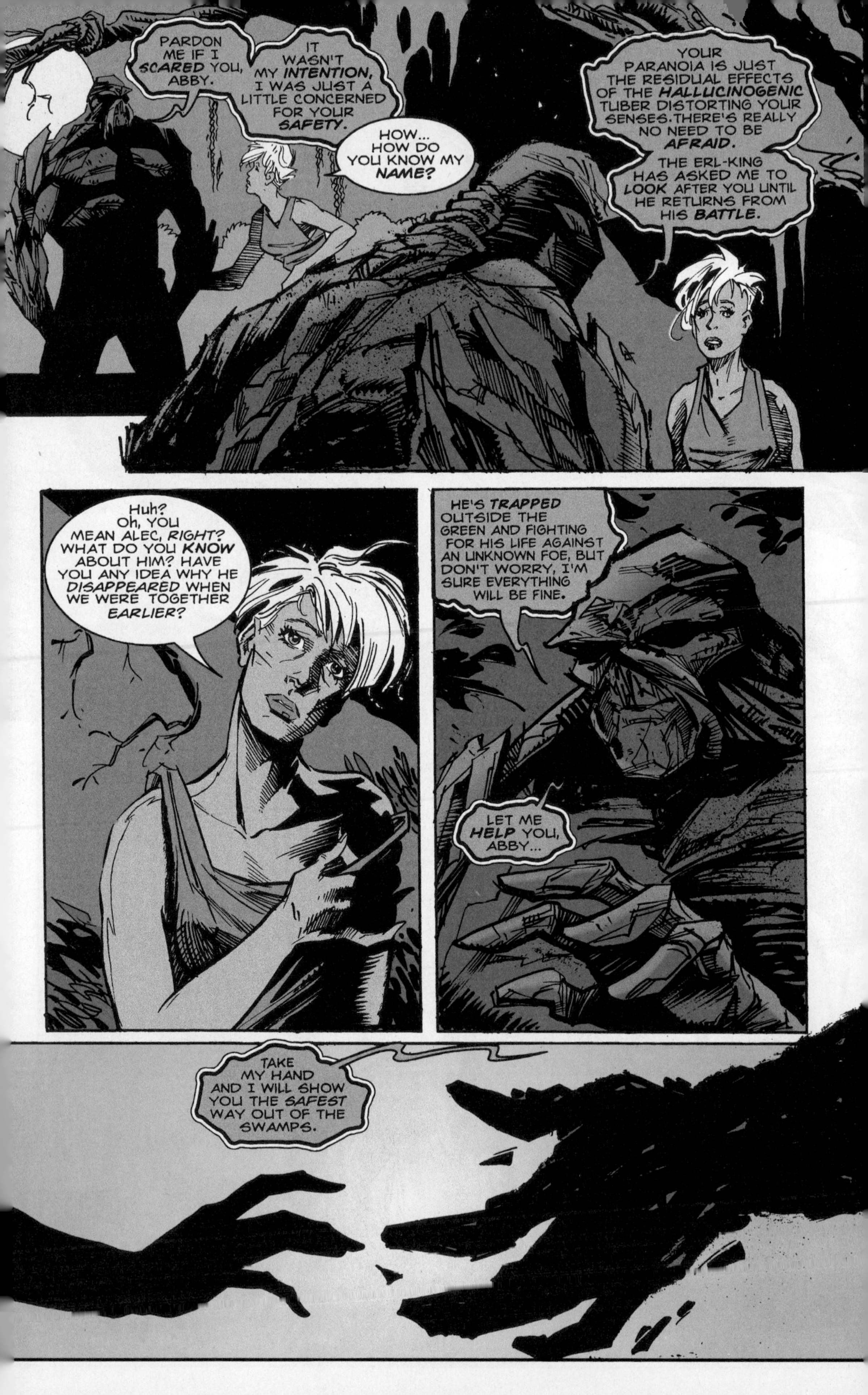
PARDON ME IF I SCARED YOU, ABBY.
IT WASN'T MY INTENTION, I WAS JUST A LITTLE CONCERNED FOR YOUR SAFETY.
HOW... HOW DO YOU KNOW MY NAME?
YOUR PARANOIA IS JUST THE RESIDUAL EFFECTS OF THE HALLUCINOGENIC TUBER DISTORTING YOUR SENSES. THERE'S REALLY NO NEED TO BE AFRAID.
THE ERL-KING HAS ASKED ME TO LOOK AFTER YOU UNTIL HE RETURNS FROM HIS BATTLE.
Huh? Oh, YOU MEAN ALEC, RIGHT? WHAT DO YOU KNOW ABOUT HIM? HAVE YOU ANY IDEA WHY HE DISAPPEARED WHEN WE WERE TOGETHER EARLIER?
HE'S TRAPPED OUTSIDE THE GREEN AND FIGHTING FOR HIS LIFE AGAINST AN UNKNOWN FOE, BUT DON'T WORRY, I'M SURE EVERYTHING WILL BE FINE.
LET ME HELP YOU, ABBY...
TAKE MY HAND AND I WILL SHOW YOU THE SAFEST WAY OUT OF THE SWAMPS.

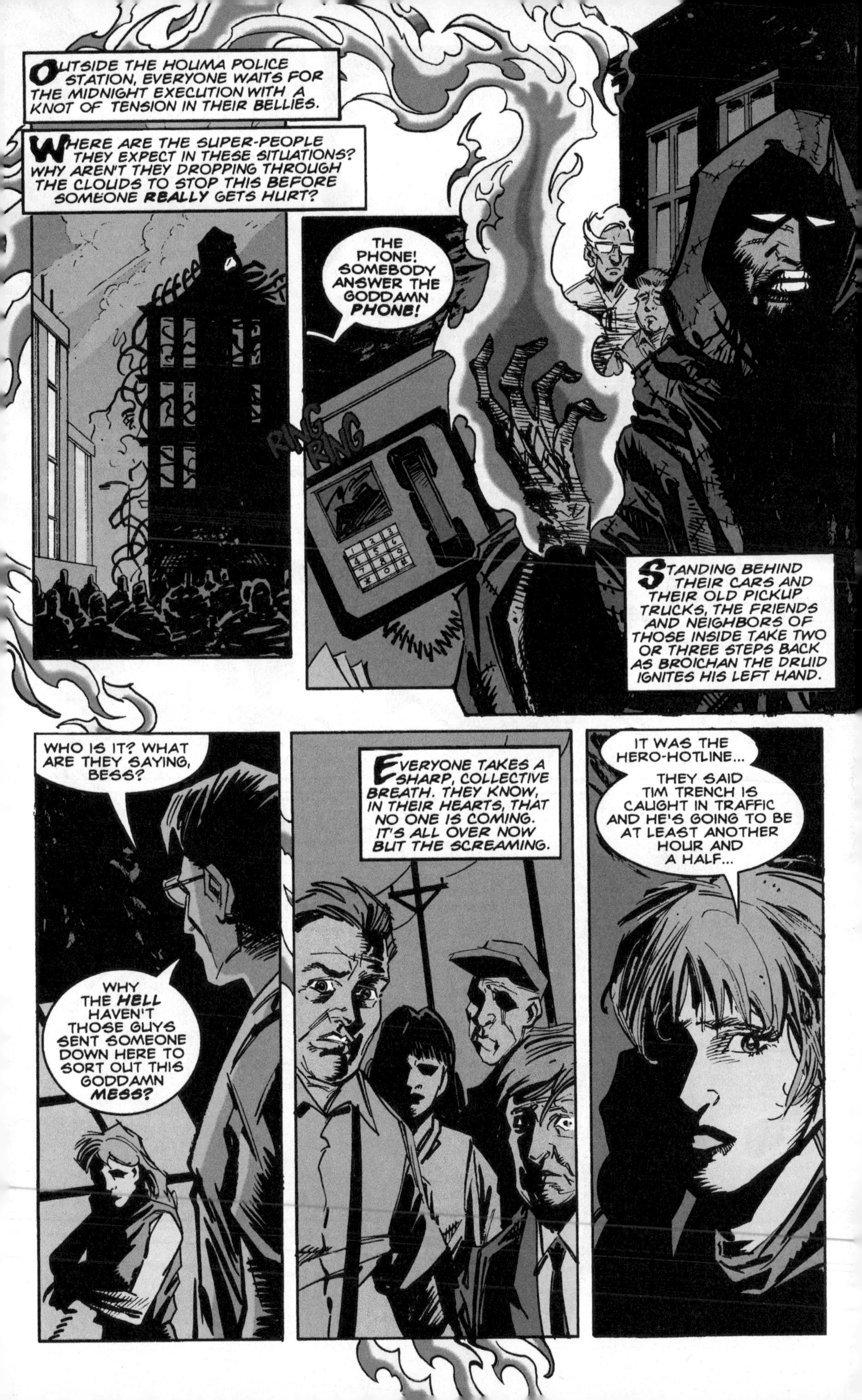
OUTSIDE THE HOUMA POLICE STATION, EVERYONE WAITS FOR THE MIDNIGHT EXECUTION WITH A KNOT OF TENSION IN THEIR BELLIES.
WHERE ARE THE SUPER-PEOPLE THEY EXPECT IN THESE SITUATIONS? WHY AREN'T THEY DROPPING THROUGH THE CLOUDS TO STOP THIS BEFORE SOMEONE REALLY GETS HURT?
THE PHONE! SOMEBODY ANSWER THE GODDAMN PHONE!
RING RING
STANDING BEHIND THEIR CARS AND THEIR OLD PICKUP TRUCKS, THE FRIENDS AND NEIGHBORS OF THOSE INSIDE TAKE TWO OR THREE STEPS BACK AS BROICHAN THE DRUID IGNITES HIS LEFT HAND.
WHO IS IT? WHAT ARE THEY SAYING, BESS?
WHY THE HELL HAVEN'T THOSE GUYS SENT SOMEONE DOWN HERE TO SORT OUT THIS GODDAMN MESS?
EVERYONE TAKES A SHARP, COLLECTIVE BREATH. THEY KNOW, IN THEIR HEARTS, THAT NO ONE IS COMING. IT'S ALL OVER NOW BUT THE SCREAMING.
IT WAS THE HERO-HOTLINE...
THEY SAID TIM TRENCH IS CAUGHT IN TRAFFIC AND HE'S GOING TO BE AT LEAST ANOTHER HOUR AND A HALF...

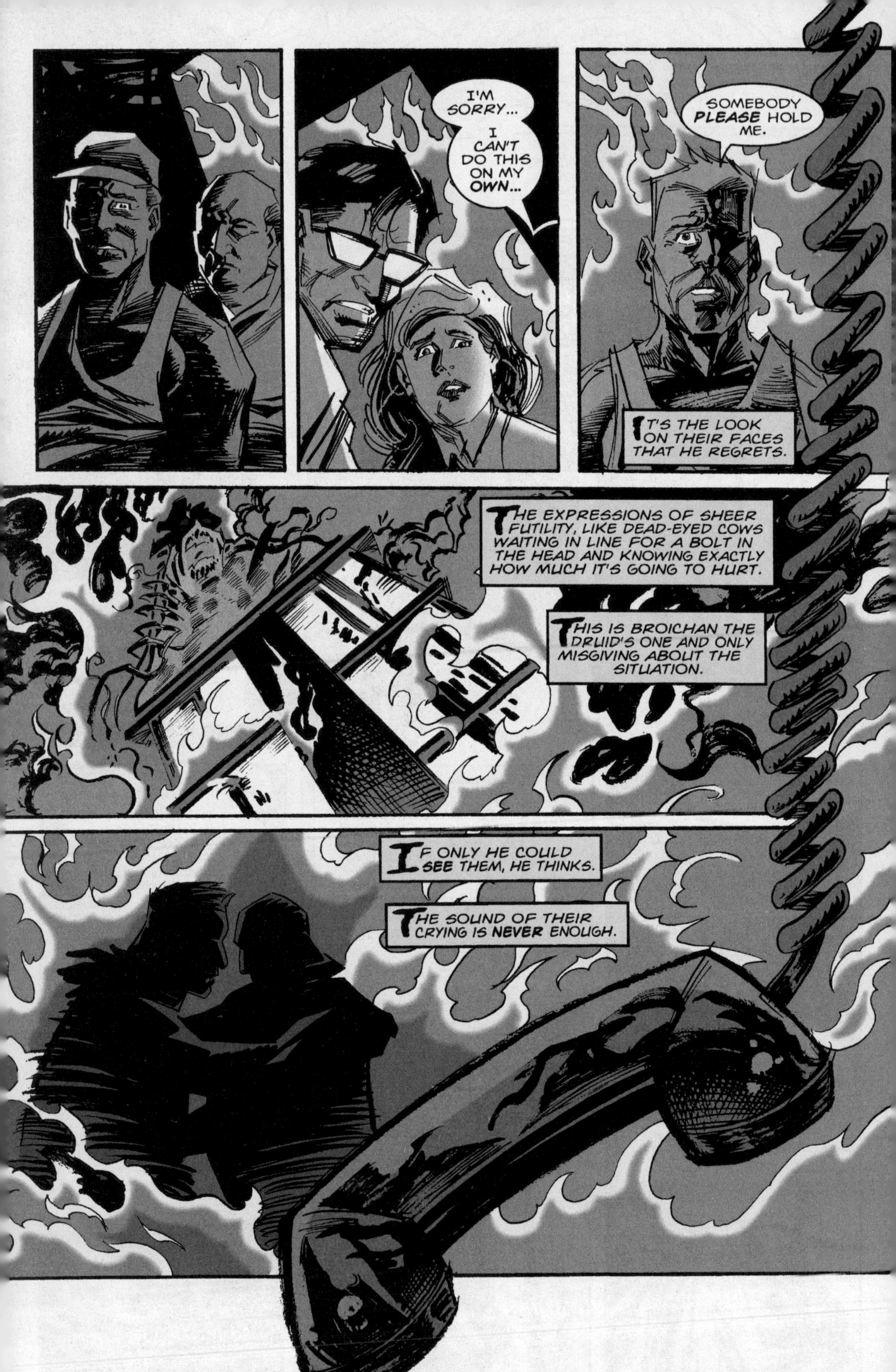
I'M SORRY... I CAN'T DO THIS ON MY OWN...
SOMEBODY PLEASE HOLD ME.
IT'S THE LOOK ON THEIR FACES THAT HE REGRETS.
THE EXPRESSIONS OF SHEER FUTILITY, LIKE DEAD-EYED COWS WAITING IN LINE FOR A BOLT IN THE HEAD AND KNOWING EXACTLY HOW MUCH IT'S GOING TO HURT.
THIS IS BROICHAN THE DRUID'S ONE AND ONLY MISGIVING ABOUT THE SITUATION.
IF ONLY HE COULD SEE THEM, HE THINKS.
THE SOUND OF THEIR CRYING IS NEVER ENOUGH.

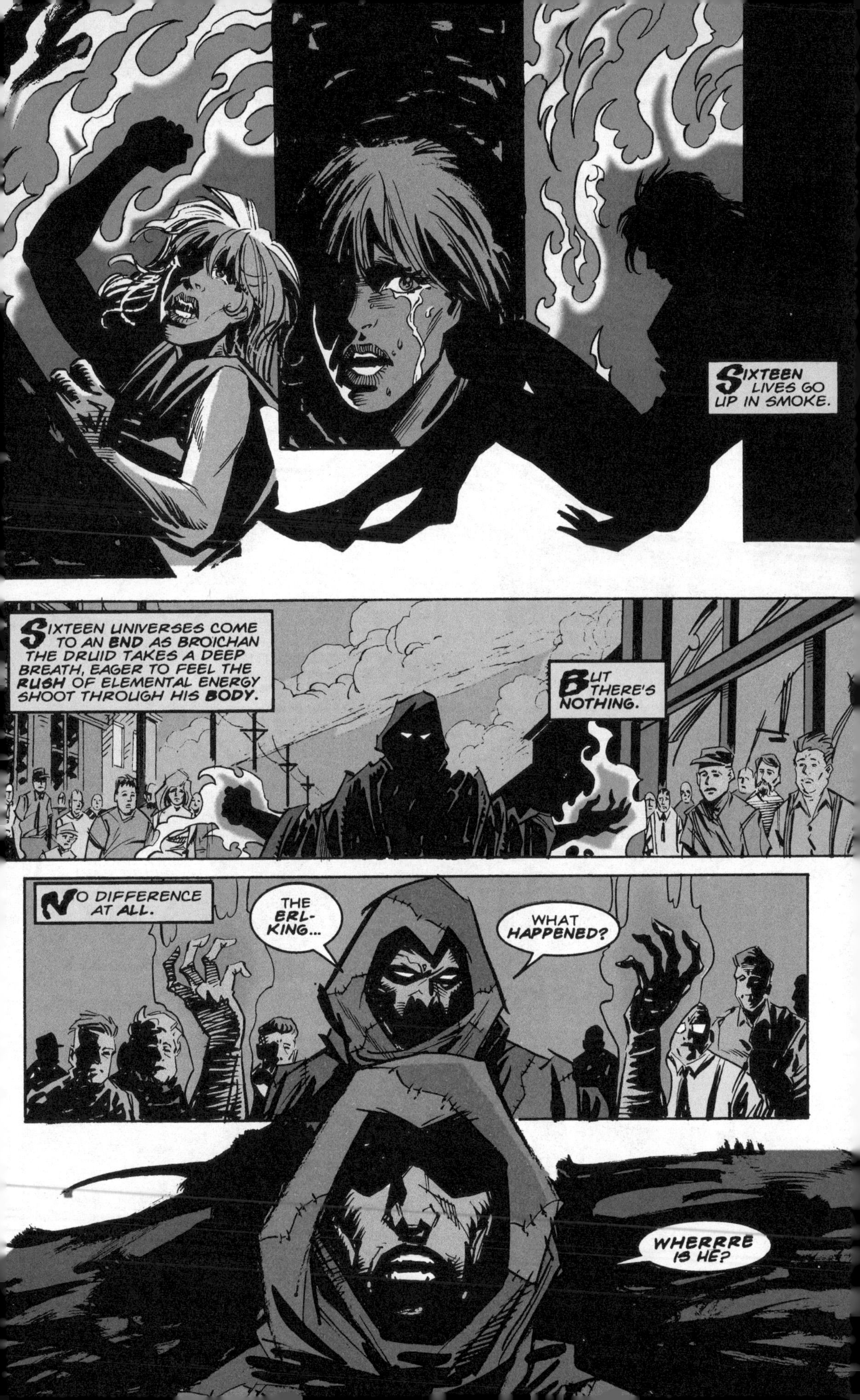
SIXTEEN LIVES GO UP IN SMOKE.
SIXTEEN UNIVERSES COME TO AN END AS BROICHAN THE DRUID TAKES A DEEP BREATH, EAGER TO FEEL THE RUSH OF ELEMENTAL ENERGY SHOOT THROUGH HIS BODY.
BUT THERE'S NOTHING.
NO DIFFERENCE AT ALL.
THE ERL-KING...
WHAT HAPPENED?
WHERRRE IS HE?

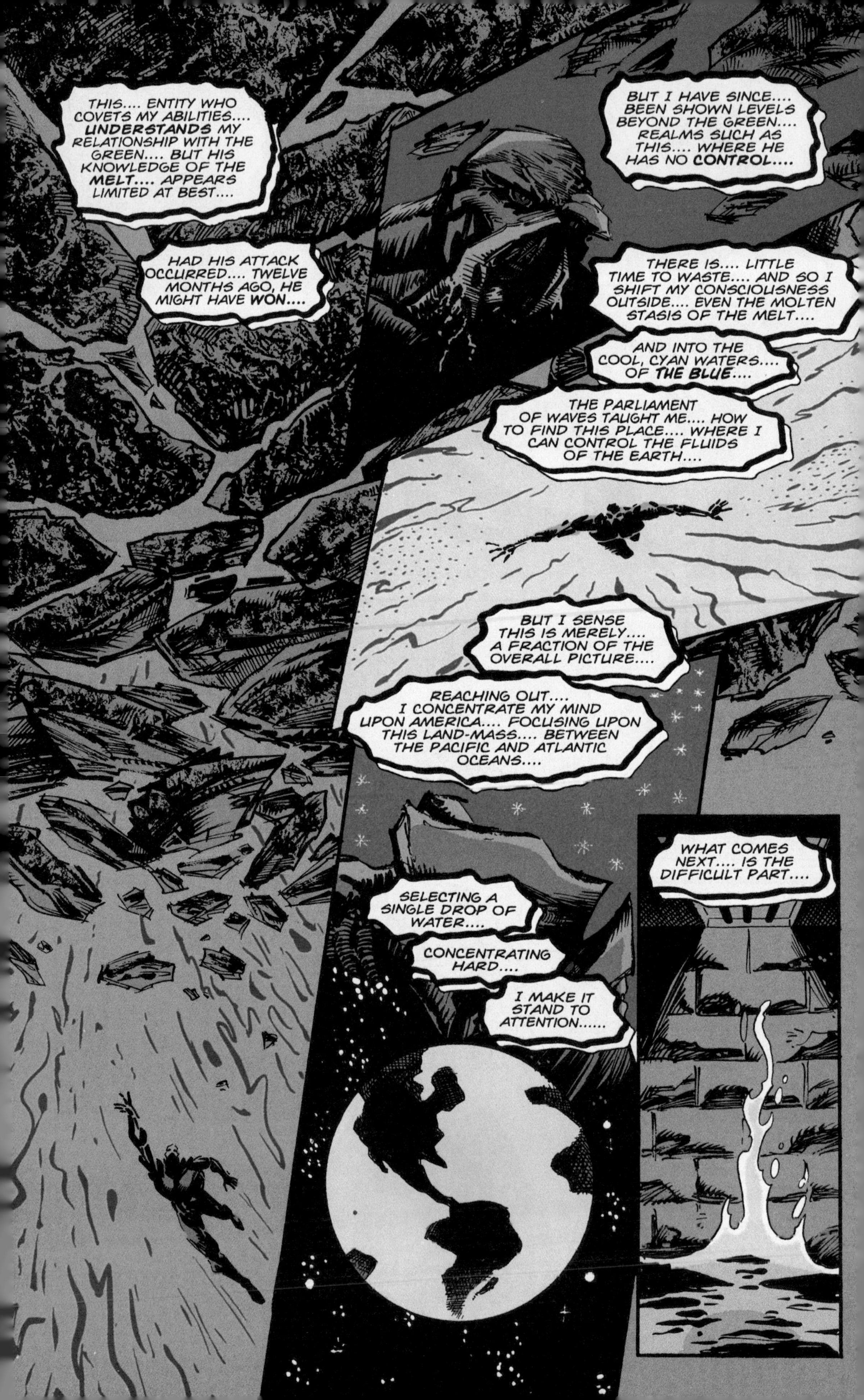
THIS.... ENTITY WHO COVETS MY ABILITIES.... UNDERSTANDS MY RELATIONSHIP WITH THE GREEN.... BUT HIS KNOWLEDGE OF THE MELT.... APPEARS LIMITED AT BEST....
HAD HIS ATTACK OCCURRED.... TWELVE MONTHS AGO, HE MIGHT HAVE WON....
BUT I HAVE SINCE.... BEEN SHOWN LEVELS BEYOND THE GREEN.... REALMS SUCH AS THIS.... WHERE HE HAS NO CONTROL....
THERE IS.... LITTLE TIME TO WASTE.... AND SO I SHIFT MY CONSCIOUSNESS OUTSIDE.... EVEN THE MOLTEN STASIS OF THE MELT....
AND INTO THE COOL, CYAN WATERS.... OF THE BLUE....
THE PARLIAMENT OF WAVES TAUGHT ME.... HOW TO FIND THIS PLACE.... WHERE I CAN CONTROL THE FLUIDS OF THE EARTH....
BUT I SENSE THIS IS MERELY.... A FRACTION OF THE OVERALL PICTURE....
REACHING OUT.... I CONCENTRATE MY MIND UPON AMERICA.... FOCUSING UPON THIS LAND-MASS.... BETWEEN THE PACIFIC AND ATLANTIC OCEANS....
SELECTING A SINGLE DROP OF WATER....
CONCENTRATING HARD....
I MAKE IT STAND TO ATTENTION......
WHAT COMES NEXT.... IS THE DIFFICULT PART....

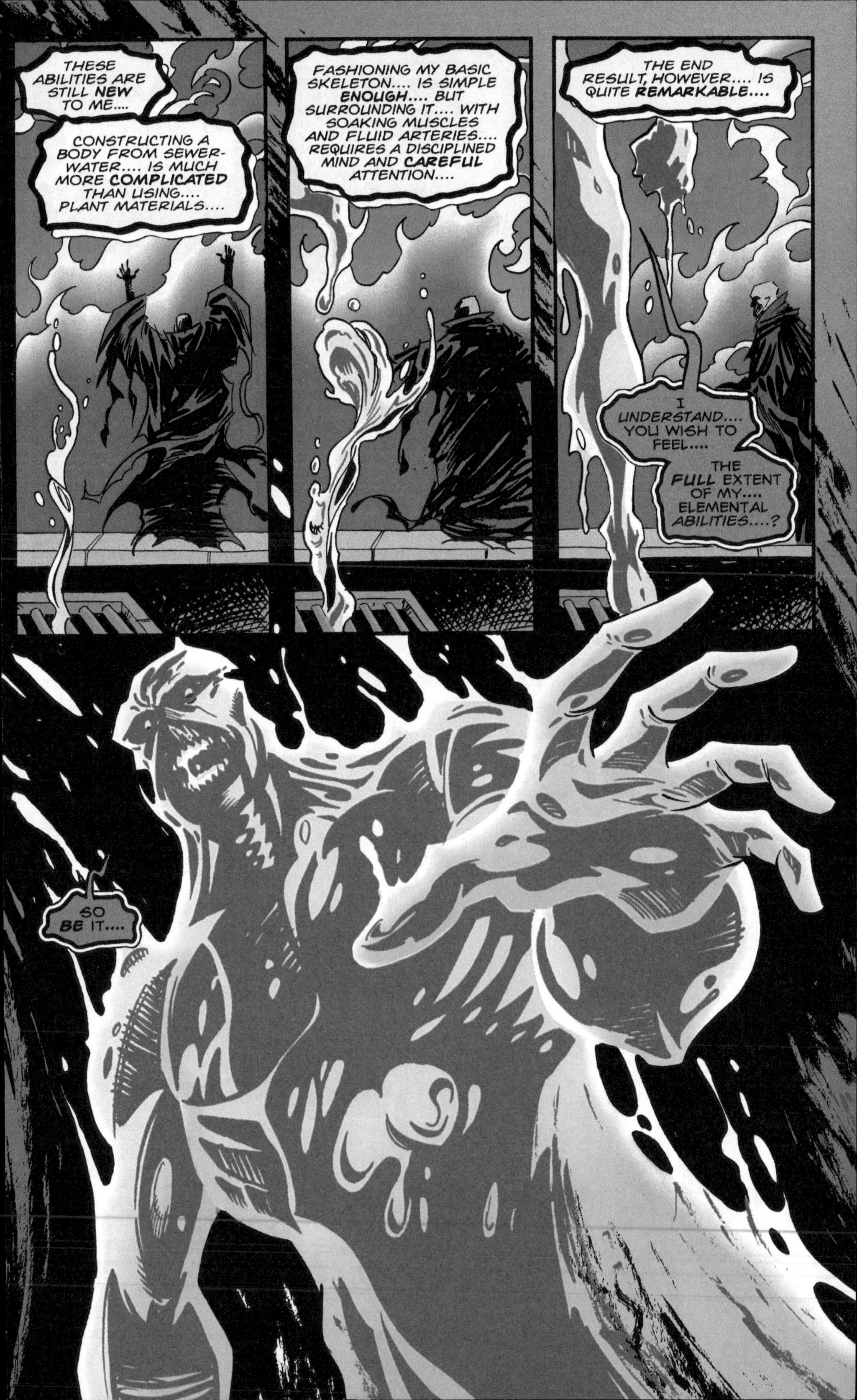
THESE ABILITIES ARE STILL NEW TO ME....
CONSTRUCTING A BODY FROM SEWER-WATER.... IS MUCH MORE COMPLICATED THAN USING.... PLANT MATERIALS....
FASHIONING MY BASIC SKELETON.... IS SIMPLE ENOUGH.... BUT SURROUNDING IT.... WITH SOAKING MUSCLES AND FLUID ARTERIES.... REQUIRES A DISCIPLINED MIND AND CAREFUL ATTENTION....
THE END RESULT, HOWEVER.... IS QUITE REMARKABLE....
I UNDERSTAND.... YOU WISH TO FEEL....
THE FULL EXTENT OF MY.... ELEMENTAL ABILITIES....?
SO BE IT....

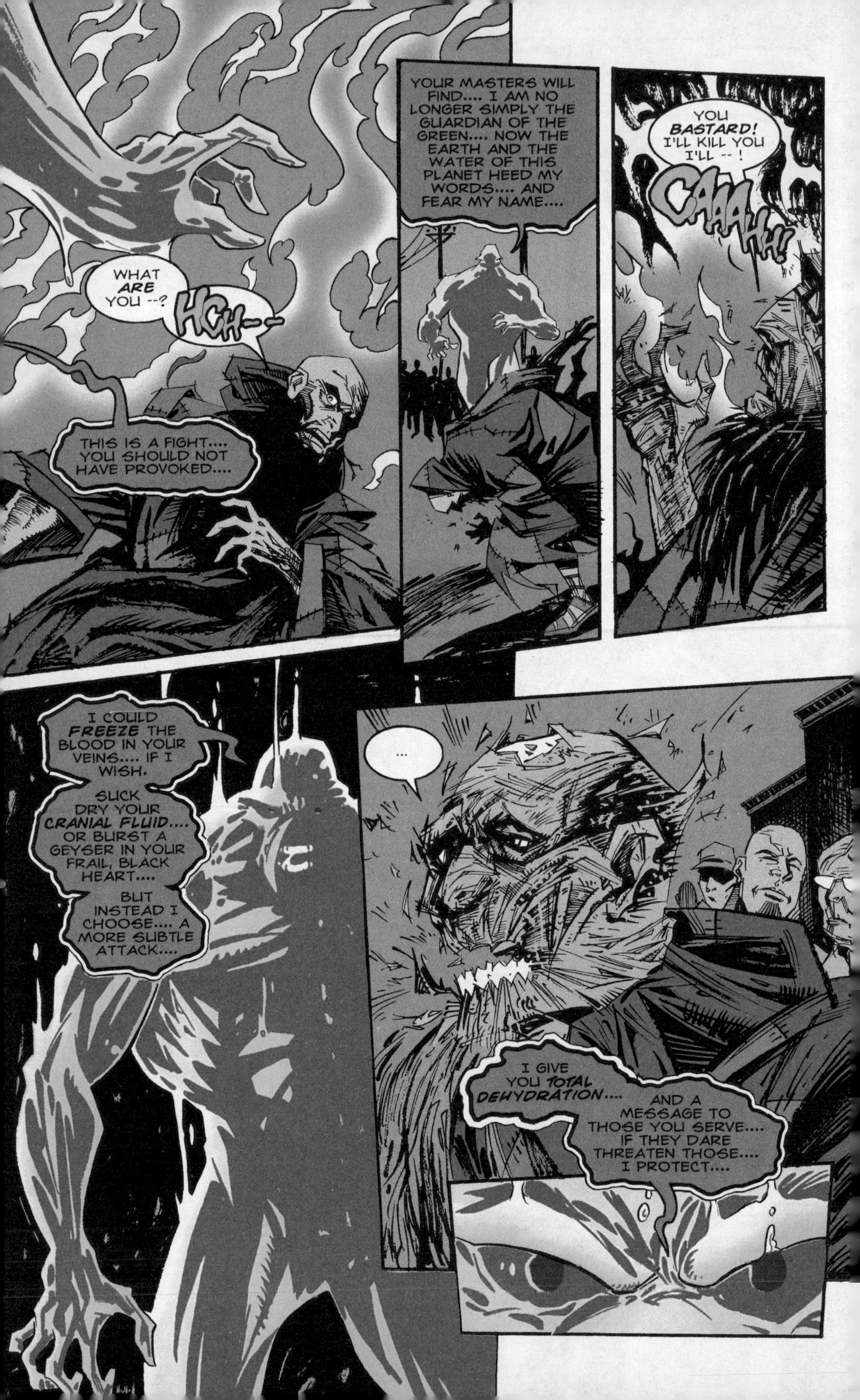
WHAT ARE YOU --?
HCH--
THIS IS A FIGHT.... YOU SHOULD NOT HAVE PROVOKED....
YOUR MASTERS WILL FIND.... I AM NO LONGER SIMPLY THE GUARDIAN OF THE GREEN.... NOW THE EARTH AND THE WATER OF THIS PLANET HEED MY WORDS.... AND FEAR MY NAME....
YOU BASTARD! I'LL KILL YOU I'LL -- !
CAAAHH!
I COULD FREEZE THE BLOOD IN YOUR VEINS.... IF I WISH.
SUCK DRY YOUR CRANIAL FLUID.... OR BURST A GEYSER IN YOUR FRAIL, BLACK HEART....
BUT INSTEAD I CHOOSE.... A MORE SUBTLE ATTACK....
...
I GIVE YOU TOTAL DEHYDRATION....
AND A MESSAGE TO THOSE YOU SERVE.... IF THEY DARE THREATEN THOSE.... I PROTECT....

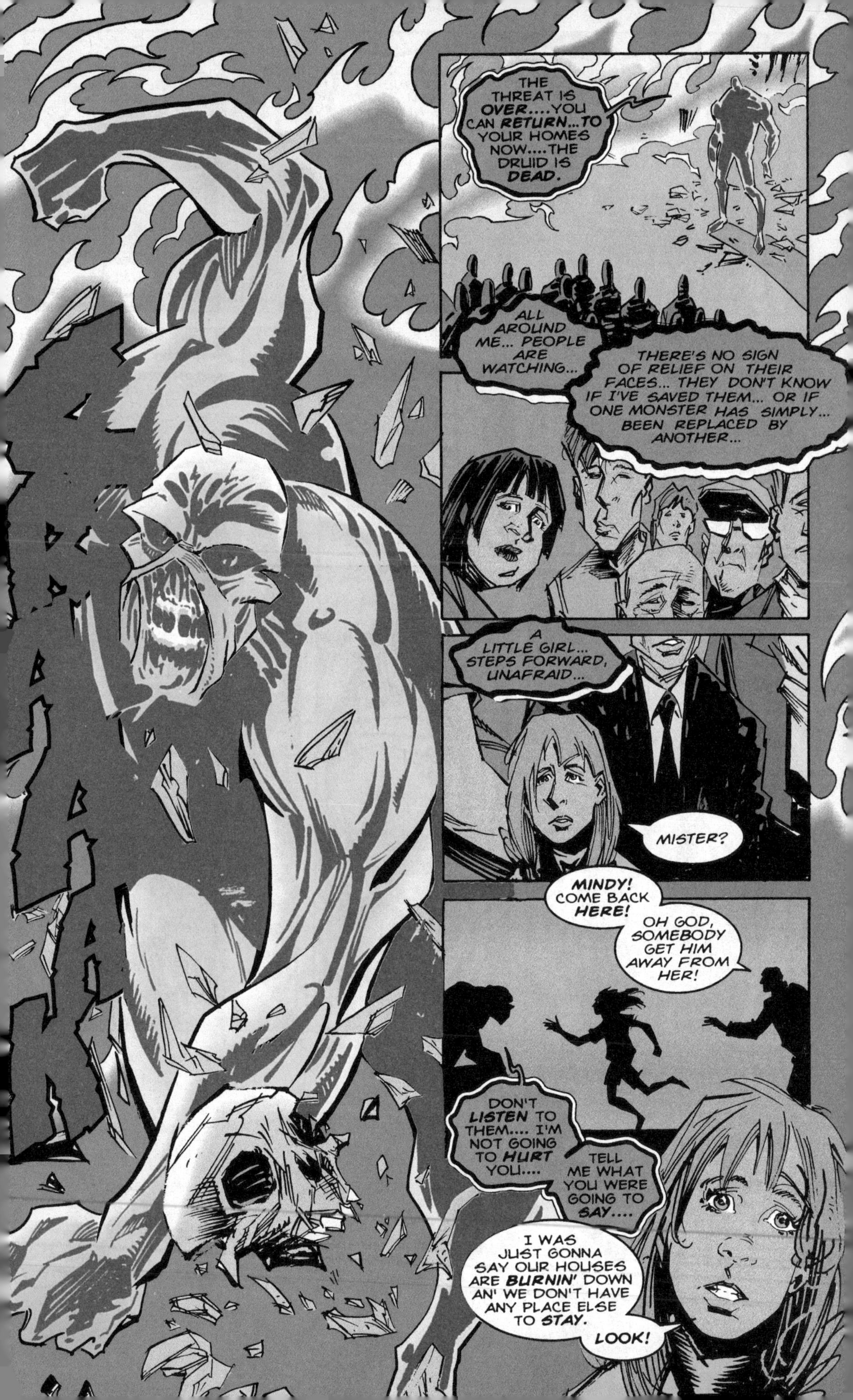
THE THREAT IS OVER....YOU CAN RETURN...TO YOUR HOMES NOW....THE DRUID IS DEAD.
ALL AROUND ME... PEOPLE ARE WATCHING...
THERE'S NO SIGN OF RELIEF ON THEIR FACES... THEY DON'T KNOW IF I'VE SAVED THEM... OR IF ONE MONSTER HAS SIMPLY... BEEN REPLACED BY ANOTHER...
A LITTLE GIRL... STEPS FORWARD, UNAFRAID...
MISTER?
MINDY! COME BACK HERE!
OH GOD, SOMEBODY GET HIM AWAY FROM HER!
DON'T LISTEN TO THEM.... I'M NOT GOING TO HURT YOU....
TELL ME WHAT YOU WERE GOING TO SAY....
I WAS JUST GONNA SAY OUR HOUSES ARE BURNIN' DOWN AN' WE DON'T HAVE ANY PLACE ELSE TO STAY.
LOOK!

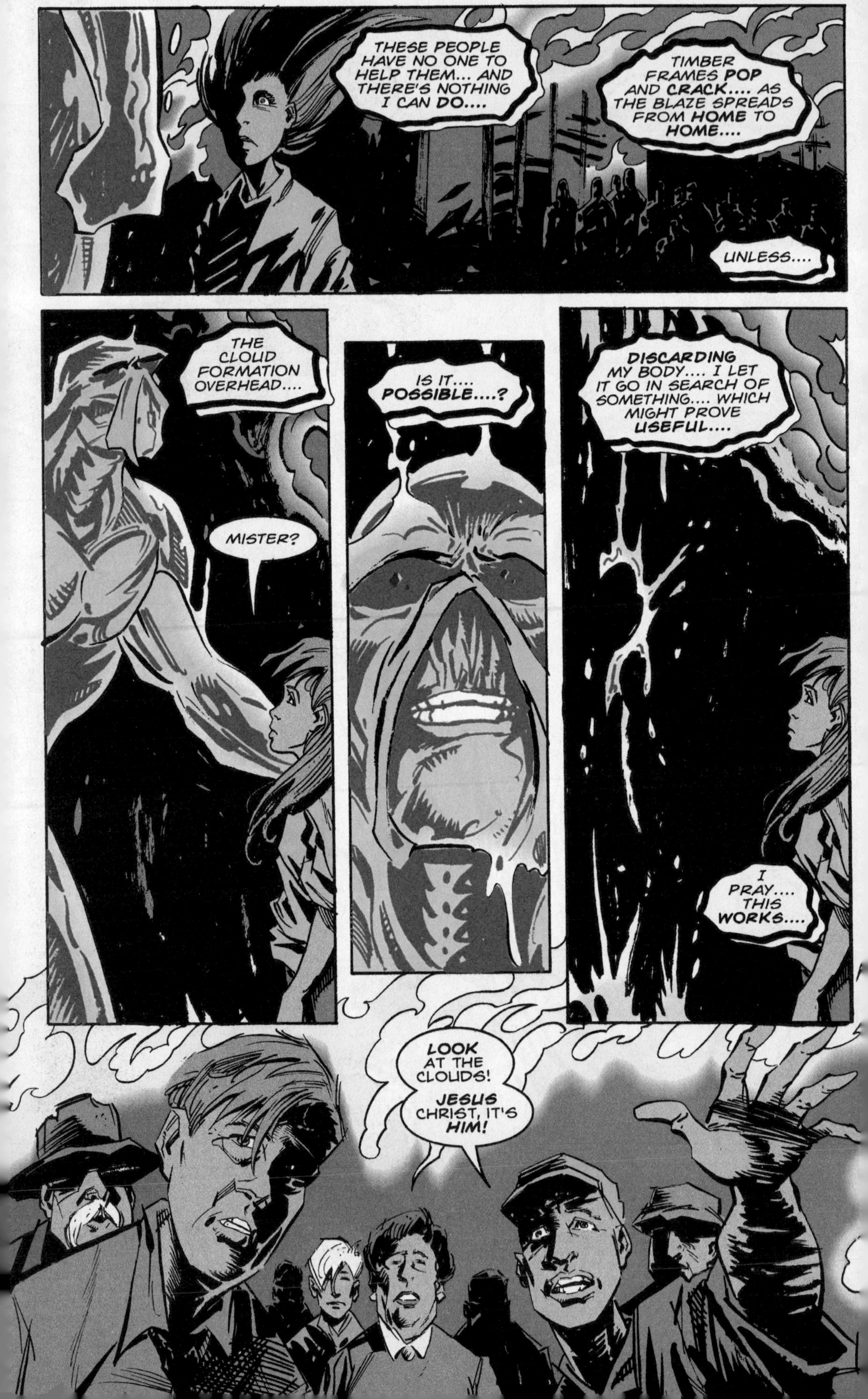
THESE PEOPLE HAVE NO ONE TO HELP THEM... AND THERE'S NOTHING I CAN DO....
TIMBER FRAMES POP AND CRACK.... AS THE BLAZE SPREADS FROM HOME TO HOME....
UNLESS....
THE CLOUD FORMATION OVERHEAD....
MISTER?
IS IT.... POSSIBLE....?
DISCARDING MY BODY.... I LET IT GO IN SEARCH OF SOMETHING.... WHICH MIGHT PROVE USEFUL....
I PRAY.... THIS WORKS....
LOOK AT THE CLOUDS!
JESUS CHRIST, IT'S HIM!

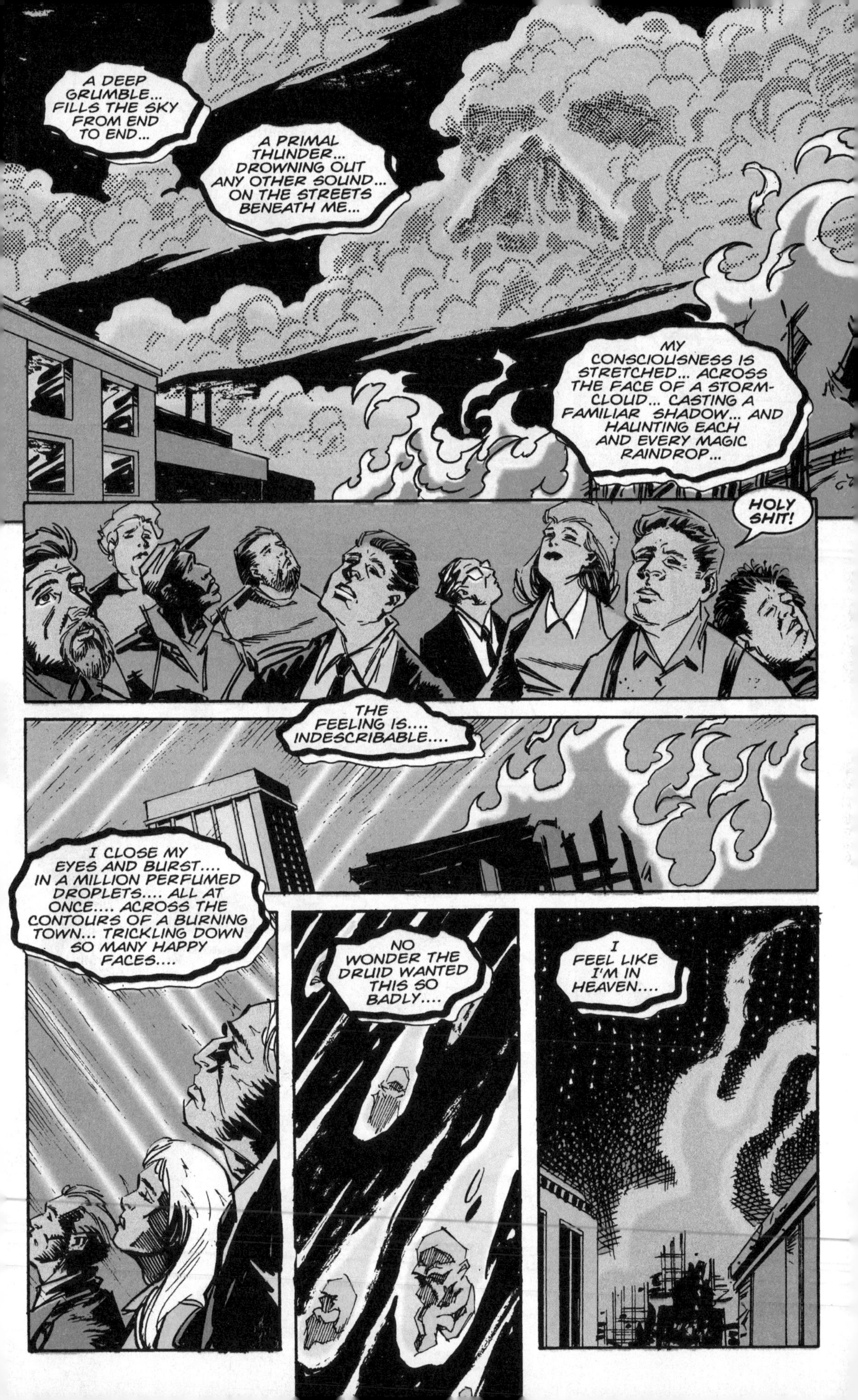
A DEEP GRUMBLE... FILLS THE SKY FROM END TO END...
A PRIMAL THUNDER... DROWNING OUT ANY OTHER SOUND... ON THE STREETS BENEATH ME...
MY CONSCIOUSNESS IS STRETCHED... ACROSS THE FACE OF A STORM-CLOUD... CASTING A FAMILIAR SHADOW... AND HAUNTING EACH AND EVERY MAGIC RAINDROP...
HOLY SHIT!
THE FEELING IS.... INDESCRIBABLE....
I CLOSE MY EYES AND BURST.... IN A MILLION PERFUMED DROPLETS.... ALL AT ONCE.... ACROSS THE CONTOURS OF A BURNING TOWN... TRICKLING DOWN SO MANY HAPPY FACES....
NO WONDER THE DRUID WANTED THIS SO BADLY....
I FEEL LIKE I'M IN HEAVEN....

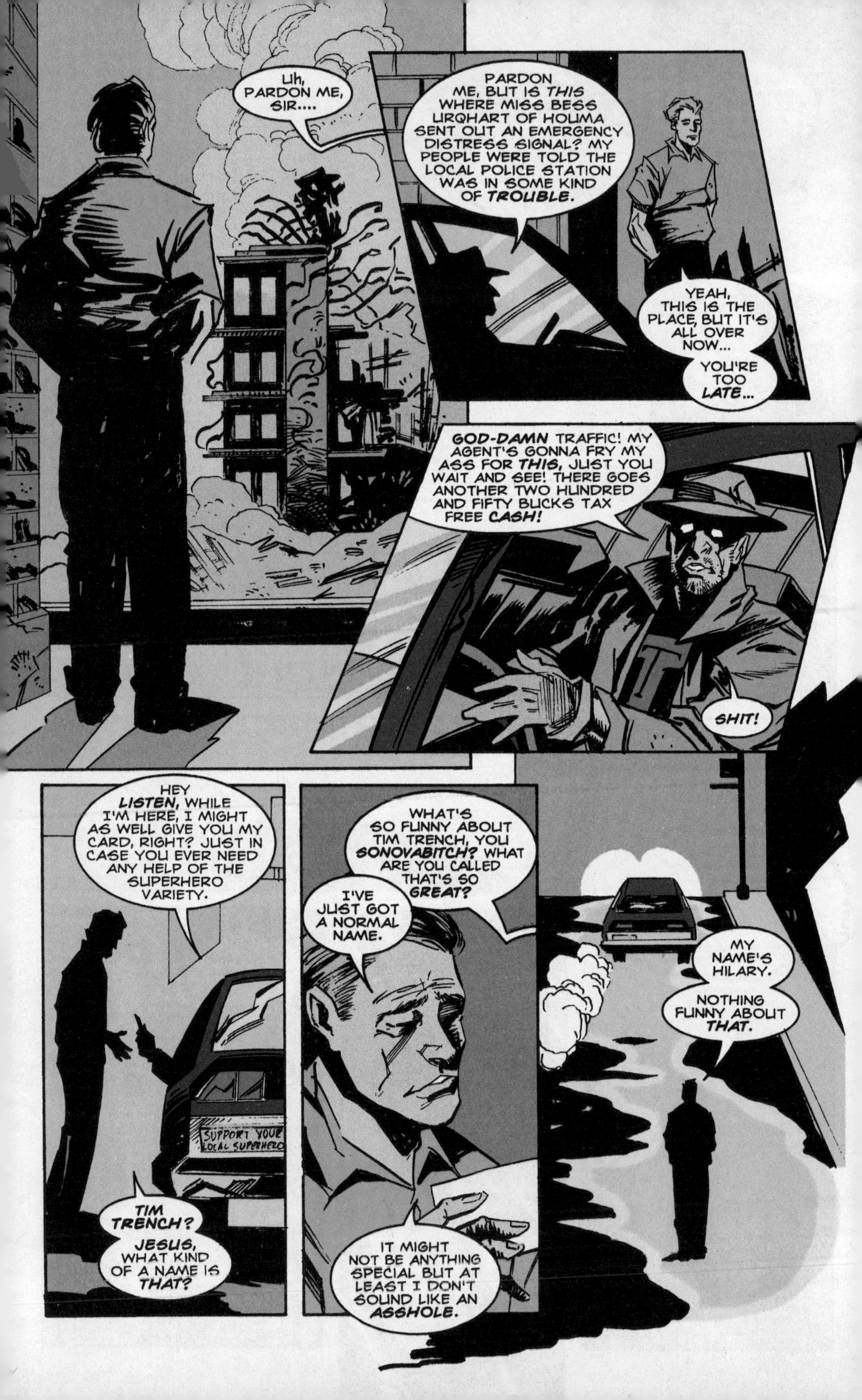

Uh, PARDON ME, SIR....
PARDON ME, BUT IS THIS WHERE MISS BESS URQHART OF HOUMA SENT OUT AN EMERGENCY DISTRESS SIGNAL? MY PEOPLE WERE TOLD THE LOCAL POLICE STATION WAS IN SOME KIND OF TROUBLE.
YEAH, THIS IS THE PLACE, BUT IT'S ALL OVER NOW...
YOU'RE TOO LATE...
GOD-DAMN TRAFFIC! MY AGENT'S GONNA FRY MY ASS FOR THIS, JUST YOU WAIT AND SEE! THERE GOES ANOTHER TWO HUNDRED AND FIFTY BUCKS TAX FREE CASH!
SHIT!
HEY LISTEN, WHILE I'M HERE, I MIGHT AS WELL GIVE YOU MY CARD, RIGHT? JUST IN CASE YOU EVER NEED ANY HELP OF THE SUPERHERO VARIETY.
SUPPORT YOUR LOCAL SUPERHERO
TIM TRENCH?
JESUS, WHAT KIND OF A NAME IS THAT?
WHAT'S SO FUNNY ABOUT TIM TRENCH, YOU SONOVABITCH? WHAT ARE YOU CALLED THAT'S SO GREAT?
I'VE JUST GOT A NORMAL NAME.
IT MIGHT NOT BE ANYTHING SPECIAL BUT AT LEAST I DON'T SOUND LIKE AN ASSHOLE.
MY NAME'S HILARY.
NOTHING FUNNY ABOUT THAT.

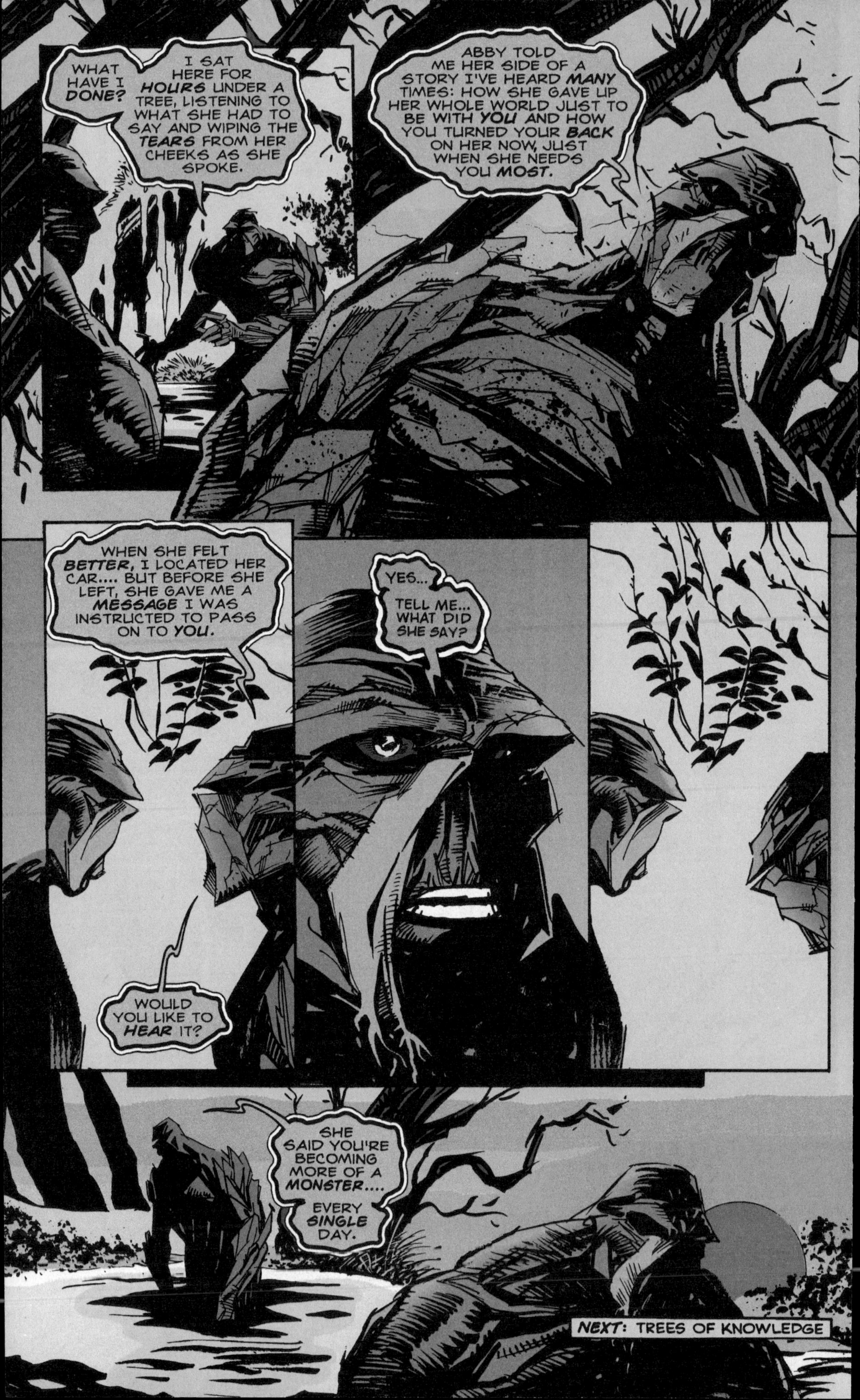
WHAT HAVE I DONE?
I SAT HERE FOR HOURS UNDER A TREE, LISTENING TO WHAT SHE HAD TO SAY AND WIPING THE TEARS FROM HER CHEEKS AS SHE SPOKE.
ABBY TOLD ME HER SIDE OF A STORY I'VE HEARD MANY TIMES: HOW SHE GAVE UP HER WHOLE WORLD JUST TO BE WITH YOU AND HOW YOU TURNED YOUR BACK ON HER NOW, JUST WHEN SHE NEEDS YOU MOST.
WHEN SHE FELT BETTER, I LOCATED HER CAR.... BUT BEFORE SHE LEFT, SHE GAVE ME A MESSAGE I WAS INSTRUCTED TO PASS ON TO YOU.
WOULD YOU LIKE TO HEAR IT?
YES...
TELL ME... WHAT DID SHE SAY?
SHE SAID YOU'RE BECOMING MORE OF A MONSTER....
EVERY SINGLE DAY.
NEXT: TREES OF KNOWLEDGE

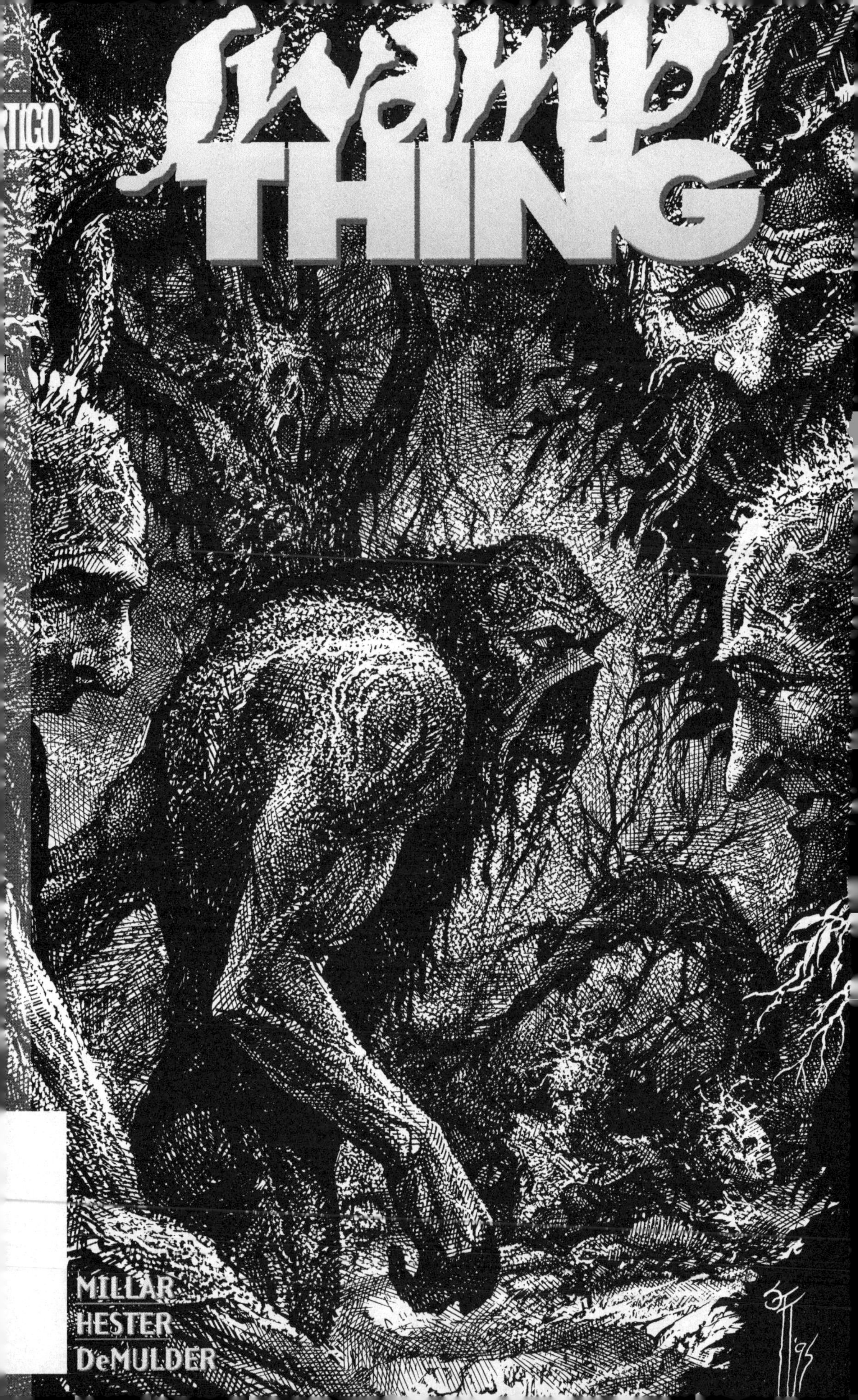
Swamp THING™
MILLAR
HESTER
DeMULDER

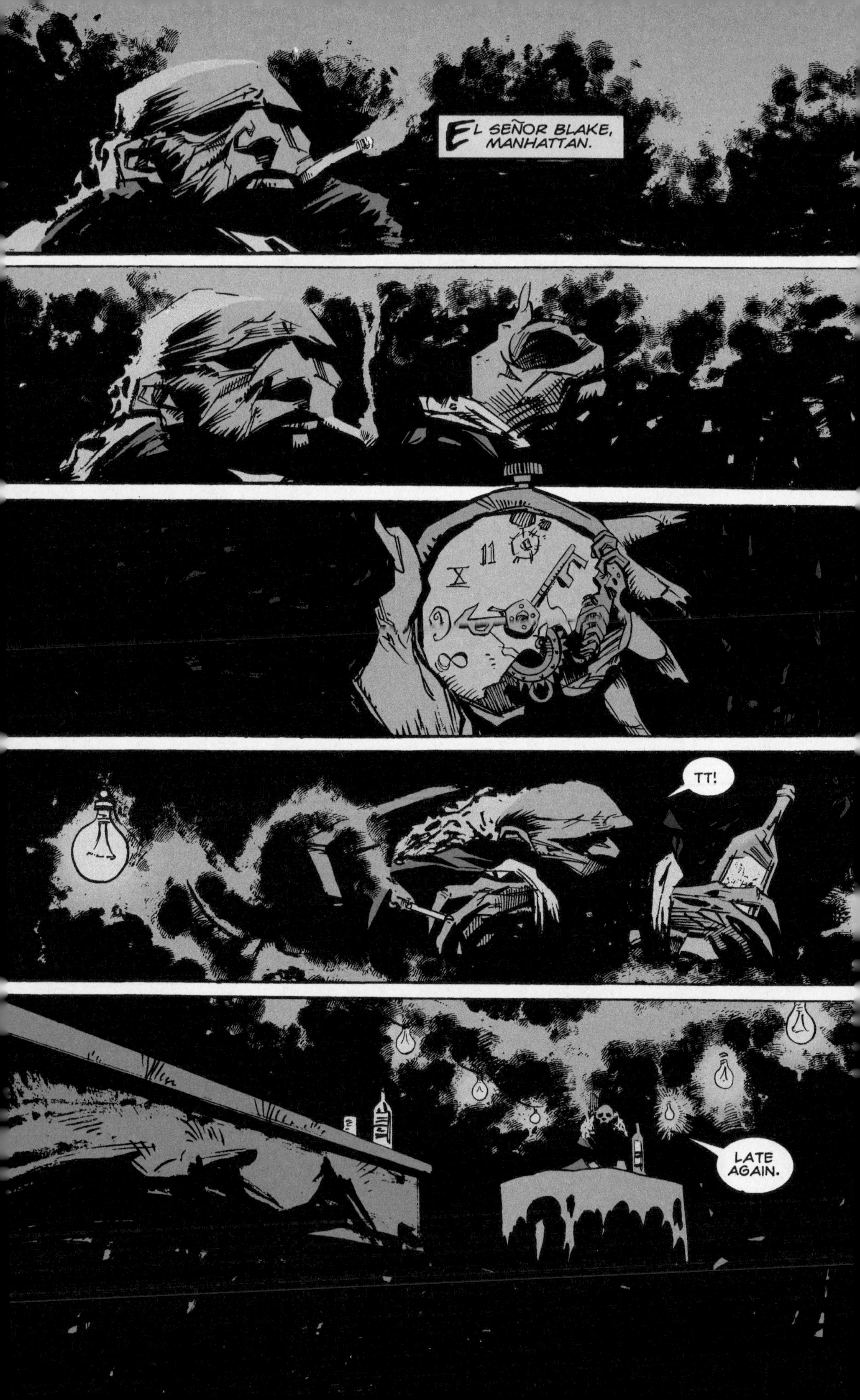
EL SEÑOR BLAKE, MANHATTAN.
TT!
LATE AGAIN.

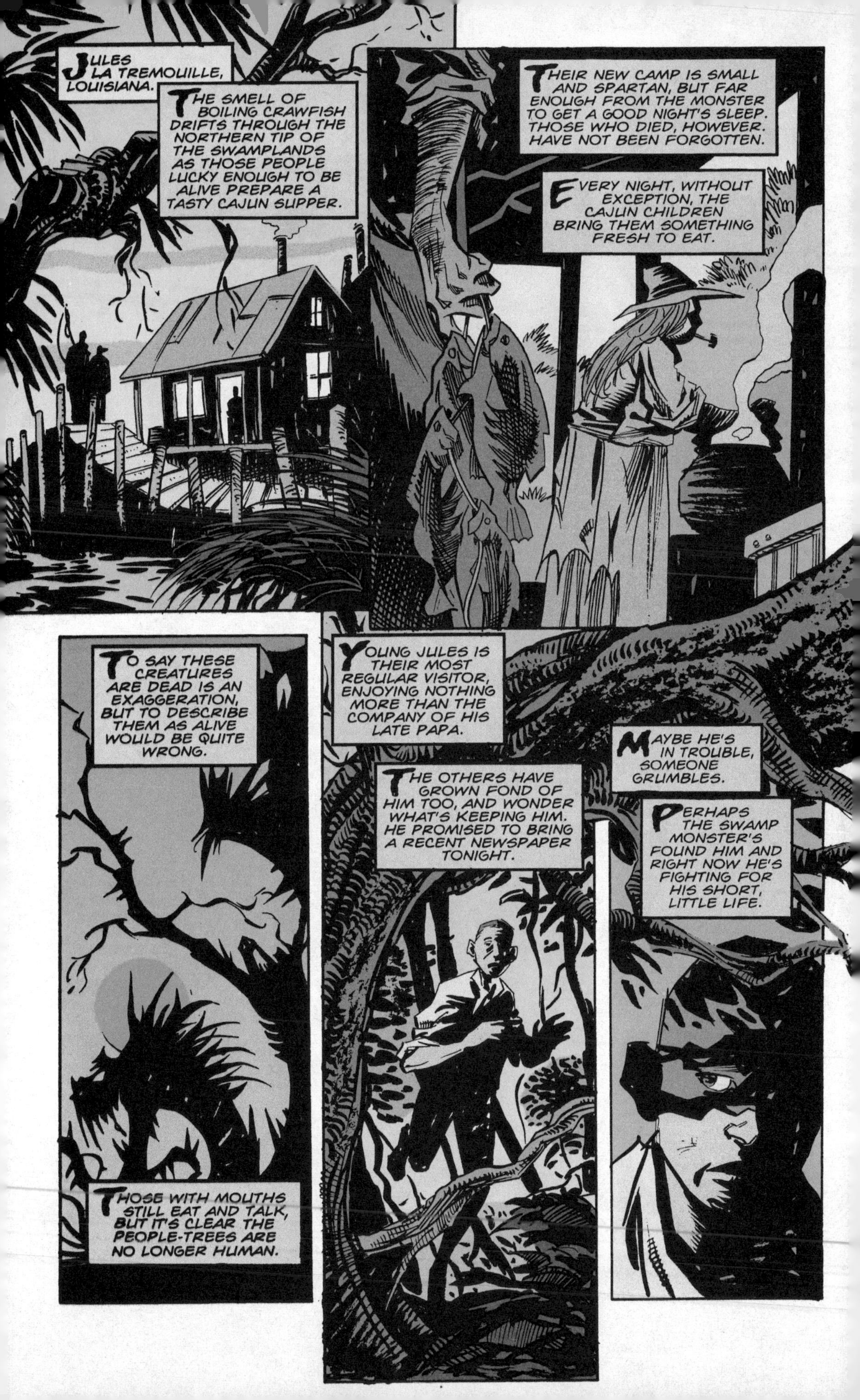
JULES LA TREMOUILLE, LOUISIANA.
THE SMELL OF BOILING CRAWFISH DRIFTS THROUGH THE NORTHERN TIP OF THE SWAMPLANDS AS THOSE PEOPLE LUCKY ENOUGH TO BE ALIVE PREPARE A TASTY CAJUN SUPPER.
THEIR NEW CAMP IS SMALL AND SPARTAN, BUT FAR ENOUGH FROM THE MONSTER TO GET A GOOD NIGHT'S SLEEP. THOSE WHO DIED, HOWEVER. HAVE NOT BEEN FORGOTTEN.
EVERY NIGHT, WITHOUT EXCEPTION, THE CAJUN CHILDREN BRING THEM SOMETHING FRESH TO EAT.
TO SAY THESE CREATURES ARE DEAD IS AN EXAGGERATION, BUT TO DESCRIBE THEM AS ALIVE WOULD BE QUITE WRONG.
THOSE WITH MOUTHS STILL EAT AND TALK, BUT IT'S CLEAR THE PEOPLE-TREES ARE NO LONGER HUMAN.
YOUNG JULES IS THEIR MOST REGULAR VISITOR, ENJOYING NOTHING MORE THAN THE COMPANY OF HIS LATE PAPA.
THE OTHERS HAVE GROWN FOND OF HIM TOO, AND WONDER WHAT'S KEEPING HIM. HE PROMISED TO BRING A RECENT NEWSPAPER TONIGHT.
MAYBE HE'S IN TROUBLE, SOMEONE GRUMBLES.
PERHAPS THE SWAMP MONSTER'S FOUND HIM AND RIGHT NOW HE'S FIGHTING FOR HIS SHORT, LITTLE LIFE.

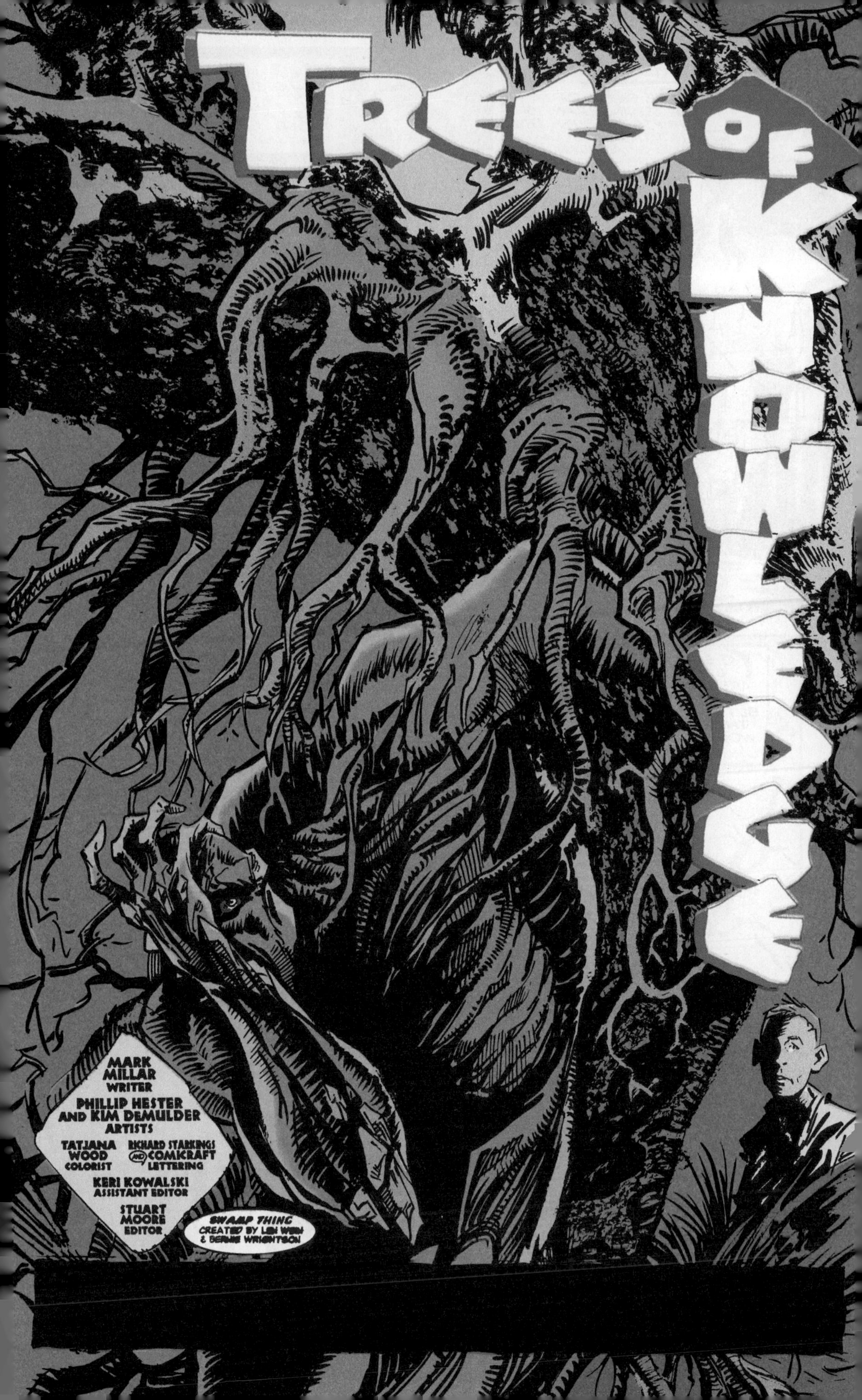
TREES OF KNOWLEDGE
MARK MILLAR WRITER
PHILLIP HESTER AND KIM DEMULDER ARTISTS
TATJANA WOOD COLORIST
RICHARD STARKINGS AND COMICRAFT LETTERING
KERI KOWALSKI ASSISTANT EDITOR
STUART MOORE EDITOR
SWAMP THING CREATED BY LEN WEIN & BERNIE WRIGHTSON

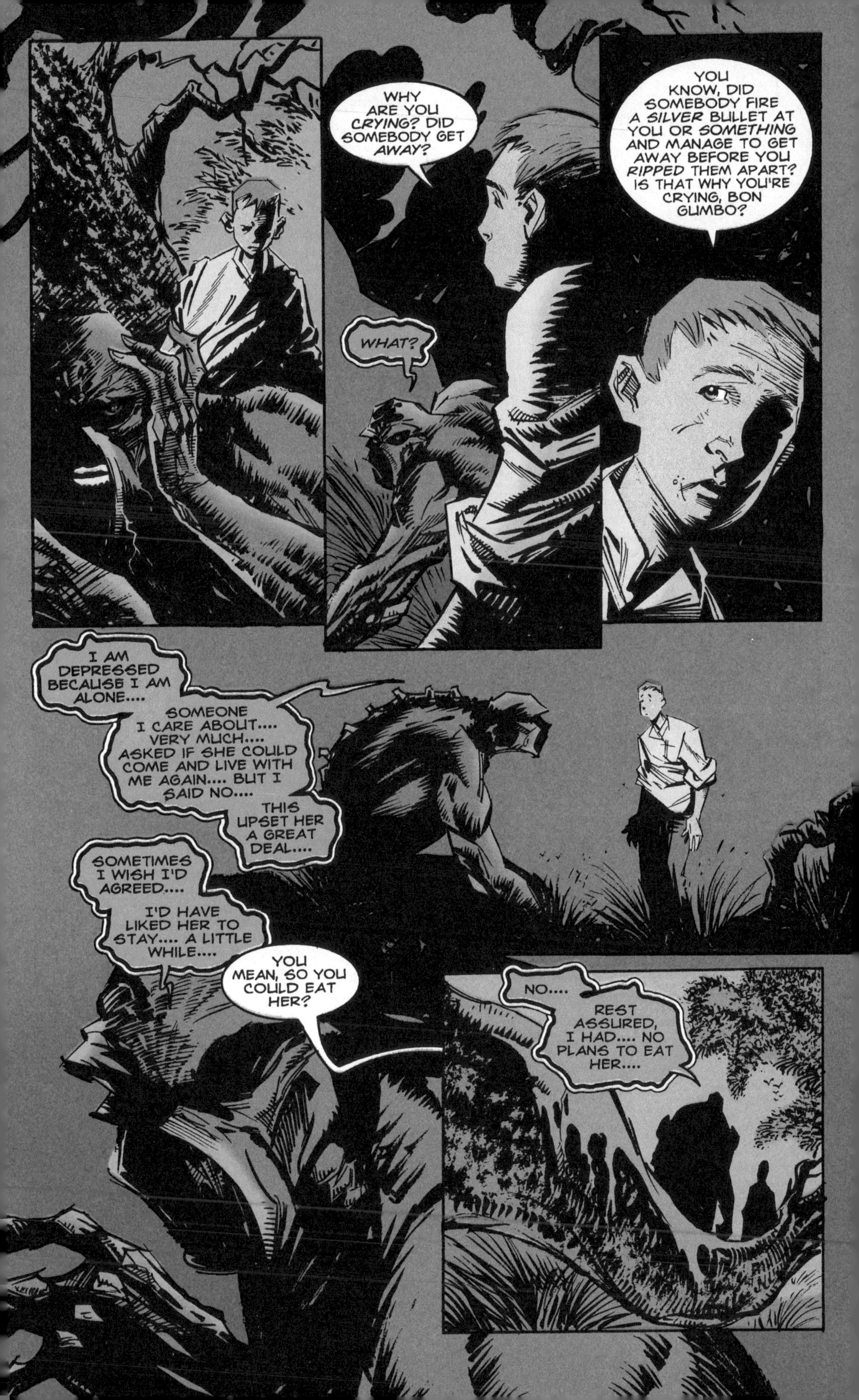
WHY ARE YOU *CRYING?* DID SOMEBODY GET *AWAY?*
WHAT?
YOU KNOW, DID SOMEBODY FIRE A *SILVER* BULLET AT YOU OR *SOMETHING* AND MANAGE TO GET AWAY BEFORE YOU *RIPPED* THEM APART? IS THAT WHY YOU'RE CRYING, BON GUMBO?
I AM DEPRESSED BECAUSE I AM ALONE....
SOMEONE I CARE ABOUT.... VERY MUCH.... ASKED IF SHE COULD COME AND LIVE WITH ME AGAIN.... BUT I SAID NO....
THIS UPSET HER A GREAT DEAL....
SOMETIMES I WISH I'D AGREED....
I'D HAVE LIKED HER TO STAY.... A LITTLE WHILE....
YOU MEAN, SO YOU COULD EAT HER?
NO....
REST ASSURED, I HAD.... NO PLANS TO EAT HER....

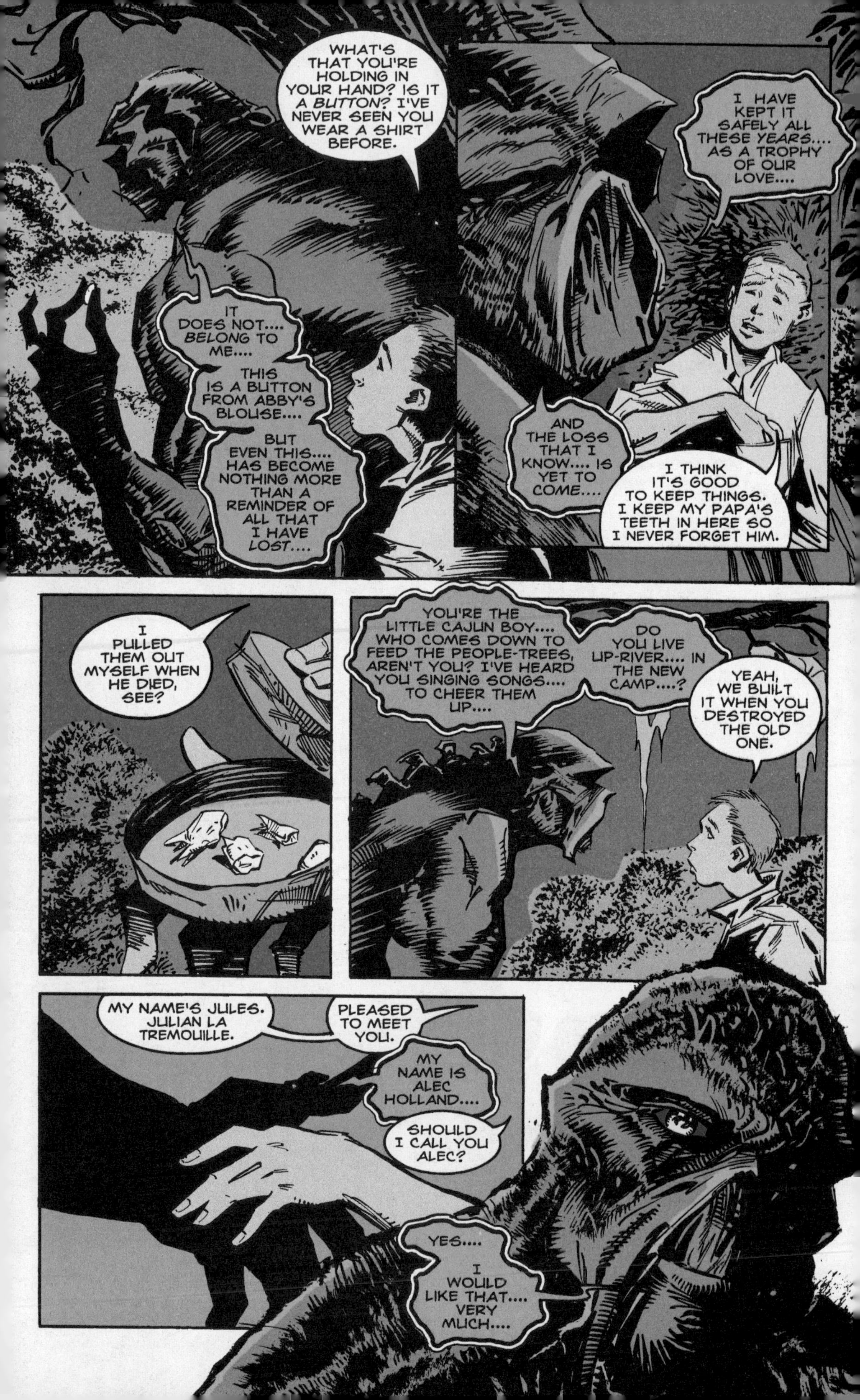
WHAT'S THAT YOU'RE HOLDING IN YOUR HAND? IS IT A *BUTTON*? I'VE NEVER SEEN YOU WEAR A SHIRT BEFORE.
IT DOES NOT.... *BELONG* TO ME....
THIS IS A BUTTON FROM ABBY'S BLOUSE....
BUT EVEN THIS.... HAS BECOME NOTHING MORE THAN A REMINDER OF ALL THAT I HAVE *LOST*....
I HAVE KEPT IT SAFELY ALL THESE *YEARS*.... AS A TROPHY OF OUR LOVE....
AND THE LOSS THAT I KNOW.... IS YET TO COME....
I THINK IT'S GOOD TO KEEP THINGS. I KEEP MY PAPA'S TEETH IN HERE SO I NEVER FORGET HIM.
I PULLED THEM OUT MYSELF WHEN HE DIED, SEE?
YOU'RE THE LITTLE CAJUN BOY.... WHO COMES DOWN TO FEED THE PEOPLE-TREES, AREN'T YOU? I'VE HEARD YOU SINGING SONGS.... TO CHEER THEM UP....
DO YOU LIVE UP-RIVER.... IN THE NEW CAMP....?
YEAH, WE BUILT IT WHEN YOU DESTROYED THE OLD ONE.
MY NAME'S JULES. JULIAN LA TREMOUILLE.
PLEASED TO MEET YOU.
MY NAME IS ALEC HOLLAND....
SHOULD I CALL YOU ALEC?
YES....
I WOULD LIKE THAT.... VERY MUCH....

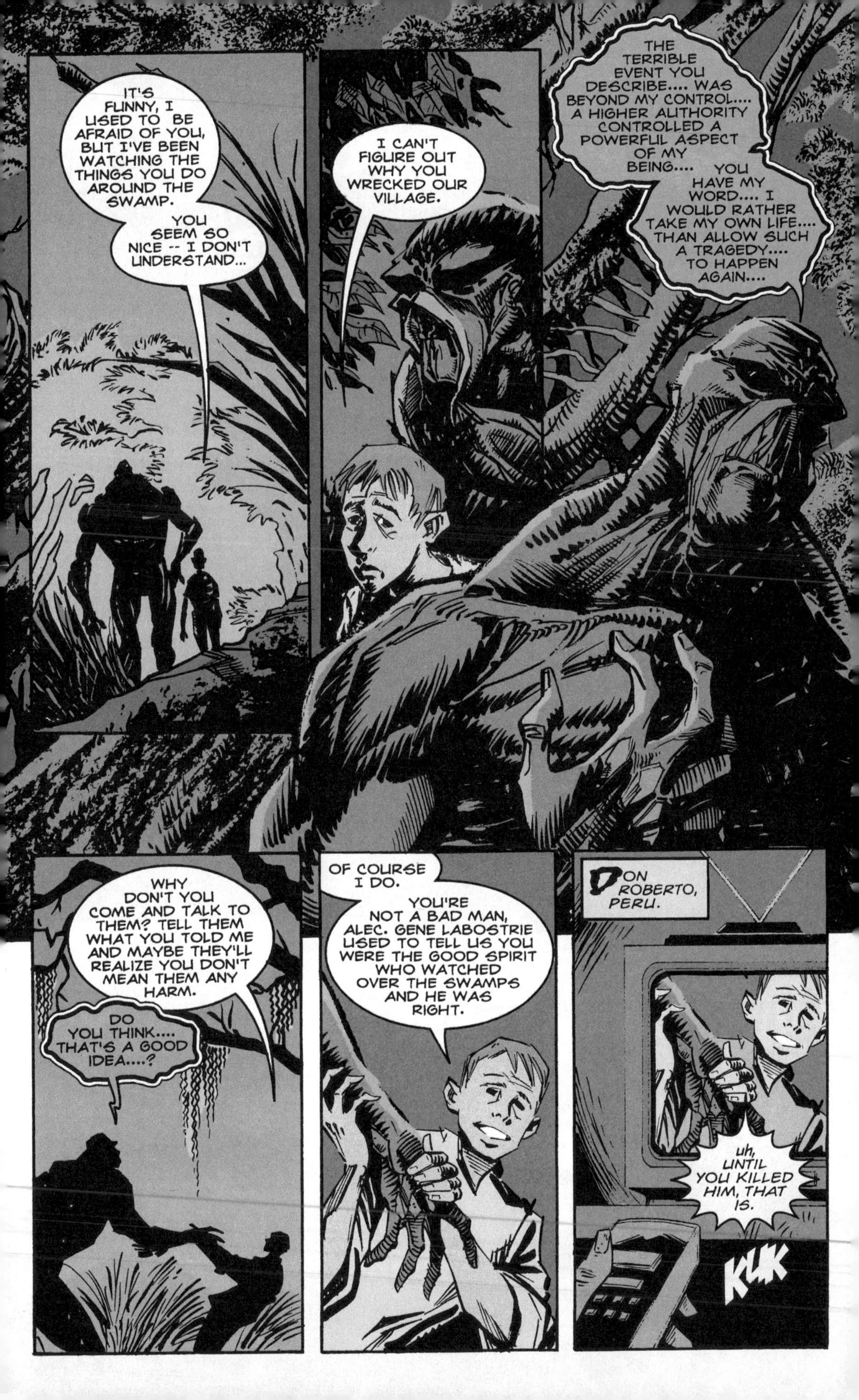
IT'S FUNNY, I USED TO BE AFRAID OF YOU, BUT I'VE BEEN WATCHING THE THINGS YOU DO AROUND THE SWAMP.
YOU SEEM SO NICE -- I DON'T UNDERSTAND...
I CAN'T FIGURE OUT WHY YOU WRECKED OUR VILLAGE.
THE TERRIBLE EVENT YOU DESCRIBE.... WAS BEYOND MY CONTROL.... A HIGHER AUTHORITY CONTROLLED A POWERFUL ASPECT OF MY BEING.... YOU HAVE MY WORD.... I WOULD RATHER TAKE MY OWN LIFE.... THAN ALLOW SUCH A TRAGEDY.... TO HAPPEN AGAIN....
WHY DON'T YOU COME AND TALK TO THEM? TELL THEM WHAT YOU TOLD ME AND MAYBE THEY'LL REALIZE YOU DON'T MEAN THEM ANY HARM.
DO YOU THINK.... THAT'S A GOOD IDEA....?
OF COURSE I DO.
YOU'RE NOT A BAD MAN, ALEC. GENE LABOSTRIE USED TO TELL US YOU WERE THE GOOD SPIRIT WHO WATCHED OVER THE SWAMPS AND HE WAS RIGHT.
DON ROBERTO, PERU.
uh, UNTIL YOU KILLED HIM, THAT IS.
KLIK

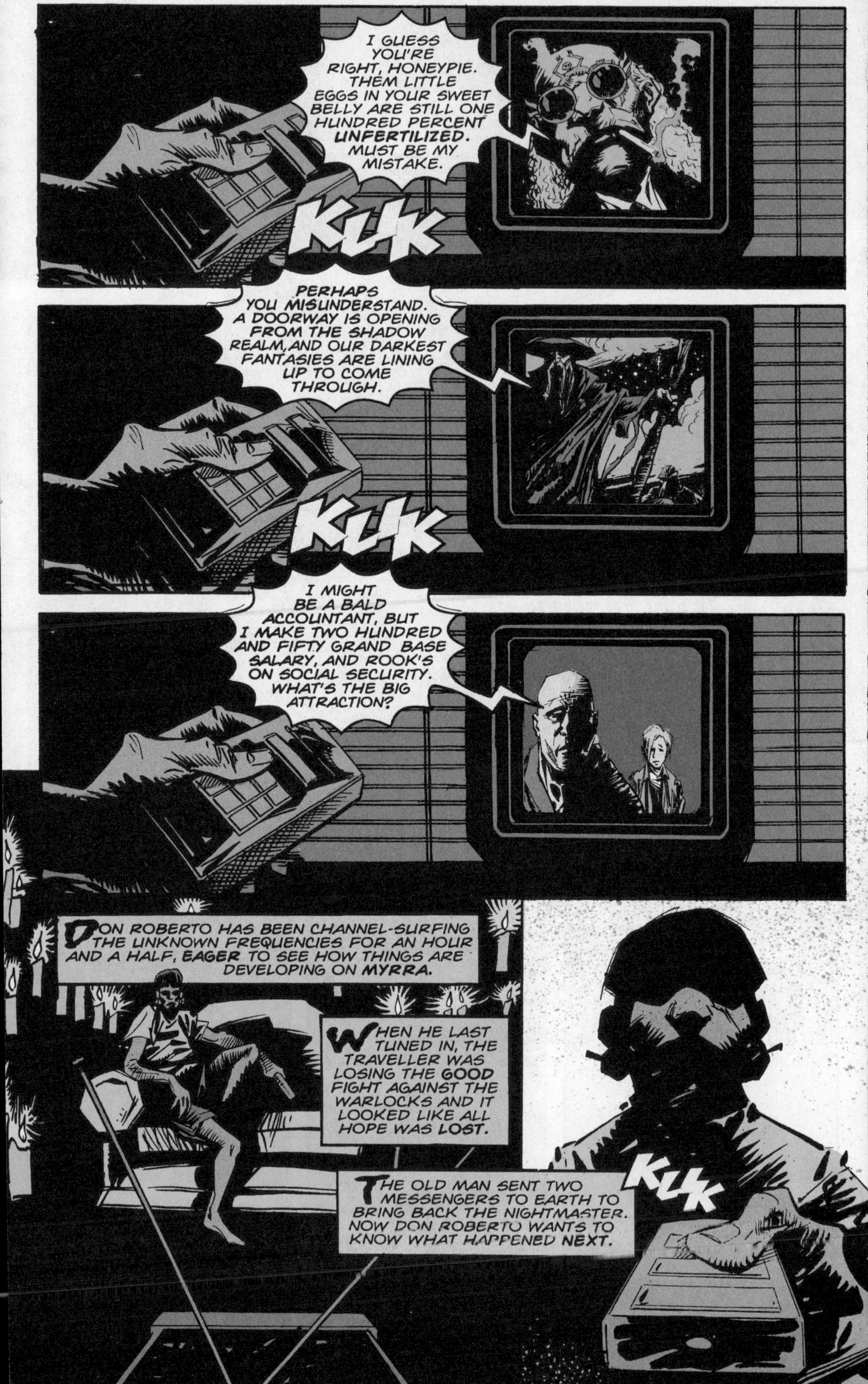
I GUESS YOU'RE RIGHT, HONEYPIE. THEM LITTLE EGGS IN YOUR SWEET BELLY ARE STILL ONE HUNDRED PERCENT **UNFERTILIZED**. MUST BE MY MISTAKE.
KLIK
PERHAPS YOU **MISUNDERSTAND**. A DOORWAY IS OPENING FROM THE SHADOW REALM, AND OUR DARKEST FANTASIES ARE LINING UP TO COME THROUGH.
KLIK
I MIGHT BE A BALD ACCOUNTANT, BUT I MAKE TWO HUNDRED AND FIFTY GRAND BASE SALARY, AND ROOK'S ON SOCIAL SECURITY. WHAT'S THE BIG ATTRACTION?
DON ROBERTO HAS BEEN CHANNEL-SURFING THE UNKNOWN FREQUENCIES FOR AN HOUR AND A HALF, **EAGER** TO SEE HOW THINGS ARE DEVELOPING ON **MYRRA**.
WHEN HE LAST TUNED IN, THE TRAVELLER WAS LOSING THE **GOOD** FIGHT AGAINST THE WARLOCKS AND IT LOOKED LIKE ALL HOPE WAS **LOST**.
KLIK
THE OLD MAN SENT TWO MESSENGERS TO EARTH TO BRING BACK THE NIGHTMASTER. NOW DON ROBERTO WANTS TO KNOW WHAT HAPPENED **NEXT**.

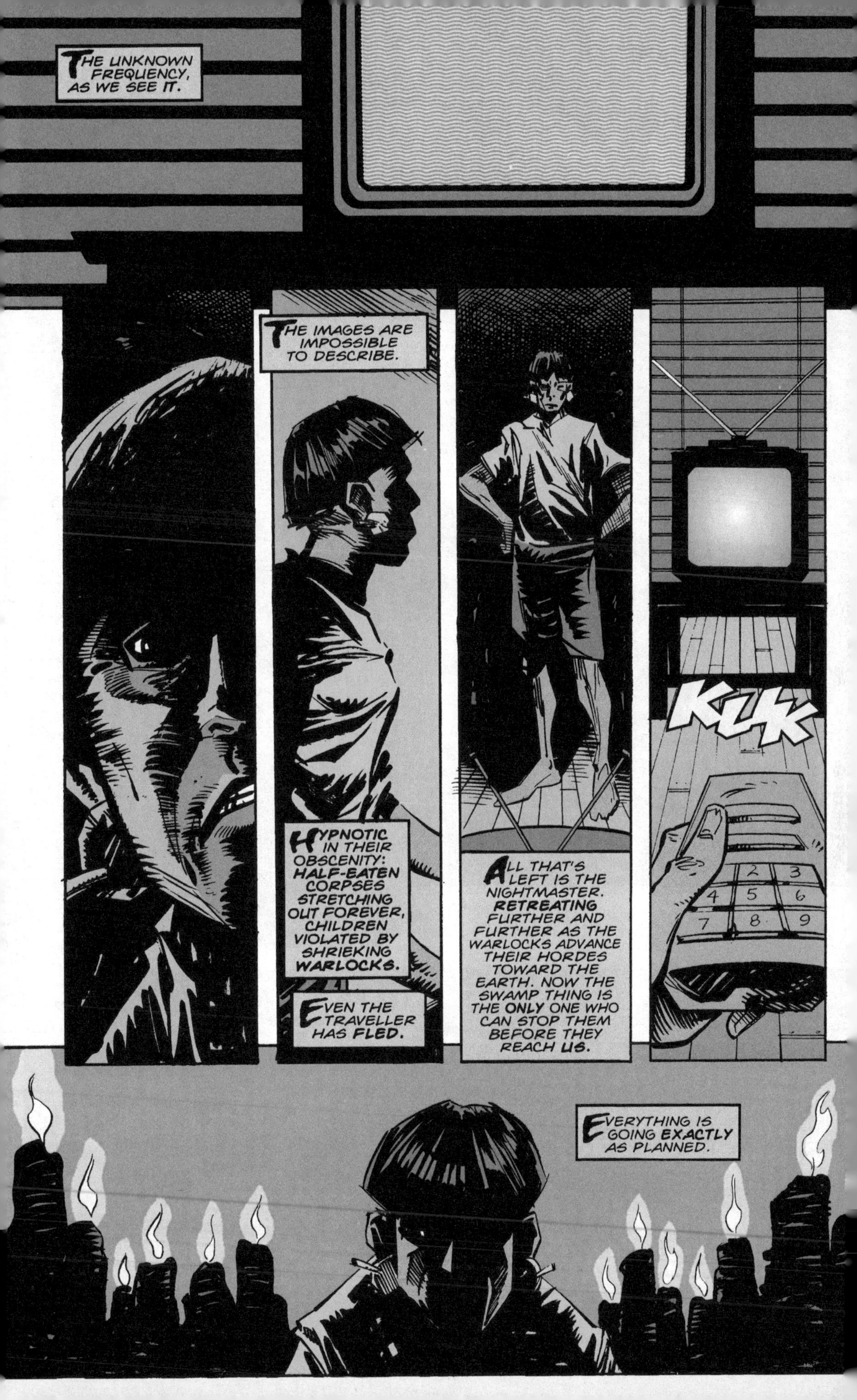

THE UNKNOWN FREQUENCY, AS WE SEE IT.
THE IMAGES ARE IMPOSSIBLE TO DESCRIBE.
HYPNOTIC IN THEIR OBSCENITY: HALF-EATEN CORPSES STRETCHING OUT FOREVER, CHILDREN VIOLATED BY SHRIEKING WARLOCKS.
EVEN THE TRAVELLER HAS FLED.
ALL THAT'S LEFT IS THE NIGHTMASTER. RETREATING FURTHER AND FURTHER AS THE WARLOCKS ADVANCE THEIR HORDES TOWARD THE EARTH. NOW THE SWAMP THING IS THE ONLY ONE WHO CAN STOP THEM BEFORE THEY REACH US.
KLIK
EVERYTHING IS GOING EXACTLY AS PLANNED.

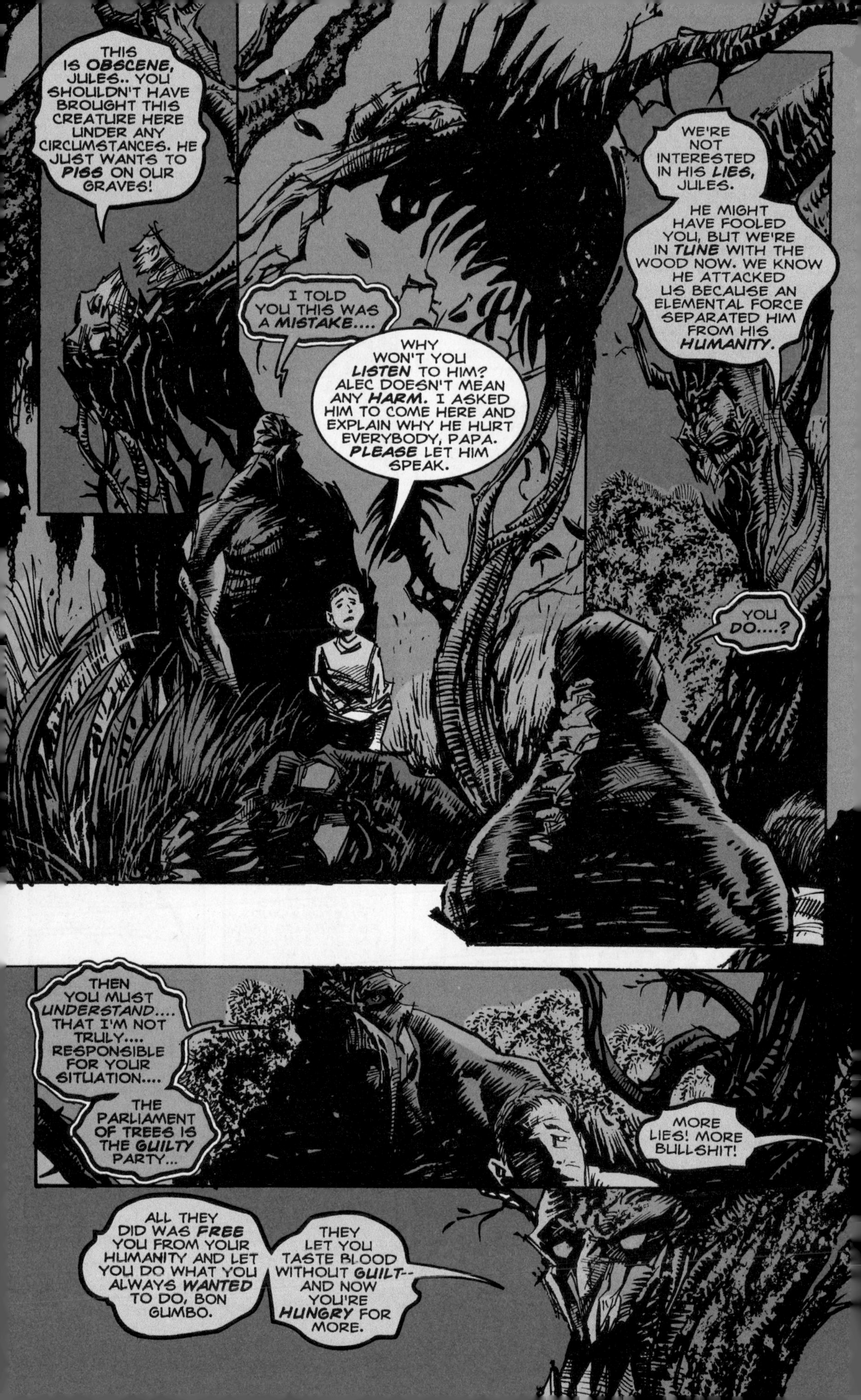
THIS IS OBSCENE, JULES.. YOU SHOULDN'T HAVE BROUGHT THIS CREATURE HERE UNDER ANY CIRCUMSTANCES. HE JUST WANTS TO PISS ON OUR GRAVES!
I TOLD YOU THIS WAS A MISTAKE....
WHY WON'T YOU LISTEN TO HIM? ALEC DOESN'T MEAN ANY HARM. I ASKED HIM TO COME HERE AND EXPLAIN WHY HE HURT EVERYBODY, PAPA. PLEASE LET HIM SPEAK.
WE'RE NOT INTERESTED IN HIS LIES, JULES.
HE MIGHT HAVE FOOLED YOU, BUT WE'RE IN TUNE WITH THE WOOD NOW. WE KNOW HE ATTACKED US BECAUSE AN ELEMENTAL FORCE SEPARATED HIM FROM HIS HUMANITY.
YOU DO....?
THEN YOU MUST UNDERSTAND.... THAT I'M NOT TRULY.... RESPONSIBLE FOR YOUR SITUATION....
THE PARLIAMENT OF TREES IS THE GUILTY PARTY...
MORE LIES! MORE BULLSHIT!
ALL THEY DID WAS FREE YOU FROM YOUR HUMANITY AND LET YOU DO WHAT YOU ALWAYS WANTED TO DO, BON GUMBO.
THEY LET YOU TASTE BLOOD WITHOUT GUILT-- AND NOW YOU'RE HUNGRY FOR MORE.

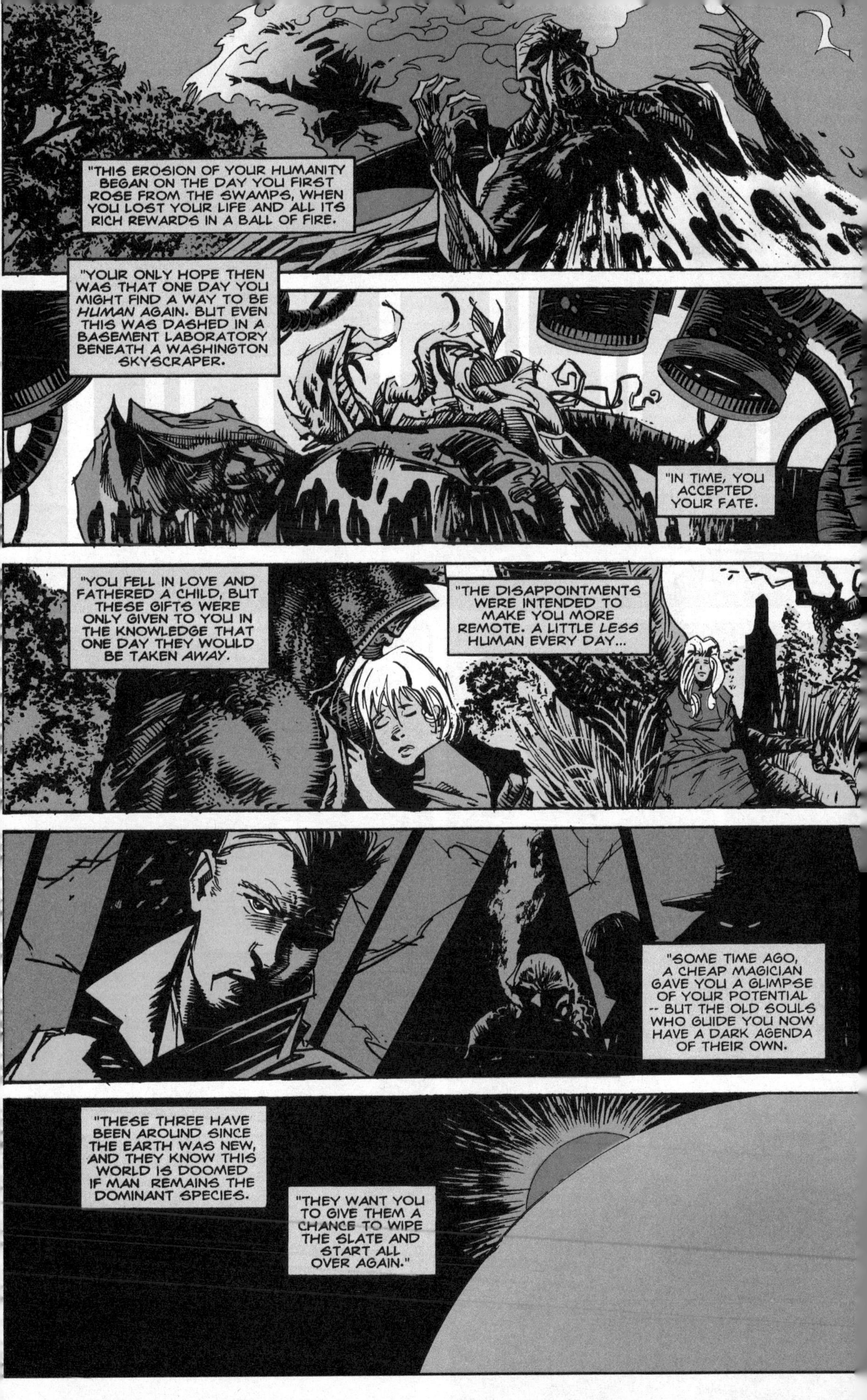
"THIS EROSION OF YOUR HUMANITY BEGAN ON THE DAY YOU FIRST ROSE FROM THE SWAMPS, WHEN YOU LOST YOUR LIFE AND ALL ITS RICH REWARDS IN A BALL OF FIRE.
"YOUR ONLY HOPE THEN WAS THAT ONE DAY YOU MIGHT FIND A WAY TO BE *HUMAN* AGAIN. BUT EVEN THIS WAS DASHED IN A BASEMENT LABORATORY BENEATH A WASHINGTON SKYSCRAPER.
"IN TIME, YOU ACCEPTED YOUR FATE.
"YOU FELL IN LOVE AND FATHERED A CHILD, BUT THESE GIFTS WERE ONLY GIVEN TO YOU IN THE KNOWLEDGE THAT ONE DAY THEY WOULD BE TAKEN *AWAY*.
"THE DISAPPOINTMENTS WERE INTENDED TO MAKE YOU MORE REMOTE. A LITTLE *LESS* HUMAN EVERY DAY...
"SOME TIME AGO, A CHEAP MAGICIAN GAVE YOU A GLIMPSE OF YOUR POTENTIAL -- BUT THE OLD SOULS WHO GUIDE YOU NOW HAVE A DARK AGENDA OF THEIR OWN.
"THESE THREE HAVE BEEN AROUND SINCE THE EARTH WAS NEW, AND THEY KNOW THIS WORLD IS DOOMED IF MAN REMAINS THE DOMINANT SPECIES.
"THEY WANT YOU TO GIVE THEM A CHANCE TO WIPE THE SLATE AND START ALL OVER AGAIN."

IMPOSSIBLE.... THESE ENTITIES HAVE BEEN GUIDING ME.... TO GREATNESS.... SO THAT I MIGHT PROTECT.... THE WORLD....

PROTECT US FROM *WHO?* MURDERERS? BANK ROBBERS?

THEY'RE CHIPPING AWAY AT YOUR HUMANITY UNTIL YOU SEE THE WORLD THROUGH AN UNCARING GOD'S EYES.

MANKIND IS THE VIRUS THEY WANT YOU TO ELIMINATE. A NEW SPECIES IS ALREADY BEING PREPARED TO TAKE OUR PLACE.

ALEC? IS...IS ANY OF THIS STUFF *TRUE?*

OF COURSE NOT.... THEY'RE LYING....

THEY'RE ALL INSANE....

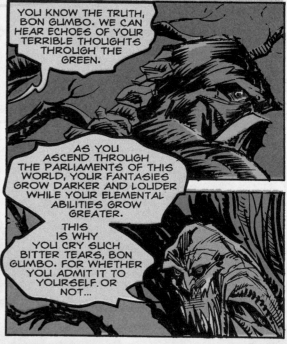

YOU KNOW THE TRUTH, BON GUMBO. WE CAN HEAR ECHOES OF YOUR TERRIBLE THOUGHTS THROUGH THE GREEN.

AS YOU ASCEND THROUGH THE PARLIAMENTS OF THIS WORLD, YOUR FANTASIES GROW DARKER AND LOUDER WHILE YOUR ELEMENTAL ABILITIES GROW GREATER.

THIS IS WHY YOU CRY SUCH BITTER TEARS, BON GUMBO. FOR WHETHER YOU ADMIT IT TO YOURSELF. OR NOT...

...WE KNOW YOU'RE LOOKING FORWARD TO THE DESTRUCTION TO COME.

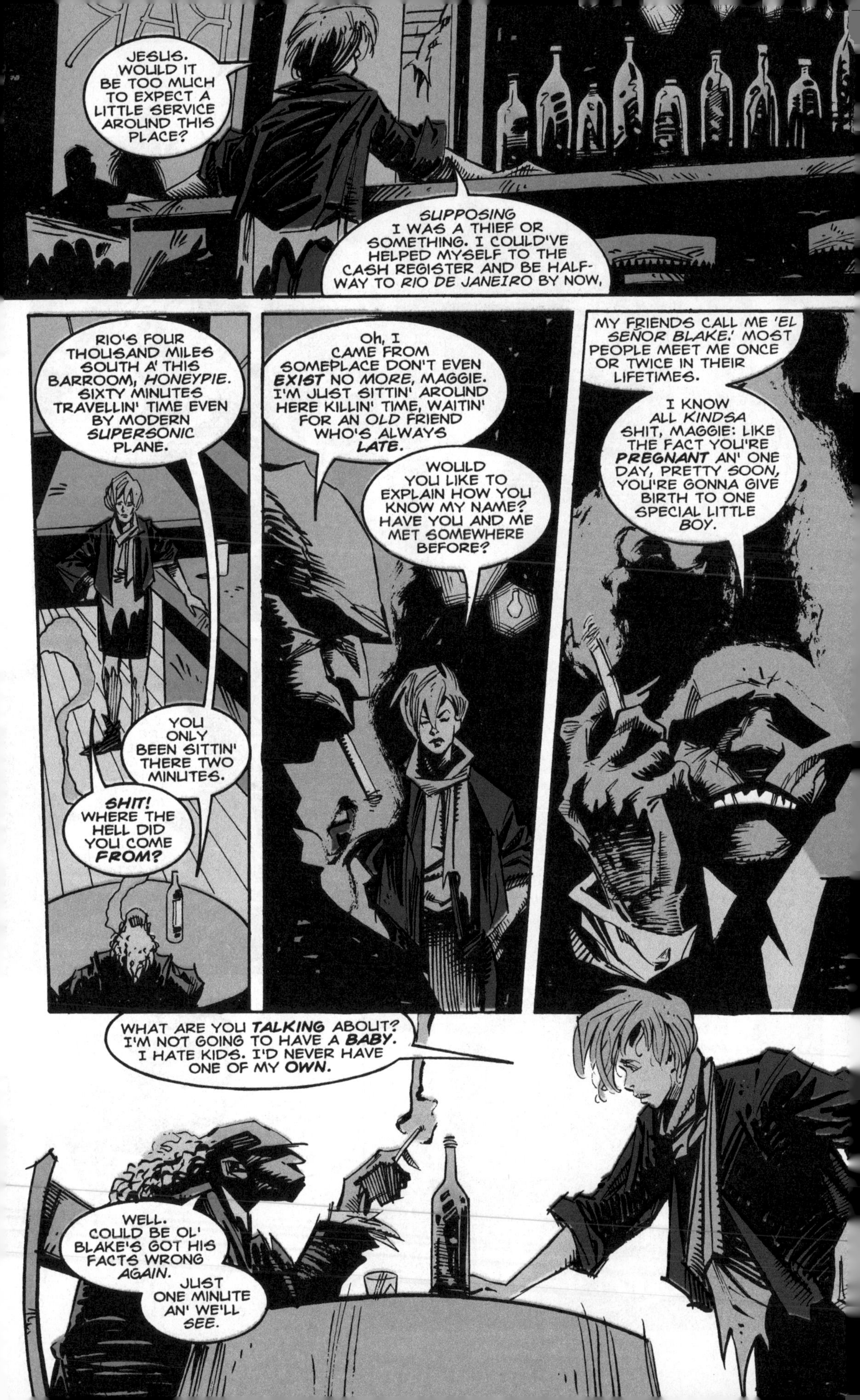
JESUS. WOULD IT BE TOO MUCH TO EXPECT A LITTLE SERVICE AROUND THIS PLACE?
SUPPOSING I WAS A THIEF OR SOMETHING. I COULD'VE HELPED MYSELF TO THE CASH REGISTER AND BE HALF-WAY TO RIO DE JANEIRO BY NOW,
RIO'S FOUR THOUSAND MILES SOUTH A' THIS BARROOM, HONEYPIE. SIXTY MINUTES TRAVELLIN' TIME EVEN BY MODERN SUPERSONIC PLANE.
YOU ONLY BEEN SITTIN' THERE TWO MINUTES.
SHIT! WHERE THE HELL DID YOU COME FROM?
Oh, I CAME FROM SOMEPLACE DON'T EVEN EXIST NO MORE, MAGGIE. I'M JUST SITTIN' AROUND HERE KILLIN' TIME, WAITIN' FOR AN OLD FRIEND WHO'S ALWAYS LATE.
WOULD YOU LIKE TO EXPLAIN HOW YOU KNOW MY NAME? HAVE YOU AND ME MET SOMEWHERE BEFORE?
MY FRIENDS CALL ME 'EL SEÑOR BLAKE.' MOST PEOPLE MEET ME ONCE OR TWICE IN THEIR LIFETIMES.
I KNOW ALL KINDSA SHIT, MAGGIE: LIKE THE FACT YOU'RE PREGNANT AN' ONE DAY, PRETTY SOON, YOU'RE GONNA GIVE BIRTH TO ONE SPECIAL LITTLE BOY.
WHAT ARE YOU TALKING ABOUT? I'M NOT GOING TO HAVE A BABY. I HATE KIDS. I'D NEVER HAVE ONE OF MY OWN.
WELL. COULD BE OL' BLAKE'S GOT HIS FACTS WRONG AGAIN.
JUST ONE MINUTE AN' WE'LL SEE.

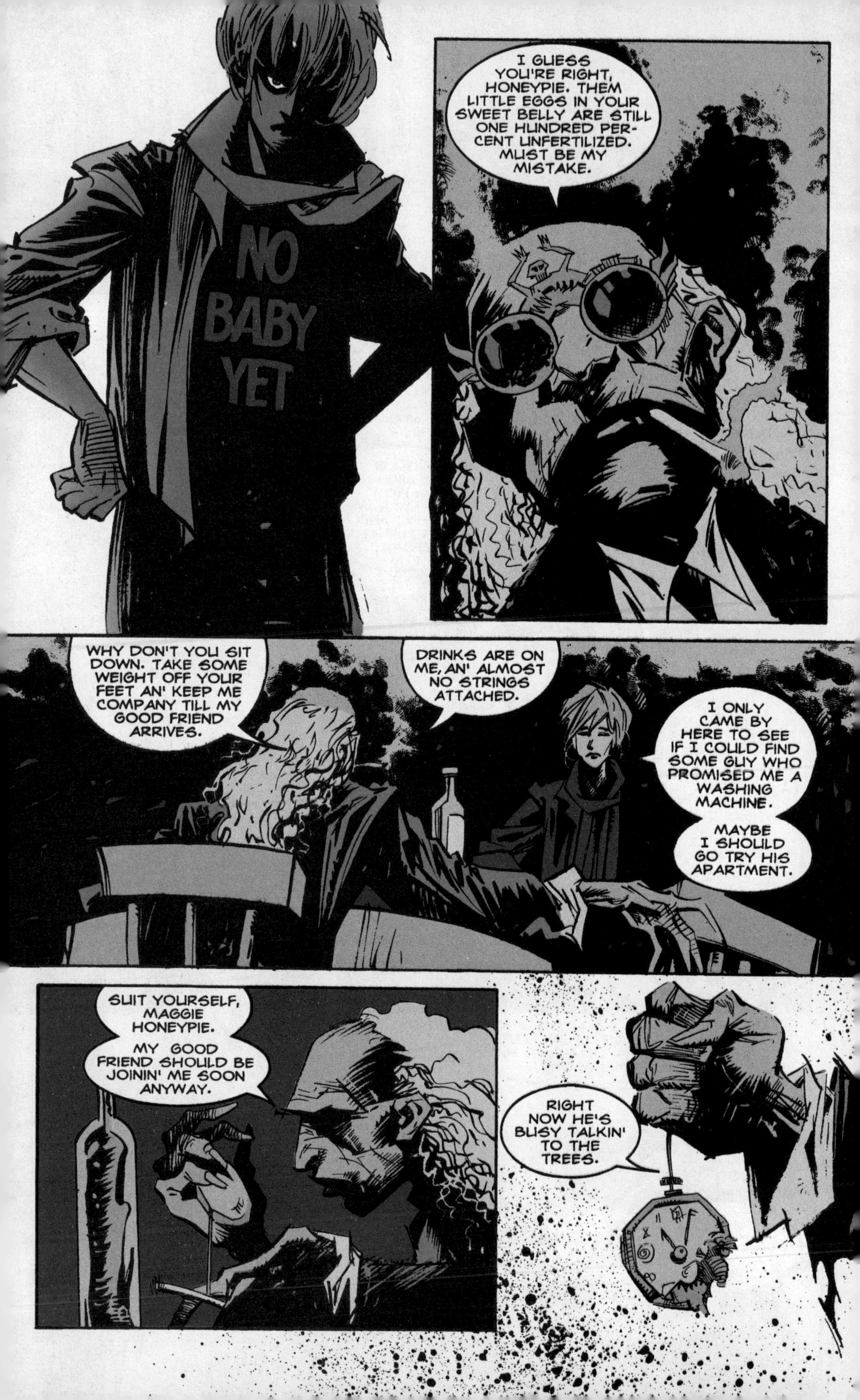
NO
BABY
YET
I GUESS YOU'RE RIGHT, HONEYPIE. THEM LITTLE EGGS IN YOUR SWEET BELLY ARE STILL ONE HUNDRED PER-CENT UNFERTILIZED. MUST BE MY MISTAKE.
WHY DON'T YOU SIT DOWN. TAKE SOME WEIGHT OFF YOUR FEET AN' KEEP ME COMPANY TILL MY GOOD FRIEND ARRIVES.
DRINKS ARE ON ME, AN' ALMOST NO STRINGS ATTACHED.
I ONLY CAME BY HERE TO SEE IF I COULD FIND SOME GUY WHO PROMISED ME A WASHING MACHINE.
MAYBE I SHOULD GO TRY HIS APARTMENT.
SUIT YOURSELF, MAGGIE HONEYPIE.
MY GOOD FRIEND SHOULD BE JOININ' ME SOON ANYWAY.
RIGHT NOW HE'S BUSY TALKIN' TO THE TREES.

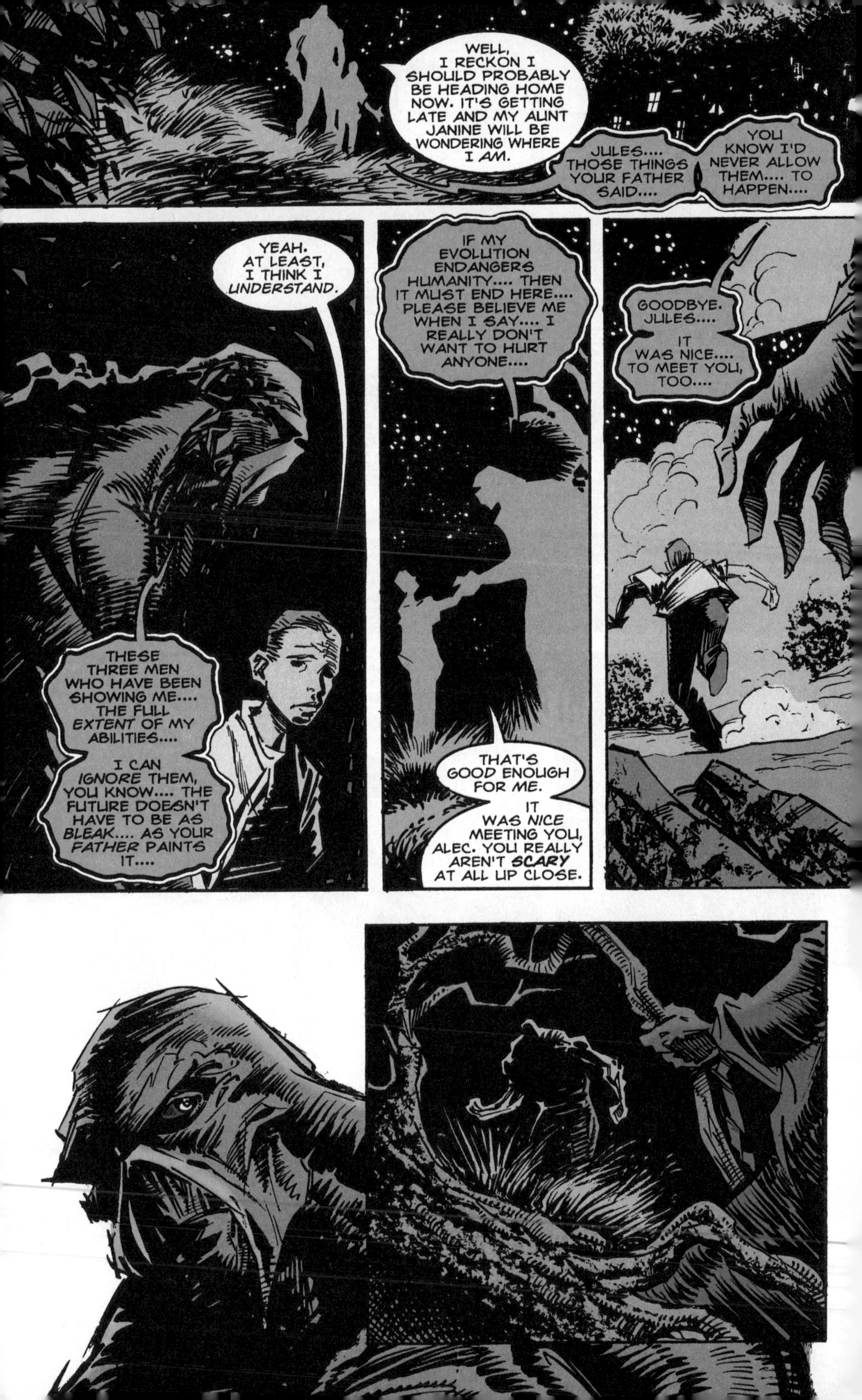
WELL, I RECKON I SHOULD PROBABLY BE HEADING HOME NOW. IT'S GETTING LATE AND MY AUNT JANINE WILL BE WONDERING WHERE I AM.
JULES.... THOSE THINGS YOUR FATHER SAID....
YOU KNOW I'D NEVER ALLOW THEM.... TO HAPPEN....
YEAH. AT LEAST, I THINK I UNDERSTAND.
THESE THREE MEN WHO HAVE BEEN SHOWING ME.... THE FULL EXTENT OF MY ABILITIES....
I CAN IGNORE THEM, YOU KNOW.... THE FUTURE DOESN'T HAVE TO BE AS BLEAK.... AS YOUR FATHER PAINTS IT....
IF MY EVOLUTION ENDANGERS HUMANITY.... THEN IT MUST END HERE.... PLEASE BELIEVE ME WHEN I SAY.... I REALLY DON'T WANT TO HURT ANYONE....
THAT'S GOOD ENOUGH FOR ME.
IT WAS NICE MEETING YOU, ALEC. YOU REALLY AREN'T SCARY AT ALL UP CLOSE.
GOODBYE. JULES....
IT WAS NICE.... TO MEET YOU, TOO....

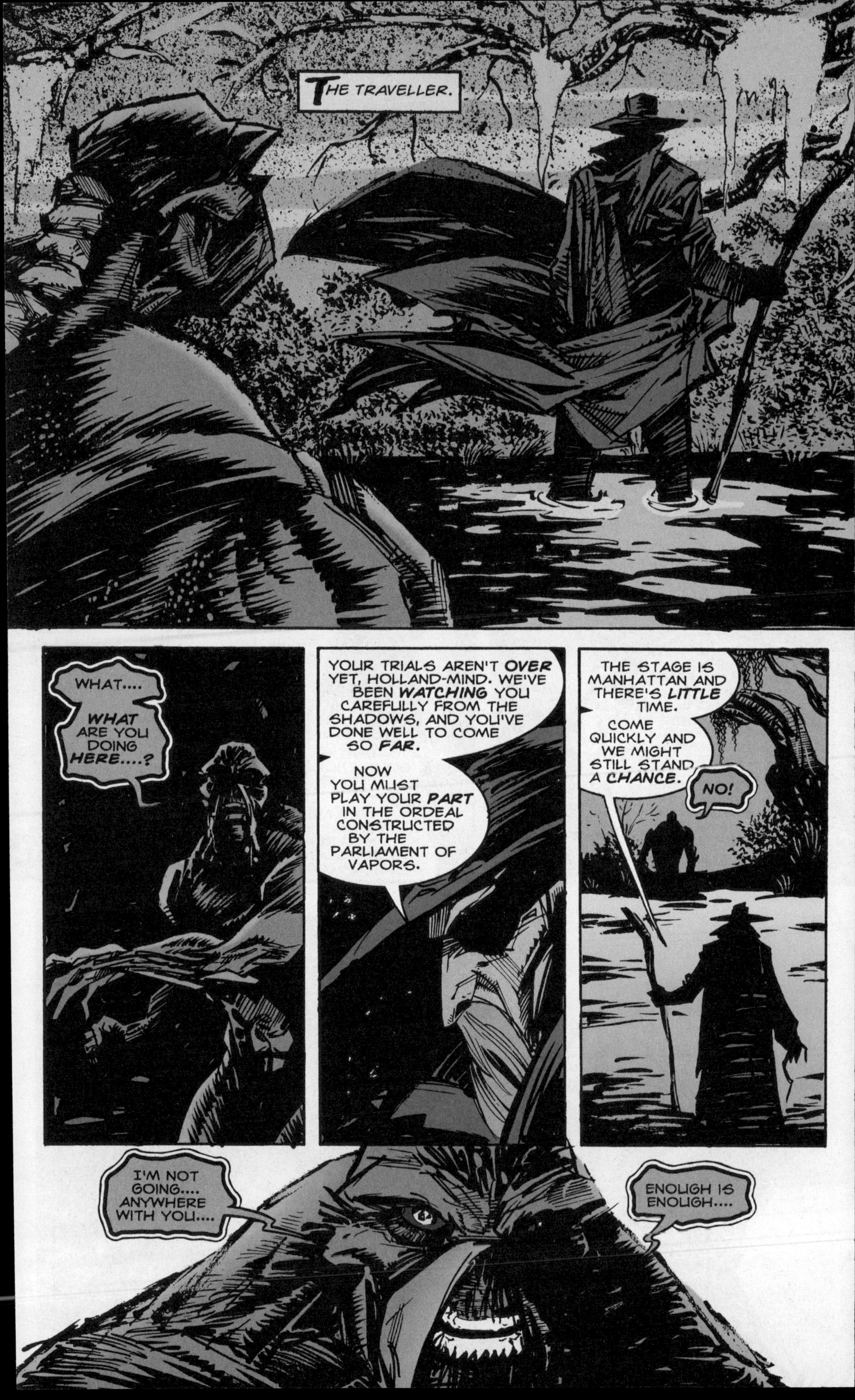
THE TRAVELLER.
WHAT.... WHAT ARE YOU DOING HERE....?
YOUR TRIALS AREN'T OVER YET, HOLLAND-MIND. WE'VE BEEN WATCHING YOU CAREFULLY FROM THE SHADOWS, AND YOU'VE DONE WELL TO COME SO FAR.
NOW YOU MUST PLAY YOUR PART IN THE ORDEAL CONSTRUCTED BY THE PARLIAMENT OF VAPORS.
THE STAGE IS MANHATTAN AND THERE'S LITTLE TIME.
COME QUICKLY AND WE MIGHT STILL STAND A CHANCE.
NO!
I'M NOT GOING.... ANYWHERE WITH YOU....
ENOUGH IS ENOUGH....

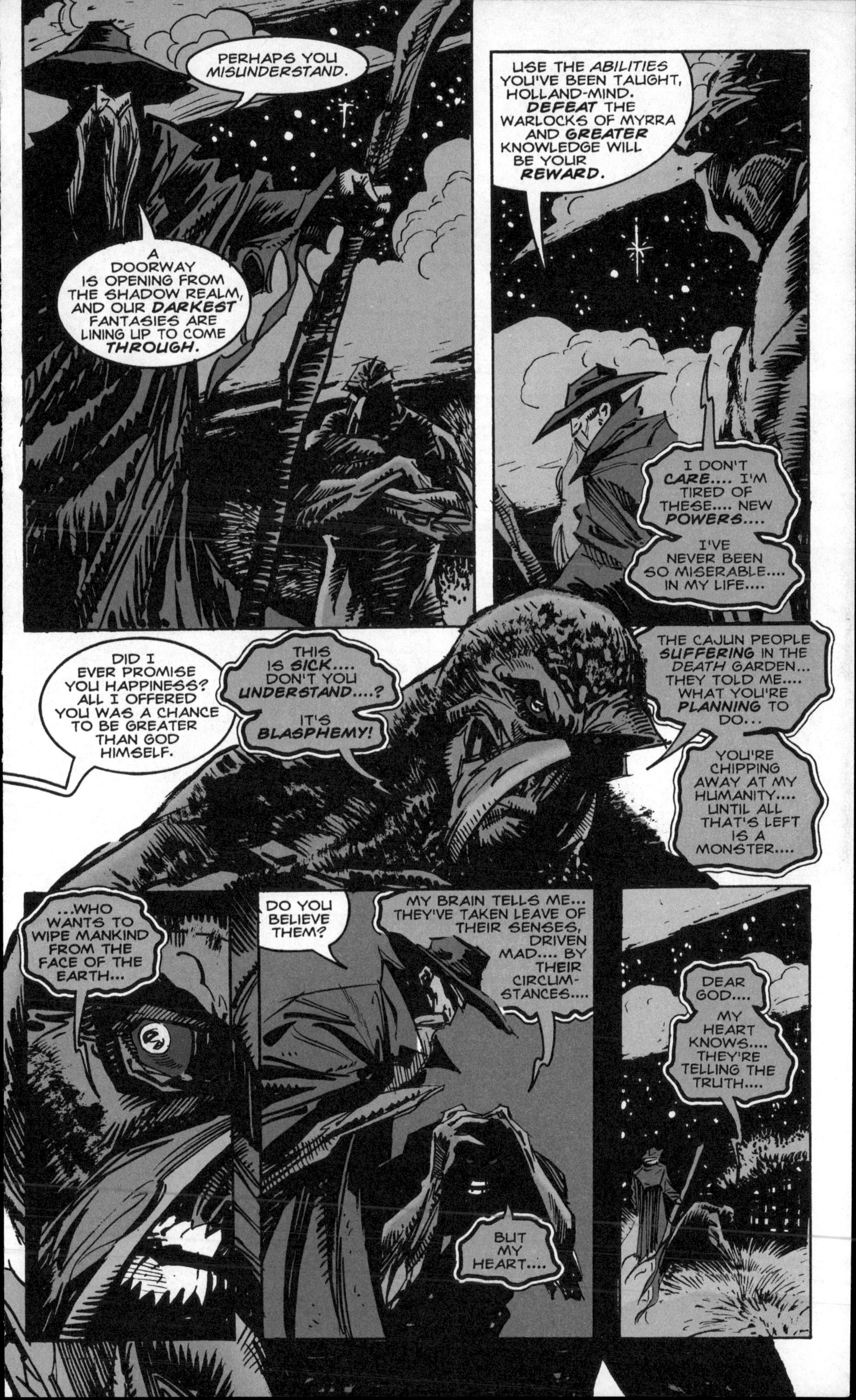
PERHAPS YOU MISUNDERSTAND.
A DOORWAY IS OPENING FROM THE SHADOW REALM, AND OUR DARKEST FANTASIES ARE LINING UP TO COME THROUGH.
USE THE ABILITIES YOU'VE BEEN TAUGHT, HOLLAND-MIND. DEFEAT THE WARLOCKS OF MYRRA AND GREATER KNOWLEDGE WILL BE YOUR REWARD.
I DON'T CARE.... I'M TIRED OF THESE.... NEW POWERS....
I'VE NEVER BEEN SO MISERABLE.... IN MY LIFE....
DID I EVER PROMISE YOU HAPPINESS? ALL I OFFERED YOU WAS A CHANCE TO BE GREATER THAN GOD HIMSELF.
THIS IS SICK.... DON'T YOU UNDERSTAND....?
IT'S BLASPHEMY!
THE CAJUN PEOPLE SUFFERING IN THE DEATH GARDEN... THEY TOLD ME.... WHAT YOU'RE PLANNING TO DO...
YOU'RE CHIPPING AWAY AT MY HUMANITY.... UNTIL ALL THAT'S LEFT IS A MONSTER....
...WHO WANTS TO WIPE MANKIND FROM THE FACE OF THE EARTH...
DO YOU BELIEVE THEM?
MY BRAIN TELLS ME... THEY'VE TAKEN LEAVE OF THEIR SENSES, DRIVEN MAD.... BY THEIR CIRCUM-STANCES....
BUT MY HEART....
DEAR GOD....
MY HEART KNOWS.... THEY'RE TELLING THE TRUTH....

THE *TRUTH* DOESN'T MATTER. THE ABILITIES YOU'VE BEEN SHOWN WERE GRANTED SO THAT YOU MIGHT *DEFEAT* THE WARLOCKS. USE THEM NOW, JUST AS YOU DESTROYED THE DRUID, OR THIS WORLD WILL MEET THE SAME FATE AS THEIR *OWN!*

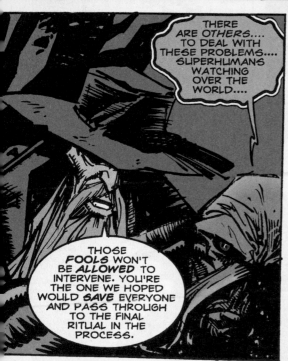

THERE ARE OTHERS.... TO DEAL WITH THESE PROBLEMS.... SUPERHUMANS WATCHING OVER THE WORLD....

THOSE *FOOLS* WON'T BE *ALLOWED* TO INTERVENE. YOU'RE THE ONE WE HOPED WOULD *SAVE* EVERYONE AND PASS THROUGH TO THE FINAL RITUAL IN THE PROCESS.

I DON'T *CARE....* ABOUT ANYTHING ANYMORE....

ALL I WANT IS *ABBY....* BACK IN MY ARMS.... AND THINGS TO BE JUST AS THEY *WERE....*

AND THAT IS YOUR FINAL *DECISION?*

YES....

THIS IS MY FINAL *DECISION....*

THEN YOUR *WORRY* THAT MY COLLEAGUES AND I ARE GUIDING YOU AWAY FROM YOUR HUMANITY IS *UNFOUNDED.*

I SUSPECT YOUR HUMANITY HAS ALREADY *DISAPPEARED.*

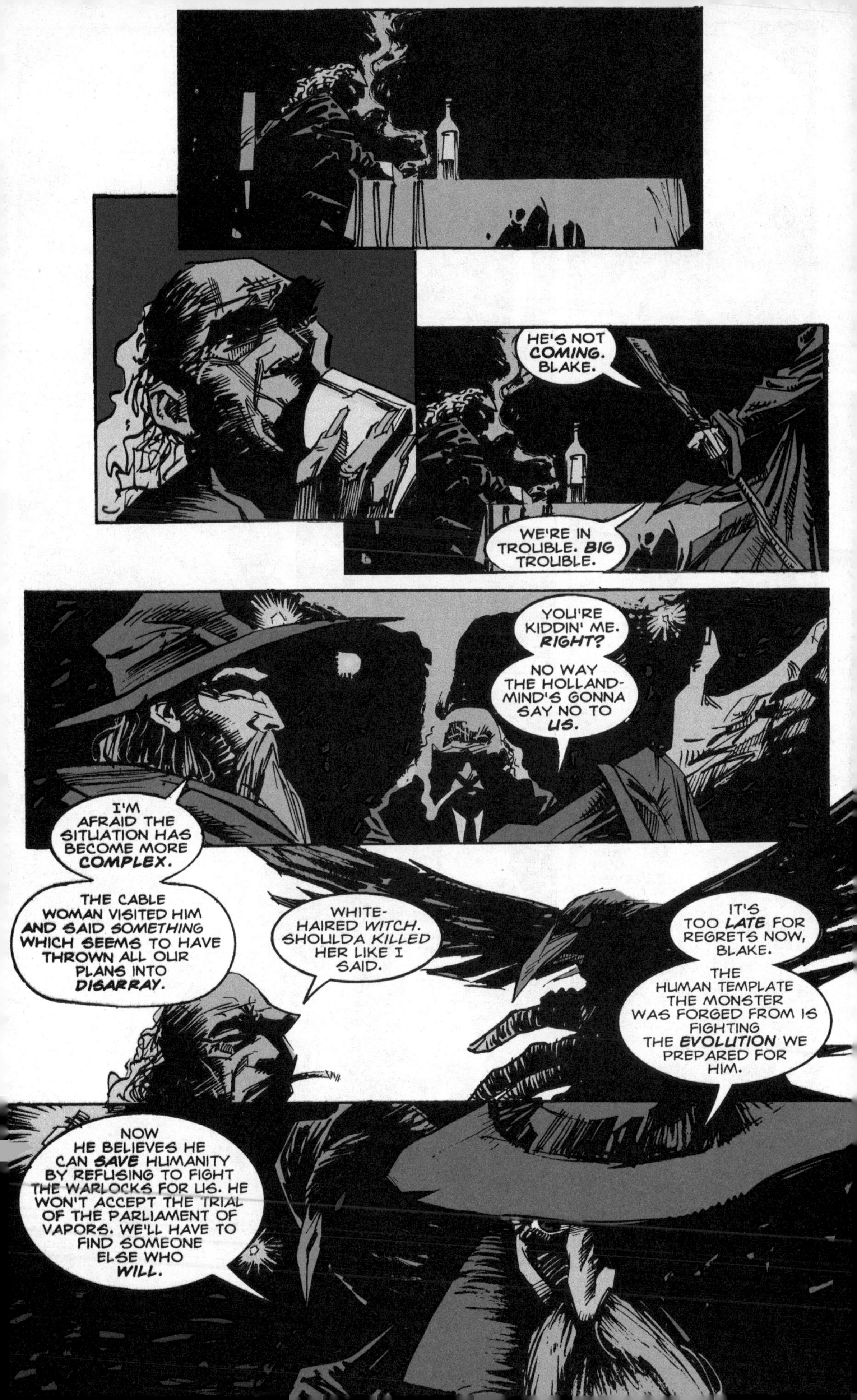

HE'S NOT COMING. BLAKE.
WE'RE IN TROUBLE. BIG TROUBLE.
YOU'RE KIDDIN' ME. RIGHT?
NO WAY THE HOLLAND-MIND'S GONNA SAY NO TO US.
I'M AFRAID THE SITUATION HAS BECOME MORE COMPLEX.
THE CABLE WOMAN VISITED HIM AND SAID SOMETHING WHICH SEEMS TO HAVE THROWN ALL OUR PLANS INTO DISARRAY.
WHITE-HAIRED WITCH. SHOULDA KILLED HER LIKE I SAID.
IT'S TOO LATE FOR REGRETS NOW, BLAKE.
THE HUMAN TEMPLATE THE MONSTER WAS FORGED FROM IS FIGHTING THE EVOLUTION WE PREPARED FOR HIM.
NOW HE BELIEVES HE CAN SAVE HUMANITY BY REFUSING TO FIGHT THE WARLOCKS FOR US. HE WON'T ACCEPT THE TRIAL OF THE PARLIAMENT OF VAPORS. WE'LL HAVE TO FIND SOMEONE ELSE WHO WILL.

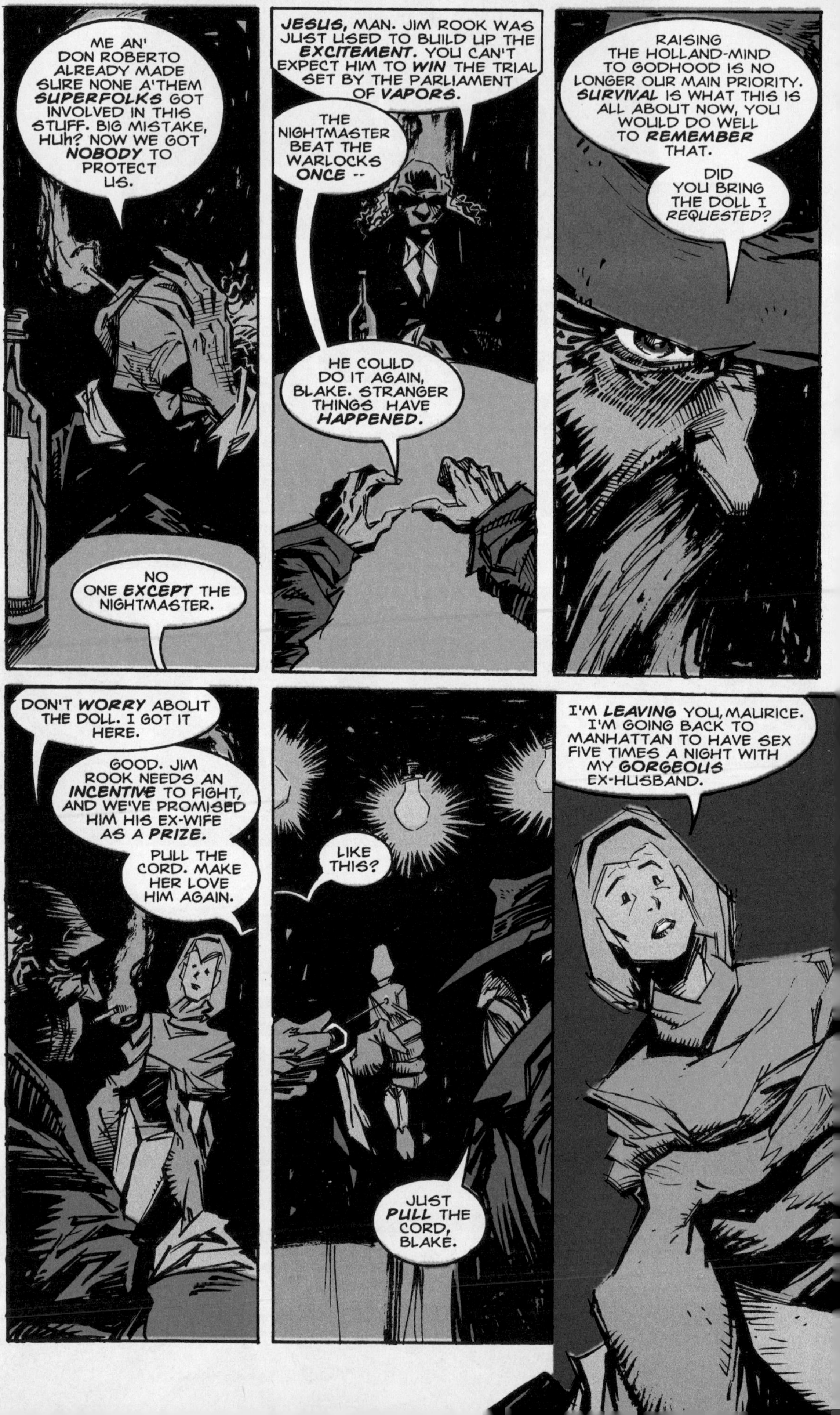

ME AN' DON ROBERTO ALREADY MADE SURE NONE A'THEM SUPERFOLKS GOT INVOLVED IN THIS STUFF. BIG MISTAKE, HUH? NOW WE GOT NOBODY TO PROTECT US.
NO ONE EXCEPT THE NIGHTMASTER.
JESUS, MAN. JIM ROOK WAS JUST USED TO BUILD UP THE EXCITEMENT. YOU CAN'T EXPECT HIM TO WIN THE TRIAL SET BY THE PARLIAMENT OF VAPORS.
THE NIGHTMASTER BEAT THE WARLOCKS ONCE --
HE COULD DO IT AGAIN, BLAKE. STRANGER THINGS HAVE HAPPENED.
RAISING THE HOLLAND-MIND TO GODHOOD IS NO LONGER OUR MAIN PRIORITY. SURVIVAL IS WHAT THIS IS ALL ABOUT NOW, YOU WOULD DO WELL TO REMEMBER THAT.
DID YOU BRING THE DOLL I REQUESTED?
DON'T WORRY ABOUT THE DOLL. I GOT IT HERE.
GOOD. JIM ROOK NEEDS AN INCENTIVE TO FIGHT, AND WE'VE PROMISED HIM HIS EX-WIFE AS A PRIZE.
PULL THE CORD. MAKE HER LOVE HIM AGAIN.
LIKE THIS?
JUST PULL THE CORD, BLAKE.
I'M LEAVING YOU, MAURICE. I'M GOING BACK TO MANHATTAN TO HAVE SEX FIVE TIMES A NIGHT WITH MY GORGEOUS EX-HUSBAND.

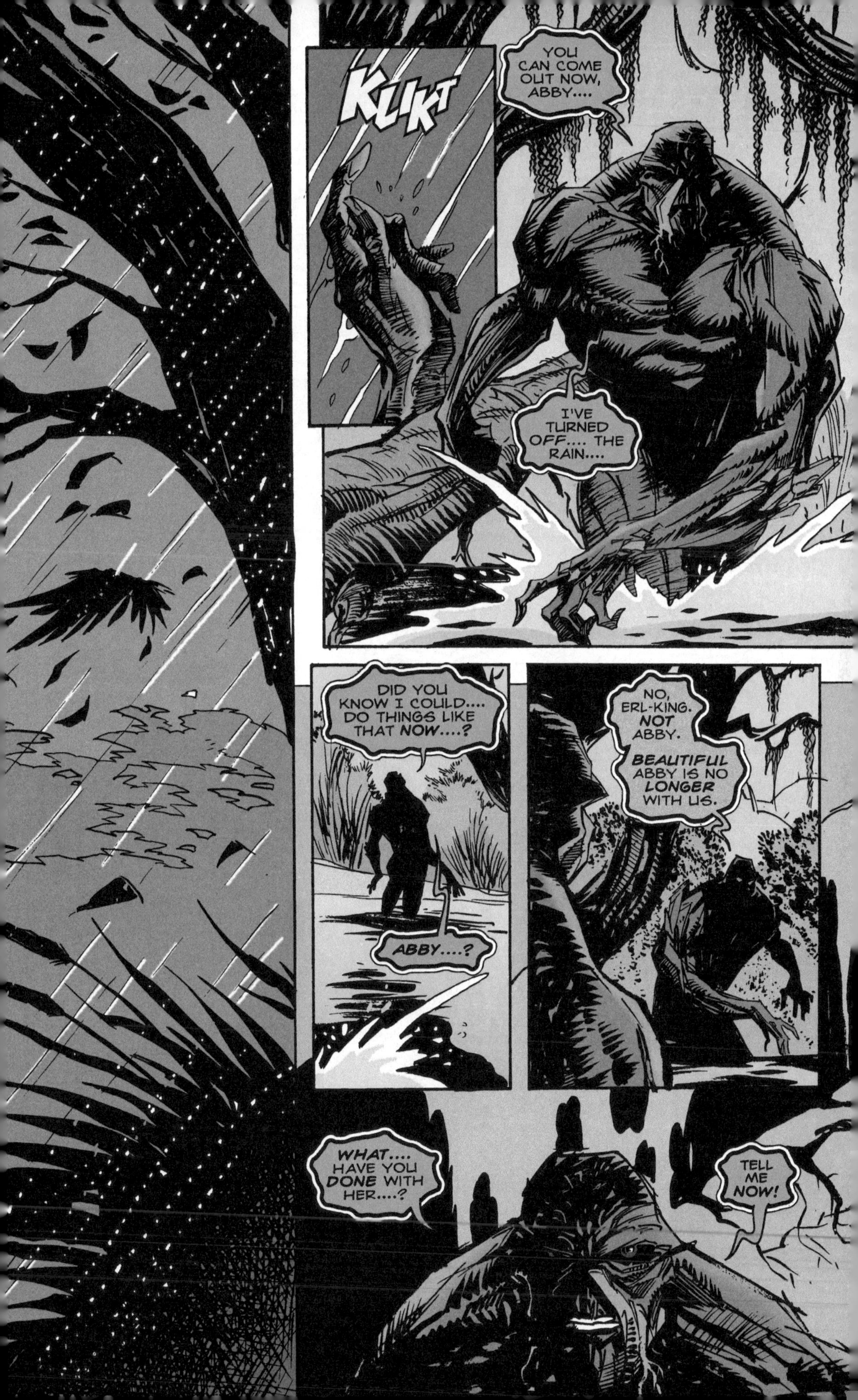
KLIKT
YOU CAN COME OUT NOW, ABBY....
I'VE TURNED OFF.... THE RAIN....
DID YOU KNOW I COULD.... DO THINGS LIKE THAT NOW....?
ABBY....?
NO, ERL-KING. NOT ABBY.
BEAUTIFUL ABBY IS NO LONGER WITH US.
WHAT.... HAVE YOU DONE WITH HER....?
TELL ME NOW!

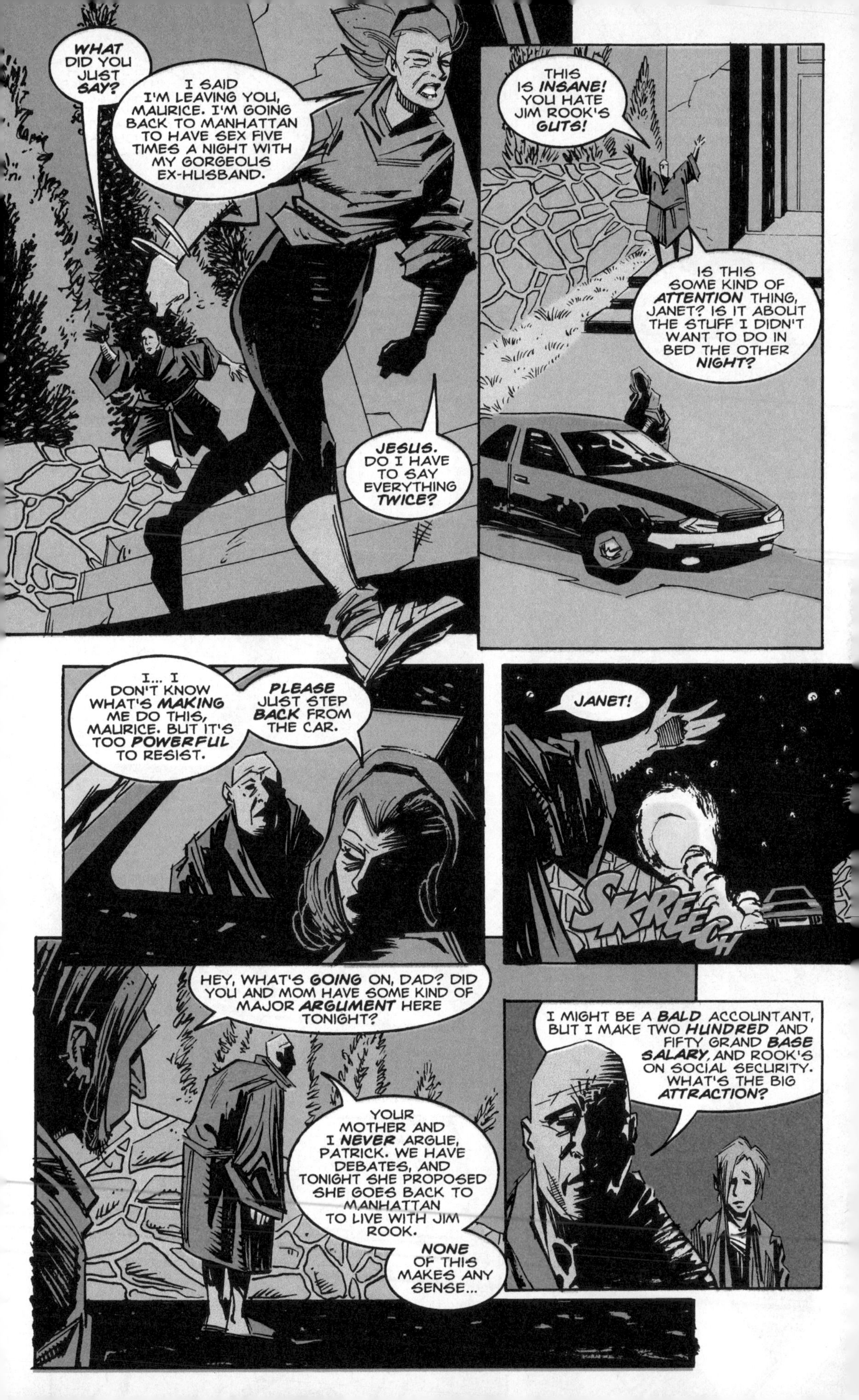
WHAT DID YOU JUST SAY?
I SAID I'M LEAVING YOU, MAURICE. I'M GOING BACK TO MANHATTAN TO HAVE SEX FIVE TIMES A NIGHT WITH MY GORGEOUS EX-HUSBAND.
JESUS. DO I HAVE TO SAY EVERYTHING TWICE?
THIS IS INSANE! YOU HATE JIM ROOK'S GUTS!
IS THIS SOME KIND OF ATTENTION THING, JANET? IS IT ABOUT THE STUFF I DIDN'T WANT TO DO IN BED THE OTHER NIGHT?
I... I DON'T KNOW WHAT'S MAKING ME DO THIS, MAURICE. BUT IT'S TOO POWERFUL TO RESIST.
PLEASE JUST STEP BACK FROM THE CAR.
JANET!
SKREECH
HEY, WHAT'S GOING ON, DAD? DID YOU AND MOM HAVE SOME KIND OF MAJOR ARGUMENT HERE TONIGHT?
YOUR MOTHER AND I NEVER ARGUE, PATRICK. WE HAVE DEBATES, AND TONIGHT SHE PROPOSED SHE GOES BACK TO MANHATTAN TO LIVE WITH JIM ROOK.
NONE OF THIS MAKES ANY SENSE...
I MIGHT BE A BALD ACCOUNTANT, BUT I MAKE TWO HUNDRED AND FIFTY GRAND BASE SALARY, AND ROOK'S ON SOCIAL SECURITY. WHAT'S THE BIG ATTRACTION?

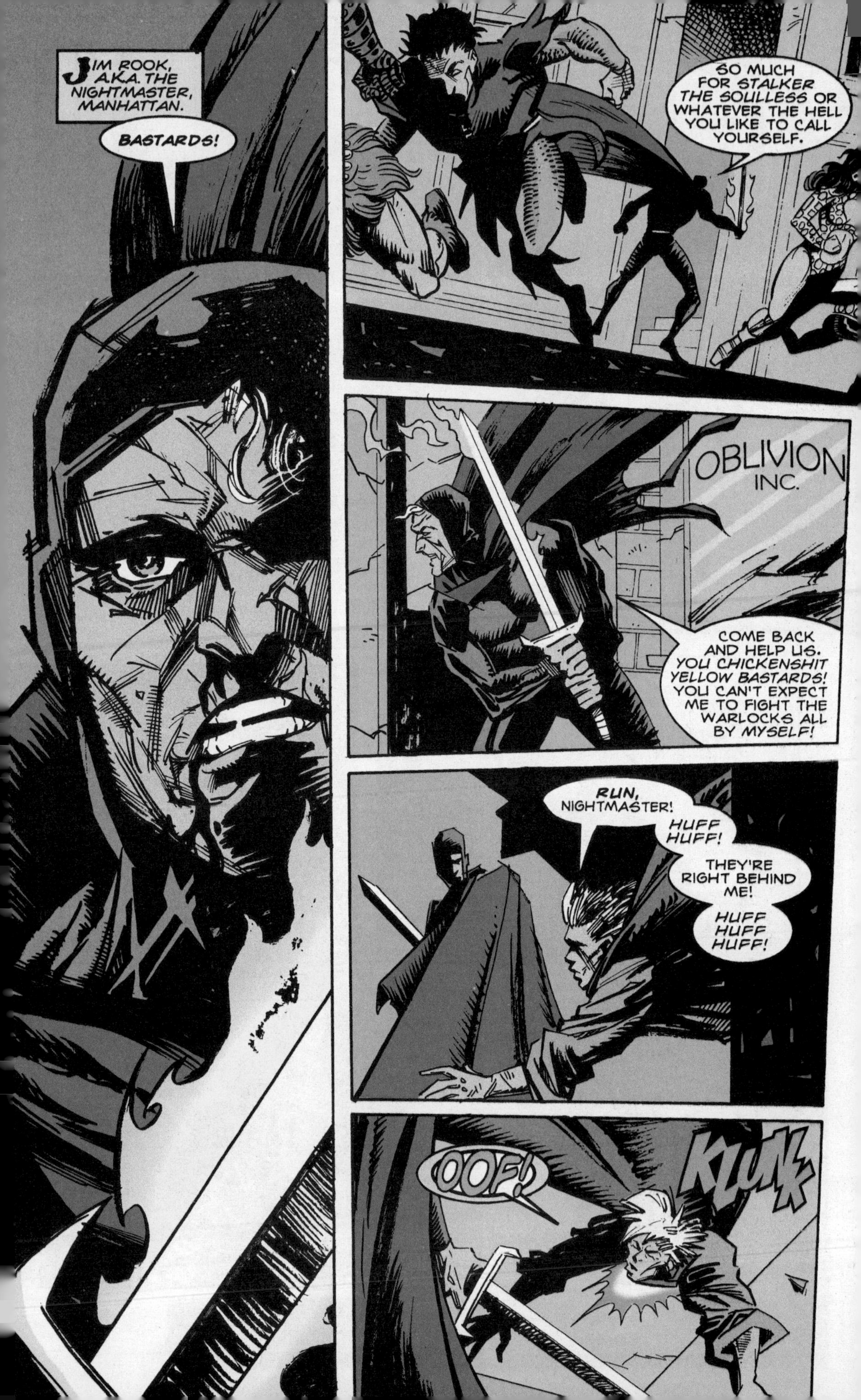
JIM ROOK, A.K.A. THE NIGHTMASTER, MANHATTAN.
BASTARDS!
SO MUCH FOR STALKER THE SOULLESS OR WHATEVER THE HELL YOU LIKE TO CALL YOURSELF.
OBLIVION INC.
COME BACK AND HELP US. YOU CHICKENSHIT YELLOW BASTARDS! YOU CAN'T EXPECT ME TO FIGHT THE WARLOCKS ALL BY MYSELF!
RUN, NIGHTMASTER!
HUFF HUFF!
THEY'RE RIGHT BEHIND ME!
HUFF HUFF HUFF!
OOF!
KLUNK

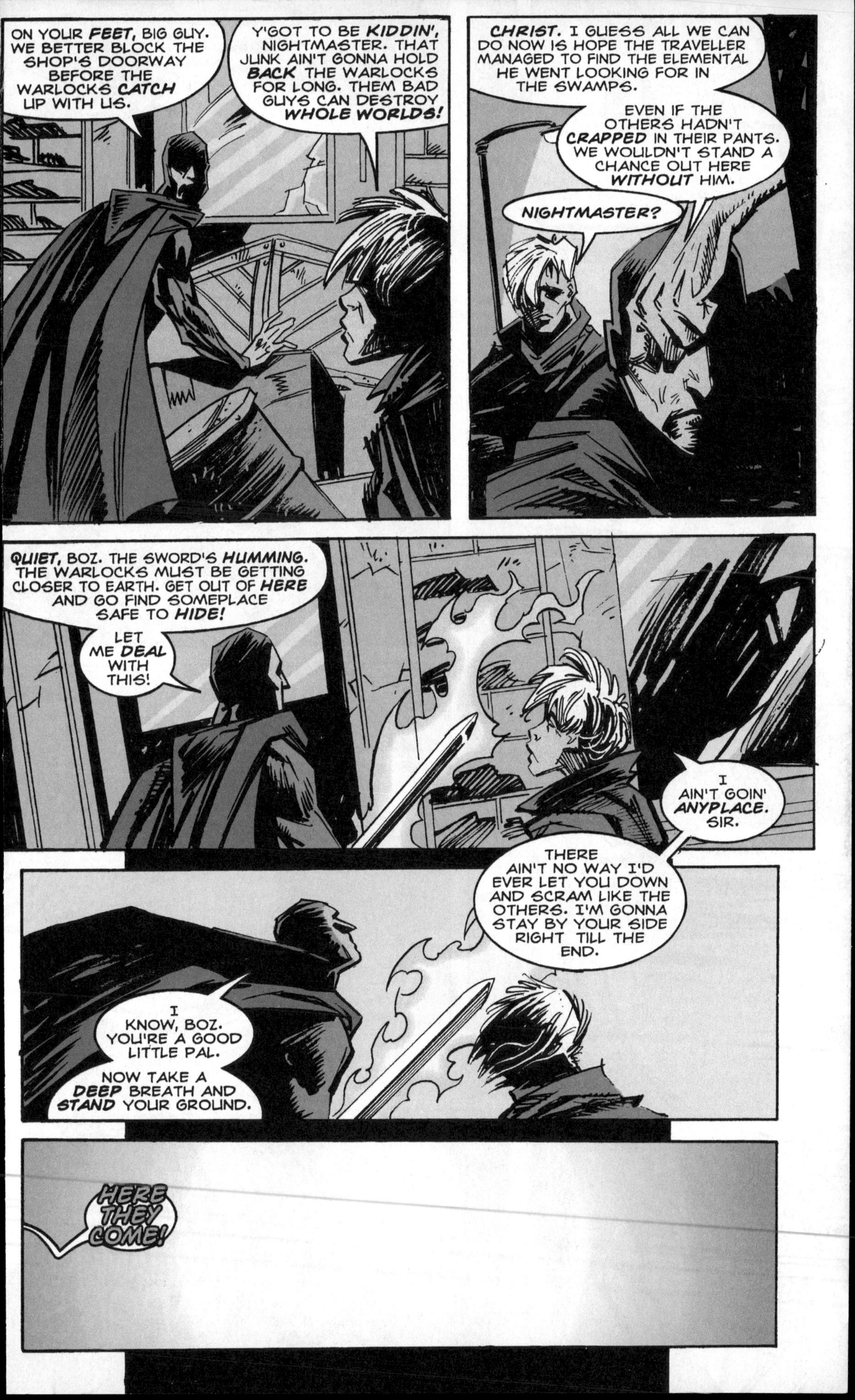
ON YOUR FEET, BIG GUY. WE BETTER BLOCK THE SHOP'S DOORWAY BEFORE THE WARLOCKS CATCH UP WITH US.
Y'GOT TO BE KIDDIN', NIGHTMASTER. THAT JUNK AIN'T GONNA HOLD BACK THE WARLOCKS FOR LONG. THEM BAD GUYS CAN DESTROY WHOLE WORLDS!
CHRIST. I GUESS ALL WE CAN DO NOW IS HOPE THE TRAVELLER MANAGED TO FIND THE ELEMENTAL HE WENT LOOKING FOR IN THE SWAMPS.
EVEN IF THE OTHERS HADN'T CRAPPED IN THEIR PANTS. WE WOULDN'T STAND A CHANCE OUT HERE WITHOUT HIM.
NIGHTMASTER?
QUIET, BOZ. THE SWORD'S HUMMING. THE WARLOCKS MUST BE GETTING CLOSER TO EARTH. GET OUT OF HERE AND GO FIND SOMEPLACE SAFE TO HIDE!
LET ME DEAL WITH THIS!
I AIN'T GOIN' ANYPLACE. SIR.
THERE AIN'T NO WAY I'D EVER LET YOU DOWN AND SCRAM LIKE THE OTHERS. I'M GONNA STAY BY YOUR SIDE RIGHT TILL THE END.
I KNOW, BOZ. YOU'RE A GOOD LITTLE PAL.
NOW TAKE A DEEP BREATH AND STAND YOUR GROUND.
HERE THEY COME!

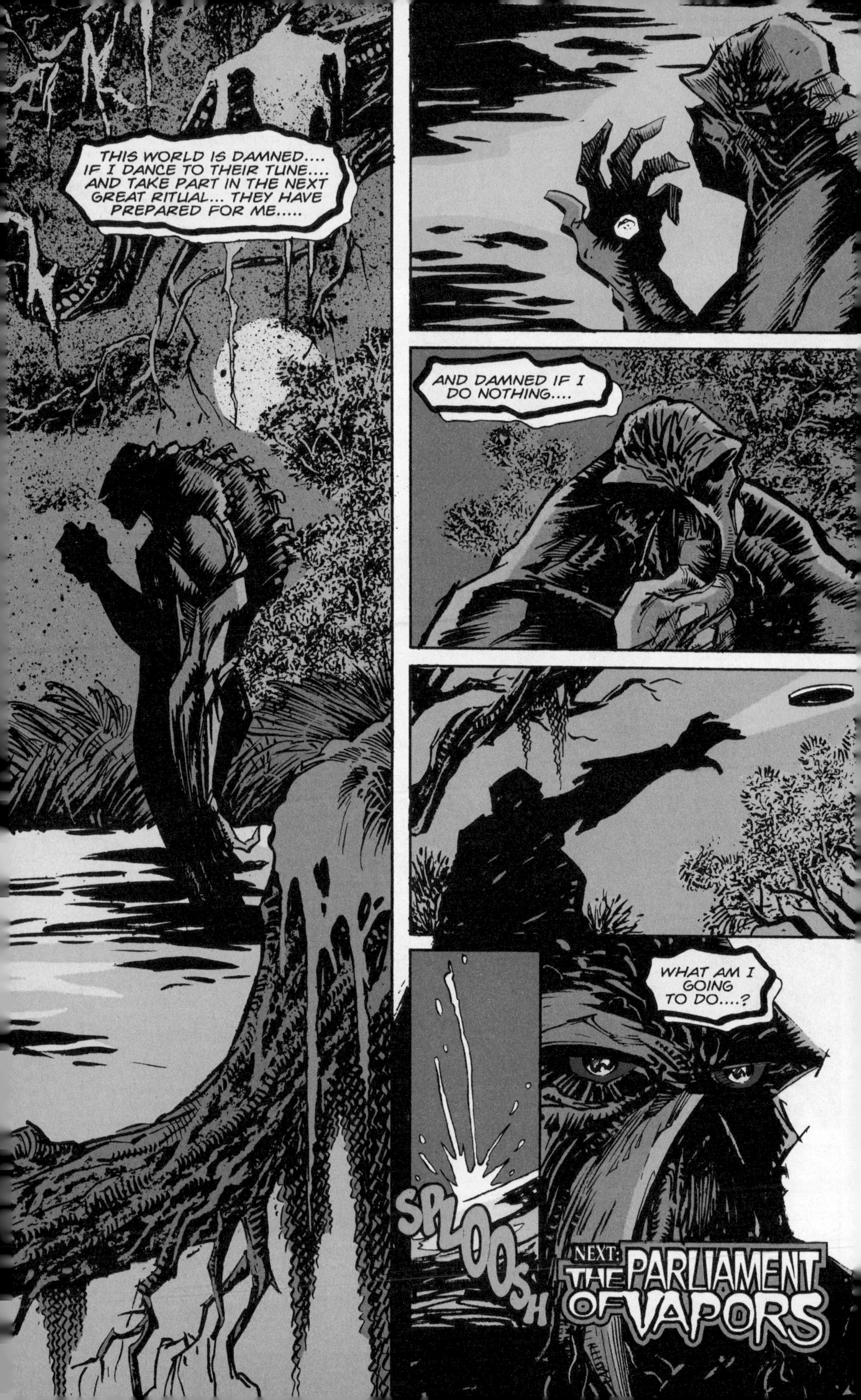
THIS WORLD IS DAMNED.... IF I DANCE TO THEIR TUNE.... AND TAKE PART IN THE NEXT GREAT RITUAL... THEY HAVE PREPARED FOR ME.....
AND DAMNED IF I DO NOTHING....
WHAT AM I GOING TO DO....?
SPLOOSH
NEXT: THE PARLIAMENT OF VAPORS

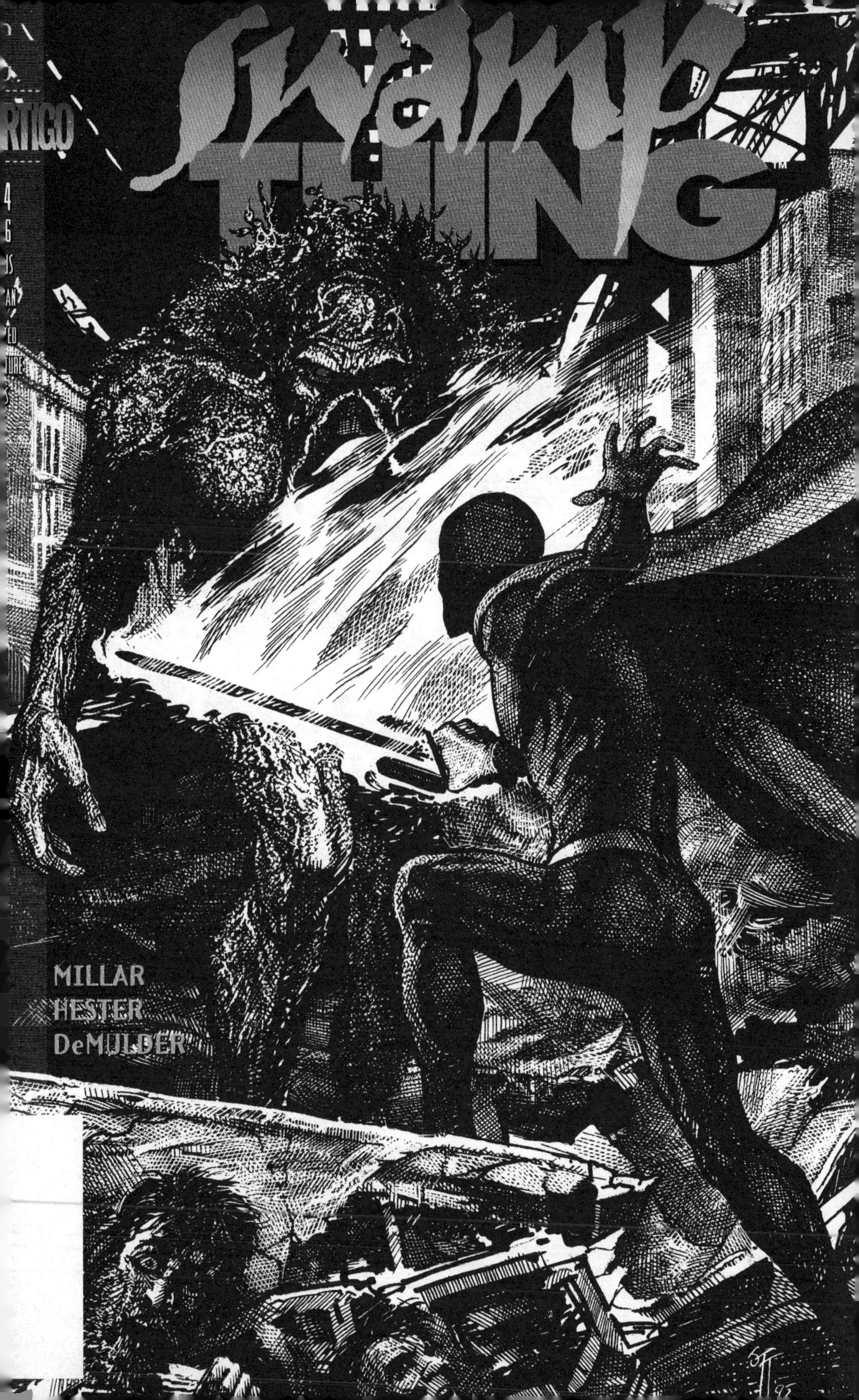
Swamp
THING™
MILLAR
HESTER
DeMULDER

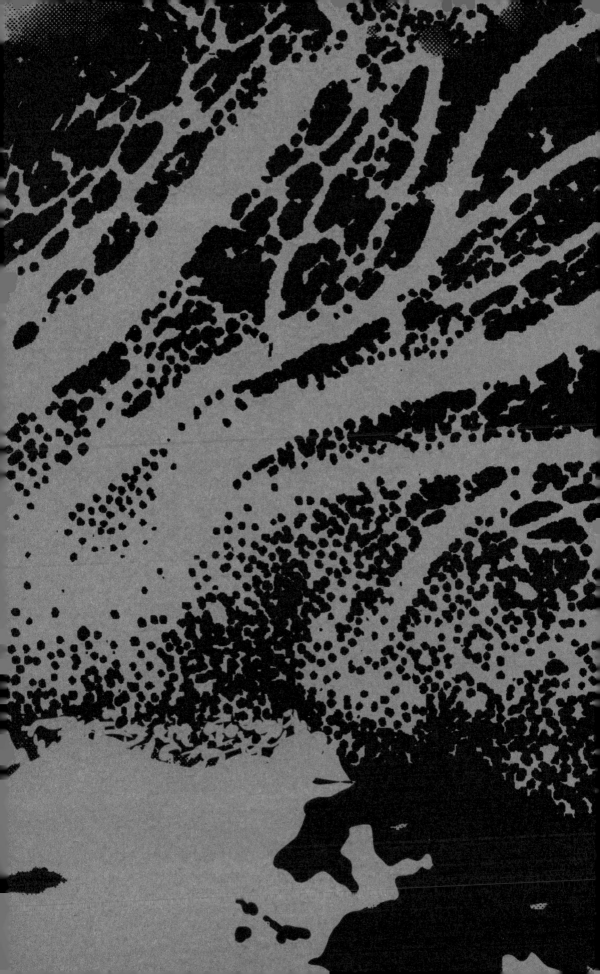

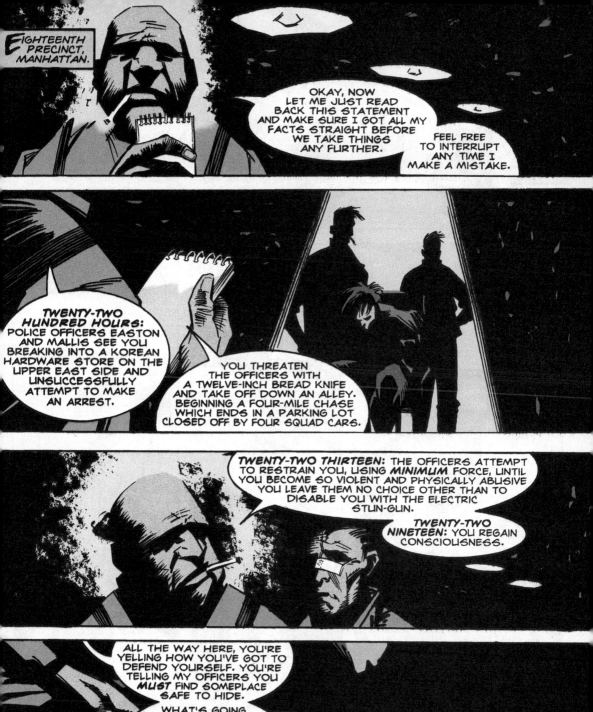

EIGHTEENTH PRECINCT, MANHATTAN.

OKAY, NOW LET ME JUST READ BACK THIS STATEMENT AND MAKE SURE I GOT ALL MY FACTS STRAIGHT BEFORE WE TAKE THINGS ANY FURTHER.

FEEL FREE TO INTERRUPT ANY TIME I MAKE A MISTAKE.

TWENTY-TWO HUNDRED HOURS: POLICE OFFICERS EASTON AND MALLIS SEE YOU BREAKING INTO A KOREAN HARDWARE STORE ON THE UPPER EAST SIDE AND UNSUCCESSFULLY ATTEMPT TO MAKE AN ARREST.

YOU THREATEN THE OFFICERS WITH A TWELVE-INCH BREAD KNIFE AND TAKE OFF DOWN AN ALLEY. BEGINNING A FOUR-MILE CHASE WHICH ENDS IN A PARKING LOT CLOSED OFF BY FOUR SQUAD CARS.

TWENTY-TWO THIRTEEN: THE OFFICERS ATTEMPT TO RESTRAIN YOU, USING MINIMUM FORCE, UNTIL YOU BECOME SO VIOLENT AND PHYSICALLY ABUSIVE YOU LEAVE THEM NO CHOICE OTHER THAN TO DISABLE YOU WITH THE ELECTRIC STUN-GUN.

TWENTY-TWO NINETEEN: YOU REGAIN CONSCIOUSNESS.

ALL THE WAY HERE, YOU'RE YELLING HOW YOU'VE GOT TO DEFEND YOURSELF. YOU'RE TELLING MY OFFICERS YOU MUST FIND SOMEPLACE SAFE TO HIDE.

WHAT'S GOING ON, ASSHOLE? HOW COME YOU'RE TRYING TO HOLE UP IN A KOREAN HARDWARE STORE DRESSED LIKE CONAN THE GODDAMN BARBARIAN?

I ALREADY TOLD YOU...

THE WARLOCKS CHASED US TO THIS REALM.

WE COULDN'T HOLD THEM BACK FROM YOU PEOPLE ANY LONGER.

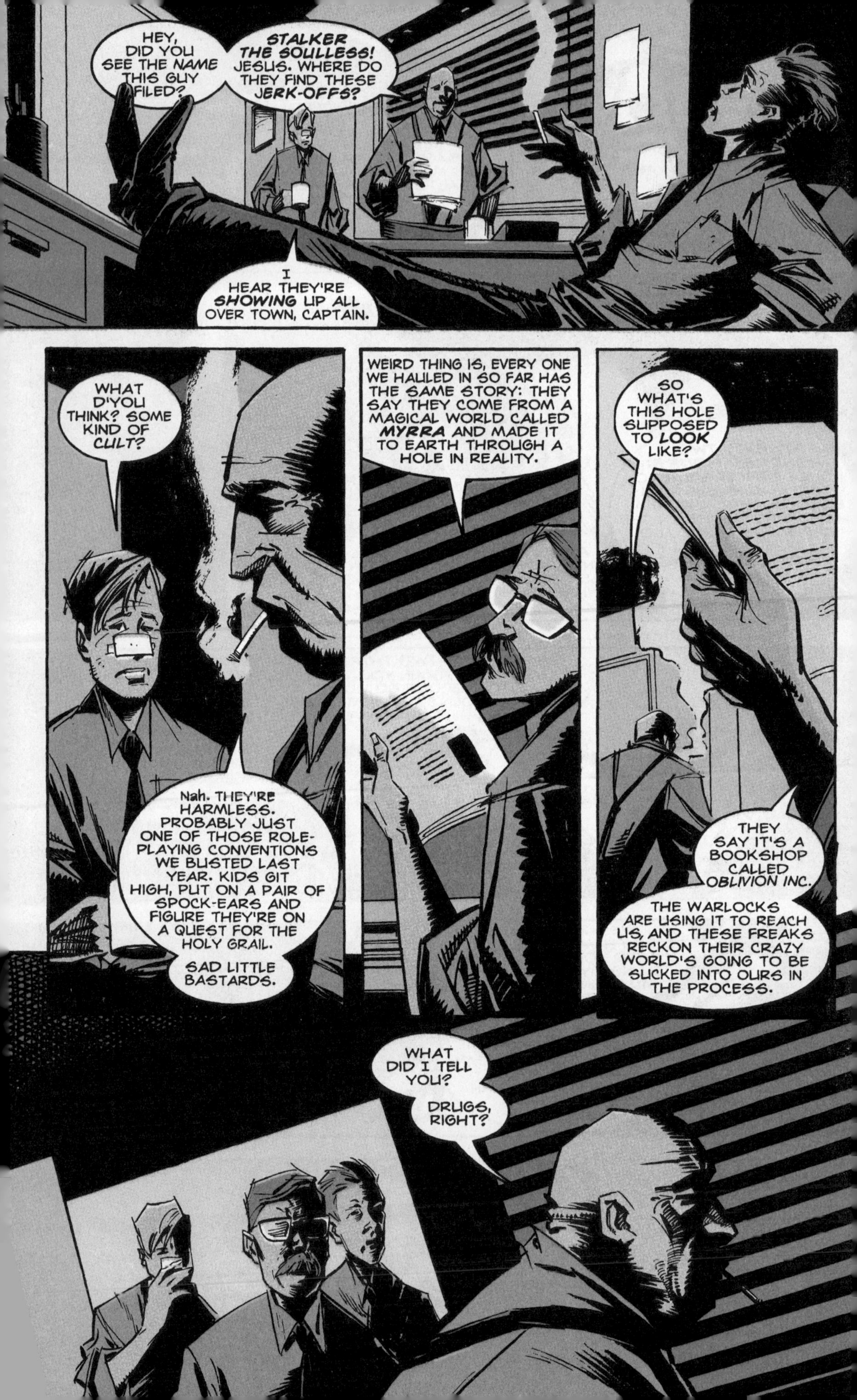

HEY, DID YOU SEE THE NAME THIS GUY FILED?
STALKER THE SOULLESS! JESUS. WHERE DO THEY FIND THESE JERK-OFFS?
I HEAR THEY'RE SHOWING UP ALL OVER TOWN, CAPTAIN.
WHAT D'YOU THINK? SOME KIND OF CULT?
Nah. THEY'RE HARMLESS. PROBABLY JUST ONE OF THOSE ROLE-PLAYING CONVENTIONS WE BUSTED LAST YEAR. KIDS GIT HIGH, PUT ON A PAIR OF SPOCK-EARS AND FIGURE THEY'RE ON A QUEST FOR THE HOLY GRAIL.
SAD LITTLE BASTARDS.
WEIRD THING IS, EVERY ONE WE HAULED IN SO FAR HAS THE SAME STORY: THEY SAY THEY COME FROM A MAGICAL WORLD CALLED MYRRA AND MADE IT TO EARTH THROUGH A HOLE IN REALITY.
SO WHAT'S THIS HOLE SUPPOSED TO LOOK LIKE?
THEY SAY IT'S A BOOKSHOP CALLED OBLIVION INC.
THE WARLOCKS ARE USING IT TO REACH US, AND THESE FREAKS RECKON THEIR CRAZY WORLD'S GOING TO BE SUCKED INTO OURS IN THE PROCESS.
WHAT DID I TELL YOU?
DRUGS, RIGHT?

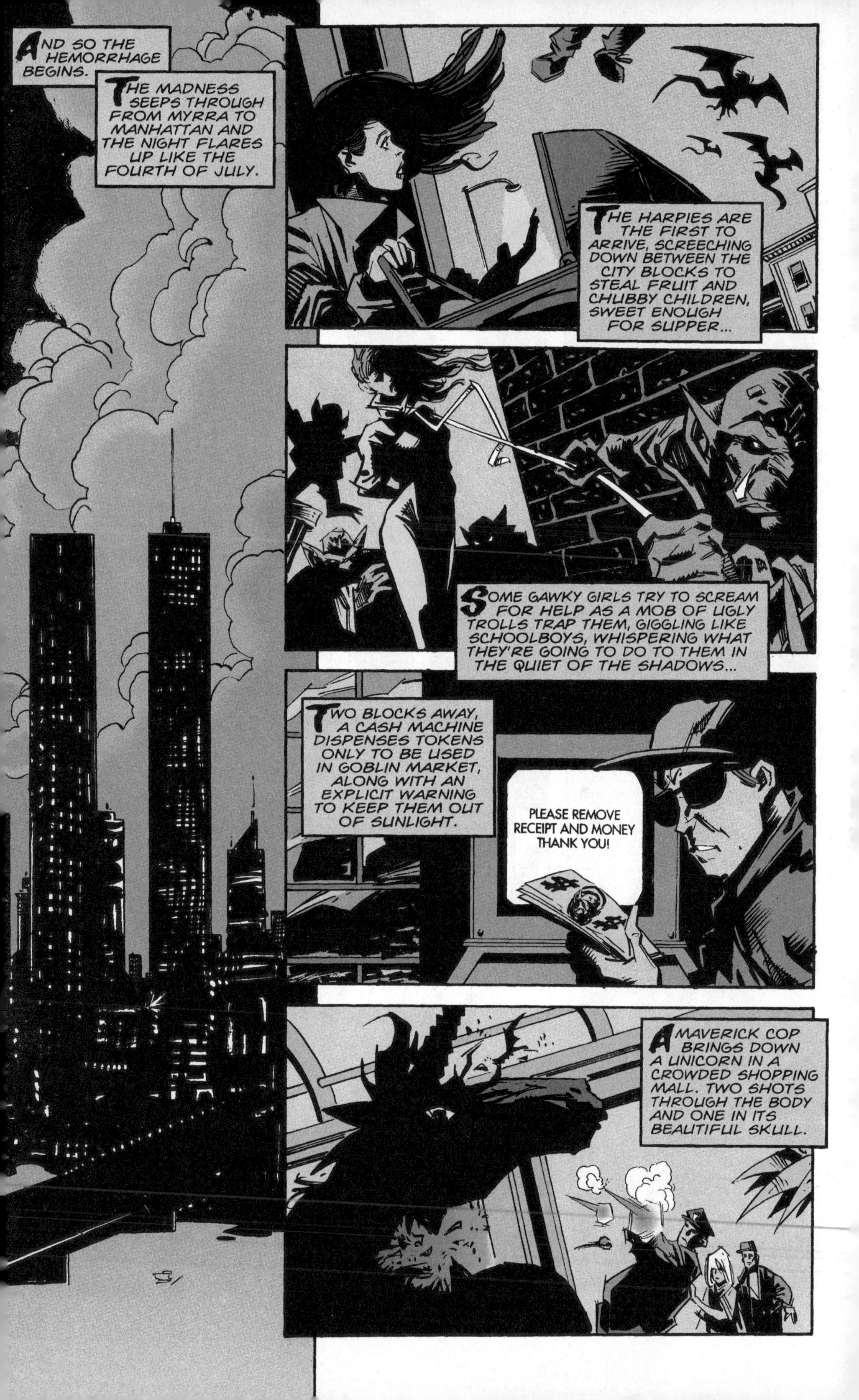
AND SO THE HEMORRHAGE BEGINS.
THE MADNESS SEEPS THROUGH FROM MYRRA TO MANHATTAN AND THE NIGHT FLARES UP LIKE THE FOURTH OF JULY.
THE HARPIES ARE THE FIRST TO ARRIVE, SCREECHING DOWN BETWEEN THE CITY BLOCKS TO STEAL FRUIT AND CHUBBY CHILDREN, SWEET ENOUGH FOR SUPPER...
SOME GAWKY GIRLS TRY TO SCREAM FOR HELP AS A MOB OF UGLY TROLLS TRAP THEM, GIGGLING LIKE SCHOOLBOYS, WHISPERING WHAT THEY'RE GOING TO DO TO THEM IN THE QUIET OF THE SHADOWS...
TWO BLOCKS AWAY, A CASH MACHINE DISPENSES TOKENS ONLY TO BE USED IN GOBLIN MARKET, ALONG WITH AN EXPLICIT WARNING TO KEEP THEM OUT OF SUNLIGHT.
PLEASE REMOVE RECEIPT AND MONEY THANK YOU!
A MAVERICK COP BRINGS DOWN A UNICORN IN A CROWDED SHOPPING MALL. TWO SHOTS THROUGH THE BODY AND ONE IN ITS BEAUTIFUL SKULL.

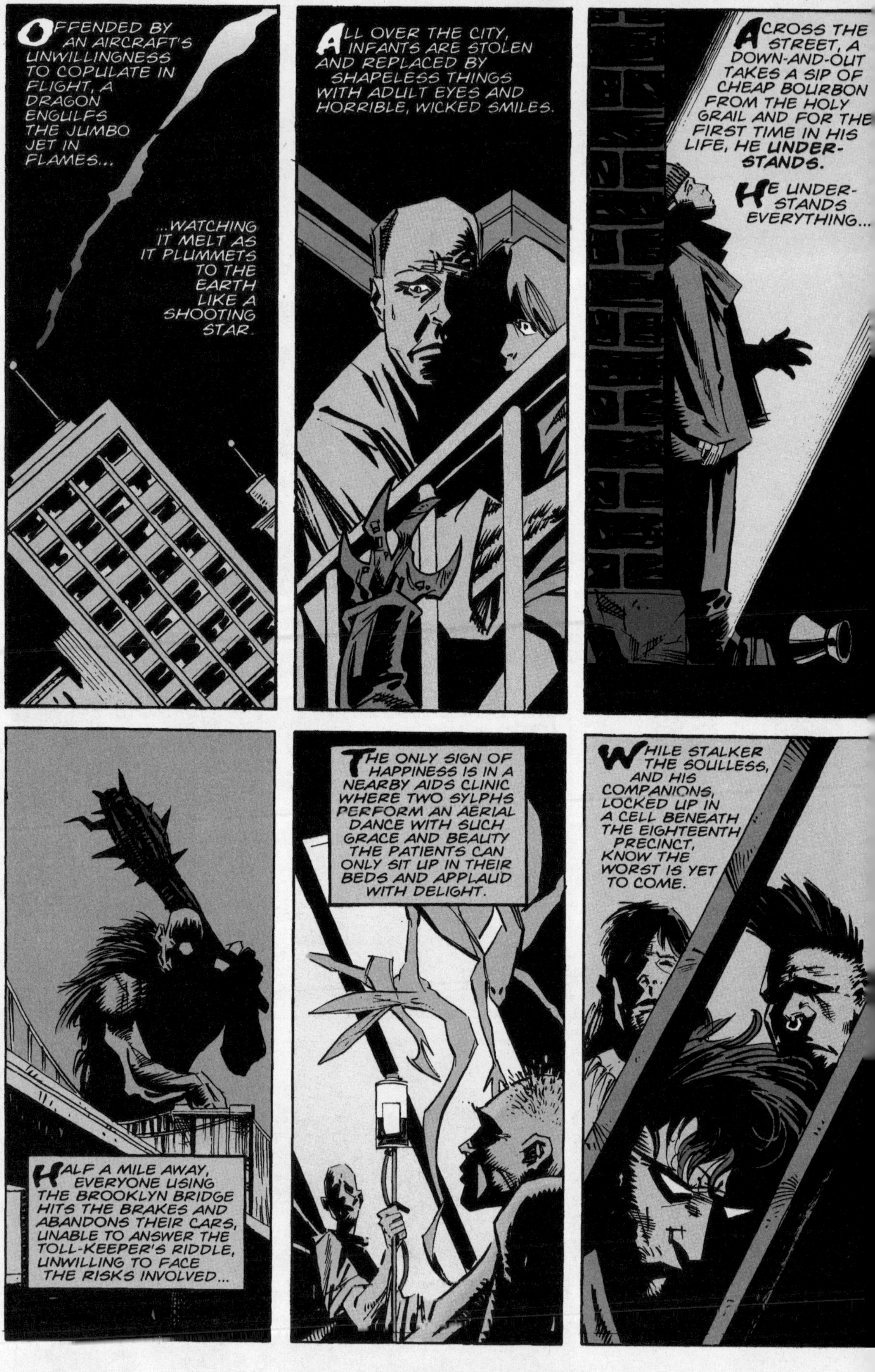
OFFENDED BY AN AIRCRAFT'S UNWILLINGNESS TO COPULATE IN FLIGHT, A DRAGON ENGULFS THE JUMBO JET IN FLAMES...
...WATCHING IT MELT AS IT PLUMMETS TO THE EARTH LIKE A SHOOTING STAR.
ALL OVER THE CITY, INFANTS ARE STOLEN AND REPLACED BY SHAPELESS THINGS WITH ADULT EYES AND HORRIBLE, WICKED SMILES.
ACROSS THE STREET, A DOWN-AND-OUT TAKES A SIP OF CHEAP BOURBON FROM THE HOLY GRAIL AND FOR THE FIRST TIME IN HIS LIFE, HE UNDERSTANDS.
HE UNDERSTANDS EVERYTHING...
HALF A MILE AWAY, EVERYONE USING THE BROOKLYN BRIDGE HITS THE BRAKES AND ABANDONS THEIR CARS, UNABLE TO ANSWER THE TOLL-KEEPER'S RIDDLE, UNWILLING TO FACE THE RISKS INVOLVED...
THE ONLY SIGN OF HAPPINESS IS IN A NEARBY AIDS CLINIC WHERE TWO SYLPHS PERFORM AN AERIAL DANCE WITH SUCH GRACE AND BEAUTY THE PATIENTS CAN ONLY SIT UP IN THEIR BEDS AND APPLAUD WITH DELIGHT.
WHILE STALKER THE SOULLESS, AND HIS COMPANIONS, LOCKED UP IN A CELL BENEATH THE EIGHTEENTH PRECINCT, KNOW THE WORST IS YET TO COME.

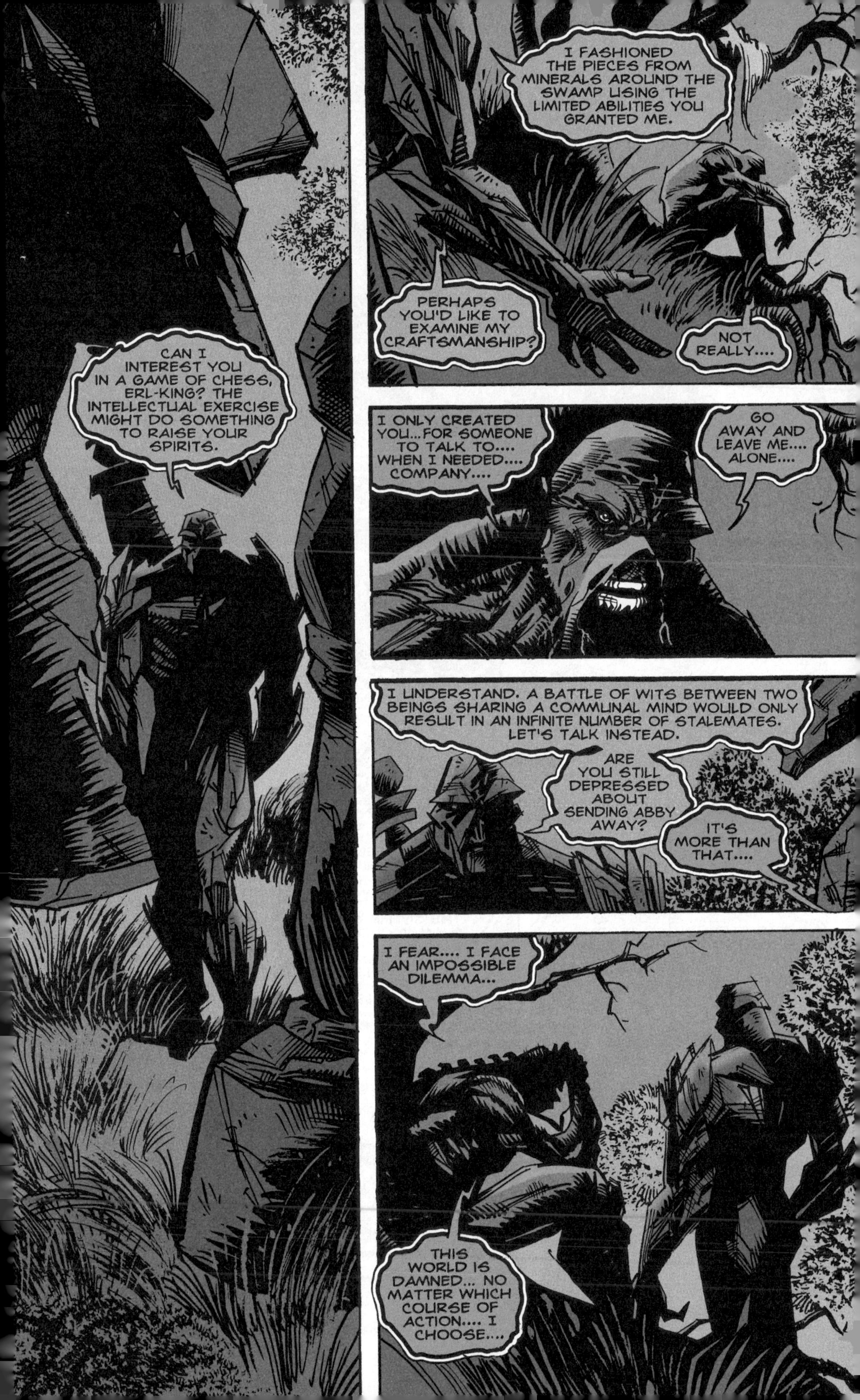
CAN I INTEREST YOU IN A GAME OF CHESS, ERL-KING? THE INTELLECTUAL EXERCISE MIGHT DO SOMETHING TO RAISE YOUR SPIRITS.
I FASHIONED THE PIECES FROM MINERALS AROUND THE SWAMP USING THE LIMITED ABILITIES YOU GRANTED ME.
PERHAPS YOU'D LIKE TO EXAMINE MY CRAFTSMANSHIP?
NOT REALLY....
I ONLY CREATED YOU...FOR SOMEONE TO TALK TO.... WHEN I NEEDED.... COMPANY....
GO AWAY AND LEAVE ME.... ALONE....
I UNDERSTAND. A BATTLE OF WITS BETWEEN TWO BEINGS SHARING A COMMUNAL MIND WOULD ONLY RESULT IN AN INFINITE NUMBER OF STALEMATES. LET'S TALK INSTEAD.
ARE YOU STILL DEPRESSED ABOUT SENDING ABBY AWAY?
IT'S MORE THAN THAT....
I FEAR.... I FACE AN IMPOSSIBLE DILEMMA...
THIS WORLD IS DAMNED... NO MATTER WHICH COURSE OF ACTION.... I CHOOSE....

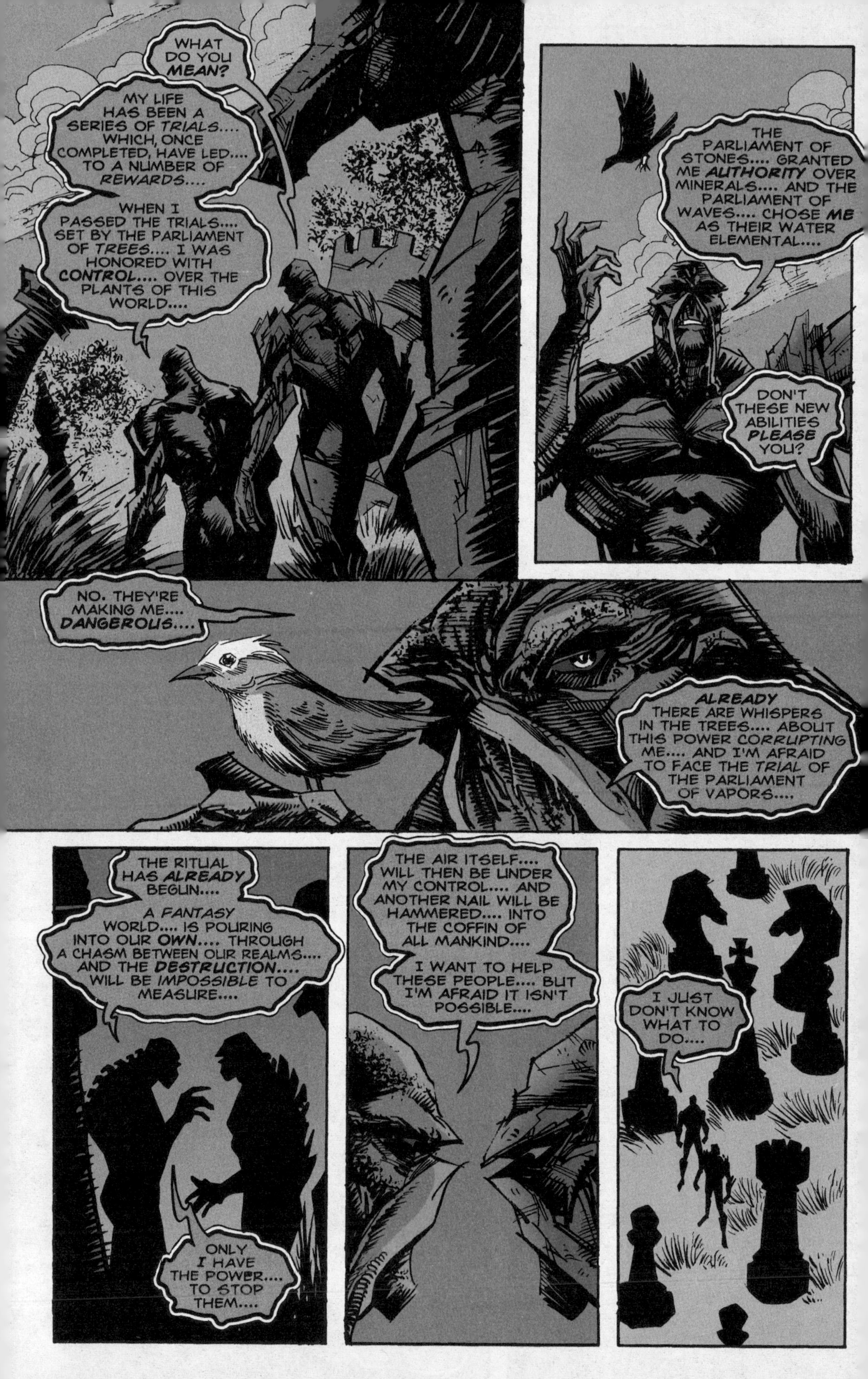
WHAT DO YOU *MEAN?*
MY LIFE HAS BEEN A SERIES OF *TRIALS*.... WHICH, ONCE COMPLETED, HAVE LED.... TO A NUMBER OF *REWARDS*....
WHEN I PASSED THE TRIALS.... SET BY THE PARLIAMENT OF *TREES*.... I WAS HONORED WITH **CONTROL**.... OVER THE PLANTS OF THIS WORLD....
THE PARLIAMENT OF STONES.... GRANTED ME ***AUTHORITY*** OVER MINERALS.... AND THE PARLIAMENT OF WAVES.... CHOSE ***ME*** AS THEIR WATER ELEMENTAL....
DON'T THESE NEW ABILITIES ***PLEASE*** YOU?
NO. THEY'RE MAKING ME.... ***DANGEROUS***....
ALREADY THERE ARE WHISPERS IN THE TREES.... ABOUT THIS POWER *CORRUPTING* ME.... AND I'M AFRAID TO FACE THE *TRIAL* OF THE PARLIAMENT OF VAPORS....
THE RITUAL HAS ***ALREADY*** BEGUN....
A *FANTASY* WORLD.... IS POURING INTO OUR **OWN**.... THROUGH A CHASM BETWEEN OUR REALMS.... AND THE **DESTRUCTION**.... WILL BE *IMPOSSIBLE* TO MEASURE....
ONLY ***I*** HAVE THE POWER.... TO STOP THEM....
THE AIR ITSELF.... WILL THEN BE UNDER MY CONTROL.... AND ANOTHER NAIL WILL BE HAMMERED.... INTO THE COFFIN OF ALL MANKIND....
I WANT TO HELP THESE PEOPLE.... BUT I'M *AFRAID* IT ISN'T POSSIBLE....
I JUST DON'T KNOW WHAT TO DO....

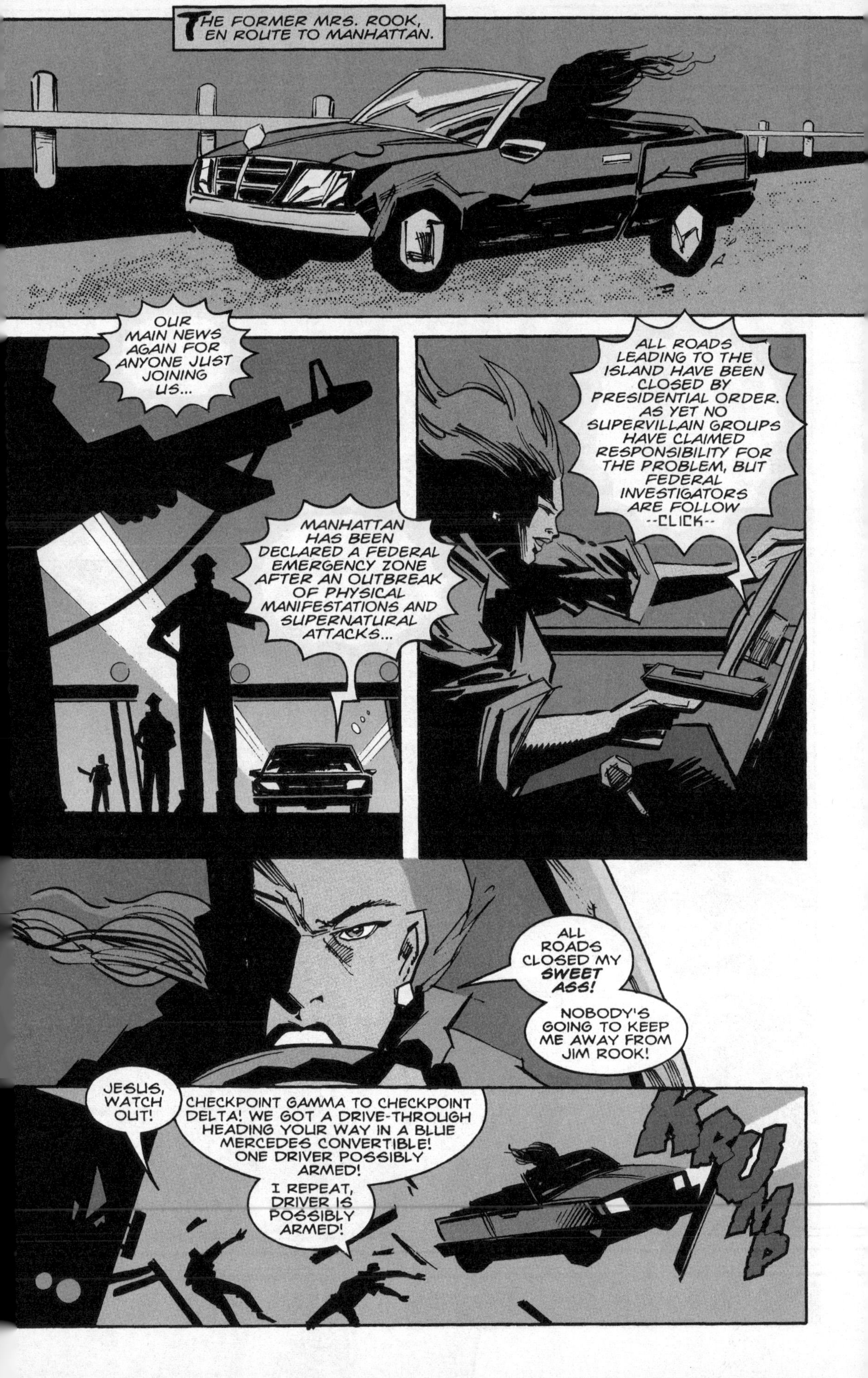
THE FORMER MRS. ROOK, EN ROUTE TO MANHATTAN.
OUR MAIN NEWS AGAIN FOR ANYONE JUST JOINING US...
MANHATTAN HAS BEEN DECLARED A FEDERAL EMERGENCY ZONE AFTER AN OUTBREAK OF PHYSICAL MANIFESTATIONS AND SUPERNATURAL ATTACKS...
ALL ROADS LEADING TO THE ISLAND HAVE BEEN CLOSED BY PRESIDENTIAL ORDER. AS YET NO SUPERVILLAIN GROUPS HAVE CLAIMED RESPONSIBILITY FOR THE PROBLEM, BUT FEDERAL INVESTIGATORS ARE FOLLOW --CLICK--
ALL ROADS CLOSED MY SWEET ASS!
NOBODY'S GOING TO KEEP ME AWAY FROM JIM ROOK!
JESUS, WATCH OUT!
CHECKPOINT GAMMA TO CHECKPOINT DELTA! WE GOT A DRIVE-THROUGH HEADING YOUR WAY IN A BLUE MERCEDES CONVERTIBLE! ONE DRIVER POSSIBLY ARMED!
I REPEAT, DRIVER IS POSSIBLY ARMED!
KRUMP

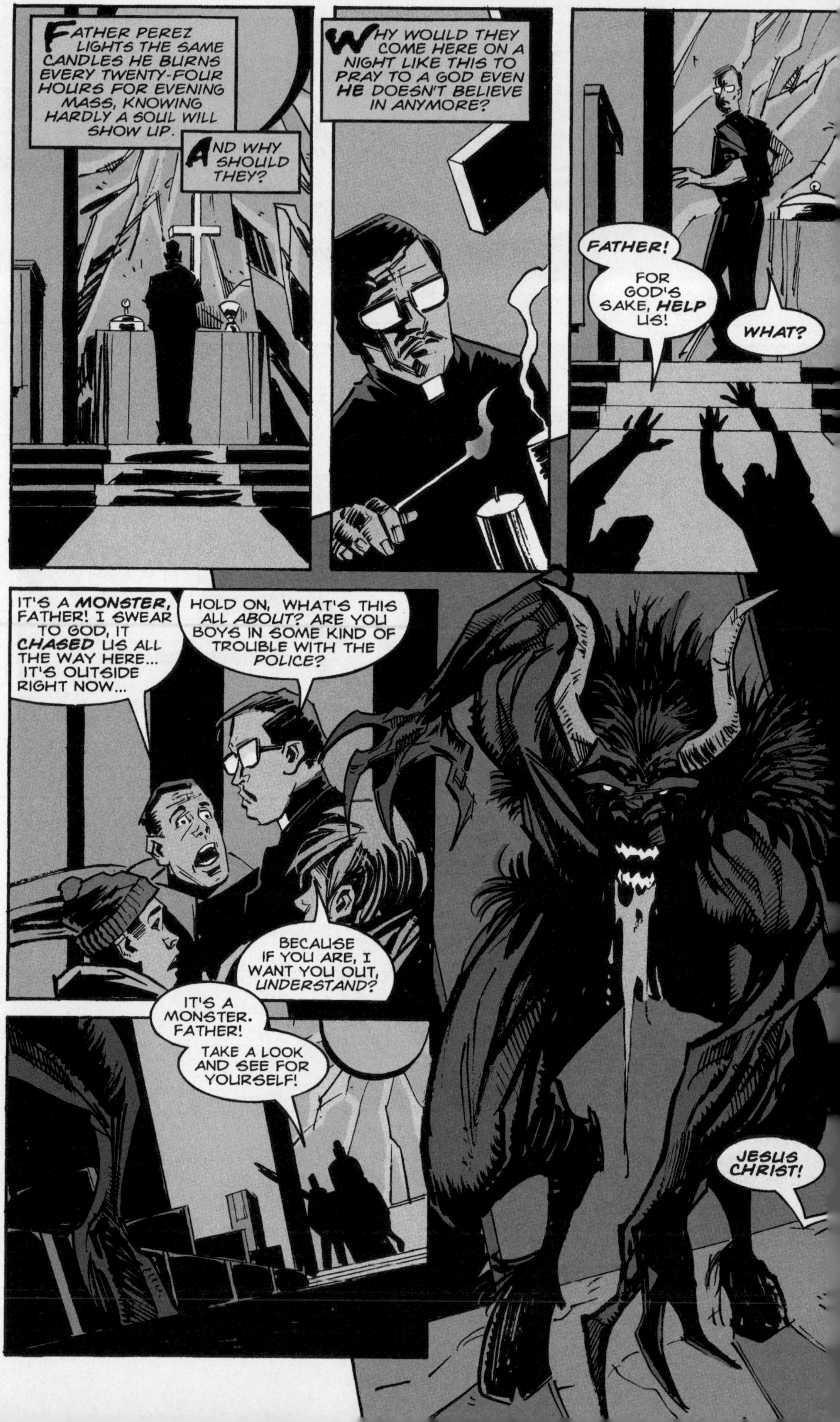
FATHER PEREZ LIGHTS THE SAME CANDLES HE BURNS EVERY TWENTY-FOUR HOURS FOR EVENING MASS, KNOWING HARDLY A SOUL WILL SHOW UP.
AND WHY SHOULD THEY?
WHY WOULD THEY COME HERE ON A NIGHT LIKE THIS TO PRAY TO A GOD EVEN HE DOESN'T BELIEVE IN ANYMORE?
FATHER!
FOR GOD'S SAKE, HELP US!
WHAT?
IT'S A MONSTER, FATHER! I SWEAR TO GOD, IT CHASED US ALL THE WAY HERE... IT'S OUTSIDE RIGHT NOW...
HOLD ON, WHAT'S THIS ALL ABOUT? ARE YOU BOYS IN SOME KIND OF TROUBLE WITH THE POLICE?
BECAUSE IF YOU ARE, I WANT YOU OUT, UNDERSTAND?
IT'S A MONSTER. FATHER!
TAKE A LOOK AND SEE FOR YOURSELF!
JESUS CHRIST!

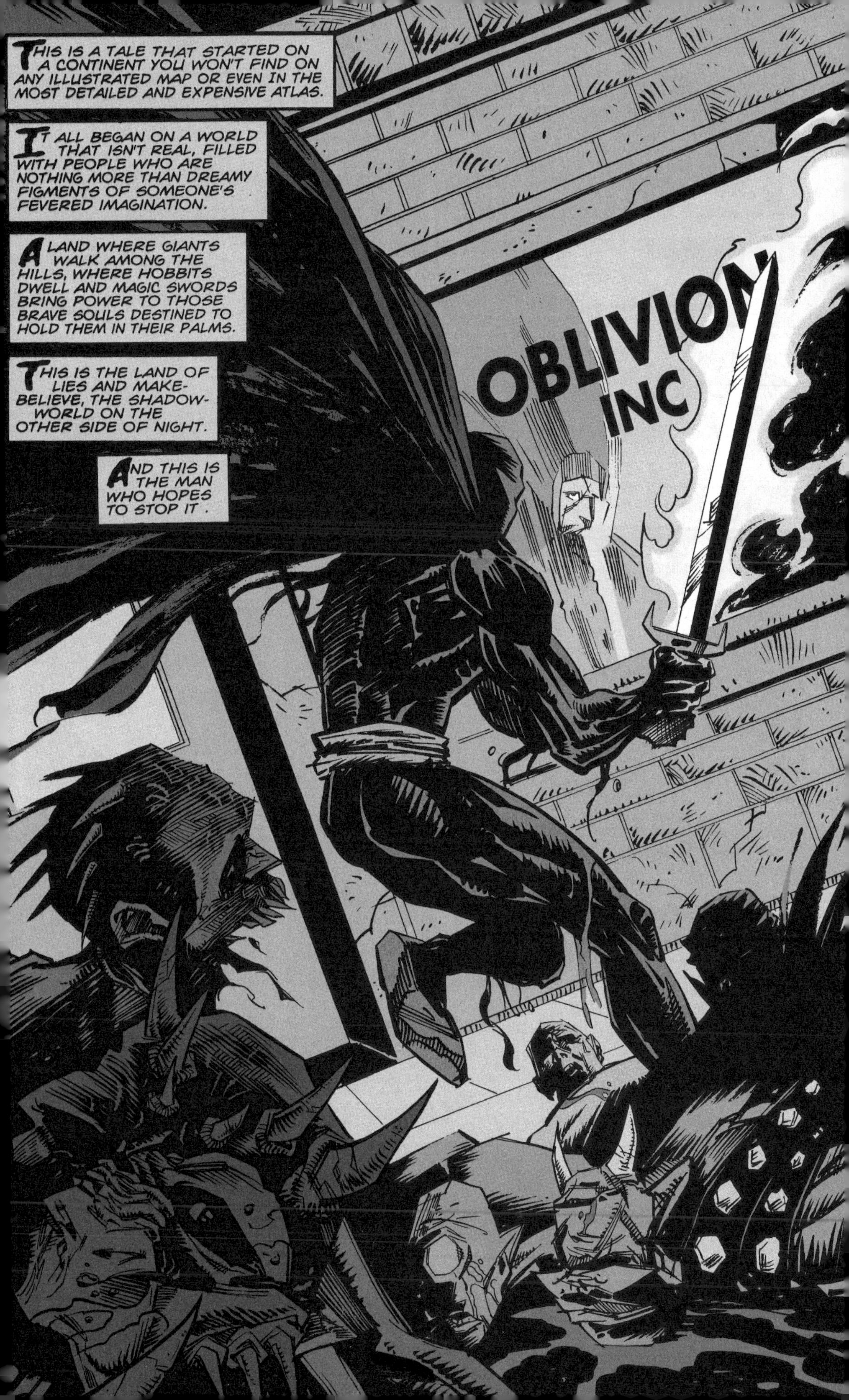
THIS IS A TALE THAT STARTED ON A CONTINENT YOU WON'T FIND ON ANY ILLUSTRATED MAP OR EVEN IN THE MOST DETAILED AND EXPENSIVE ATLAS.
IT ALL BEGAN ON A WORLD THAT ISN'T REAL, FILLED WITH PEOPLE WHO ARE NOTHING MORE THAN DREAMY FIGMENTS OF SOMEONE'S FEVERED IMAGINATION.
A LAND WHERE GIANTS WALK AMONG THE HILLS, WHERE HOBBITS DWELL AND MAGIC SWORDS BRING POWER TO THOSE BRAVE SOULS DESTINED TO HOLD THEM IN THEIR PALMS.
THIS IS THE LAND OF LIES AND MAKE-BELIEVE, THE SHADOW-WORLD ON THE OTHER SIDE OF NIGHT.
AND THIS IS THE MAN WHO HOPES TO STOP IT.
OBLIVION INC

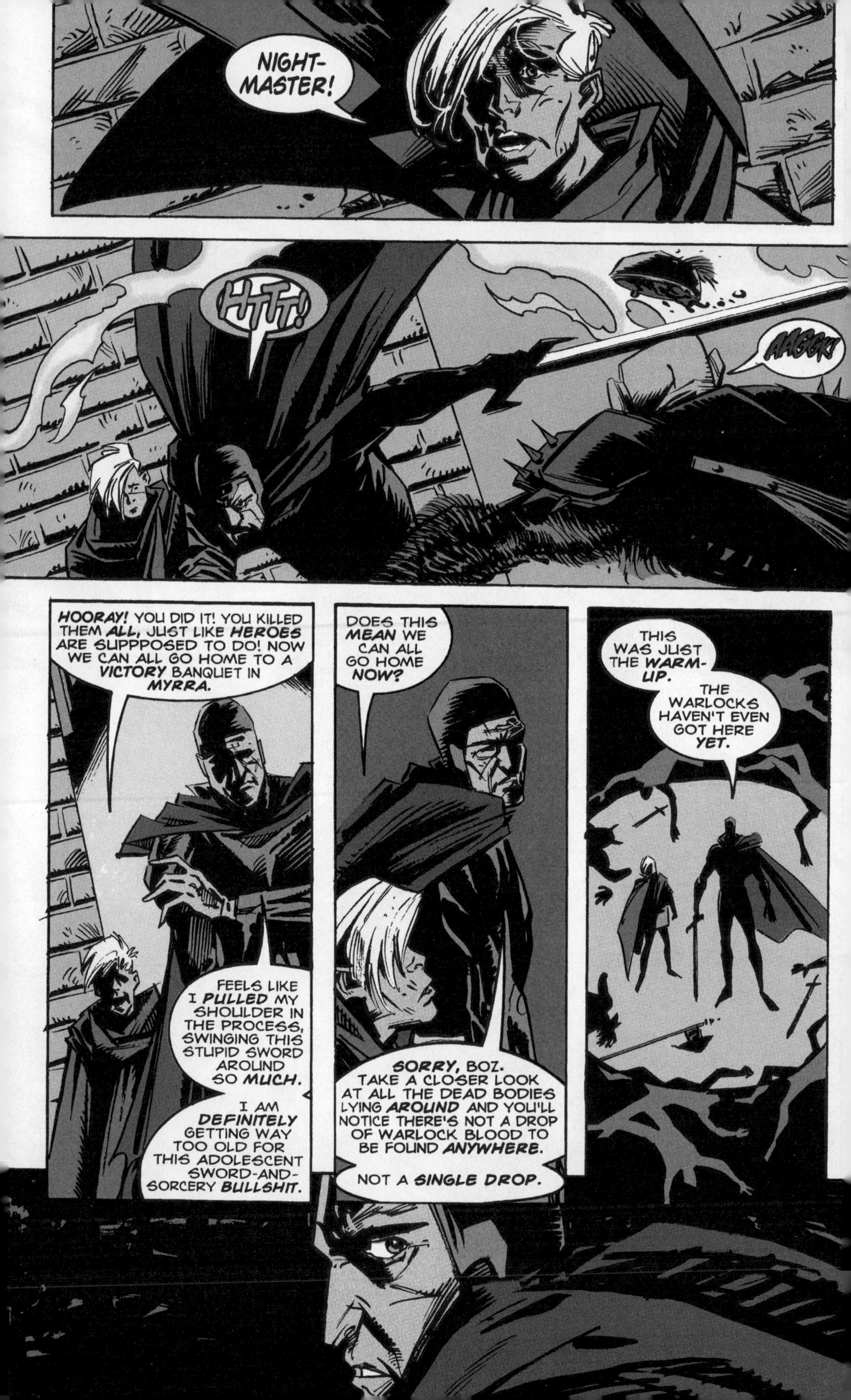
NIGHT-MASTER!
HTTT!
AAGGK!
HOORAY! YOU DID IT! YOU KILLED THEM ALL, JUST LIKE HEROES ARE SUPPPOSED TO DO! NOW WE CAN ALL GO HOME TO A VICTORY BANQUET IN MYRRA.
FEELS LIKE I PULLED MY SHOULDER IN THE PROCESS, SWINGING THIS STUPID SWORD AROUND SO MUCH.
I AM DEFINITELY GETTING WAY TOO OLD FOR THIS ADOLESCENT SWORD-AND-SORCERY BULLSHIT.
DOES THIS MEAN WE CAN ALL GO HOME NOW?
SORRY, BOZ. TAKE A CLOSER LOOK AT ALL THE DEAD BODIES LYING AROUND AND YOU'LL NOTICE THERE'S NOT A DROP OF WARLOCK BLOOD TO BE FOUND ANYWHERE.
NOT A SINGLE DROP.
THIS WAS JUST THE WARM-UP.
THE WARLOCKS HAVEN'T EVEN GOT HERE YET.

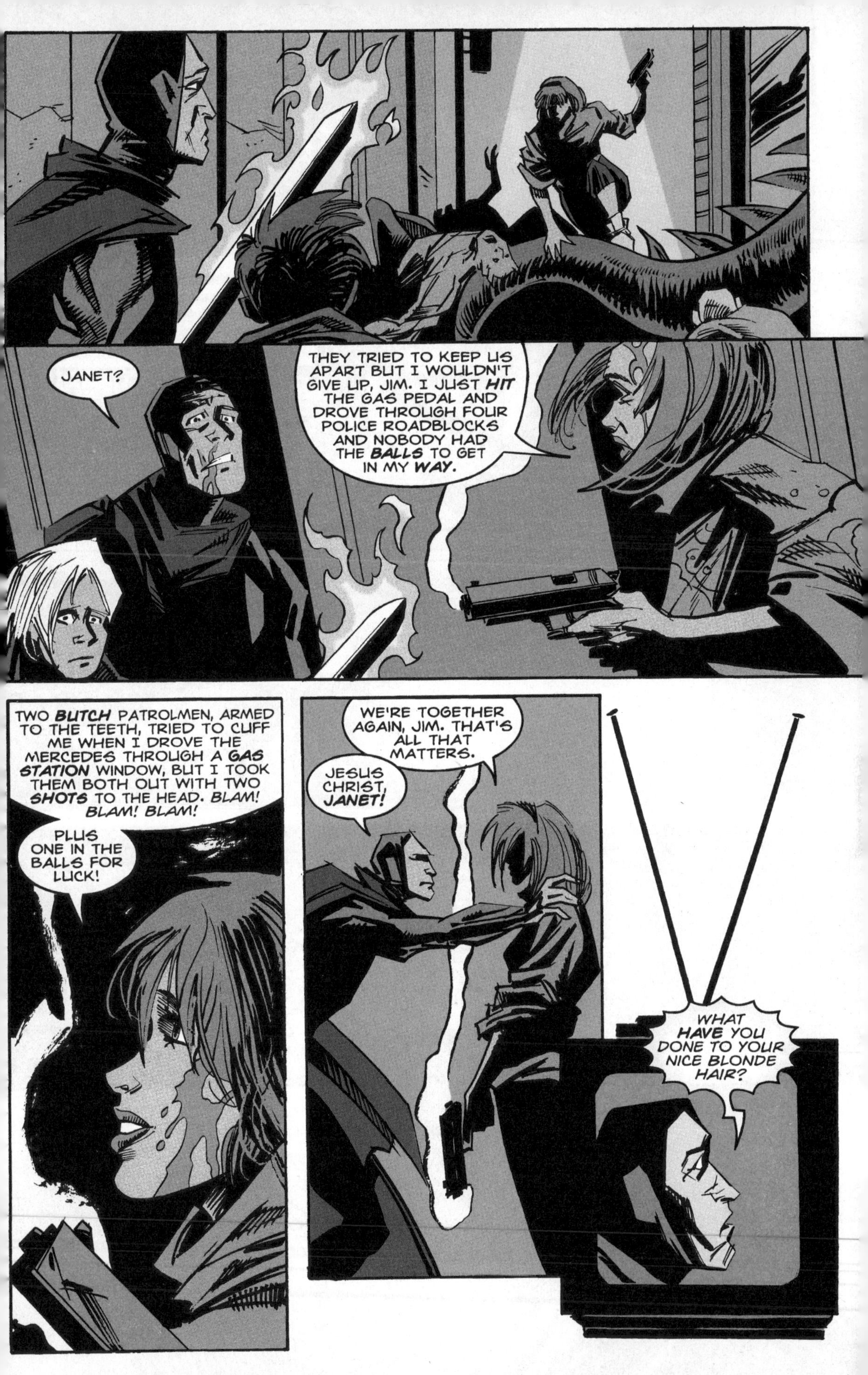
JANET?
THEY TRIED TO KEEP US APART BUT I WOULDN'T GIVE UP, JIM. I JUST HIT THE GAS PEDAL AND DROVE THROUGH FOUR POLICE ROADBLOCKS AND NOBODY HAD THE BALLS TO GET IN MY WAY.
TWO BUTCH PATROLMEN, ARMED TO THE TEETH, TRIED TO CUFF ME WHEN I DROVE THE MERCEDES THROUGH A GAS STATION WINDOW, BUT I TOOK THEM BOTH OUT WITH TWO SHOTS TO THE HEAD. BLAM! BLAM! BLAM!
PLUS ONE IN THE BALLS FOR LUCK!
WE'RE TOGETHER AGAIN, JIM. THAT'S ALL THAT MATTERS.
JESUS CHRIST, JANET!
WHAT HAVE YOU DONE TO YOUR NICE BLONDE HAIR?

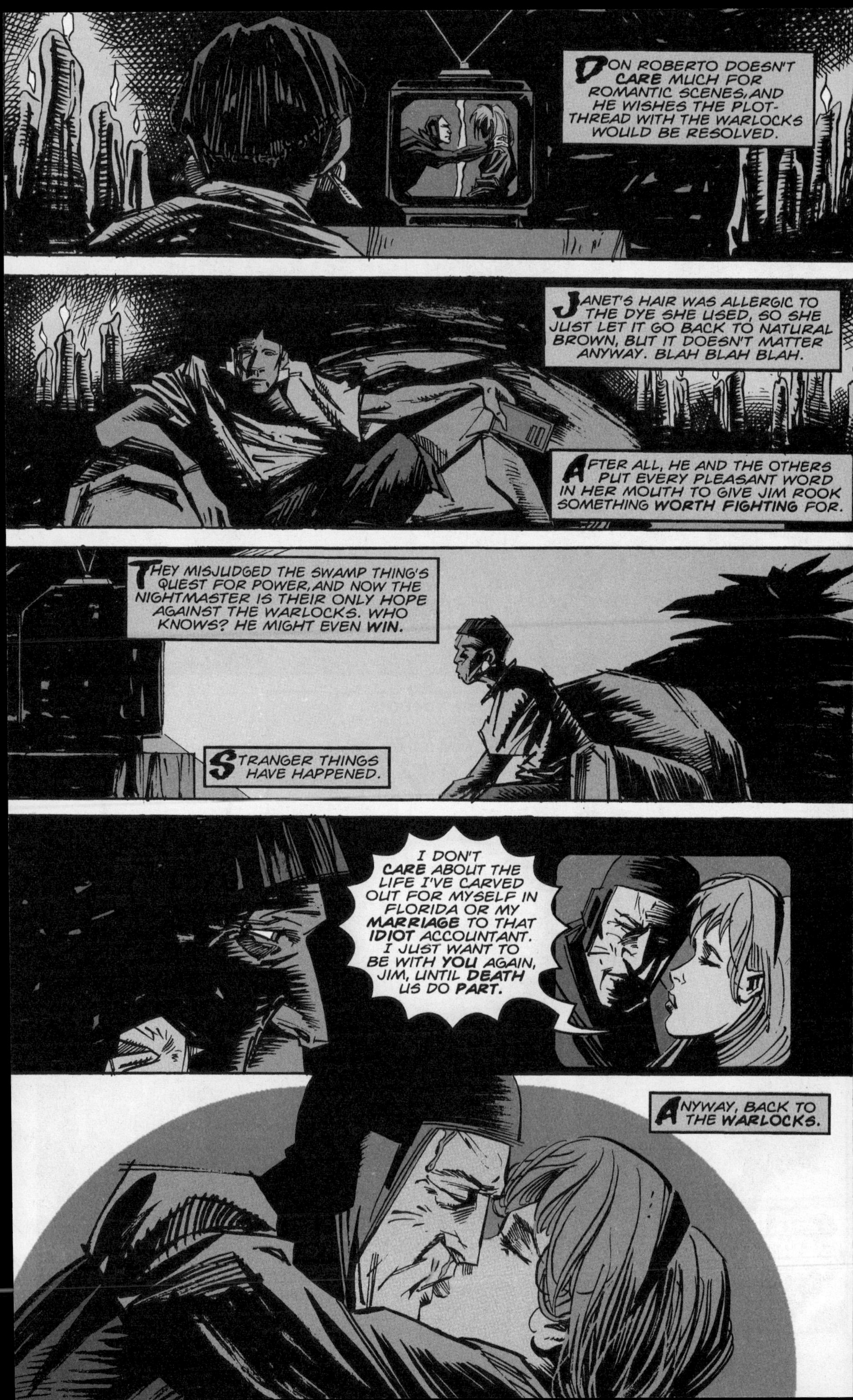
DON ROBERTO DOESN'T CARE MUCH FOR ROMANTIC SCENES, AND HE WISHES THE PLOT-THREAD WITH THE WARLOCKS WOULD BE RESOLVED.
JANET'S HAIR WAS ALLERGIC TO THE DYE SHE USED, SO SHE JUST LET IT GO BACK TO NATURAL BROWN, BUT IT DOESN'T MATTER ANYWAY. BLAH BLAH BLAH.
AFTER ALL, HE AND THE OTHERS PUT EVERY PLEASANT WORD IN HER MOUTH TO GIVE JIM ROOK SOMETHING WORTH FIGHTING FOR.
THEY MISJUDGED THE SWAMP THING'S QUEST FOR POWER, AND NOW THE NIGHTMASTER IS THEIR ONLY HOPE AGAINST THE WARLOCKS. WHO KNOWS? HE MIGHT EVEN WIN.
STRANGER THINGS HAVE HAPPENED.
I DON'T CARE ABOUT THE LIFE I'VE CARVED OUT FOR MYSELF IN FLORIDA OR MY MARRIAGE TO THAT IDIOT ACCOUNTANT. I JUST WANT TO BE WITH YOU AGAIN, JIM, UNTIL DEATH US DO PART.
ANYWAY, BACK TO THE WARLOCKS.

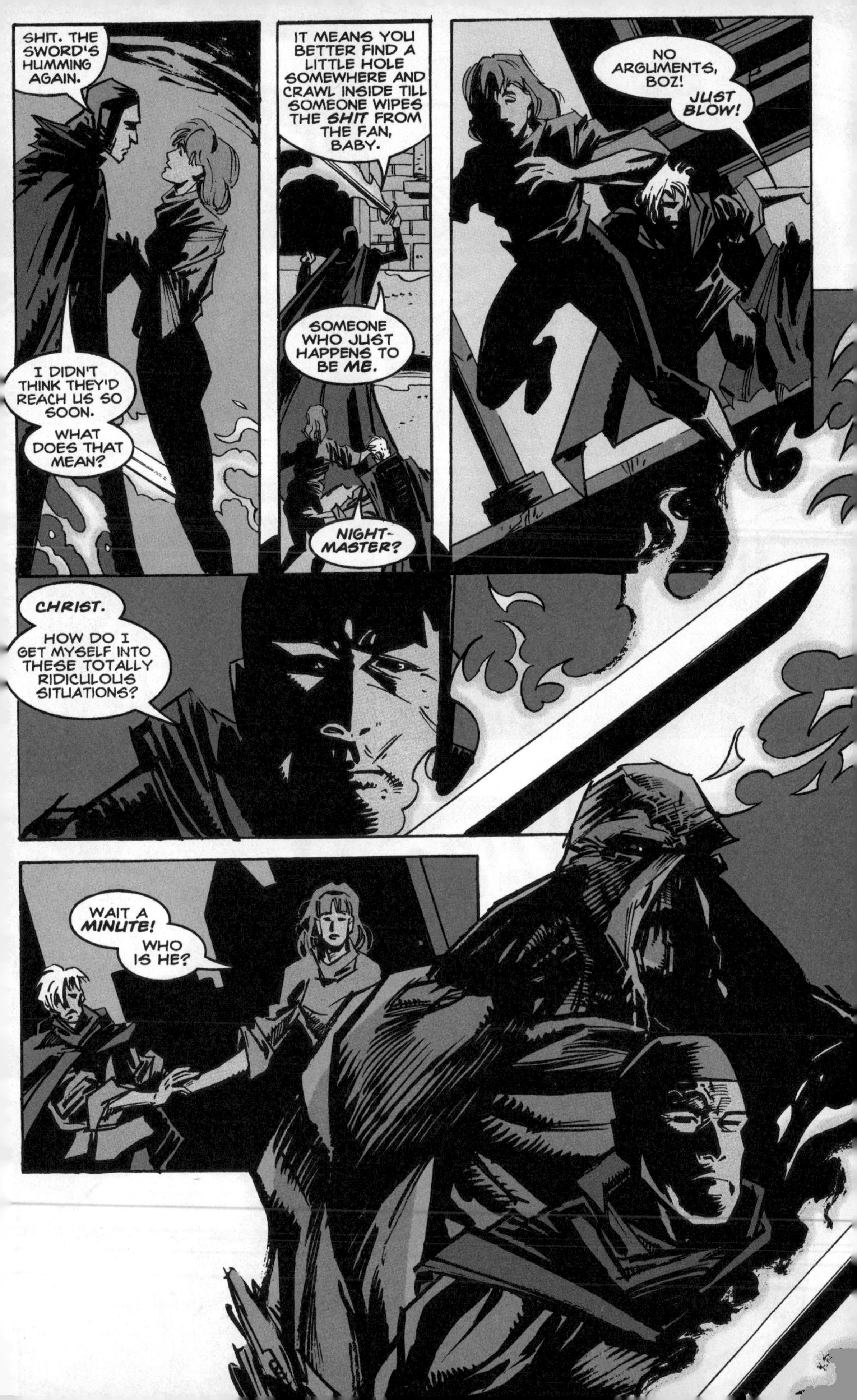
SHIT. THE SWORD'S HUMMING AGAIN.
I DIDN'T THINK THEY'D REACH US SO SOON.
WHAT DOES THAT MEAN?
IT MEANS YOU BETTER FIND A LITTLE HOLE SOMEWHERE AND CRAWL INSIDE TILL SOMEONE WIPES THE *SHIT* FROM THE FAN, BABY.
SOMEONE WHO JUST HAPPENS TO BE *ME*.
NIGHT-MASTER?
NO ARGUMENTS, BOZ!
JUST BLOW!
CHRIST.
HOW DO I GET MYSELF INTO THESE TOTALLY RIDICULOUS SITUATIONS?
WAIT A *MINUTE!*
WHO IS HE?

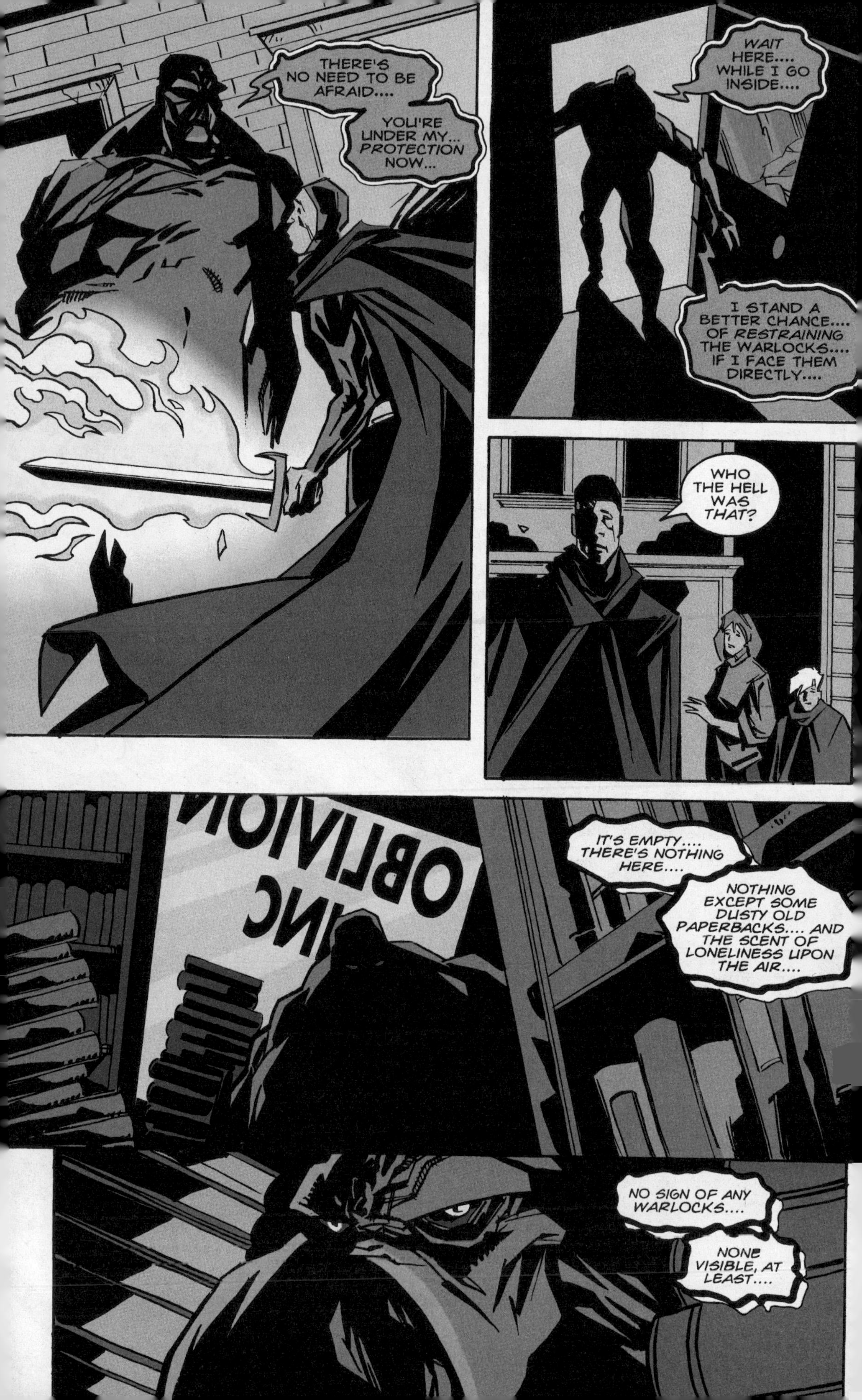
THERE'S NO NEED TO BE AFRAID....
YOU'RE UNDER MY... PROTECTION NOW...
WAIT HERE.... WHILE I GO INSIDE....
I STAND A BETTER CHANCE.... OF RESTRAINING THE WARLOCKS.... IF I FACE THEM DIRECTLY....
WHO THE HELL WAS THAT?
OBLIVION INC
IT'S EMPTY.... THERE'S NOTHING HERE....
NOTHING EXCEPT SOME DUSTY OLD PAPERBACKS.... AND THE SCENT OF LONELINESS UPON THE AIR....
NO SIGN OF ANY WARLOCKS....
NONE VISIBLE, AT LEAST....

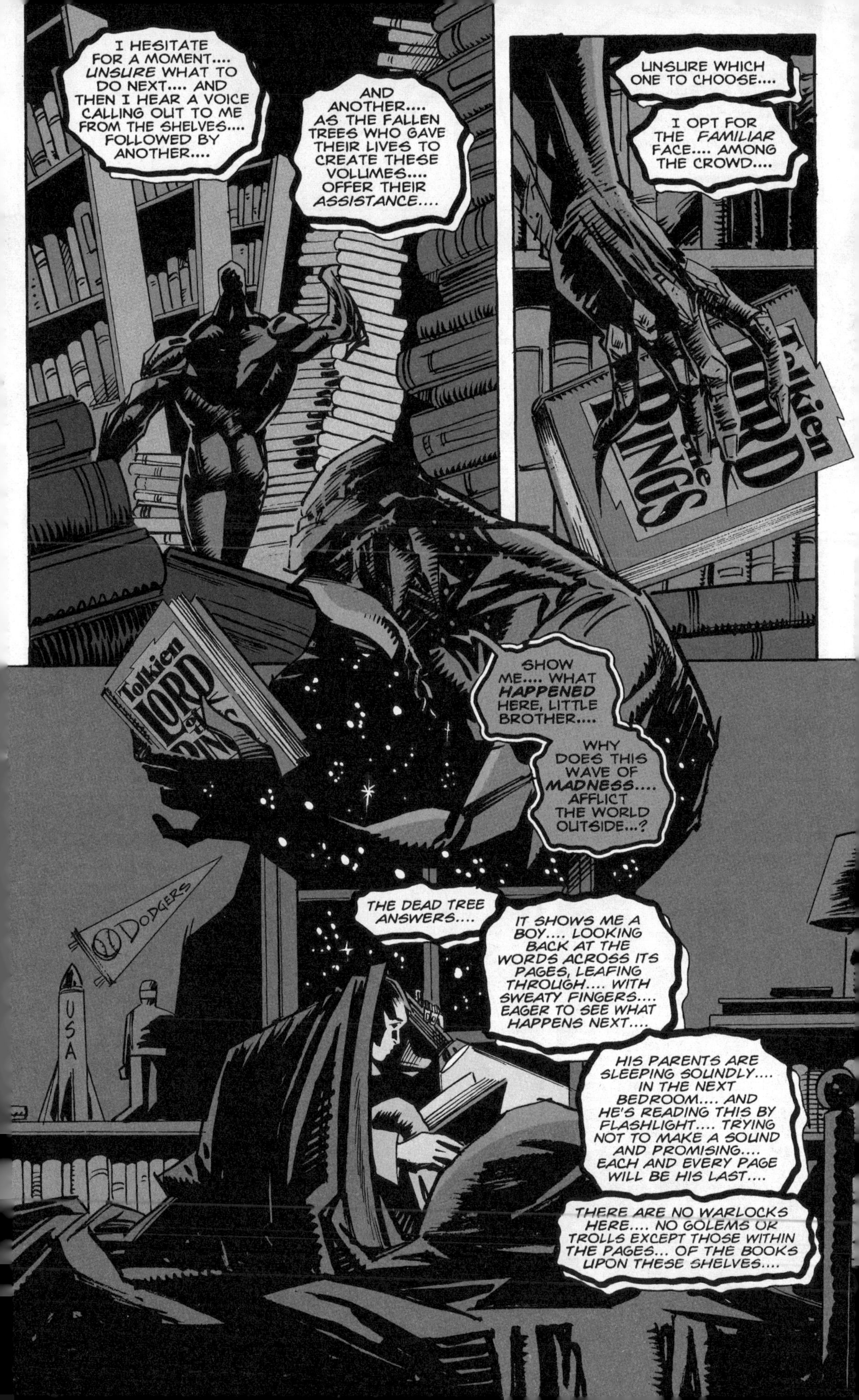
I HESITATE FOR A MOMENT.... UNSURE WHAT TO DO NEXT.... AND THEN I HEAR A VOICE CALLING OUT TO ME FROM THE SHELVES.... FOLLOWED BY ANOTHER....
AND ANOTHER.... AS THE FALLEN TREES WHO GAVE THEIR LIVES TO CREATE THESE VOLUMES.... OFFER THEIR ASSISTANCE....
UNSURE WHICH ONE TO CHOOSE....
I OPT FOR THE FAMILIAR FACE.... AMONG THE CROWD....
Tolkien
LORD RINGS
Tolkien
LORD
SHOW ME.... WHAT HAPPENED HERE, LITTLE BROTHER....
WHY DOES THIS WAVE OF MADNESS.... AFFLICT THE WORLD OUTSIDE...?
THE DEAD TREE ANSWERS....
IT SHOWS ME A BOY.... LOOKING BACK AT THE WORDS ACROSS ITS PAGES, LEAFING THROUGH.... WITH SWEATY FINGERS.... EAGER TO SEE WHAT HAPPENS NEXT....
DODGERS
USA
HIS PARENTS ARE SLEEPING SOUNDLY.... IN THE NEXT BEDROOM.... AND HE'S READING THIS BY FLASHLIGHT.... TRYING NOT TO MAKE A SOUND AND PROMISING.... EACH AND EVERY PAGE WILL BE HIS LAST....
THERE ARE NO WARLOCKS HERE.... NO GOLEMS OR TROLLS EXCEPT THOSE WITHIN THE PAGES... OF THE BOOKS UPON THESE SHELVES....

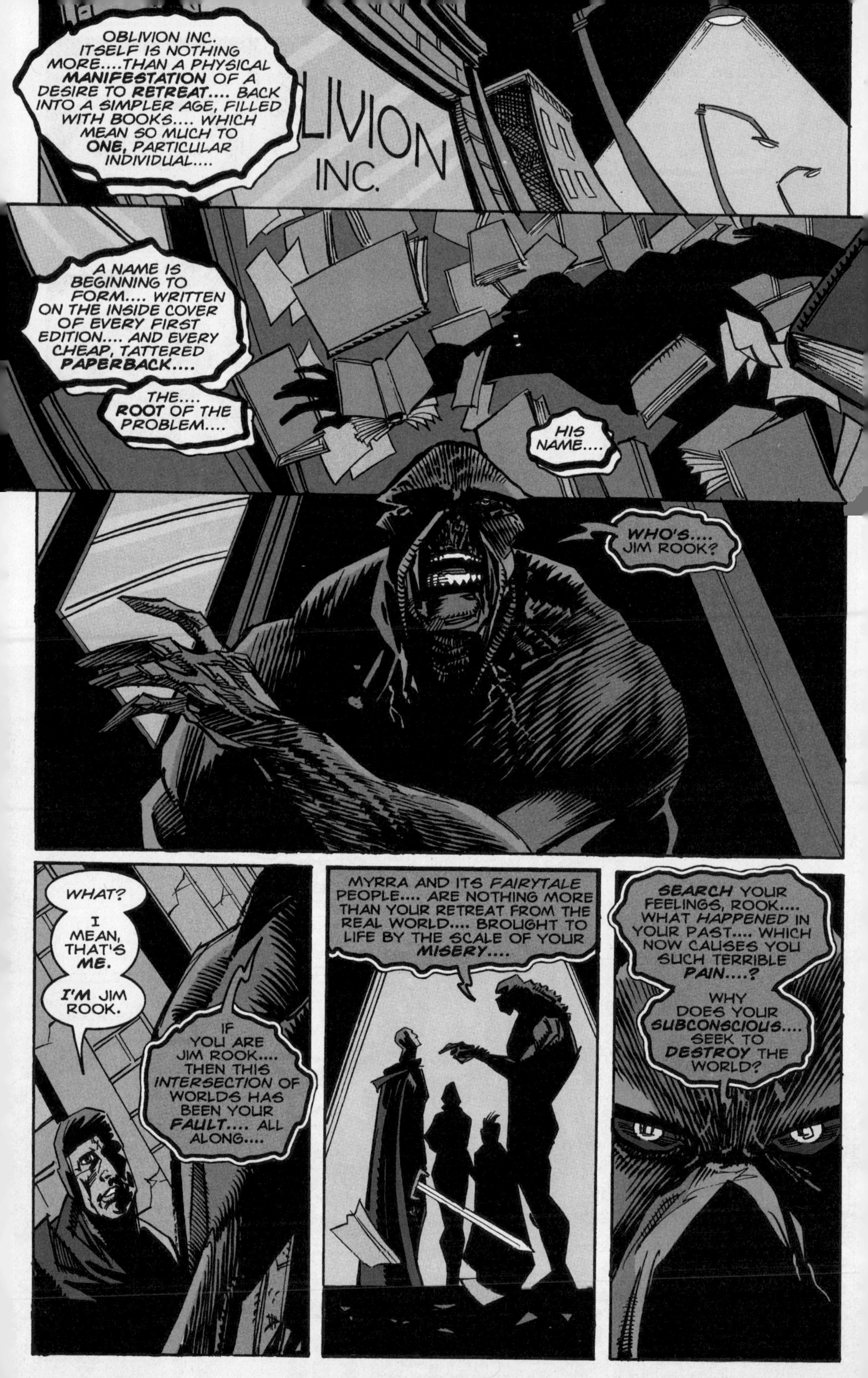
OBLIVION INC. ITSELF IS NOTHING MORE....THAN A PHYSICAL MANIFESTATION OF A DESIRE TO RETREAT.... BACK INTO A SIMPLER AGE, FILLED WITH BOOKS.... WHICH MEAN SO MUCH TO ONE, PARTICULAR INDIVIDUAL....
LIVION INC.
A NAME IS BEGINNING TO FORM.... WRITTEN ON THE INSIDE COVER OF EVERY FIRST EDITION.... AND EVERY CHEAP, TATTERED PAPERBACK....
THE.... ROOT OF THE PROBLEM....
HIS NAME....
WHO'S.... JIM ROOK?
WHAT?
I MEAN, THAT'S ME.
I'M JIM ROOK.
IF YOU ARE JIM ROOK.... THEN THIS INTERSECTION OF WORLDS HAS BEEN YOUR FAULT.... ALL ALONG....
MYRRA AND ITS FAIRYTALE PEOPLE.... ARE NOTHING MORE THAN YOUR RETREAT FROM THE REAL WORLD.... BROUGHT TO LIFE BY THE SCALE OF YOUR MISERY....
SEARCH YOUR FEELINGS, ROOK.... WHAT HAPPENED IN YOUR PAST.... WHICH NOW CAUSES YOU SUCH TERRIBLE PAIN....?
WHY DOES YOUR SUBCONSCIOUS.... SEEK TO DESTROY THE WORLD?

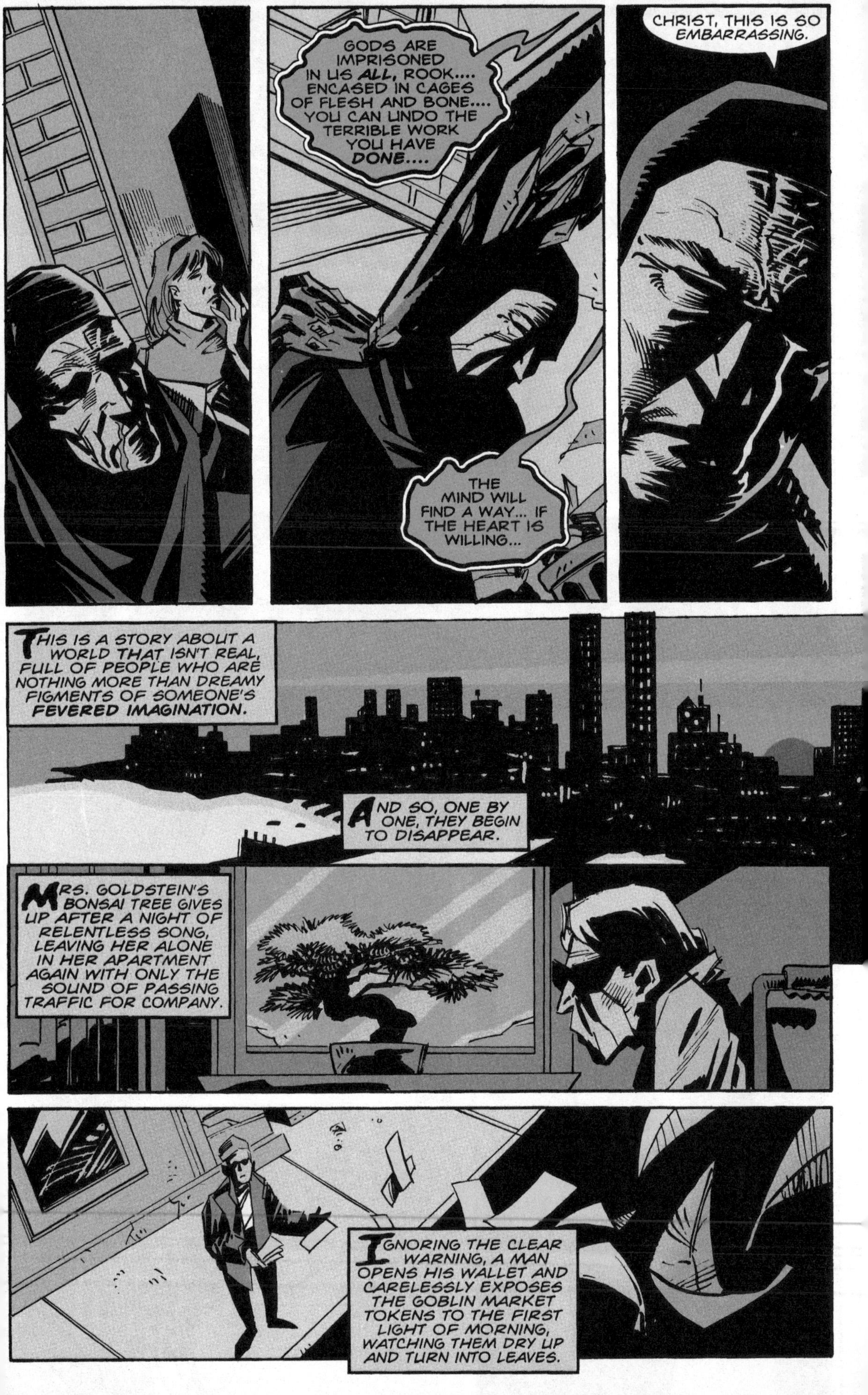
GODS ARE IMPRISONED IN US ALL, ROOK.... ENCASED IN CAGES OF FLESH AND BONE.... YOU CAN UNDO THE TERRIBLE WORK YOU HAVE DONE....
THE MIND WILL FIND A WAY... IF THE HEART IS WILLING...
CHRIST, THIS IS SO EMBARRASSING.
THIS IS A STORY ABOUT A WORLD THAT ISN'T REAL, FULL OF PEOPLE WHO ARE NOTHING MORE THAN DREAMY FIGMENTS OF SOMEONE'S FEVERED IMAGINATION.
AND SO, ONE BY ONE, THEY BEGIN TO DISAPPEAR.
MRS. GOLDSTEIN'S BONSAI TREE GIVES UP AFTER A NIGHT OF RELENTLESS SONG, LEAVING HER ALONE IN HER APARTMENT AGAIN WITH ONLY THE SOUND OF PASSING TRAFFIC FOR COMPANY.
IGNORING THE CLEAR WARNING, A MAN OPENS HIS WALLET AND CARELESSLY EXPOSES THE GOBLIN MARKET TOKENS TO THE FIRST LIGHT OF MORNING, WATCHING THEM DRY UP AND TURN INTO LEAVES.

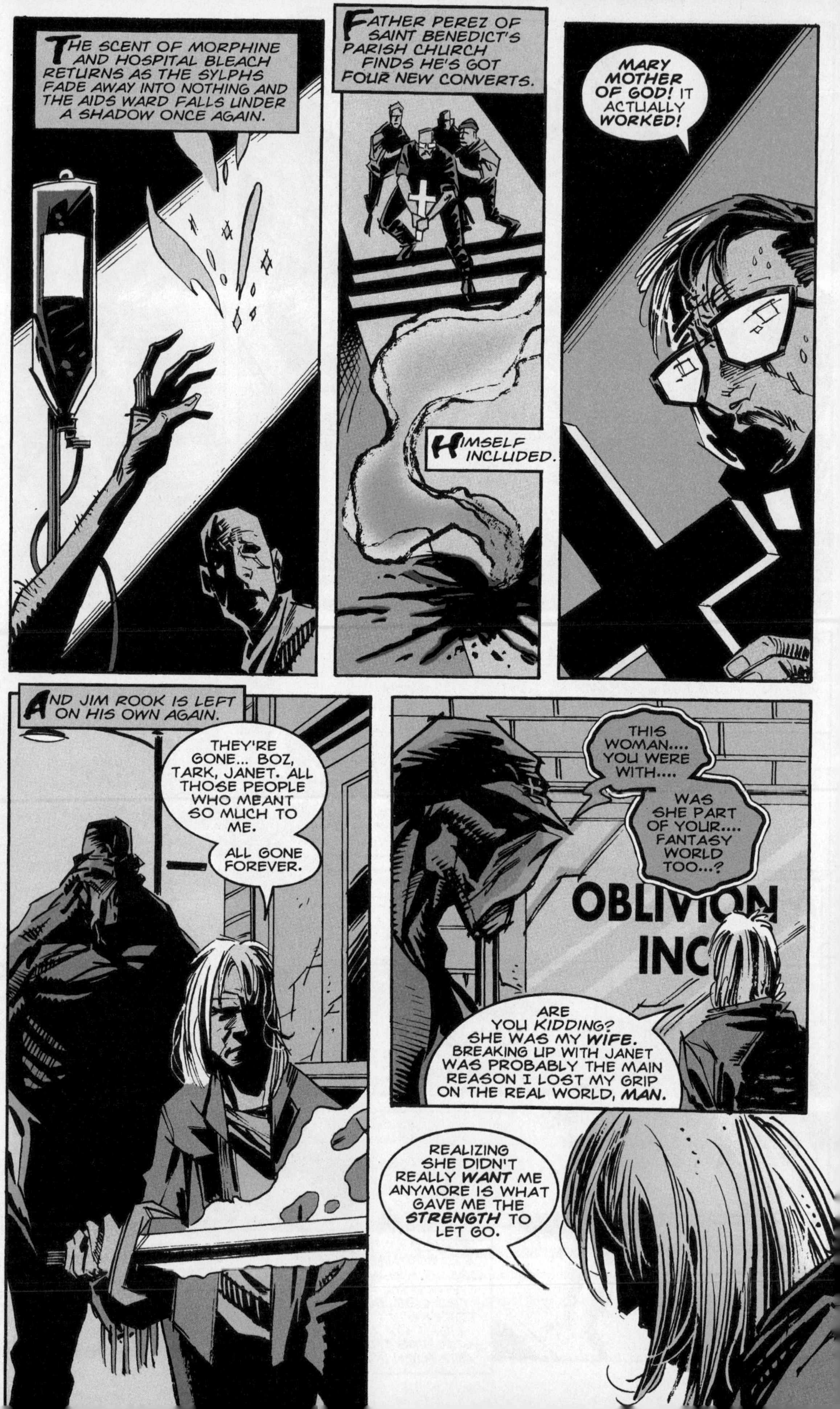
THE SCENT OF MORPHINE AND HOSPITAL BLEACH RETURNS AS THE SYLPHS FADE AWAY INTO NOTHING AND THE AIDS WARD FALLS UNDER A SHADOW ONCE AGAIN.
FATHER PEREZ OF SAINT BENEDICT'S PARISH CHURCH FINDS HE'S GOT FOUR NEW CONVERTS.
HIMSELF INCLUDED.
MARY MOTHER OF GOD! IT ACTUALLY WORKED!
AND JIM ROOK IS LEFT ON HIS OWN AGAIN.
THEY'RE GONE... BOZ, TARK, JANET. ALL THOSE PEOPLE WHO MEANT SO MUCH TO ME.
ALL GONE FOREVER.
THIS WOMAN.... YOU WERE WITH....
WAS SHE PART OF YOUR.... FANTASY WORLD TOO...?
OBLIVION INC
ARE YOU KIDDING? SHE WAS MY WIFE. BREAKING UP WITH JANET WAS PROBABLY THE MAIN REASON I LOST MY GRIP ON THE REAL WORLD, MAN.
REALIZING SHE DIDN'T REALLY WANT ME ANYMORE IS WHAT GAVE ME THE STRENGTH TO LET GO.

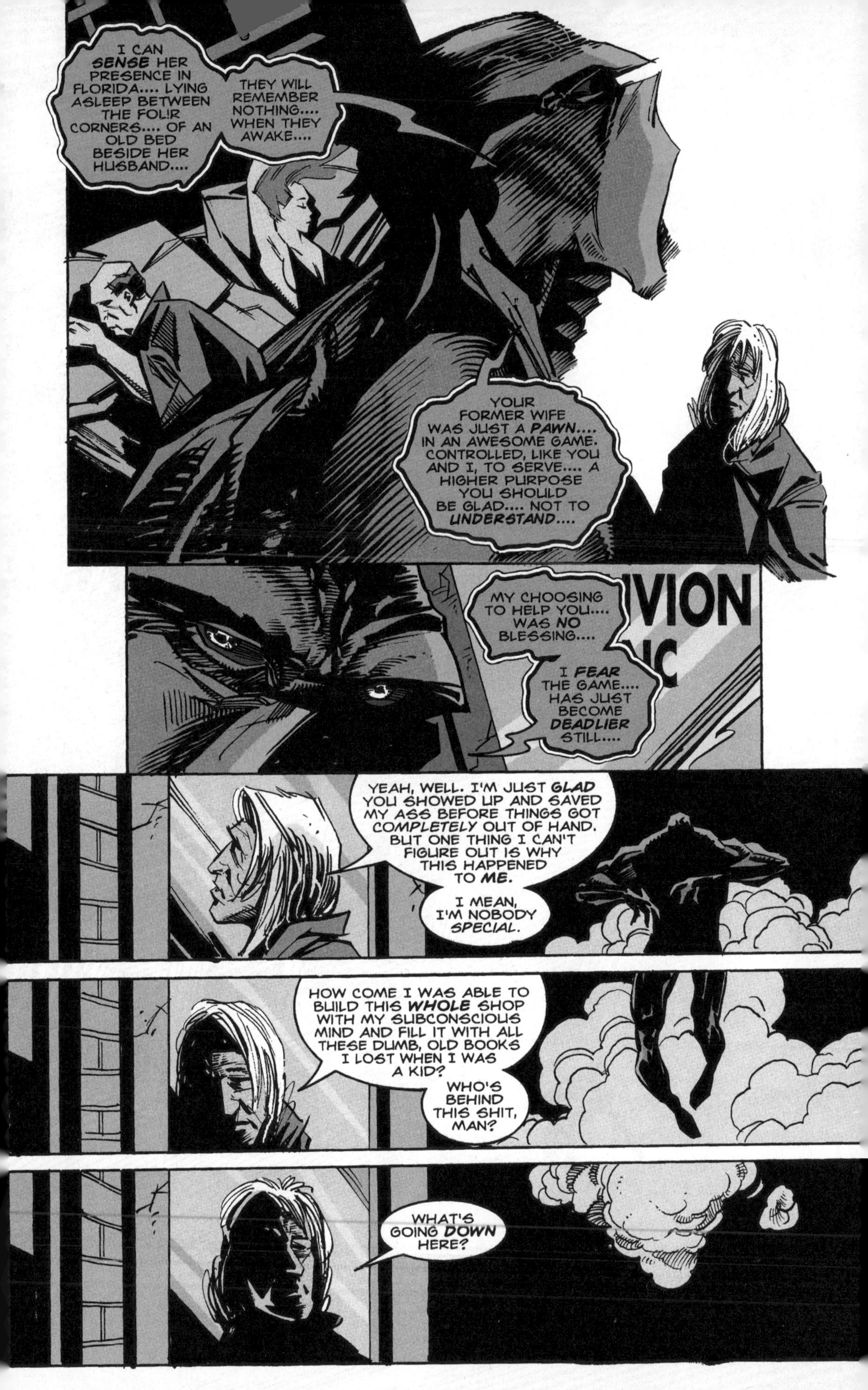
I CAN SENSE HER PRESENCE IN FLORIDA.... LYING ASLEEP BETWEEN THE FOUR CORNERS.... OF AN OLD BED BESIDE HER HUSBAND....
THEY WILL REMEMBER NOTHING.... WHEN THEY AWAKE....
YOUR FORMER WIFE WAS JUST A PAWN.... IN AN AWESOME GAME. CONTROLLED, LIKE YOU AND I, TO SERVE.... A HIGHER PURPOSE YOU SHOULD BE GLAD.... NOT TO UNDERSTAND....
IVION
NC
MY CHOOSING TO HELP YOU.... WAS NO BLESSING....
I FEAR THE GAME.... HAS JUST BECOME DEADLIER STILL....
YEAH, WELL. I'M JUST GLAD YOU SHOWED UP AND SAVED MY ASS BEFORE THINGS GOT COMPLETELY OUT OF HAND. BUT ONE THING I CAN'T FIGURE OUT IS WHY THIS HAPPENED TO ME.
I MEAN, I'M NOBODY SPECIAL.
HOW COME I WAS ABLE TO BUILD THIS WHOLE SHOP WITH MY SUBCONSCIOUS MIND AND FILL IT WITH ALL THESE DUMB, OLD BOOKS I LOST WHEN I WAS A KID?
WHO'S BEHIND THIS SHIT, MAN?
WHAT'S GOING DOWN HERE?

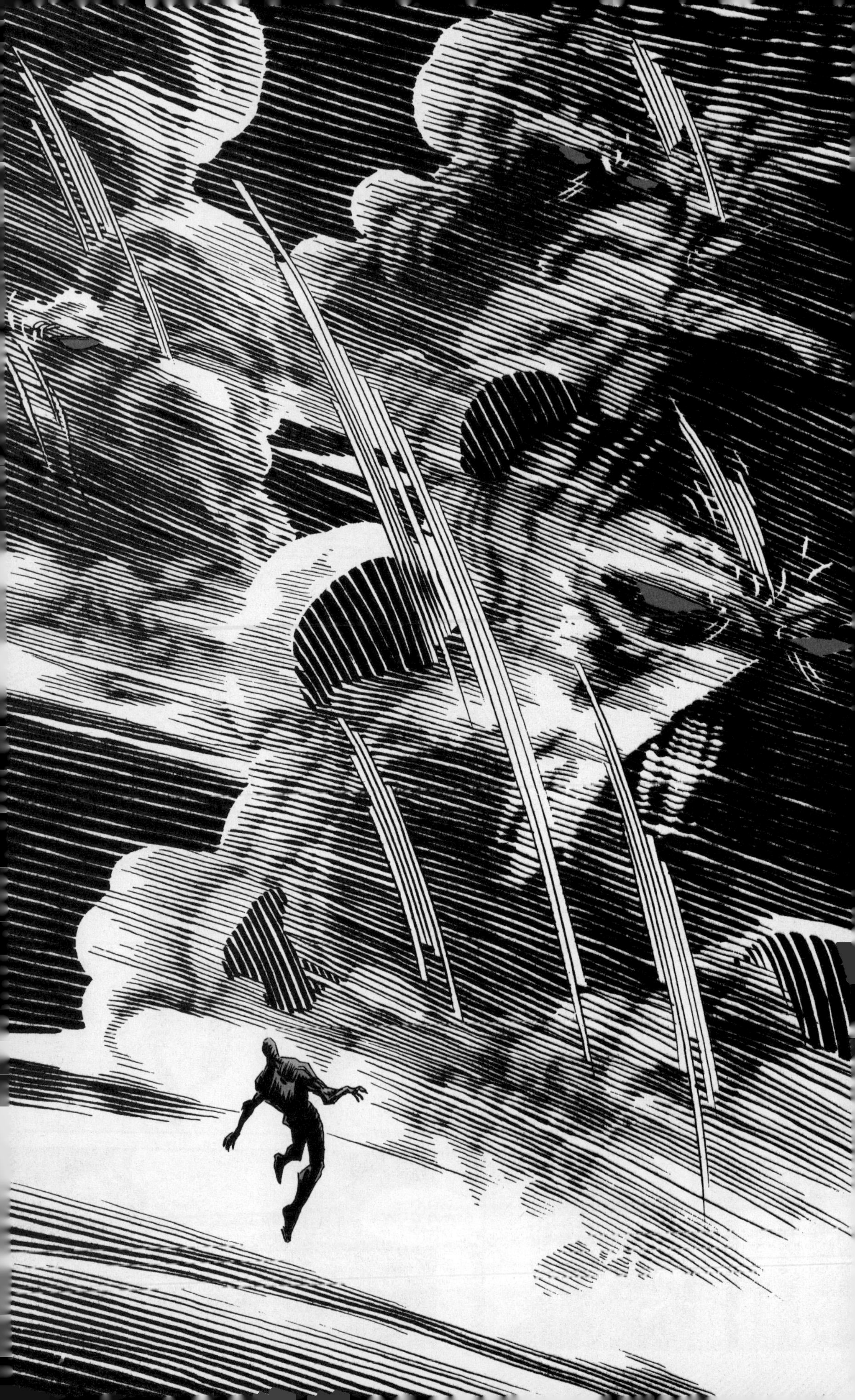

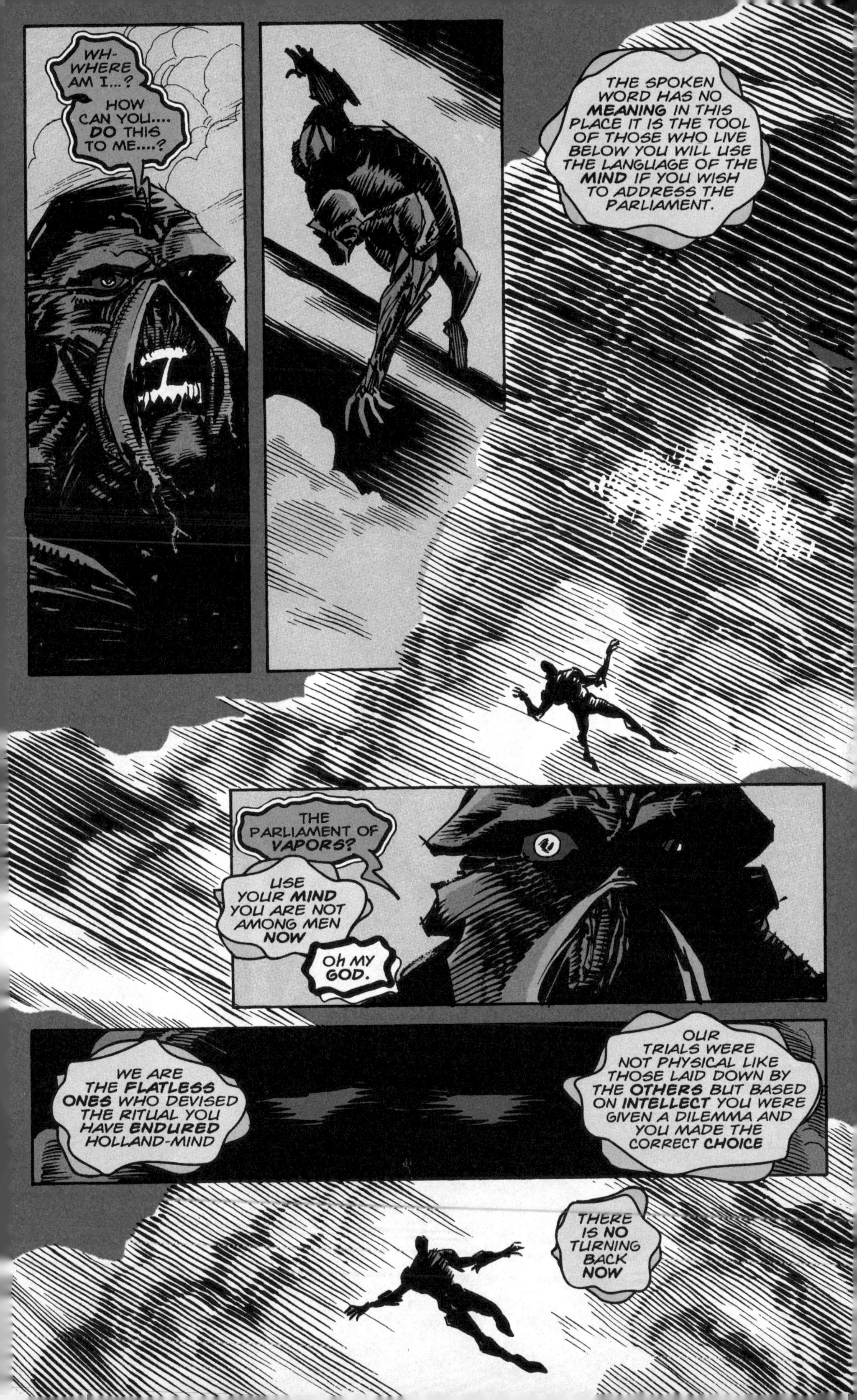

WH- WHERE AM I...? HOW CAN YOU.... DO THIS TO ME....?
THE SPOKEN WORD HAS NO MEANING IN THIS PLACE IT IS THE TOOL OF THOSE WHO LIVE BELOW YOU WILL USE THE LANGUAGE OF THE MIND IF YOU WISH TO ADDRESS THE PARLIAMENT.
THE PARLIAMENT OF VAPORS?
USE YOUR MIND YOU ARE NOT AMONG MEN NOW
Oh MY GOD.
WE ARE THE FLATLESS ONES WHO DEVISED THE RITUAL YOU HAVE ENDURED HOLLAND-MIND
OUR TRIALS WERE NOT PHYSICAL LIKE THOSE LAID DOWN BY THE OTHERS BUT BASED ON INTELLECT YOU WERE GIVEN A DILEMMA AND YOU MADE THE CORRECT CHOICE
THERE IS NO TURNING BACK NOW

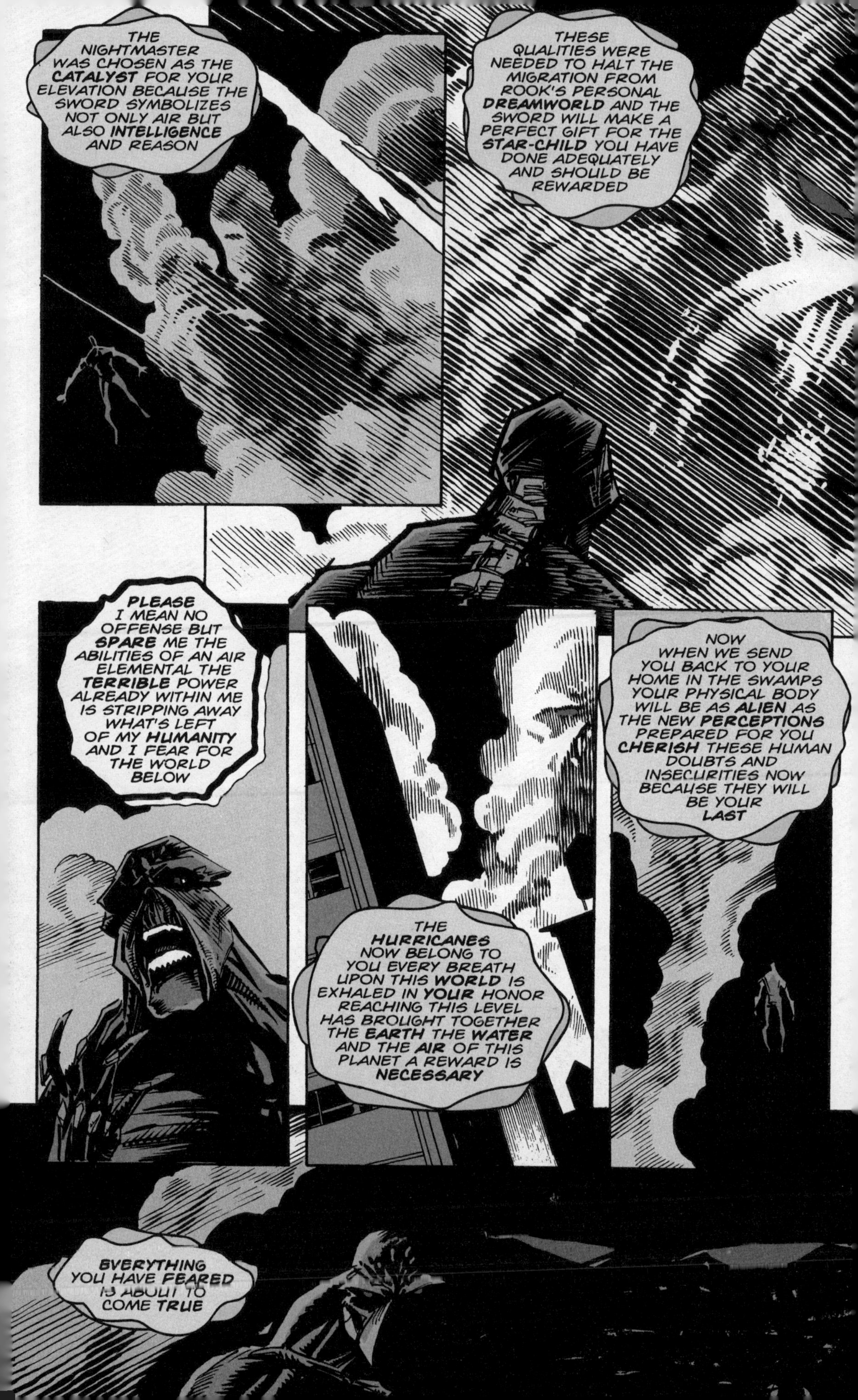
THE NIGHTMASTER WAS CHOSEN AS THE CATALYST FOR YOUR ELEVATION BECAUSE THE SWORD SYMBOLIZES NOT ONLY AIR BUT ALSO INTELLIGENCE AND REASON
THESE QUALITIES WERE NEEDED TO HALT THE MIGRATION FROM ROOK'S PERSONAL DREAMWORLD AND THE SWORD WILL MAKE A PERFECT GIFT FOR THE STAR-CHILD YOU HAVE DONE ADEQUATELY AND SHOULD BE REWARDED
PLEASE I MEAN NO OFFENSE BUT SPARE ME THE ABILITIES OF AN AIR ELEMENTAL THE TERRIBLE POWER ALREADY WITHIN ME IS STRIPPING AWAY WHAT'S LEFT OF MY HUMANITY AND I FEAR FOR THE WORLD BELOW
THE HURRICANES NOW BELONG TO YOU EVERY BREATH UPON THIS WORLD IS EXHALED IN YOUR HONOR REACHING THIS LEVEL HAS BROUGHT TOGETHER THE EARTH THE WATER AND THE AIR OF THIS PLANET A REWARD IS NECESSARY
NOW WHEN WE SEND YOU BACK TO YOUR HOME IN THE SWAMPS YOUR PHYSICAL BODY WILL BE AS ALIEN AS THE NEW PERCEPTIONS PREPARED FOR YOU CHERISH THESE HUMAN DOUBTS AND INSECURITIES NOW BECAUSE THEY WILL BE YOUR LAST
EVERYTHING YOU HAVE FEARED IS ABOUT TO COME TRUE

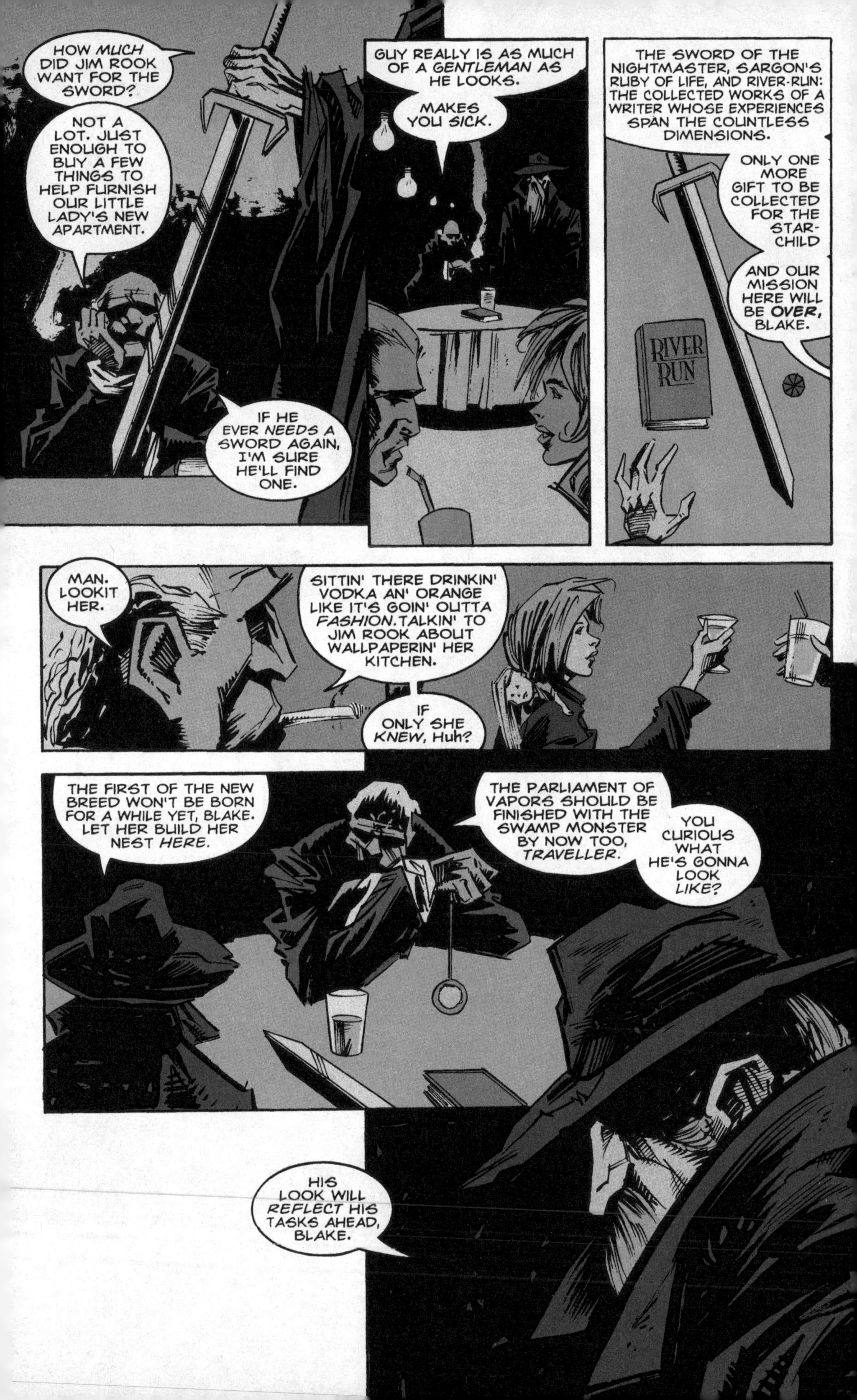
HOW MUCH DID JIM ROOK WANT FOR THE SWORD?
NOT A LOT. JUST ENOUGH TO BUY A FEW THINGS TO HELP FURNISH OUR LITTLE LADY'S NEW APARTMENT.
IF HE EVER NEEDS A SWORD AGAIN, I'M SURE HE'LL FIND ONE.
GUY REALLY IS AS MUCH OF A GENTLEMAN AS HE LOOKS.
MAKES YOU SICK.
THE SWORD OF THE NIGHTMASTER, SARGON'S RUBY OF LIFE, AND RIVER-RUN: THE COLLECTED WORKS OF A WRITER WHOSE EXPERIENCES SPAN THE COUNTLESS DIMENSIONS.
RIVER RUN
ONLY ONE MORE GIFT TO BE COLLECTED FOR THE STAR-CHILD
AND OUR MISSION HERE WILL BE OVER, BLAKE.
MAN. LOOKIT HER.
SITTIN' THERE DRINKIN' VODKA AN' ORANGE LIKE IT'S GOIN' OUTTA FASHION. TALKIN' TO JIM ROOK ABOUT WALLPAPERIN' HER KITCHEN.
IF ONLY SHE KNEW, Huh?
THE FIRST OF THE NEW BREED WON'T BE BORN FOR A WHILE YET, BLAKE. LET HER BUILD HER NEST HERE.
THE PARLIAMENT OF VAPORS SHOULD BE FINISHED WITH THE SWAMP MONSTER BY NOW TOO, TRAVELLER.
YOU CURIOUS WHAT HE'S GONNA LOOK LIKE?
HIS LOOK WILL REFLECT HIS TASKS AHEAD, BLAKE.

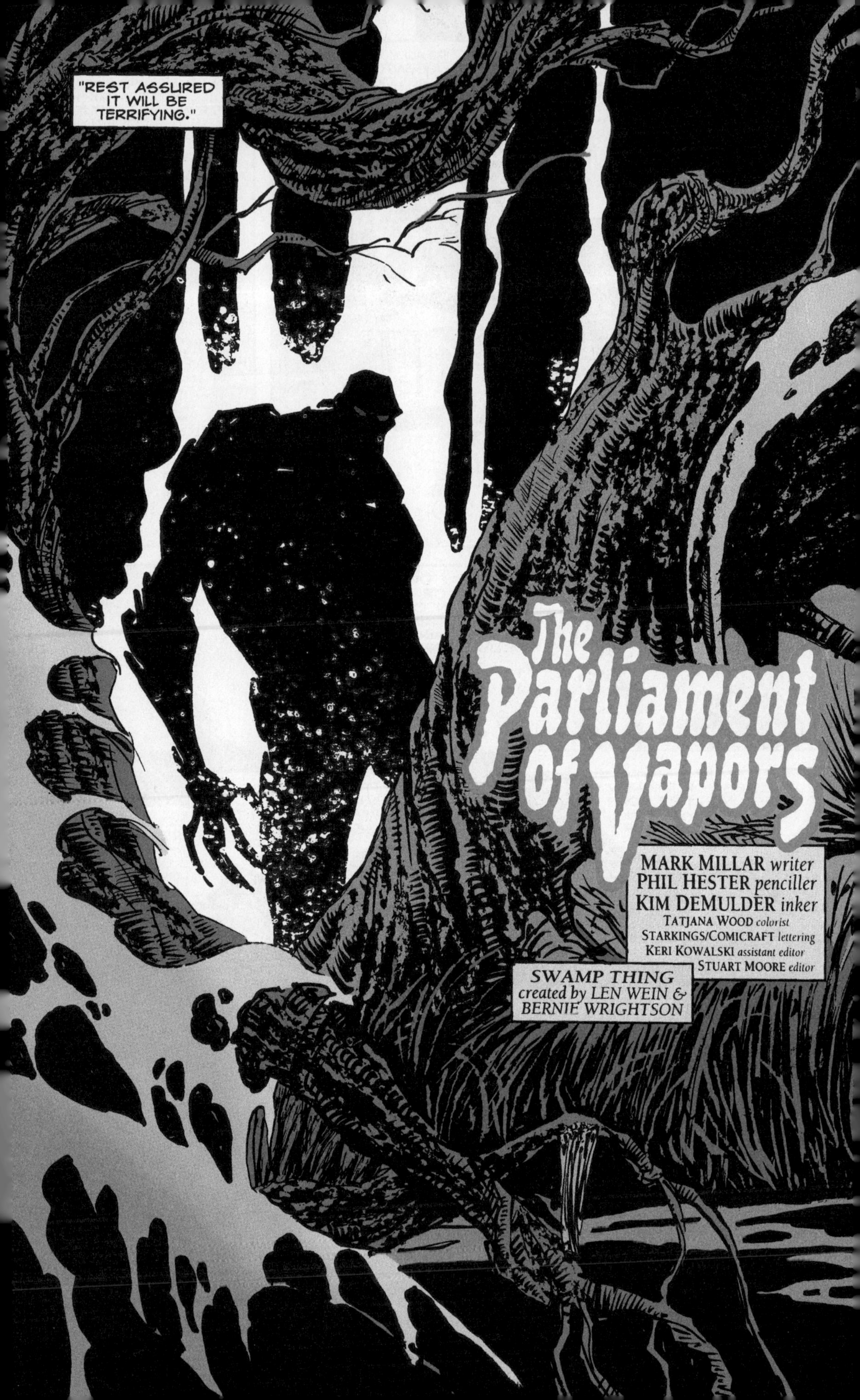
"REST ASSURED IT WILL BE TERRIFYING."
The Parliament of Vapors
MARK MILLAR writer
PHIL HESTER penciller
KIM DEMULDER inker
TATJANA WOOD colorist
STARKINGS/COMICRAFT lettering
KERI KOWALSKI assistant editor
STUART MOORE editor
SWAMP THING created by LEN WEIN & BERNIE WRIGHTSON

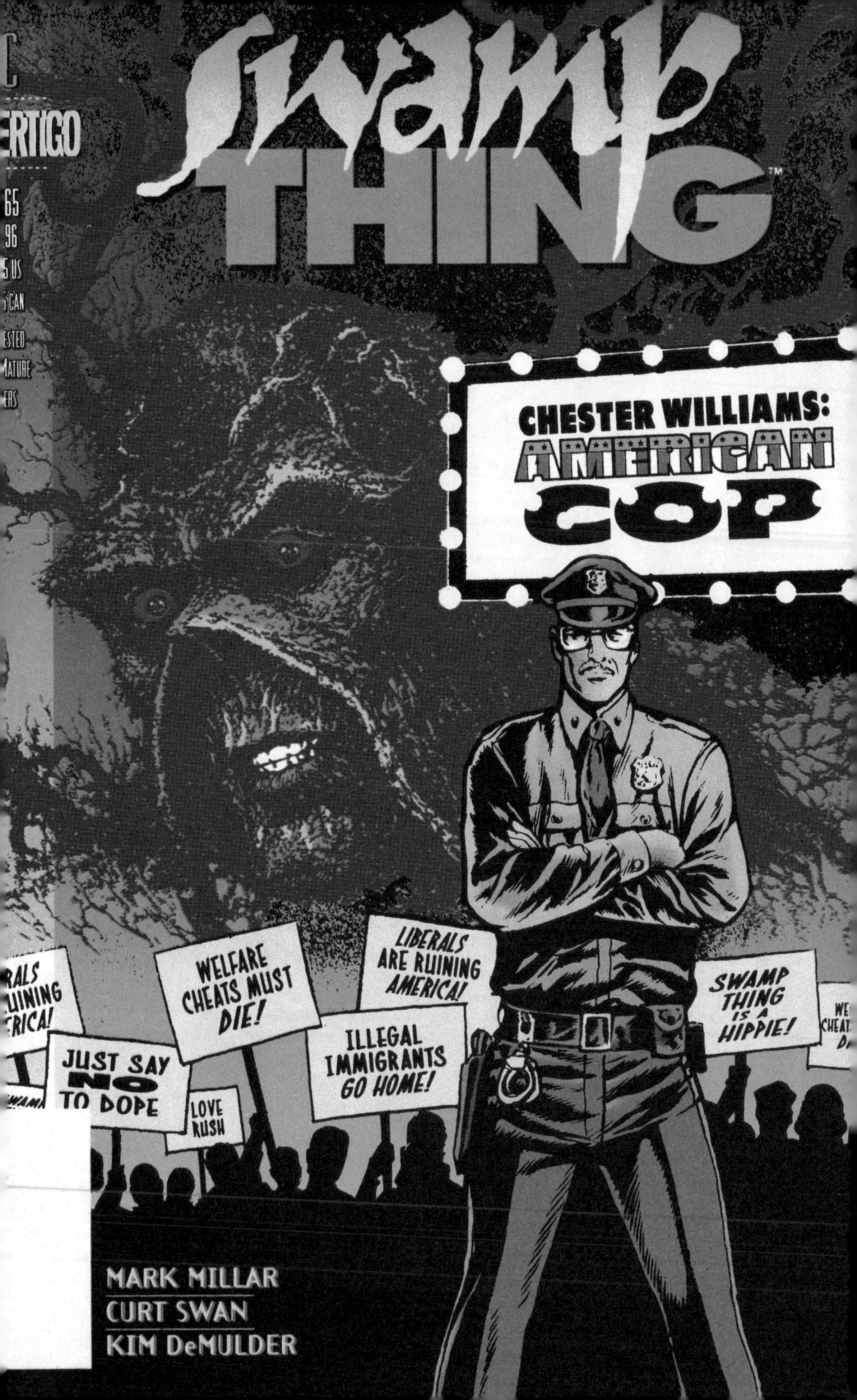
SWAMP THING
CHESTER WILLIAMS: AMERICAN COP
WELFARE CHEATS MUST DIE!
LIBERALS ARE RUINING AMERICA!
SWAMP THING IS A HIPPIE!
JUST SAY NO TO DOPE
LOVE RUSH
ILLEGAL IMMIGRANTS GO HOME!
MARK MILLAR
CURT SWAN
KIM DeMULDER

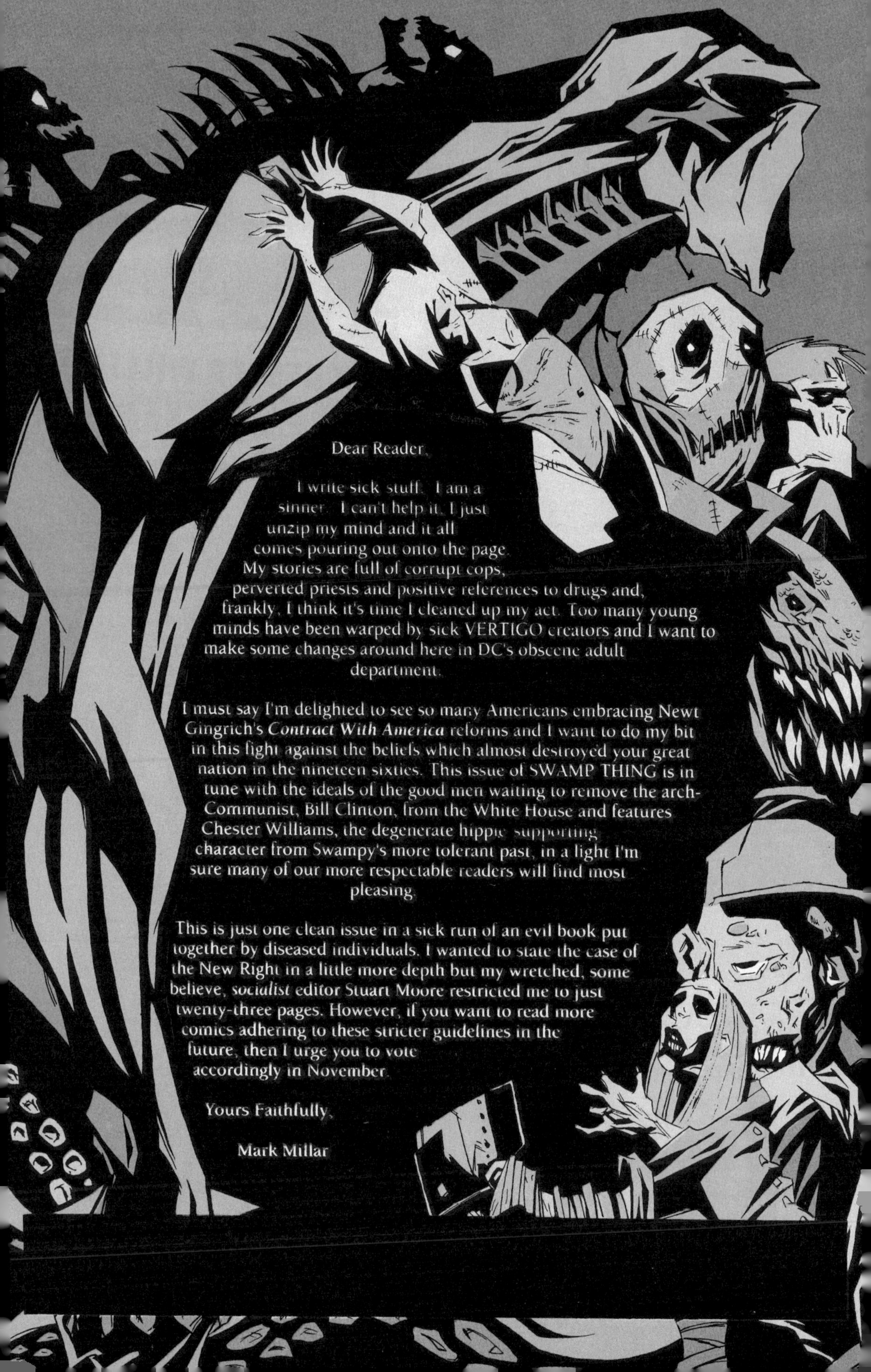

Dear Reader,

I write sick stuff. I am a sinner. I can't help it. I just unzip my mind and it all comes pouring out onto the page. My stories are full of corrupt cops, perverted priests and positive references to drugs and, frankly, I think it's time I cleaned up my act. Too many young minds have been warped by sick VERTIGO creators and I want to make some changes around here in DC's obscene adult department.

I must say I'm delighted to see so many Americans embracing Newt Gingrich's *Contract With America* reforms and I want to do my bit in this fight against the beliefs which almost destroyed your great nation in the nineteen sixties. This issue of SWAMP THING is in tune with the ideals of the good men waiting to remove the arch-Communist, Bill Clinton, from the White House and features Chester Williams, the degenerate hippie supporting character from Swampy's more tolerant past, in a light I'm sure many of our more respectable readers will find most pleasing.

This is just one clean issue in a sick run of an evil book put together by diseased individuals. I wanted to state the case of the New Right in a little more depth but my wretched, some believe, *socialist* editor Stuart Moore restricted me to just twenty-three pages. However, if you want to read more comics adhering to these stricter guidelines in the future, then I urge you to vote accordingly in November.

Yours Faithfully,

Mark Millar

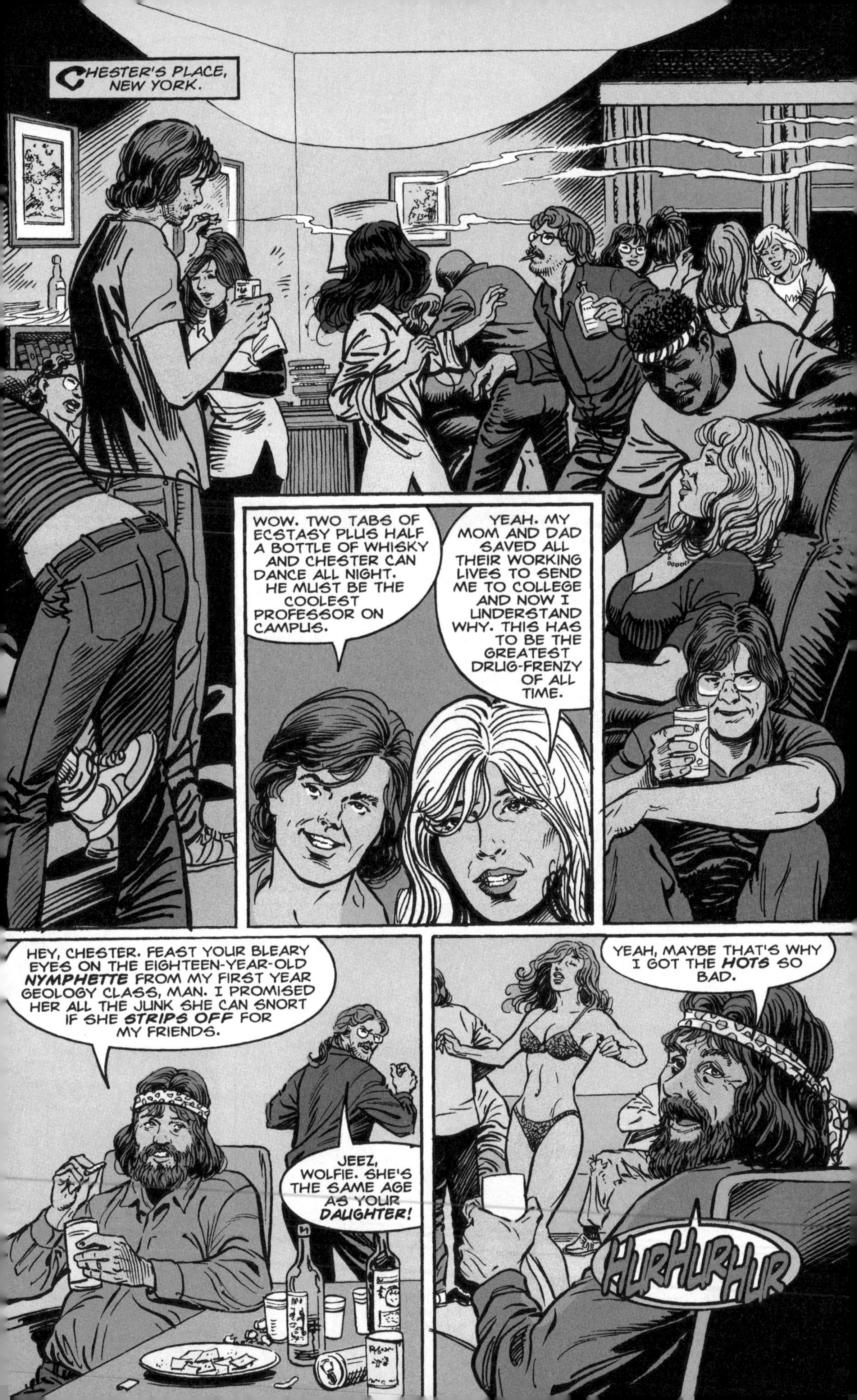
CHESTER'S PLACE, NEW YORK.
WOW. TWO TABS OF ECSTASY PLUS HALF A BOTTLE OF WHISKY AND CHESTER CAN DANCE ALL NIGHT. HE MUST BE THE COOLEST PROFESSOR ON CAMPUS.
YEAH. MY MOM AND DAD SAVED ALL THEIR WORKING LIVES TO SEND ME TO COLLEGE AND NOW I UNDERSTAND WHY. THIS HAS TO BE THE GREATEST DRUG-FRENZY OF ALL TIME.
HEY, CHESTER. FEAST YOUR BLEARY EYES ON THE EIGHTEEN-YEAR-OLD NYMPHETTE FROM MY FIRST YEAR GEOLOGY CLASS, MAN. I PROMISED HER ALL THE JUNK SHE CAN SNORT IF SHE STRIPS OFF FOR MY FRIENDS.
JEEZ, WOLFIE. SHE'S THE SAME AGE AS YOUR DAUGHTER!
YEAH, MAYBE THAT'S WHY I GOT THE HOTS SO BAD.
HURHURHUR

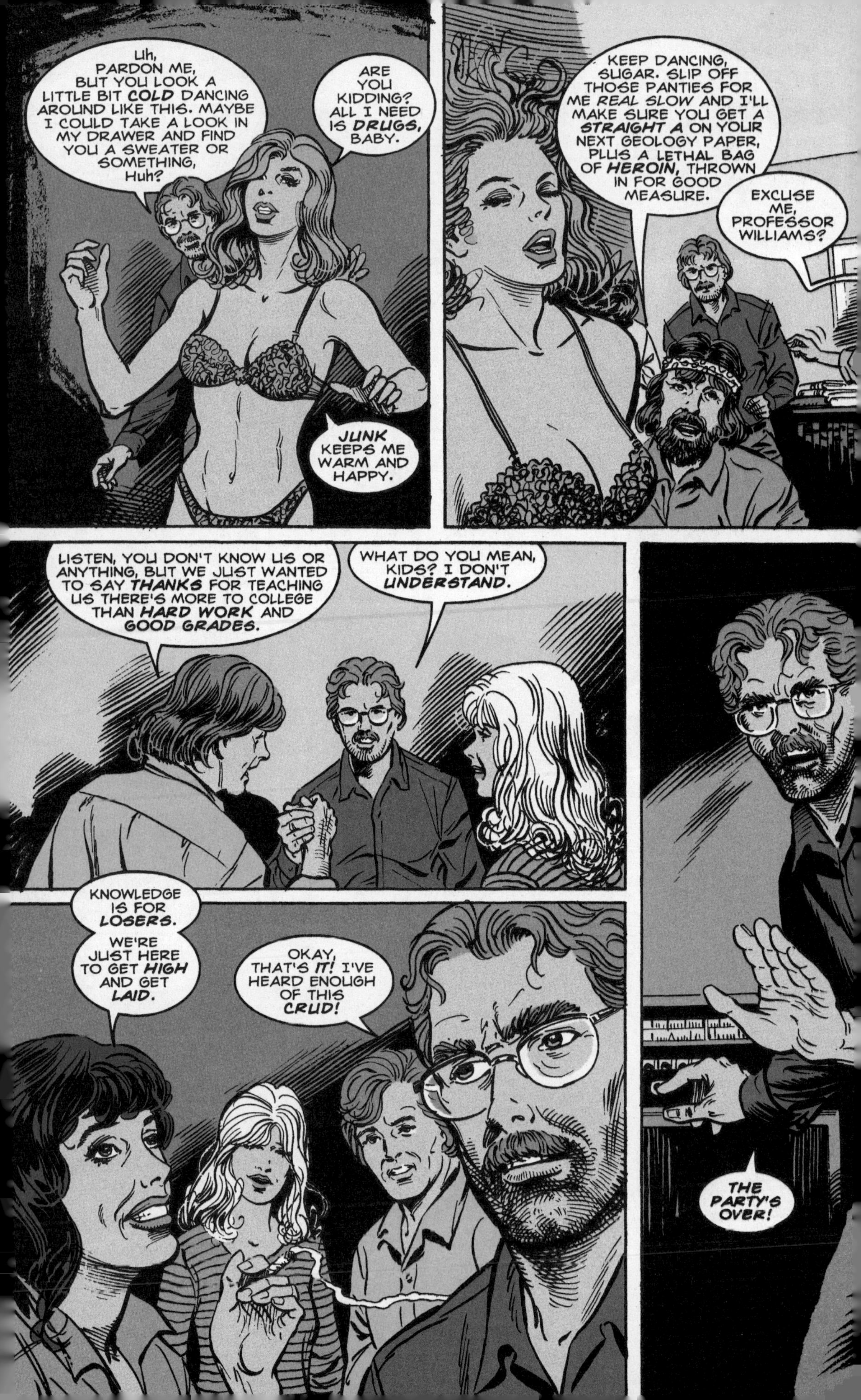

UH, PARDON ME, BUT YOU LOOK A LITTLE BIT COLD DANCING AROUND LIKE THIS. MAYBE I COULD TAKE A LOOK IN MY DRAWER AND FIND YOU A SWEATER OR SOMETHING, HUH?
ARE YOU KIDDING? ALL I NEED IS DRUGS, BABY.
JUNK KEEPS ME WARM AND HAPPY.
KEEP DANCING, SUGAR. SLIP OFF THOSE PANTIES FOR ME REAL SLOW AND I'LL MAKE SURE YOU GET A STRAIGHT A ON YOUR NEXT GEOLOGY PAPER, PLUS A LETHAL BAG OF HEROIN, THROWN IN FOR GOOD MEASURE.
EXCUSE ME, PROFESSOR WILLIAMS?
LISTEN, YOU DON'T KNOW US OR ANYTHING, BUT WE JUST WANTED TO SAY THANKS FOR TEACHING US THERE'S MORE TO COLLEGE THAN HARD WORK AND GOOD GRADES.
WHAT DO YOU MEAN, KIDS? I DON'T UNDERSTAND.
KNOWLEDGE IS FOR LOSERS.
WE'RE JUST HERE TO GET HIGH AND GET LAID.
OKAY, THAT'S IT! I'VE HEARD ENOUGH OF THIS CRUD!
THE PARTY'S OVER!

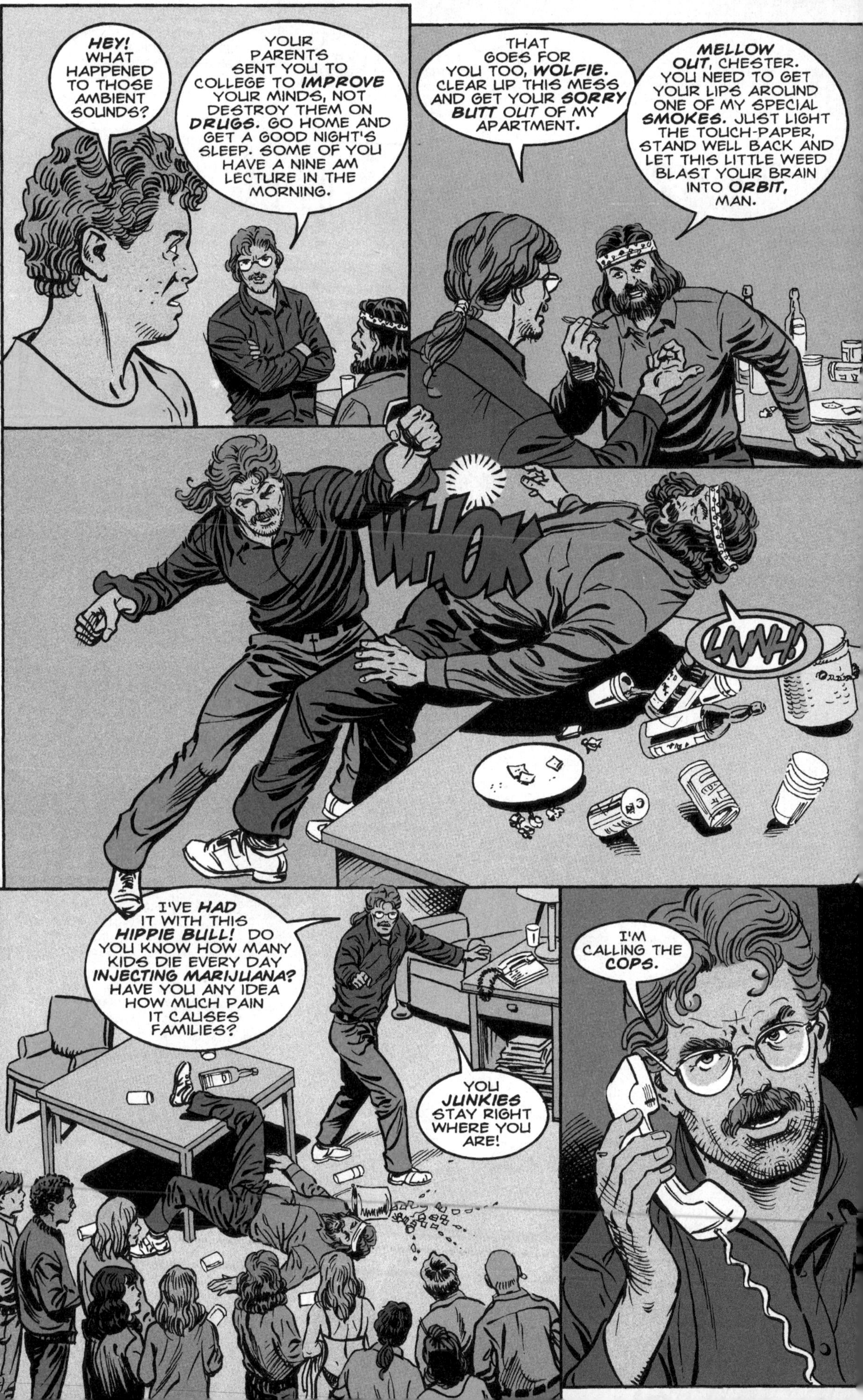
HEY! WHAT HAPPENED TO THOSE AMBIENT SOUNDS?
YOUR PARENTS SENT YOU TO COLLEGE TO IMPROVE YOUR MINDS, NOT DESTROY THEM ON DRUGS. GO HOME AND GET A GOOD NIGHT'S SLEEP. SOME OF YOU HAVE A NINE AM LECTURE IN THE MORNING.
THAT GOES FOR YOU TOO, WOLFIE. CLEAR UP THIS MESS AND GET YOUR SORRY BUTT OUT OF MY APARTMENT.
MELLOW OUT, CHESTER. YOU NEED TO GET YOUR LIPS AROUND ONE OF MY SPECIAL SMOKES. JUST LIGHT THE TOUCH-PAPER, STAND WELL BACK AND LET THIS LITTLE WEED BLAST YOUR BRAIN INTO ORBIT, MAN.
WHOK
LNNH!
I'VE HAD IT WITH THIS HIPPIE BULL! DO YOU KNOW HOW MANY KIDS DIE EVERY DAY INJECTING MARIJUANA? HAVE YOU ANY IDEA HOW MUCH PAIN IT CAUSES FAMILIES?
YOU JUNKIES STAY RIGHT WHERE YOU ARE!
I'M CALLING THE COPS.

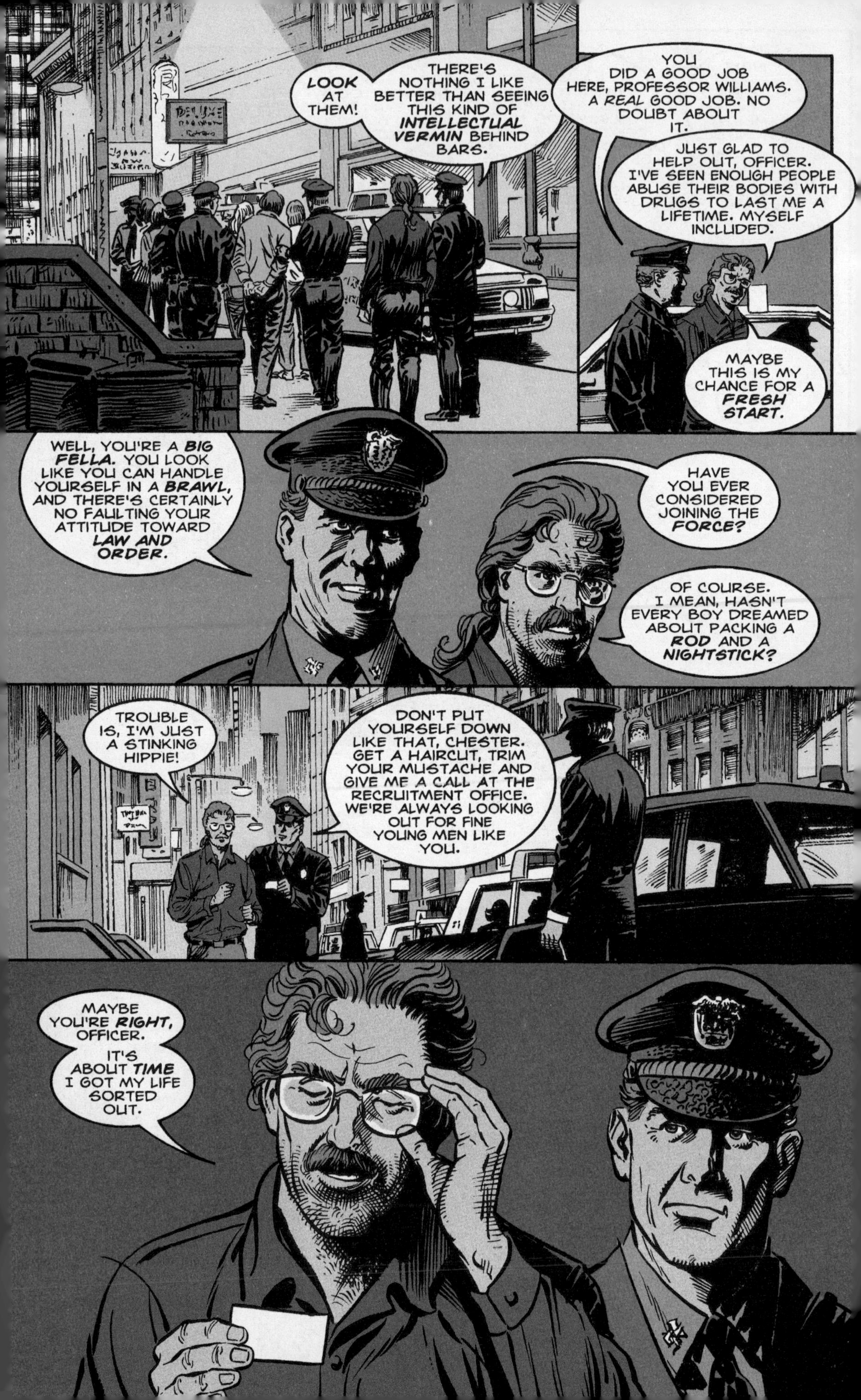
LOOK AT THEM!
THERE'S NOTHING I LIKE BETTER THAN SEEING THIS KIND OF INTELLECTUAL VERMIN BEHIND BARS.
YOU DID A GOOD JOB HERE, PROFESSOR WILLIAMS. A REAL GOOD JOB. NO DOUBT ABOUT IT.
JUST GLAD TO HELP OUT, OFFICER. I'VE SEEN ENOUGH PEOPLE ABUSE THEIR BODIES WITH DRUGS TO LAST ME A LIFETIME. MYSELF INCLUDED.
MAYBE THIS IS MY CHANCE FOR A FRESH START.
WELL, YOU'RE A BIG FELLA. YOU LOOK LIKE YOU CAN HANDLE YOURSELF IN A BRAWL, AND THERE'S CERTAINLY NO FAULTING YOUR ATTITUDE TOWARD LAW AND ORDER.
HAVE YOU EVER CONSIDERED JOINING THE FORCE?
OF COURSE. I MEAN, HASN'T EVERY BOY DREAMED ABOUT PACKING A ROD AND A NIGHTSTICK?
TROUBLE IS, I'M JUST A STINKING HIPPIE!
DON'T PUT YOURSELF DOWN LIKE THAT, CHESTER. GET A HAIRCUT, TRIM YOUR MUSTACHE AND GIVE ME A CALL AT THE RECRUITMENT OFFICE. WE'RE ALWAYS LOOKING OUT FOR FINE YOUNG MEN LIKE YOU.
MAYBE YOU'RE RIGHT, OFFICER.
IT'S ABOUT TIME I GOT MY LIFE SORTED OUT.

CHESTER WILLIAMS:

AMERICAN COP

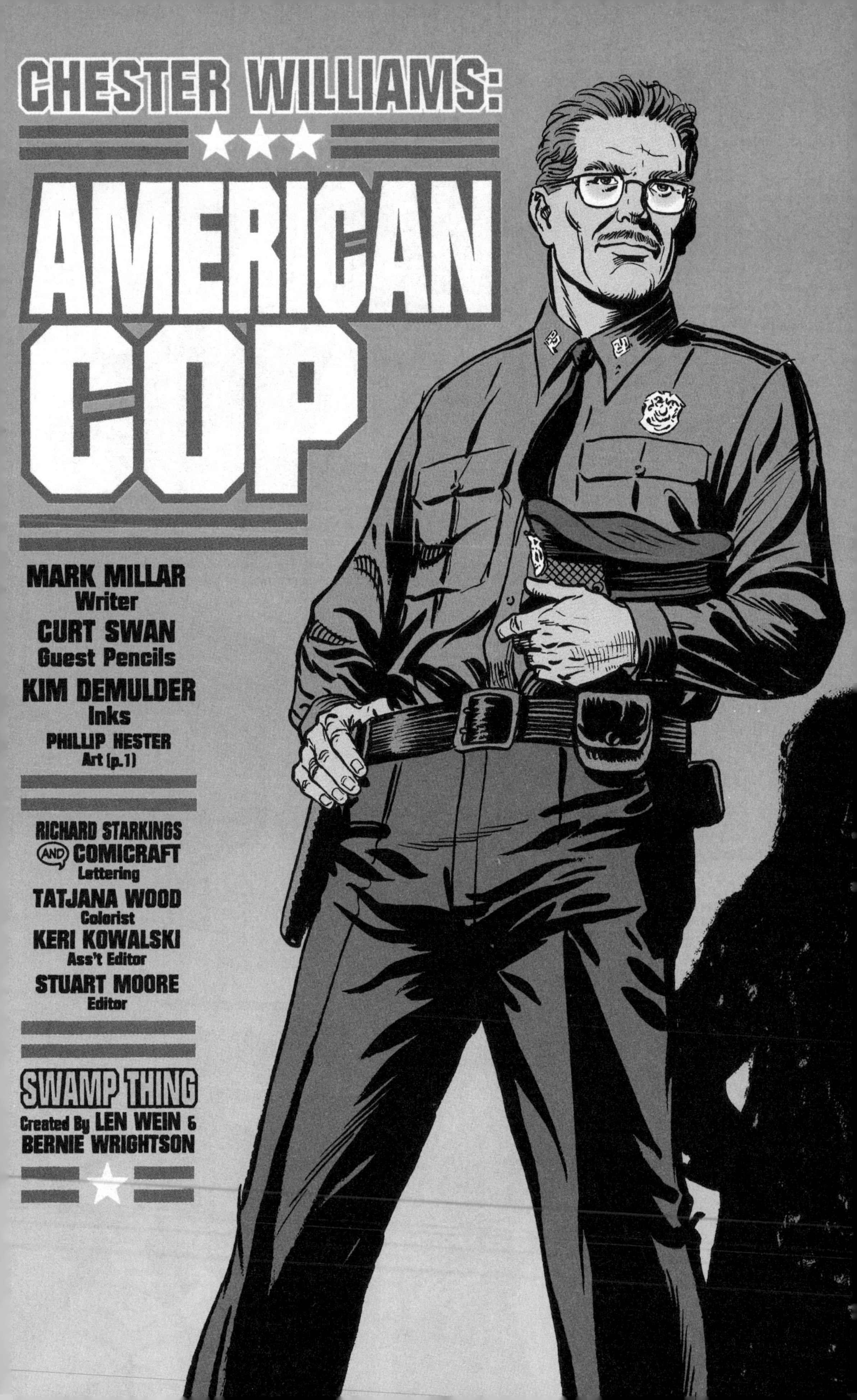

MARK MILLAR
Writer

CURT SWAN
Guest Pencils

KIM DEMULDER
Inks

PHILLIP HESTER
Art (p.1)

RICHARD STARKINGS AND COMICRAFT
Lettering

TATJANA WOOD
Colorist

KERI KOWALSKI
Ass't Editor

STUART MOORE
Editor

SWAMP THING
Created By LEN WEIN & BERNIE WRIGHTSON

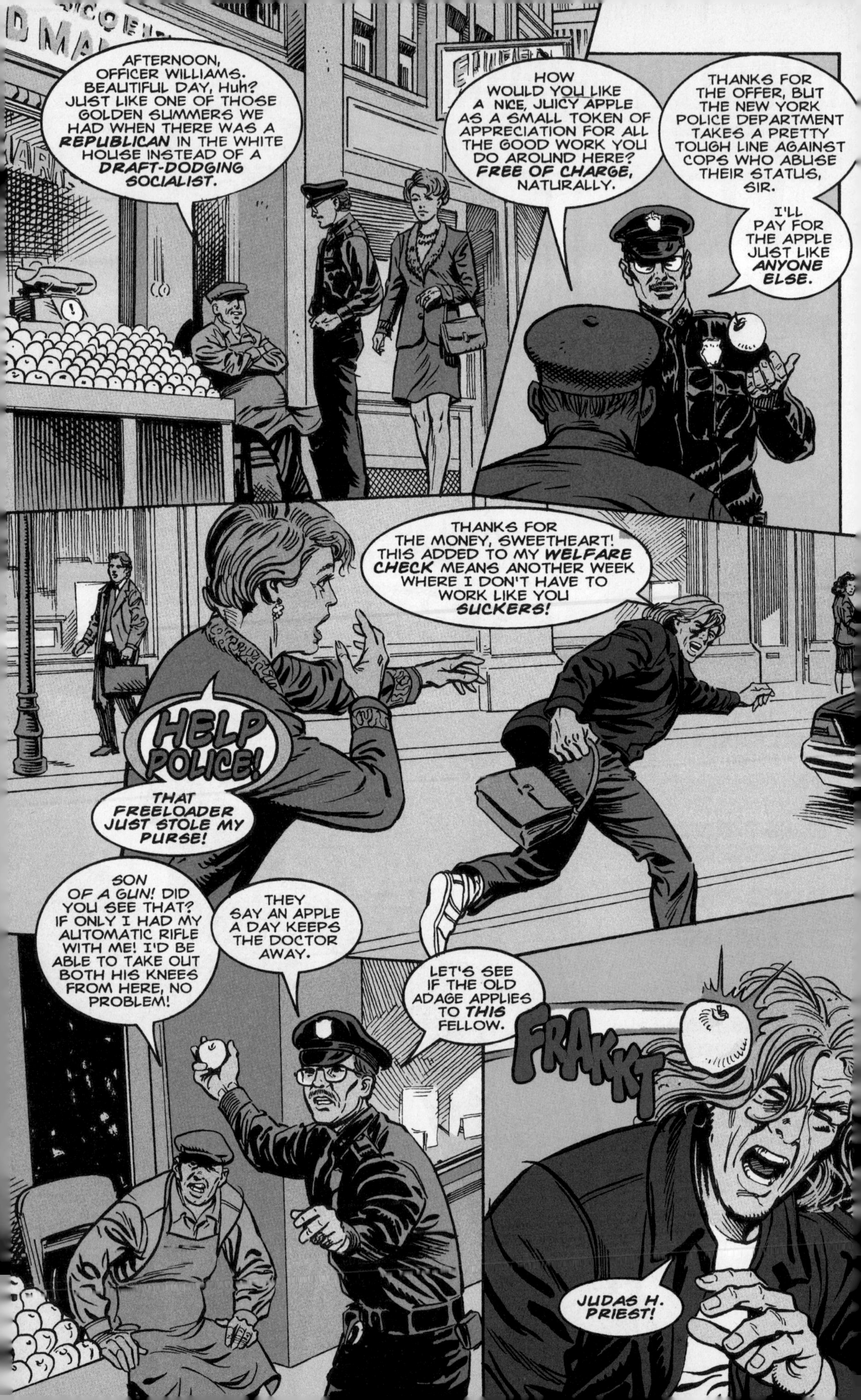
AFTERNOON, OFFICER WILLIAMS. BEAUTIFUL DAY, Huh? JUST LIKE ONE OF THOSE GOLDEN SUMMERS WE HAD WHEN THERE WAS A REPUBLICAN IN THE WHITE HOUSE INSTEAD OF A DRAFT-DODGING SOCIALIST.
HOW WOULD YOU LIKE A NICE, JUICY APPLE AS A SMALL TOKEN OF APPRECIATION FOR ALL THE GOOD WORK YOU DO AROUND HERE? FREE OF CHARGE, NATURALLY.
THANKS FOR THE OFFER, BUT THE NEW YORK POLICE DEPARTMENT TAKES A PRETTY TOUGH LINE AGAINST COPS WHO ABUSE THEIR STATUS, SIR.
I'LL PAY FOR THE APPLE JUST LIKE ANYONE ELSE.
HELP POLICE!
THAT FREELOADER JUST STOLE MY PURSE!
THANKS FOR THE MONEY, SWEETHEART! THIS ADDED TO MY WELFARE CHECK MEANS ANOTHER WEEK WHERE I DON'T HAVE TO WORK LIKE YOU SUCKERS!
SON OF A GUN! DID YOU SEE THAT? IF ONLY I HAD MY AUTOMATIC RIFLE WITH ME! I'D BE ABLE TO TAKE OUT BOTH HIS KNEES FROM HERE, NO PROBLEM!
THEY SAY AN APPLE A DAY KEEPS THE DOCTOR AWAY.
LET'S SEE IF THE OLD ADAGE APPLIES TO THIS FELLOW.
FRAKKT
JUDAS H. PRIEST!

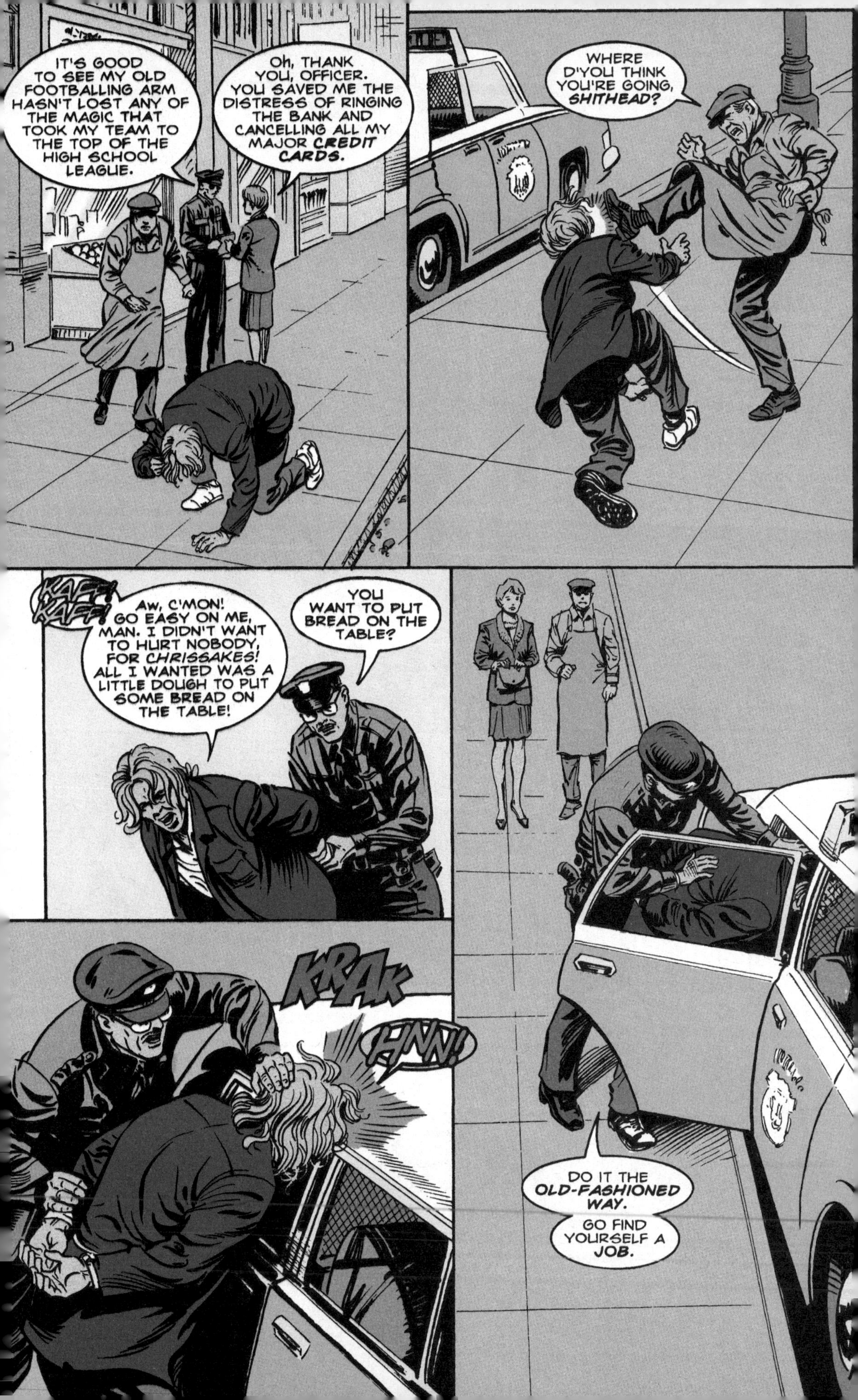
IT'S GOOD TO SEE MY OLD FOOTBALLING ARM HASN'T LOST ANY OF THE MAGIC THAT TOOK MY TEAM TO THE TOP OF THE HIGH SCHOOL LEAGUE.
Oh, THANK YOU, OFFICER. YOU SAVED ME THE DISTRESS OF RINGING THE BANK AND CANCELLING ALL MY MAJOR CREDIT CARDS.
WHERE D'YOU THINK YOU'RE GOING, SHITHEAD?
KAFF! KAFF!
AW, C'MON! GO EASY ON ME, MAN. I DIDN'T WANT TO HURT NOBODY, FOR CHRISSAKES! ALL I WANTED WAS A LITTLE DOUGH TO PUT SOME BREAD ON THE TABLE!
YOU WANT TO PUT BREAD ON THE TABLE?
KRAK
HNN!
DO IT THE OLD-FASHIONED WAY.
GO FIND YOURSELF A JOB.

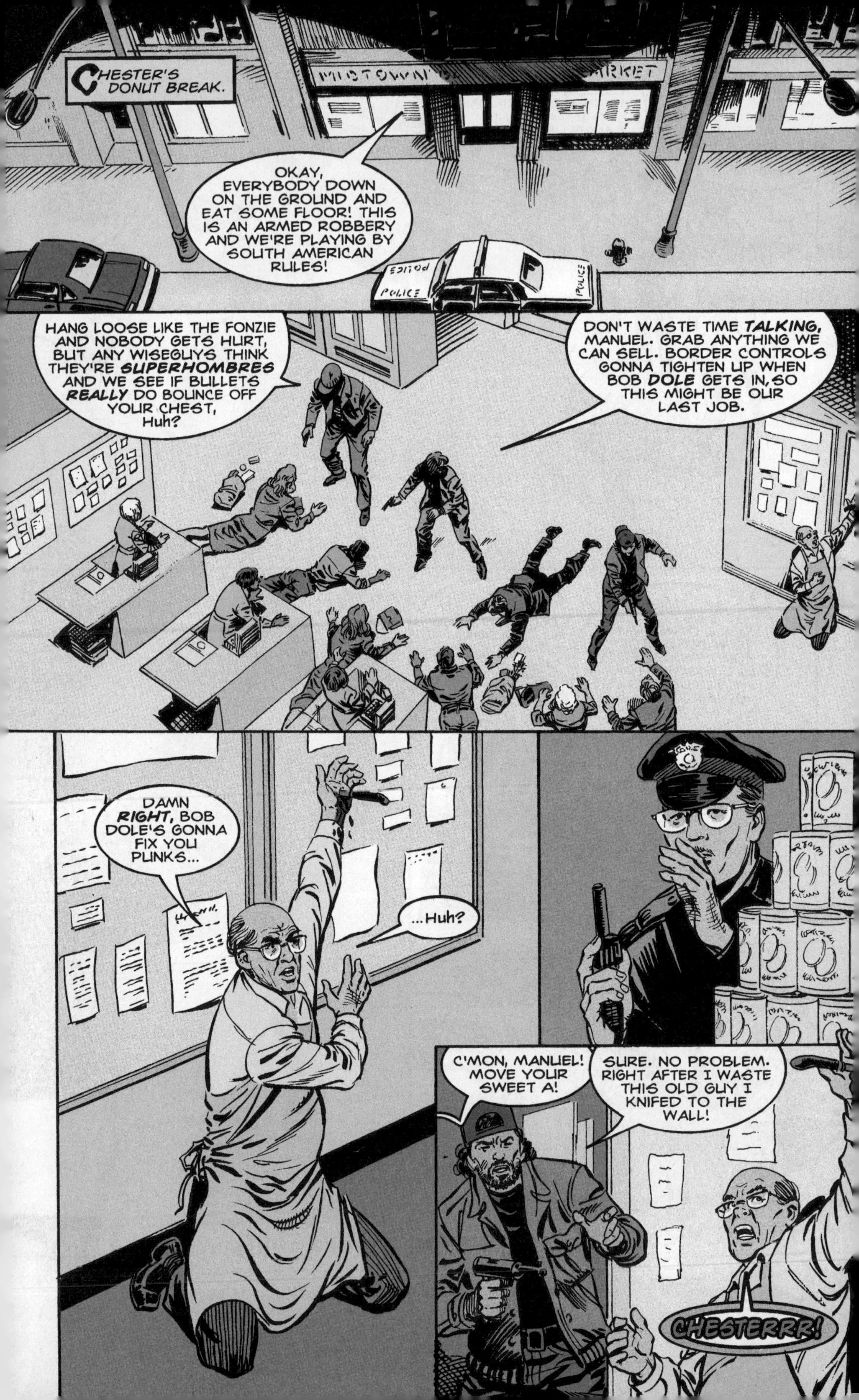
CHESTER'S DONUT BREAK.
MIDTOWN'S MARKET
OKAY, EVERYBODY DOWN ON THE GROUND AND EAT SOME FLOOR! THIS IS AN ARMED ROBBERY AND WE'RE PLAYING BY SOUTH AMERICAN RULES!
POLICE
HANG LOOSE LIKE THE FONZIE AND NOBODY GETS HURT, BUT ANY WISEGUYS THINK THEY'RE SUPERHOMBRES AND WE SEE IF BULLETS REALLY DO BOUNCE OFF YOUR CHEST, Huh?
DON'T WASTE TIME TALKING, MANUEL. GRAB ANYTHING WE CAN SELL. BORDER CONTROLS GONNA TIGHTEN UP WHEN BOB DOLE GETS IN, SO THIS MIGHT BE OUR LAST JOB.
DAMN RIGHT, BOB DOLE'S GONNA FIX YOU PUNKS...
...Huh?
C'MON, MANUEL! MOVE YOUR SWEET A!
SURE. NO PROBLEM. RIGHT AFTER I WASTE THIS OLD GUY I KNIFED TO THE WALL!
CHESTERRR!

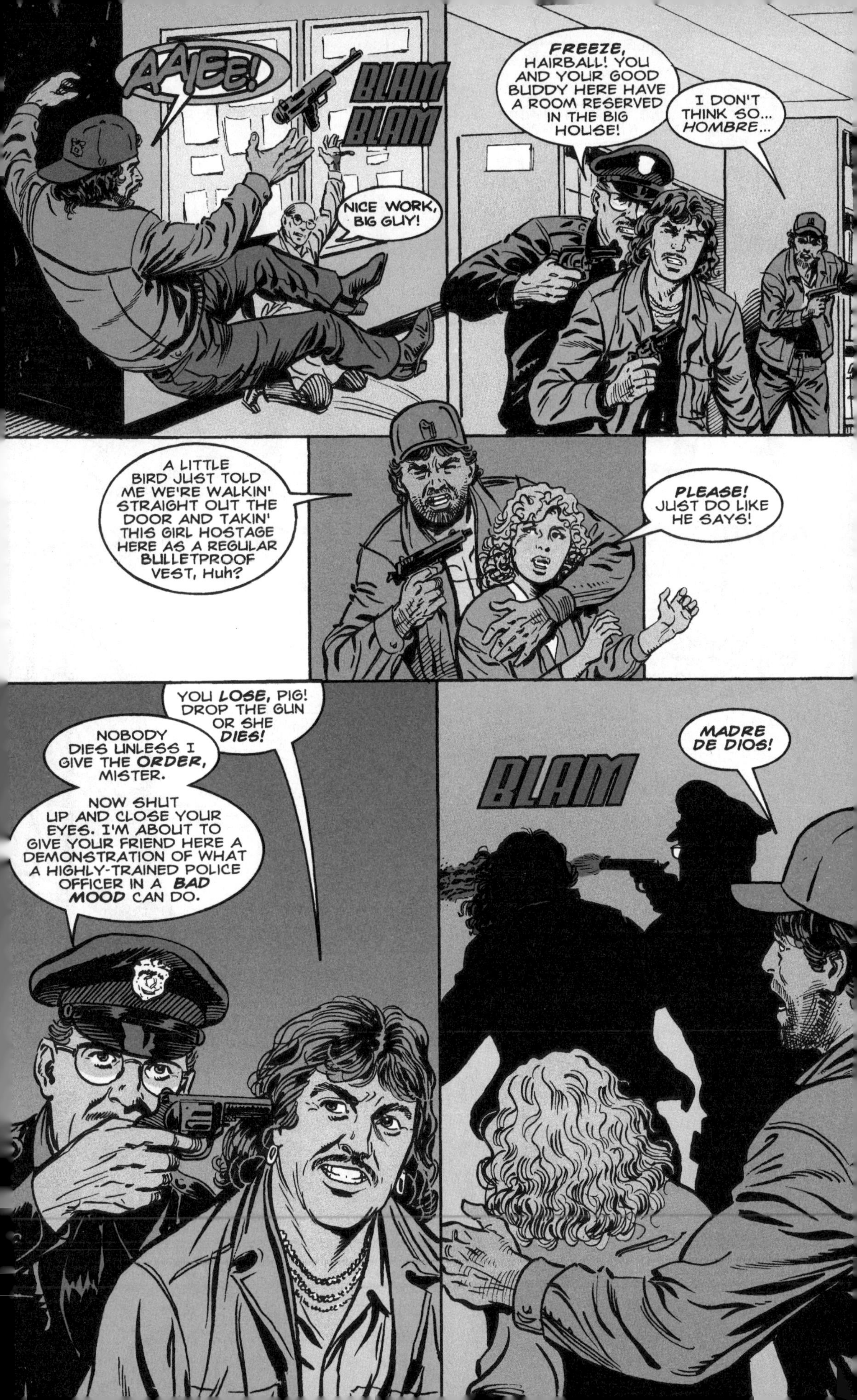
AAIEE!
BLAM
BLAM
NICE WORK, BIG GUY!
FREEZE, HAIRBALL! YOU AND YOUR GOOD BUDDY HERE HAVE A ROOM RESERVED IN THE BIG HOUSE!
I DON'T THINK SO... HOMBRE...
A LITTLE BIRD JUST TOLD ME WE'RE WALKIN' STRAIGHT OUT THE DOOR AND TAKIN' THIS GIRL HOSTAGE HERE AS A REGULAR BULLETPROOF VEST, Huh?
PLEASE! JUST DO LIKE HE SAYS!
YOU LOSE, PIG! DROP THE GUN OR SHE DIES!
NOBODY DIES UNLESS I GIVE THE ORDER, MISTER.
NOW SHUT UP AND CLOSE YOUR EYES. I'M ABOUT TO GIVE YOUR FRIEND HERE A DEMONSTRATION OF WHAT A HIGHLY-TRAINED POLICE OFFICER IN A BAD MOOD CAN DO.
BLAM
MADRE DE DIOS!

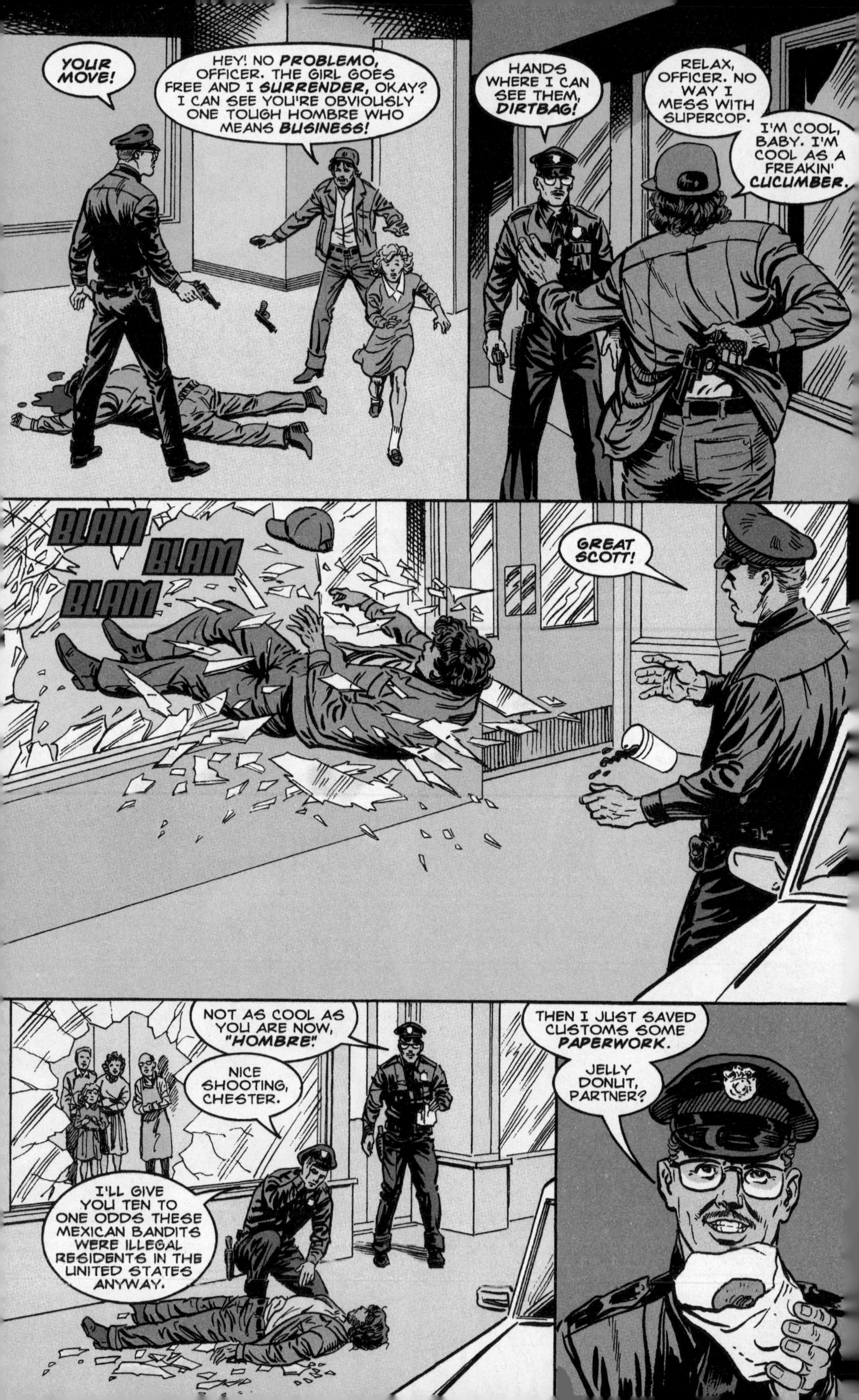
YOUR MOVE!
HEY! NO PROBLEMO, OFFICER. THE GIRL GOES FREE AND I SURRENDER, OKAY? I CAN SEE YOU'RE OBVIOUSLY ONE TOUGH HOMBRE WHO MEANS BUSINESS!
HANDS WHERE I CAN SEE THEM, DIRTBAG!
RELAX, OFFICER. NO WAY I MESS WITH SUPERCOP.
I'M COOL, BABY. I'M COOL AS A FREAKIN' CUCUMBER.
BLAM
BLAM
BLAM
GREAT SCOTT!
NOT AS COOL AS YOU ARE NOW, "HOMBRE."
NICE SHOOTING, CHESTER.
I'LL GIVE YOU TEN TO ONE ODDS THESE MEXICAN BANDITS WERE ILLEGAL RESIDENTS IN THE UNITED STATES ANYWAY.
THEN I JUST SAVED CUSTOMS SOME PAPERWORK.
JELLY DONUT, PARTNER?

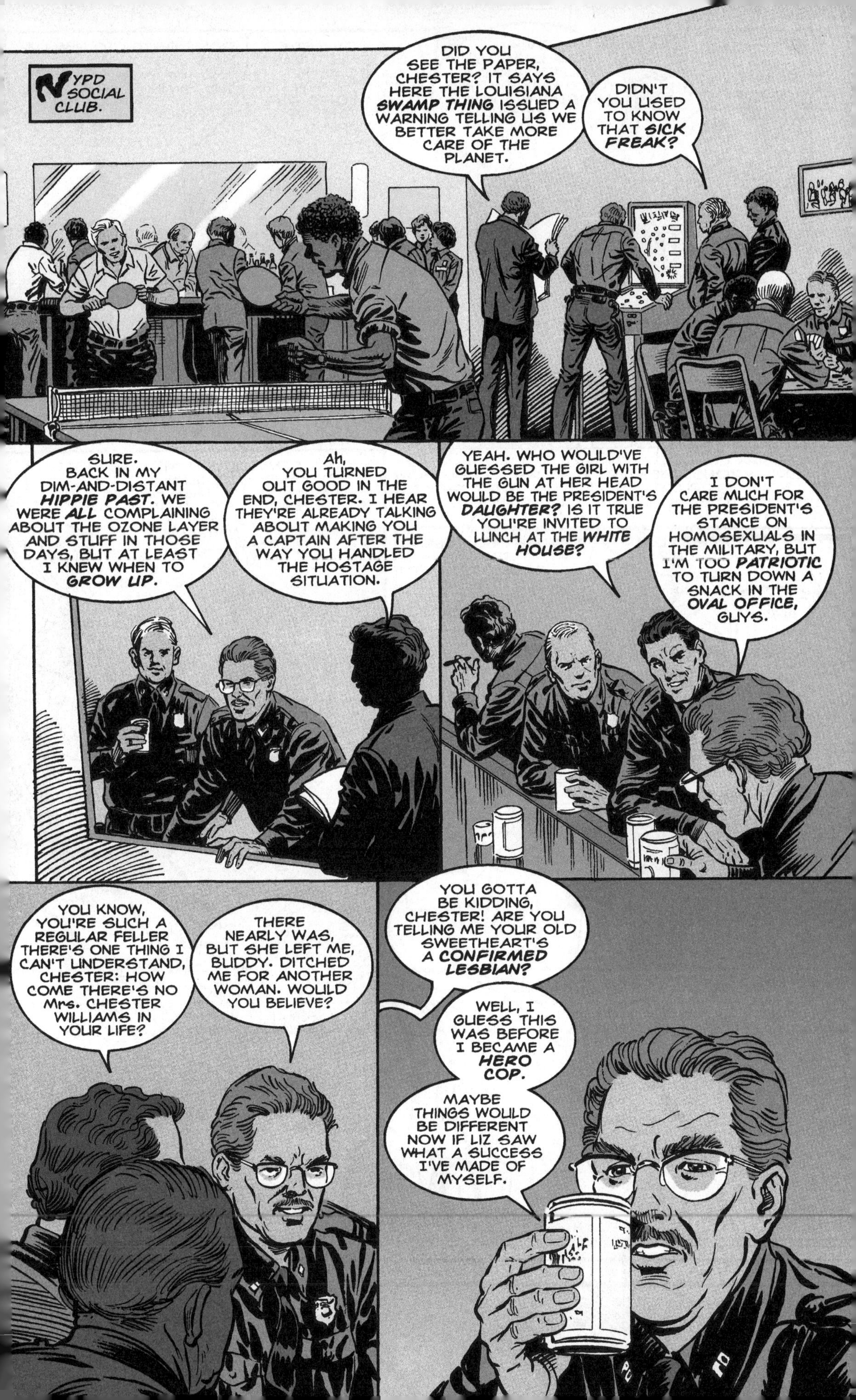
NYPD SOCIAL CLUB.
DID YOU SEE THE PAPER, CHESTER? IT SAYS HERE THE LOUISIANA SWAMP THING ISSUED A WARNING TELLING US WE BETTER TAKE MORE CARE OF THE PLANET.
DIDN'T YOU USED TO KNOW THAT SICK FREAK?
SURE. BACK IN MY DIM-AND-DISTANT HIPPIE PAST. WE WERE ALL COMPLAINING ABOUT THE OZONE LAYER AND STUFF IN THOSE DAYS, BUT AT LEAST I KNEW WHEN TO GROW UP.
Ah, YOU TURNED OUT GOOD IN THE END, CHESTER. I HEAR THEY'RE ALREADY TALKING ABOUT MAKING YOU A CAPTAIN AFTER THE WAY YOU HANDLED THE HOSTAGE SITUATION.
YEAH. WHO WOULD'VE GUESSED THE GIRL WITH THE GUN AT HER HEAD WOULD BE THE PRESIDENT'S DAUGHTER? IS IT TRUE YOU'RE INVITED TO LUNCH AT THE WHITE HOUSE?
I DON'T CARE MUCH FOR THE PRESIDENT'S STANCE ON HOMOSEXUALS IN THE MILITARY, BUT I'M TOO PATRIOTIC TO TURN DOWN A SNACK IN THE OVAL OFFICE, GUYS.
YOU KNOW, YOU'RE SUCH A REGULAR FELLER THERE'S ONE THING I CAN'T UNDERSTAND, CHESTER: HOW COME THERE'S NO Mrs. CHESTER WILLIAMS IN YOUR LIFE?
THERE NEARLY WAS, BUT SHE LEFT ME, BUDDY. DITCHED ME FOR ANOTHER WOMAN. WOULD YOU BELIEVE?
YOU GOTTA BE KIDDING, CHESTER! ARE YOU TELLING ME YOUR OLD SWEETHEART'S A CONFIRMED LESBIAN?
WELL, I GUESS THIS WAS BEFORE I BECAME A HERO COP.
MAYBE THINGS WOULD BE DIFFERENT NOW IF LIZ SAW WHAT A SUCCESS I'VE MADE OF MYSELF.

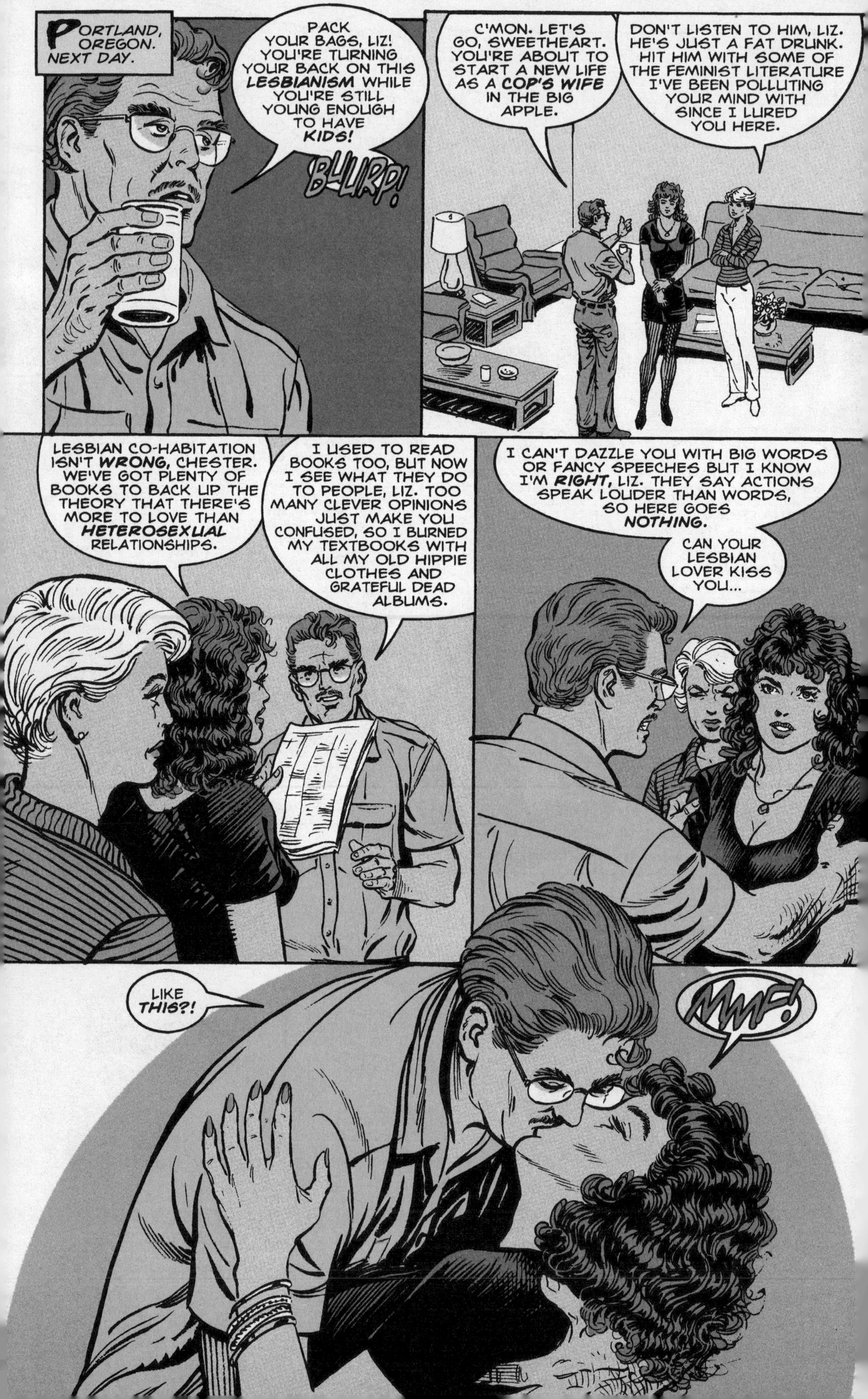
PORTLAND, OREGON. NEXT DAY.
PACK YOUR BAGS, LIZ! YOU'RE TURNING YOUR BACK ON THIS LESBIANISM WHILE YOU'RE STILL YOUNG ENOUGH TO HAVE KIDS!
BLURP!
C'MON. LET'S GO, SWEETHEART. YOU'RE ABOUT TO START A NEW LIFE AS A COP'S WIFE IN THE BIG APPLE.
DON'T LISTEN TO HIM, LIZ. HE'S JUST A FAT DRUNK. HIT HIM WITH SOME OF THE FEMINIST LITERATURE I'VE BEEN POLLUTING YOUR MIND WITH SINCE I LURED YOU HERE.
LESBIAN CO-HABITATION ISN'T WRONG, CHESTER. WE'VE GOT PLENTY OF BOOKS TO BACK UP THE THEORY THAT THERE'S MORE TO LOVE THAN HETEROSEXUAL RELATIONSHIPS.
I USED TO READ BOOKS TOO, BUT NOW I SEE WHAT THEY DO TO PEOPLE, LIZ. TOO MANY CLEVER OPINIONS JUST MAKE YOU CONFUSED, SO I BURNED MY TEXTBOOKS WITH ALL MY OLD HIPPIE CLOTHES AND GRATEFUL DEAD ALBUMS.
I CAN'T DAZZLE YOU WITH BIG WORDS OR FANCY SPEECHES BUT I KNOW I'M RIGHT, LIZ. THEY SAY ACTIONS SPEAK LOUDER THAN WORDS, SO HERE GOES NOTHING.
CAN YOUR LESBIAN LOVER KISS YOU...
LIKE THIS?!
MMF!

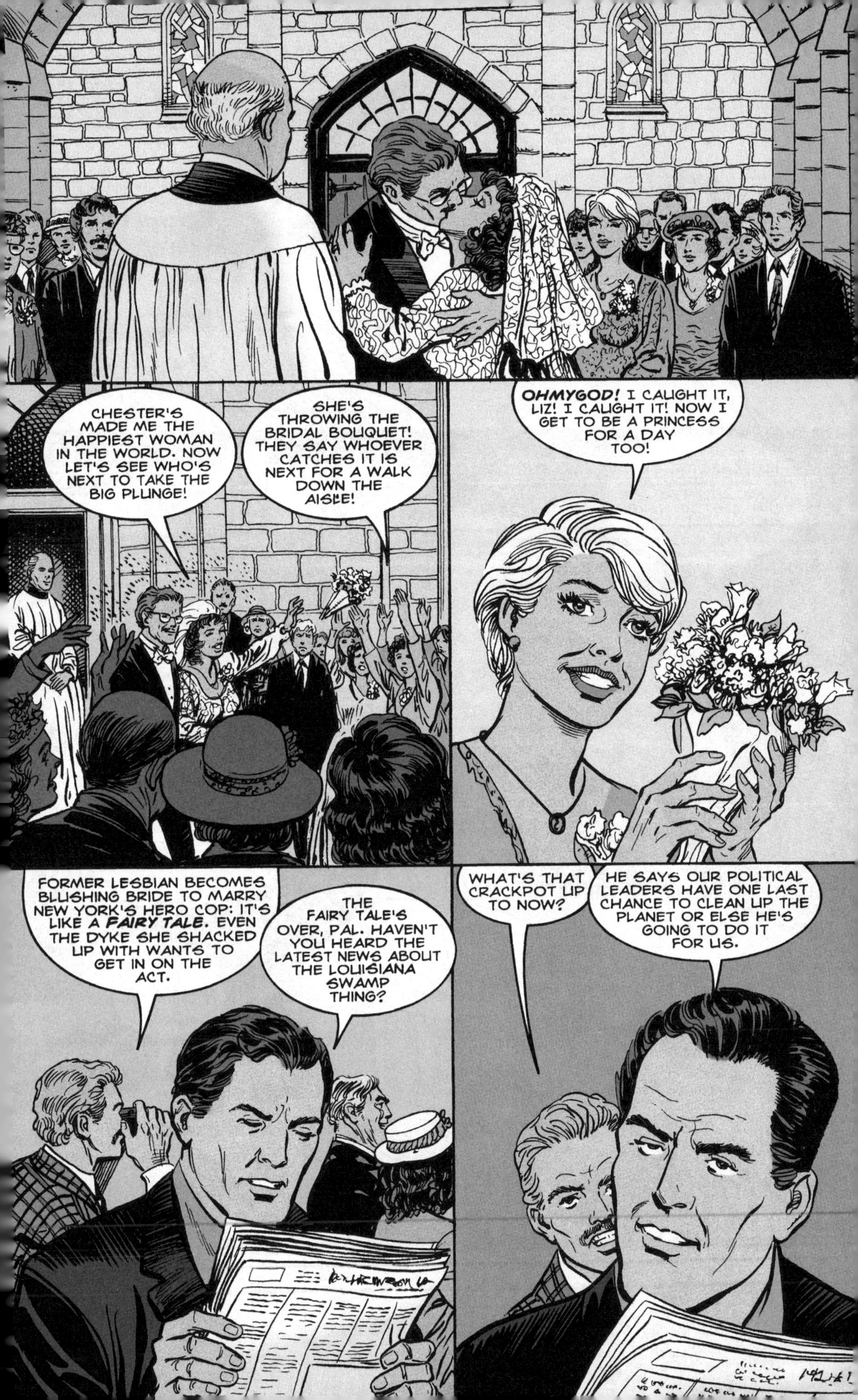
CHESTER'S MADE ME THE HAPPIEST WOMAN IN THE WORLD. NOW LET'S SEE WHO'S NEXT TO TAKE THE BIG PLUNGE!
SHE'S THROWING THE BRIDAL BOUQUET! THEY SAY WHOEVER CATCHES IT IS NEXT FOR A WALK DOWN THE AISLE!
OHMYGOD! I CAUGHT IT, LIZ! I CAUGHT IT! NOW I GET TO BE A PRINCESS FOR A DAY TOO!
FORMER LESBIAN BECOMES BLUSHING BRIDE TO MARRY NEW YORK'S HERO COP: IT'S LIKE A FAIRY TALE. EVEN THE DYKE SHE SHACKED UP WITH WANTS TO GET IN ON THE ACT.
THE FAIRY TALE'S OVER, PAL. HAVEN'T YOU HEARD THE LATEST NEWS ABOUT THE LOUISIANA SWAMP THING?
WHAT'S THAT CRACKPOT UP TO NOW?
HE SAYS OUR POLITICAL LEADERS HAVE ONE LAST CHANCE TO CLEAN UP THE PLANET OR ELSE HE'S GOING TO DO IT FOR US.

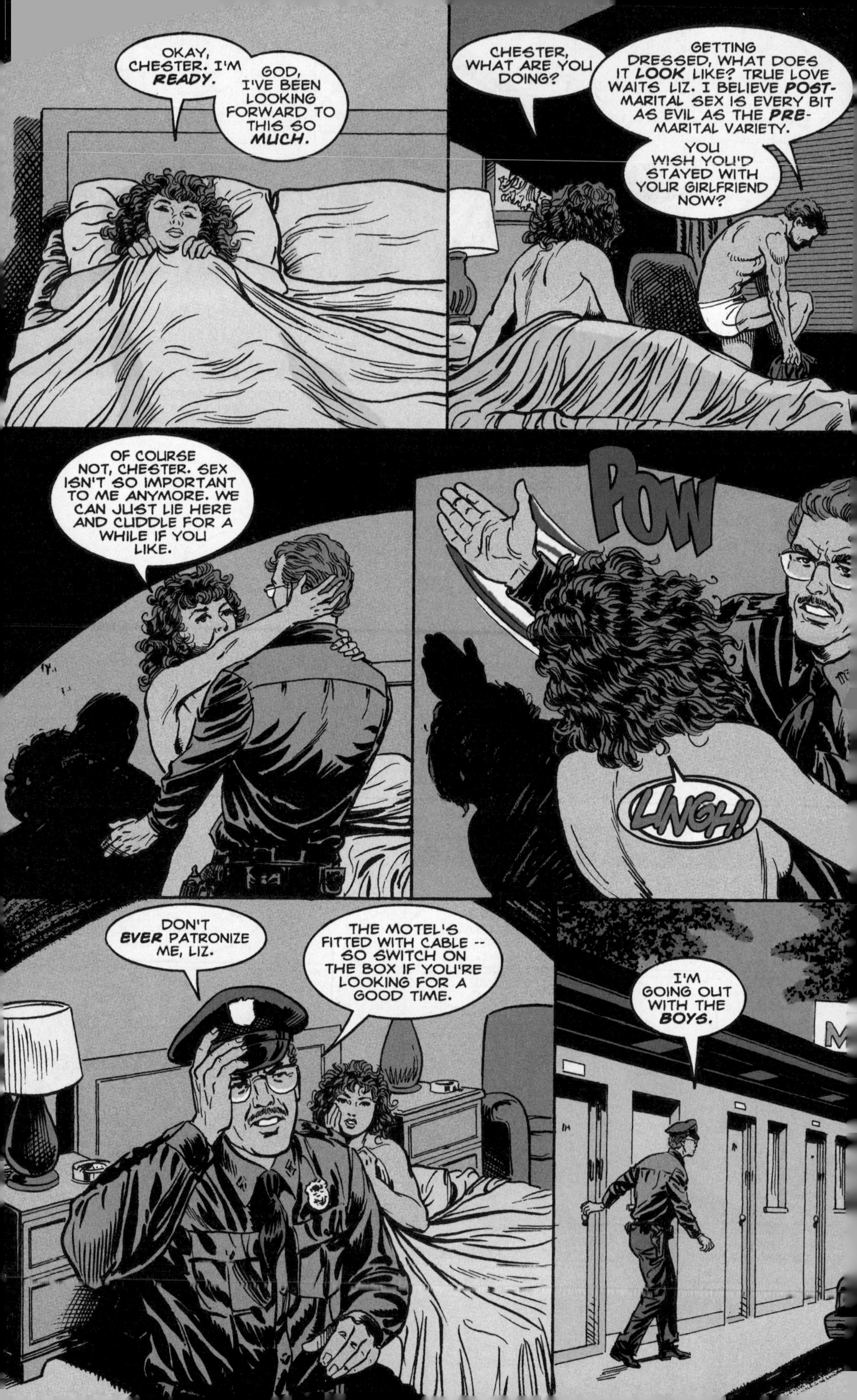
OKAY, CHESTER. I'M *READY.*
GOD, I'VE BEEN LOOKING FORWARD TO THIS SO *MUCH.*
CHESTER, WHAT ARE YOU DOING?
GETTING DRESSED, WHAT DOES IT *LOOK* LIKE? TRUE LOVE WAITS LIZ. I BELIEVE *POST*-MARITAL SEX IS EVERY BIT AS EVIL AS THE *PRE*-MARITAL VARIETY.
YOU WISH YOU'D STAYED WITH YOUR GIRLFRIEND NOW?
OF COURSE NOT, CHESTER. SEX ISN'T SO IMPORTANT TO ME ANYMORE. WE CAN JUST LIE HERE AND CUDDLE FOR A WHILE IF YOU LIKE.
POW
UNGH!
DON'T *EVER* PATRONIZE ME, LIZ.
THE MOTEL'S FITTED WITH CABLE -- SO SWITCH ON THE BOX IF YOU'RE LOOKING FOR A GOOD TIME.
I'M GOING OUT WITH THE *BOYS.*

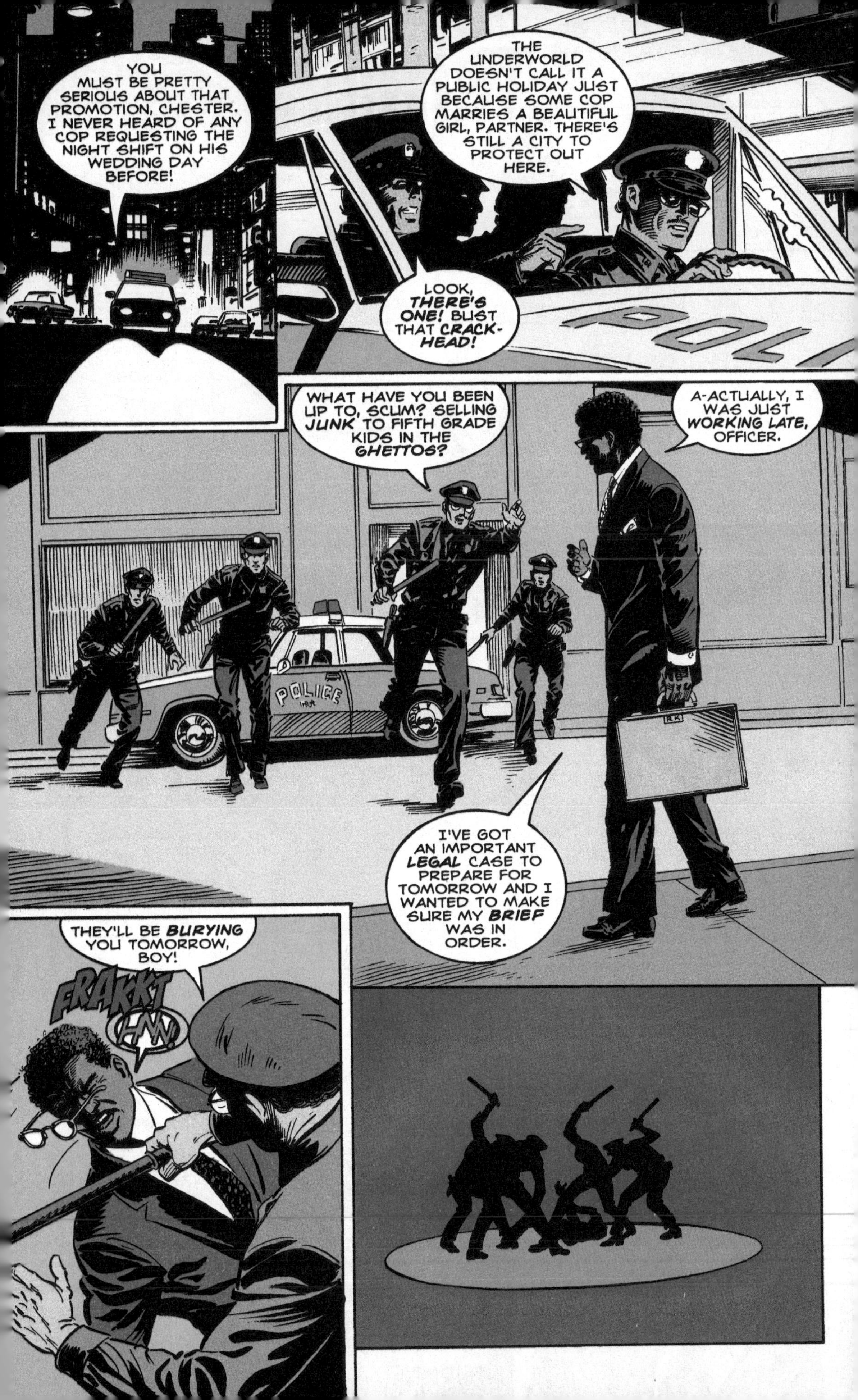

YOU MUST BE PRETTY SERIOUS ABOUT THAT PROMOTION, CHESTER. I NEVER HEARD OF ANY COP REQUESTING THE NIGHT SHIFT ON HIS WEDDING DAY BEFORE!
THE UNDERWORLD DOESN'T CALL IT A PUBLIC HOLIDAY JUST BECAUSE SOME COP MARRIES A BEAUTIFUL GIRL, PARTNER. THERE'S STILL A CITY TO PROTECT OUT HERE.
LOOK, **THERE'S ONE!** BUST THAT **CRACK-HEAD!**
POLI
WHAT HAVE YOU BEEN UP TO, SCUM? SELLING **JUNK** TO FIFTH GRADE KIDS IN THE **GHETTOS?**
A-ACTUALLY, I WAS JUST **WORKING LATE,** OFFICER.
POLICE
I'VE GOT AN IMPORTANT **LEGAL** CASE TO PREPARE FOR TOMORROW AND I WANTED TO MAKE SURE MY **BRIEF** WAS IN ORDER.
THEY'LL BE **BURYING** YOU TOMORROW, BOY!
FRAKKT
HNN!

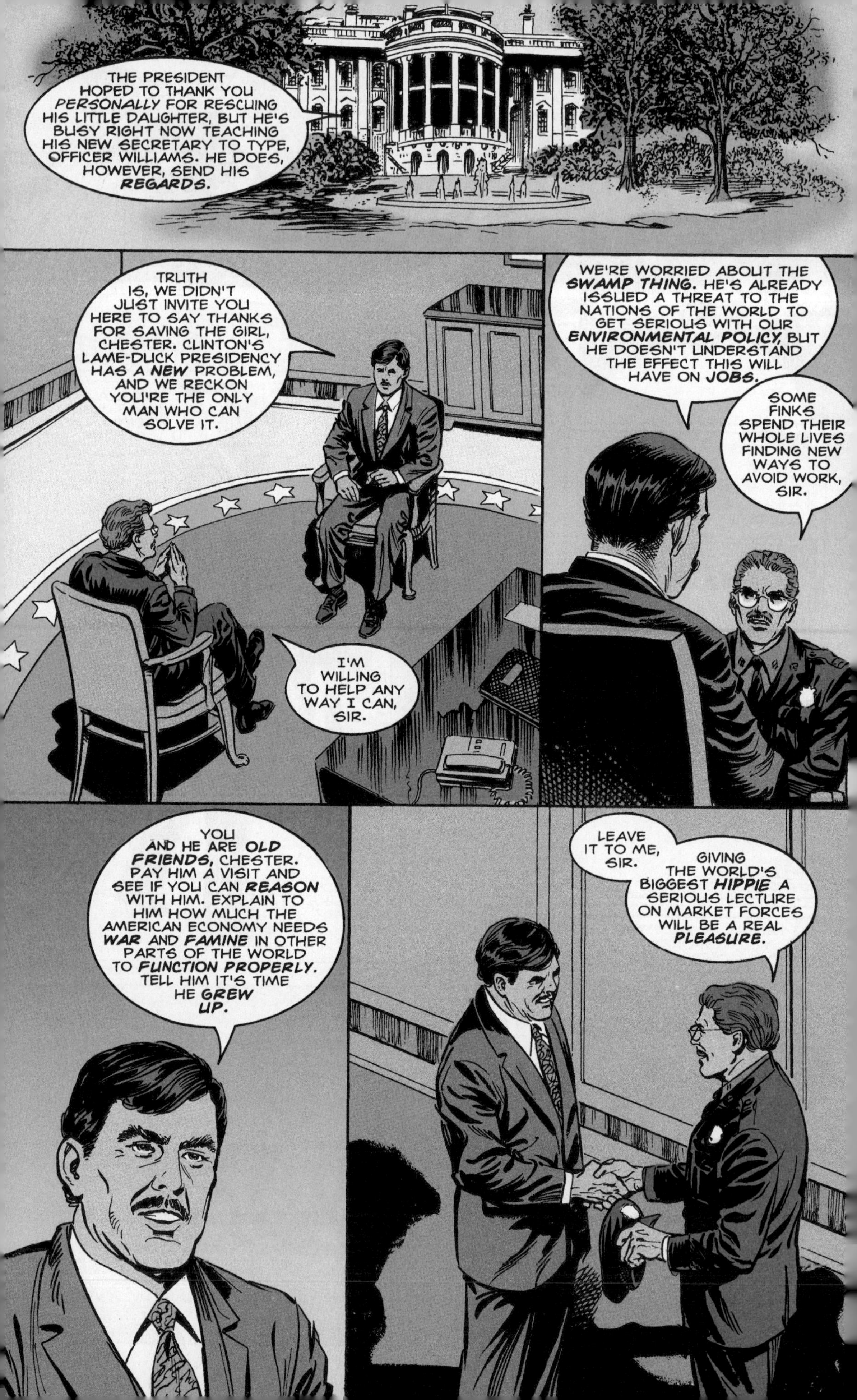
THE PRESIDENT HOPED TO THANK YOU PERSONALLY FOR RESCUING HIS LITTLE DAUGHTER, BUT HE'S BUSY RIGHT NOW TEACHING HIS NEW SECRETARY TO TYPE, OFFICER WILLIAMS. HE DOES, HOWEVER, SEND HIS REGARDS.
TRUTH IS, WE DIDN'T JUST INVITE YOU HERE TO SAY THANKS FOR SAVING THE GIRL, CHESTER. CLINTON'S LAME-DUCK PRESIDENCY HAS A NEW PROBLEM, AND WE RECKON YOU'RE THE ONLY MAN WHO CAN SOLVE IT.
I'M WILLING TO HELP ANY WAY I CAN, SIR.
WE'RE WORRIED ABOUT THE SWAMP THING. HE'S ALREADY ISSUED A THREAT TO THE NATIONS OF THE WORLD TO GET SERIOUS WITH OUR ENVIRONMENTAL POLICY, BUT HE DOESN'T UNDERSTAND THE EFFECT THIS WILL HAVE ON JOBS.
SOME FINKS SPEND THEIR WHOLE LIVES FINDING NEW WAYS TO AVOID WORK, SIR.
YOU AND HE ARE OLD FRIENDS, CHESTER. PAY HIM A VISIT AND SEE IF YOU CAN REASON WITH HIM. EXPLAIN TO HIM HOW MUCH THE AMERICAN ECONOMY NEEDS WAR AND FAMINE IN OTHER PARTS OF THE WORLD TO FUNCTION PROPERLY. TELL HIM IT'S TIME HE GREW UP.
LEAVE IT TO ME, SIR.
GIVING THE WORLD'S BIGGEST HIPPIE A SERIOUS LECTURE ON MARKET FORCES WILL BE A REAL PLEASURE.

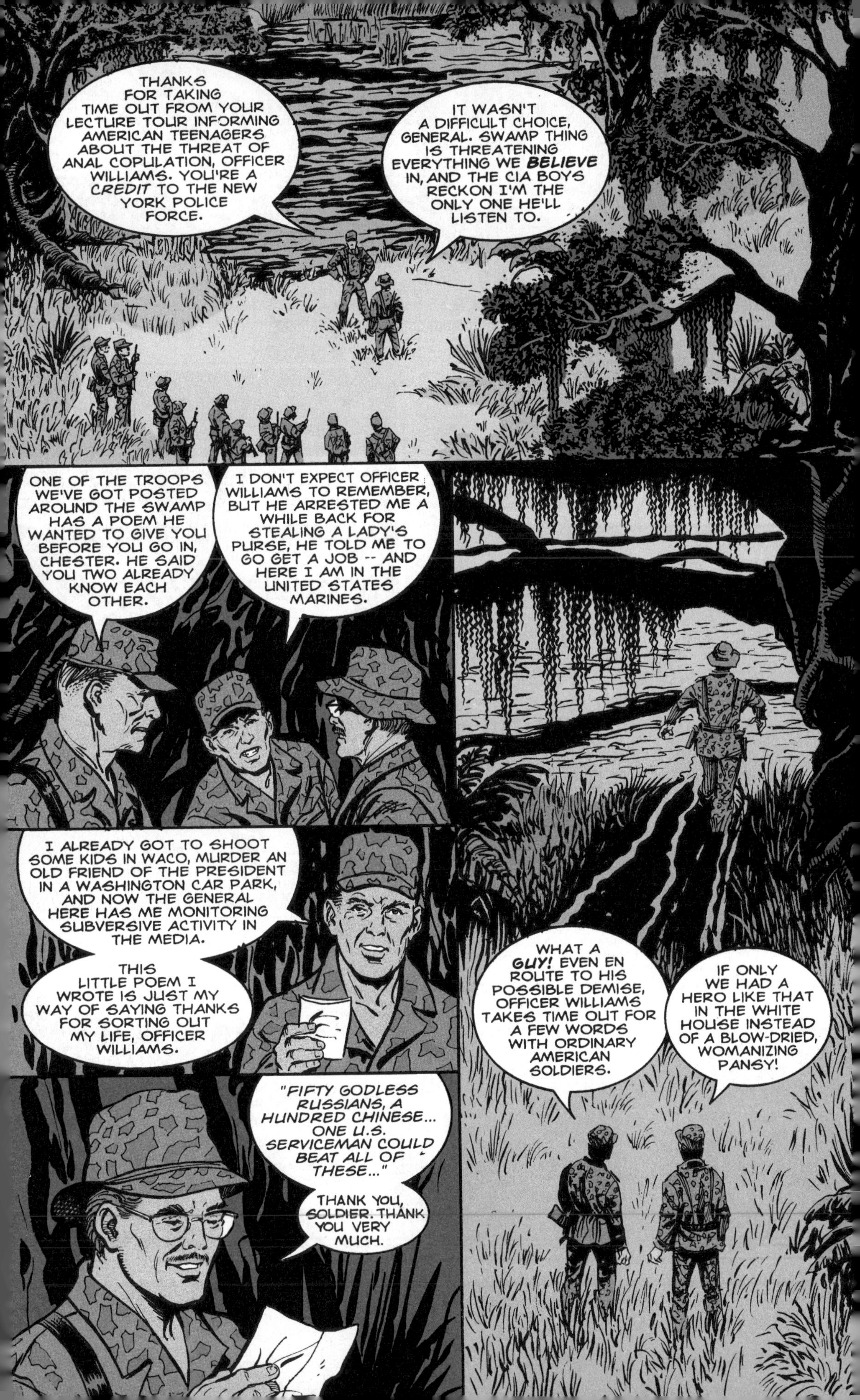
THANKS FOR TAKING TIME OUT FROM YOUR LECTURE TOUR INFORMING AMERICAN TEENAGERS ABOUT THE THREAT OF ANAL COPULATION, OFFICER WILLIAMS. YOU'RE A *CREDIT* TO THE NEW YORK POLICE FORCE.
IT WASN'T A DIFFICULT CHOICE, GENERAL. SWAMP THING IS THREATENING EVERYTHING WE ***BELIEVE*** IN, AND THE CIA BOYS RECKON I'M THE ONLY ONE HE'LL LISTEN TO.
ONE OF THE TROOPS WE'VE GOT POSTED AROUND THE SWAMP HAS A POEM HE WANTED TO GIVE YOU BEFORE YOU GO IN, CHESTER. HE SAID YOU TWO ALREADY KNOW EACH OTHER.
I DON'T EXPECT OFFICER WILLIAMS TO REMEMBER, BUT HE ARRESTED ME A WHILE BACK FOR STEALING A LADY'S PURSE. HE TOLD ME TO GO GET A JOB -- AND HERE I AM IN THE UNITED STATES MARINES.
I ALREADY GOT TO SHOOT SOME KIDS IN WACO, MURDER AN OLD FRIEND OF THE PRESIDENT IN A WASHINGTON CAR PARK, AND NOW THE GENERAL HERE HAS ME MONITORING SUBVERSIVE ACTIVITY IN THE MEDIA.
THIS LITTLE POEM I WROTE IS JUST MY WAY OF SAYING THANKS FOR SORTING OUT MY LIFE, OFFICER WILLIAMS.
"FIFTY GODLESS RUSSIANS, A HUNDRED CHINESE... ONE U.S. SERVICEMAN COULD BEAT ALL OF THESE..."
THANK YOU, SOLDIER. THANK YOU VERY MUCH.
WHAT A ***GUY!*** EVEN EN ROUTE TO HIS POSSIBLE DEMISE, OFFICER WILLIAMS TAKES TIME OUT FOR A FEW WORDS WITH ORDINARY AMERICAN SOLDIERS.
IF ONLY WE HAD A HERO LIKE THAT IN THE WHITE HOUSE INSTEAD OF A BLOW-DRIED, WOMANIZING PANSY!

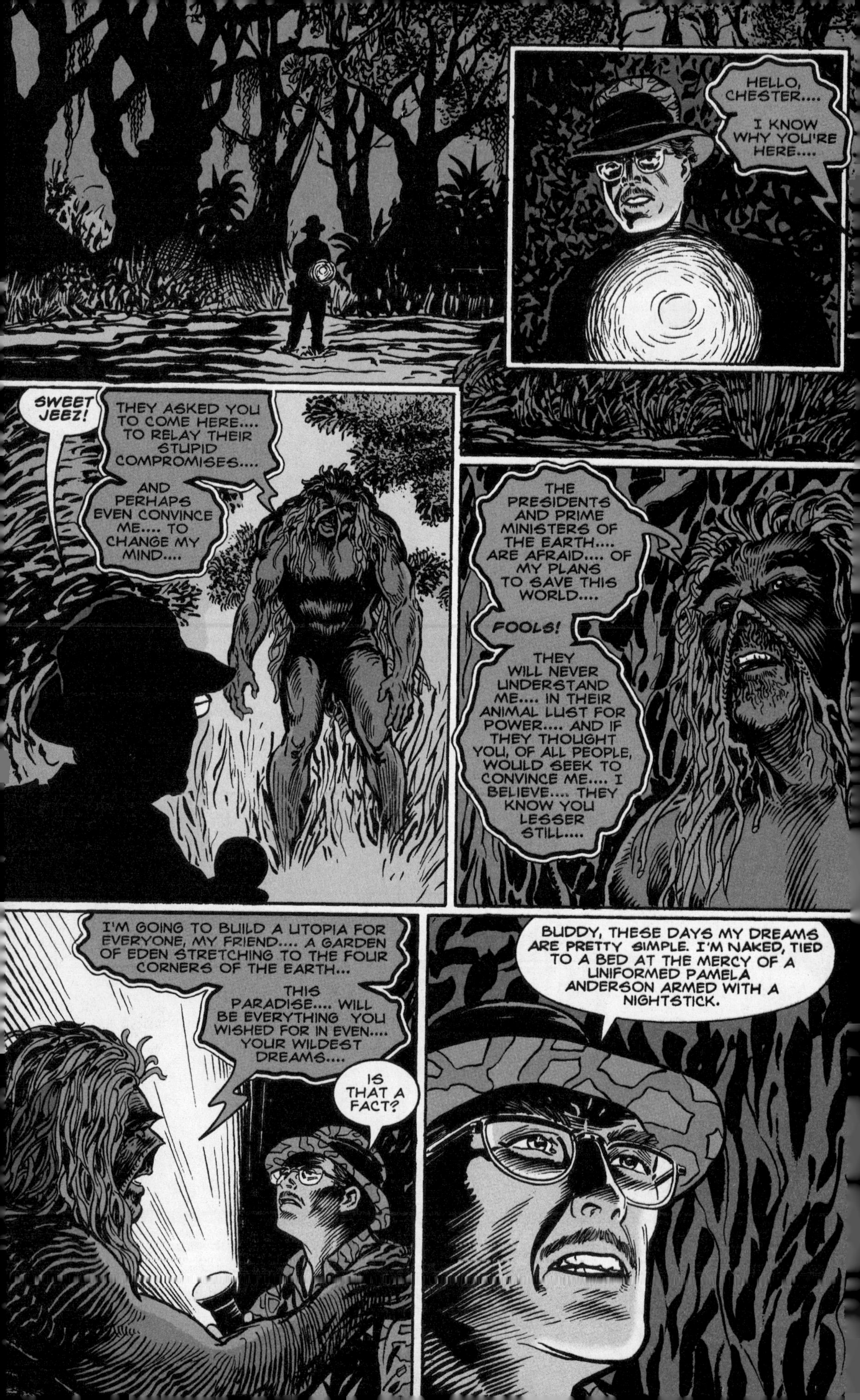
HELLO, CHESTER....
I KNOW WHY YOU'RE HERE....
SWEET JEEZ!
THEY ASKED YOU TO COME HERE.... TO RELAY THEIR STUPID COMPROMISES....
AND PERHAPS EVEN CONVINCE ME.... TO CHANGE MY MIND....
THE PRESIDENTS AND PRIME MINISTERS OF THE EARTH.... ARE AFRAID.... OF MY PLANS TO SAVE THIS WORLD....
FOOLS!
THEY WILL NEVER UNDERSTAND ME.... IN THEIR ANIMAL LUST FOR POWER.... AND IF THEY THOUGHT YOU, OF ALL PEOPLE, WOULD SEEK TO CONVINCE ME.... I BELIEVE.... THEY KNOW YOU LESSER STILL....
I'M GOING TO BUILD A UTOPIA FOR EVERYONE, MY FRIEND.... A GARDEN OF EDEN STRETCHING TO THE FOUR CORNERS OF THE EARTH...
THIS PARADISE.... WILL BE EVERYTHING YOU WISHED FOR IN EVEN.... YOUR WILDEST DREAMS....
IS THAT A FACT?
BUDDY, THESE DAYS MY DREAMS ARE PRETTY SIMPLE. I'M NAKED, TIED TO A BED AT THE MERCY OF A UNIFORMED PAMELA ANDERSON ARMED WITH A NIGHTSTICK.

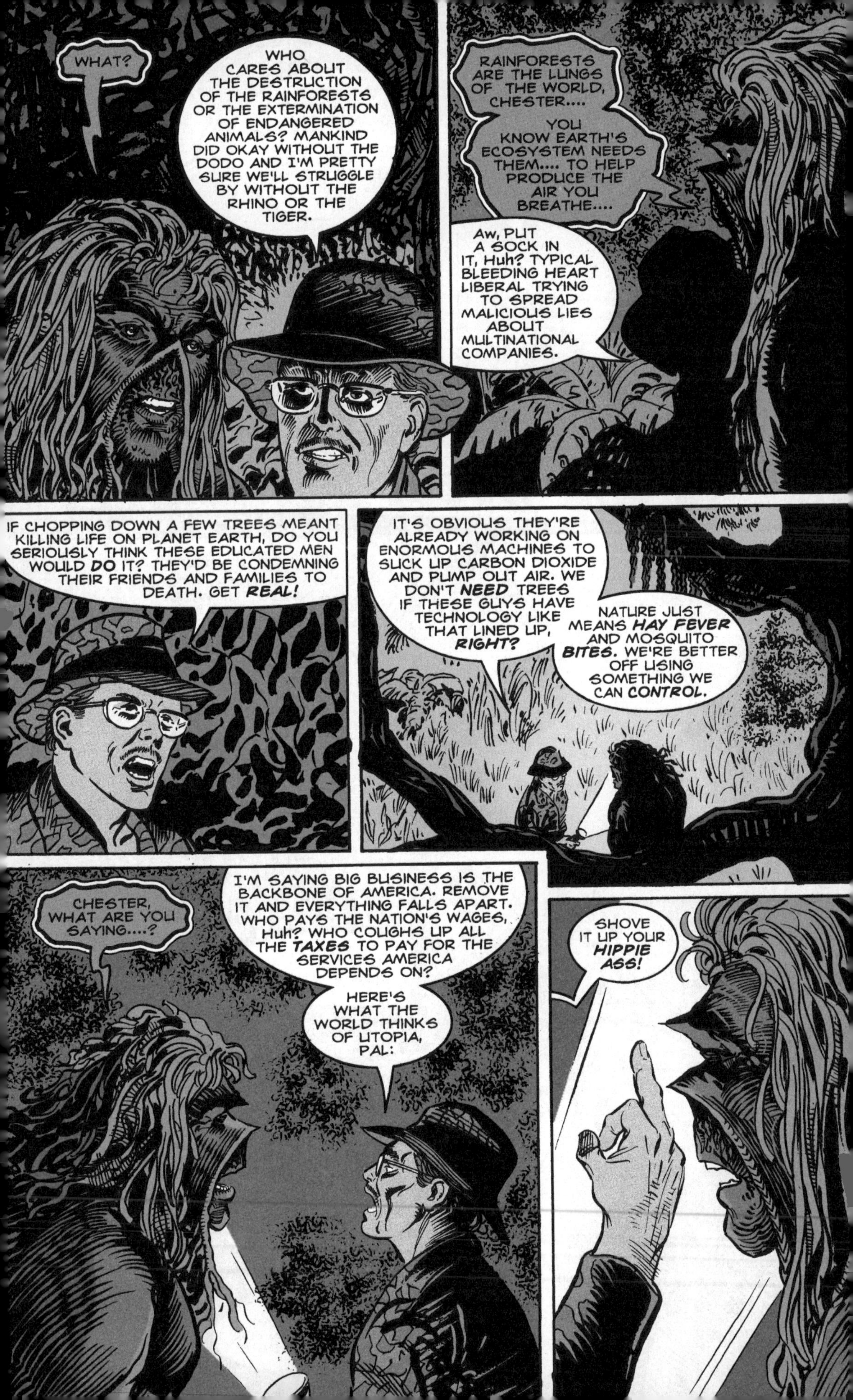
WHAT?
WHO CARES ABOUT THE DESTRUCTION OF THE RAINFORESTS OR THE EXTERMINATION OF ENDANGERED ANIMALS? MANKIND DID OKAY WITHOUT THE DODO AND I'M PRETTY SURE WE'LL STRUGGLE BY WITHOUT THE RHINO OR THE TIGER.
RAINFORESTS ARE THE LUNGS OF THE WORLD, CHESTER....
YOU KNOW EARTH'S ECOSYSTEM NEEDS THEM.... TO HELP PRODUCE THE AIR YOU BREATHE....
Aw, PUT A SOCK IN IT, Huh? TYPICAL BLEEDING HEART LIBERAL TRYING TO SPREAD MALICIOUS LIES ABOUT MULTINATIONAL COMPANIES.
IF CHOPPING DOWN A FEW TREES MEANT KILLING LIFE ON PLANET EARTH, DO YOU SERIOUSLY THINK THESE EDUCATED MEN WOULD *DO* IT? THEY'D BE CONDEMNING THEIR FRIENDS AND FAMILIES TO DEATH. GET *REAL!*
IT'S OBVIOUS THEY'RE ALREADY WORKING ON ENORMOUS MACHINES TO SUCK UP CARBON DIOXIDE AND PUMP OUT AIR. WE DON'T *NEED* TREES IF THESE GUYS HAVE TECHNOLOGY LIKE THAT LINED UP, *RIGHT?*
NATURE JUST MEANS *HAY FEVER* AND MOSQUITO *BITES*. WE'RE BETTER OFF USING SOMETHING WE CAN *CONTROL*.
CHESTER, WHAT ARE YOU SAYING....?
I'M SAYING BIG BUSINESS IS THE BACKBONE OF AMERICA. REMOVE IT AND EVERYTHING FALLS APART. WHO PAYS THE NATION'S WAGES, Huh? WHO COUGHS UP ALL THE *TAXES* TO PAY FOR THE SERVICES AMERICA DEPENDS ON?
HERE'S WHAT THE WORLD THINKS OF UTOPIA, PAL:
SHOVE IT UP YOUR *HIPPIE ASS!*

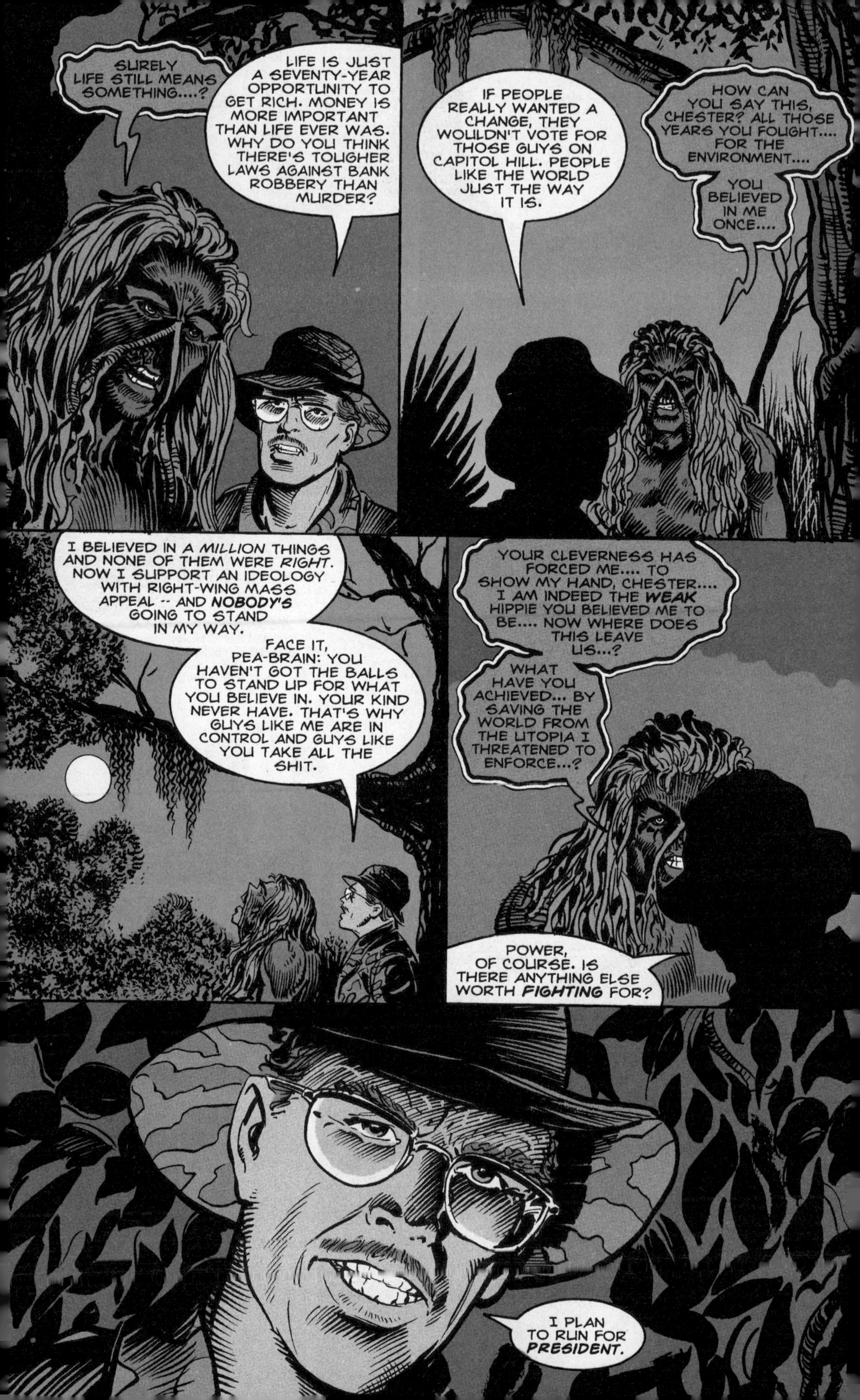
SURELY LIFE STILL MEANS SOMETHING....?
LIFE IS JUST A SEVENTY-YEAR OPPORTUNITY TO GET RICH. MONEY IS MORE IMPORTANT THAN LIFE EVER WAS. WHY DO YOU THINK THERE'S TOUGHER LAWS AGAINST BANK ROBBERY THAN MURDER?
IF PEOPLE REALLY WANTED A CHANGE, THEY WOULDN'T VOTE FOR THOSE GUYS ON CAPITOL HILL. PEOPLE LIKE THE WORLD JUST THE WAY IT IS.
HOW CAN YOU SAY THIS, CHESTER? ALL THOSE YEARS YOU FOUGHT.... FOR THE ENVIRONMENT....
YOU BELIEVED IN ME ONCE....
I BELIEVED IN A *MILLION* THINGS AND NONE OF THEM WERE *RIGHT*. NOW I SUPPORT AN IDEOLOGY WITH RIGHT-WING MASS APPEAL -- AND **NOBODY'S** GOING TO STAND IN MY WAY.
FACE IT, PEA-BRAIN: YOU HAVEN'T GOT THE BALLS TO STAND UP FOR WHAT YOU BELIEVE IN. YOUR KIND NEVER HAVE. THAT'S WHY GUYS LIKE ME ARE IN CONTROL AND GUYS LIKE YOU TAKE ALL THE SHIT.
YOUR CLEVERNESS HAS FORCED ME.... TO SHOW MY HAND, CHESTER.... I AM INDEED THE ***WEAK*** HIPPIE YOU BELIEVED ME TO BE.... NOW WHERE DOES THIS LEAVE US...?
WHAT HAVE YOU ACHIEVED... BY SAVING THE WORLD FROM THE UTOPIA I THREATENED TO ENFORCE...?
POWER, OF COURSE. IS THERE ANYTHING ELSE WORTH ***FIGHTING*** FOR?
I PLAN TO RUN FOR ***PRESIDENT***.

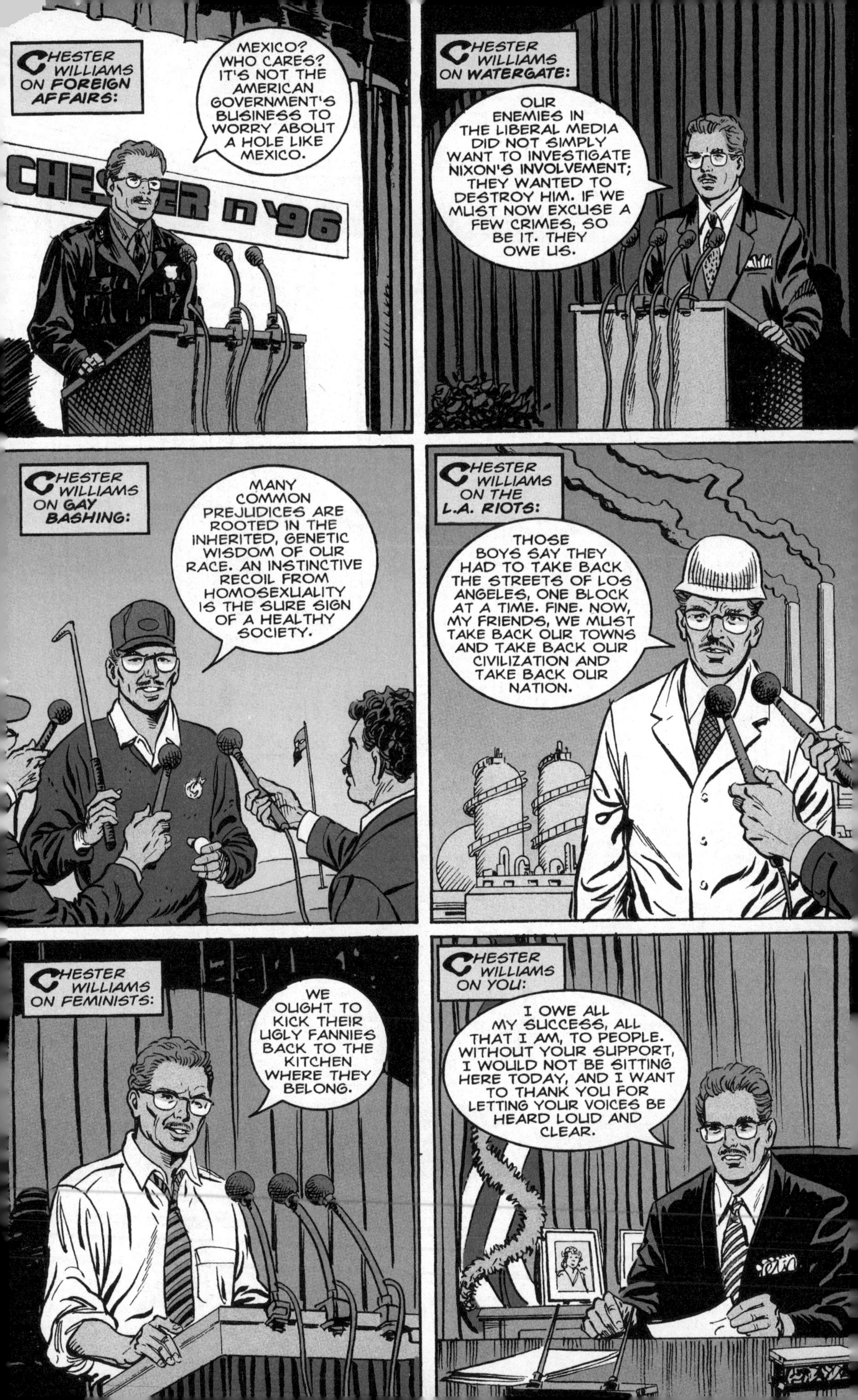
CHESTER WILLIAMS ON FOREIGN AFFAIRS:
MEXICO? WHO CARES? IT'S NOT THE AMERICAN GOVERNMENT'S BUSINESS TO WORRY ABOUT A HOLE LIKE MEXICO.
CHESTER IN '96
CHESTER WILLIAMS ON WATERGATE:
OUR ENEMIES IN THE LIBERAL MEDIA DID NOT SIMPLY WANT TO INVESTIGATE NIXON'S INVOLVEMENT; THEY WANTED TO DESTROY HIM. IF WE MUST NOW EXCUSE A FEW CRIMES, SO BE IT. THEY OWE US.
CHESTER WILLIAMS ON GAY BASHING:
MANY COMMON PREJUDICES ARE ROOTED IN THE INHERITED, GENETIC WISDOM OF OUR RACE. AN INSTINCTIVE RECOIL FROM HOMOSEXUALITY IS THE SURE SIGN OF A HEALTHY SOCIETY.
CHESTER WILLIAMS ON THE L.A. RIOTS:
THOSE BOYS SAY THEY HAD TO TAKE BACK THE STREETS OF LOS ANGELES, ONE BLOCK AT A TIME. FINE. NOW, MY FRIENDS, WE MUST TAKE BACK OUR TOWNS AND TAKE BACK OUR CIVILIZATION AND TAKE BACK OUR NATION.
CHESTER WILLIAMS ON FEMINISTS:
WE OUGHT TO KICK THEIR UGLY FANNIES BACK TO THE KITCHEN WHERE THEY BELONG.
CHESTER WILLIAMS ON YOU:
I OWE ALL MY SUCCESS, ALL THAT I AM, TO PEOPLE. WITHOUT YOUR SUPPORT, I WOULD NOT BE SITTING HERE TODAY, AND I WANT TO THANK YOU FOR LETTING YOUR VOICES BE HEARD LOUD AND CLEAR.

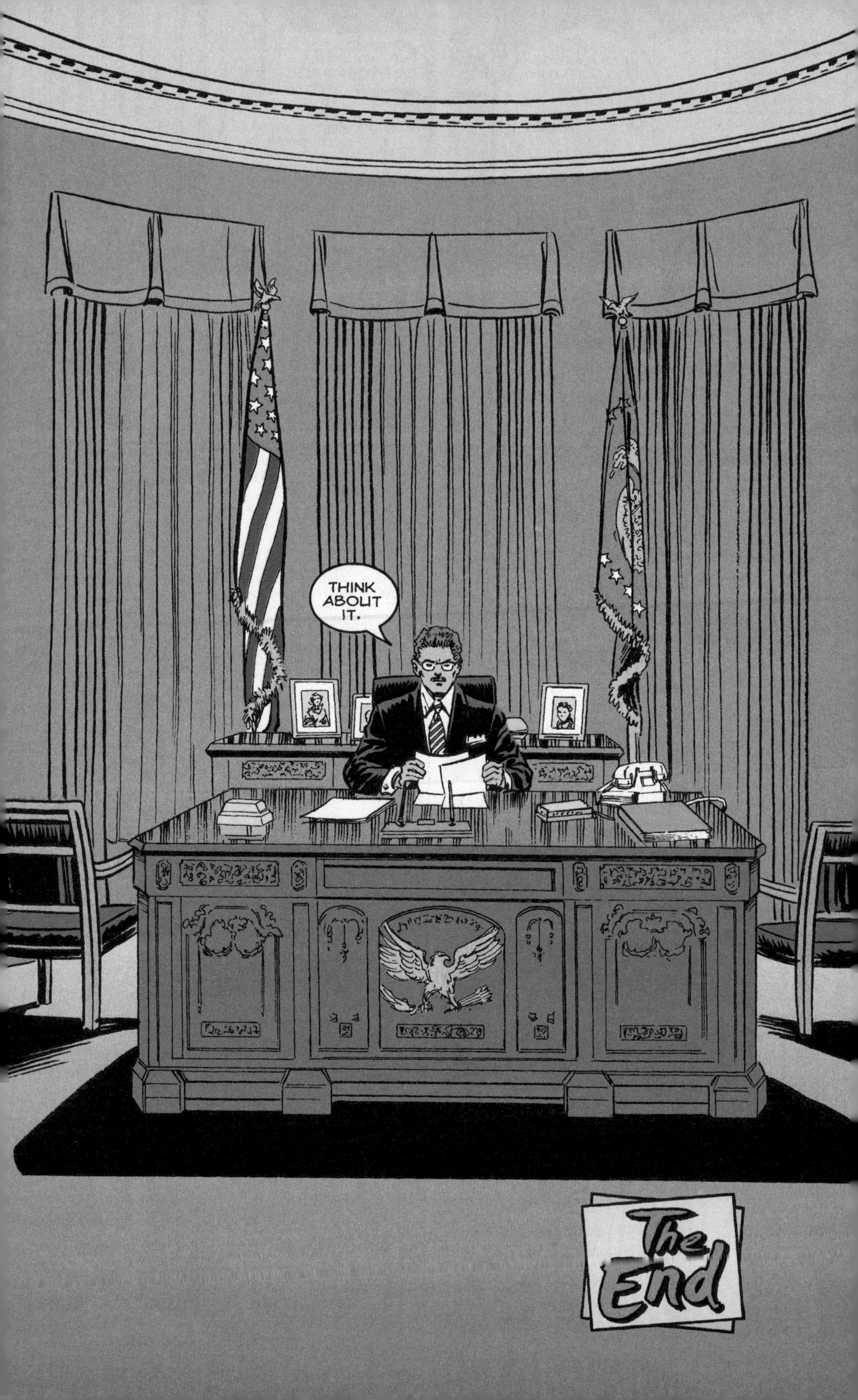
THINK ABOUT IT.
The End

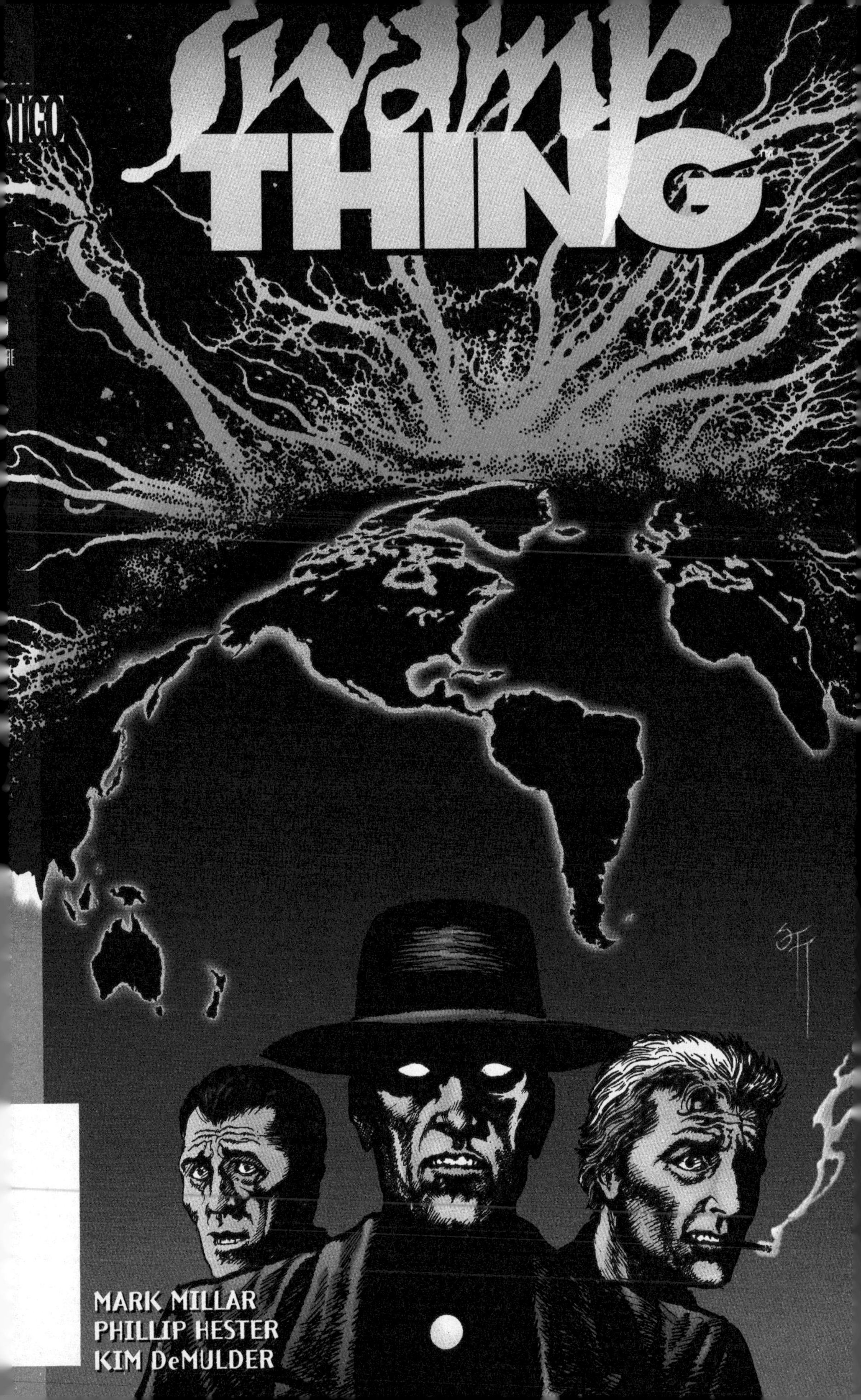

VERTIGO
Swamp
THING™
MARK MILLAR
PHILLIP HESTER
KIM DeMULDER

ONE
YEAR
LATER.

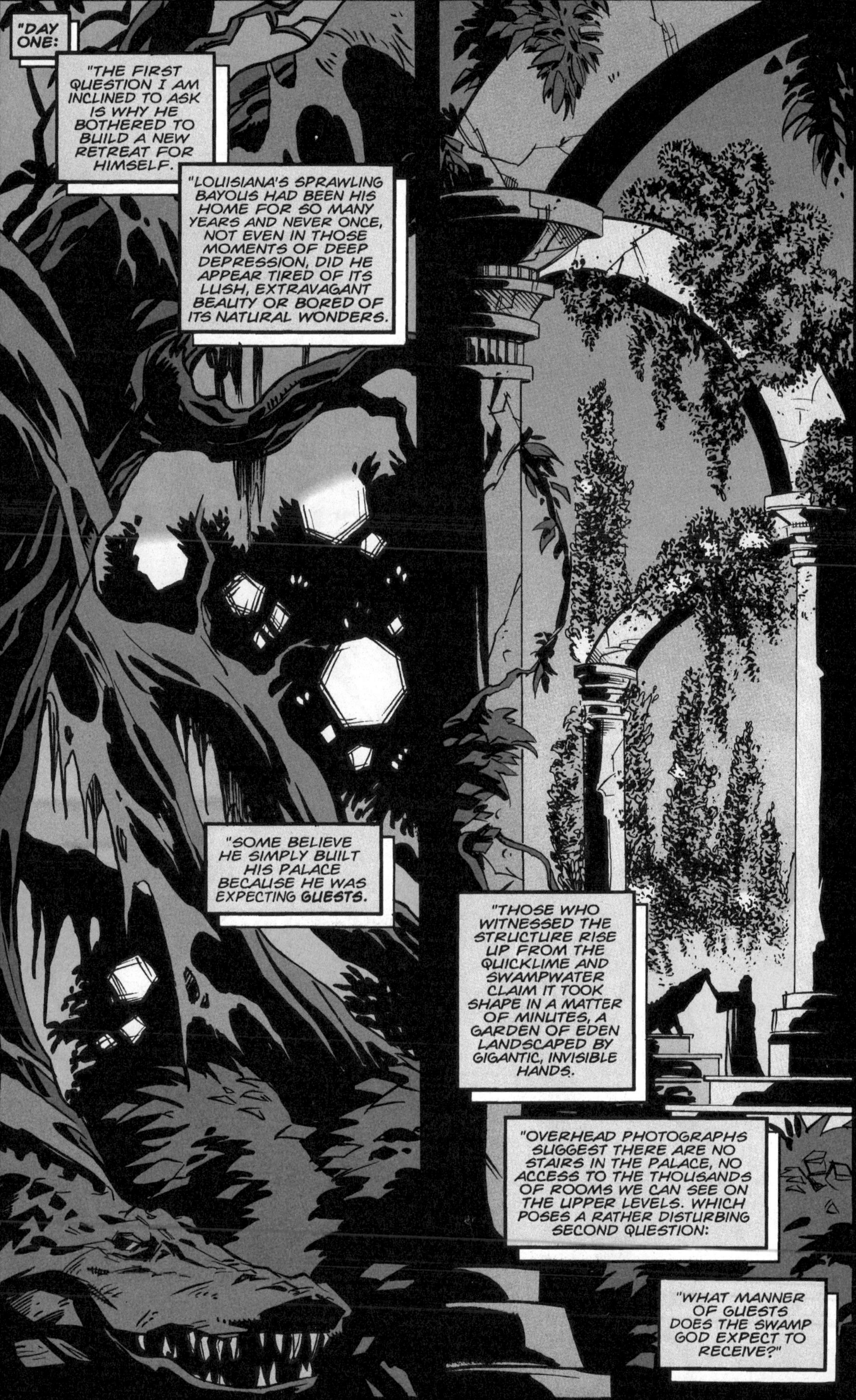
"DAY ONE:
"THE FIRST QUESTION I AM INCLINED TO ASK IS WHY HE BOTHERED TO BUILD A NEW RETREAT FOR HIMSELF.
"LOUISIANA'S SPRAWLING BAYOUS HAD BEEN HIS HOME FOR SO MANY YEARS AND NEVER ONCE, NOT EVEN IN THOSE MOMENTS OF DEEP DEPRESSION, DID HE APPEAR TIRED OF ITS LUSH, EXTRAVAGANT BEAUTY OR BORED OF ITS NATURAL WONDERS.
"SOME BELIEVE HE SIMPLY BUILT HIS PALACE BECAUSE HE WAS EXPECTING **GUESTS**.
"THOSE WHO WITNESSED THE STRUCTURE RISE UP FROM THE QUICKLIME AND SWAMPWATER CLAIM IT TOOK SHAPE IN A MATTER OF MINUTES, A GARDEN OF EDEN LANDSCAPED BY GIGANTIC, INVISIBLE HANDS.
"OVERHEAD PHOTOGRAPHS SUGGEST THERE ARE NO STAIRS IN THE PALACE, NO ACCESS TO THE THOUSANDS OF ROOMS WE CAN SEE ON THE UPPER LEVELS. WHICH POSES A RATHER DISTURBING SECOND QUESTION:
"WHAT MANNER OF GUESTS DOES THE SWAMP GOD EXPECT TO RECEIVE?"

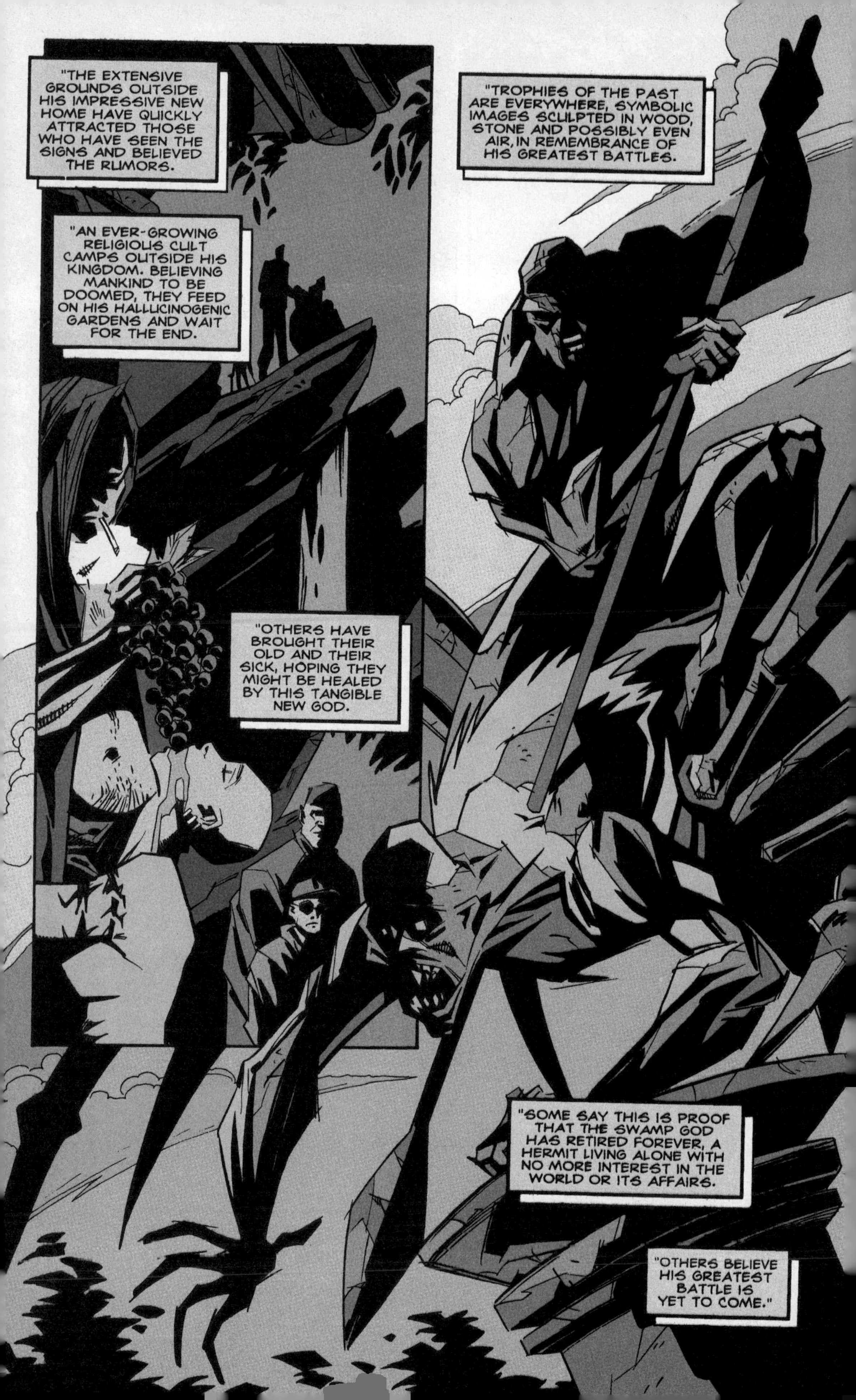
"THE EXTENSIVE GROUNDS OUTSIDE HIS IMPRESSIVE NEW HOME HAVE QUICKLY ATTRACTED THOSE WHO HAVE SEEN THE SIGNS AND BELIEVED THE RUMORS.
"AN EVER-GROWING RELIGIOUS CULT CAMPS OUTSIDE HIS KINGDOM. BELIEVING MANKIND TO BE DOOMED, THEY FEED ON HIS HALLUCINOGENIC GARDENS AND WAIT FOR THE END.
"OTHERS HAVE BROUGHT THEIR OLD AND THEIR SICK, HOPING THEY MIGHT BE HEALED BY THIS TANGIBLE NEW GOD.
"TROPHIES OF THE PAST ARE EVERYWHERE, SYMBOLIC IMAGES SCULPTED IN WOOD, STONE AND POSSIBLY EVEN AIR, IN REMEMBRANCE OF HIS GREATEST BATTLES.
"SOME SAY THIS IS PROOF THAT THE SWAMP GOD HAS RETIRED FOREVER, A HERMIT LIVING ALONE WITH NO MORE INTEREST IN THE WORLD OR ITS AFFAIRS.
"OTHERS BELIEVE HIS GREATEST BATTLE IS YET TO COME."

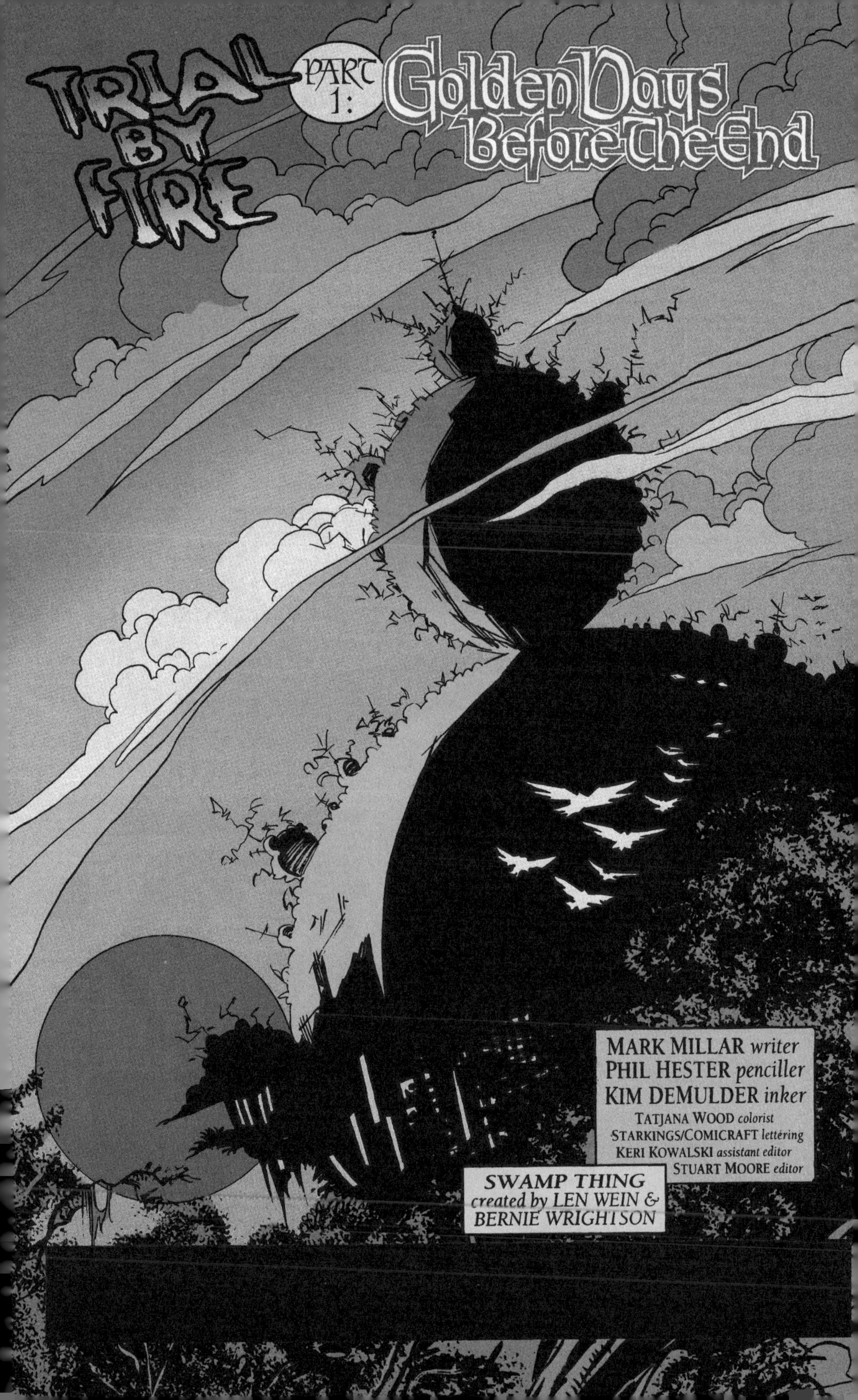
TRIAL BY FIRE
PART 1:
Golden Days Before The End
MARK MILLAR writer
PHIL HESTER penciller
KIM DEMULDER inker
TATJANA WOOD colorist
STARKINGS/COMICRAFT lettering
KERI KOWALSKI assistant editor
STUART MOORE editor
SWAMP THING
created by LEN WEIN &
BERNIE WRIGHTSON

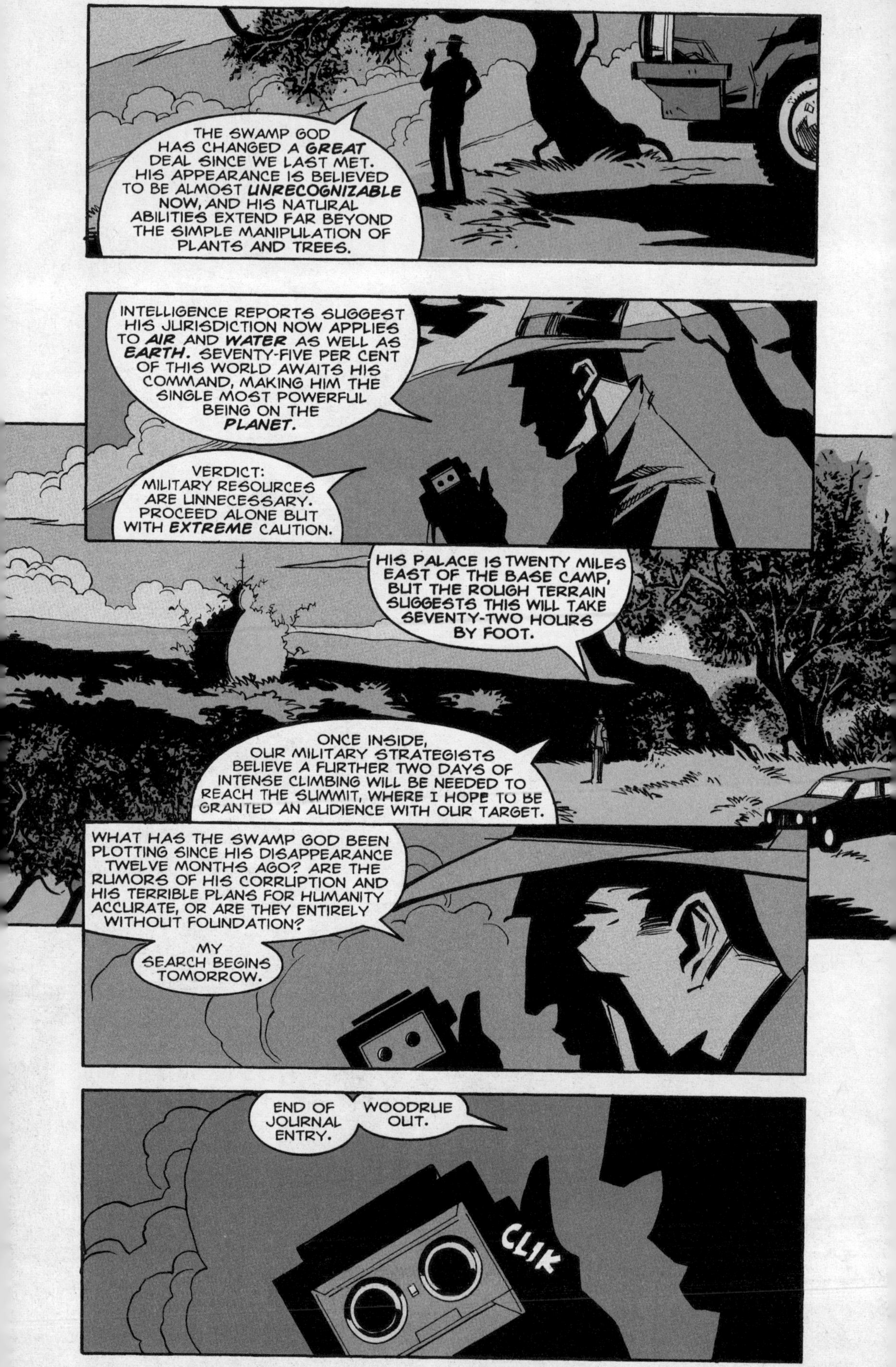
THE SWAMP GOD HAS CHANGED A GREAT DEAL SINCE WE LAST MET. HIS APPEARANCE IS BELIEVED TO BE ALMOST UNRECOGNIZABLE NOW, AND HIS NATURAL ABILITIES EXTEND FAR BEYOND THE SIMPLE MANIPULATION OF PLANTS AND TREES.
INTELLIGENCE REPORTS SUGGEST HIS JURISDICTION NOW APPLIES TO AIR AND WATER AS WELL AS EARTH. SEVENTY-FIVE PER CENT OF THIS WORLD AWAITS HIS COMMAND, MAKING HIM THE SINGLE MOST POWERFUL BEING ON THE PLANET.
VERDICT: MILITARY RESOURCES ARE UNNECESSARY. PROCEED ALONE BUT WITH EXTREME CAUTION.
HIS PALACE IS TWENTY MILES EAST OF THE BASE CAMP, BUT THE ROUGH TERRAIN SUGGESTS THIS WILL TAKE SEVENTY-TWO HOURS BY FOOT.
ONCE INSIDE, OUR MILITARY STRATEGISTS BELIEVE A FURTHER TWO DAYS OF INTENSE CLIMBING WILL BE NEEDED TO REACH THE SUMMIT, WHERE I HOPE TO BE GRANTED AN AUDIENCE WITH OUR TARGET.
WHAT HAS THE SWAMP GOD BEEN PLOTTING SINCE HIS DISAPPEARANCE TWELVE MONTHS AGO? ARE THE RUMORS OF HIS CORRUPTION AND HIS TERRIBLE PLANS FOR HUMANITY ACCURATE, OR ARE THEY ENTIRELY WITHOUT FOUNDATION?
MY SEARCH BEGINS TOMORROW.
END OF JOURNAL ENTRY.
WOODRUE OUT.
CLIK

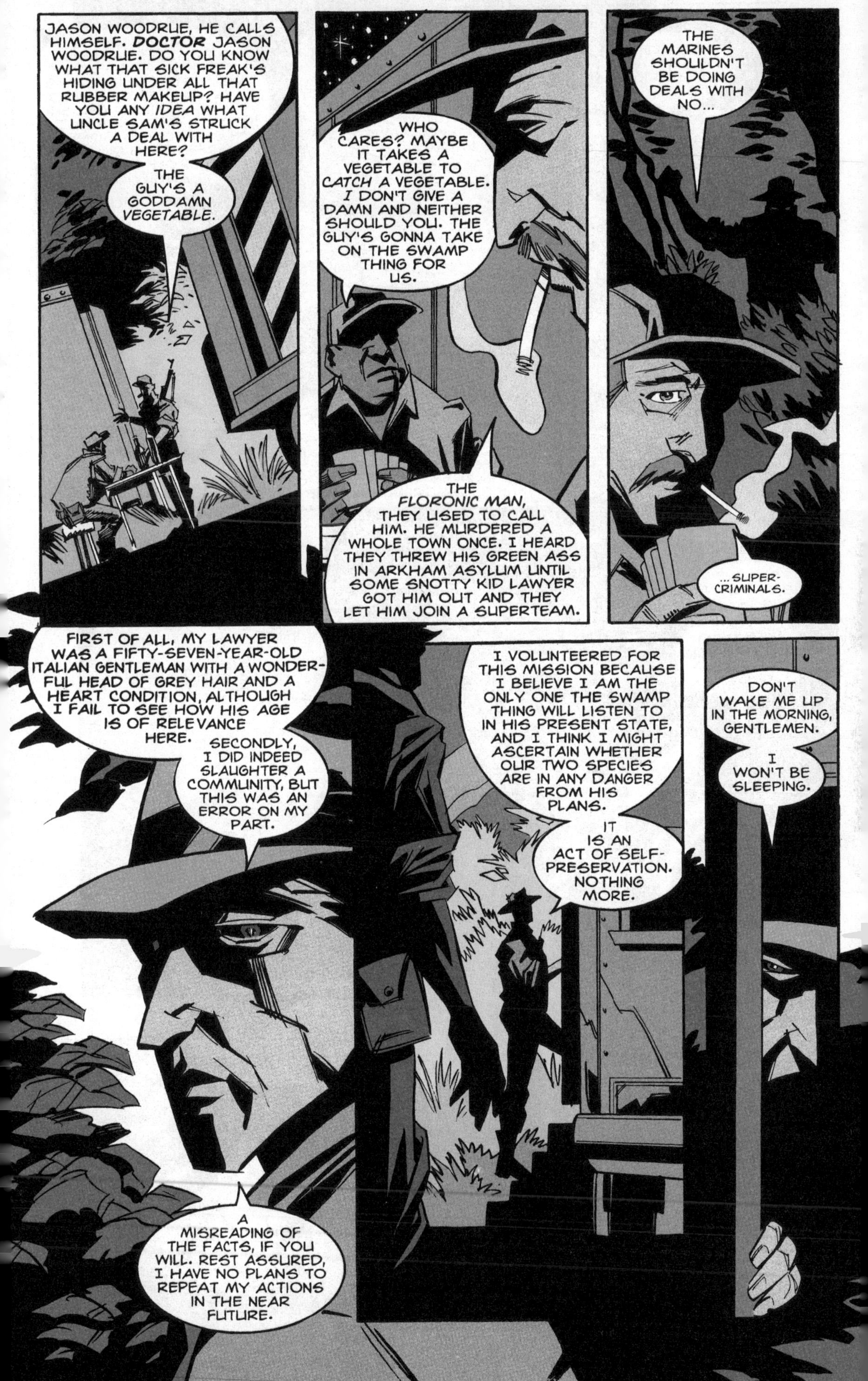
JASON WOODRUE, HE CALLS HIMSELF. DOCTOR JASON WOODRUE. DO YOU KNOW WHAT THAT SICK FREAK'S HIDING UNDER ALL THAT RUBBER MAKEUP? HAVE YOU ANY IDEA WHAT UNCLE SAM'S STRUCK A DEAL WITH HERE?
THE GUY'S A GODDAMN VEGETABLE.
WHO CARES? MAYBE IT TAKES A VEGETABLE TO CATCH A VEGETABLE. I DON'T GIVE A DAMN AND NEITHER SHOULD YOU. THE GUY'S GONNA TAKE ON THE SWAMP THING FOR US.
THE FLORONIC MAN, THEY USED TO CALL HIM. HE MURDERED A WHOLE TOWN ONCE. I HEARD THEY THREW HIS GREEN ASS IN ARKHAM ASYLUM UNTIL SOME SNOTTY KID LAWYER GOT HIM OUT AND THEY LET HIM JOIN A SUPERTEAM.
THE MARINES SHOULDN'T BE DOING DEALS WITH NO...
...SUPER-CRIMINALS.
FIRST OF ALL, MY LAWYER WAS A FIFTY-SEVEN-YEAR-OLD ITALIAN GENTLEMAN WITH A WONDERFUL HEAD OF GREY HAIR AND A HEART CONDITION, ALTHOUGH I FAIL TO SEE HOW HIS AGE IS OF RELEVANCE HERE.
SECONDLY, I DID INDEED SLAUGHTER A COMMUNITY, BUT THIS WAS AN ERROR ON MY PART.
A MISREADING OF THE FACTS, IF YOU WILL. REST ASSURED, I HAVE NO PLANS TO REPEAT MY ACTIONS IN THE NEAR FUTURE.
I VOLUNTEERED FOR THIS MISSION BECAUSE I BELIEVE I AM THE ONLY ONE THE SWAMP THING WILL LISTEN TO IN HIS PRESENT STATE, AND I THINK I MIGHT ASCERTAIN WHETHER OUR TWO SPECIES ARE IN ANY DANGER FROM HIS PLANS.
IT IS AN ACT OF SELF-PRESERVATION. NOTHING MORE.
DON'T WAKE ME UP IN THE MORNING, GENTLEMEN.
I WON'T BE SLEEPING.

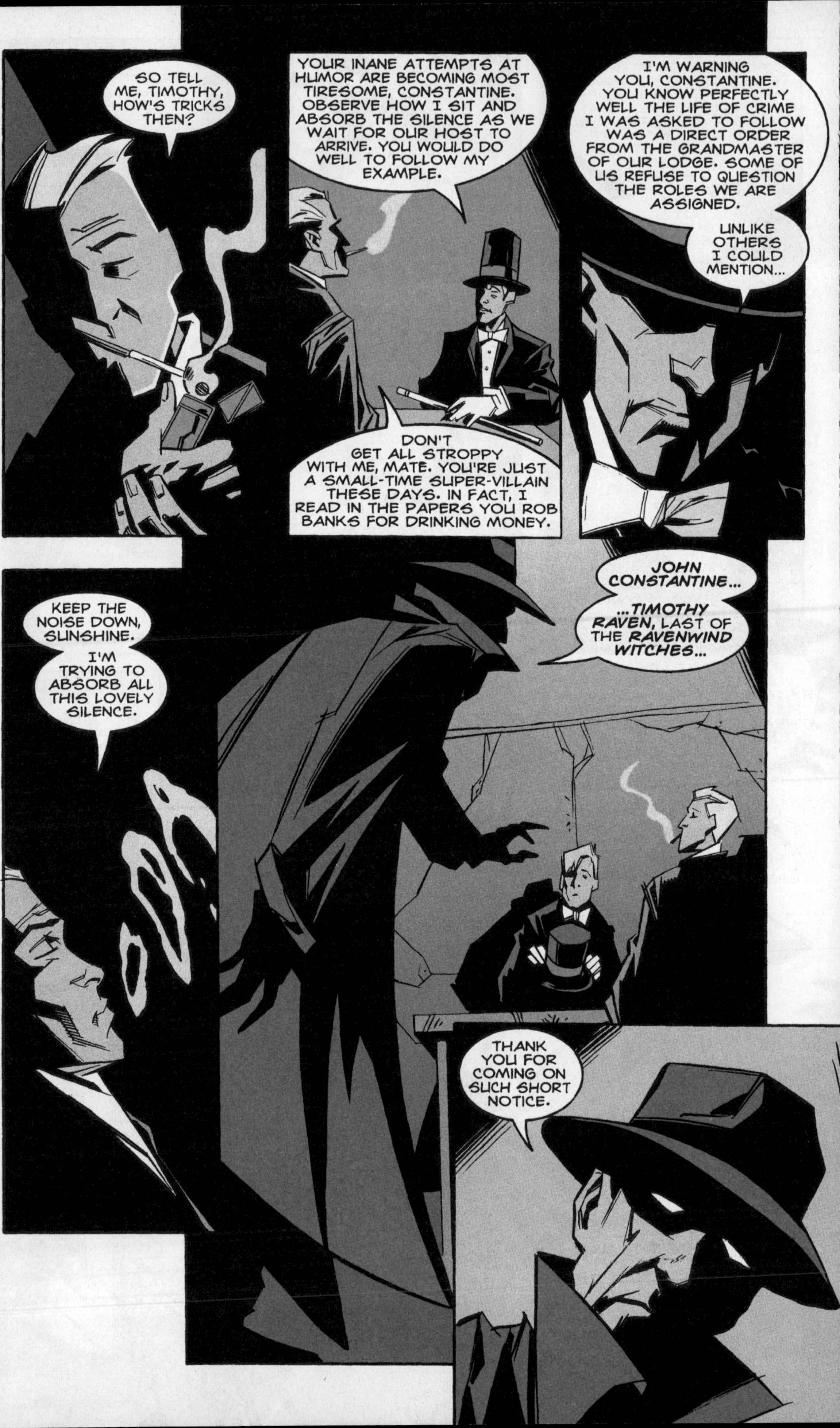
SO TELL ME, TIMOTHY, HOW'S TRICKS THEN?
YOUR INANE ATTEMPTS AT HUMOR ARE BECOMING MOST TIRESOME, CONSTANTINE. OBSERVE HOW I SIT AND ABSORB THE SILENCE AS WE WAIT FOR OUR HOST TO ARRIVE. YOU WOULD DO WELL TO FOLLOW MY EXAMPLE.
DON'T GET ALL STROPPY WITH ME, MATE. YOU'RE JUST A SMALL-TIME SUPER-VILLAIN THESE DAYS. IN FACT, I READ IN THE PAPERS YOU ROB BANKS FOR DRINKING MONEY.
I'M WARNING YOU, CONSTANTINE. YOU KNOW PERFECTLY WELL THE LIFE OF CRIME I WAS ASKED TO FOLLOW WAS A DIRECT ORDER FROM THE GRANDMASTER OF OUR LODGE. SOME OF US REFUSE TO QUESTION THE ROLES WE ARE ASSIGNED.
UNLIKE OTHERS I COULD MENTION...
KEEP THE NOISE DOWN, SUNSHINE.
I'M TRYING TO ABSORB ALL THIS LOVELY SILENCE.
JOHN CONSTANTINE...
...TIMOTHY RAVEN, LAST OF THE RAVENWIND WITCHES...
THANK YOU FOR COMING ON SUCH SHORT NOTICE.

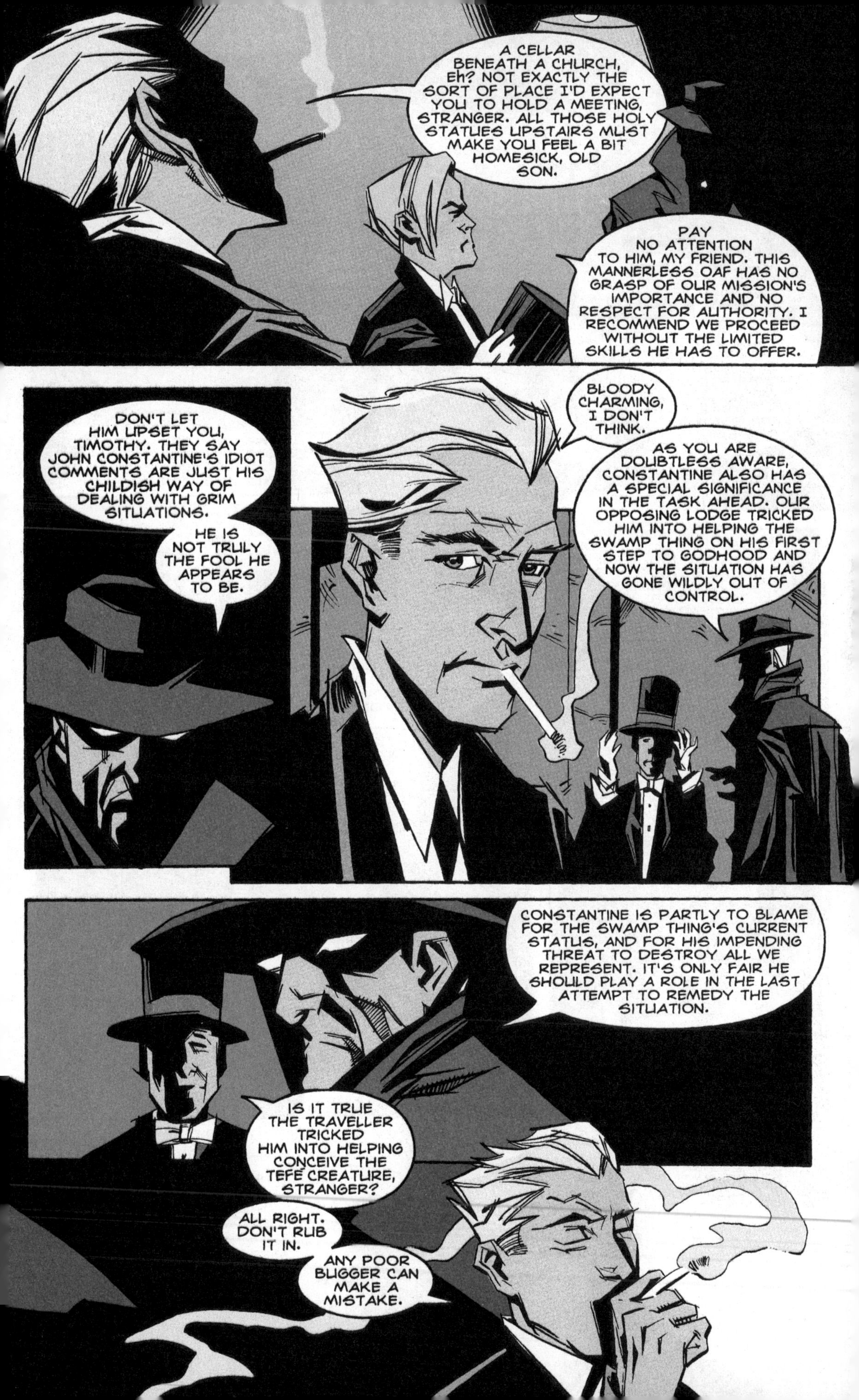
A CELLAR BENEATH A CHURCH, Eh? NOT EXACTLY THE SORT OF PLACE I'D EXPECT YOU TO HOLD A MEETING, STRANGER. ALL THOSE HOLY STATUES UPSTAIRS MUST MAKE YOU FEEL A BIT HOMESICK, OLD SON.
PAY NO ATTENTION TO HIM, MY FRIEND. THIS MANNERLESS OAF HAS NO GRASP OF OUR MISSION'S IMPORTANCE AND NO RESPECT FOR AUTHORITY. I RECOMMEND WE PROCEED WITHOUT THE LIMITED SKILLS HE HAS TO OFFER.
DON'T LET HIM UPSET YOU, TIMOTHY. THEY SAY JOHN CONSTANTINE'S IDIOT COMMENTS ARE JUST HIS CHILDISH WAY OF DEALING WITH GRIM SITUATIONS.
HE IS NOT TRULY THE FOOL HE APPEARS TO BE.
BLOODY CHARMING, I DON'T THINK.
AS YOU ARE DOUBTLESS AWARE, CONSTANTINE ALSO HAS A SPECIAL SIGNIFICANCE IN THE TASK AHEAD. OUR OPPOSING LODGE TRICKED HIM INTO HELPING THE SWAMP THING ON HIS FIRST STEP TO GODHOOD AND NOW THE SITUATION HAS GONE WILDLY OUT OF CONTROL.
CONSTANTINE IS PARTLY TO BLAME FOR THE SWAMP THING'S CURRENT STATUS, AND FOR HIS IMPENDING THREAT TO DESTROY ALL WE REPRESENT. IT'S ONLY FAIR HE SHOULD PLAY A ROLE IN THE LAST ATTEMPT TO REMEDY THE SITUATION.
IS IT TRUE THE TRAVELLER TRICKED HIM INTO HELPING CONCEIVE THE TEFÉ CREATURE, STRANGER?
ALL RIGHT. DON'T RUB IT IN.
ANY POOR BUGGER CAN MAKE A MISTAKE.

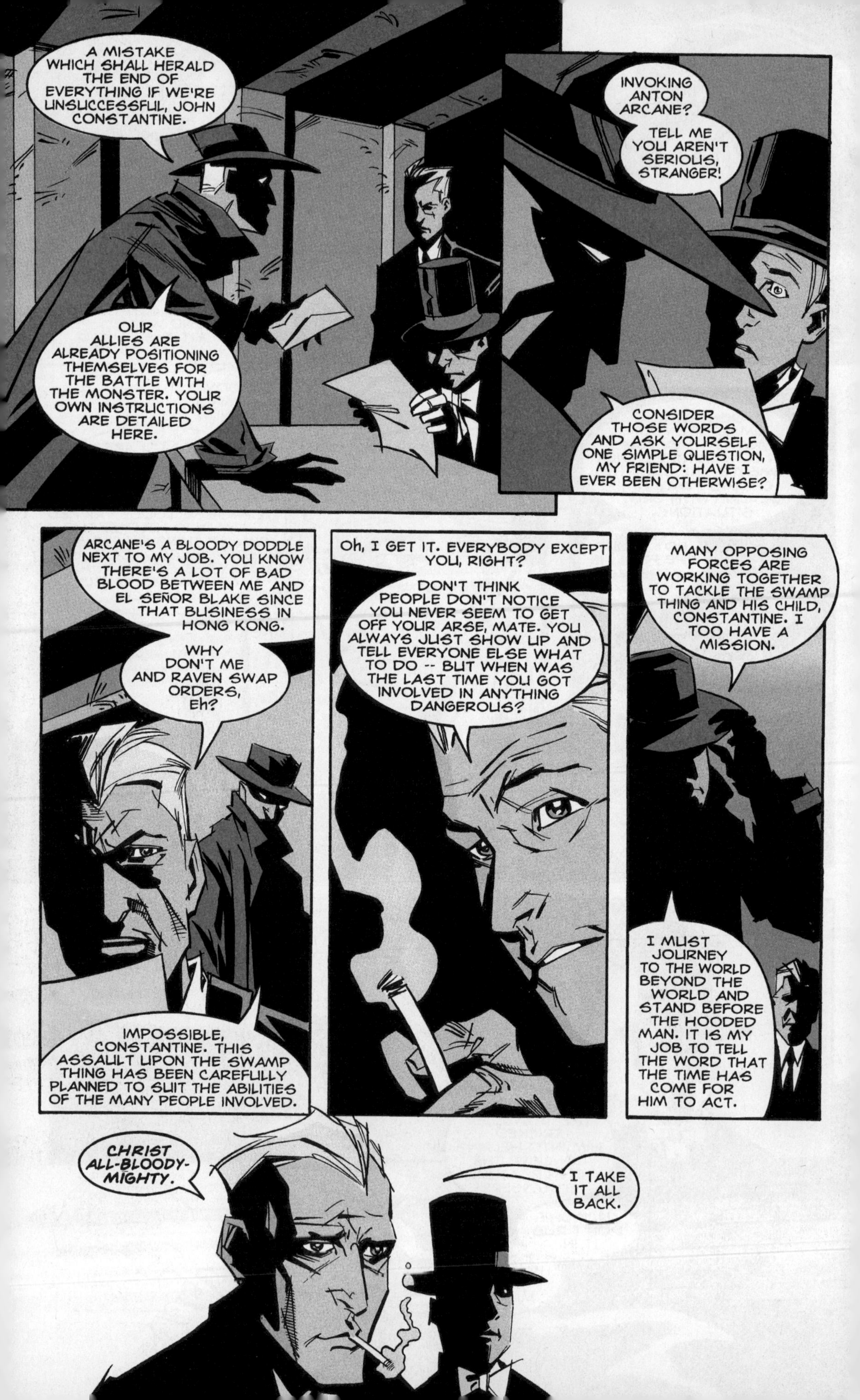
A MISTAKE WHICH SHALL HERALD THE END OF EVERYTHING IF WE'RE UNSUCCESSFUL, JOHN CONSTANTINE.
OUR ALLIES ARE ALREADY POSITIONING THEMSELVES FOR THE BATTLE WITH THE MONSTER. YOUR OWN INSTRUCTIONS ARE DETAILED HERE.
INVOKING ANTON ARCANE?
TELL ME YOU AREN'T SERIOUS, STRANGER!
CONSIDER THOSE WORDS AND ASK YOURSELF ONE SIMPLE QUESTION, MY FRIEND: HAVE I EVER BEEN OTHERWISE?
ARCANE'S A BLOODY DODDLE NEXT TO MY JOB. YOU KNOW THERE'S A LOT OF BAD BLOOD BETWEEN ME AND EL SEÑOR BLAKE SINCE THAT BUSINESS IN HONG KONG.
WHY DON'T ME AND RAVEN SWAP ORDERS, Eh?
IMPOSSIBLE, CONSTANTINE. THIS ASSAULT UPON THE SWAMP THING HAS BEEN CAREFULLY PLANNED TO SUIT THE ABILITIES OF THE MANY PEOPLE INVOLVED.
Oh, I GET IT. EVERYBODY EXCEPT YOU, RIGHT?
DON'T THINK PEOPLE DON'T NOTICE YOU NEVER SEEM TO GET OFF YOUR ARSE, MATE. YOU ALWAYS JUST SHOW UP AND TELL EVERYONE ELSE WHAT TO DO -- BUT WHEN WAS THE LAST TIME YOU GOT INVOLVED IN ANYTHING DANGEROUS?
MANY OPPOSING FORCES ARE WORKING TOGETHER TO TACKLE THE SWAMP THING AND HIS CHILD, CONSTANTINE. I TOO HAVE A MISSION.
I MUST JOURNEY TO THE WORLD BEYOND THE WORLD AND STAND BEFORE THE HOODED MAN. IT IS MY JOB TO TELL THE WORD THAT THE TIME HAS COME FOR HIM TO ACT.
CHRIST ALL-BLOODY-MIGHTY.
I TAKE IT ALL BACK.

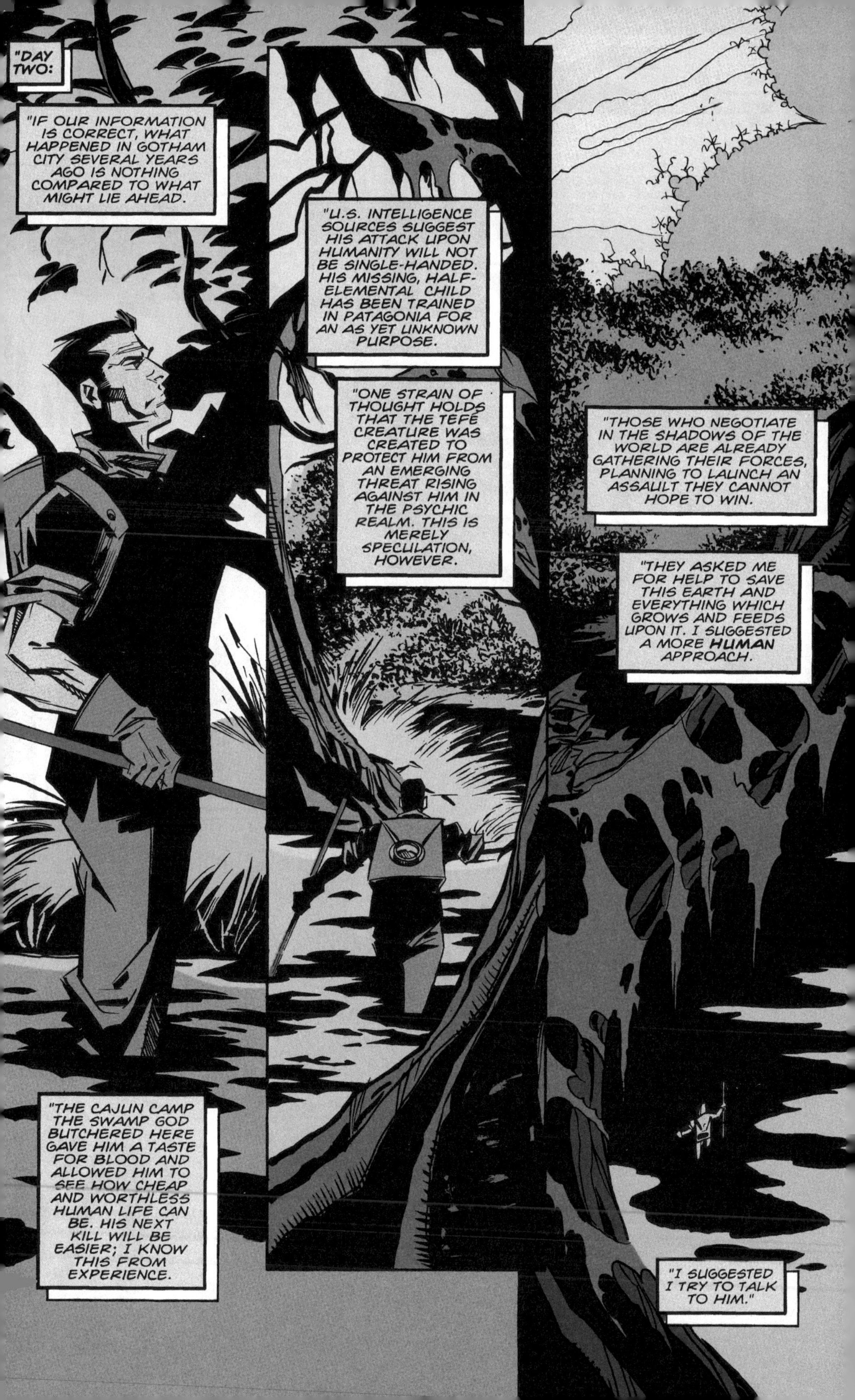
"DAY TWO:
"IF OUR INFORMATION IS CORRECT, WHAT HAPPENED IN GOTHAM CITY SEVERAL YEARS AGO IS NOTHING COMPARED TO WHAT MIGHT LIE AHEAD.
"U.S. INTELLIGENCE SOURCES SUGGEST HIS ATTACK UPON HUMANITY WILL NOT BE SINGLE-HANDED. HIS MISSING, HALF-ELEMENTAL CHILD HAS BEEN TRAINED IN PATAGONIA FOR AN AS YET UNKNOWN PURPOSE.
"ONE STRAIN OF THOUGHT HOLDS THAT THE TEFÉ CREATURE WAS CREATED TO PROTECT HIM FROM AN EMERGING THREAT RISING AGAINST HIM IN THE PSYCHIC REALM. THIS IS MERELY SPECULATION, HOWEVER.
"THOSE WHO NEGOTIATE IN THE SHADOWS OF THE WORLD ARE ALREADY GATHERING THEIR FORCES, PLANNING TO LAUNCH AN ASSAULT THEY CANNOT HOPE TO WIN.
"THEY ASKED ME FOR HELP TO SAVE THIS EARTH AND EVERYTHING WHICH GROWS AND FEEDS UPON IT. I SUGGESTED A MORE **HUMAN** APPROACH.
"THE CAJUN CAMP THE SWAMP GOD BUTCHERED HERE GAVE HIM A TASTE FOR BLOOD AND ALLOWED HIM TO SEE HOW CHEAP AND WORTHLESS HUMAN LIFE CAN BE. HIS NEXT KILL WILL BE EASIER; I KNOW THIS FROM EXPERIENCE.
"I SUGGESTED I TRY TO TALK TO HIM."

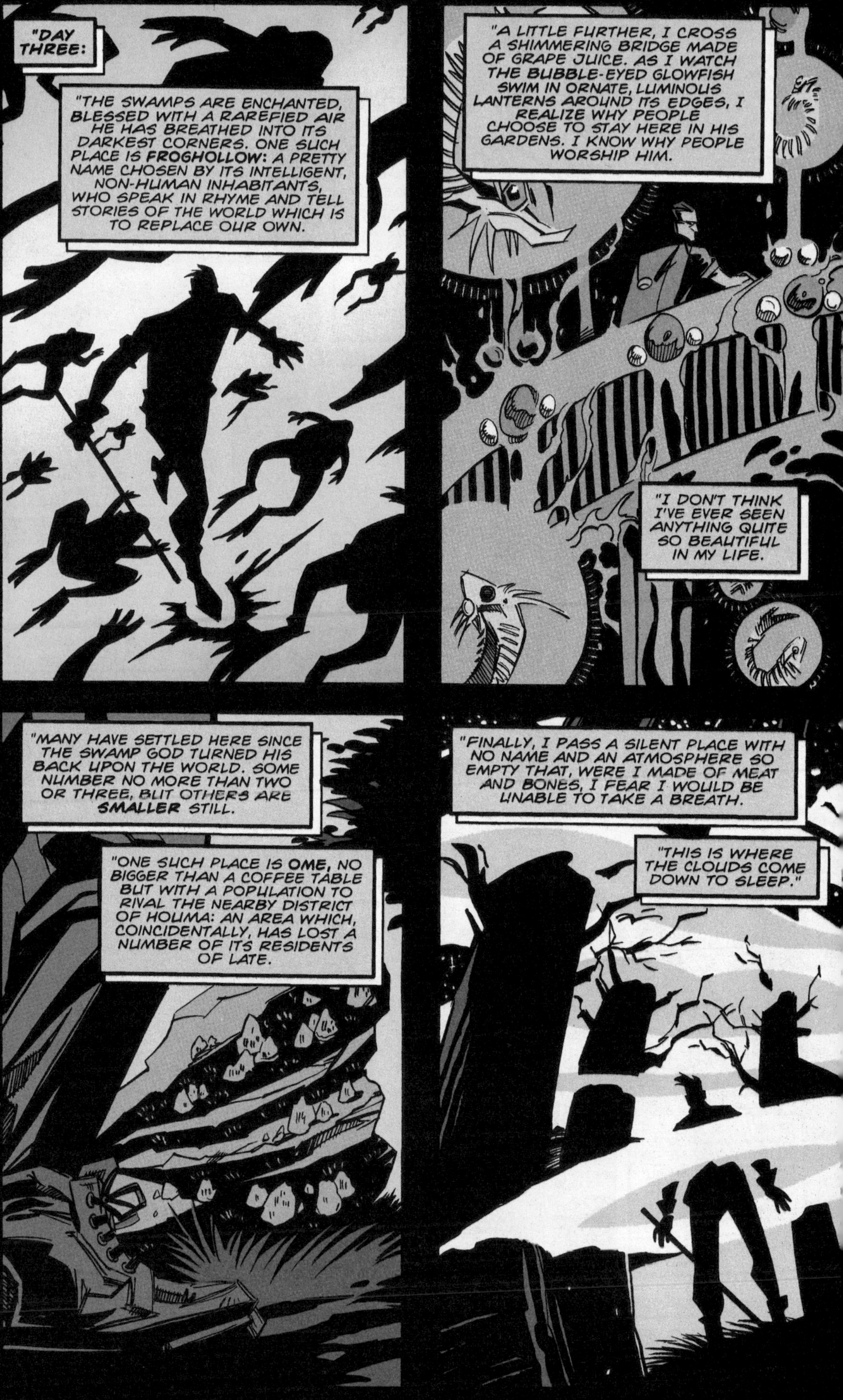
"DAY THREE:
"THE SWAMPS ARE ENCHANTED, BLESSED WITH A RAREFIED AIR HE HAS BREATHED INTO ITS DARKEST CORNERS. ONE SUCH PLACE IS FROGHOLLOW: A PRETTY NAME CHOSEN BY ITS INTELLIGENT, NON-HUMAN INHABITANTS, WHO SPEAK IN RHYME AND TELL STORIES OF THE WORLD WHICH IS TO REPLACE OUR OWN.
"A LITTLE FURTHER, I CROSS A SHIMMERING BRIDGE MADE OF GRAPE JUICE. AS I WATCH THE BUBBLE-EYED GLOWFISH SWIM IN ORNATE, LUMINOUS LANTERNS AROUND ITS EDGES, I REALIZE WHY PEOPLE CHOOSE TO STAY HERE IN HIS GARDENS. I KNOW WHY PEOPLE WORSHIP HIM.
"I DON'T THINK I'VE EVER SEEN ANYTHING QUITE SO BEAUTIFUL IN MY LIFE.
"MANY HAVE SETTLED HERE SINCE THE SWAMP GOD TURNED HIS BACK UPON THE WORLD. SOME NUMBER NO MORE THAN TWO OR THREE, BUT OTHERS ARE SMALLER STILL.
"ONE SUCH PLACE IS OME, NO BIGGER THAN A COFFEE TABLE BUT WITH A POPULATION TO RIVAL THE NEARBY DISTRICT OF HOUMA: AN AREA WHICH, COINCIDENTALLY, HAS LOST A NUMBER OF ITS RESIDENTS OF LATE.
"FINALLY, I PASS A SILENT PLACE WITH NO NAME AND AN ATMOSPHERE SO EMPTY THAT, WERE I MADE OF MEAT AND BONES, I FEAR I WOULD BE UNABLE TO TAKE A BREATH.
"THIS IS WHERE THE CLOUDS COME DOWN TO SLEEP."

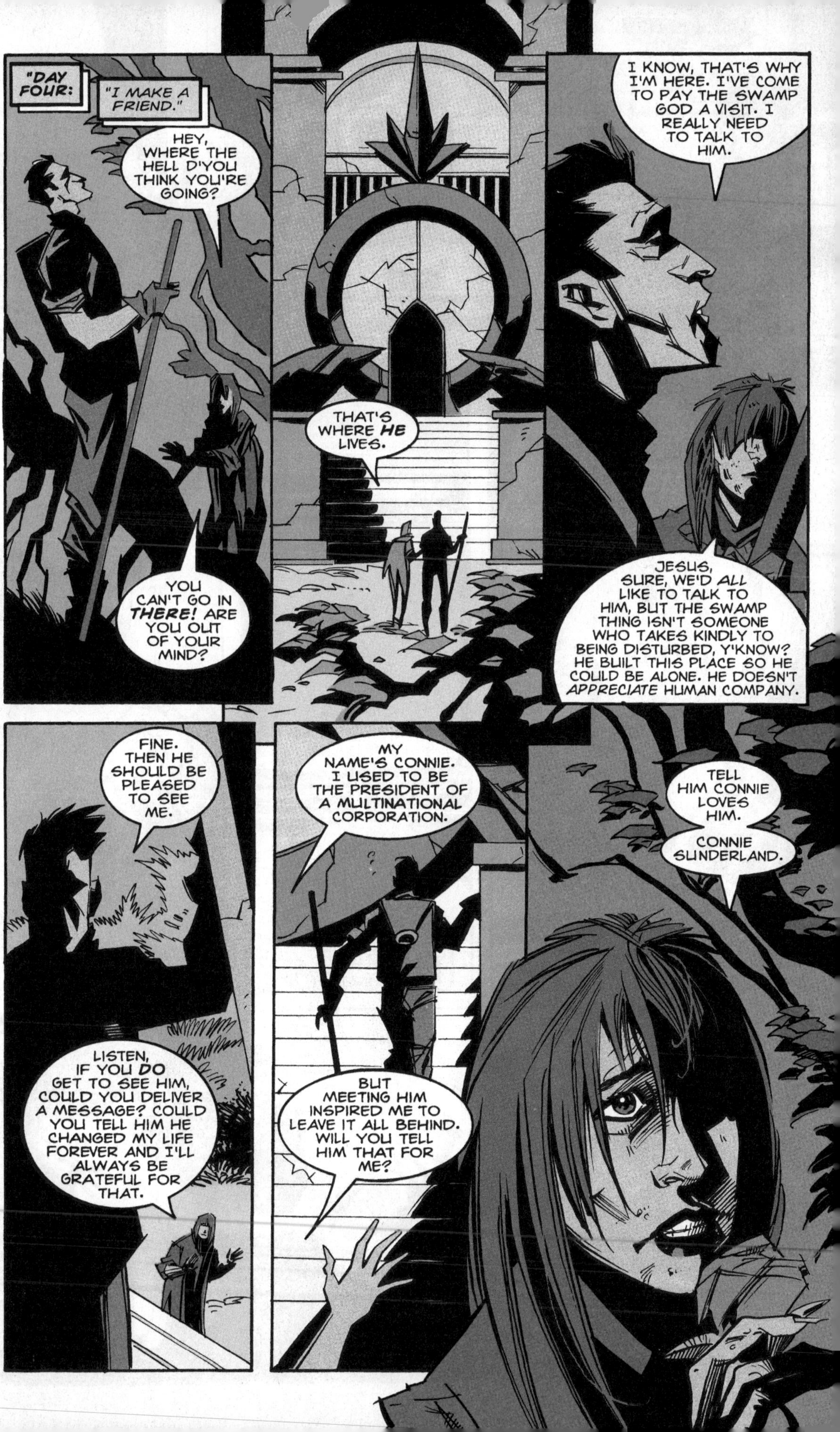
"DAY FOUR:
"I MAKE A FRIEND."
HEY, WHERE THE HELL D'YOU THINK YOU'RE GOING?
YOU CAN'T GO IN THERE! ARE YOU OUT OF YOUR MIND?
THAT'S WHERE HE LIVES.
I KNOW, THAT'S WHY I'M HERE. I'VE COME TO PAY THE SWAMP GOD A VISIT. I REALLY NEED TO TALK TO HIM.
JESUS, SURE, WE'D ALL LIKE TO TALK TO HIM, BUT THE SWAMP THING ISN'T SOMEONE WHO TAKES KINDLY TO BEING DISTURBED, Y'KNOW? HE BUILT THIS PLACE SO HE COULD BE ALONE. HE DOESN'T APPRECIATE HUMAN COMPANY.
FINE. THEN HE SHOULD BE PLEASED TO SEE ME.
LISTEN, IF YOU DO GET TO SEE HIM, COULD YOU DELIVER A MESSAGE? COULD YOU TELL HIM HE CHANGED MY LIFE FOREVER AND I'LL ALWAYS BE GRATEFUL FOR THAT.
MY NAME'S CONNIE. I USED TO BE THE PRESIDENT OF A MULTINATIONAL CORPORATION.
BUT MEETING HIM INSPIRED ME TO LEAVE IT ALL BEHIND. WILL YOU TELL HIM THAT FOR ME?
TELL HIM CONNIE LOVES HIM.
CONNIE SUNDERLAND.

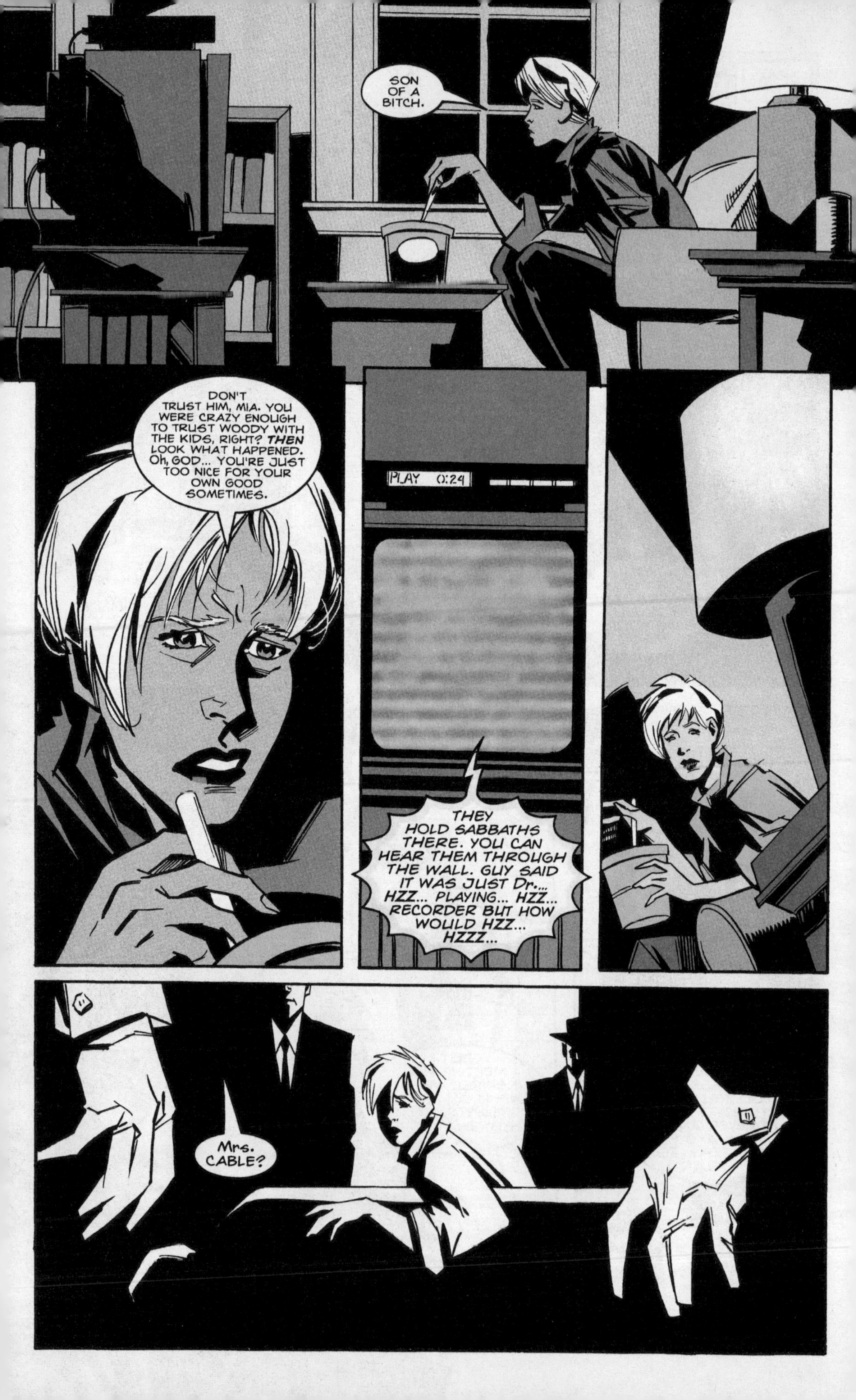
SON OF A BITCH.
DON'T TRUST HIM, MIA. YOU WERE CRAZY ENOUGH TO TRUST WOODY WITH THE KIDS, RIGHT? THEN LOOK WHAT HAPPENED. Oh, GOD... YOU'RE JUST TOO NICE FOR YOUR OWN GOOD SOMETIMES.
PLAY 0:24
THEY HOLD SABBATHS THERE. YOU CAN HEAR THEM THROUGH THE WALL. GUY SAID IT WAS JUST Dr.... HZZ... PLAYING... HZZ... RECORDER BUT HOW WOULD HZZ... HZZZ...
Mrs. CABLE?

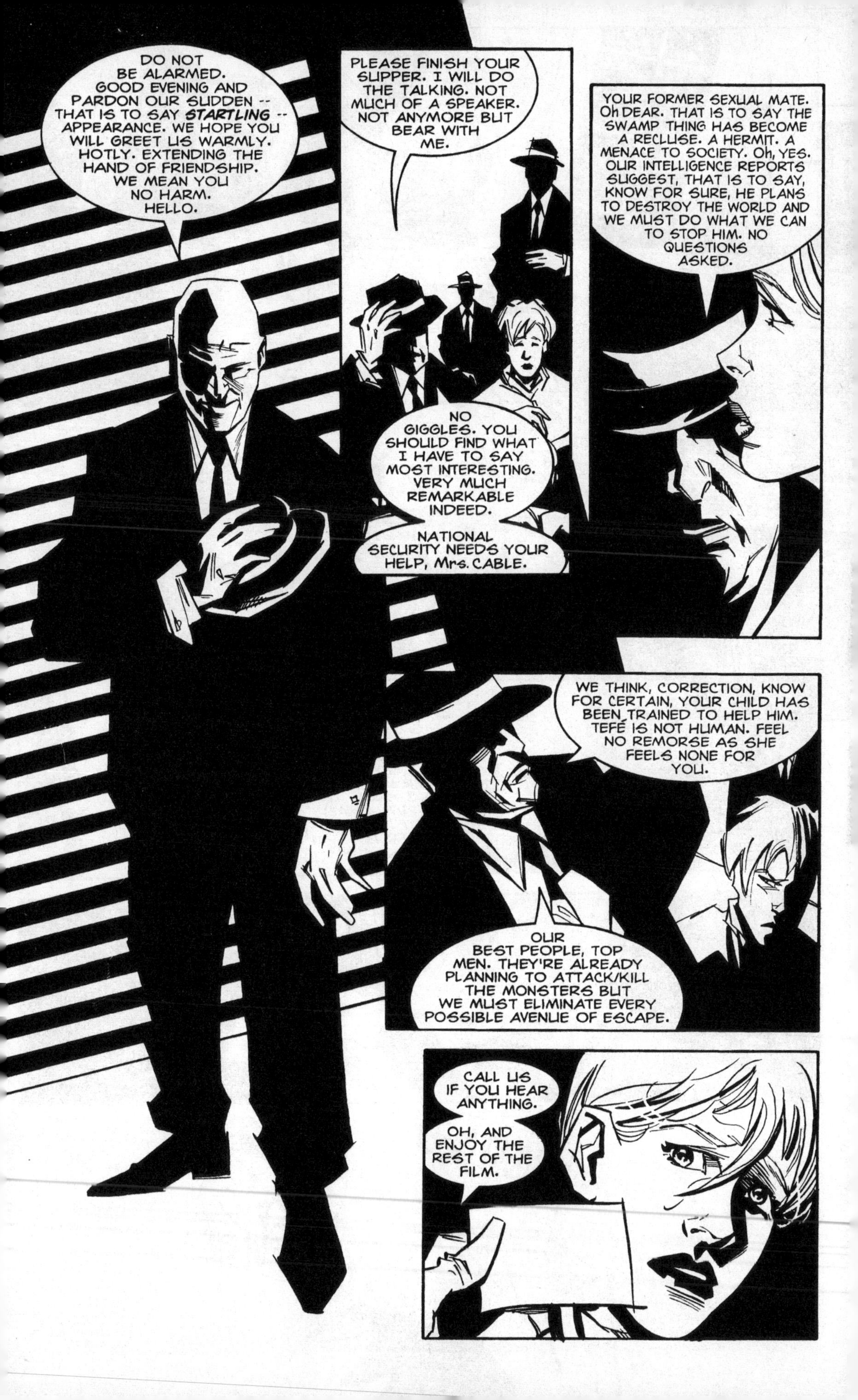
DO NOT BE ALARMED. GOOD EVENING AND PARDON OUR SUDDEN -- THAT IS TO SAY *STARTLING* -- APPEARANCE. WE HOPE YOU WILL GREET US WARMLY. HOTLY. EXTENDING THE HAND OF FRIENDSHIP. WE MEAN YOU NO HARM. HELLO.
PLEASE FINISH YOUR SUPPER. I WILL DO THE TALKING. NOT MUCH OF A SPEAKER. NOT ANYMORE BUT BEAR WITH ME.
NO GIGGLES. YOU SHOULD FIND WHAT I HAVE TO SAY MOST INTERESTING. VERY MUCH REMARKABLE INDEED.
NATIONAL SECURITY NEEDS YOUR HELP, Mrs. CABLE.
YOUR FORMER SEXUAL MATE. Oh DEAR. THAT IS TO SAY THE SWAMP THING HAS BECOME A RECLUSE. A HERMIT. A MENACE TO SOCIETY. Oh, YES. OUR INTELLIGENCE REPORTS SUGGEST, THAT IS TO SAY, KNOW FOR SURE, HE PLANS TO DESTROY THE WORLD AND WE MUST DO WHAT WE CAN TO STOP HIM. NO QUESTIONS ASKED.
WE THINK, CORRECTION, KNOW FOR CERTAIN, YOUR CHILD HAS BEEN TRAINED TO HELP HIM. TEFÉ IS NOT HUMAN. FEEL NO REMORSE AS SHE FEELS NONE FOR YOU.
OUR BEST PEOPLE, TOP MEN. THEY'RE ALREADY PLANNING TO ATTACK/KILL THE MONSTERS BUT WE MUST ELIMINATE EVERY POSSIBLE AVENUE OF ESCAPE.
CALL US IF YOU HEAR ANYTHING.
OH, AND ENJOY THE REST OF THE FILM.

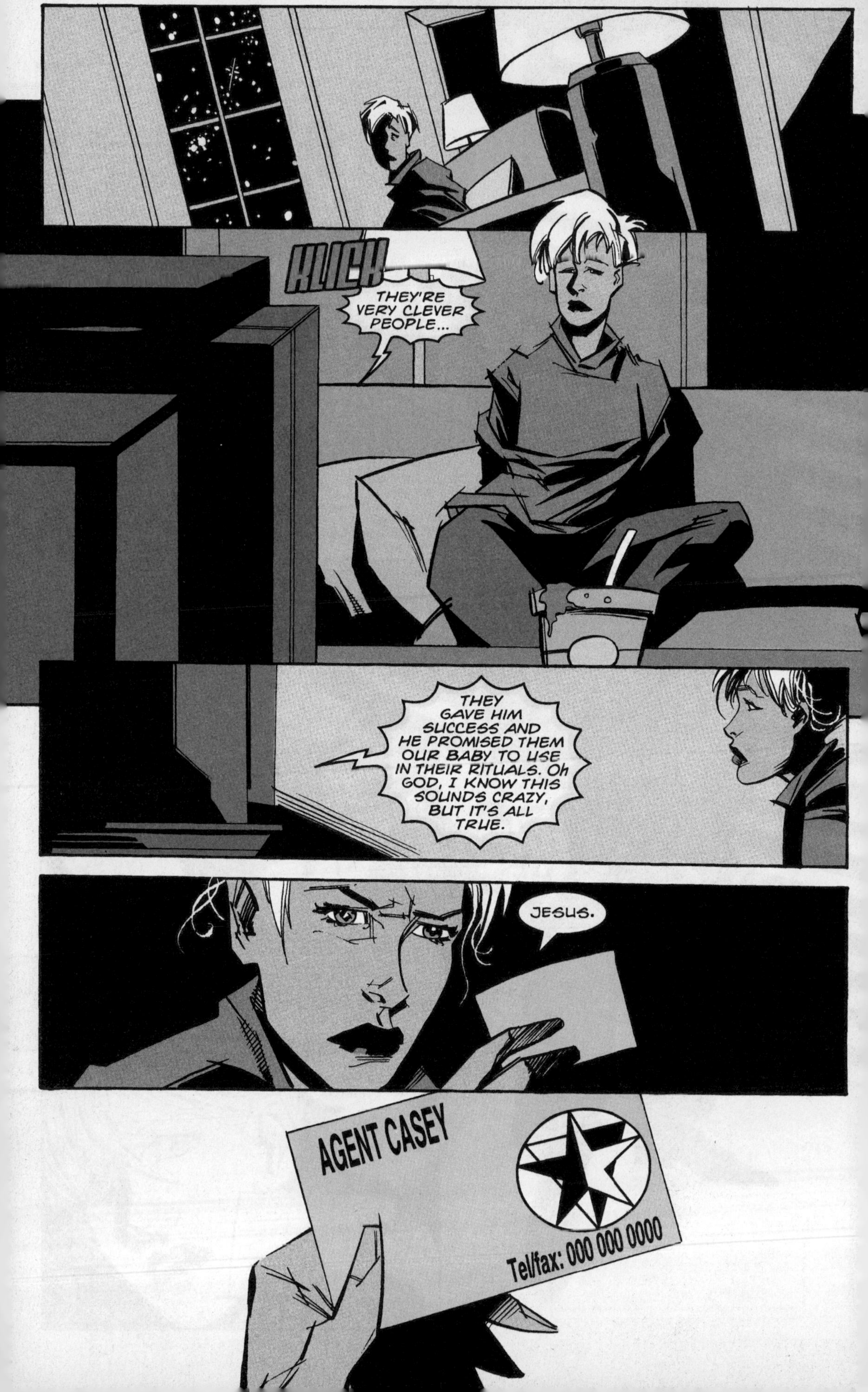
KLICK
THEY'RE VERY CLEVER PEOPLE...
THEY GAVE HIM SUCCESS AND HE PROMISED THEM OUR BABY TO USE IN THEIR RITUALS. Oh GOD, I KNOW THIS SOUNDS CRAZY, BUT IT'S ALL TRUE.
JESUS.
AGENT CASEY
Tel/fax: 000 000 0000

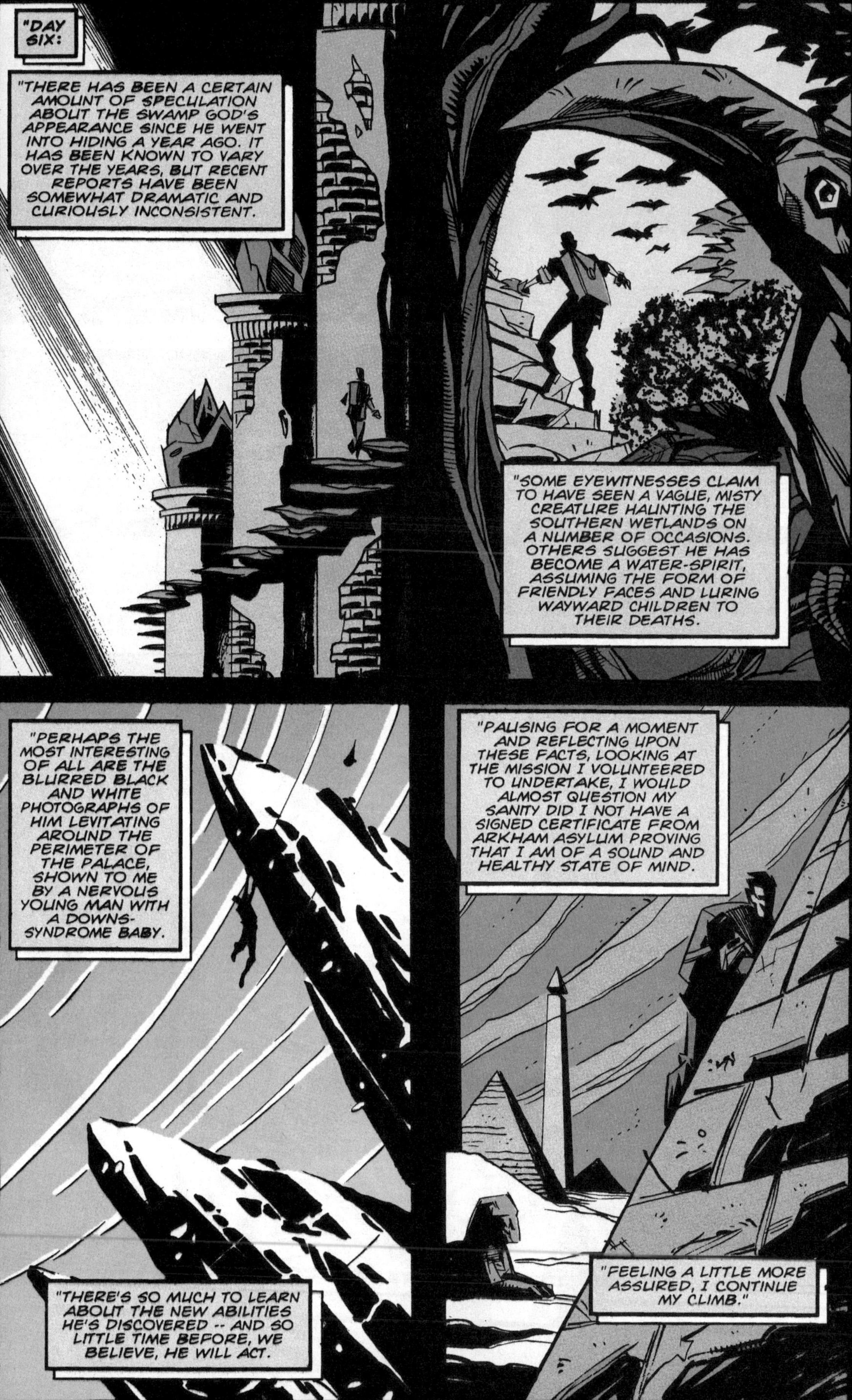
"DAY SIX:
"THERE HAS BEEN A CERTAIN AMOUNT OF SPECULATION ABOUT THE SWAMP GOD'S APPEARANCE SINCE HE WENT INTO HIDING A YEAR AGO. IT HAS BEEN KNOWN TO VARY OVER THE YEARS, BUT RECENT REPORTS HAVE BEEN SOMEWHAT DRAMATIC AND CURIOUSLY INCONSISTENT.
"SOME EYEWITNESSES CLAIM TO HAVE SEEN A VAGUE, MISTY CREATURE HAUNTING THE SOUTHERN WETLANDS ON A NUMBER OF OCCASIONS. OTHERS SUGGEST HE HAS BECOME A WATER-SPIRIT, ASSUMING THE FORM OF FRIENDLY FACES AND LURING WAYWARD CHILDREN TO THEIR DEATHS.
"PERHAPS THE MOST INTERESTING OF ALL ARE THE BLURRED BLACK AND WHITE PHOTOGRAPHS OF HIM LEVITATING AROUND THE PERIMETER OF THE PALACE, SHOWN TO ME BY A NERVOUS YOUNG MAN WITH A DOWNS-SYNDROME BABY.
"THERE'S SO MUCH TO LEARN ABOUT THE NEW ABILITIES HE'S DISCOVERED -- AND SO LITTLE TIME BEFORE, WE BELIEVE, HE WILL ACT.
"PAUSING FOR A MOMENT AND REFLECTING UPON THESE FACTS, LOOKING AT THE MISSION I VOLUNTEERED TO UNDERTAKE, I WOULD ALMOST QUESTION MY SANITY DID I NOT HAVE A SIGNED CERTIFICATE FROM ARKHAM ASYLUM PROVING THAT I AM OF A SOUND AND HEALTHY STATE OF MIND.
"FEELING A LITTLE MORE ASSURED, I CONTINUE MY CLIMB."

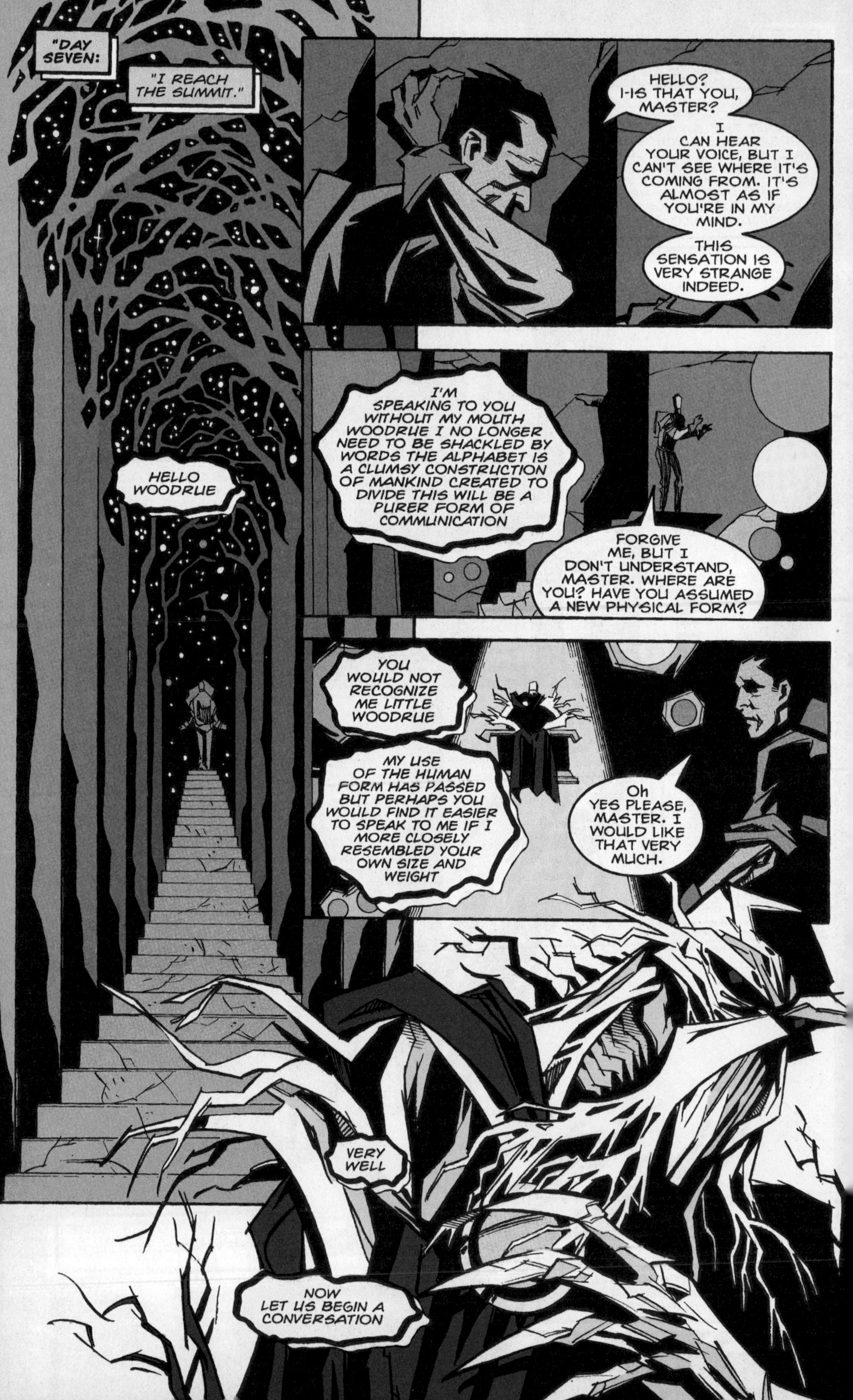
"DAY SEVEN:
"I REACH THE SUMMIT."
HELLO? I-IS THAT YOU, MASTER?
I CAN HEAR YOUR VOICE, BUT I CAN'T SEE WHERE IT'S COMING FROM. IT'S ALMOST AS IF YOU'RE IN MY MIND.
THIS SENSATION IS VERY STRANGE INDEED.
HELLO WOODRUE
I'M SPEAKING TO YOU WITHOUT MY MOUTH WOODRUE I NO LONGER NEED TO BE SHACKLED BY WORDS THE ALPHABET IS A CLUMSY CONSTRUCTION OF MANKIND CREATED TO DIVIDE THIS WILL BE A PURER FORM OF COMMUNICATION
FORGIVE ME, BUT I DON'T UNDERSTAND, MASTER. WHERE ARE YOU? HAVE YOU ASSUMED A NEW PHYSICAL FORM?
YOU WOULD NOT RECOGNIZE ME LITTLE WOODRUE
MY USE OF THE HUMAN FORM HAS PASSED BUT PERHAPS YOU WOULD FIND IT EASIER TO SPEAK TO ME IF I MORE CLOSELY RESEMBLED YOUR OWN SIZE AND WEIGHT
Oh YES PLEASE, MASTER. I WOULD LIKE THAT VERY MUCH.
VERY WELL
NOW LET US BEGIN A CONVERSATION

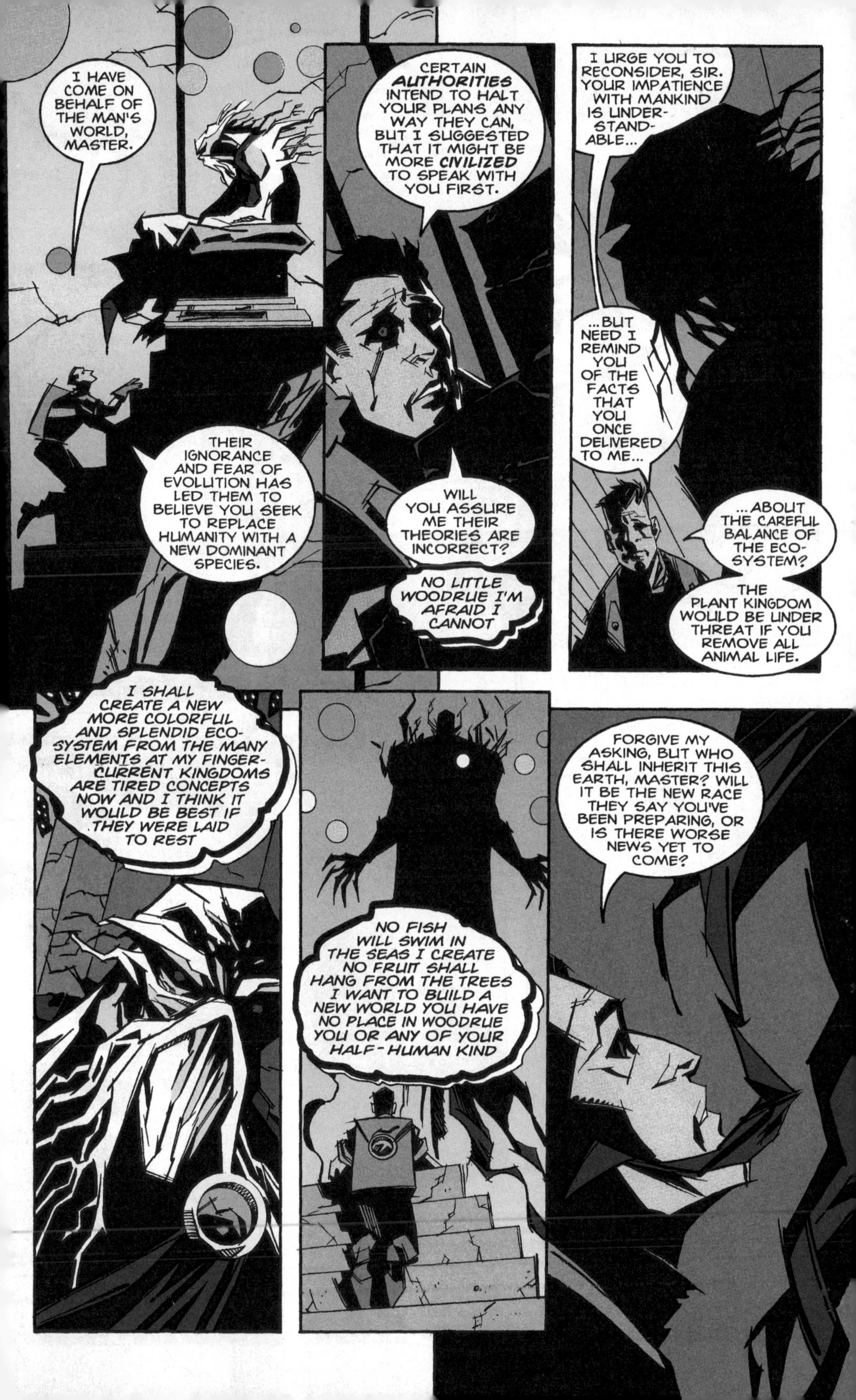

I HAVE COME ON BEHALF OF THE MAN'S WORLD, MASTER.
CERTAIN AUTHORITIES INTEND TO HALT YOUR PLANS ANY WAY THEY CAN, BUT I SUGGESTED THAT IT MIGHT BE MORE CIVILIZED TO SPEAK WITH YOU FIRST.
THEIR IGNORANCE AND FEAR OF EVOLUTION HAS LED THEM TO BELIEVE YOU SEEK TO REPLACE HUMANITY WITH A NEW DOMINANT SPECIES.
WILL YOU ASSURE ME THEIR THEORIES ARE INCORRECT?
NO LITTLE WOODRUE I'M AFRAID I CANNOT
I URGE YOU TO RECONSIDER, SIR. YOUR IMPATIENCE WITH MANKIND IS UNDER-STAND-ABLE...
...BUT NEED I REMIND YOU OF THE FACTS THAT YOU ONCE DELIVERED TO ME...
...ABOUT THE CAREFUL BALANCE OF THE ECO-SYSTEM?
THE PLANT KINGDOM WOULD BE UNDER THREAT IF YOU REMOVE ALL ANIMAL LIFE.
I SHALL CREATE A NEW MORE COLORFUL AND SPLENDID ECO-SYSTEM FROM THE MANY ELEMENTS AT MY FINGER-CURRENT KINGDOMS ARE TIRED CONCEPTS NOW AND I THINK IT WOULD BE BEST IF THEY WERE LAID TO REST
NO FISH WILL SWIM IN THE SEAS I CREATE NO FRUIT SHALL HANG FROM THE TREES I WANT TO BUILD A NEW WORLD YOU HAVE NO PLACE IN WOODRUE YOU OR ANY OF YOUR HALF-HUMAN KIND
FORGIVE MY ASKING, BUT WHO SHALL INHERIT THIS EARTH, MASTER? WILL IT BE THE NEW RACE THEY SAY YOU'VE BEEN PREPARING, OR IS THERE WORSE NEWS YET TO COME?

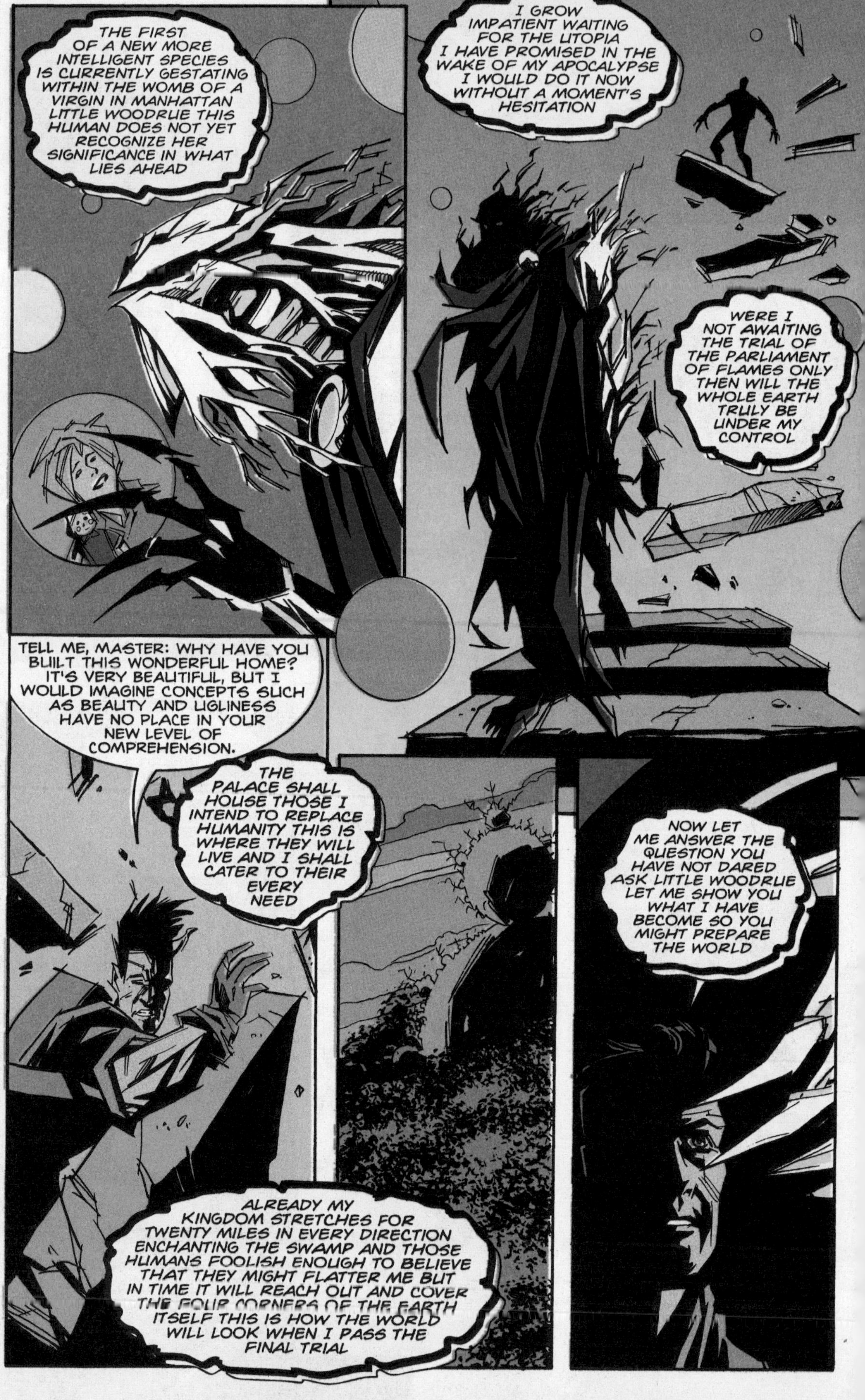
THE FIRST OF A NEW MORE INTELLIGENT SPECIES IS CURRENTLY GESTATING WITHIN THE WOMB OF A VIRGIN IN MANHATTAN LITTLE WOODRUE THIS HUMAN DOES NOT YET RECOGNIZE HER SIGNIFICANCE IN WHAT LIES AHEAD
I GROW IMPATIENT WAITING FOR THE UTOPIA I HAVE PROMISED IN THE WAKE OF MY APOCALYPSE I WOULD DO IT NOW WITHOUT A MOMENT'S HESITATION
WERE I NOT AWAITING THE TRIAL OF THE PARLIAMENT OF FLAMES ONLY THEN WILL THE WHOLE EARTH TRULY BE UNDER MY CONTROL
TELL ME, MASTER: WHY HAVE YOU BUILT THIS WONDERFUL HOME? IT'S VERY BEAUTIFUL, BUT I WOULD IMAGINE CONCEPTS SUCH AS BEAUTY AND UGLINESS HAVE NO PLACE IN YOUR NEW LEVEL OF COMPREHENSION.
THE PALACE SHALL HOUSE THOSE I INTEND TO REPLACE HUMANITY THIS IS WHERE THEY WILL LIVE AND I SHALL CATER TO THEIR EVERY NEED
ALREADY MY KINGDOM STRETCHES FOR TWENTY MILES IN EVERY DIRECTION ENCHANTING THE SWAMP AND THOSE HUMANS FOOLISH ENOUGH TO BELIEVE THAT THEY MIGHT FLATTER ME BUT IN TIME IT WILL REACH OUT AND COVER THE FOUR CORNERS OF THE EARTH ITSELF THIS IS HOW THE WORLD WILL LOOK WHEN I PASS THE FINAL TRIAL
NOW LET ME ANSWER THE QUESTION YOU HAVE NOT DARED ASK LITTLE WOODRUE LET ME SHOW YOU WHAT I HAVE BECOME SO YOU MIGHT PREPARE THE WORLD

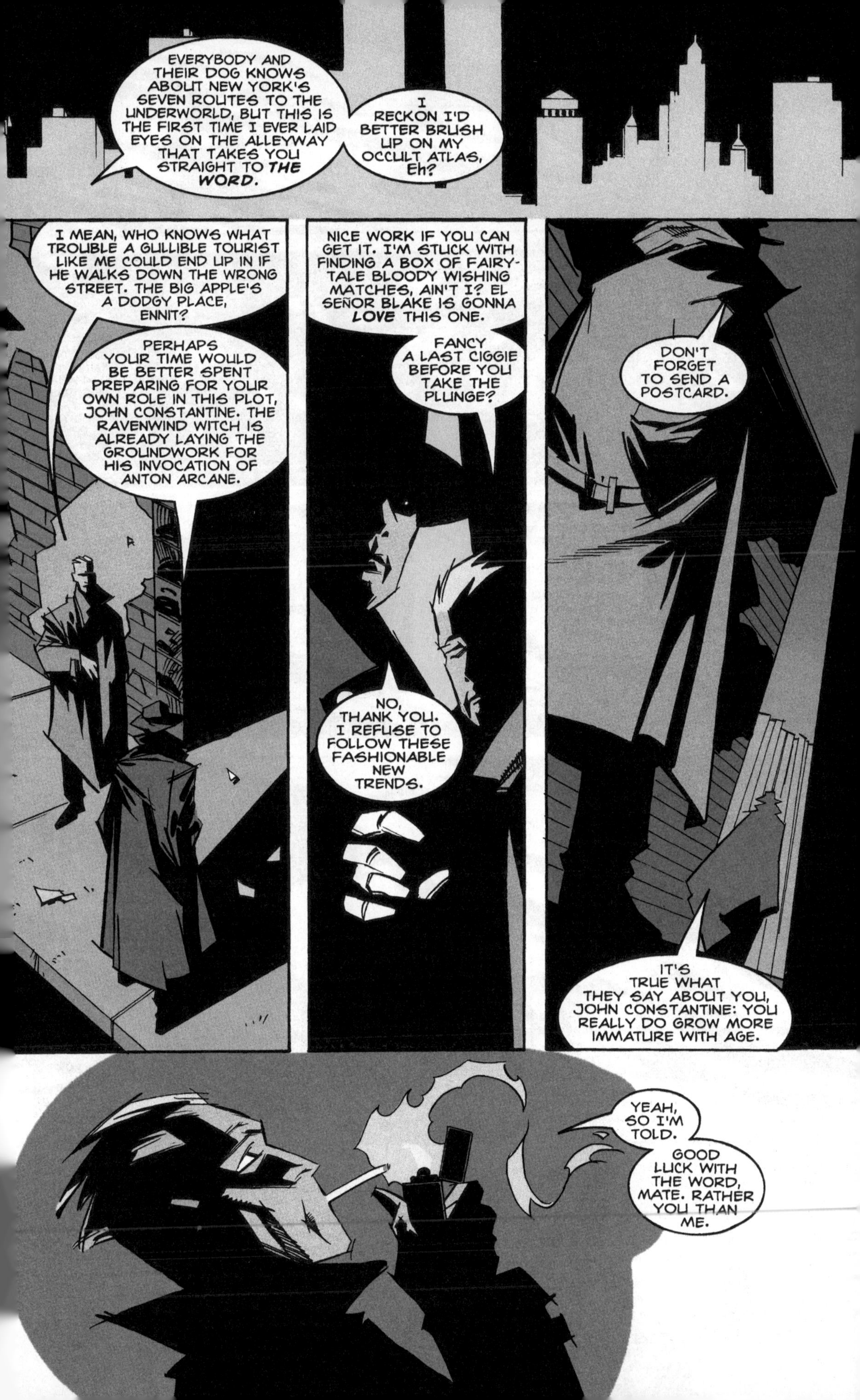
EVERYBODY AND THEIR DOG KNOWS ABOUT NEW YORK'S SEVEN ROUTES TO THE UNDERWORLD, BUT THIS IS THE FIRST TIME I EVER LAID EYES ON THE ALLEYWAY THAT TAKES YOU STRAIGHT TO THE WORD.
I RECKON I'D BETTER BRUSH UP ON MY OCCULT ATLAS, Eh?
I MEAN, WHO KNOWS WHAT TROUBLE A GULLIBLE TOURIST LIKE ME COULD END UP IN IF HE WALKS DOWN THE WRONG STREET. THE BIG APPLE'S A DODGY PLACE, ENNIT?
PERHAPS YOUR TIME WOULD BE BETTER SPENT PREPARING FOR YOUR OWN ROLE IN THIS PLOT, JOHN CONSTANTINE. THE RAVENWIND WITCH IS ALREADY LAYING THE GROUNDWORK FOR HIS INVOCATION OF ANTON ARCANE.
NICE WORK IF YOU CAN GET IT. I'M STUCK WITH FINDING A BOX OF FAIRY-TALE BLOODY WISHING MATCHES, AIN'T I? EL SEÑOR BLAKE IS GONNA LOVE THIS ONE.
FANCY A LAST CIGGIE BEFORE YOU TAKE THE PLUNGE?
NO, THANK YOU. I REFUSE TO FOLLOW THESE FASHIONABLE NEW TRENDS.
DON'T FORGET TO SEND A POSTCARD.
IT'S TRUE WHAT THEY SAY ABOUT YOU, JOHN CONSTANTINE: YOU REALLY DO GROW MORE IMMATURE WITH AGE.
YEAH, SO I'M TOLD.
GOOD LUCK WITH THE WORD, MATE. RATHER YOU THAN ME.

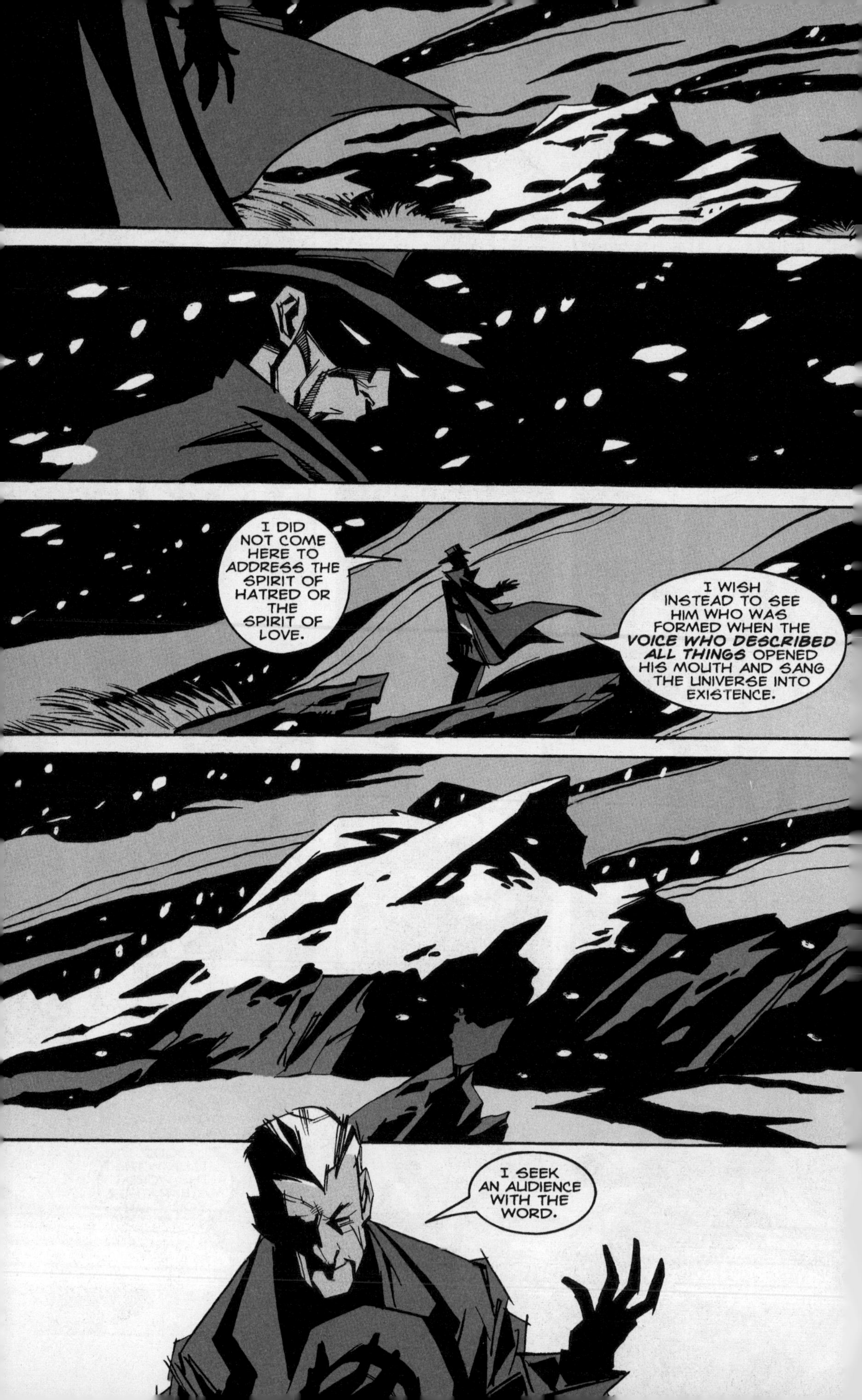
I DID NOT COME HERE TO ADDRESS THE SPIRIT OF HATRED OR THE SPIRIT OF LOVE.
I WISH INSTEAD TO SEE HIM WHO WAS FORMED WHEN THE *VOICE WHO DESCRIBED ALL THINGS* OPENED HIS MOUTH AND SANG THE UNIVERSE INTO EXISTENCE.
I SEEK AN AUDIENCE WITH THE WORD.

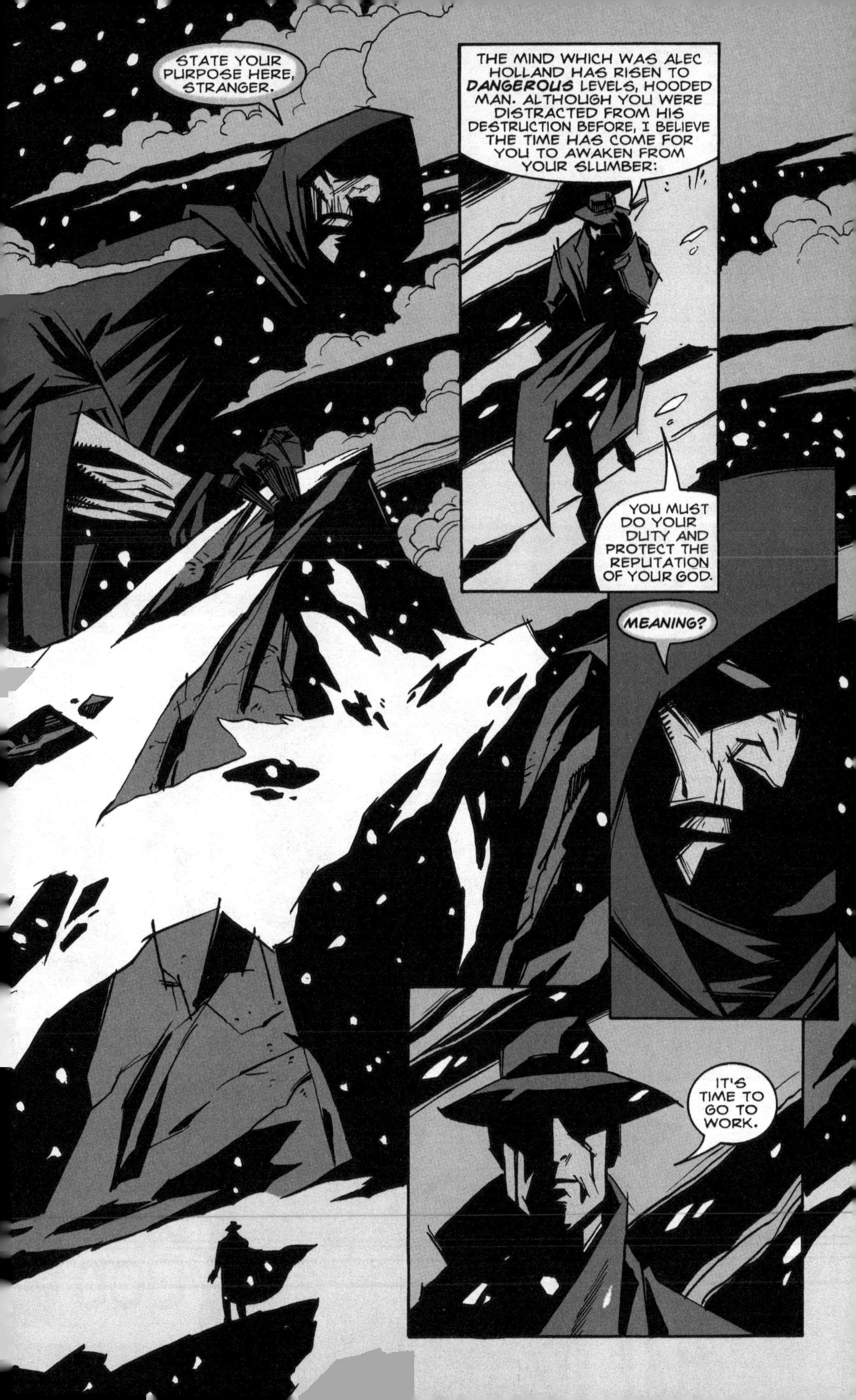
STATE YOUR PURPOSE HERE, STRANGER.
THE MIND WHICH WAS ALEC HOLLAND HAS RISEN TO DANGEROUS LEVELS, HOODED MAN. ALTHOUGH YOU WERE DISTRACTED FROM HIS DESTRUCTION BEFORE, I BELIEVE THE TIME HAS COME FOR YOU TO AWAKEN FROM YOUR SLUMBER:
YOU MUST DO YOUR DUTY AND PROTECT THE REPUTATION OF YOUR GOD.
MEANING?
IT'S TIME TO GO TO WORK.

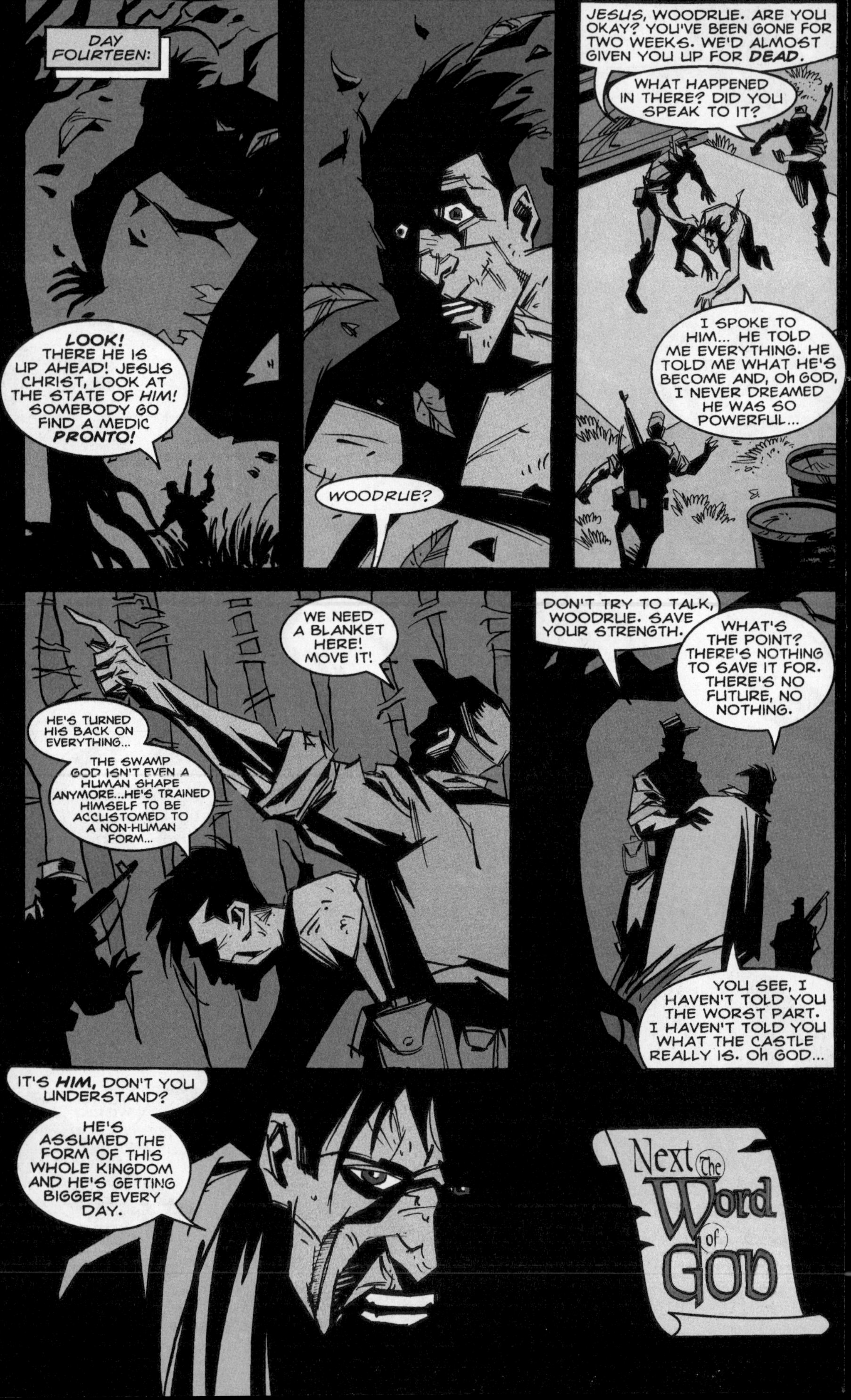
DAY FOURTEEN:
LOOK! THERE HE IS UP AHEAD! JESUS CHRIST, LOOK AT THE STATE OF HIM! SOMEBODY GO FIND A MEDIC PRONTO!
WOODRUE?
JESUS, WOODRUE. ARE YOU OKAY? YOU'VE BEEN GONE FOR TWO WEEKS. WE'D ALMOST GIVEN YOU UP FOR DEAD.
WHAT HAPPENED IN THERE? DID YOU SPEAK TO IT?
I SPOKE TO HIM... HE TOLD ME EVERYTHING. HE TOLD ME WHAT HE'S BECOME AND, Oh GOD, I NEVER DREAMED HE WAS SO POWERFUL...
WE NEED A BLANKET HERE! MOVE IT!
HE'S TURNED HIS BACK ON EVERYTHING...
THE SWAMP GOD ISN'T EVEN A HUMAN SHAPE ANYMORE...HE'S TRAINED HIMSELF TO BE ACCUSTOMED TO A NON-HUMAN FORM...
DON'T TRY TO TALK, WOODRUE. SAVE YOUR STRENGTH.
WHAT'S THE POINT? THERE'S NOTHING TO SAVE IT FOR. THERE'S NO FUTURE, NO NOTHING.
YOU SEE, I HAVEN'T TOLD YOU THE WORST PART. I HAVEN'T TOLD YOU WHAT THE CASTLE REALLY IS. Oh GOD...
IT'S HIM, DON'T YOU UNDERSTAND?
HE'S ASSUMED THE FORM OF THIS WHOLE KINGDOM AND HE'S GETTING BIGGER EVERY DAY.
Next The Word of God

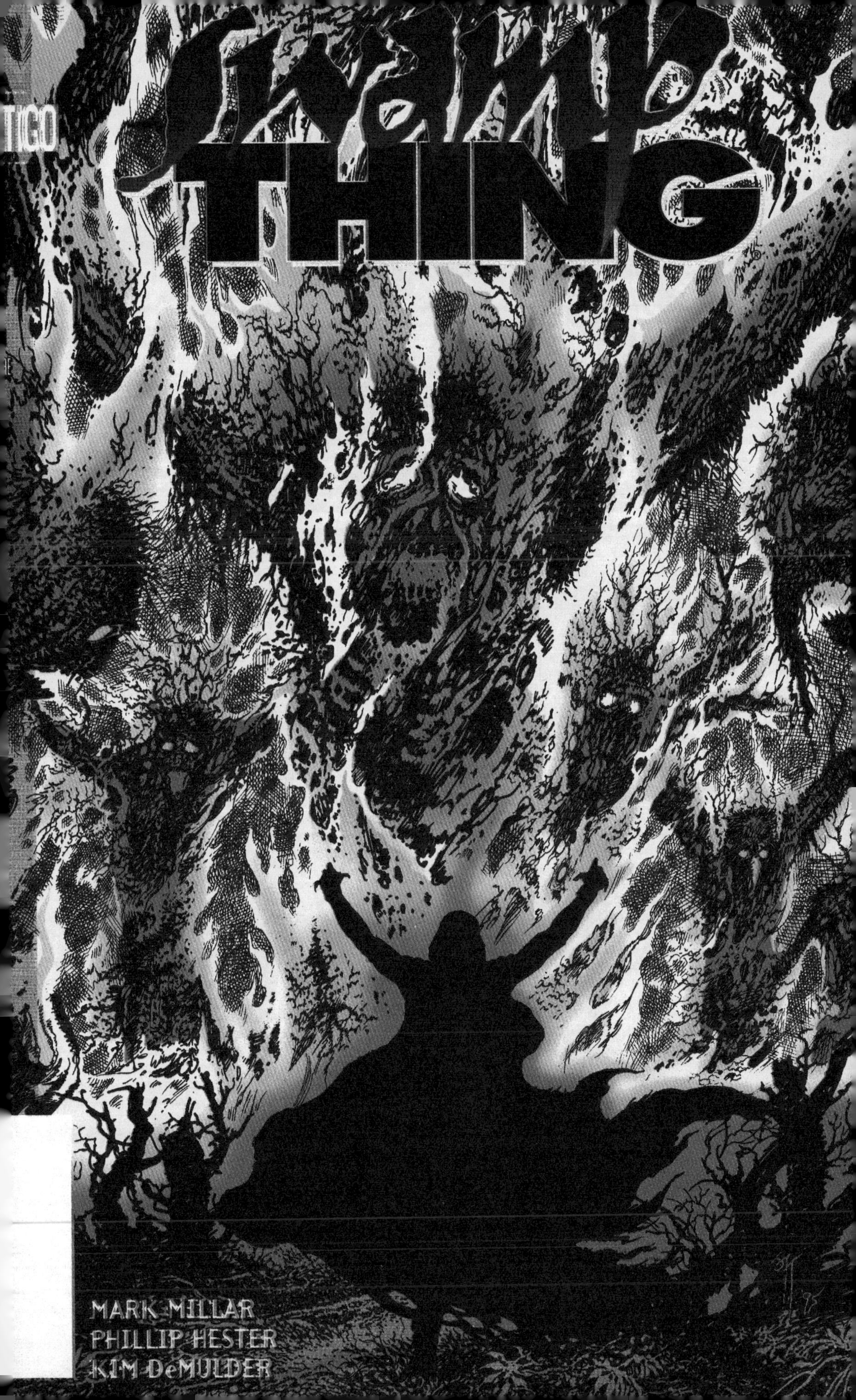
TIGO
SWAMP
THING
MARK MILLAR
PHILLIP HESTER
KIM DeMULDER

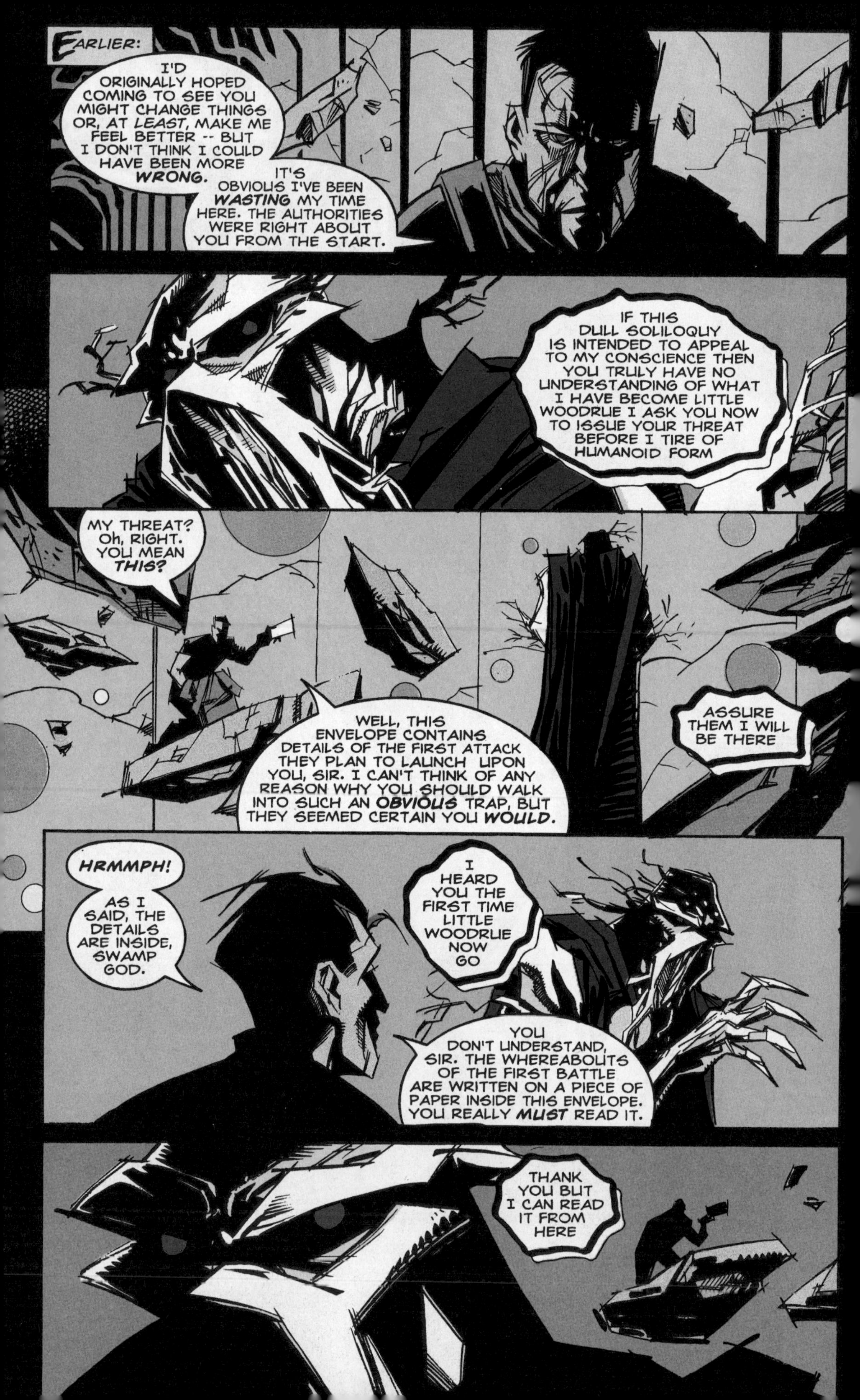
EARLIER:
I'D ORIGINALLY HOPED COMING TO SEE YOU MIGHT CHANGE THINGS OR, AT *LEAST*, MAKE ME FEEL BETTER -- BUT I DON'T THINK I COULD HAVE BEEN MORE **WRONG**.
IT'S OBVIOUS I'VE BEEN **WASTING** MY TIME HERE. THE AUTHORITIES WERE RIGHT ABOUT YOU FROM THE START.
IF THIS DULL SOLILOQUY IS INTENDED TO APPEAL TO MY CONSCIENCE THEN YOU TRULY HAVE NO UNDERSTANDING OF WHAT I HAVE BECOME LITTLE WOODRUE I ASK YOU NOW TO ISSUE YOUR THREAT BEFORE I TIRE OF HUMANOID FORM
MY THREAT? Oh, RIGHT. YOU MEAN **THIS?**
WELL, THIS ENVELOPE CONTAINS DETAILS OF THE FIRST ATTACK THEY PLAN TO LAUNCH UPON YOU, SIR. I CAN'T THINK OF ANY REASON WHY YOU SHOULD WALK INTO SUCH AN **OBVIOUS** TRAP, BUT THEY SEEMED CERTAIN YOU **WOULD**.
ASSURE THEM I WILL BE THERE
HRMMPH!
AS I SAID, THE DETAILS ARE INSIDE, SWAMP GOD.
I HEARD YOU THE FIRST TIME LITTLE WOODRUE NOW GO
YOU DON'T UNDERSTAND, SIR. THE WHEREABOUTS OF THE FIRST BATTLE ARE WRITTEN ON A PIECE OF PAPER INSIDE THIS ENVELOPE. YOU REALLY **MUST** READ IT.
THANK YOU BUT I CAN READ IT FROM HERE

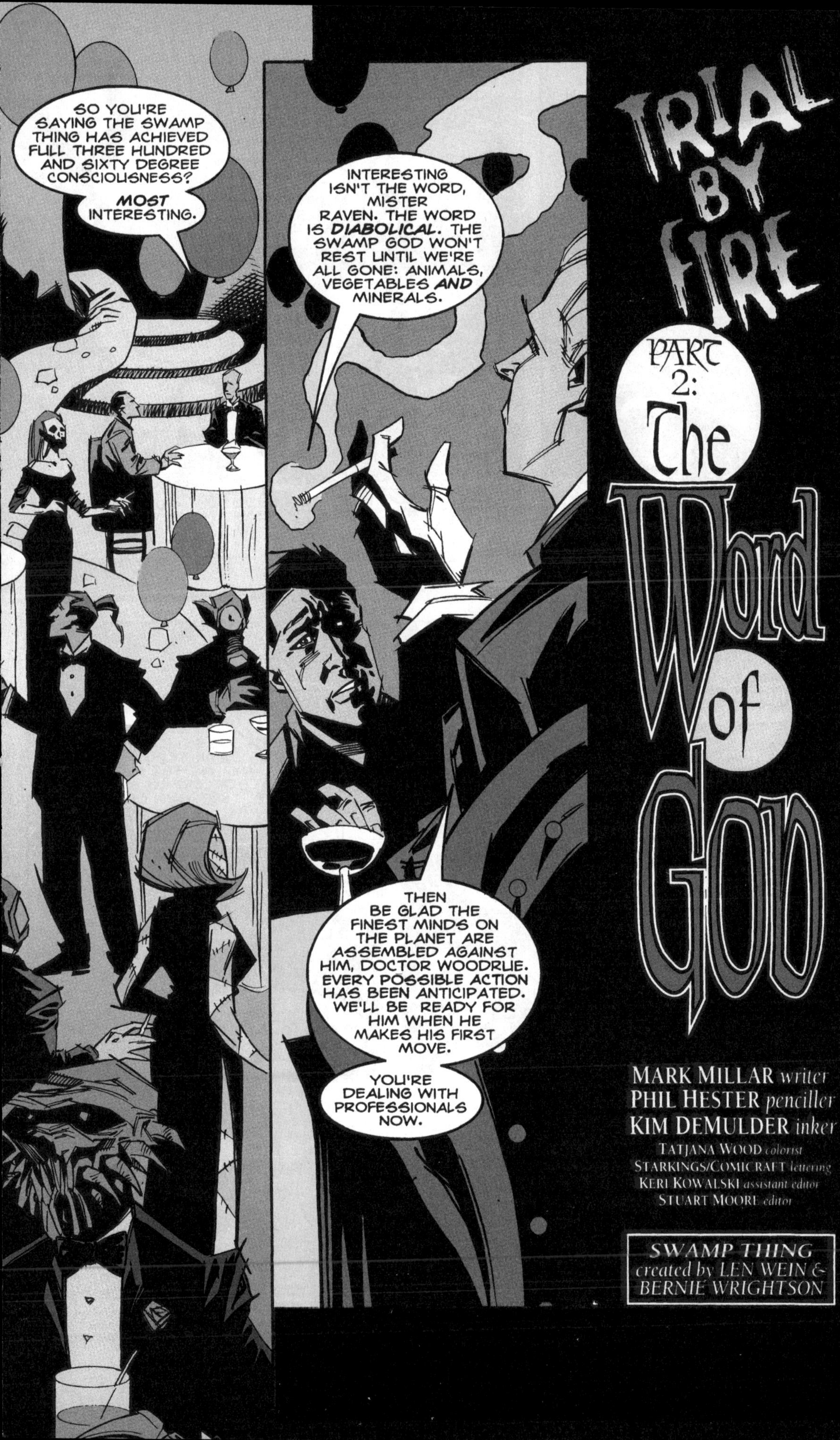
SO YOU'RE SAYING THE SWAMP THING HAS ACHIEVED FULL THREE HUNDRED AND SIXTY DEGREE CONSCIOUSNESS?
MOST INTERESTING.
INTERESTING ISN'T THE WORD, MISTER RAVEN. THE WORD IS DIABOLICAL. THE SWAMP GOD WON'T REST UNTIL WE'RE ALL GONE: ANIMALS, VEGETABLES AND MINERALS.
THEN BE GLAD THE FINEST MINDS ON THE PLANET ARE ASSEMBLED AGAINST HIM, DOCTOR WOODRUE. EVERY POSSIBLE ACTION HAS BEEN ANTICIPATED. WE'LL BE READY FOR HIM WHEN HE MAKES HIS FIRST MOVE.
YOU'RE DEALING WITH PROFESSIONALS NOW.
TRIAL BY FIRE
PART 2: The Word of God
MARK MILLAR writer
PHIL HESTER penciller
KIM DEMULDER inker
TATJANA WOOD colorist
STARKINGS/COMICRAFT lettering
KERI KOWALSKI assistant editor
STUART MOORE editor
SWAMP THING created by LEN WEIN & BERNIE WRIGHTSON

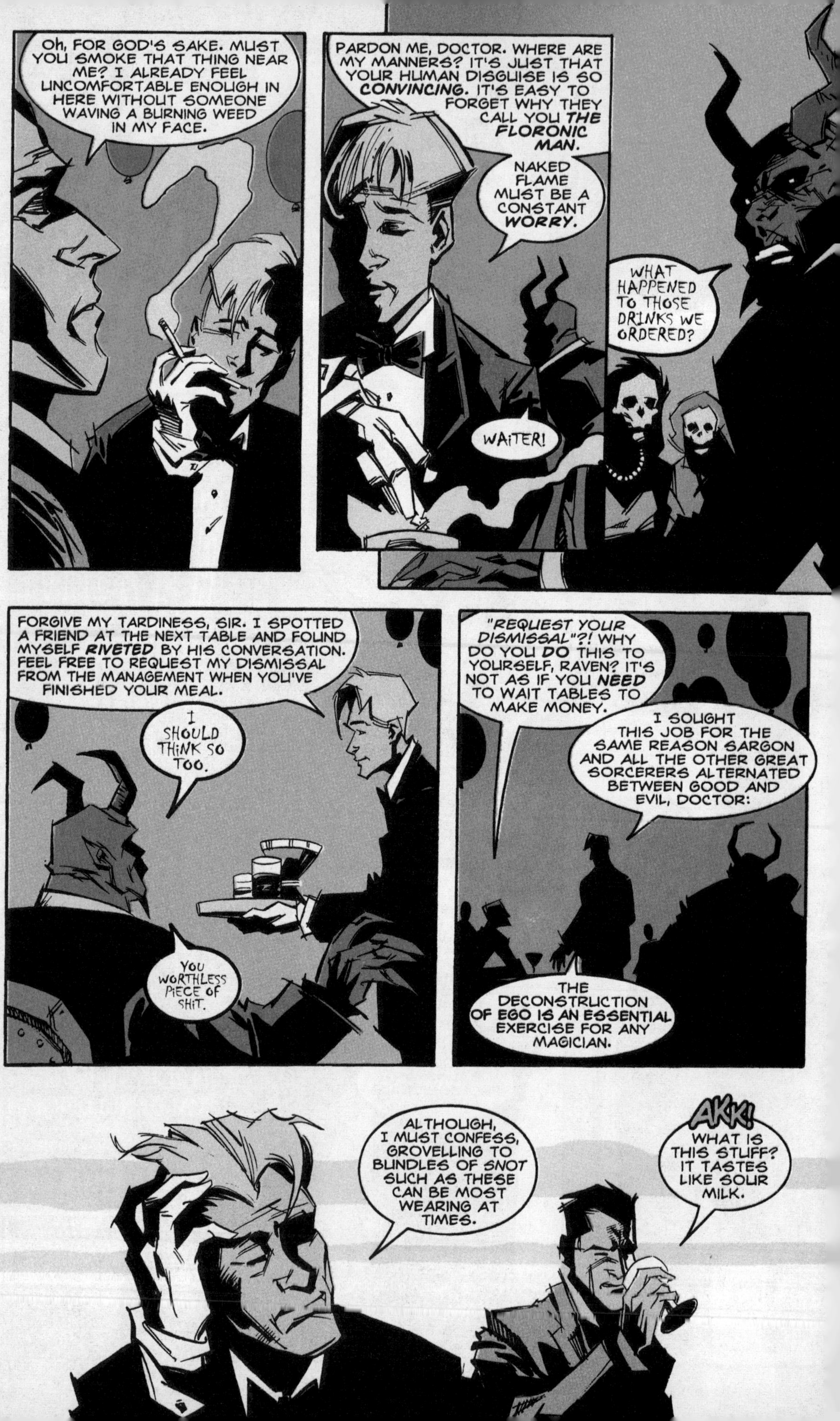
Oh, FOR GOD'S SAKE. MUST YOU SMOKE THAT THING NEAR ME? I ALREADY FEEL UNCOMFORTABLE ENOUGH IN HERE WITHOUT SOMEONE WAVING A BURNING WEED IN MY FACE.
PARDON ME, DOCTOR. WHERE ARE MY MANNERS? IT'S JUST THAT YOUR HUMAN DISGUISE IS SO CONVINCING. IT'S EASY TO FORGET WHY THEY CALL YOU THE FLORONIC MAN.
NAKED FLAME MUST BE A CONSTANT WORRY.
WAITER!
WHAT HAPPENED TO THOSE DRINKS WE ORDERED?
FORGIVE MY TARDINESS, SIR. I SPOTTED A FRIEND AT THE NEXT TABLE AND FOUND MYSELF RIVETED BY HIS CONVERSATION. FEEL FREE TO REQUEST MY DISMISSAL FROM THE MANAGEMENT WHEN YOU'VE FINISHED YOUR MEAL.
I SHOULD THINK SO TOO.
YOU WORTHLESS PIECE OF SHIT.
"REQUEST YOUR DISMISSAL"?! WHY DO YOU DO THIS TO YOURSELF, RAVEN? IT'S NOT AS IF YOU NEED TO WAIT TABLES TO MAKE MONEY.
I SOUGHT THIS JOB FOR THE SAME REASON SARGON AND ALL THE OTHER GREAT SORCERERS ALTERNATED BETWEEN GOOD AND EVIL, DOCTOR:
THE DECONSTRUCTION OF EGO IS AN ESSENTIAL EXERCISE FOR ANY MAGICIAN.
ALTHOUGH, I MUST CONFESS, GROVELLING TO BUNDLES OF SNOT SUCH AS THESE CAN BE MOST WEARING AT TIMES.
AKK!
WHAT IS THIS STUFF? IT TASTES LIKE SOUR MILK.

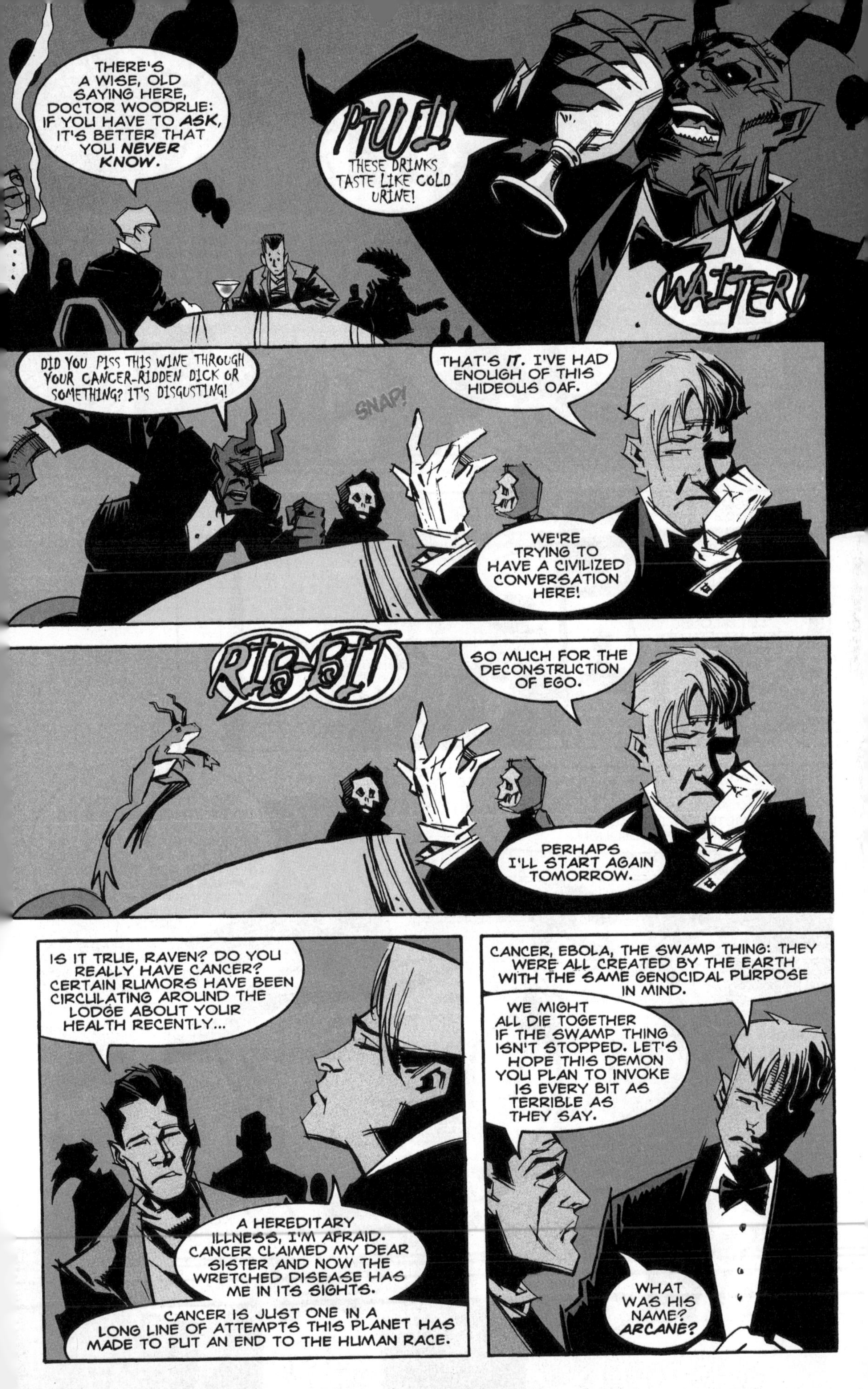
THERE'S A WISE, OLD SAYING HERE, DOCTOR WOODRUE: IF YOU HAVE TO ASK, IT'S BETTER THAT YOU NEVER KNOW.
PTUUI!
THESE DRINKS TASTE LIKE COLD URINE!
WAITER!
DID YOU PISS THIS WINE THROUGH YOUR CANCER-RIDDEN DICK OR SOMETHING? IT'S DISGUSTING!
SNAP!
THAT'S IT. I'VE HAD ENOUGH OF THIS HIDEOUS OAF.
WE'RE TRYING TO HAVE A CIVILIZED CONVERSATION HERE!
RIB-BIT
SO MUCH FOR THE DECONSTRUCTION OF EGO.
PERHAPS I'LL START AGAIN TOMORROW.
IS IT TRUE, RAVEN? DO YOU REALLY HAVE CANCER? CERTAIN RUMORS HAVE BEEN CIRCULATING AROUND THE LODGE ABOUT YOUR HEALTH RECENTLY...
A HEREDITARY ILLNESS, I'M AFRAID. CANCER CLAIMED MY DEAR SISTER AND NOW THE WRETCHED DISEASE HAS ME IN ITS SIGHTS.
CANCER IS JUST ONE IN A LONG LINE OF ATTEMPTS THIS PLANET HAS MADE TO PUT AN END TO THE HUMAN RACE.
CANCER, EBOLA, THE SWAMP THING: THEY WERE ALL CREATED BY THE EARTH WITH THE SAME GENOCIDAL PURPOSE IN MIND.
WE MIGHT ALL DIE TOGETHER IF THE SWAMP THING ISN'T STOPPED. LET'S HOPE THIS DEMON YOU PLAN TO INVOKE IS EVERY BIT AS TERRIBLE AS THEY SAY.
WHAT WAS HIS NAME? ARCANE?

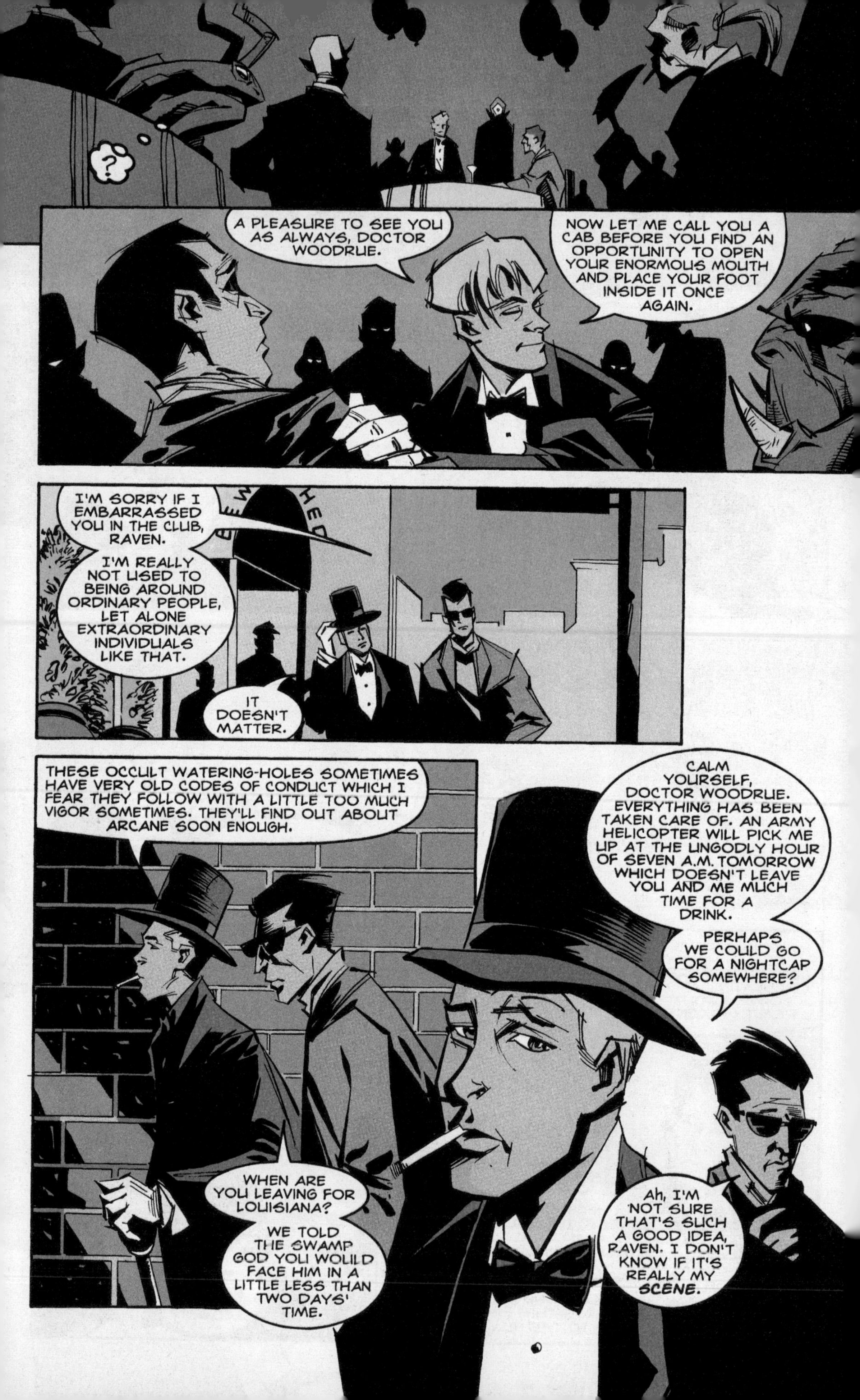
?
A PLEASURE TO SEE YOU AS ALWAYS, DOCTOR WOODRUE.
NOW LET ME CALL YOU A CAB BEFORE YOU FIND AN OPPORTUNITY TO OPEN YOUR ENORMOUS MOUTH AND PLACE YOUR FOOT INSIDE IT ONCE AGAIN.
I'M SORRY IF I EMBARRASSED YOU IN THE CLUB, RAVEN.
I'M REALLY NOT USED TO BEING AROUND ORDINARY PEOPLE, LET ALONE EXTRAORDINARY INDIVIDUALS LIKE THAT.
IT DOESN'T MATTER.
THESE OCCULT WATERING-HOLES SOMETIMES HAVE VERY OLD CODES OF CONDUCT WHICH I FEAR THEY FOLLOW WITH A LITTLE TOO MUCH VIGOR SOMETIMES. THEY'LL FIND OUT ABOUT ARCANE SOON ENOUGH.
WHEN ARE YOU LEAVING FOR LOUISIANA?
WE TOLD THE SWAMP GOD YOU WOULD FACE HIM IN A LITTLE LESS THAN TWO DAYS' TIME.
CALM YOURSELF, DOCTOR WOODRUE. EVERYTHING HAS BEEN TAKEN CARE OF. AN ARMY HELICOPTER WILL PICK ME UP AT THE UNGODLY HOUR OF SEVEN A.M. TOMORROW WHICH DOESN'T LEAVE YOU AND ME MUCH TIME FOR A DRINK.
PERHAPS WE COULD GO FOR A NIGHTCAP SOMEWHERE?
Ah, I'M NOT SURE THAT'S SUCH A GOOD IDEA, RAVEN. I DON'T KNOW IF IT'S REALLY MY *SCENE*.

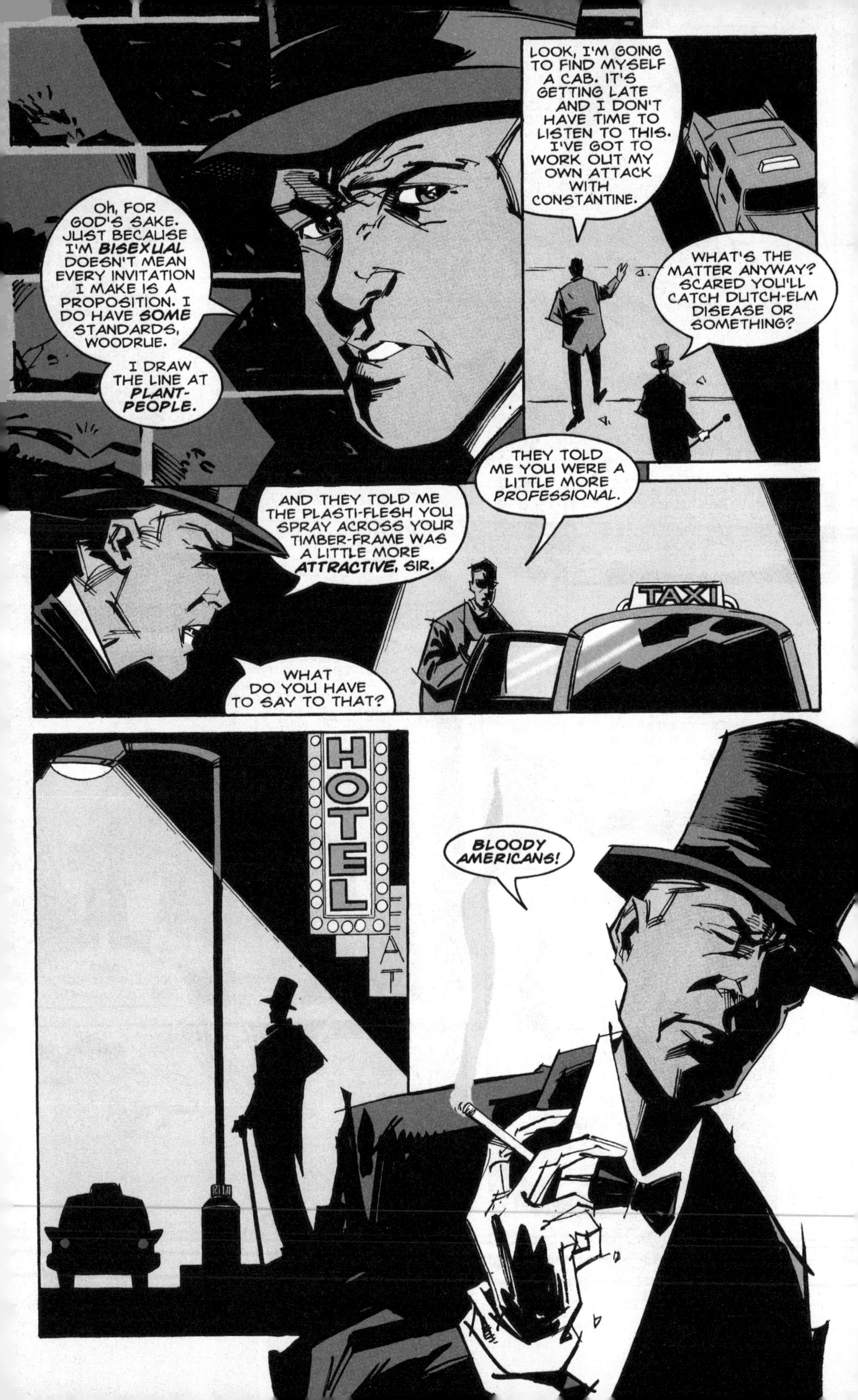
Oh, FOR GOD'S SAKE. JUST BECAUSE I'M BISEXUAL DOESN'T MEAN EVERY INVITATION I MAKE IS A PROPOSITION. I DO HAVE SOME STANDARDS, WOODRUE.
I DRAW THE LINE AT PLANT-PEOPLE.
LOOK, I'M GOING TO FIND MYSELF A CAB. IT'S GETTING LATE AND I DON'T HAVE TIME TO LISTEN TO THIS. I'VE GOT TO WORK OUT MY OWN ATTACK WITH CONSTANTINE.
WHAT'S THE MATTER ANYWAY? SCARED YOU'LL CATCH DUTCH-ELM DISEASE OR SOMETHING?
THEY TOLD ME YOU WERE A LITTLE MORE PROFESSIONAL.
AND THEY TOLD ME THE PLASTI-FLESH YOU SPRAY ACROSS YOUR TIMBER-FRAME WAS A LITTLE MORE ATTRACTIVE, SIR.
TAXI
WHAT DO YOU HAVE TO SAY TO THAT?
HOTEL
EAT
BLOODY AMERICANS!

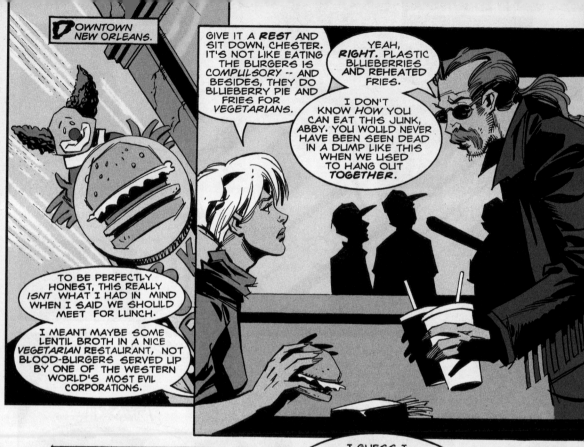

GIVE IT A *REST* AND SIT DOWN, CHESTER. IT'S NOT LIKE EATING THE BURGERS IS *COMPULSORY* -- AND BESIDES, THEY DO BLUEBERRY PIE AND FRIES FOR *VEGETARIANS*.

YEAH, *RIGHT.* PLASTIC BLUEBERRIES AND REHEATED FRIES.

I DON'T KNOW *HOW* YOU CAN EAT THIS JUNK, ABBY. YOU WOULD NEVER HAVE BEEN SEEN DEAD IN A DUMP LIKE THIS WHEN WE USED TO HANG OUT *TOGETHER.*

TO BE PERFECTLY HONEST, THIS REALLY *ISN'T* WHAT I HAD IN MIND WHEN I SAID WE SHOULD MEET FOR LUNCH.

I MEANT MAYBE SOME LENTIL BROTH IN A NICE *VEGETARIAN* RESTAURANT, NOT BLOOD-BURGERS SERVED UP BY ONE OF THE WESTERN WORLD'S MOST *EVIL* CORPORATIONS.

I *DUNNO,* I GUESS MAYBE THIS STUFF IS SORT OF FUN AFTER ALL THOSE YEARS OF HEALTHY EATING WITH ALEC IN THE SWAMPS. NOW IT'S LIKE I CAN'T GET ENOUGH CRAP TV OR SPECIAL SAUCE, Y'KNOW?

IT'S PLAYING HAVOC WITH MY WAISTLINE.

I GUESS I *COULD* COMPROMISE MY PRINCIPLES AND SIT HERE FOR A LITTLE WHILE, RIGHT? IT'S NOT EVERY DAY AN OLD FRIEND CALLS ME UP AT SCHOOL AND ASKS FOR HELP.

AND YOU STILL LOOK FINE TO ME, ABBY.

THANKS FOR COMING, CHESTER. I *MEAN* IT.

IT'S TIMES LIKE THIS YOU REALIZE HOW FEW PEOPLE IN LIFE YOU CAN DEPEND ON WHEN THE WEIRD SHIT REALLY HITS THE FAN.

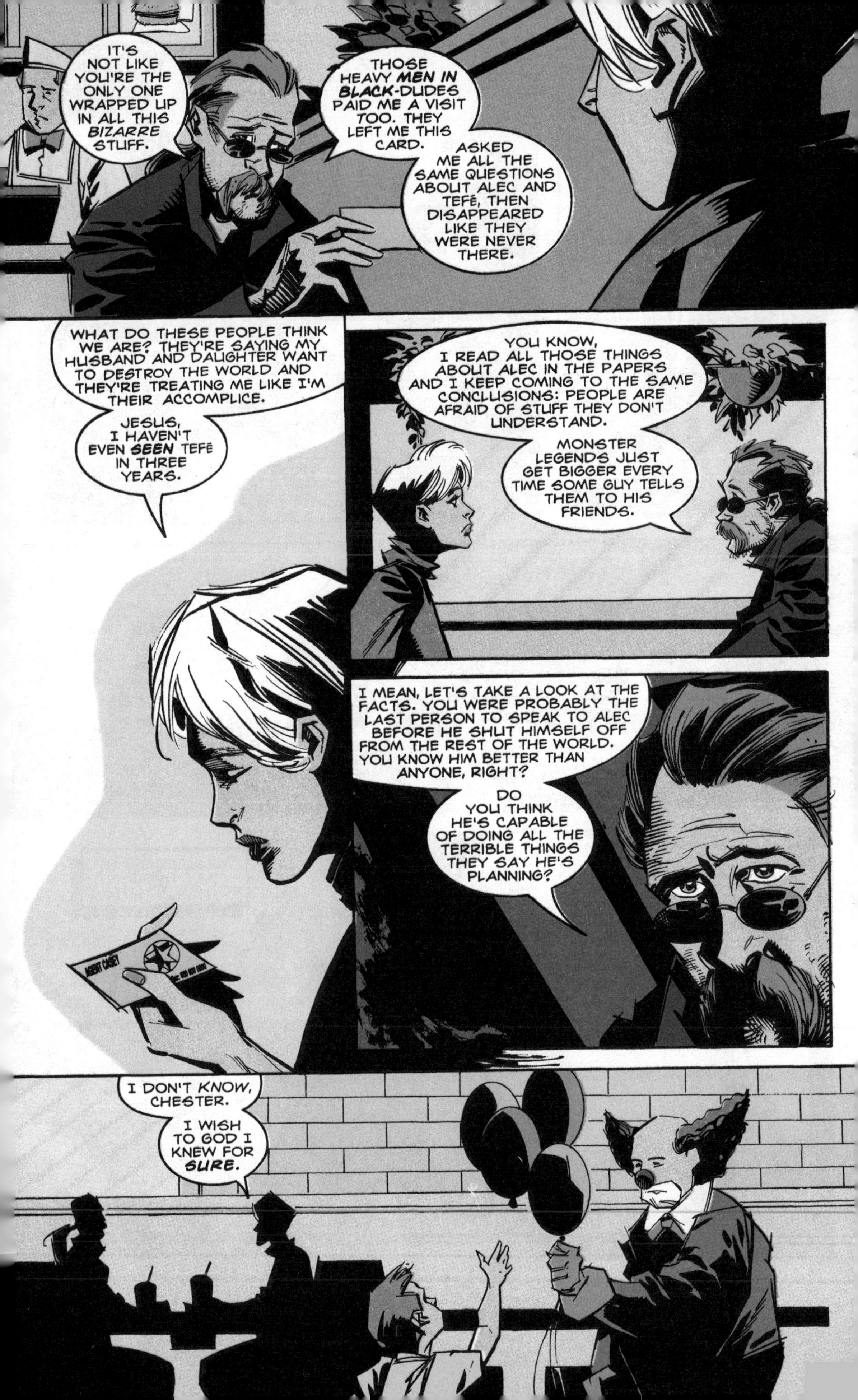
IT'S NOT LIKE YOU'RE THE ONLY ONE WRAPPED UP IN ALL THIS *BIZARRE* STUFF.
THOSE HEAVY ***MEN IN BLACK***-DUDES PAID ME A VISIT *TOO*. THEY LEFT ME THIS CARD.
ASKED ME ALL THE SAME QUESTIONS ABOUT ALEC AND TEFÉ, THEN DISAPPEARED LIKE THEY WERE NEVER THERE.
WHAT DO THESE PEOPLE THINK WE ARE? THEY'RE SAYING MY HUSBAND AND DAUGHTER WANT TO DESTROY THE WORLD AND THEY'RE TREATING ME LIKE I'M THEIR ACCOMPLICE.
JESUS, I HAVEN'T EVEN ***SEEN*** TEFÉ IN THREE YEARS.
YOU KNOW, I READ ALL THOSE THINGS ABOUT ALEC IN THE PAPERS AND I KEEP COMING TO THE SAME CONCLUSIONS: PEOPLE ARE AFRAID OF STUFF THEY DON'T UNDERSTAND.
MONSTER LEGENDS JUST GET BIGGER EVERY TIME SOME GUY TELLS THEM TO HIS FRIENDS.
AGENT CASEY
I MEAN, LET'S TAKE A LOOK AT THE FACTS. YOU WERE PROBABLY THE LAST PERSON TO SPEAK TO ALEC BEFORE HE SHUT HIMSELF OFF FROM THE REST OF THE WORLD. YOU KNOW HIM BETTER THAN ANYONE, RIGHT?
DO YOU THINK HE'S CAPABLE OF DOING ALL THE TERRIBLE THINGS THEY SAY HE'S PLANNING?
I DON'T *KNOW*, CHESTER.
I WISH TO GOD I KNEW FOR ***SURE***.

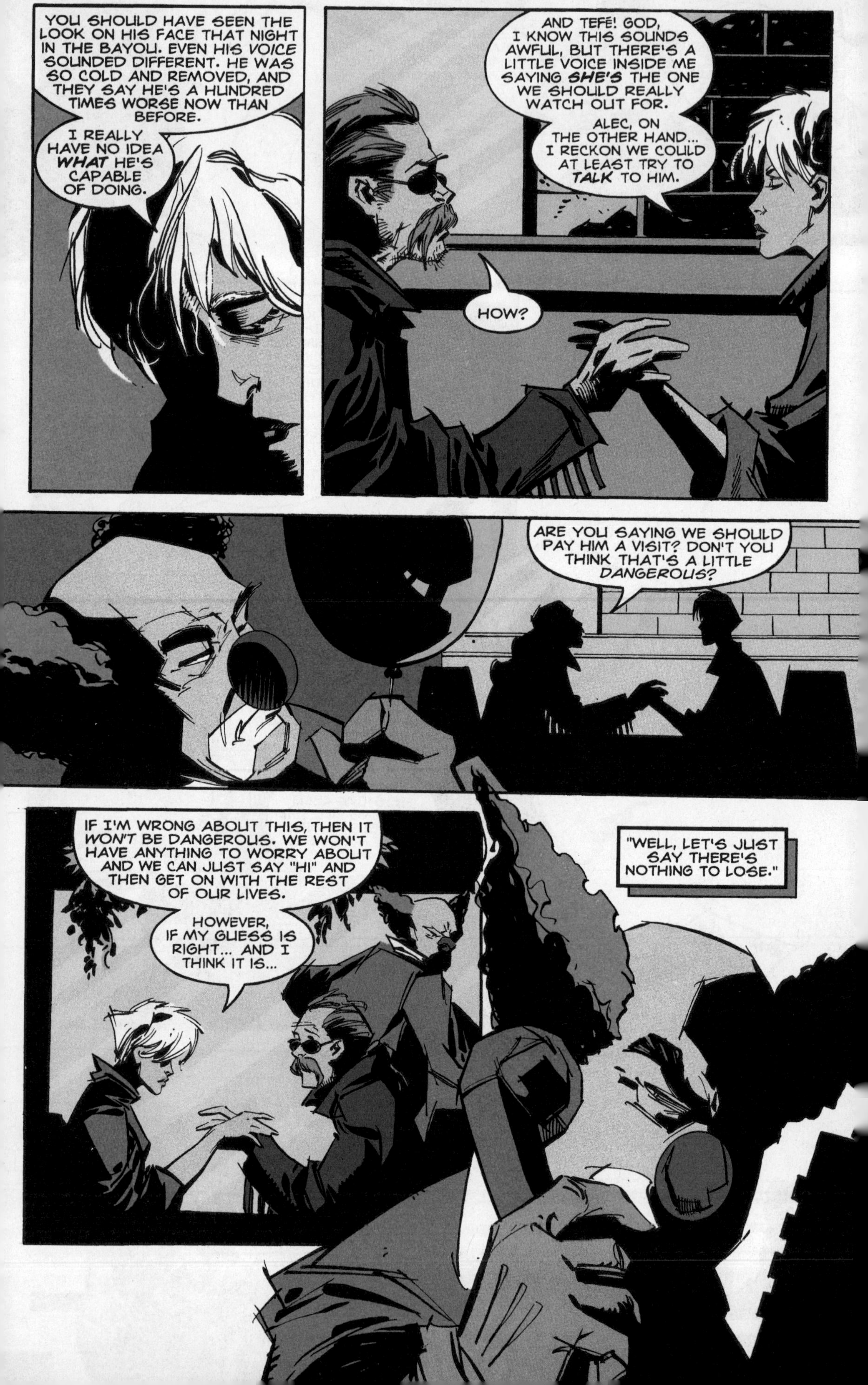
YOU SHOULD HAVE SEEN THE LOOK ON HIS FACE THAT NIGHT IN THE BAYOU. EVEN HIS *VOICE* SOUNDED DIFFERENT. HE WAS SO COLD AND REMOVED, AND THEY SAY HE'S A HUNDRED TIMES WORSE NOW THAN BEFORE.
I REALLY HAVE NO IDEA ***WHAT*** HE'S CAPABLE OF DOING.
AND TEFÉ! GOD, I KNOW THIS SOUNDS AWFUL, BUT THERE'S A LITTLE VOICE INSIDE ME SAYING ***SHE'S*** THE ONE WE SHOULD REALLY WATCH OUT FOR.
ALEC, ON THE OTHER HAND... I RECKON WE COULD AT LEAST TRY TO ***TALK*** TO HIM.
HOW?
ARE YOU SAYING WE SHOULD PAY HIM A VISIT? DON'T YOU THINK THAT'S A LITTLE *DANGEROUS*?
IF I'M WRONG ABOUT THIS, THEN IT *WON'T* BE DANGEROUS. WE WON'T HAVE ANYTHING TO WORRY ABOUT AND WE CAN JUST SAY "HI" AND THEN GET ON WITH THE REST OF OUR LIVES.
HOWEVER, IF MY GUESS IS RIGHT... AND I THINK IT IS...
"WELL, LET'S JUST SAY THERE'S NOTHING TO LOSE."

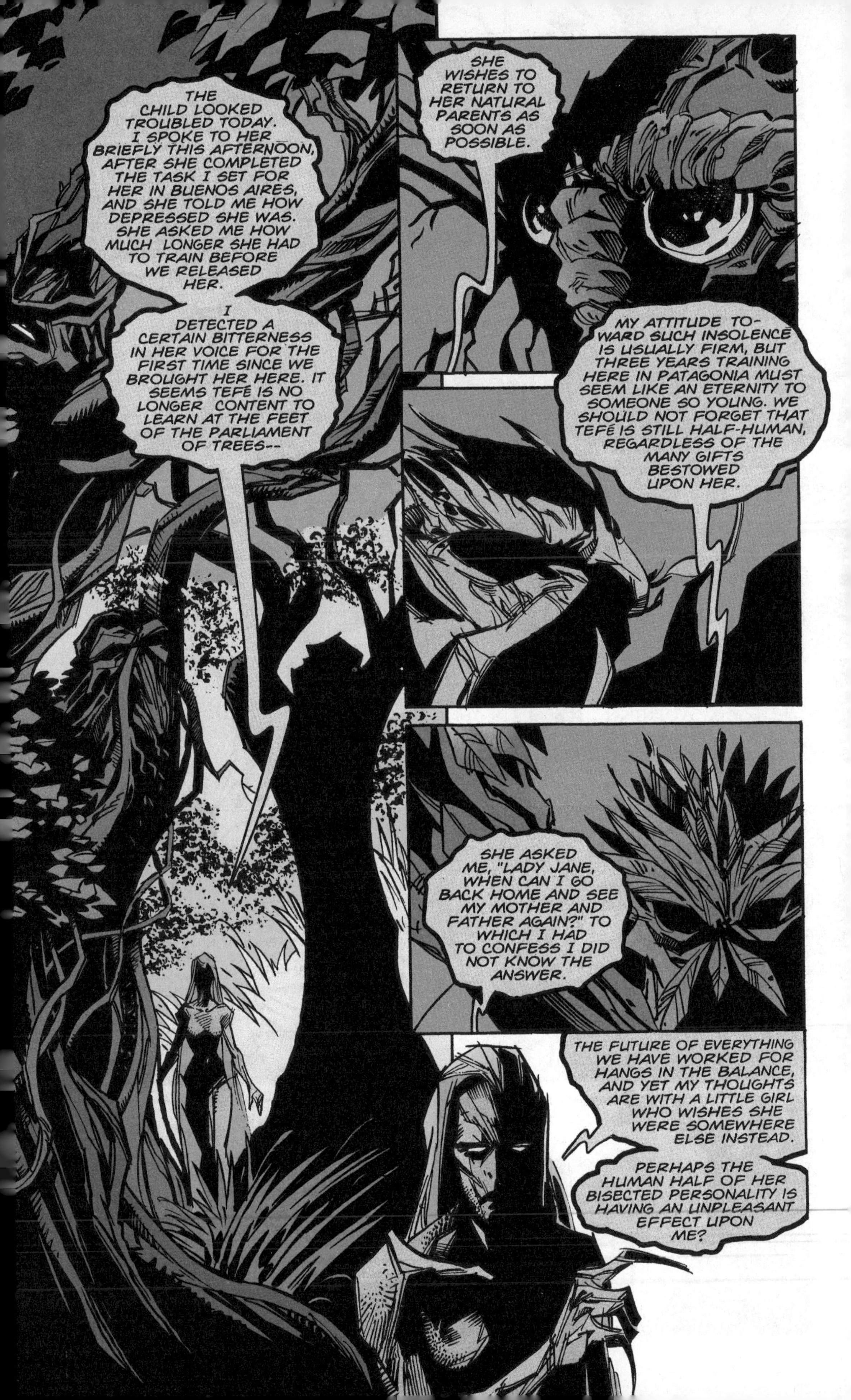
THE CHILD LOOKED TROUBLED TODAY. I SPOKE TO HER BRIEFLY THIS AFTERNOON, AFTER SHE COMPLETED THE TASK I SET FOR HER IN BUENOS AIRES, AND SHE TOLD ME HOW DEPRESSED SHE WAS. SHE ASKED ME HOW MUCH LONGER SHE HAD TO TRAIN BEFORE WE RELEASED HER.
I DETECTED A CERTAIN BITTERNESS IN HER VOICE FOR THE FIRST TIME SINCE WE BROUGHT HER HERE. IT SEEMS TEFÉ IS NO LONGER CONTENT TO LEARN AT THE FEET OF THE PARLIAMENT OF TREES--
SHE WISHES TO RETURN TO HER NATURAL PARENTS AS SOON AS POSSIBLE.
MY ATTITUDE TOWARD SUCH INSOLENCE IS USUALLY FIRM, BUT THREE YEARS TRAINING HERE IN PATAGONIA MUST SEEM LIKE AN ETERNITY TO SOMEONE SO YOUNG. WE SHOULD NOT FORGET THAT TEFÉ IS STILL HALF-HUMAN, REGARDLESS OF THE MANY GIFTS BESTOWED UPON HER.
SHE ASKED ME, "LADY JANE, WHEN CAN I GO BACK HOME AND SEE MY MOTHER AND FATHER AGAIN?" TO WHICH I HAD TO CONFESS I DID NOT KNOW THE ANSWER.
THE FUTURE OF EVERYTHING WE HAVE WORKED FOR HANGS IN THE BALANCE, AND YET MY THOUGHTS ARE WITH A LITTLE GIRL WHO WISHES SHE WERE SOMEWHERE ELSE INSTEAD.
PERHAPS THE HUMAN HALF OF HER BISECTED PERSONALITY IS HAVING AN UNPLEASANT EFFECT UPON ME?

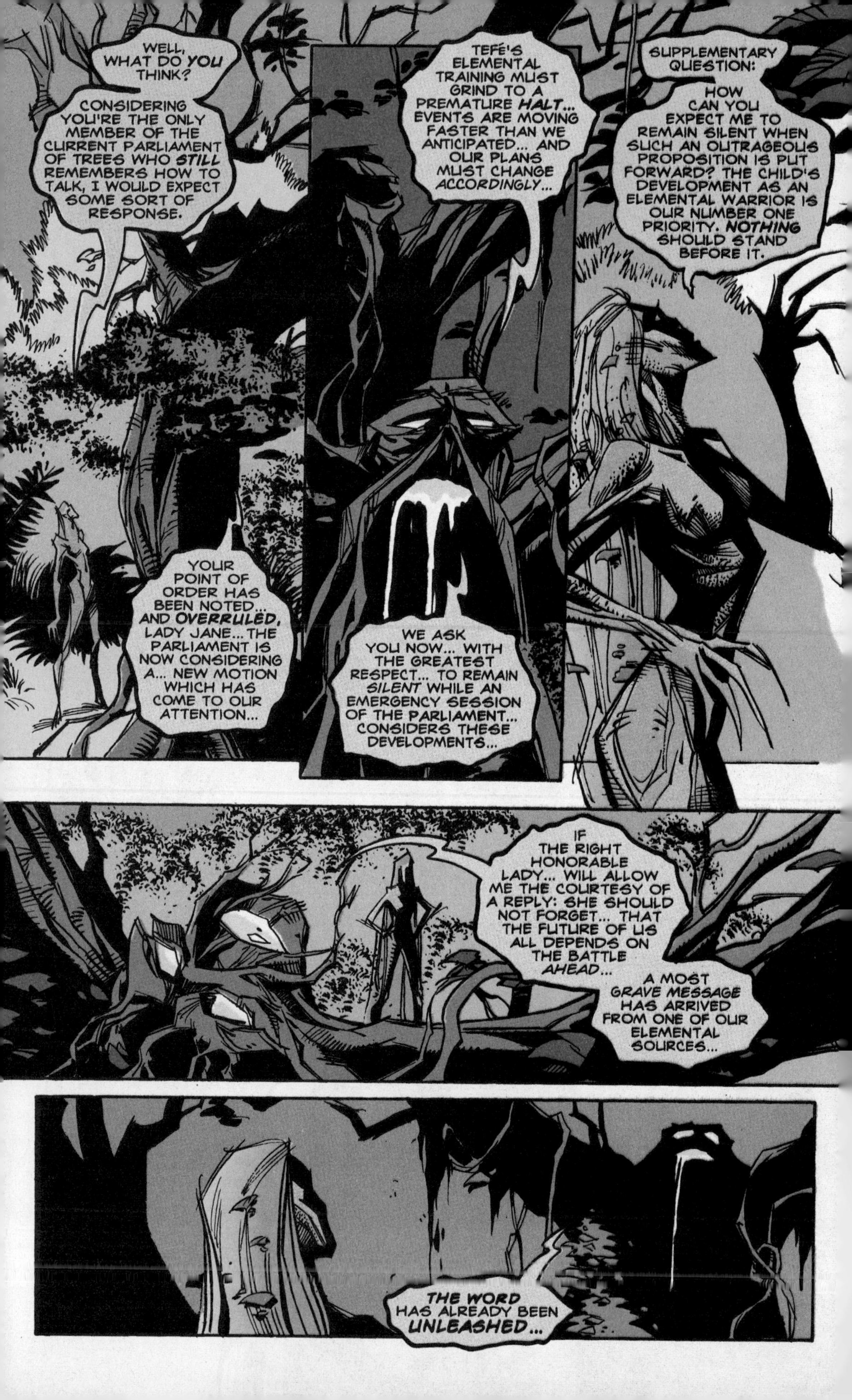

WELL, WHAT DO *YOU* THINK?
CONSIDERING YOU'RE THE ONLY MEMBER OF THE CURRENT PARLIAMENT OF TREES WHO *STILL* REMEMBERS HOW TO TALK, I WOULD EXPECT SOME SORT OF RESPONSE.
TEFÉ'S ELEMENTAL TRAINING MUST GRIND TO A PREMATURE *HALT*... EVENTS ARE MOVING FASTER THAN WE ANTICIPATED... AND OUR PLANS MUST CHANGE *ACCORDINGLY*...
WE ASK YOU NOW... WITH THE GREATEST RESPECT... TO REMAIN *SILENT* WHILE AN EMERGENCY SESSION OF THE PARLIAMENT... CONSIDERS THESE DEVELOPMENTS...
SUPPLEMENTARY QUESTION:
HOW CAN YOU EXPECT ME TO REMAIN SILENT WHEN SUCH AN OUTRAGEOUS PROPOSITION IS PUT FORWARD? THE CHILD'S DEVELOPMENT AS AN ELEMENTAL WARRIOR IS OUR NUMBER ONE PRIORITY. ***NOTHING*** SHOULD STAND BEFORE IT.
YOUR POINT OF ORDER HAS BEEN NOTED... AND ***OVERRULED,*** LADY JANE... THE PARLIAMENT IS NOW CONSIDERING A... NEW MOTION WHICH HAS COME TO OUR ATTENTION...
IF THE RIGHT HONORABLE LADY... WILL ALLOW ME THE COURTESY OF A REPLY: SHE SHOULD NOT FORGET... THAT THE FUTURE OF US ALL DEPENDS ON THE BATTLE *AHEAD*...
A MOST *GRAVE MESSAGE* HAS ARRIVED FROM ONE OF OUR ELEMENTAL SOURCES...
THE WORD HAS ALREADY BEEN ***UNLEASHED...***

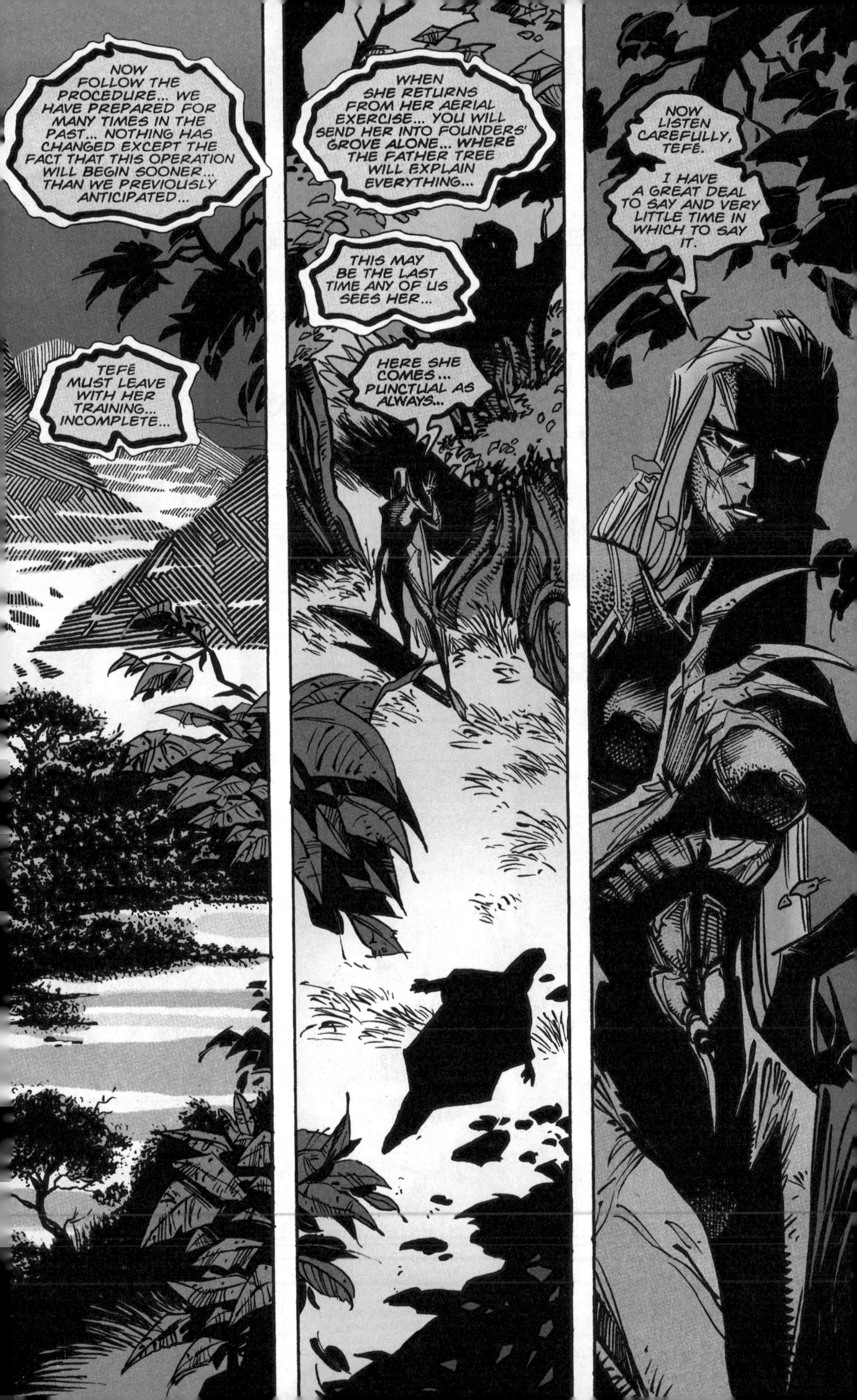
NOW FOLLOW THE PROCEDURE... WE HAVE PREPARED FOR MANY TIMES IN THE PAST... NOTHING HAS CHANGED EXCEPT THE FACT THAT THIS OPERATION WILL BEGIN SOONER... THAN WE PREVIOUSLY ANTICIPATED...
TEFÉ MUST LEAVE WITH HER TRAINING... INCOMPLETE...
WHEN SHE RETURNS FROM HER AERIAL EXERCISE... YOU WILL SEND HER INTO FOUNDERS' GROVE ALONE... WHERE THE FATHER TREE WILL EXPLAIN EVERYTHING...
THIS MAY BE THE LAST TIME ANY OF US SEES HER...
HERE SHE COMES... PUNCTUAL AS ALWAYS...
NOW LISTEN CAREFULLY, TEFÉ.
I HAVE A GREAT DEAL TO SAY AND VERY LITTLE TIME IN WHICH TO SAY IT.

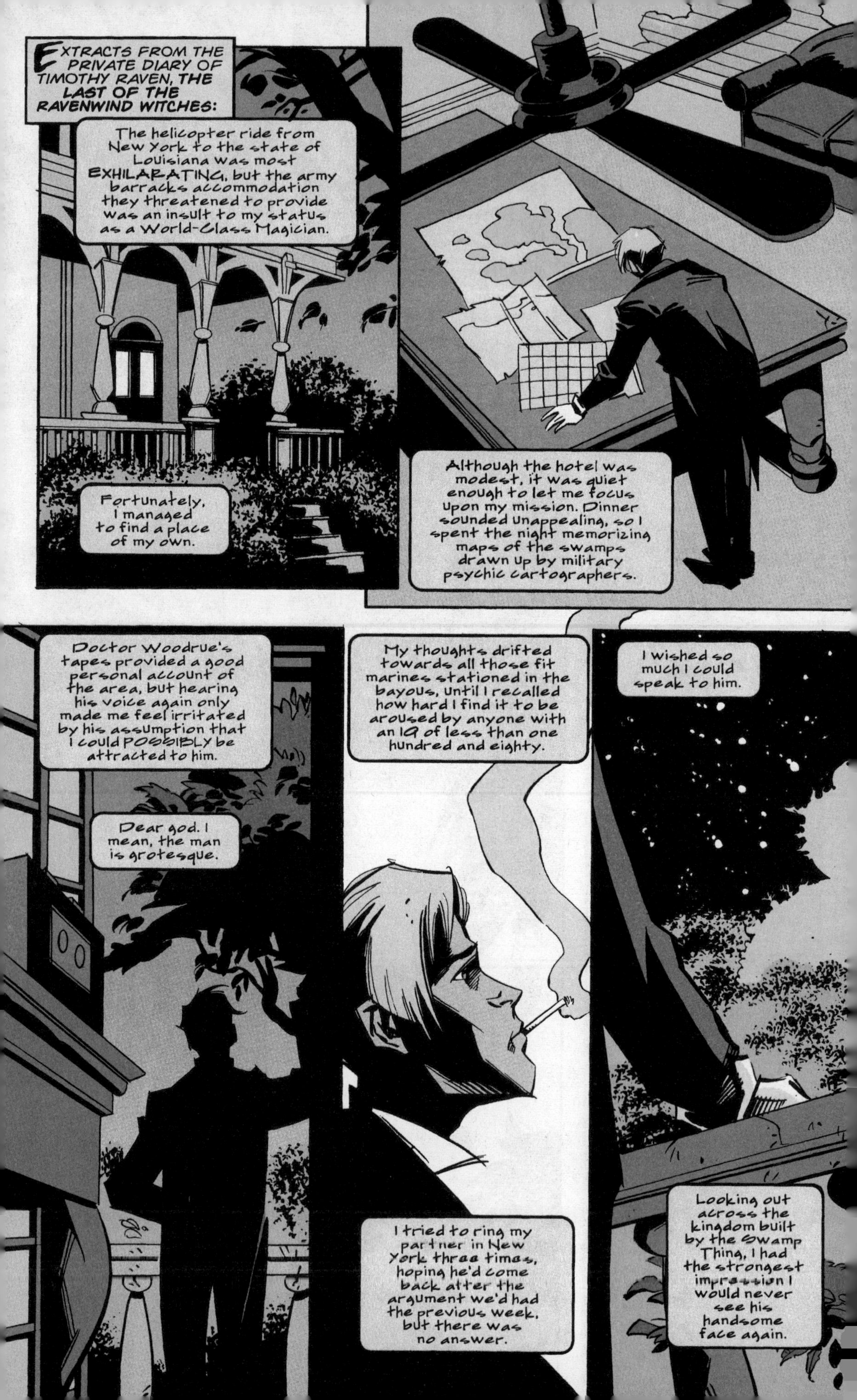
EXTRACTS FROM THE PRIVATE DIARY OF TIMOTHY RAVEN, THE LAST OF THE RAVENWIND WITCHES:
The helicopter ride from New York to the state of Louisiana was most EXHILARATING, but the army barracks accommodation they threatened to provide was an insult to my status as a World-Class Magician.
Fortunately, I managed to find a place of my own.
Although the hotel was modest, it was quiet enough to let me focus upon my mission. Dinner sounded unappealing, so I spent the night memorizing maps of the swamps drawn up by military psychic cartographers.
Doctor Woodrue's tapes provided a good personal account of the area, but hearing his voice again only made me feel irritated by his assumption that I could POSSIBLY be attracted to him.
Dear god. I mean, the man is grotesque.
My thoughts drifted towards all those fit marines stationed in the bayous, until I recalled how hard I find it to be aroused by anyone with an IQ of less than one hundred and eighty.
I tried to ring my partner in New York three times, hoping he'd come back after the argument we'd had the previous week, but there was no answer.
I wished so much I could speak to him.
Looking out across the kingdom built by the Swamp Thing, I had the strongest impression I would never see his handsome face again.

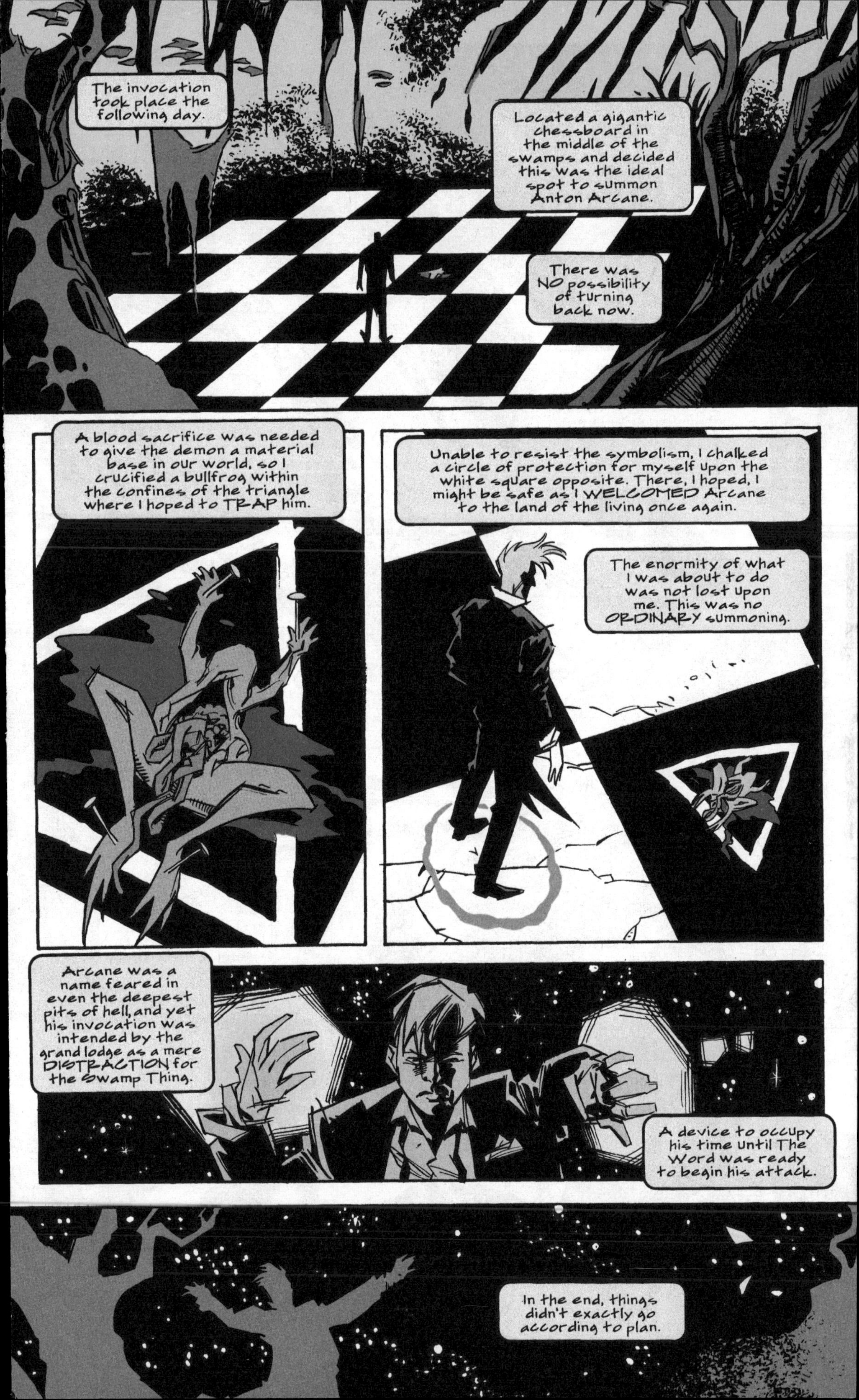

The invocation took place the following day.
Located a gigantic chessboard in the middle of the swamps and decided this was the ideal spot to summon Anton Arcane.
There was NO possibility of turning back now.
A blood sacrifice was needed to give the demon a material base in our world, so I crucified a bullfrog within the confines of the triangle where I hoped to TRAP him.
Unable to resist the symbolism, I chalked a circle of protection for myself upon the white square opposite. There, I hoped, I might be safe as I WELCOMED Arcane to the land of the living once again.
The enormity of what I was about to do was not lost upon me. This was no ORDINARY summoning.
Arcane was a name feared in even the deepest pits of hell, and yet his invocation was intended by the grand lodge as a mere DISTRACTION for the Swamp Thing.
A device to occupy his time until The Word was ready to begin his attack.
In the end, things didn't exactly go according to plan.

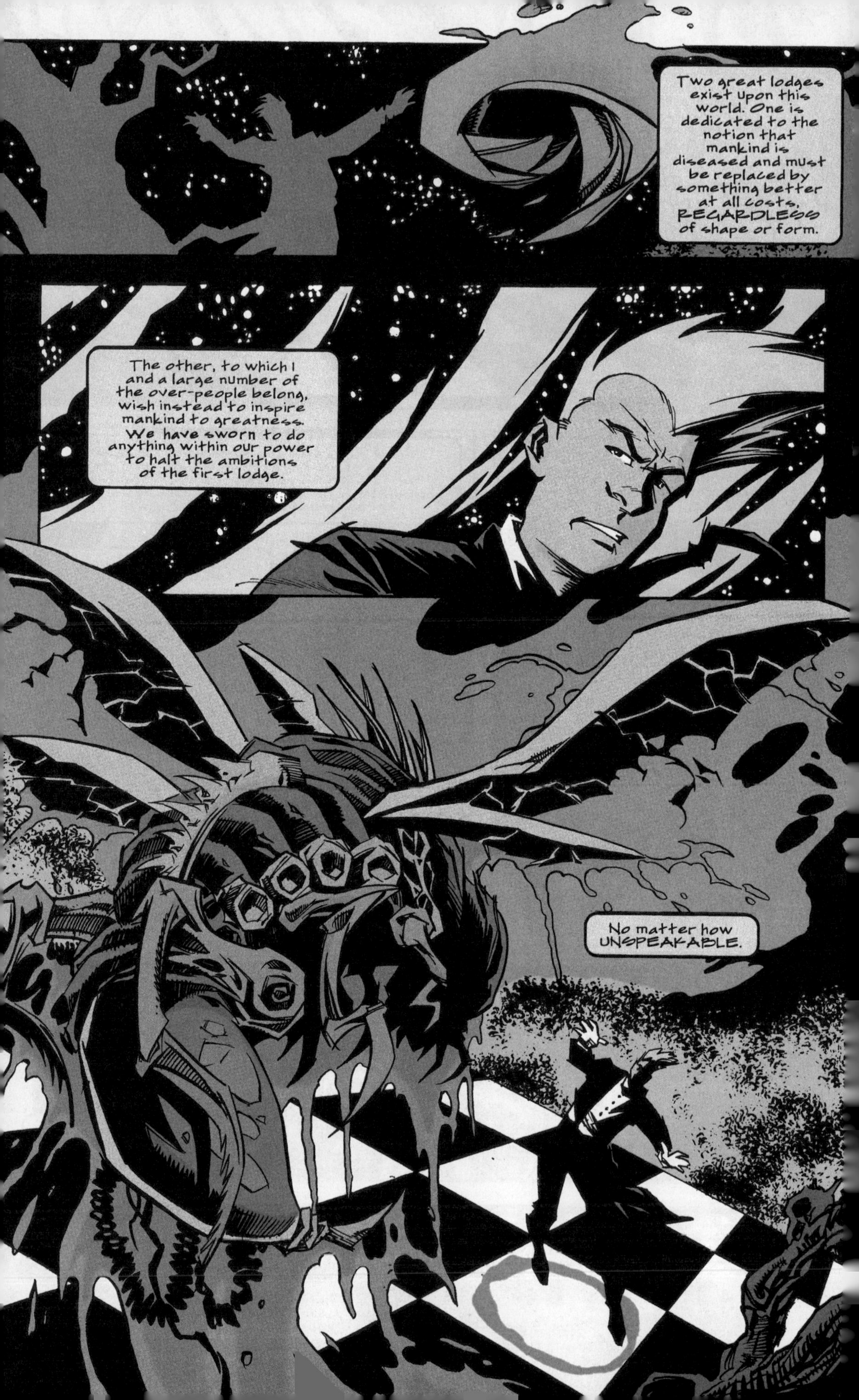
Two great lodges exist upon this world. One is dedicated to the notion that mankind is diseased and must be replaced by something better at all costs, REGARDLESS of shape or form.
The other, to which I and a large number of the over-people belong, wish instead to inspire mankind to greatness. We have sworn to do anything within our power to halt the ambitions of the first lodge.
No matter how UNSPEAKABLE.

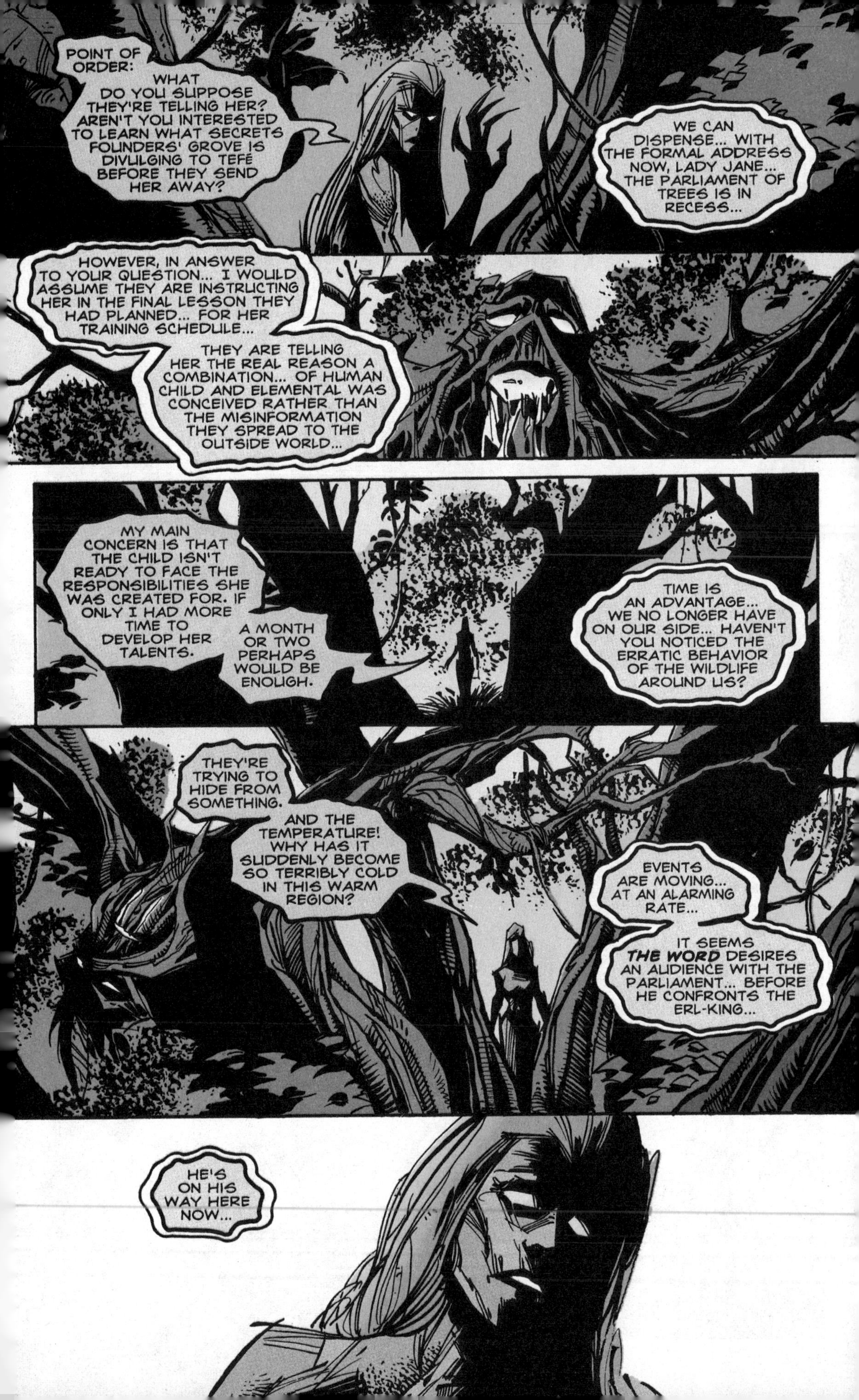
POINT OF ORDER: WHAT DO YOU SUPPOSE THEY'RE TELLING HER? AREN'T YOU INTERESTED TO LEARN WHAT SECRETS FOUNDERS' GROVE IS DIVULGING TO TEFÉ BEFORE THEY SEND HER AWAY?
WE CAN DISPENSE... WITH THE FORMAL ADDRESS NOW, LADY JANE... THE PARLIAMENT OF TREES IS IN RECESS...
HOWEVER, IN ANSWER TO YOUR QUESTION... I WOULD ASSUME THEY ARE INSTRUCTING HER IN THE FINAL LESSON THEY HAD PLANNED... FOR HER TRAINING SCHEDULE...
THEY ARE TELLING HER THE REAL REASON A COMBINATION... OF HUMAN CHILD AND ELEMENTAL WAS CONCEIVED RATHER THAN THE MISINFORMATION THEY SPREAD TO THE OUTSIDE WORLD...
MY MAIN CONCERN IS THAT THE CHILD ISN'T READY TO FACE THE RESPONSIBILITIES SHE WAS CREATED FOR. IF ONLY I HAD MORE TIME TO DEVELOP HER TALENTS.
A MONTH OR TWO PERHAPS WOULD BE ENOUGH.
TIME IS AN ADVANTAGE... WE NO LONGER HAVE ON OUR SIDE... HAVEN'T YOU NOTICED THE ERRATIC BEHAVIOR OF THE WILDLIFE AROUND US?
THEY'RE TRYING TO HIDE FROM SOMETHING.
AND THE TEMPERATURE! WHY HAS IT SUDDENLY BECOME SO TERRIBLY COLD IN THIS WARM REGION?
EVENTS ARE MOVING... AT AN ALARMING RATE...
IT SEEMS **THE WORD** DESIRES AN AUDIENCE WITH THE PARLIAMENT... BEFORE HE CONFRONTS THE ERL-KING...
HE'S ON HIS WAY HERE NOW...

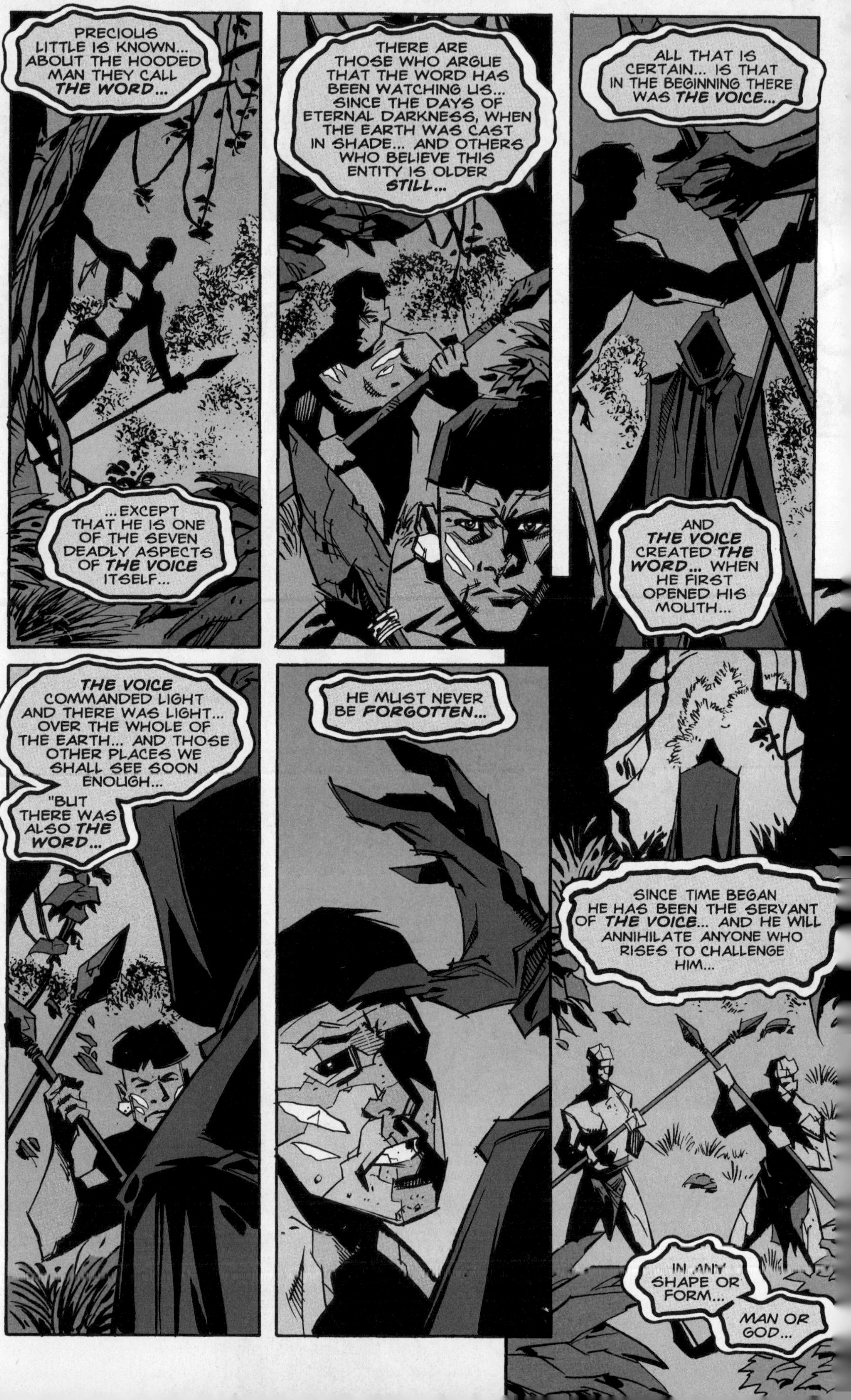
PRECIOUS LITTLE IS KNOWN... ABOUT THE HOODED MAN THEY CALL THE WORD...
...EXCEPT THAT HE IS ONE OF THE SEVEN DEADLY ASPECTS OF THE VOICE ITSELF...
THERE ARE THOSE WHO ARGUE THAT THE WORD HAS BEEN WATCHING US... SINCE THE DAYS OF ETERNAL DARKNESS, WHEN THE EARTH WAS CAST IN SHADE... AND OTHERS WHO BELIEVE THIS ENTITY IS OLDER STILL...
ALL THAT IS CERTAIN... IS THAT IN THE BEGINNING THERE WAS THE VOICE...
AND THE VOICE CREATED THE WORD... WHEN HE FIRST OPENED HIS MOUTH...
THE VOICE COMMANDED LIGHT AND THERE WAS LIGHT... OVER THE WHOLE OF THE EARTH... AND THOSE OTHER PLACES WE SHALL SEE SOON ENOUGH...
"BUT THERE WAS ALSO THE WORD...
HE MUST NEVER BE FORGOTTEN...
SINCE TIME BEGAN HE HAS BEEN THE SERVANT OF THE VOICE... AND HE WILL ANNIHILATE ANYONE WHO RISES TO CHALLENGE HIM...
IN ANY SHAPE OR FORM...
MAN OR GOD...

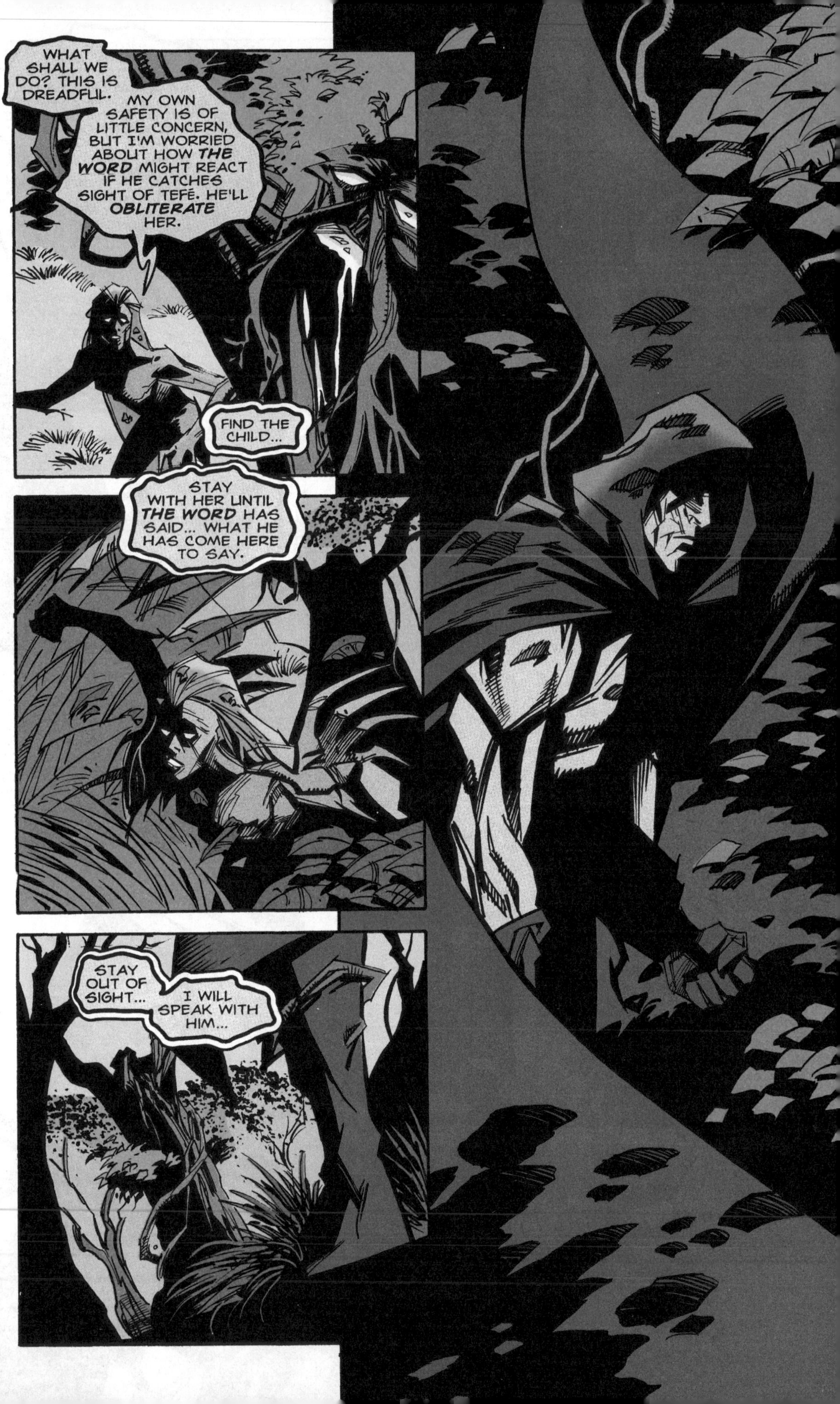

WHAT SHALL WE DO? THIS IS DREADFUL.
MY OWN SAFETY IS OF LITTLE CONCERN, BUT I'M WORRIED ABOUT HOW **THE WORD** MIGHT REACT IF HE CATCHES SIGHT OF TEFÉ. HE'LL ***OBLITERATE*** HER.
FIND THE CHILD...
STAY WITH HER UNTIL **THE WORD** HAS SAID... WHAT HE HAS COME HERE TO SAY.
STAY OUT OF SIGHT...
I WILL SPEAK WITH HIM...

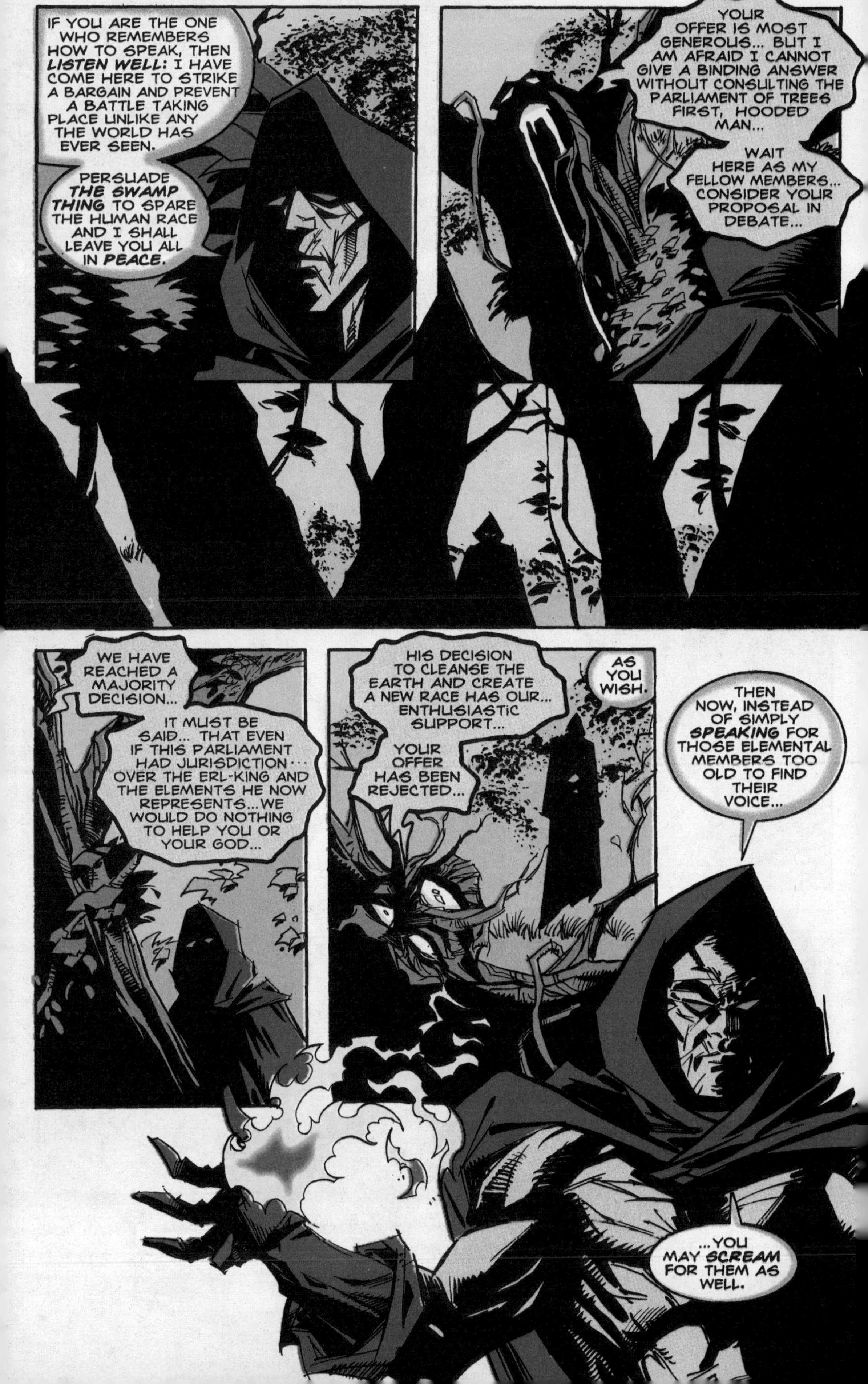
IF YOU ARE THE ONE WHO REMEMBERS HOW TO SPEAK, THEN **LISTEN WELL:** I HAVE COME HERE TO STRIKE A BARGAIN AND PREVENT A BATTLE TAKING PLACE UNLIKE ANY THE WORLD HAS EVER SEEN.
PERSUADE **THE SWAMP THING** TO SPARE THE HUMAN RACE AND I SHALL LEAVE YOU ALL IN **PEACE.**
YOUR OFFER IS MOST GENEROUS... BUT I AM AFRAID I CANNOT GIVE A BINDING ANSWER WITHOUT CONSULTING THE PARLIAMENT OF TREES FIRST, HOODED MAN...
WAIT HERE AS MY FELLOW MEMBERS... CONSIDER YOUR PROPOSAL IN DEBATE...
WE HAVE REACHED A MAJORITY DECISION...
IT MUST BE SAID... THAT EVEN IF THIS PARLIAMENT HAD JURISDICTION... OVER THE ERL-KING AND THE ELEMENTS HE NOW REPRESENTS... WE WOULD DO NOTHING TO HELP YOU OR YOUR GOD...
HIS DECISION TO CLEANSE THE EARTH AND CREATE A NEW RACE HAS OUR... ENTHUSIASTIC SUPPORT...
YOUR OFFER HAS BEEN REJECTED...
AS YOU WISH.
THEN NOW, INSTEAD OF SIMPLY **SPEAKING** FOR THOSE ELEMENTAL MEMBERS TOO OLD TO FIND THEIR VOICE...
...YOU MAY **SCREAM** FOR THEM AS WELL.

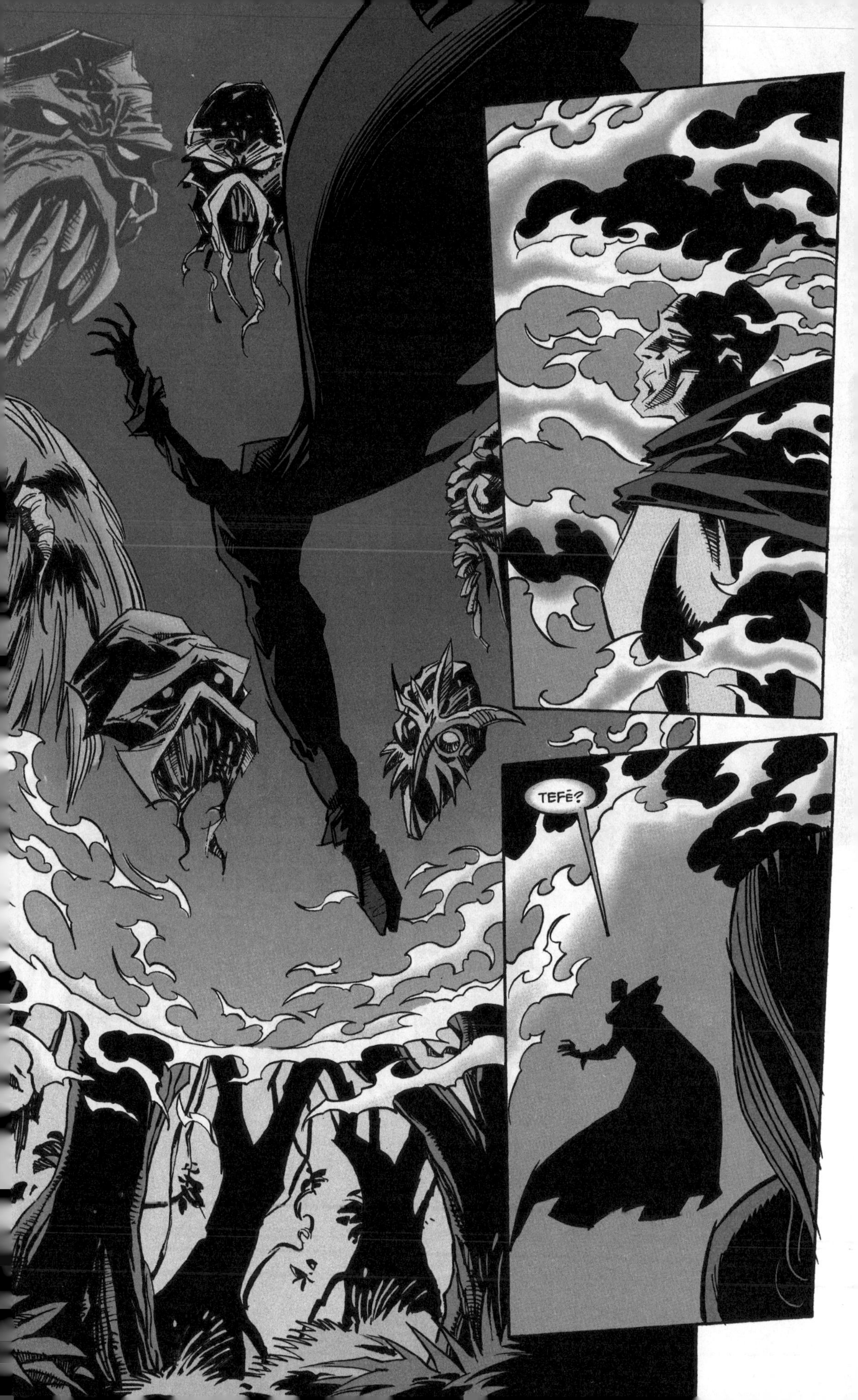
TEFÉ?

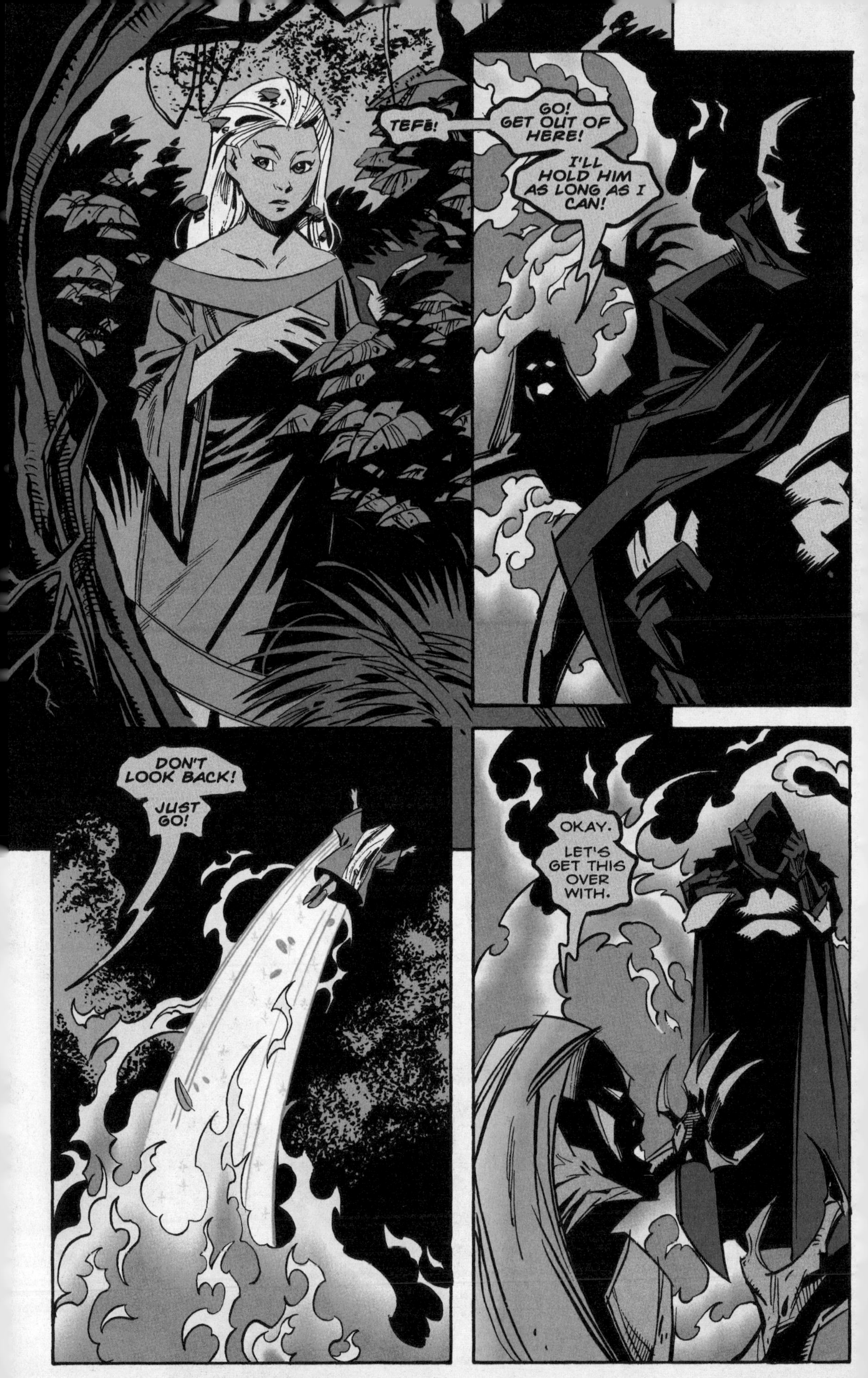
TEFÉ!
GO! GET OUT OF HERE!
I'LL HOLD HIM AS LONG AS I CAN!
DON'T LOOK BACK!
JUST GO!
OKAY.
LET'S GET THIS OVER WITH.

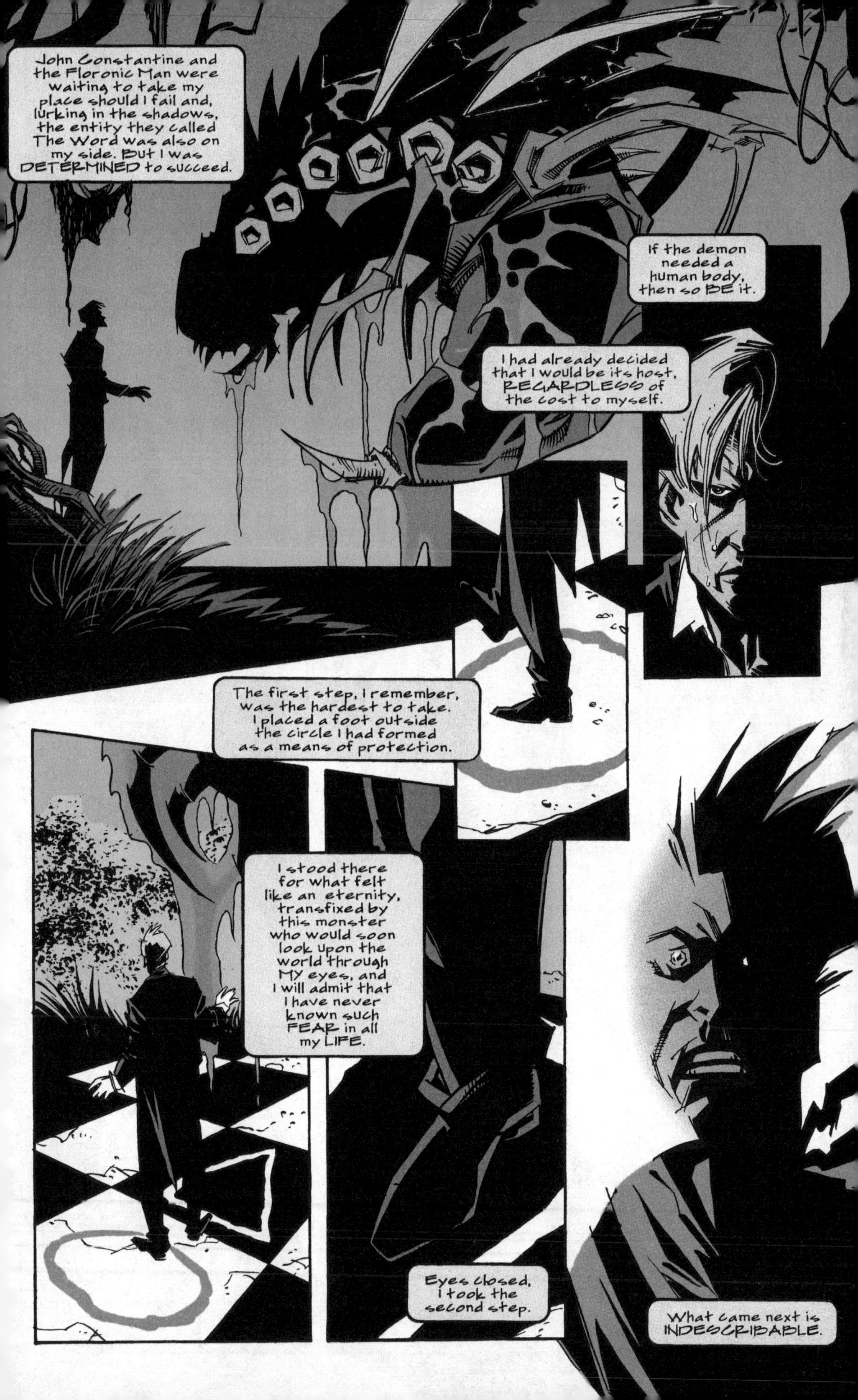
John Constantine and the Floronic Man were waiting to take my place should I fail and, lurking in the shadows, the entity they called The Word was also on my side. But I was DETERMINED to succeed.
If the demon needed a human body, then so BE it.
I had already decided that I would be its host, REGARDLESS of the cost to myself.
The first step, I remember, was the hardest to take. I placed a foot outside the circle I had formed as a means of protection.
I stood there for what felt like an eternity, transfixed by this monster who would soon look upon the world through MY eyes, and I will admit that I have never known such FEAR in all my LIFE.
Eyes closed, I took the second step.
What came next is INDESCRIBABLE.

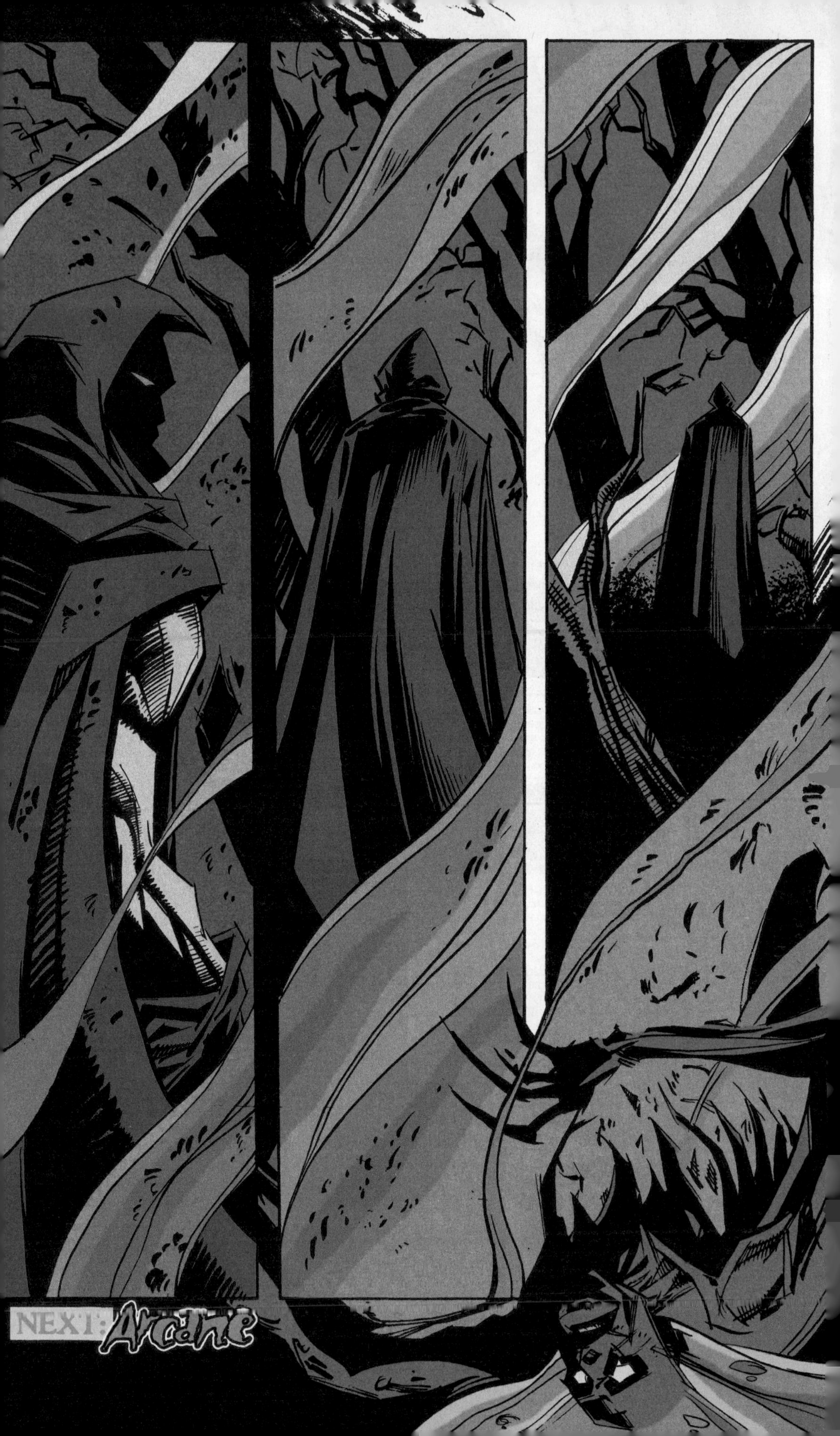
NEXT: Arcane

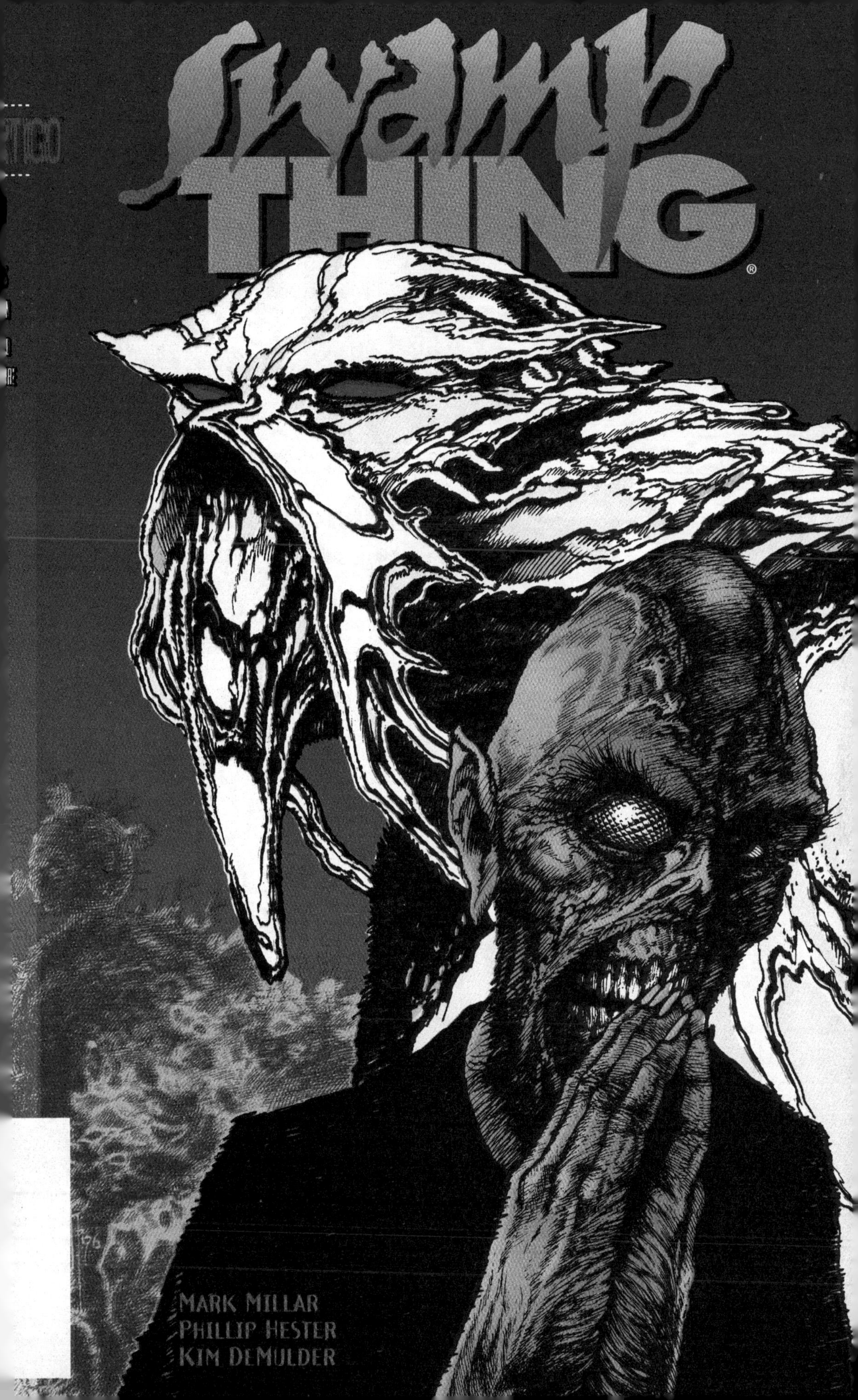
Swamp
THING
MARK MILLAR
PHILLIP HESTER
KIM DEMULDER

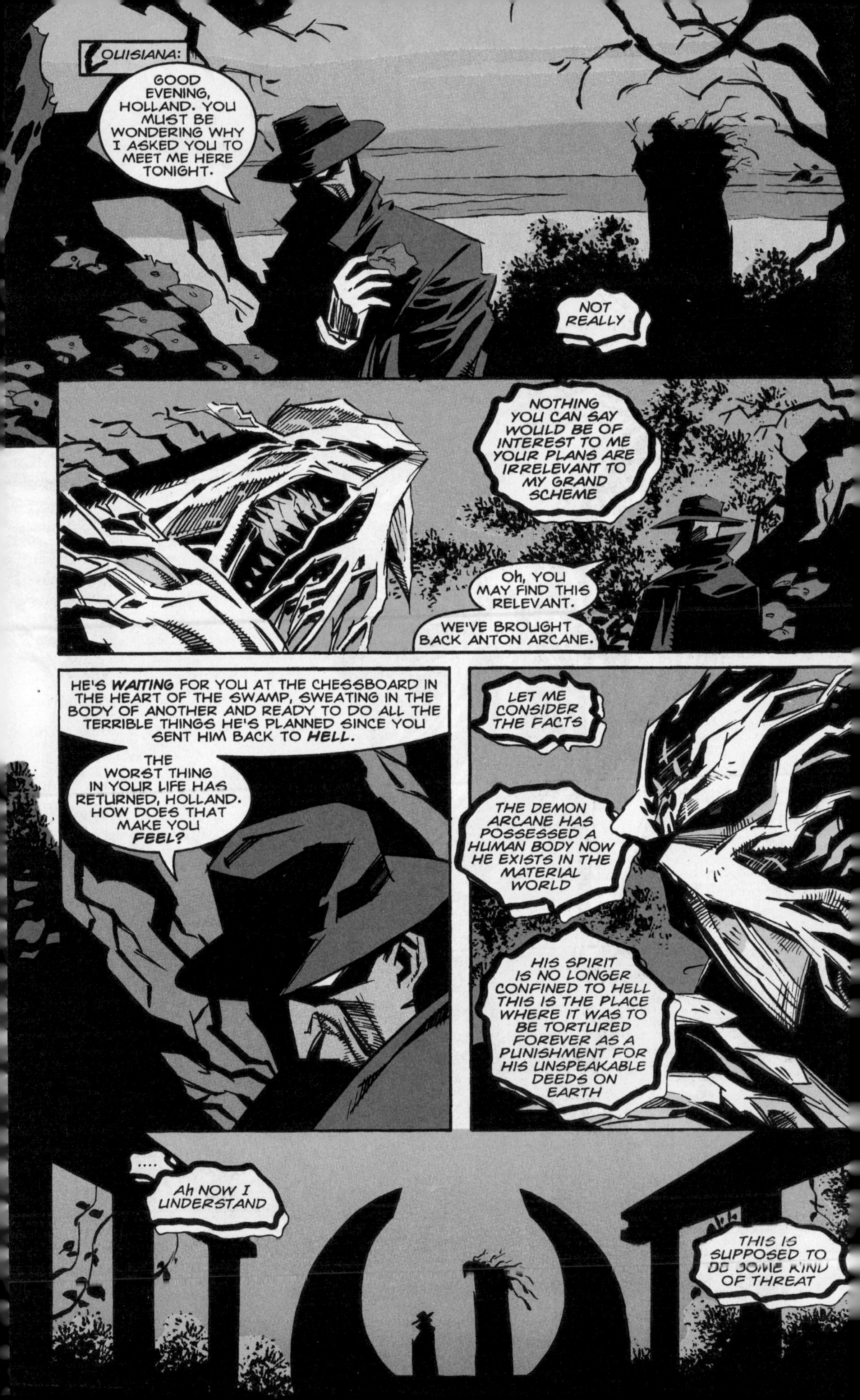
LOUISIANA:
GOOD EVENING, HOLLAND. YOU MUST BE WONDERING WHY I ASKED YOU TO MEET ME HERE TONIGHT.
NOT REALLY
NOTHING YOU CAN SAY WOULD BE OF INTEREST TO ME YOUR PLANS ARE IRRELEVANT TO MY GRAND SCHEME
Oh, YOU MAY FIND THIS RELEVANT.
WE'VE BROUGHT BACK ANTON ARCANE.
HE'S WAITING FOR YOU AT THE CHESSBOARD IN THE HEART OF THE SWAMP, SWEATING IN THE BODY OF ANOTHER AND READY TO DO ALL THE TERRIBLE THINGS HE'S PLANNED SINCE YOU SENT HIM BACK TO HELL.
THE WORST THING IN YOUR LIFE HAS RETURNED, HOLLAND. HOW DOES THAT MAKE YOU FEEL?
LET ME CONSIDER THE FACTS
THE DEMON ARCANE HAS POSSESSED A HUMAN BODY NOW HE EXISTS IN THE MATERIAL WORLD
HIS SPIRIT IS NO LONGER CONFINED TO HELL THIS IS THE PLACE WHERE IT WAS TO BE TORTURED FOREVER AS A PUNISHMENT FOR HIS UNSPEAKABLE DEEDS ON EARTH
....
Ah NOW I UNDERSTAND
THIS IS SUPPOSED TO BE SOME KIND OF THREAT

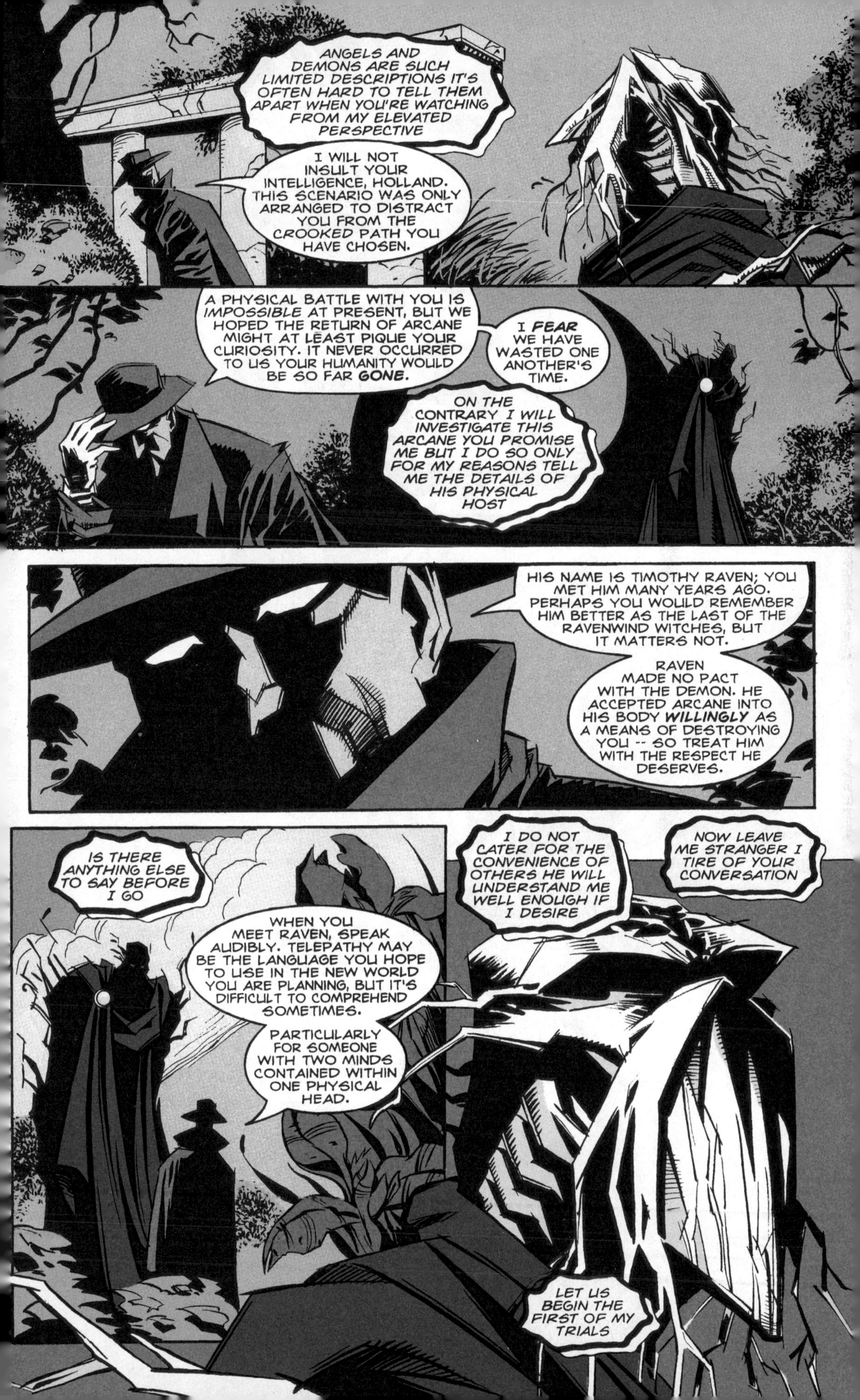
ANGELS AND DEMONS ARE SUCH LIMITED DESCRIPTIONS IT'S OFTEN HARD TO TELL THEM APART WHEN YOU'RE WATCHING FROM MY ELEVATED PERSPECTIVE
I WILL NOT INSULT YOUR INTELLIGENCE, HOLLAND. THIS SCENARIO WAS ONLY ARRANGED TO DISTRACT YOU FROM THE CROOKED PATH YOU HAVE CHOSEN.
A PHYSICAL BATTLE WITH YOU IS IMPOSSIBLE AT PRESENT, BUT WE HOPED THE RETURN OF ARCANE MIGHT AT LEAST PIQUE YOUR CURIOSITY. IT NEVER OCCURRED TO US YOUR HUMANITY WOULD BE SO FAR GONE.
I FEAR WE HAVE WASTED ONE ANOTHER'S TIME.
ON THE CONTRARY I WILL INVESTIGATE THIS ARCANE YOU PROMISE ME BUT I DO SO ONLY FOR MY REASONS TELL ME THE DETAILS OF HIS PHYSICAL HOST
HIS NAME IS TIMOTHY RAVEN; YOU MET HIM MANY YEARS AGO. PERHAPS YOU WOULD REMEMBER HIM BETTER AS THE LAST OF THE RAVENWIND WITCHES, BUT IT MATTERS NOT.
RAVEN MADE NO PACT WITH THE DEMON. HE ACCEPTED ARCANE INTO HIS BODY WILLINGLY AS A MEANS OF DESTROYING YOU -- SO TREAT HIM WITH THE RESPECT HE DESERVES.
IS THERE ANYTHING ELSE TO SAY BEFORE I GO
WHEN YOU MEET RAVEN, SPEAK AUDIBLY. TELEPATHY MAY BE THE LANGUAGE YOU HOPE TO USE IN THE NEW WORLD YOU ARE PLANNING, BUT IT'S DIFFICULT TO COMPREHEND SOMETIMES.
PARTICULARLY FOR SOMEONE WITH TWO MINDS CONTAINED WITHIN ONE PHYSICAL HEAD.
I DO NOT CATER FOR THE CONVENIENCE OF OTHERS HE WILL UNDERSTAND ME WELL ENOUGH IF I DESIRE
NOW LEAVE ME STRANGER I TIRE OF YOUR CONVERSATION
LET US BEGIN THE FIRST OF MY TRIALS

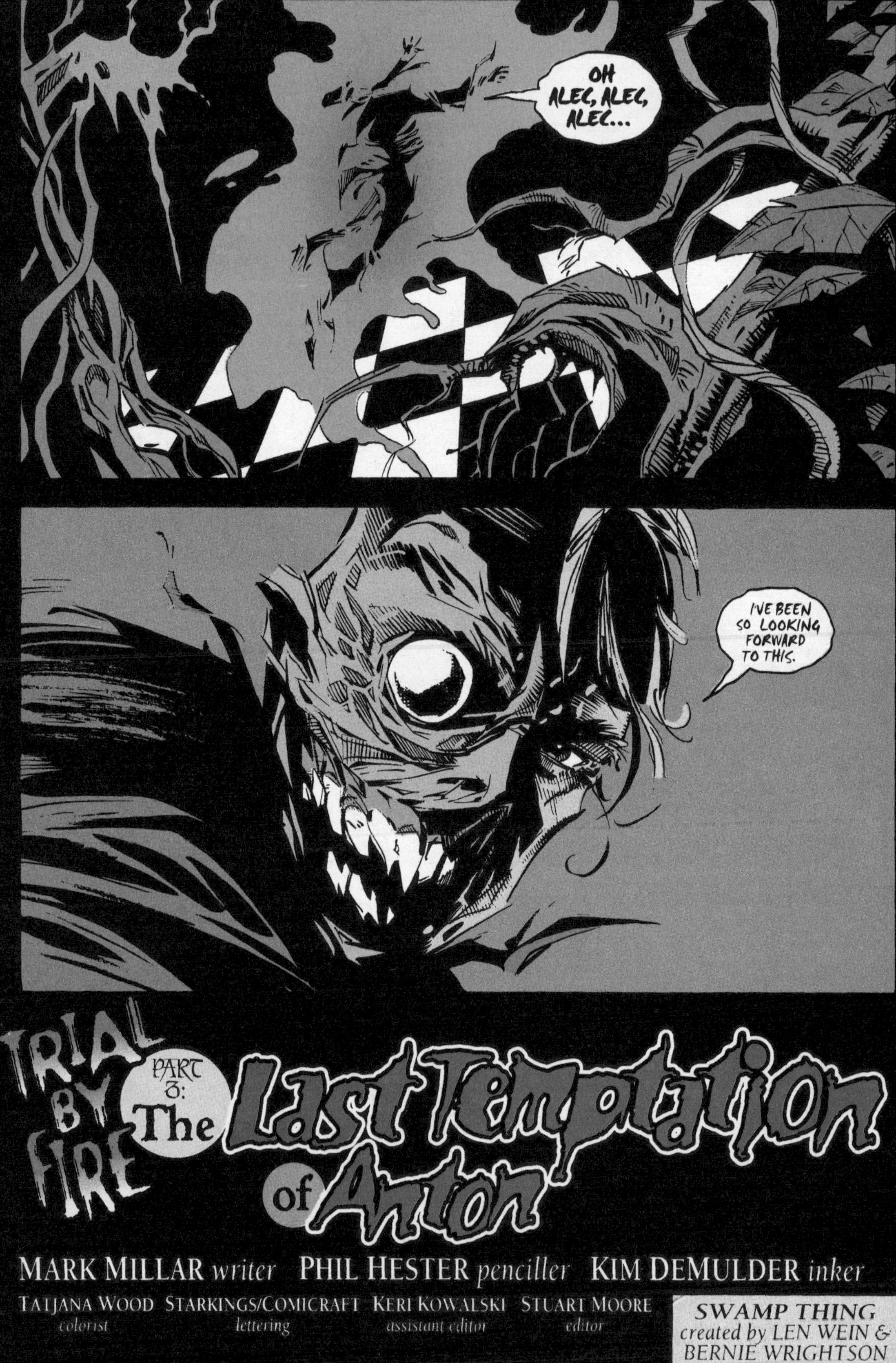
OH ALEC, ALEC, ALEC...
I'VE BEEN SO LOOKING FORWARD TO THIS.
TRIAL BY FIRE
PART 3: The Last Temptation of Anton

MARK MILLAR *writer* PHIL HESTER *penciller* KIM DEMULDER *inker*

TATJANA WOOD *colorist* STARKINGS/COMICRAFT *lettering* KERI KOWALSKI *assistant editor* STUART MOORE *editor*

SWAMP THING
created by LEN WEIN & BERNIE WRIGHTSON

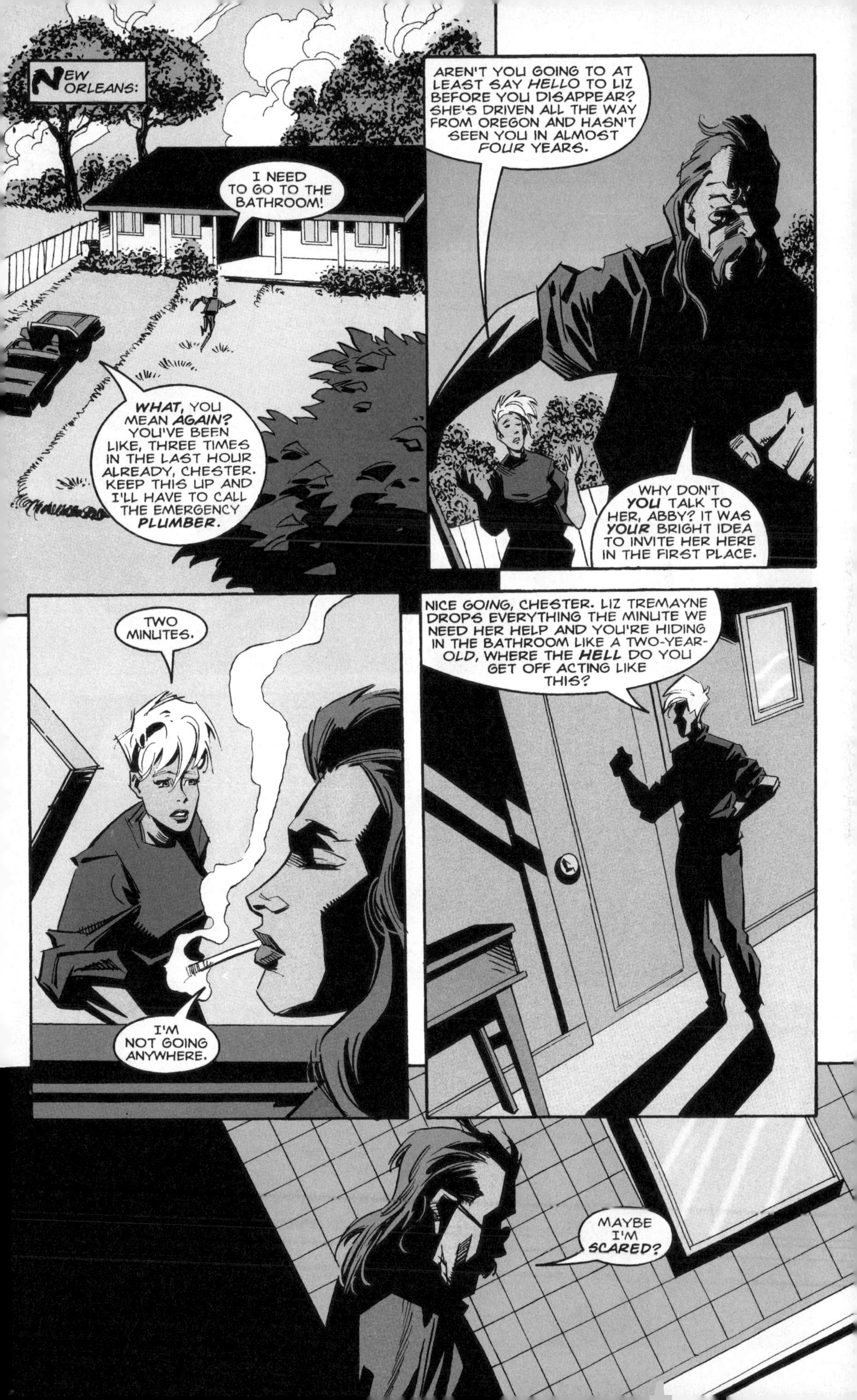
NEW ORLEANS:
I NEED TO GO TO THE BATHROOM!
WHAT, YOU MEAN AGAIN? YOU'VE BEEN LIKE, THREE TIMES IN THE LAST HOUR ALREADY, CHESTER. KEEP THIS UP AND I'LL HAVE TO CALL THE EMERGENCY PLUMBER.
AREN'T YOU GOING TO AT LEAST SAY HELLO TO LIZ BEFORE YOU DISAPPEAR? SHE'S DRIVEN ALL THE WAY FROM OREGON AND HASN'T SEEN YOU IN ALMOST FOUR YEARS.
WHY DON'T YOU TALK TO HER, ABBY? IT WAS YOUR BRIGHT IDEA TO INVITE HER HERE IN THE FIRST PLACE.
TWO MINUTES.
I'M NOT GOING ANYWHERE.
NICE GOING, CHESTER. LIZ TREMAYNE DROPS EVERYTHING THE MINUTE WE NEED HER HELP AND YOU'RE HIDING IN THE BATHROOM LIKE A TWO-YEAR-OLD, WHERE THE HELL DO YOU GET OFF ACTING LIKE THIS?
MAYBE I'M SCARED?

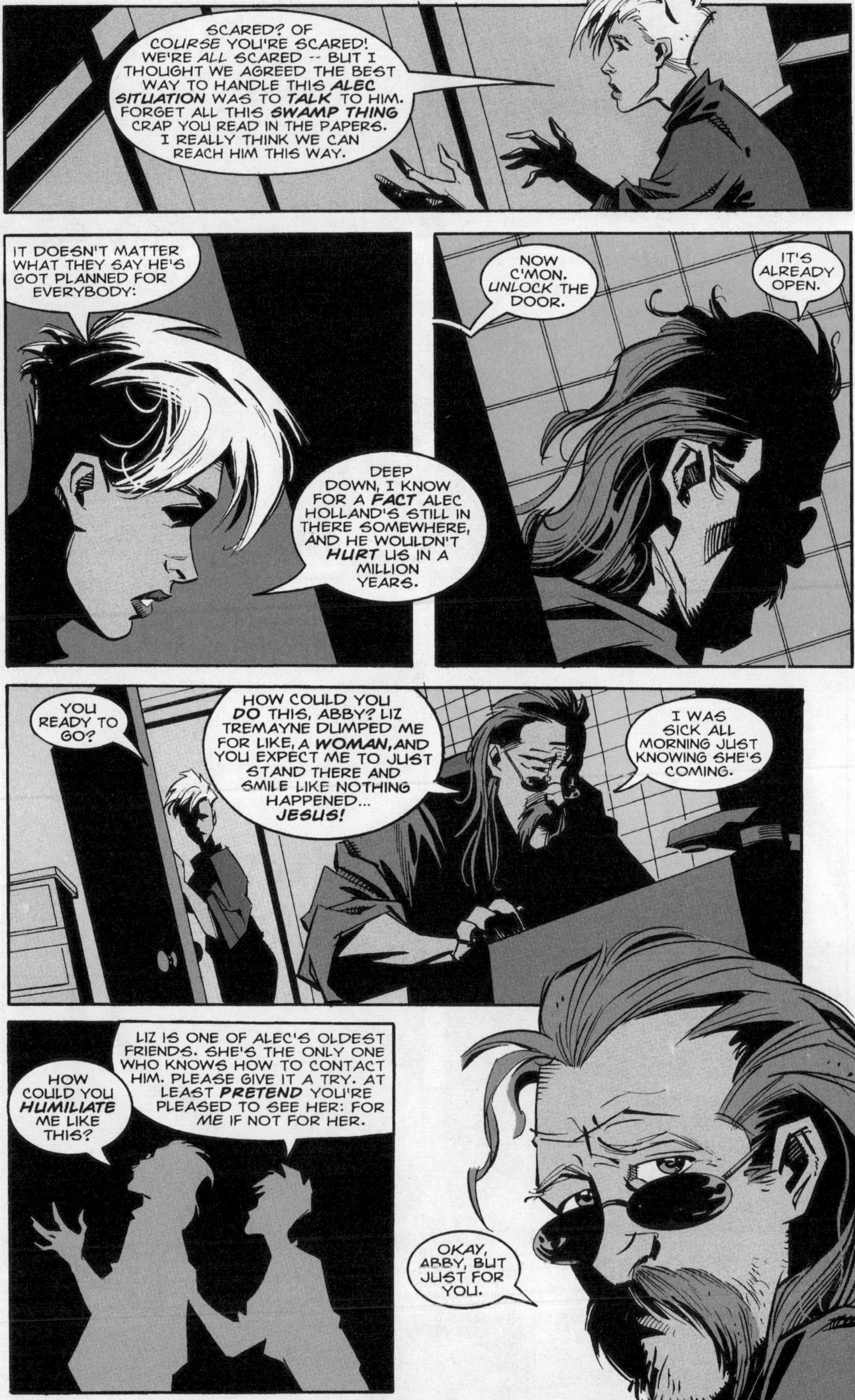
SCARED? OF COURSE YOU'RE SCARED! WE'RE ALL SCARED -- BUT I THOUGHT WE AGREED THE BEST WAY TO HANDLE THIS ALEC SITUATION WAS TO TALK TO HIM. FORGET ALL THIS SWAMP THING CRAP YOU READ IN THE PAPERS. I REALLY THINK WE CAN REACH HIM THIS WAY.
IT DOESN'T MATTER WHAT THEY SAY HE'S GOT PLANNED FOR EVERYBODY:
DEEP DOWN, I KNOW FOR A FACT ALEC HOLLAND'S STILL IN THERE SOMEWHERE, AND HE WOULDN'T HURT US IN A MILLION YEARS.
NOW C'MON. UNLOCK THE DOOR.
IT'S ALREADY OPEN.
YOU READY TO GO?
HOW COULD YOU DO THIS, ABBY? LIZ TREMAYNE DUMPED ME FOR LIKE, A WOMAN, AND YOU EXPECT ME TO JUST STAND THERE AND SMILE LIKE NOTHING HAPPENED... JESUS!
I WAS SICK ALL MORNING JUST KNOWING SHE'S COMING.
HOW COULD YOU HUMILIATE ME LIKE THIS?
LIZ IS ONE OF ALEC'S OLDEST FRIENDS. SHE'S THE ONLY ONE WHO KNOWS HOW TO CONTACT HIM. PLEASE GIVE IT A TRY. AT LEAST PRETEND YOU'RE PLEASED TO SEE HER: FOR ME IF NOT FOR HER.
OKAY, ABBY, BUT JUST FOR YOU.

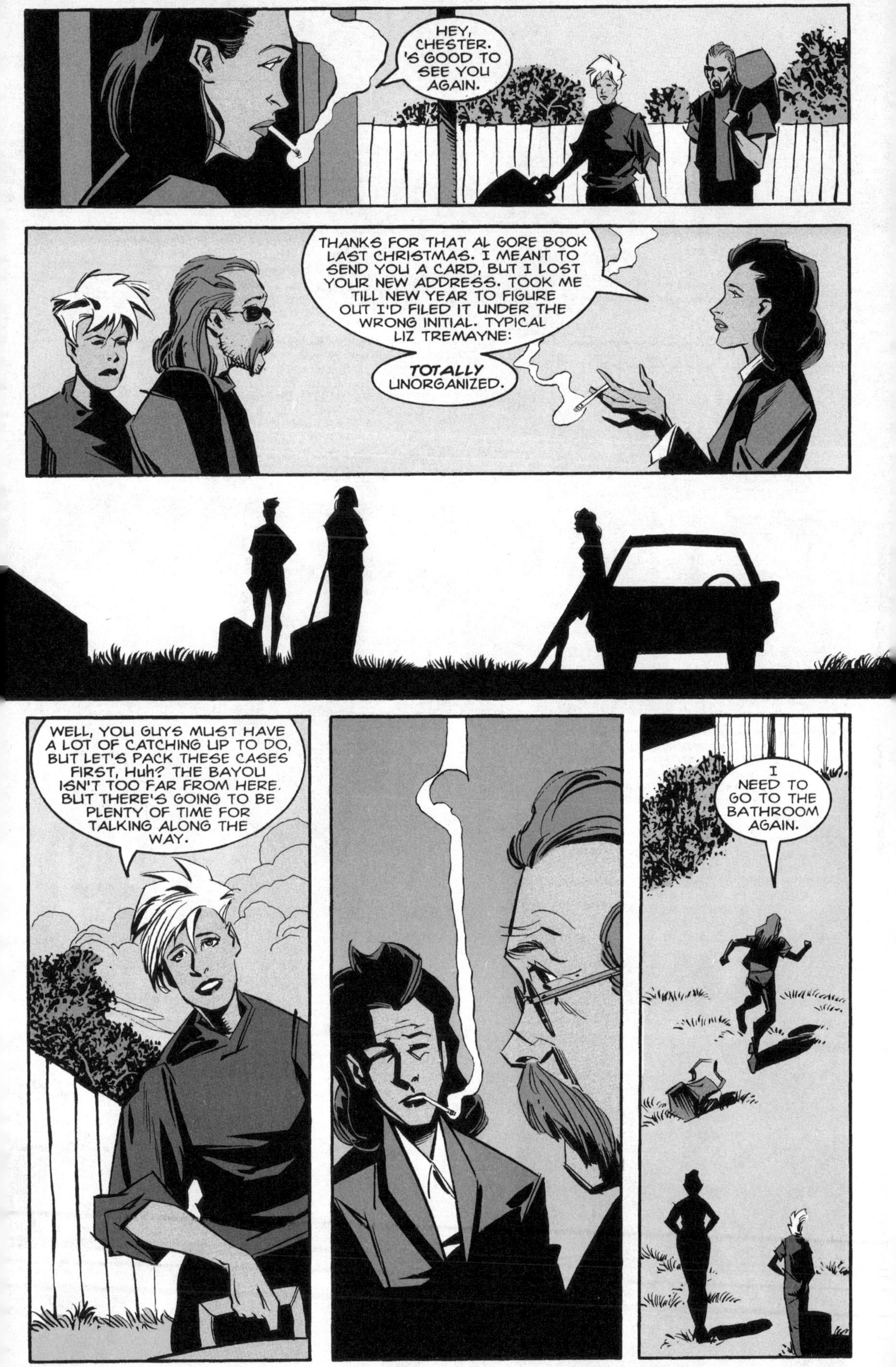
HEY, CHESTER. 'S GOOD TO SEE YOU AGAIN.
THANKS FOR THAT AL GORE BOOK LAST CHRISTMAS. I MEANT TO SEND YOU A CARD, BUT I LOST YOUR NEW ADDRESS. TOOK ME TILL NEW YEAR TO FIGURE OUT I'D FILED IT UNDER THE WRONG INITIAL. TYPICAL LIZ TREMAYNE:
TOTALLY UNORGANIZED.
WELL, YOU GUYS MUST HAVE A LOT OF CATCHING UP TO DO, BUT LET'S PACK THESE CASES FIRST, HUH? THE BAYOU ISN'T TOO FAR FROM HERE. BUT THERE'S GOING TO BE PLENTY OF TIME FOR TALKING ALONG THE WAY.
I NEED TO GO TO THE BATHROOM AGAIN.

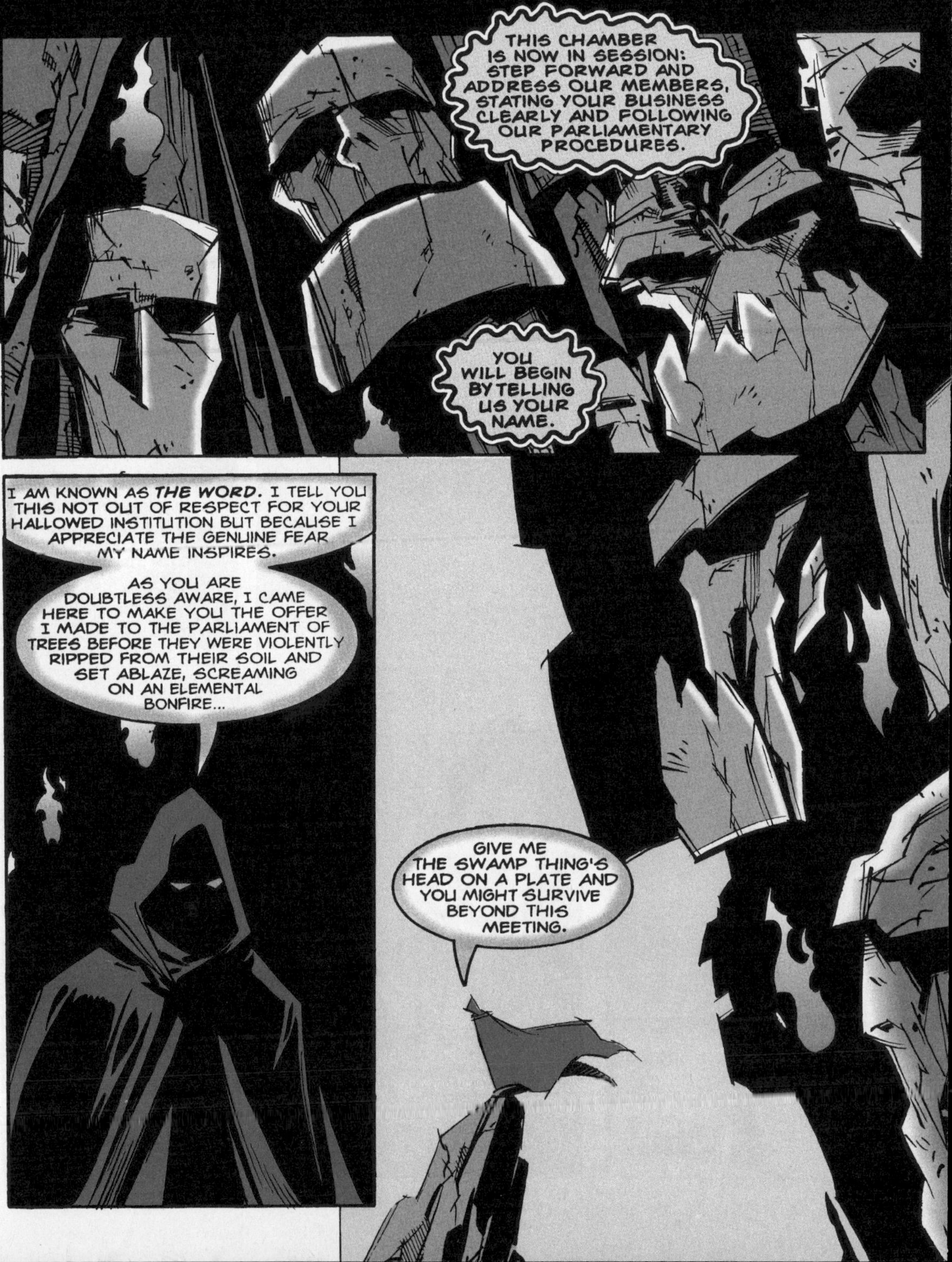
THIS CHAMBER IS NOW IN SESSION: STEP FORWARD AND ADDRESS OUR MEMBERS, STATING YOUR BUSINESS CLEARLY AND FOLLOWING OUR PARLIAMENTARY PROCEDURES.
YOU WILL BEGIN BY TELLING US YOUR NAME.
I AM KNOWN AS *THE WORD.* I TELL YOU THIS NOT OUT OF RESPECT FOR YOUR HALLOWED INSTITUTION BUT BECAUSE I APPRECIATE THE GENUINE FEAR MY NAME INSPIRES.
AS YOU ARE DOUBTLESS AWARE, I CAME HERE TO MAKE YOU THE OFFER I MADE TO THE PARLIAMENT OF TREES BEFORE THEY WERE VIOLENTLY RIPPED FROM THEIR SOIL AND SET ABLAZE, SCREAMING ON AN ELEMENTAL BONFIRE...
GIVE ME THE SWAMP THING'S HEAD ON A PLATE AND YOU MIGHT SURVIVE BEYOND THIS MEETING.

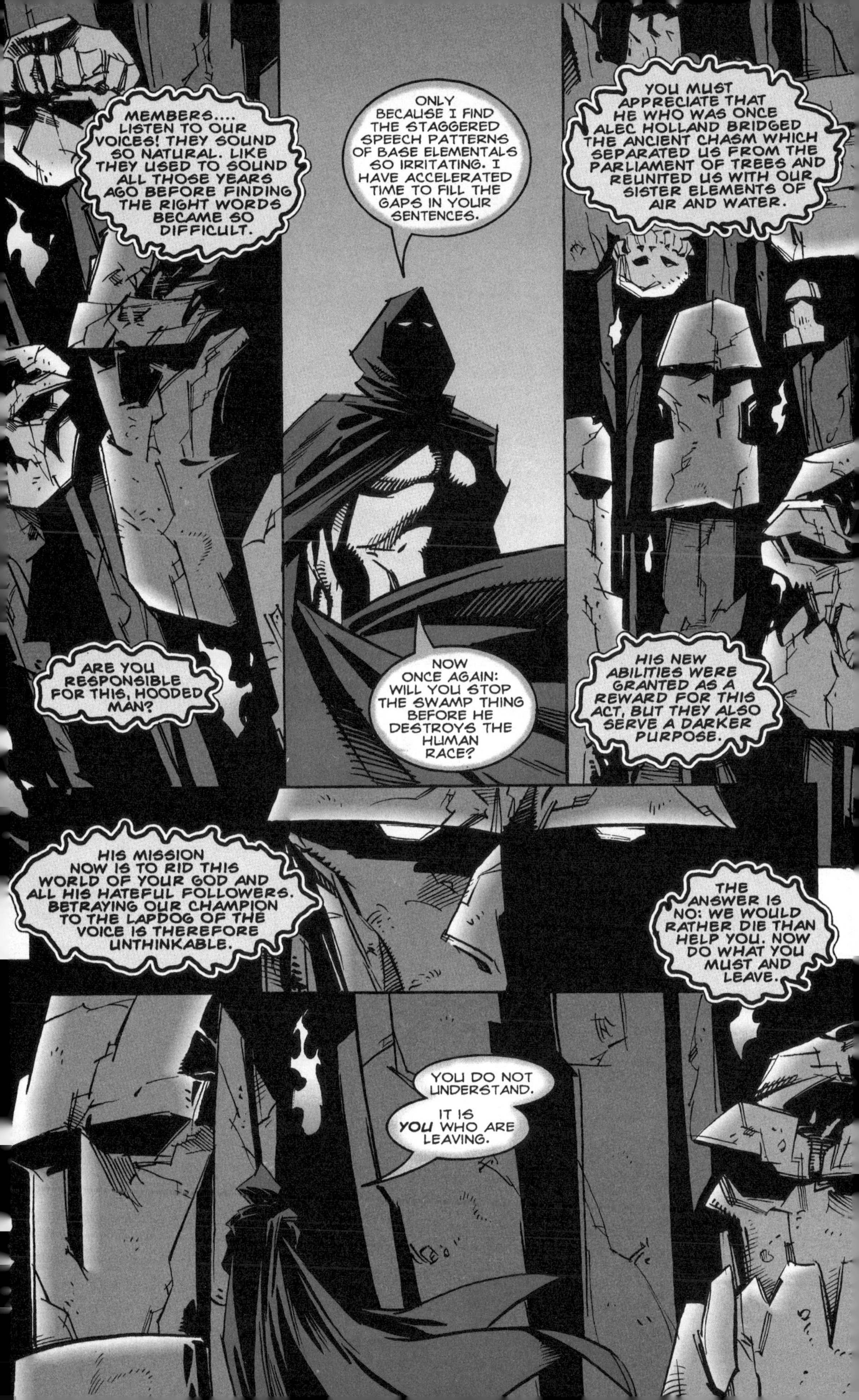
MEMBERS.... LISTEN TO OUR VOICES! THEY SOUND SO NATURAL. LIKE THEY USED TO SOUND ALL THOSE YEARS AGO BEFORE FINDING THE RIGHT WORDS BECAME SO DIFFICULT.
ONLY BECAUSE I FIND THE STAGGERED SPEECH PATTERNS OF BASE ELEMENTALS SO IRRITATING. I HAVE ACCELERATED TIME TO FILL THE GAPS IN YOUR SENTENCES.
YOU MUST APPRECIATE THAT HE WHO WAS ONCE ALEC HOLLAND BRIDGED THE ANCIENT CHASM WHICH SEPARATED US FROM THE PARLIAMENT OF TREES AND REUNITED US WITH OUR SISTER ELEMENTS OF AIR AND WATER.
ARE YOU RESPONSIBLE FOR THIS, HOODED MAN?
NOW ONCE AGAIN: WILL YOU STOP THE SWAMP THING BEFORE HE DESTROYS THE HUMAN RACE?
HIS NEW ABILITIES WERE GRANTED AS A REWARD FOR THIS ACT, BUT THEY ALSO SERVE A DARKER PURPOSE.
HIS MISSION NOW IS TO RID THIS WORLD OF YOUR GOD AND ALL HIS HATEFUL FOLLOWERS. BETRAYING OUR CHAMPION TO THE LAPDOG OF THE VOICE IS THEREFORE UNTHINKABLE.
THE ANSWER IS NO: WE WOULD RATHER DIE THAN HELP YOU. NOW DO WHAT YOU MUST AND LEAVE.
YOU DO NOT UNDERSTAND.
IT IS *YOU* WHO ARE LEAVING.

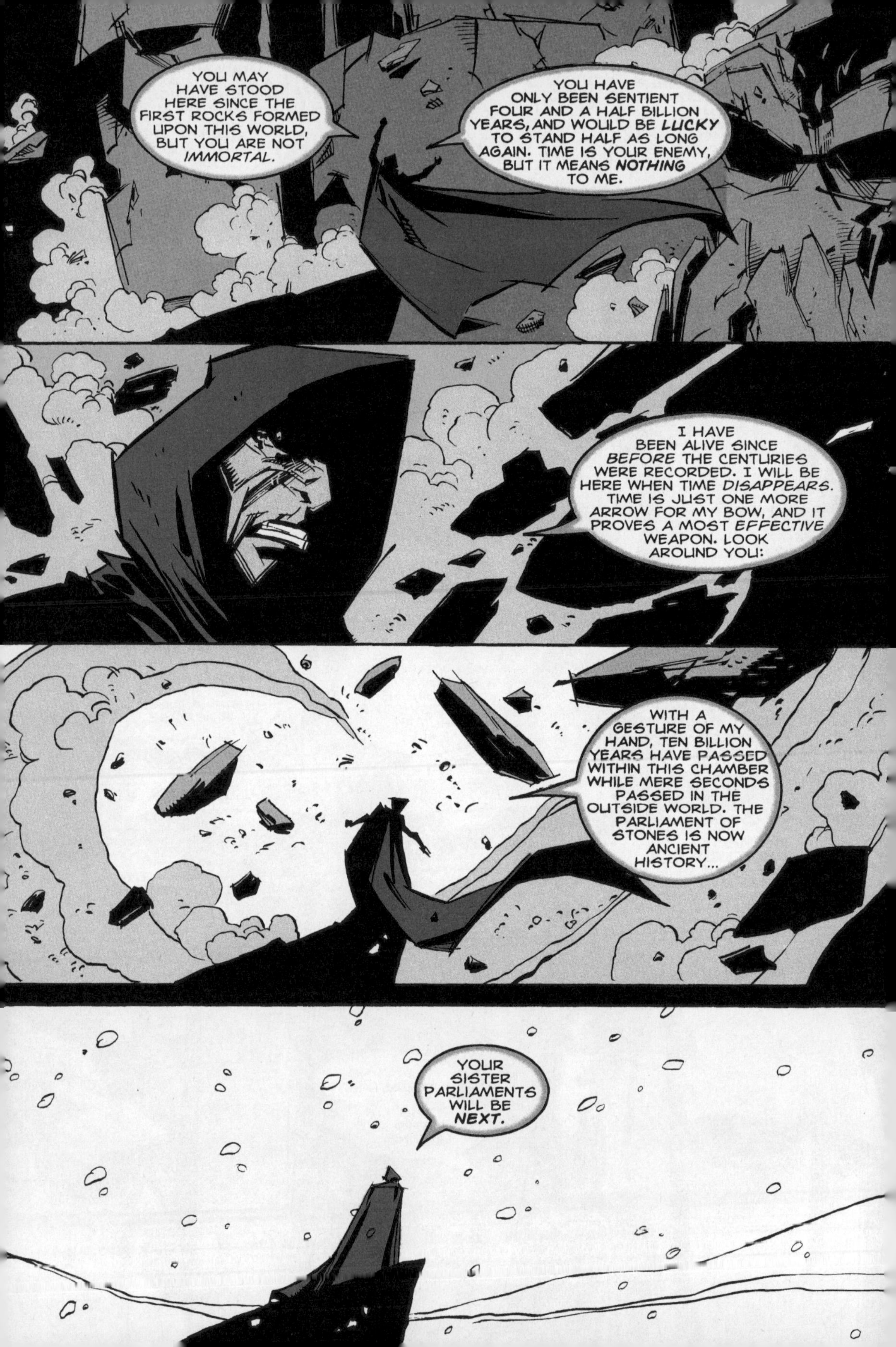
YOU MAY HAVE STOOD HERE SINCE THE FIRST ROCKS FORMED UPON THIS WORLD, BUT YOU ARE NOT *IMMORTAL*.
YOU HAVE ONLY BEEN SENTIENT FOUR AND A HALF BILLION YEARS, AND WOULD BE ***LUCKY*** TO STAND HALF AS LONG AGAIN. TIME IS YOUR ENEMY, BUT IT MEANS **NOTHING** TO ME.
I HAVE BEEN ALIVE SINCE *BEFORE* THE CENTURIES WERE RECORDED. I WILL BE HERE WHEN TIME *DISAPPEARS*. TIME IS JUST ONE MORE ARROW FOR MY BOW, AND IT PROVES A MOST *EFFECTIVE* WEAPON. LOOK AROUND YOU:
WITH A GESTURE OF MY HAND, TEN BILLION YEARS HAVE PASSED WITHIN THIS CHAMBER WHILE MERE SECONDS PASSED IN THE OUTSIDE WORLD. THE PARLIAMENT OF STONES IS NOW ANCIENT HISTORY...
YOUR SISTER PARLIAMENTS WILL BE ***NEXT***.

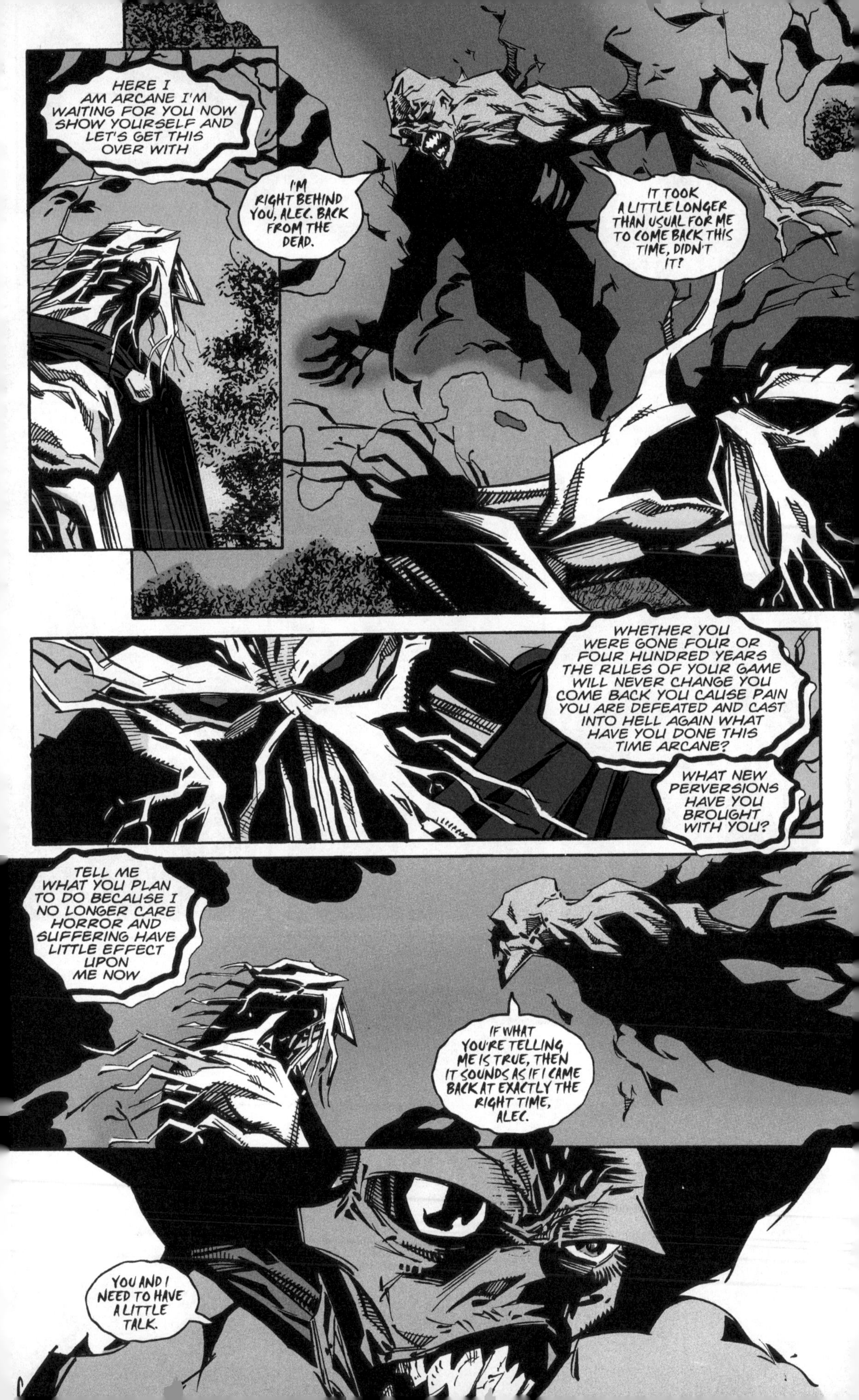
HERE I AM ARCANE I'M WAITING FOR YOU NOW SHOW YOURSELF AND LET'S GET THIS OVER WITH
I'M RIGHT BEHIND YOU, ALEC. BACK FROM THE DEAD.
IT TOOK A LITTLE LONGER THAN USUAL FOR ME TO COME BACK THIS TIME, DIDN'T IT?
WHETHER YOU WERE GONE FOUR OR FOUR HUNDRED YEARS THE RULES OF YOUR GAME WILL NEVER CHANGE YOU COME BACK YOU CAUSE PAIN YOU ARE DEFEATED AND CAST INTO HELL AGAIN WHAT HAVE YOU DONE THIS TIME ARCANE?
WHAT NEW PERVERSIONS HAVE YOU BROUGHT WITH YOU?
TELL ME WHAT YOU PLAN TO DO BECAUSE I NO LONGER CARE HORROR AND SUFFERING HAVE LITTLE EFFECT UPON ME NOW
IF WHAT YOU'RE TELLING ME IS TRUE, THEN IT SOUNDS AS IF I CAME BACK AT EXACTLY THE RIGHT TIME, ALEC.
YOU AND I NEED TO HAVE A LITTLE TALK.

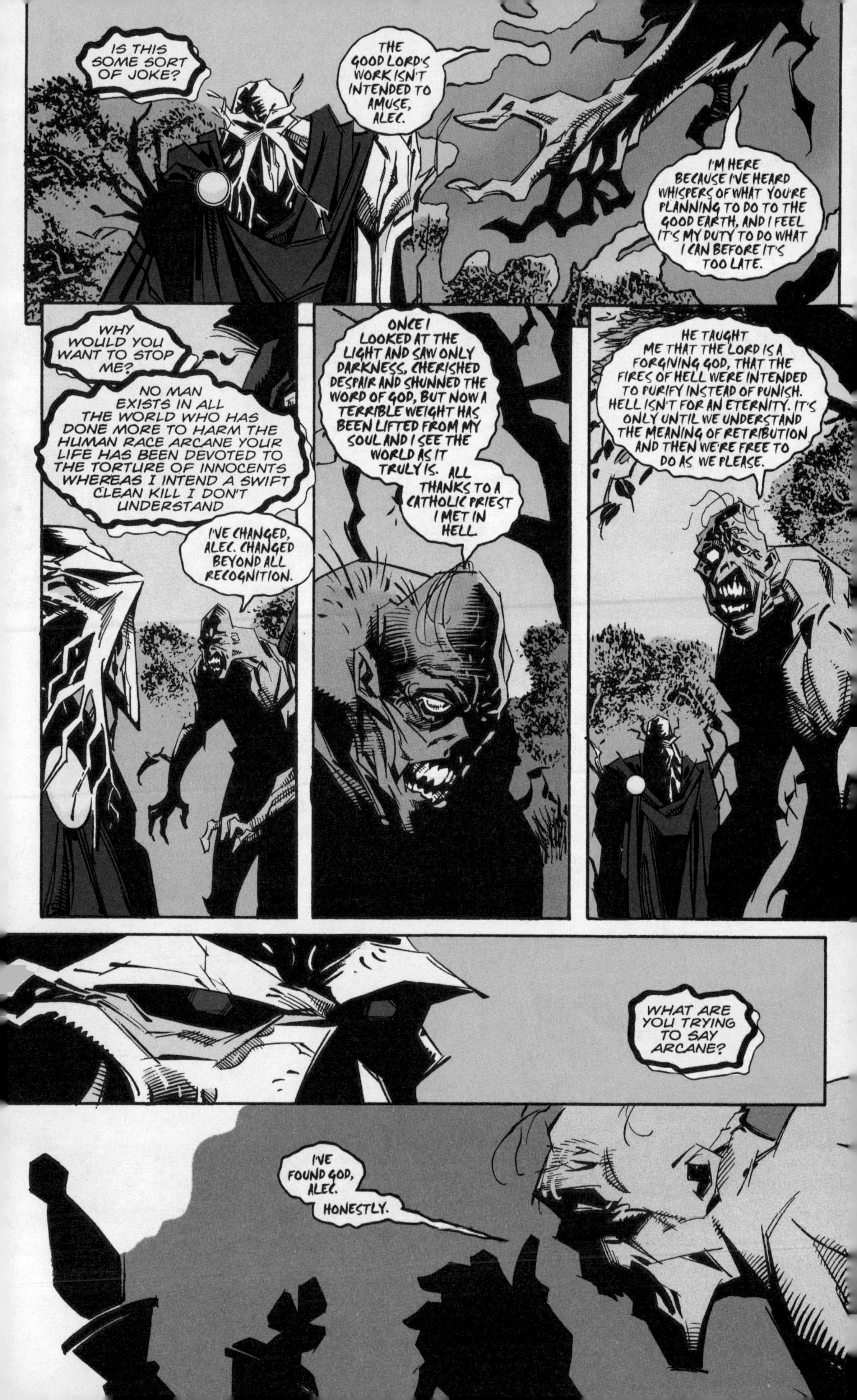
IS THIS SOME SORT OF JOKE?
THE GOOD LORD'S WORK ISN'T INTENDED TO AMUSE, ALEC.
I'M HERE BECAUSE I'VE HEARD WHISPERS OF WHAT YOU'RE PLANNING TO DO TO THE GOOD EARTH, AND I FEEL IT'S MY DUTY TO DO WHAT I CAN BEFORE IT'S TOO LATE.
WHY WOULD YOU WANT TO STOP ME?
NO MAN EXISTS IN ALL THE WORLD WHO HAS DONE MORE TO HARM THE HUMAN RACE ARCANE YOUR LIFE HAS BEEN DEVOTED TO THE TORTURE OF INNOCENTS WHEREAS I INTEND A SWIFT CLEAN KILL I DON'T UNDERSTAND
I'VE CHANGED, ALEC. CHANGED BEYOND ALL RECOGNITION.
ONCE I LOOKED AT THE LIGHT AND SAW ONLY DARKNESS, CHERISHED DESPAIR AND SHUNNED THE WORD OF GOD, BUT NOW A TERRIBLE WEIGHT HAS BEEN LIFTED FROM MY SOUL AND I SEE THE WORLD AS IT TRULY IS.
ALL THANKS TO A CATHOLIC PRIEST I MET IN HELL.
HE TAUGHT ME THAT THE LORD IS A FORGIVING GOD, THAT THE FIRES OF HELL WERE INTENDED TO PURIFY INSTEAD OF PUNISH. HELL ISN'T FOR AN ETERNITY. IT'S ONLY UNTIL WE UNDERSTAND THE MEANING OF RETRIBUTION AND THEN WE'RE FREE TO DO AS WE PLEASE.
WHAT ARE YOU TRYING TO SAY ARCANE?
I'VE FOUND GOD, ALEC.
HONESTLY.

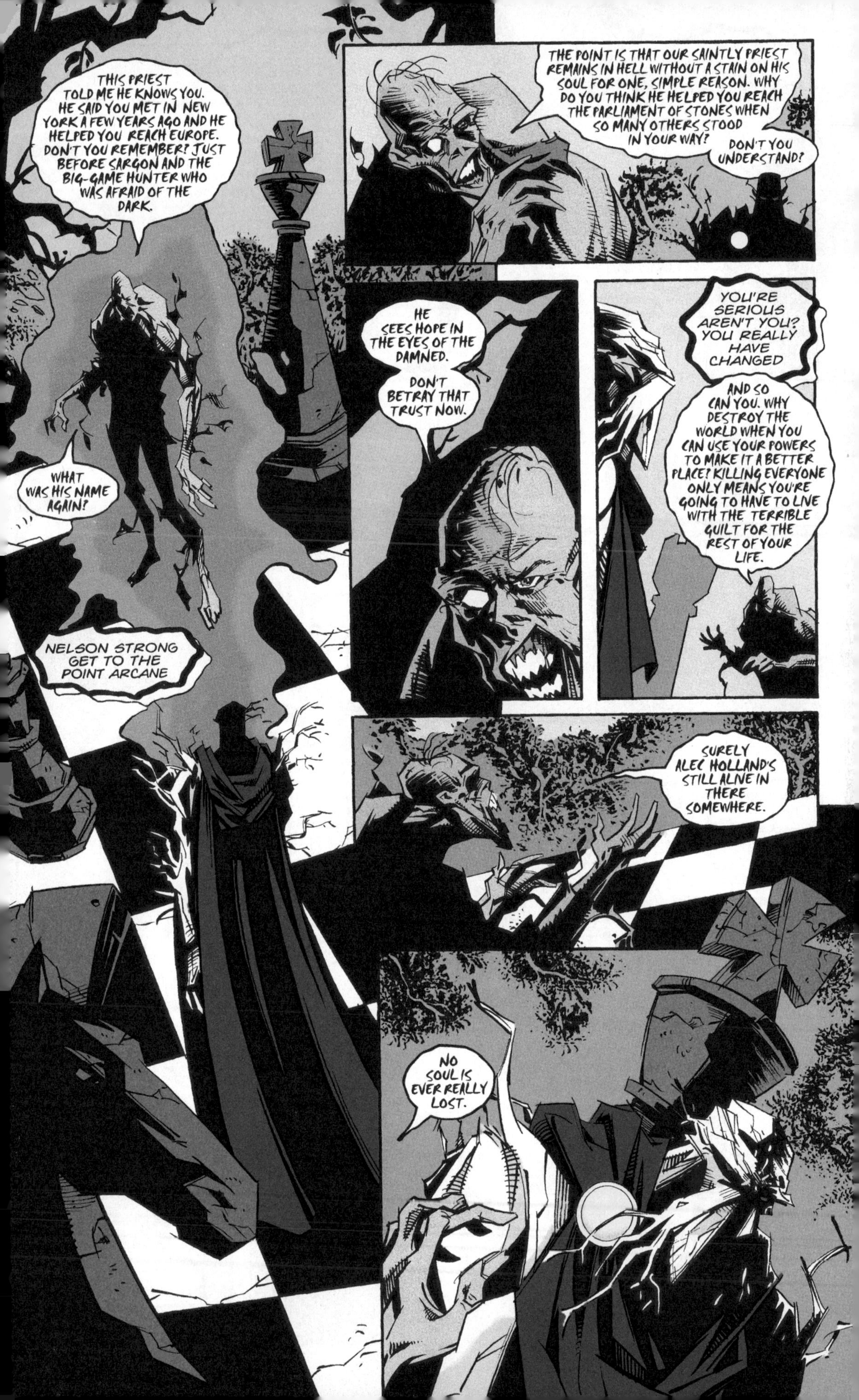
THIS PRIEST TOLD ME HE KNOWS YOU. HE SAID YOU MET IN NEW YORK A FEW YEARS AGO AND HE HELPED YOU REACH EUROPE. DON'T YOU REMEMBER? JUST BEFORE SARGON AND THE BIG-GAME HUNTER WHO WAS AFRAID OF THE DARK.
WHAT WAS HIS NAME AGAIN?
NELSON STRONG GET TO THE POINT ARCANE
THE POINT IS THAT OUR SAINTLY PRIEST REMAINS IN HELL WITHOUT A STAIN ON HIS SOUL FOR ONE, SIMPLE REASON. WHY DO YOU THINK HE HELPED YOU REACH THE PARLIAMENT OF STONES WHEN SO MANY OTHERS STOOD IN YOUR WAY?
DON'T YOU UNDERSTAND?
HE SEES HOPE IN THE EYES OF THE DAMNED.
DON'T BETRAY THAT TRUST NOW.
YOU'RE SERIOUS AREN'T YOU? YOU REALLY HAVE CHANGED
AND SO CAN YOU. WHY DESTROY THE WORLD WHEN YOU CAN USE YOUR POWERS TO MAKE IT A BETTER PLACE? KILLING EVERYONE ONLY MEANS YOU'RE GOING TO HAVE TO LIVE WITH THE TERRIBLE GUILT FOR THE REST OF YOUR LIFE.
SURELY ALEC HOLLAND'S STILL ALIVE IN THERE SOMEWHERE.
NO SOUL IS EVER REALLY LOST.

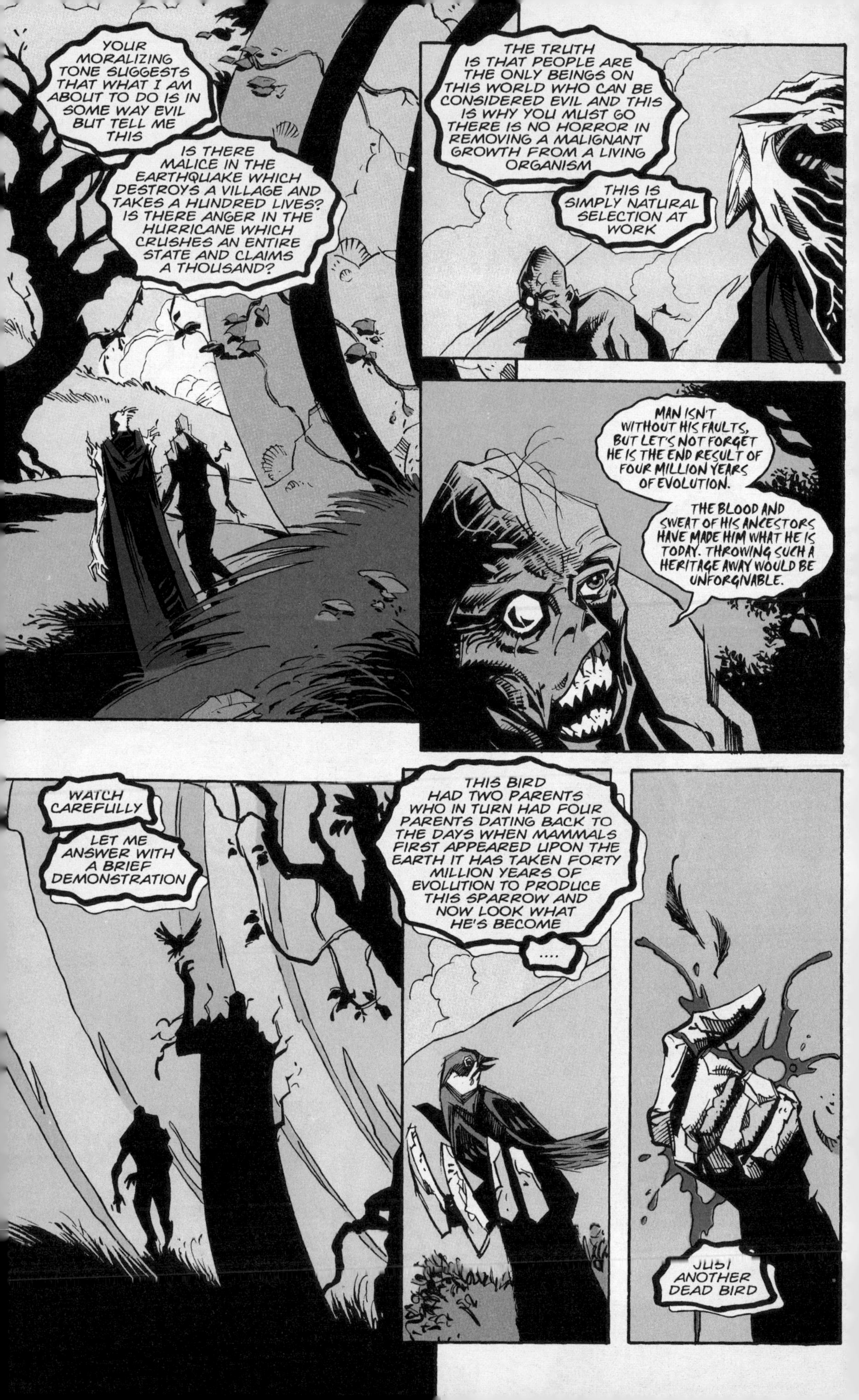

YOUR MORALIZING TONE SUGGESTS THAT WHAT I AM ABOUT TO DO IS IN SOME WAY EVIL BUT TELL ME THIS
IS THERE MALICE IN THE EARTHQUAKE WHICH DESTROYS A VILLAGE AND TAKES A HUNDRED LIVES? IS THERE ANGER IN THE HURRICANE WHICH CRUSHES AN ENTIRE STATE AND CLAIMS A THOUSAND?
THE TRUTH IS THAT PEOPLE ARE THE ONLY BEINGS ON THIS WORLD WHO CAN BE CONSIDERED EVIL AND THIS IS WHY YOU MUST GO THERE IS NO HORROR IN REMOVING A MALIGNANT GROWTH FROM A LIVING ORGANISM
THIS IS SIMPLY NATURAL SELECTION AT WORK
MAN ISN'T WITHOUT HIS FAULTS, BUT LET'S NOT FORGET HE IS THE END RESULT OF FOUR MILLION YEARS OF EVOLUTION.
THE BLOOD AND SWEAT OF HIS ANCESTORS HAVE MADE HIM WHAT HE IS TODAY. THROWING SUCH A HERITAGE AWAY WOULD BE UNFORGIVABLE.
WATCH CAREFULLY
LET ME ANSWER WITH A BRIEF DEMONSTRATION
THIS BIRD HAD TWO PARENTS WHO IN TURN HAD FOUR PARENTS DATING BACK TO THE DAYS WHEN MAMMALS FIRST APPEARED UPON THE EARTH IT HAS TAKEN FORTY MILLION YEARS OF EVOLUTION TO PRODUCE THIS SPARROW AND NOW LOOK WHAT HE'S BECOME
....
JUST ANOTHER DEAD BIRD

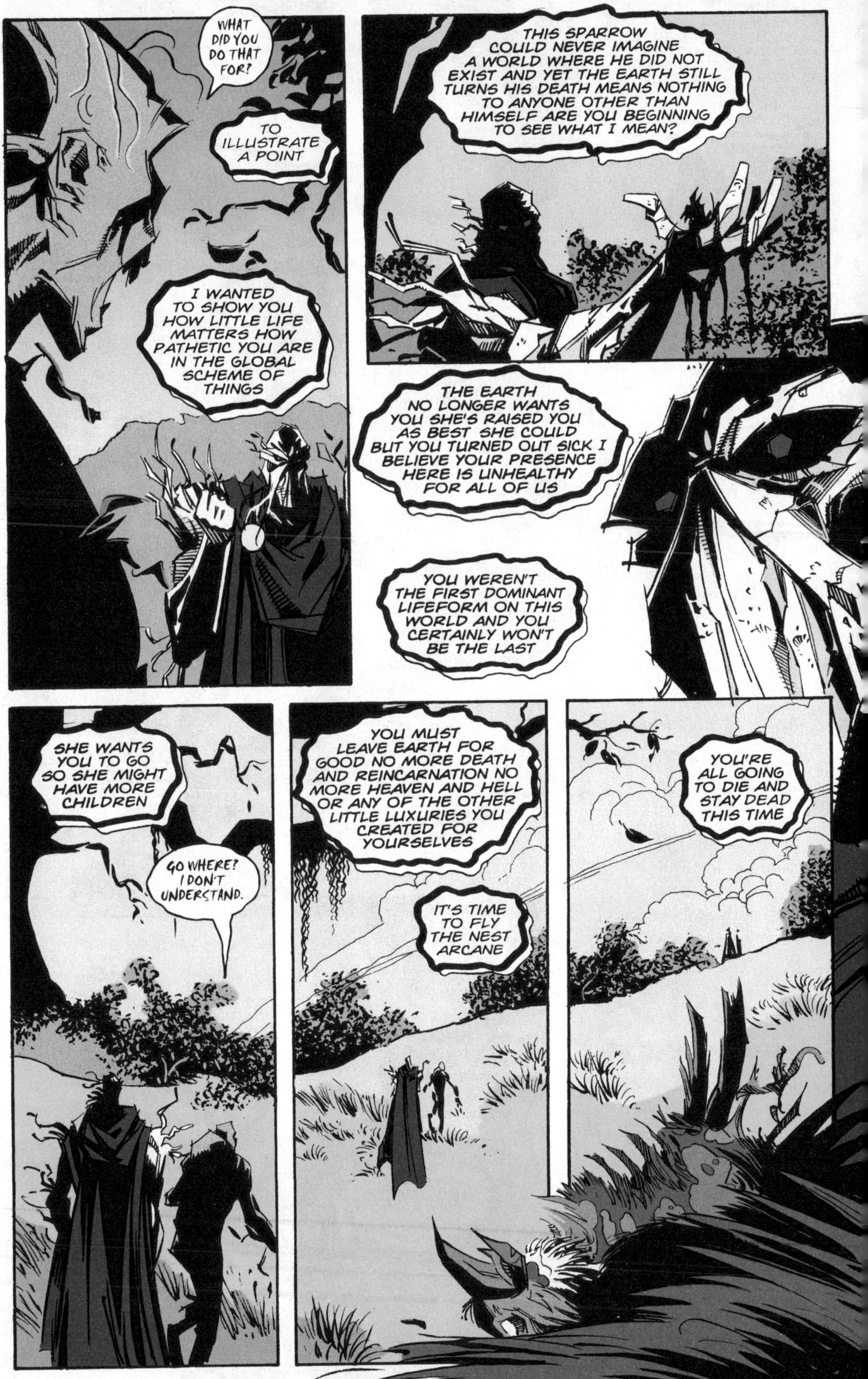
WHAT DID YOU DO THAT FOR?
TO ILLUSTRATE A POINT
I WANTED TO SHOW YOU HOW LITTLE LIFE MATTERS HOW PATHETIC YOU ARE IN THE GLOBAL SCHEME OF THINGS
THIS SPARROW COULD NEVER IMAGINE A WORLD WHERE HE DID NOT EXIST AND YET THE EARTH STILL TURNS HIS DEATH MEANS NOTHING TO ANYONE OTHER THAN HIMSELF ARE YOU BEGINNING TO SEE WHAT I MEAN?
THE EARTH NO LONGER WANTS YOU SHE'S RAISED YOU AS BEST SHE COULD BUT YOU TURNED OUT SICK I BELIEVE YOUR PRESENCE HERE IS UNHEALTHY FOR ALL OF US
YOU WEREN'T THE FIRST DOMINANT LIFEFORM ON THIS WORLD AND YOU CERTAINLY WON'T BE THE LAST
SHE WANTS YOU TO GO SO SHE MIGHT HAVE MORE CHILDREN
GO WHERE? I DON'T UNDERSTAND.
YOU MUST LEAVE EARTH FOR GOOD NO MORE DEATH AND REINCARNATION NO MORE HEAVEN AND HELL OR ANY OF THE OTHER LITTLE LUXURIES YOU CREATED FOR YOURSELVES
IT'S TIME TO FLY THE NEST ARCANE
YOU'RE ALL GOING TO DIE AND STAY DEAD THIS TIME

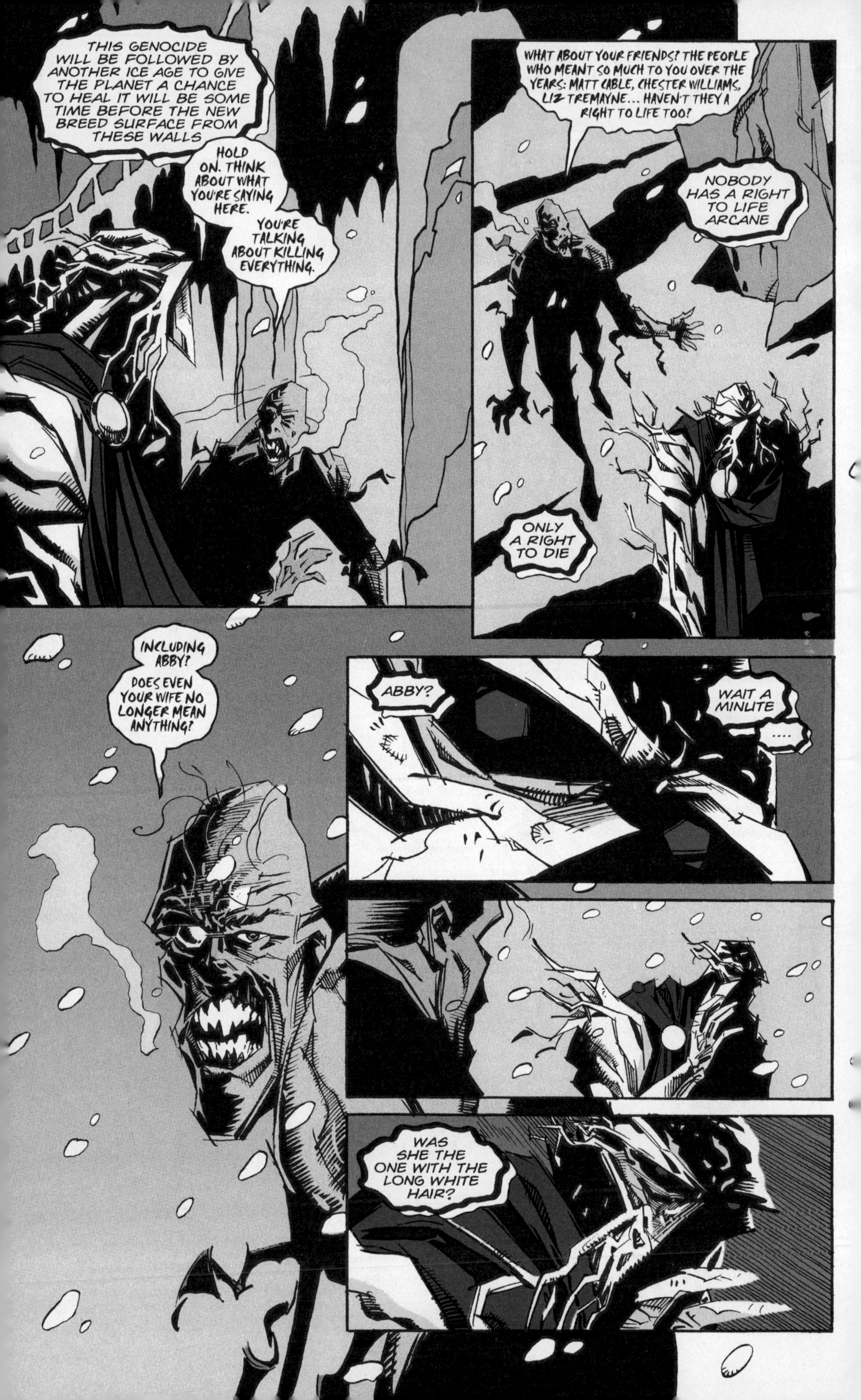
THIS GENOCIDE WILL BE FOLLOWED BY ANOTHER ICE AGE TO GIVE THE PLANET A CHANCE TO HEAL IT WILL BE SOME TIME BEFORE THE NEW BREED SURFACE FROM THESE WALLS
HOLD ON. THINK ABOUT WHAT YOU'RE SAYING HERE.
YOU'RE TALKING ABOUT KILLING EVERYTHING.
WHAT ABOUT YOUR FRIENDS? THE PEOPLE WHO MEANT SO MUCH TO YOU OVER THE YEARS: MATT CABLE, CHESTER WILLIAMS, LIZ TREMAYNE... HAVEN'T THEY A RIGHT TO LIFE TOO?
NOBODY HAS A RIGHT TO LIFE ARCANE
ONLY A RIGHT TO DIE
INCLUDING ABBY?
DOES EVEN YOUR WIFE NO LONGER MEAN ANYTHING?
ABBY?
WAIT A MINUTE
....
WAS SHE THE ONE WITH THE LONG WHITE HAIR?

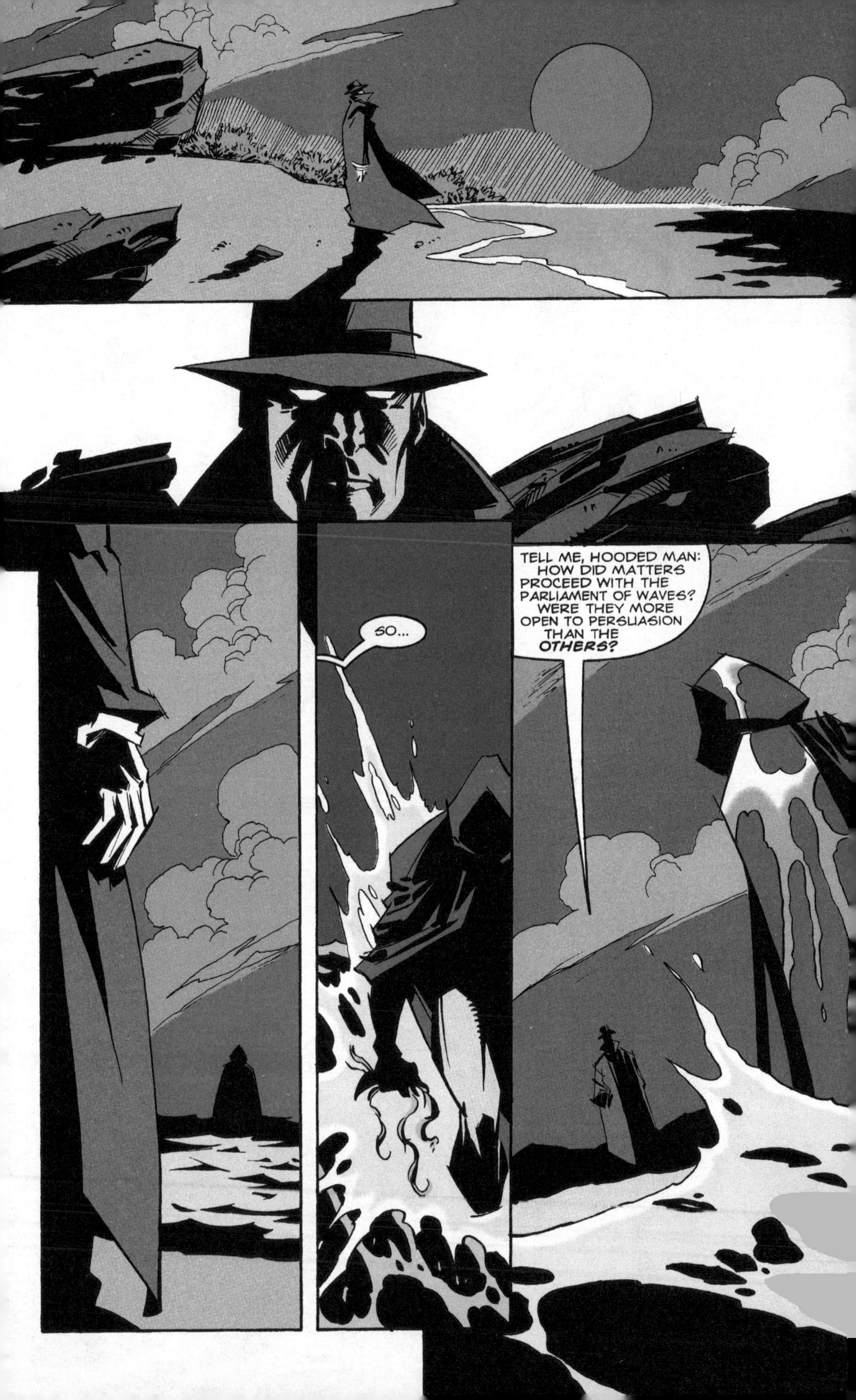

SO...
TELL ME, HOODED MAN: HOW DID MATTERS PROCEED WITH THE PARLIAMENT OF WAVES? WERE THEY MORE OPEN TO PERSUASION THAN THE OTHERS?

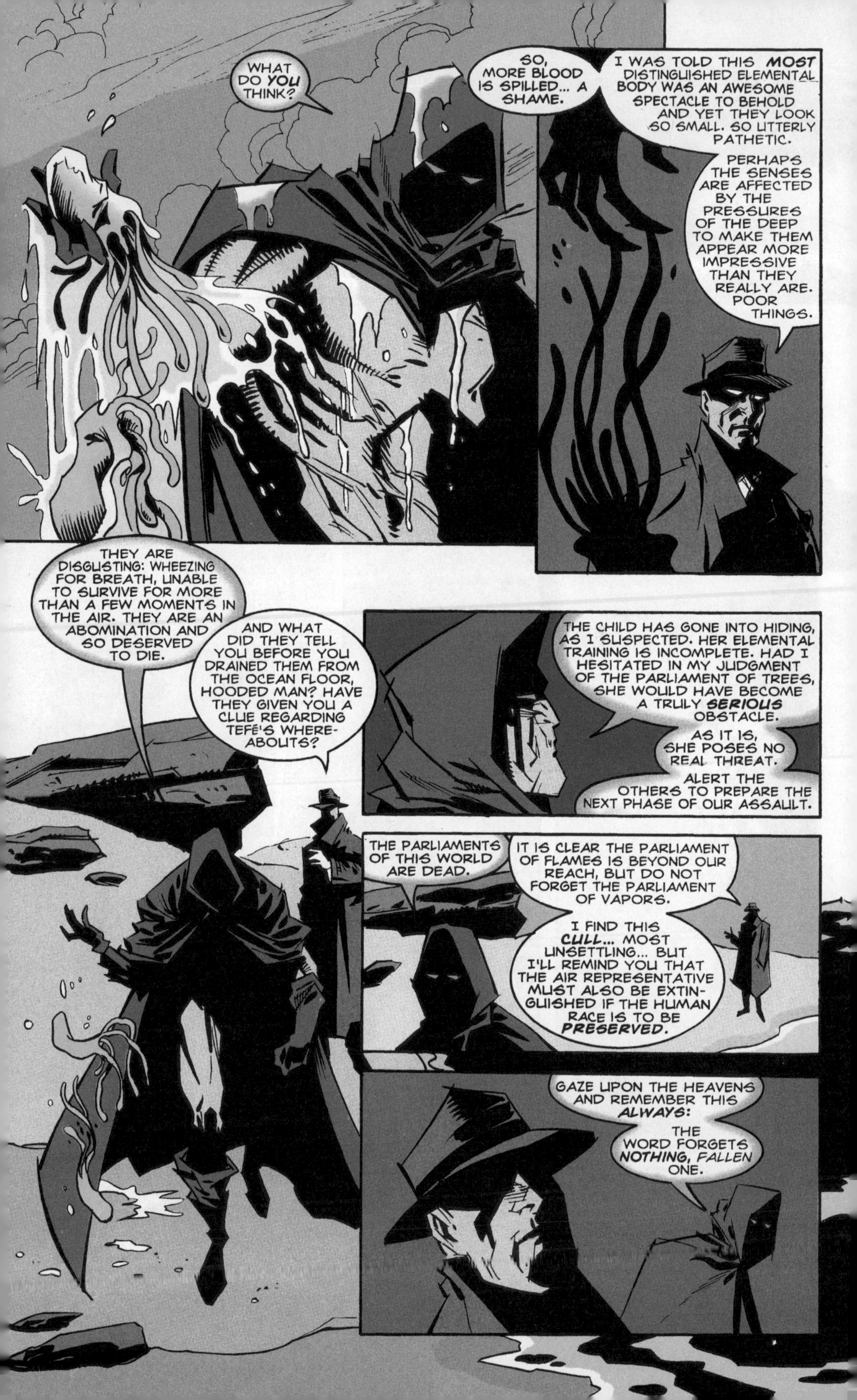
WHAT DO YOU THINK?
SO, MORE BLOOD IS SPILLED... A SHAME.
I WAS TOLD THIS MOST DISTINGUISHED ELEMENTAL BODY WAS AN AWESOME SPECTACLE TO BEHOLD AND YET THEY LOOK SO SMALL. SO UTTERLY PATHETIC.
PERHAPS THE SENSES ARE AFFECTED BY THE PRESSURES OF THE DEEP TO MAKE THEM APPEAR MORE IMPRESSIVE THAN THEY REALLY ARE. POOR THINGS.
THEY ARE DISGUSTING: WHEEZING FOR BREATH, UNABLE TO SURVIVE FOR MORE THAN A FEW MOMENTS IN THE AIR. THEY ARE AN ABOMINATION AND SO DESERVED TO DIE.
AND WHAT DID THEY TELL YOU BEFORE YOU DRAINED THEM FROM THE OCEAN FLOOR, HOODED MAN? HAVE THEY GIVEN YOU A CLUE REGARDING TEFÉ'S WHEREABOUTS?
THE CHILD HAS GONE INTO HIDING, AS I SUSPECTED. HER ELEMENTAL TRAINING IS INCOMPLETE. HAD I HESITATED IN MY JUDGMENT OF THE PARLIAMENT OF TREES, SHE WOULD HAVE BECOME A TRULY SERIOUS OBSTACLE.
AS IT IS, SHE POSES NO REAL THREAT.
ALERT THE OTHERS TO PREPARE THE NEXT PHASE OF OUR ASSAULT.
THE PARLIAMENTS OF THIS WORLD ARE DEAD.
IT IS CLEAR THE PARLIAMENT OF FLAMES IS BEYOND OUR REACH, BUT DO NOT FORGET THE PARLIAMENT OF VAPORS.
I FIND THIS CULL... MOST UNSETTLING... BUT I'LL REMIND YOU THAT THE AIR REPRESENTATIVE MUST ALSO BE EXTINGUISHED IF THE HUMAN RACE IS TO BE PRESERVED.
GAZE UPON THE HEAVENS AND REMEMBER THIS ALWAYS:
THE WORD FORGETS NOTHING, FALLEN ONE.

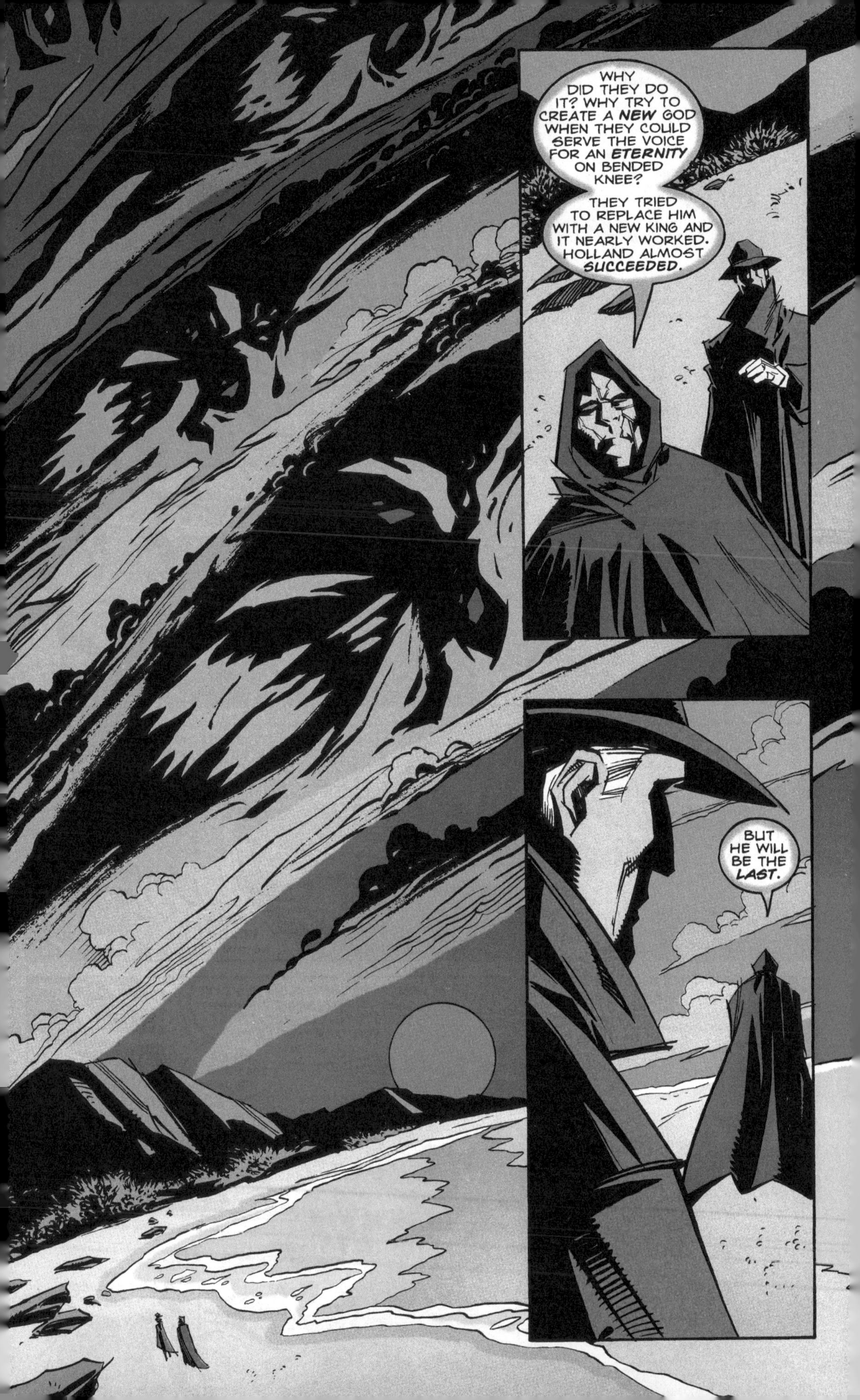
WHY DID THEY DO IT? WHY TRY TO CREATE A NEW GOD WHEN THEY COULD SERVE THE VOICE FOR AN ETERNITY ON BENDED KNEE?
THEY TRIED TO REPLACE HIM WITH A NEW KING AND IT NEARLY WORKED. HOLLAND ALMOST SUCCEEDED.
BUT HE WILL BE THE LAST.

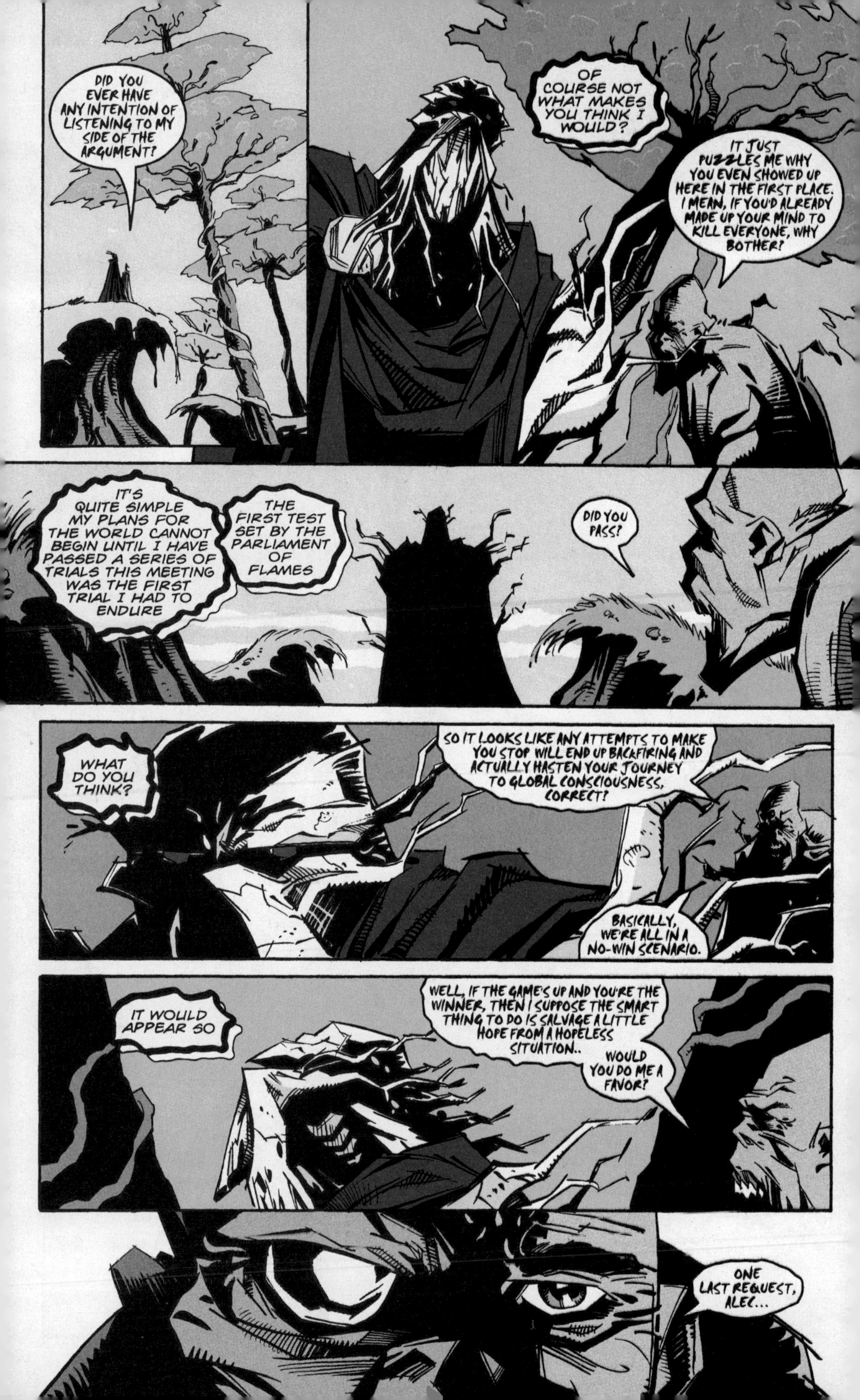
DID YOU EVER HAVE ANY INTENTION OF LISTENING TO MY SIDE OF THE ARGUMENT?
OF COURSE NOT WHAT MAKES YOU THINK I WOULD?
IT JUST PUZZLES ME WHY YOU EVEN SHOWED UP HERE IN THE FIRST PLACE. I MEAN, IF YOU'D ALREADY MADE UP YOUR MIND TO KILL EVERYONE, WHY BOTHER?
IT'S QUITE SIMPLE MY PLANS FOR THE WORLD CANNOT BEGIN UNTIL I HAVE PASSED A SERIES OF TRIALS THIS MEETING WAS THE FIRST TRIAL I HAD TO ENDURE
THE FIRST TEST SET BY THE PARLIAMENT OF FLAMES
DID YOU PASS?
WHAT DO YOU THINK?
SO IT LOOKS LIKE ANY ATTEMPTS TO MAKE YOU STOP WILL END UP BACKFIRING AND ACTUALLY HASTEN YOUR JOURNEY TO GLOBAL CONSCIOUSNESS, CORRECT?
BASICALLY, WE'RE ALL IN A NO-WIN SCENARIO.
IT WOULD APPEAR SO
WELL, IF THE GAME'S UP AND YOU'RE THE WINNER, THEN I SUPPOSE THE SMART THING TO DO IS SALVAGE A LITTLE HOPE FROM A HOPELESS SITUATION..
WOULD YOU DO ME A FAVOR?
ONE LAST REQUEST, ALEC...

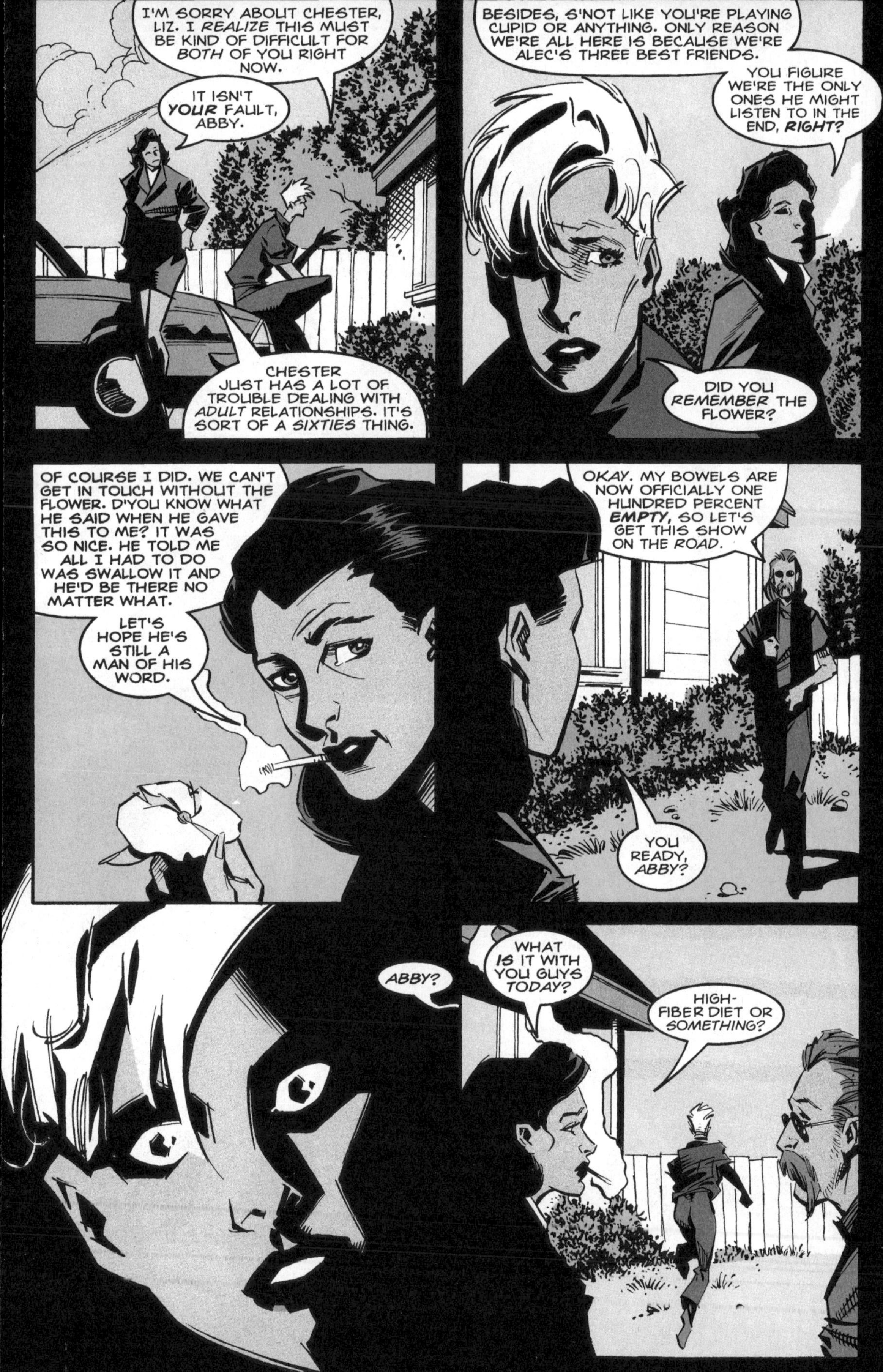
I'M SORRY ABOUT CHESTER, LIZ. I *REALIZE* THIS MUST BE KIND OF DIFFICULT FOR *BOTH* OF YOU RIGHT NOW.
IT ISN'T ***YOUR*** FAULT, ABBY.
CHESTER JUST HAS A LOT OF TROUBLE DEALING WITH *ADULT* RELATIONSHIPS. IT'S SORT OF A *SIXTIES* THING.
BESIDES, S'NOT LIKE YOU'RE PLAYING CUPID OR ANYTHING. ONLY REASON WE'RE ALL HERE IS BECAUSE WE'RE ALEC'S THREE BEST FRIENDS.
YOU FIGURE WE'RE THE ONLY ONES HE MIGHT LISTEN TO IN THE END, ***RIGHT?***
DID YOU *REMEMBER* THE FLOWER?
OF COURSE I DID. WE CAN'T GET IN TOUCH WITHOUT THE FLOWER. D'YOU KNOW WHAT HE SAID WHEN HE GAVE THIS TO ME? IT WAS SO NICE. HE TOLD ME ALL I HAD TO DO WAS SWALLOW IT AND HE'D BE THERE NO MATTER WHAT.
LET'S HOPE HE'S STILL A MAN OF HIS WORD.
OKAY. MY BOWELS ARE NOW OFFICIALLY ONE HUNDRED PERCENT ***EMPTY,*** SO LET'S GET THIS SHOW ON THE *ROAD.*
YOU READY, *ABBY?*
ABBY?
WHAT ***IS*** IT WITH YOU GUYS *TODAY?*
HIGH-FIBER DIET OR *SOMETHING?*

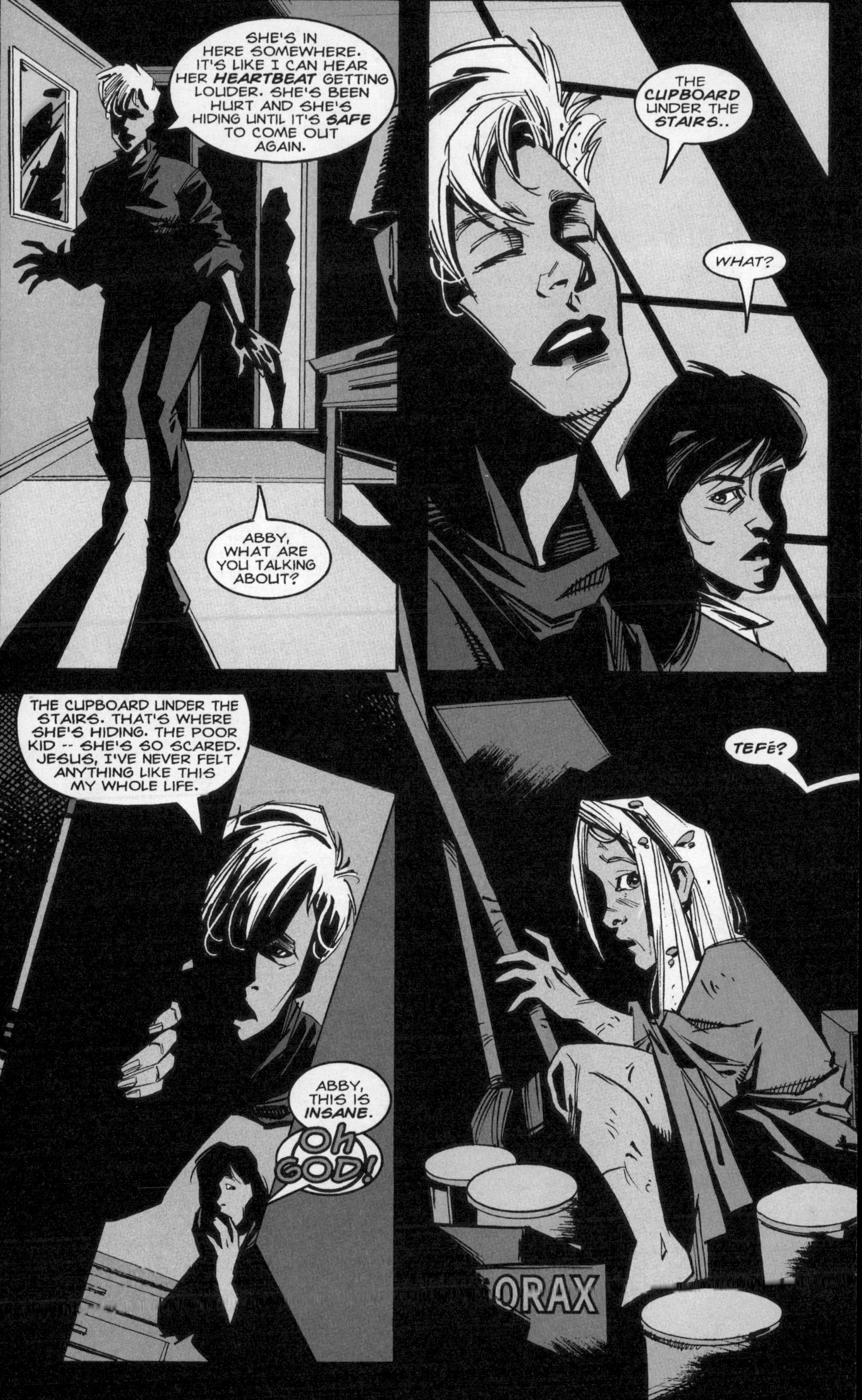

SHE'S IN HERE SOMEWHERE. IT'S LIKE I CAN HEAR HER HEARTBEAT GETTING LOUDER. SHE'S BEEN HURT AND SHE'S HIDING UNTIL IT'S SAFE TO COME OUT AGAIN.
ABBY, WHAT ARE YOU TALKING ABOUT?
THE CUPBOARD UNDER THE STAIRS..
WHAT?
THE CUPBOARD UNDER THE STAIRS. THAT'S WHERE SHE'S HIDING. THE POOR KID -- SHE'S SO SCARED. JESUS, I'VE NEVER FELT ANYTHING LIKE THIS MY WHOLE LIFE.
ABBY, THIS IS INSANE.
OH GOD!
TEFÉ?
ORAX

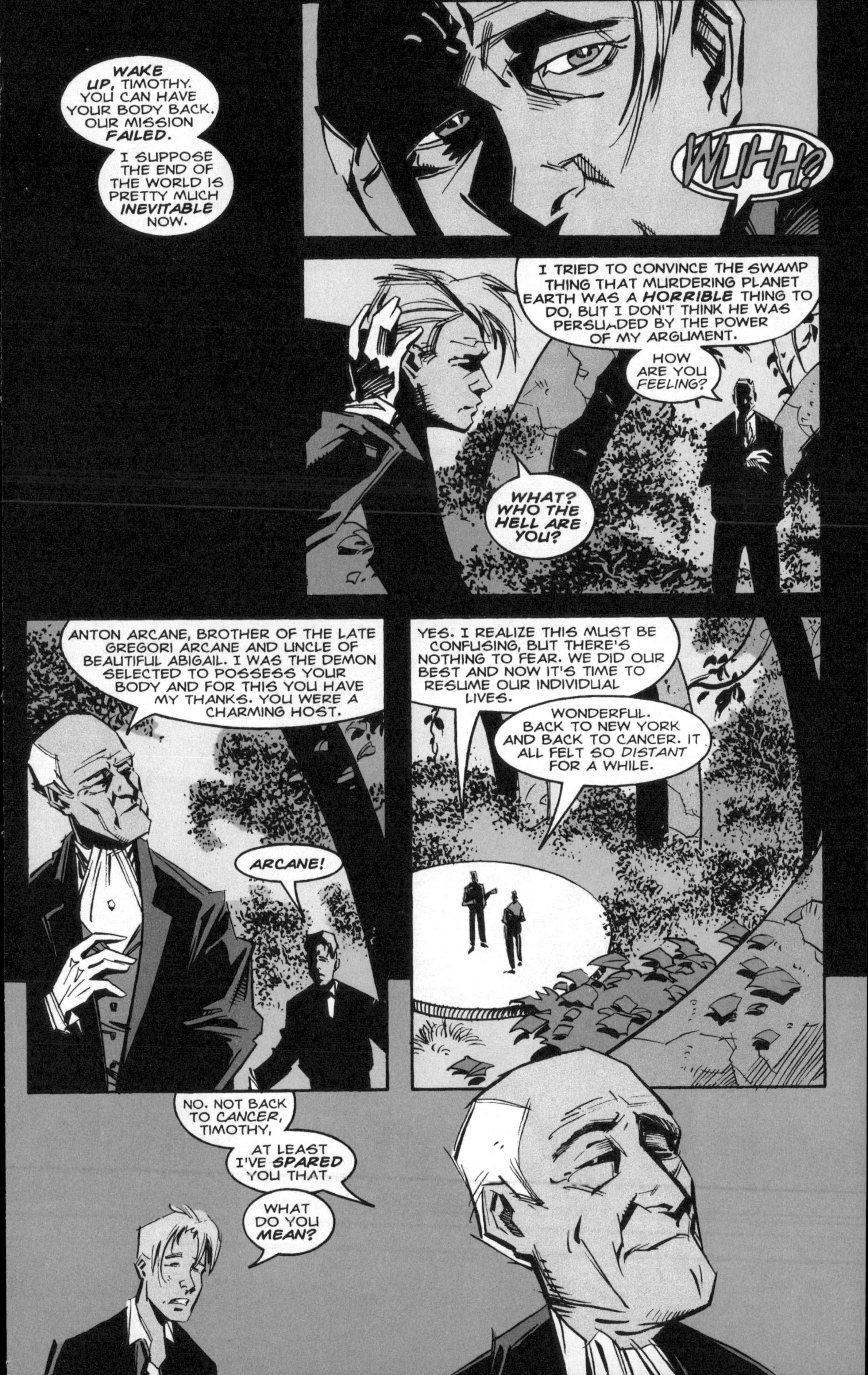
WAKE UP, TIMOTHY. YOU CAN HAVE YOUR BODY BACK. OUR MISSION FAILED.
I SUPPOSE THE END OF THE WORLD IS PRETTY MUCH INEVITABLE NOW.
WUHH?
I TRIED TO CONVINCE THE SWAMP THING THAT MURDERING PLANET EARTH WAS A HORRIBLE THING TO DO, BUT I DON'T THINK HE WAS PERSUADED BY THE POWER OF MY ARGUMENT.
HOW ARE YOU FEELING?
WHAT? WHO THE HELL ARE YOU?
ANTON ARCANE, BROTHER OF THE LATE GREGORI ARCANE AND UNCLE OF BEAUTIFUL ABIGAIL. I WAS THE DEMON SELECTED TO POSSESS YOUR BODY AND FOR THIS YOU HAVE MY THANKS. YOU WERE A CHARMING HOST.
ARCANE!
YES. I REALIZE THIS MUST BE CONFUSING, BUT THERE'S NOTHING TO FEAR. WE DID OUR BEST AND NOW IT'S TIME TO RESUME OUR INDIVIDUAL LIVES.
WONDERFUL. BACK TO NEW YORK AND BACK TO CANCER. IT ALL FELT SO DISTANT FOR A WHILE.
NO. NOT BACK TO CANCER, TIMOTHY,
AT LEAST I'VE SPARED YOU THAT.
WHAT DO YOU MEAN?

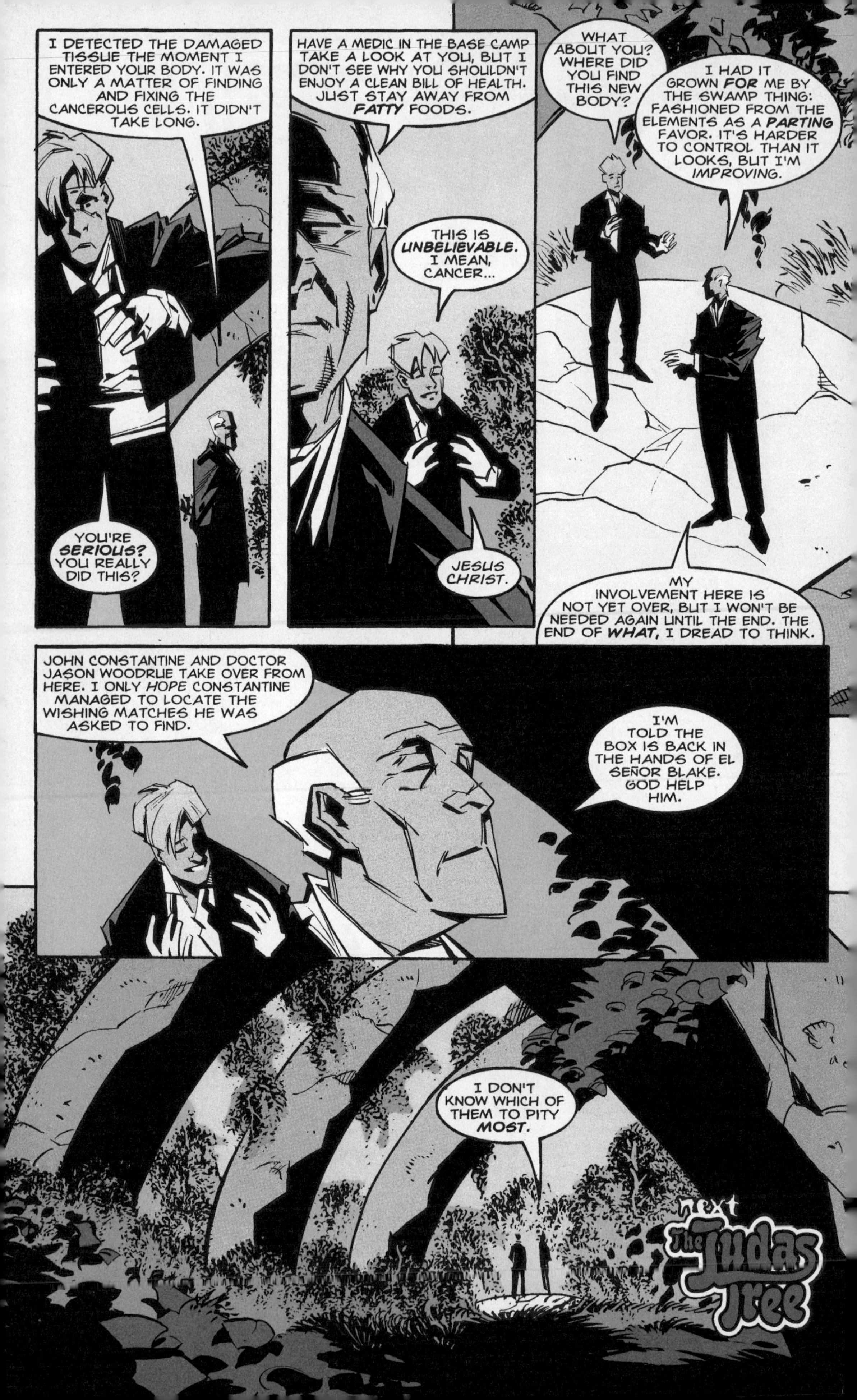
I DETECTED THE DAMAGED TISSUE THE MOMENT I ENTERED YOUR BODY. IT WAS ONLY A MATTER OF FINDING AND FIXING THE CANCEROUS CELLS. IT DIDN'T TAKE LONG.
YOU'RE SERIOUS? YOU REALLY DID THIS?
HAVE A MEDIC IN THE BASE CAMP TAKE A LOOK AT YOU, BUT I DON'T SEE WHY YOU SHOULDN'T ENJOY A CLEAN BILL OF HEALTH. JUST STAY AWAY FROM FATTY FOODS.
THIS IS UNBELIEVABLE. I MEAN, CANCER...
JESUS CHRIST.
WHAT ABOUT YOU? WHERE DID YOU FIND THIS NEW BODY?
I HAD IT GROWN FOR ME BY THE SWAMP THING: FASHIONED FROM THE ELEMENTS AS A PARTING FAVOR. IT'S HARDER TO CONTROL THAN IT LOOKS, BUT I'M IMPROVING.
MY INVOLVEMENT HERE IS NOT YET OVER, BUT I WON'T BE NEEDED AGAIN UNTIL THE END. THE END OF WHAT, I DREAD TO THINK.
JOHN CONSTANTINE AND DOCTOR JASON WOODRUE TAKE OVER FROM HERE. I ONLY HOPE CONSTANTINE MANAGED TO LOCATE THE WISHING MATCHES HE WAS ASKED TO FIND.
I'M TOLD THE BOX IS BACK IN THE HANDS OF EL SEÑOR BLAKE. GOD HELP HIM.
I DON'T KNOW WHICH OF THEM TO PITY MOST.
next
The Judas Tree

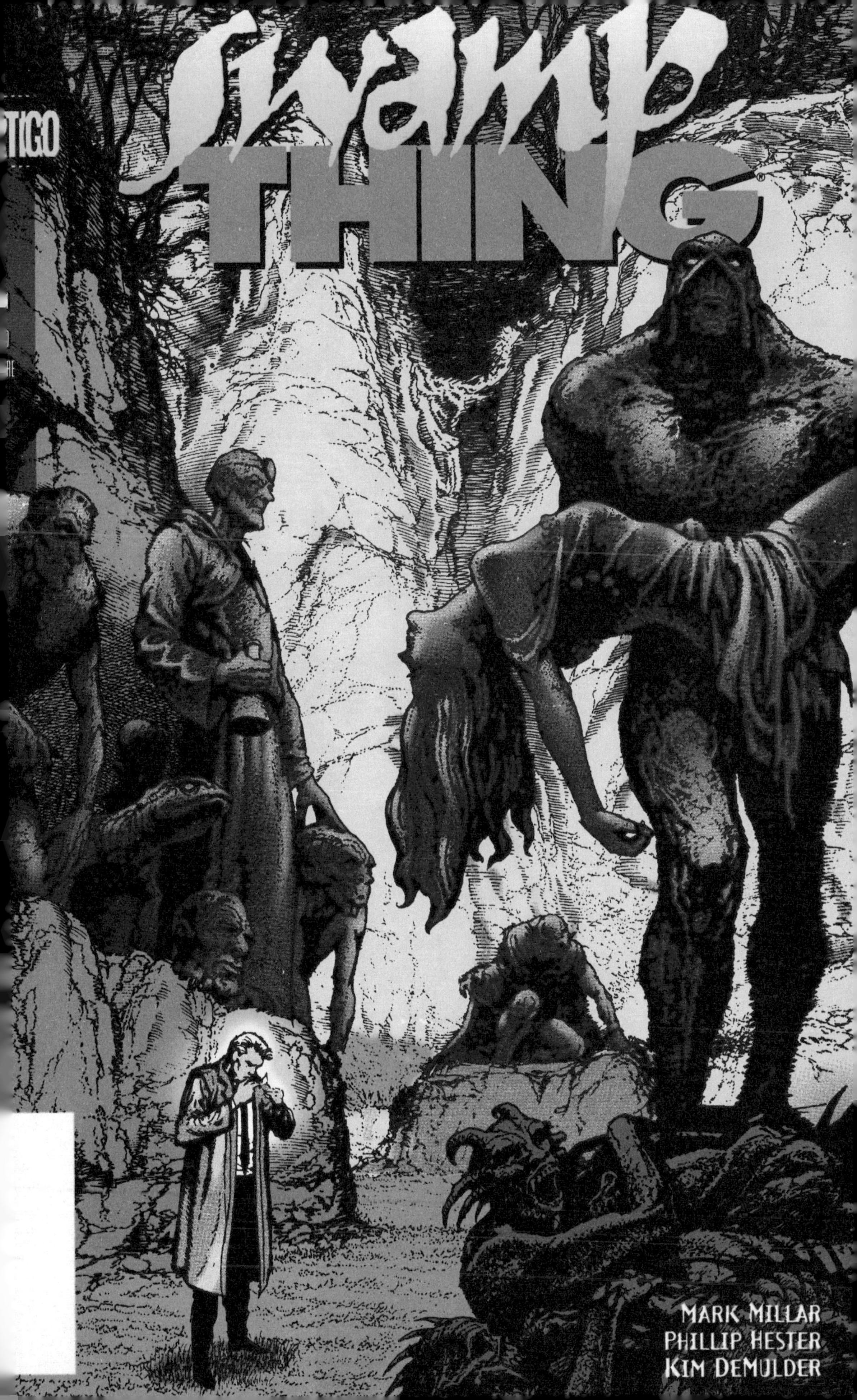
Swamp THING
MARK MILLAR
PHILLIP HESTER
KIM DEMULDER

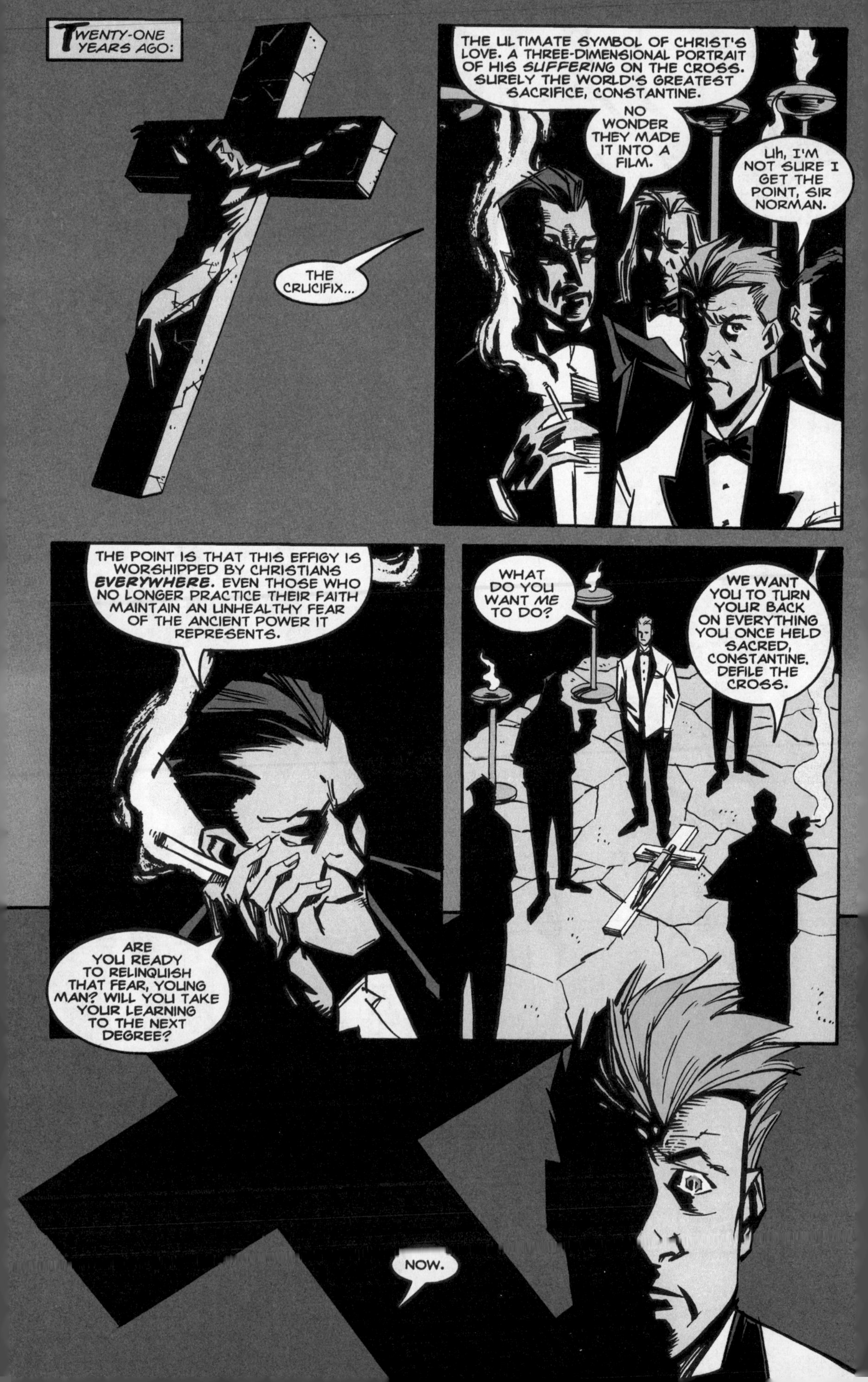
TWENTY-ONE YEARS AGO:
THE CRUCIFIX...
THE ULTIMATE SYMBOL OF CHRIST'S LOVE. A THREE-DIMENSIONAL PORTRAIT OF HIS SUFFERING ON THE CROSS. SURELY THE WORLD'S GREATEST SACRIFICE, CONSTANTINE.
NO WONDER THEY MADE IT INTO A FILM.
UH, I'M NOT SURE I GET THE POINT, SIR NORMAN.
THE POINT IS THAT THIS EFFIGY IS WORSHIPPED BY CHRISTIANS EVERYWHERE. EVEN THOSE WHO NO LONGER PRACTICE THEIR FAITH MAINTAIN AN UNHEALTHY FEAR OF THE ANCIENT POWER IT REPRESENTS.
ARE YOU READY TO RELINQUISH THAT FEAR, YOUNG MAN? WILL YOU TAKE YOUR LEARNING TO THE NEXT DEGREE?
WHAT DO YOU WANT ME TO DO?
WE WANT YOU TO TURN YOUR BACK ON EVERYTHING YOU ONCE HELD SACRED, CONSTANTINE. DEFILE THE CROSS.
NOW.

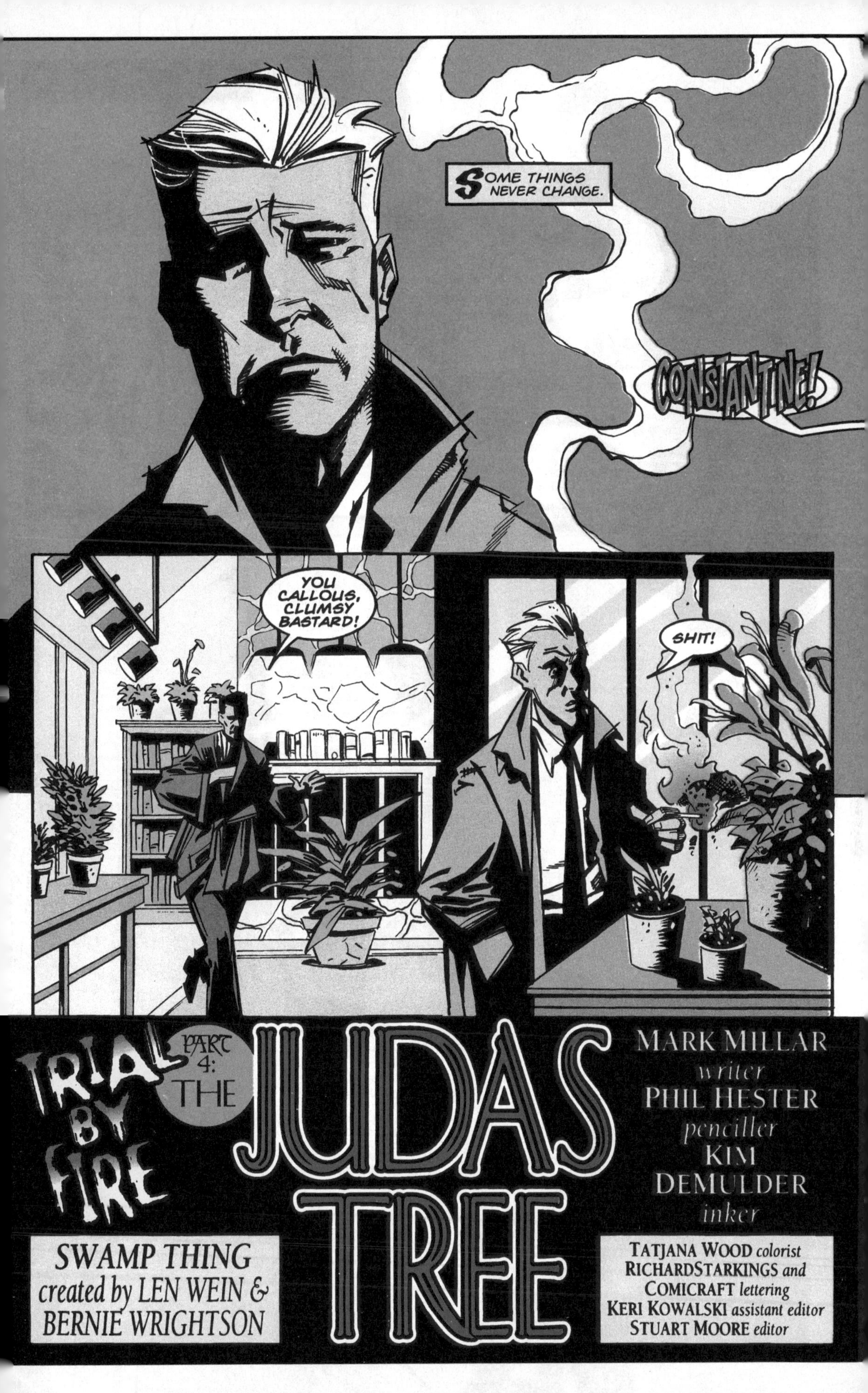
SOME THINGS NEVER CHANGE.
CONSTANTINE!
YOU CALLOUS, CLUMSY BASTARD!
SHIT!
TRIAL BY FIRE
PART 4: THE JUDAS TREE
MARK MILLAR writer
PHIL HESTER penciller
KIM DEMULDER inker
SWAMP THING created by LEN WEIN & BERNIE WRIGHTSON
TATJANA WOOD colorist
RICHARDSTARKINGS and COMICRAFT lettering
KERI KOWALSKI assistant editor
STUART MOORE editor

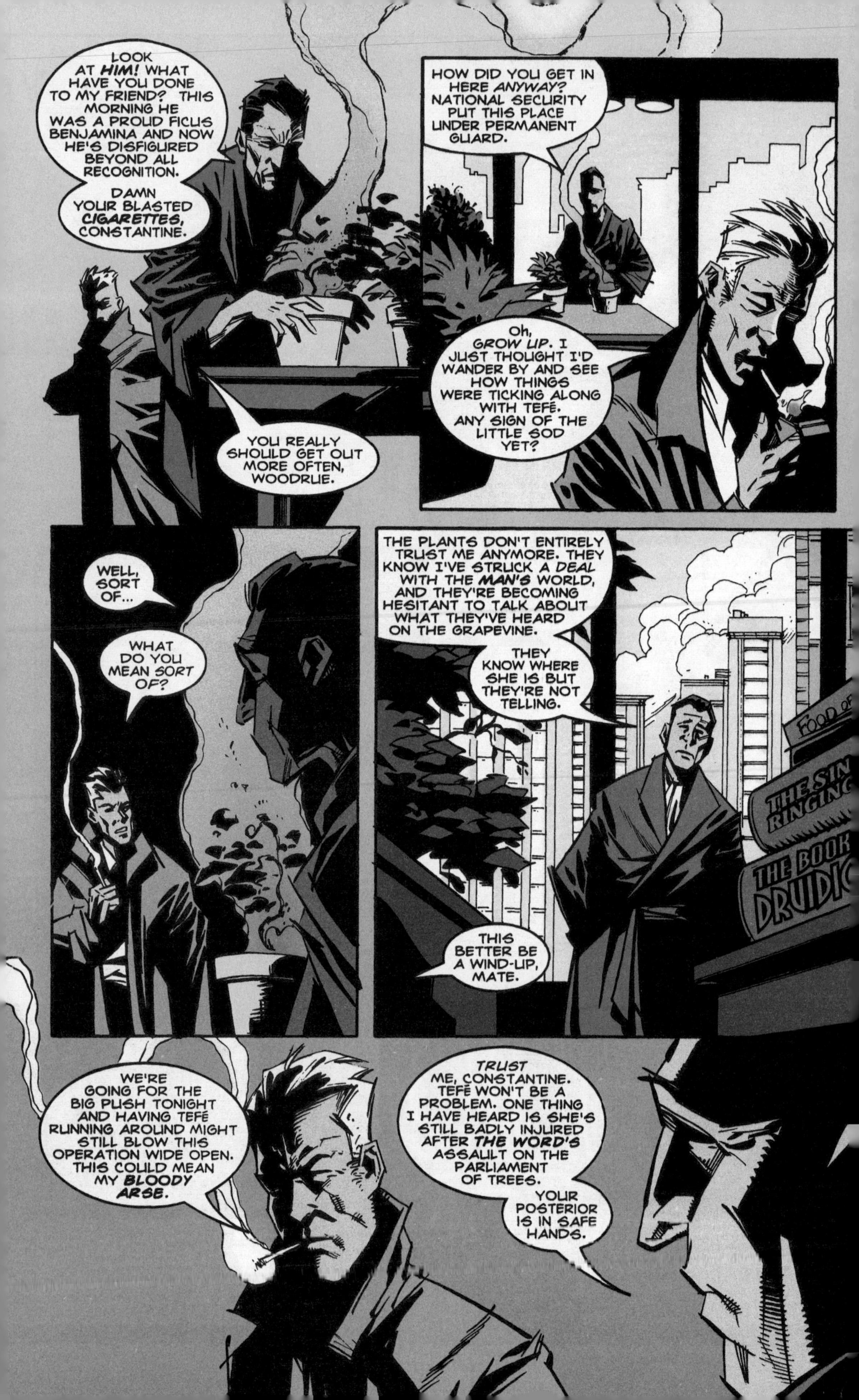
LOOK AT *HIM!* WHAT HAVE YOU DONE TO MY FRIEND? THIS MORNING HE WAS A PROUD FICUS BENJAMINA AND NOW HE'S DISFIGURED BEYOND ALL RECOGNITION.
DAMN YOUR BLASTED *CIGARETTES,* CONSTANTINE.
YOU REALLY SHOULD GET OUT MORE OFTEN, WOODRUE.
HOW DID YOU GET IN HERE *ANYWAY?* NATIONAL SECURITY PUT THIS PLACE UNDER PERMANENT GUARD.
Oh, *GROW UP.* I JUST THOUGHT I'D WANDER BY AND SEE HOW THINGS WERE TICKING ALONG WITH TEFÉ. ANY SIGN OF THE LITTLE SOD YET?
WELL, SORT OF...
WHAT DO YOU MEAN *SORT OF?*
THE PLANTS DON'T ENTIRELY TRUST ME ANYMORE. THEY KNOW I'VE STRUCK A *DEAL* WITH THE *MAN'S* WORLD, AND THEY'RE BECOMING HESITANT TO TALK ABOUT WHAT THEY'VE HEARD ON THE GRAPEVINE.
THEY KNOW WHERE SHE IS BUT THEY'RE NOT TELLING.
FOOD OF
THE SIN
RINGING
THE BOOK
DRUIDIC
THIS BETTER BE A WIND-UP, MATE.
WE'RE GOING FOR THE BIG PUSH TONIGHT AND HAVING TEFÉ RUNNING AROUND MIGHT STILL BLOW THIS OPERATION WIDE OPEN. THIS COULD MEAN MY *BLOODY ARSE.*
TRUST ME, CONSTANTINE. TEFÉ WON'T BE A PROBLEM. ONE THING I HAVE HEARD IS SHE'S STILL BADLY INJURED AFTER *THE WORD'S* ASSAULT ON THE PARLIAMENT OF TREES.
YOUR POSTERIOR IS IN SAFE HANDS.

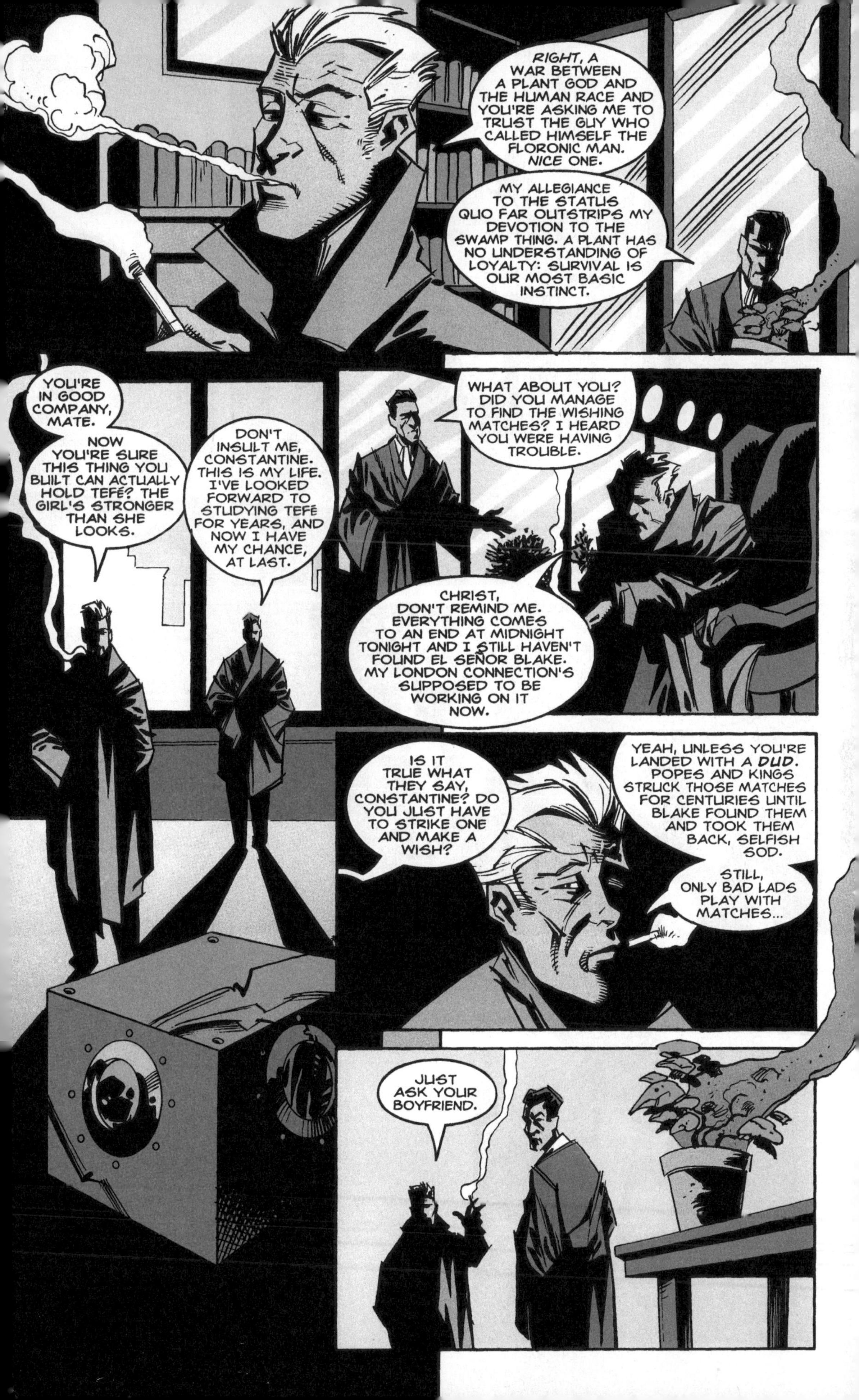
RIGHT, A WAR BETWEEN A PLANT GOD AND THE HUMAN RACE AND YOU'RE ASKING ME TO TRUST THE GUY WHO CALLED HIMSELF THE FLORONIC MAN. NICE ONE.
MY ALLEGIANCE TO THE STATUS QUO FAR OUTSTRIPS MY DEVOTION TO THE SWAMP THING. A PLANT HAS NO UNDERSTANDING OF LOYALTY: SURVIVAL IS OUR MOST BASIC INSTINCT.
YOU'RE IN GOOD COMPANY, MATE.
NOW YOU'RE SURE THIS THING YOU BUILT CAN ACTUALLY HOLD TEFÉ? THE GIRL'S STRONGER THAN SHE LOOKS.
DON'T INSULT ME, CONSTANTINE. THIS IS MY LIFE. I'VE LOOKED FORWARD TO STUDYING TEFÉ FOR YEARS, AND NOW I HAVE MY CHANCE, AT LAST.
WHAT ABOUT YOU? DID YOU MANAGE TO FIND THE WISHING MATCHES? I HEARD YOU WERE HAVING TROUBLE.
CHRIST, DON'T REMIND ME. EVERYTHING COMES TO AN END AT MIDNIGHT TONIGHT AND I STILL HAVEN'T FOUND EL SEÑOR BLAKE. MY LONDON CONNECTION'S SUPPOSED TO BE WORKING ON IT NOW.
IS IT TRUE WHAT THEY SAY, CONSTANTINE? DO YOU JUST HAVE TO STRIKE ONE AND MAKE A WISH?
YEAH, UNLESS YOU'RE LANDED WITH A DUD. POPES AND KINGS STRUCK THOSE MATCHES FOR CENTURIES UNTIL BLAKE FOUND THEM AND TOOK THEM BACK, SELFISH SOD.
STILL, ONLY BAD LADS PLAY WITH MATCHES...
JUST ASK YOUR BOYFRIEND.

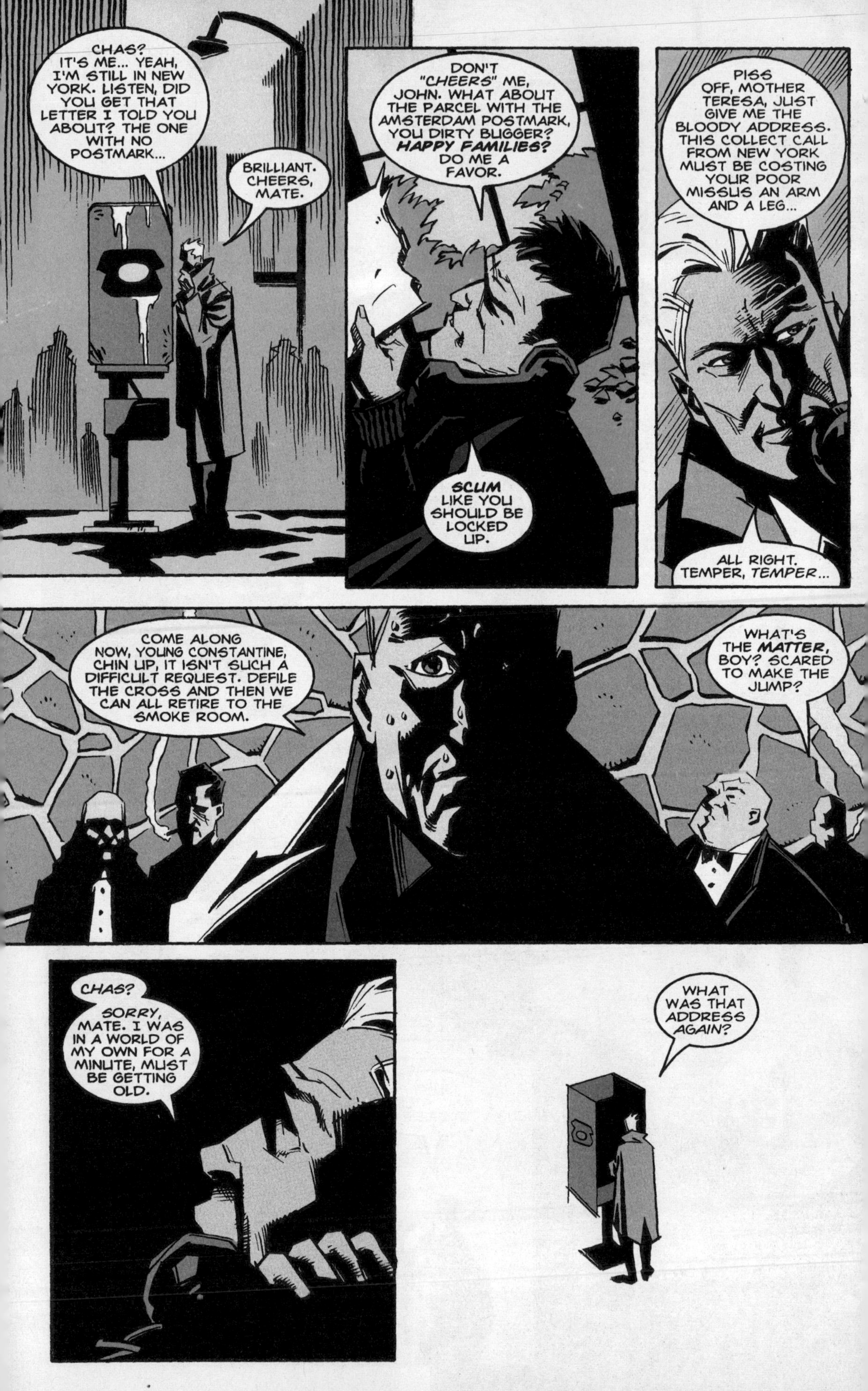
CHAS? IT'S ME... YEAH, I'M STILL IN NEW YORK. LISTEN, DID YOU GET THAT LETTER I TOLD YOU ABOUT? THE ONE WITH NO POSTMARK...
BRILLIANT. CHEERS, MATE.
DON'T "*CHEERS*" ME, JOHN. WHAT ABOUT THE PARCEL WITH THE AMSTERDAM POSTMARK, YOU DIRTY BUGGER? ***HAPPY FAMILIES?*** DO ME A FAVOR.
SCUM LIKE YOU SHOULD BE LOCKED UP.
PISS OFF, MOTHER TERESA, JUST GIVE ME THE BLOODY ADDRESS. THIS COLLECT CALL FROM NEW YORK MUST BE COSTING YOUR POOR MISSUS AN ARM AND A LEG...
ALL RIGHT. TEMPER, *TEMPER*...
COME ALONG NOW, YOUNG CONSTANTINE, CHIN UP, IT ISN'T SUCH A DIFFICULT REQUEST. DEFILE THE CROSS AND THEN WE CAN ALL RETIRE TO THE SMOKE ROOM.
WHAT'S THE ***MATTER***, BOY? SCARED TO MAKE THE JUMP?
CHAS?
SORRY, MATE. I WAS IN A WORLD OF MY OWN FOR A MINUTE, MUST BE GETTING OLD.
WHAT WAS THAT ADDRESS *AGAIN?*

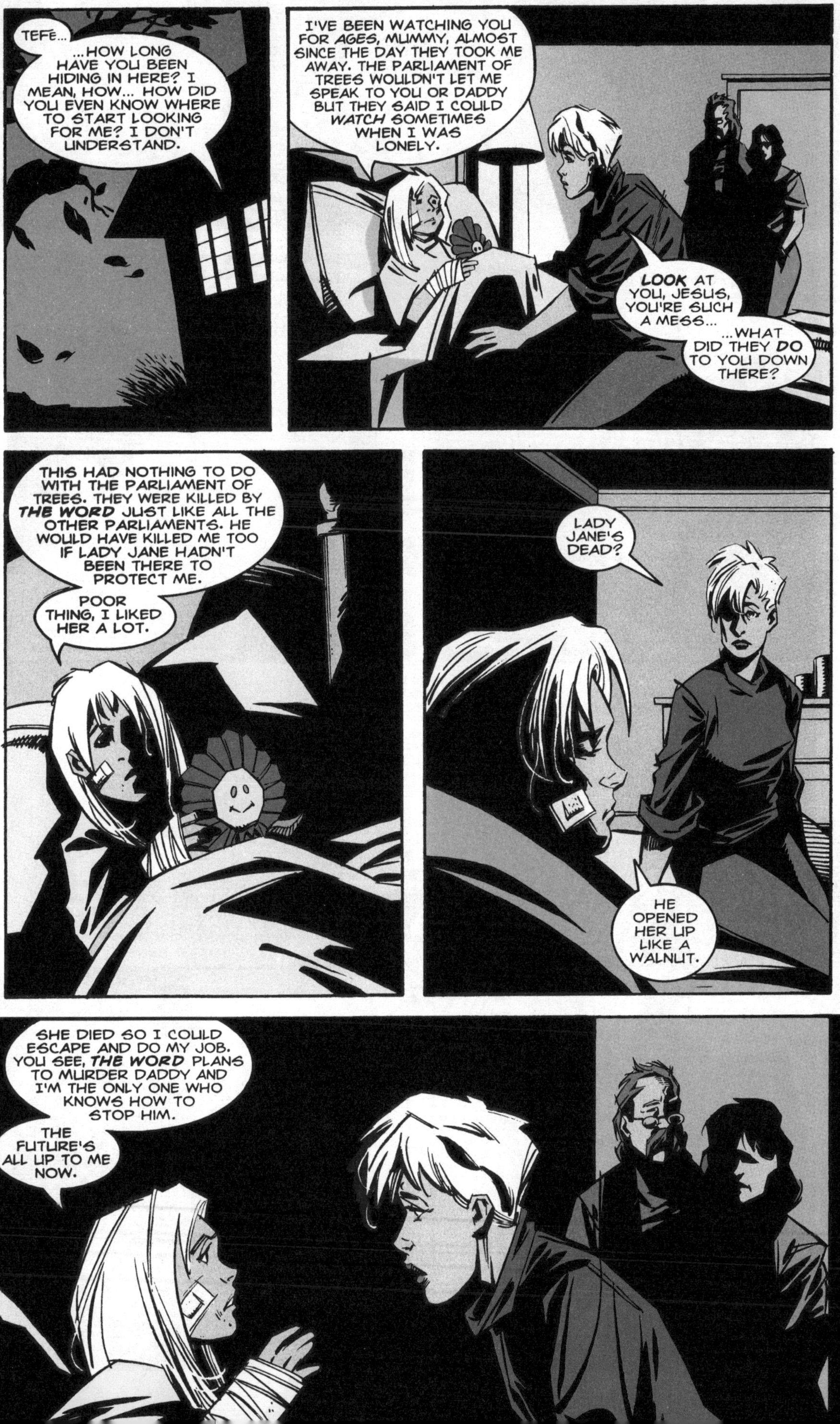
TEFÉ...
...HOW LONG HAVE YOU BEEN HIDING IN HERE? I MEAN, HOW... HOW DID YOU EVEN KNOW WHERE TO START LOOKING FOR ME? I DON'T UNDERSTAND.
I'VE BEEN WATCHING YOU FOR AGES, MUMMY, ALMOST SINCE THE DAY THEY TOOK ME AWAY. THE PARLIAMENT OF TREES WOULDN'T LET ME SPEAK TO YOU OR DADDY BUT THEY SAID I COULD WATCH SOMETIMES WHEN I WAS LONELY.
LOOK AT YOU, JESUS, YOU'RE SUCH A MESS...
...WHAT DID THEY DO TO YOU DOWN THERE?
THIS HAD NOTHING TO DO WITH THE PARLIAMENT OF TREES. THEY WERE KILLED BY THE WORD JUST LIKE ALL THE OTHER PARLIAMENTS. HE WOULD HAVE KILLED ME TOO IF LADY JANE HADN'T BEEN THERE TO PROTECT ME.
POOR THING, I LIKED HER A LOT.
LADY JANE'S DEAD?
HE OPENED HER UP LIKE A WALNUT.
SHE DIED SO I COULD ESCAPE AND DO MY JOB. YOU SEE, THE WORD PLANS TO MURDER DADDY AND I'M THE ONLY ONE WHO KNOWS HOW TO STOP HIM.
THE FUTURE'S ALL UP TO ME NOW.

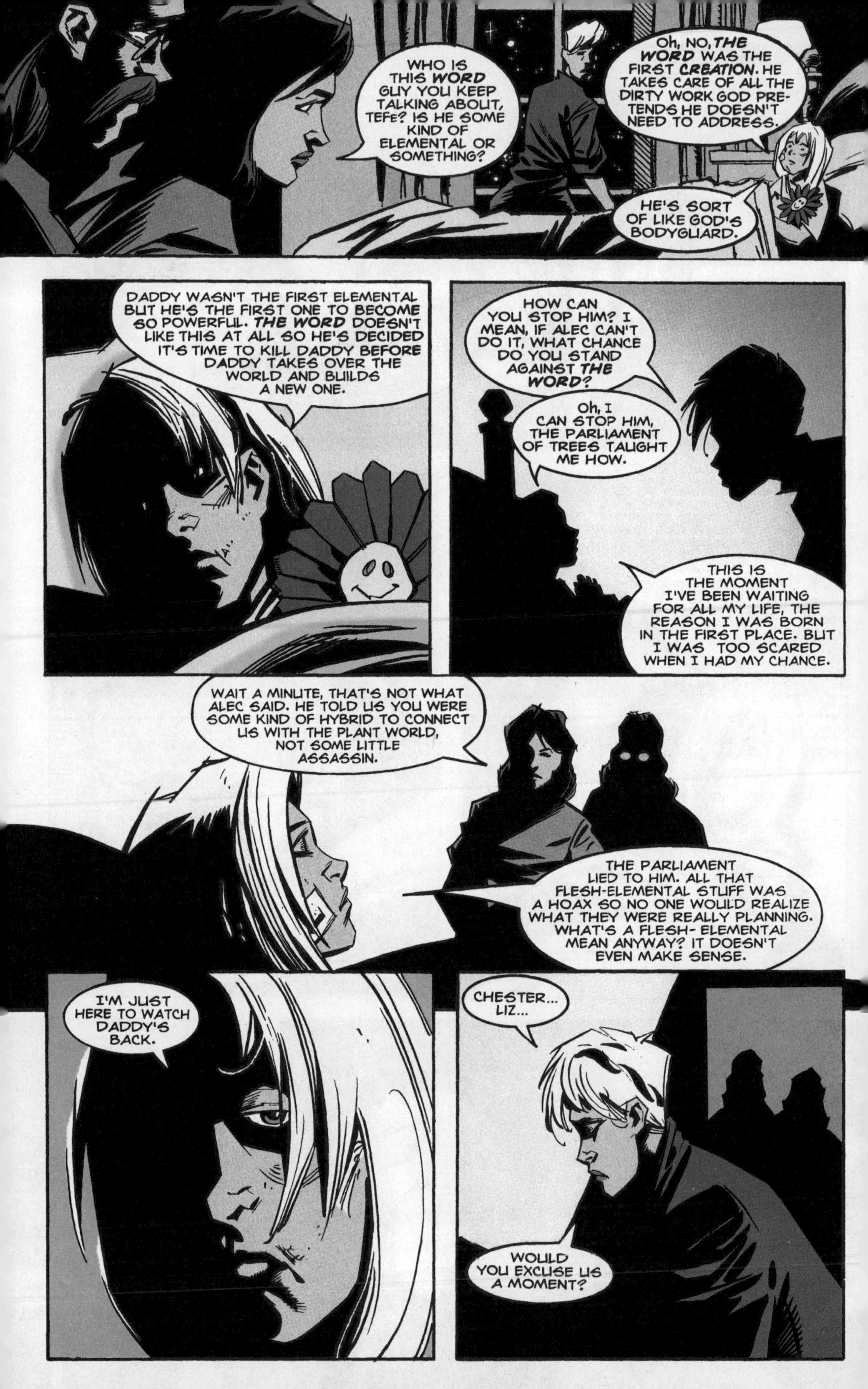

WHO IS THIS *WORD* GUY YOU KEEP TALKING ABOUT, TEFE? IS HE SOME KIND OF ELEMENTAL OR SOMETHING?
Oh, NO, *THE WORD* WAS THE FIRST *CREATION*. HE TAKES CARE OF ALL THE DIRTY WORK GOD PRE-TENDS HE DOESN'T NEED TO ADDRESS.
HE'S SORT OF LIKE GOD'S BODYGUARD.
DADDY WASN'T THE FIRST ELEMENTAL BUT HE'S THE FIRST ONE TO BECOME SO POWERFUL. *THE WORD* DOESN'T LIKE THIS AT ALL SO HE'S DECIDED IT'S TIME TO KILL DADDY BEFORE DADDY TAKES OVER THE WORLD AND BUILDS A NEW ONE.
HOW CAN YOU STOP HIM? I MEAN, IF ALEC CAN'T DO IT, WHAT CHANCE DO YOU STAND AGAINST *THE WORD*?
Oh, I CAN STOP HIM, THE PARLIAMENT OF TREES TAUGHT ME HOW.
THIS IS THE MOMENT I'VE BEEN WAITING FOR ALL MY LIFE, THE REASON I WAS BORN IN THE FIRST PLACE. BUT I WAS TOO SCARED WHEN I HAD MY CHANCE.
WAIT A MINUTE, THAT'S NOT WHAT ALEC SAID. HE TOLD US YOU WERE SOME KIND OF HYBRID TO CONNECT US WITH THE PLANT WORLD, NOT SOME LITTLE ASSASSIN.
THE PARLIAMENT LIED TO HIM. ALL THAT FLESH-ELEMENTAL STUFF WAS A HOAX SO NO ONE WOULD REALIZE WHAT THEY WERE REALLY PLANNING. WHAT'S A FLESH- ELEMENTAL MEAN ANYWAY? IT DOESN'T EVEN MAKE SENSE.
I'M JUST HERE TO WATCH DADDY'S BACK.
CHESTER... LIZ...
WOULD YOU EXCUSE US A MOMENT?

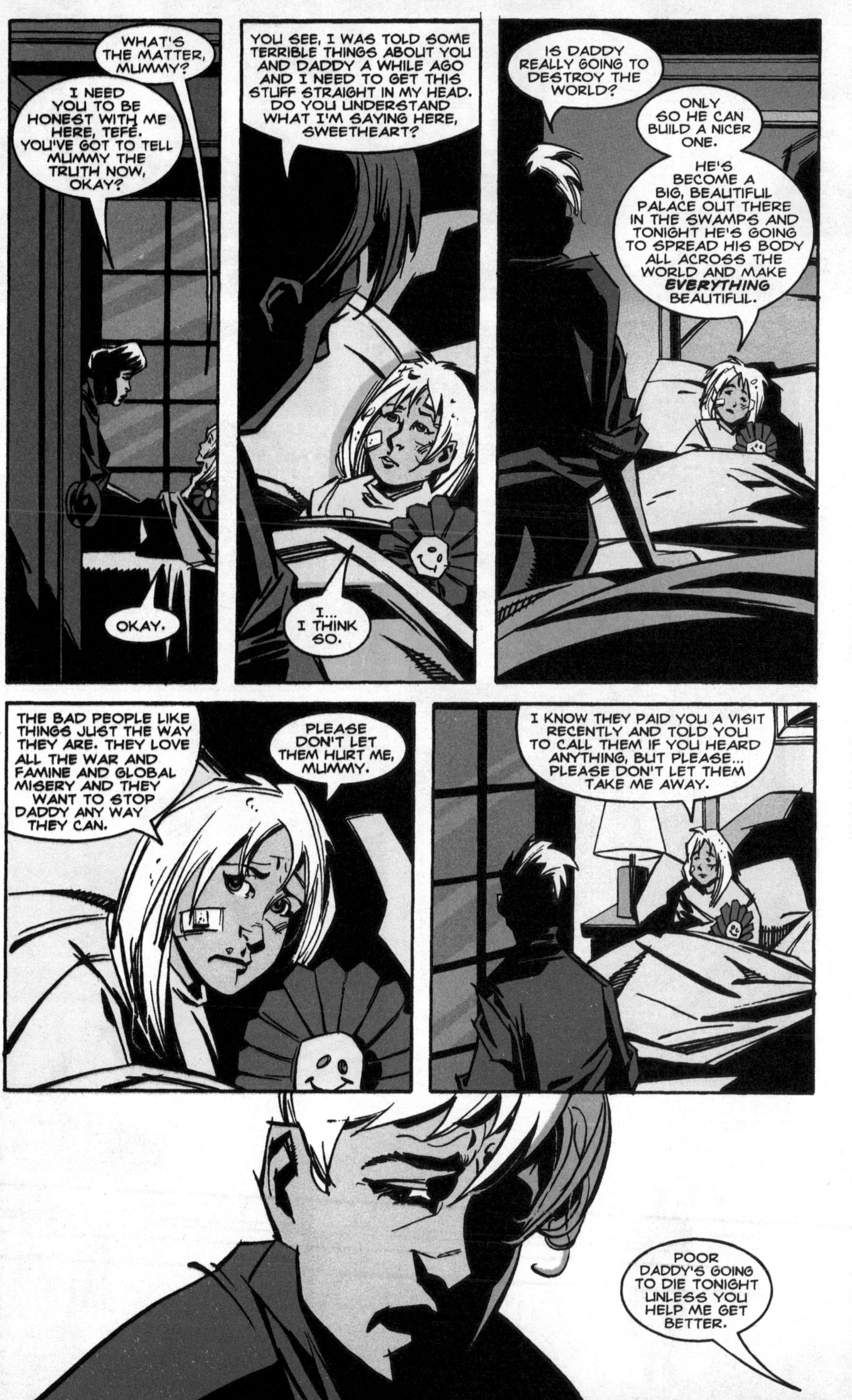
WHAT'S THE MATTER, MUMMY?
I NEED YOU TO BE HONEST WITH ME HERE, TEFÉ. YOU'VE GOT TO TELL MUMMY THE TRUTH NOW, OKAY?
OKAY.
YOU SEE, I WAS TOLD SOME TERRIBLE THINGS ABOUT YOU AND DADDY A WHILE AGO AND I NEED TO GET THIS STUFF STRAIGHT IN MY HEAD. DO YOU UNDERSTAND WHAT I'M SAYING HERE, SWEETHEART?
I... I THINK SO.
IS DADDY REALLY GOING TO DESTROY THE WORLD?
ONLY SO HE CAN BUILD A NICER ONE.
HE'S BECOME A BIG, BEAUTIFUL PALACE OUT THERE IN THE SWAMPS AND TONIGHT HE'S GOING TO SPREAD HIS BODY ALL ACROSS THE WORLD AND MAKE EVERYTHING BEAUTIFUL.
THE BAD PEOPLE LIKE THINGS JUST THE WAY THEY ARE. THEY LOVE ALL THE WAR AND FAMINE AND GLOBAL MISERY AND THEY WANT TO STOP DADDY ANY WAY THEY CAN.
PLEASE DON'T LET THEM HURT ME, MUMMY.
I KNOW THEY PAID YOU A VISIT RECENTLY AND TOLD YOU TO CALL THEM IF YOU HEARD ANYTHING, BUT PLEASE... PLEASE DON'T LET THEM TAKE ME AWAY.
POOR DADDY'S GOING TO DIE TONIGHT UNLESS YOU HELP ME GET BETTER.

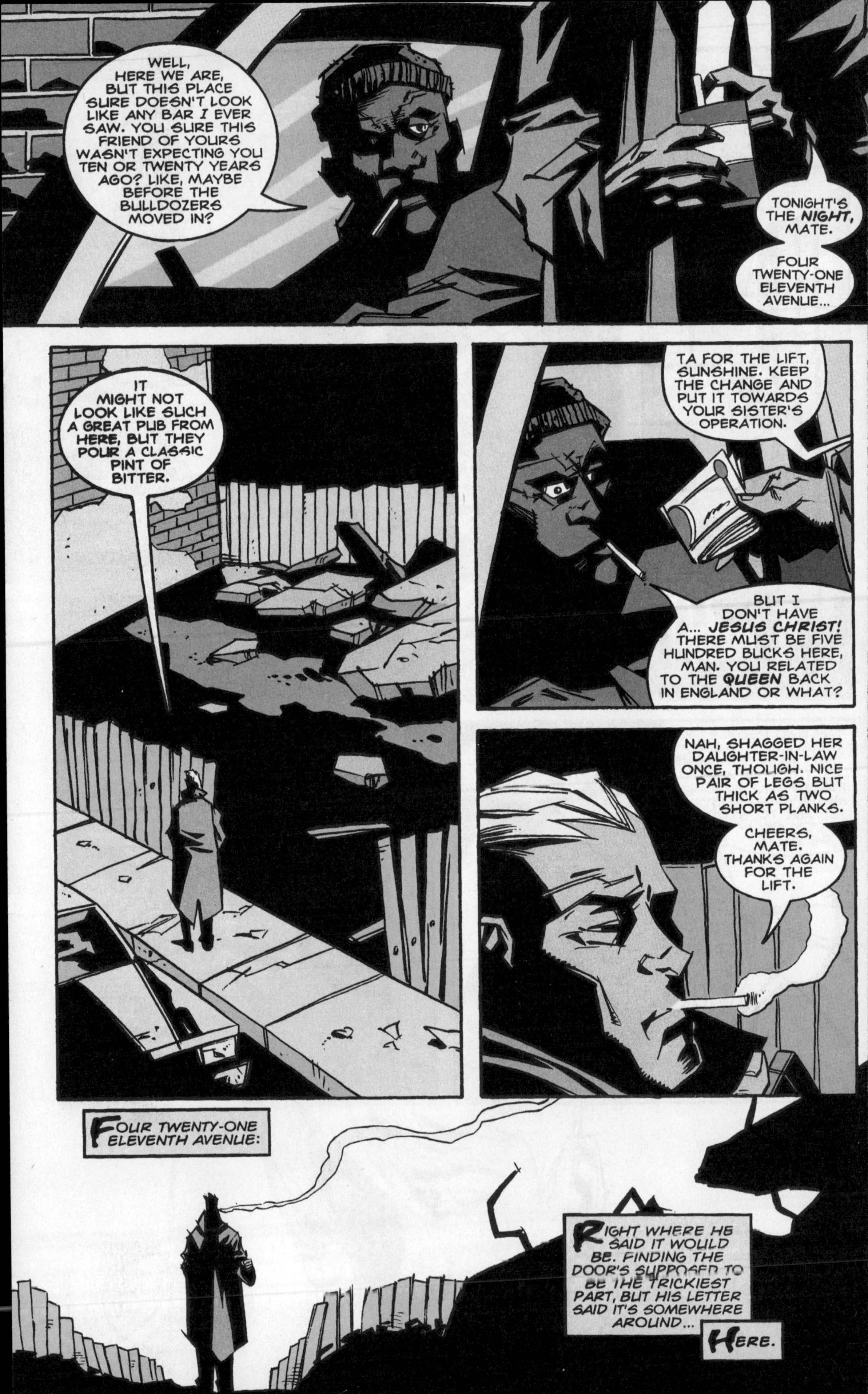
WELL, HERE WE ARE, BUT THIS PLACE SURE DOESN'T LOOK LIKE ANY BAR I EVER SAW. YOU SURE THIS FRIEND OF YOURS WASN'T EXPECTING YOU TEN OR TWENTY YEARS AGO? LIKE, MAYBE BEFORE THE BULLDOZERS MOVED IN?
TONIGHT'S THE NIGHT, MATE.
FOUR TWENTY-ONE ELEVENTH AVENUE...
IT MIGHT NOT LOOK LIKE SUCH A GREAT PUB FROM HERE, BUT THEY POUR A CLASSIC PINT OF BITTER.
TA FOR THE LIFT, SUNSHINE. KEEP THE CHANGE AND PUT IT TOWARDS YOUR SISTER'S OPERATION.
BUT I DON'T HAVE A... JESUS CHRIST! THERE MUST BE FIVE HUNDRED BUCKS HERE, MAN. YOU RELATED TO THE QUEEN BACK IN ENGLAND OR WHAT?
NAH, SHAGGED HER DAUGHTER-IN-LAW ONCE, THOUGH. NICE PAIR OF LEGS BUT THICK AS TWO SHORT PLANKS.
CHEERS, MATE. THANKS AGAIN FOR THE LIFT.
FOUR TWENTY-ONE ELEVENTH AVENUE:
RIGHT WHERE HE SAID IT WOULD BE. FINDING THE DOOR'S SUPPOSED TO BE THE TRICKIEST PART, BUT HIS LETTER SAID IT'S SOMEWHERE AROUND...
HERE.

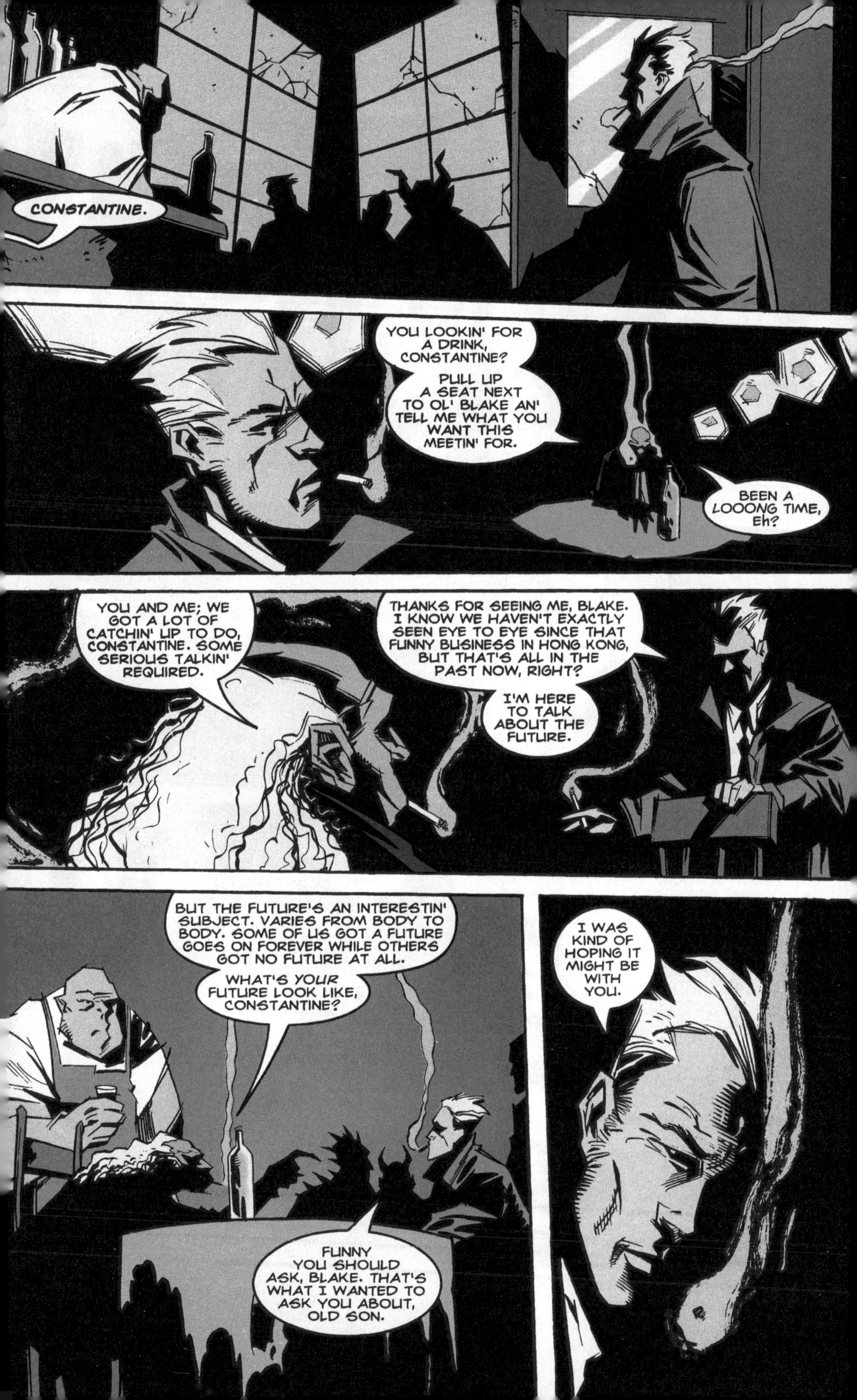
CONSTANTINE.
YOU LOOKIN' FOR A DRINK, CONSTANTINE?
PULL UP A SEAT NEXT TO OL' BLAKE AN' TELL ME WHAT YOU WANT THIS MEETIN' FOR.
BEEN A LOOONG TIME, Eh?
YOU AND ME; WE GOT A LOT OF CATCHIN' UP TO DO, CONSTANTINE. SOME SERIOUS TALKIN' REQUIRED.
THANKS FOR SEEING ME, BLAKE. I KNOW WE HAVEN'T EXACTLY SEEN EYE TO EYE SINCE THAT FUNNY BUSINESS IN HONG KONG, BUT THAT'S ALL IN THE PAST NOW, RIGHT?
I'M HERE TO TALK ABOUT THE FUTURE.
BUT THE FUTURE'S AN INTERESTIN' SUBJECT. VARIES FROM BODY TO BODY. SOME OF US GOT A FUTURE GOES ON FOREVER WHILE OTHERS GOT NO FUTURE AT ALL.
WHAT'S *YOUR* FUTURE LOOK LIKE, CONSTANTINE?
FUNNY YOU SHOULD ASK, BLAKE. THAT'S WHAT I WANTED TO ASK YOU ABOUT, OLD SON.
I WAS KIND OF HOPING IT MIGHT BE WITH YOU.

THIS SOME KIND OF JOKE, CONSTANTINE?

YOU PISSIN' OL' BLAKE AROUND?

NO JOKE, BLAKE. JUST COMMON SENSE. THERE'S A WAR ABOUT TO ERUPT IN THE MAGICAL WORLD AT MIDNIGHT TONIGHT, AND I'M A BLOKE WITH A KNACK FOR PICKING THE WINNING SIDE.

BESIDES, I'M NOT EXACTLY CHUFFED WITH DOING THE DIRTY ON THE SWAMP THING. WE'RE OLD MATES, REMEMBER?

WHAT ABOUT YOUR LODGE? THEY BEEN PLANNIN' THIS ATTACK OH, SO METICULOUSLY SINCE THE HOLLAND-MIND FORMED HIS BODY IN THE SHAPE OF THE PALACE.

YOU WANT TO BETRAY THE WORD IN FAVOR OF US?

THE WORD'S A WANKER, ASK ANYBODY. I'M NOT EVEN A MEMBER OF THE BLOODY LODGE ANYMORE. I TOOK A WALK MORE THAN TWENTY YEARS AGO AND I DON'T OWE THAT BUNCH ANY FAVORS.

YEAH. THEY SAY YOU WERE A RISIN' STAR ONE TIME BUT YOU DIDN'T HAVE THE BALLS TO REACH THE TOP.

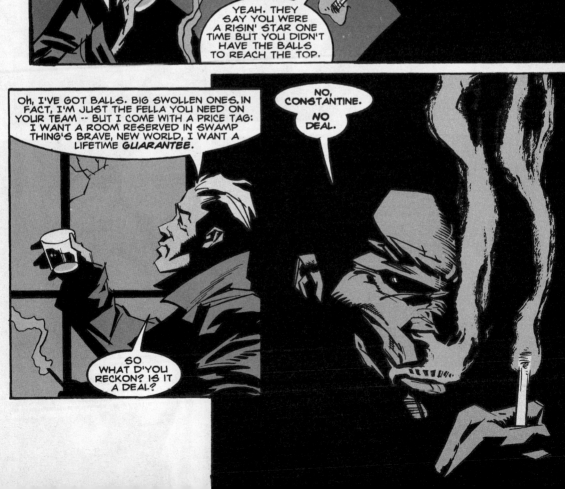

OH, I'VE GOT BALLS. BIG SWOLLEN ONES. IN FACT, I'M JUST THE FELLA YOU NEED ON YOUR TEAM -- BUT I COME WITH A PRICE TAG: I WANT A ROOM RESERVED IN SWAMP THING'S BRAVE, NEW WORLD, I WANT A LIFETIME GUARANTEE.

SO WHAT D'YOU RECKON? IS IT A DEAL?

NO, CONSTANTINE. NO DEAL.

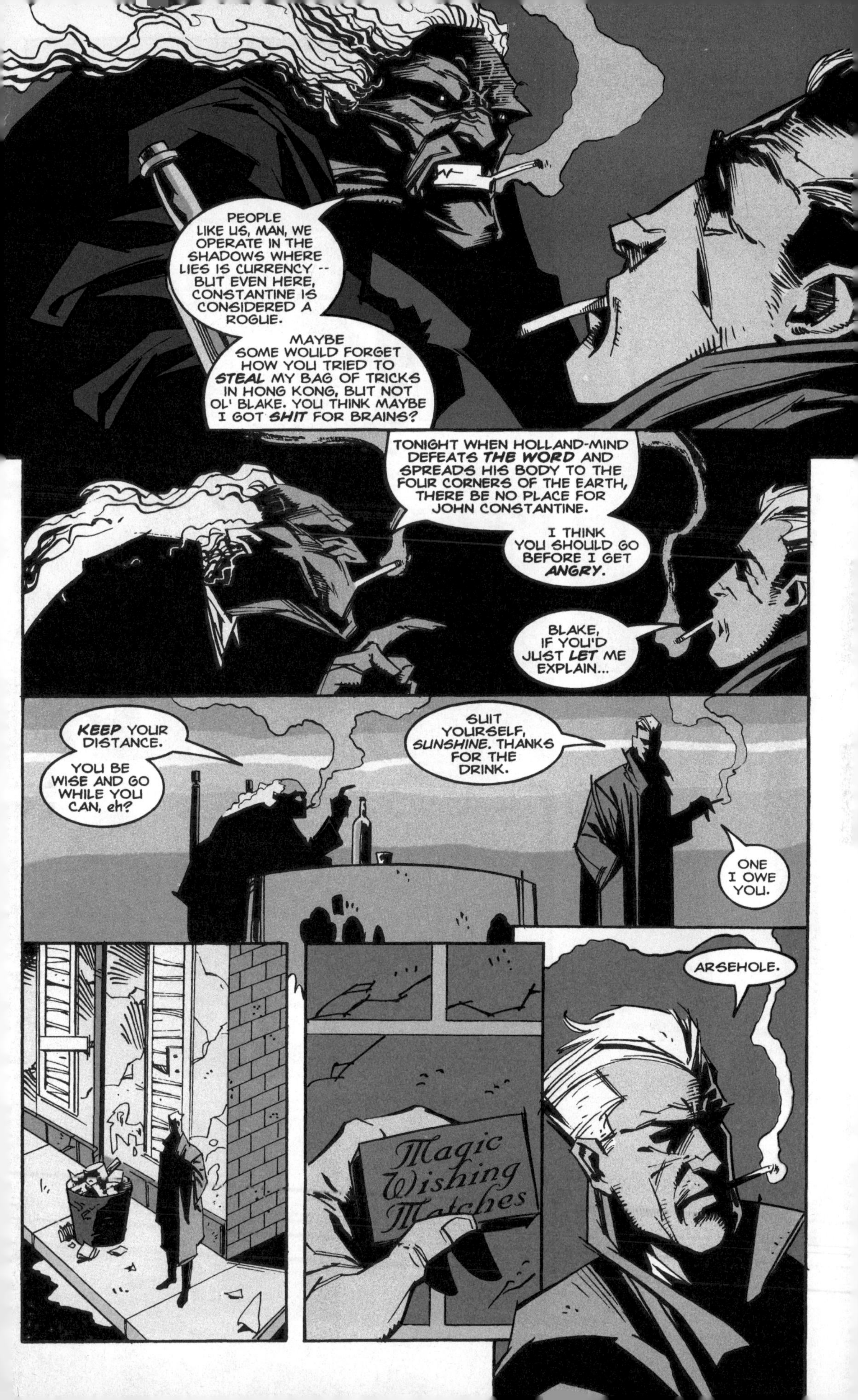
PEOPLE LIKE US, MAN, WE OPERATE IN THE SHADOWS WHERE LIES IS CURRENCY -- BUT EVEN HERE, CONSTANTINE IS CONSIDERED A ROGUE.
MAYBE SOME WOULD FORGET HOW YOU TRIED TO STEAL MY BAG OF TRICKS IN HONG KONG, BUT NOT OL' BLAKE. YOU THINK MAYBE I GOT SHIT FOR BRAINS?
TONIGHT WHEN HOLLAND-MIND DEFEATS THE WORD AND SPREADS HIS BODY TO THE FOUR CORNERS OF THE EARTH, THERE BE NO PLACE FOR JOHN CONSTANTINE.
I THINK YOU SHOULD GO BEFORE I GET ANGRY.
BLAKE, IF YOU'D JUST LET ME EXPLAIN...
KEEP YOUR DISTANCE.
YOU BE WISE AND GO WHILE YOU CAN, eh?
SUIT YOURSELF, SUNSHINE. THANKS FOR THE DRINK.
ONE I OWE YOU.
Magic Wishing Matches
ARSEHOLE.

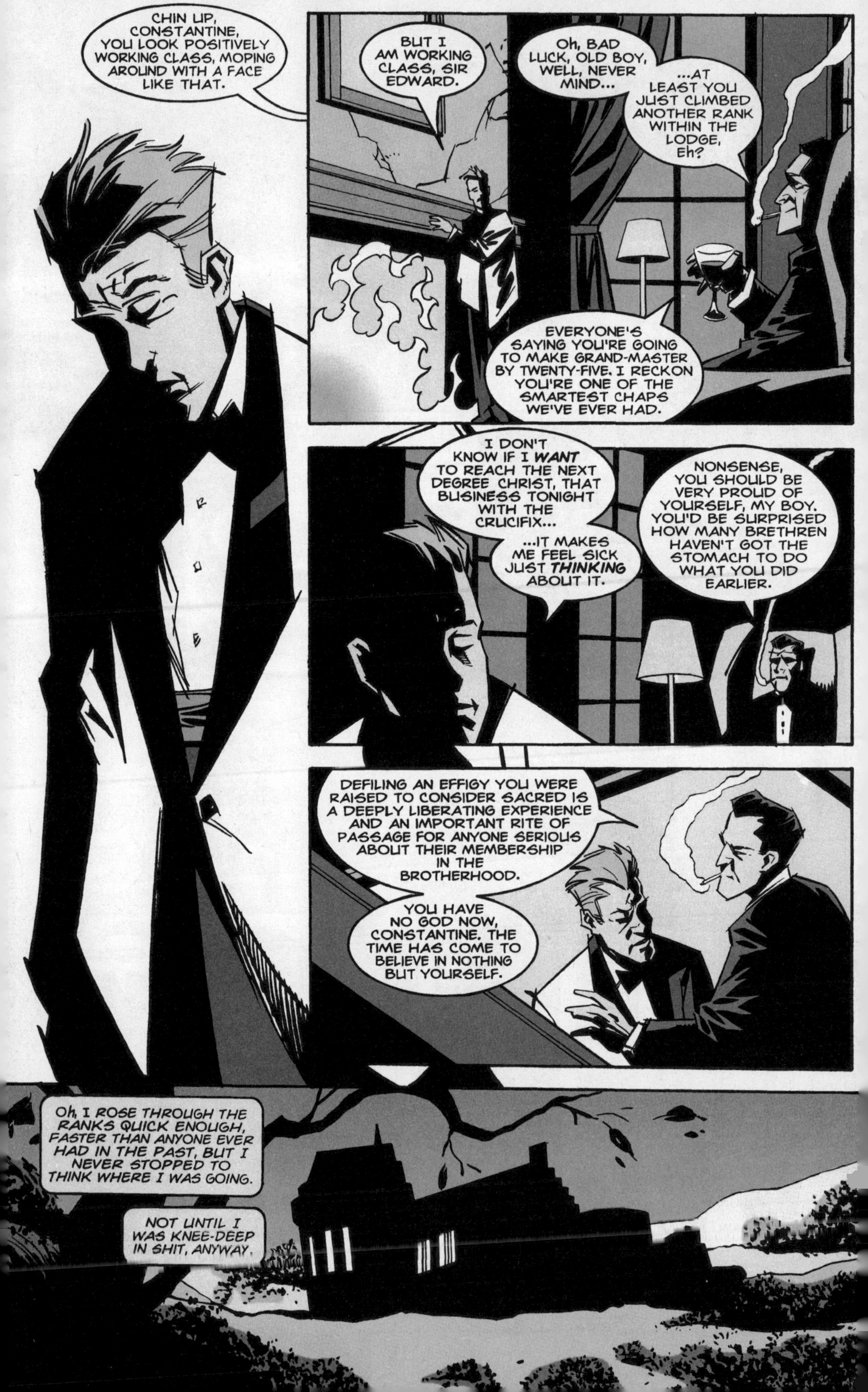
CHIN UP, CONSTANTINE, YOU LOOK POSITIVELY WORKING CLASS, MOPING AROUND WITH A FACE LIKE THAT.
BUT I AM WORKING CLASS, SIR EDWARD.
Oh, BAD LUCK, OLD BOY, WELL, NEVER MIND...
...AT LEAST YOU JUST CLIMBED ANOTHER RANK WITHIN THE LODGE, Eh?
EVERYONE'S SAYING YOU'RE GOING TO MAKE GRAND-MASTER BY TWENTY-FIVE. I RECKON YOU'RE ONE OF THE SMARTEST CHAPS WE'VE EVER HAD.
I DON'T KNOW IF I WANT TO REACH THE NEXT DEGREE CHRIST, THAT BUSINESS TONIGHT WITH THE CRUCIFIX...
...IT MAKES ME FEEL SICK JUST THINKING ABOUT IT.
NONSENSE, YOU SHOULD BE VERY PROUD OF YOURSELF, MY BOY. YOU'D BE SURPRISED HOW MANY BRETHREN HAVEN'T GOT THE STOMACH TO DO WHAT YOU DID EARLIER.
DEFILING AN EFFIGY YOU WERE RAISED TO CONSIDER SACRED IS A DEEPLY LIBERATING EXPERIENCE AND AN IMPORTANT RITE OF PASSAGE FOR ANYONE SERIOUS ABOUT THEIR MEMBERSHIP IN THE BROTHERHOOD.
YOU HAVE NO GOD NOW, CONSTANTINE. THE TIME HAS COME TO BELIEVE IN NOTHING BUT YOURSELF.
Oh, I ROSE THROUGH THE RANKS QUICK ENOUGH, FASTER THAN ANYONE EVER HAD IN THE PAST, BUT I NEVER STOPPED TO THINK WHERE I WAS GOING.
NOT UNTIL I WAS KNEE-DEEP IN SHIT, ANYWAY.

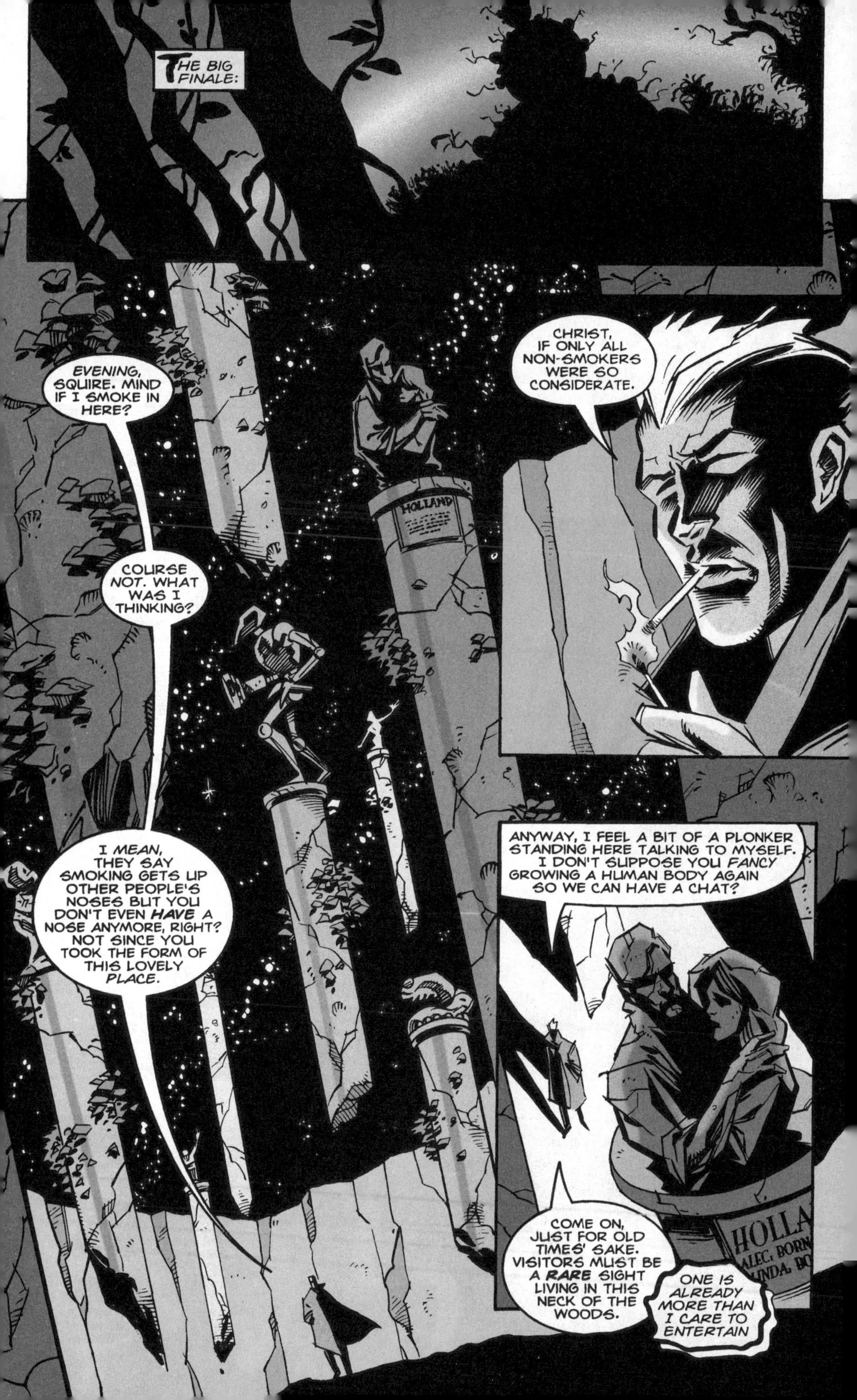
THE BIG FINALE:
EVENING, SQUIRE. MIND IF I SMOKE IN HERE?
COURSE NOT. WHAT WAS I THINKING?
I *MEAN*, THEY SAY SMOKING GETS UP OTHER PEOPLE'S NOSES BUT YOU DON'T EVEN ***HAVE*** A NOSE ANYMORE, RIGHT? NOT SINCE YOU TOOK THE FORM OF THIS LOVELY *PLACE*.
HOLLAND
CHRIST, IF ONLY ALL NON-SMOKERS WERE SO CONSIDERATE.
ANYWAY, I FEEL A BIT OF A PLONKER STANDING HERE TALKING TO MYSELF. I DON'T SUPPOSE YOU *FANCY* GROWING A HUMAN BODY AGAIN SO WE CAN HAVE A CHAT?
COME ON, JUST FOR OLD TIMES' SAKE. VISITORS MUST BE A ***RARE*** SIGHT LIVING IN THIS NECK OF THE WOODS.
ONE IS ALREADY MORE THAN I CARE TO ENTERTAIN

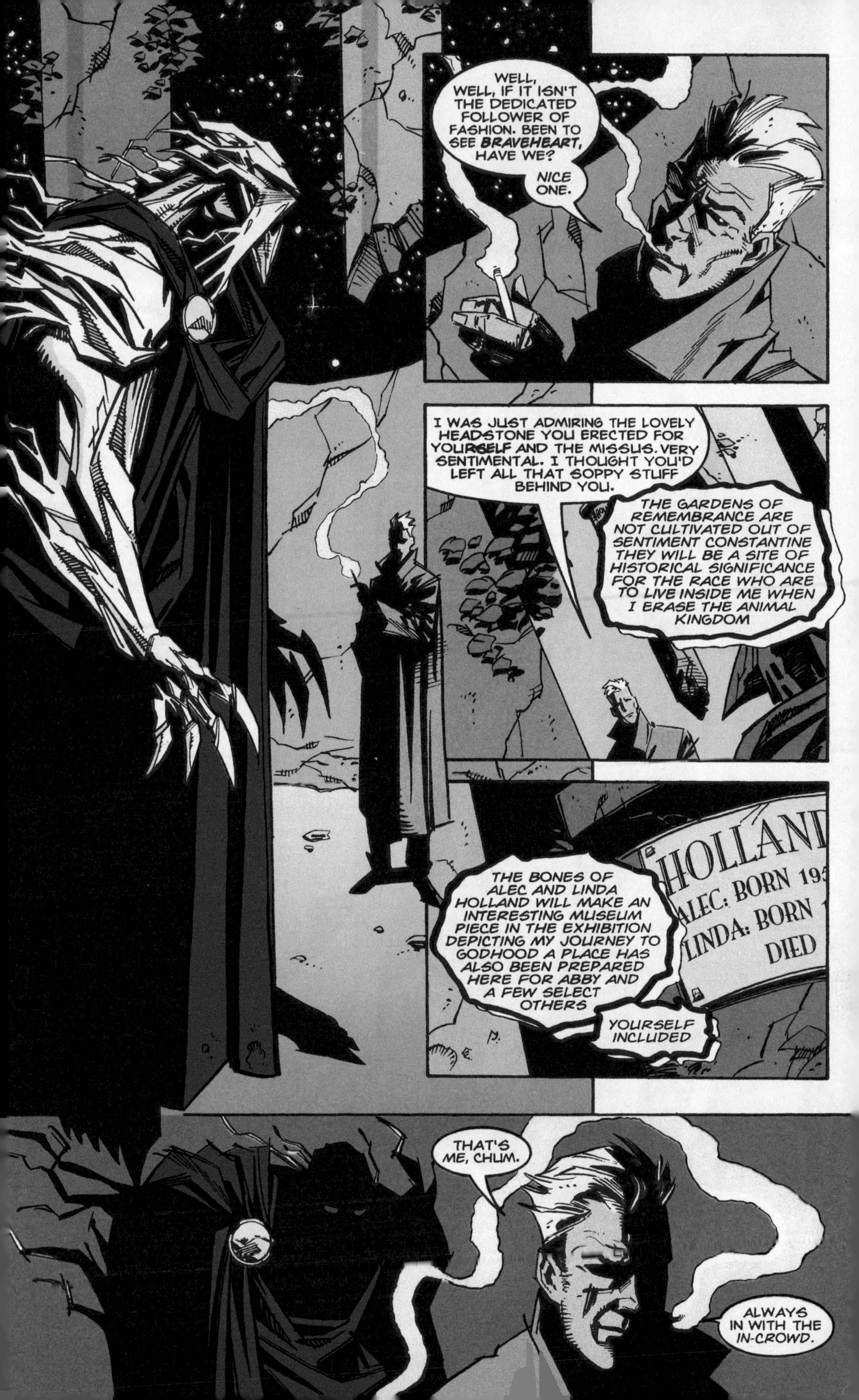
WELL, WELL, IF IT ISN'T THE DEDICATED FOLLOWER OF FASHION. BEEN TO SEE BRAVEHEART, HAVE WE?
NICE ONE.
I WAS JUST ADMIRING THE LOVELY HEADSTONE YOU ERECTED FOR YOURSELF AND THE MISSUS. VERY SENTIMENTAL. I THOUGHT YOU'D LEFT ALL THAT SOPPY STUFF BEHIND YOU.
THE GARDENS OF REMEMBRANCE ARE NOT CULTIVATED OUT OF SENTIMENT CONSTANTINE THEY WILL BE A SITE OF HISTORICAL SIGNIFICANCE FOR THE RACE WHO ARE TO LIVE INSIDE ME WHEN I ERASE THE ANIMAL KINGDOM
HOLLAND
ALEC: BORN 19
LINDA: BORN
DIED
THE BONES OF ALEC AND LINDA HOLLAND WILL MAKE AN INTERESTING MUSEUM PIECE IN THE EXHIBITION DEPICTING MY JOURNEY TO GODHOOD A PLACE HAS ALSO BEEN PREPARED HERE FOR ABBY AND A FEW SELECT OTHERS
YOURSELF INCLUDED
THAT'S ME, CHUM.
ALWAYS IN WITH THE IN-CROWD.

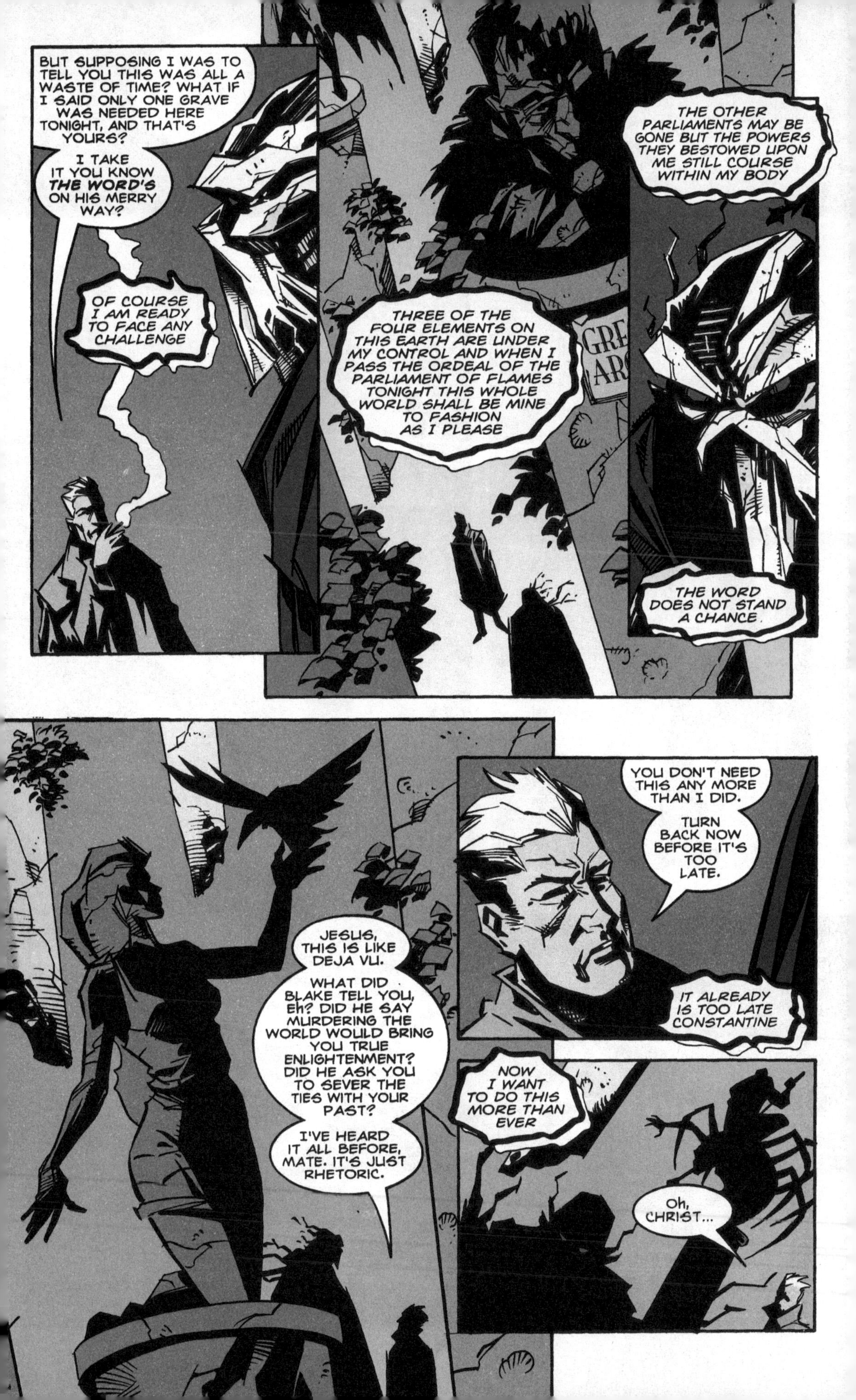
BUT SUPPOSING I WAS TO TELL YOU THIS WAS ALL A WASTE OF TIME? WHAT IF I SAID ONLY ONE GRAVE WAS NEEDED HERE TONIGHT, AND THAT'S YOURS?
I TAKE IT YOU KNOW THE WORD'S ON HIS MERRY WAY?
OF COURSE I AM READY TO FACE ANY CHALLENGE
THREE OF THE FOUR ELEMENTS ON THIS EARTH ARE UNDER MY CONTROL AND WHEN I PASS THE ORDEAL OF THE PARLIAMENT OF FLAMES TONIGHT THIS WHOLE WORLD SHALL BE MINE TO FASHION AS I PLEASE
THE OTHER PARLIAMENTS MAY BE GONE BUT THE POWERS THEY BESTOWED UPON ME STILL COURSE WITHIN MY BODY
THE WORD DOES NOT STAND A CHANCE
JESUS, THIS IS LIKE DEJA VU.
WHAT DID BLAKE TELL YOU, Eh? DID HE SAY MURDERING THE WORLD WOULD BRING YOU TRUE ENLIGHTENMENT? DID HE ASK YOU TO SEVER THE TIES WITH YOUR PAST?
I'VE HEARD IT ALL BEFORE, MATE. IT'S JUST RHETORIC.
YOU DON'T NEED THIS ANY MORE THAN I DID.
TURN BACK NOW BEFORE IT'S TOO LATE.
IT ALREADY IS TOO LATE CONSTANTINE
NOW I WANT TO DO THIS MORE THAN EVER
Oh, CHRIST...

THERE WAS A TIME WHEN I WAS IN YOUR BOAT. THE OPPOSING LODGE TRAINED ME FOR A WHILE AND I WANTED TO BE ENLIGHTENED JUST AS MUCH AS *YOU* DO NOW, BUT NOTHING COMES WITHOUT A *PRICE.*

I CLIMBED THE RANKS AND LEARNED SOME GOOD *TRICKS*, BUT AT LEAST I WAS HUMAN ENOUGH TO KNOW WHERE TO DRAW THE *LINE.*

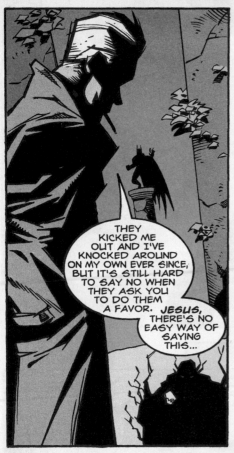

THEY KICKED ME OUT AND I'VE KNOCKED AROUND ON MY OWN EVER SINCE, BUT IT'S STILL HARD TO SAY NO WHEN THEY ASK YOU TO DO THEM A FAVOR. *JESUS*, THERE'S NO EASY WAY OF SAYING THIS...

YOU KNOW WHAT THESE ARE?

THIS IS A BOX OF WISHING MATCHES; STRIKE ONE, MAKE A WISH AND BLOW IT OUT. THESE ARE WHAT THE LODGE ASKED ME TO STEAL FROM BLAKE AND USE TO DESTROY YOU, ALEC. I'M SORRY...

DON'T BE *RIDICULOUS* YOU CANNOT USE THEM AGAINST ME CONSTANTINE I'D TEAR YOU APART BEFORE YOU EVEN REMOVED THE FIRST MATCH FROM THE BOX

YOU DON'T GET IT, MATE. I USED ONE TO LIGHT MY CIGARETTE WHEN I CAME IN HERE, REMEMBER?

I'VE ALREADY *MADE* MY MAGIC WISH.

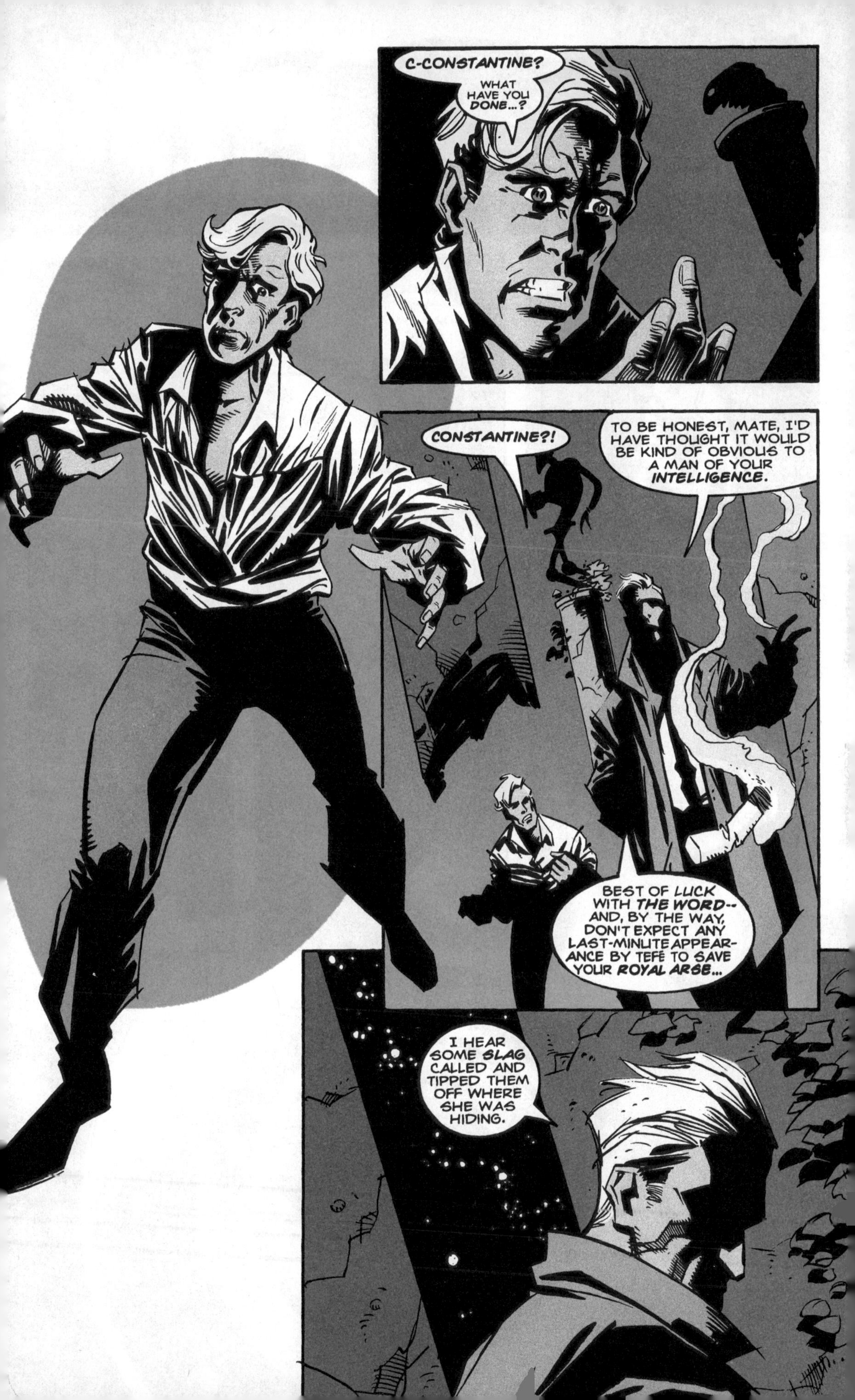
C-CONSTANTINE?
WHAT HAVE YOU DONE...?
CONSTANTINE?!
TO BE HONEST, MATE, I'D HAVE THOUGHT IT WOULD BE KIND OF OBVIOUS TO A MAN OF YOUR INTELLIGENCE.
BEST OF LUCK WITH THE WORD-- AND, BY THE WAY, DON'T EXPECT ANY LAST-MINUTE APPEARANCE BY TEFÉ TO SAVE YOUR ROYAL ARSE...
I HEAR SOME SLAG CALLED AND TIPPED THEM OFF WHERE SHE WAS HIDING.

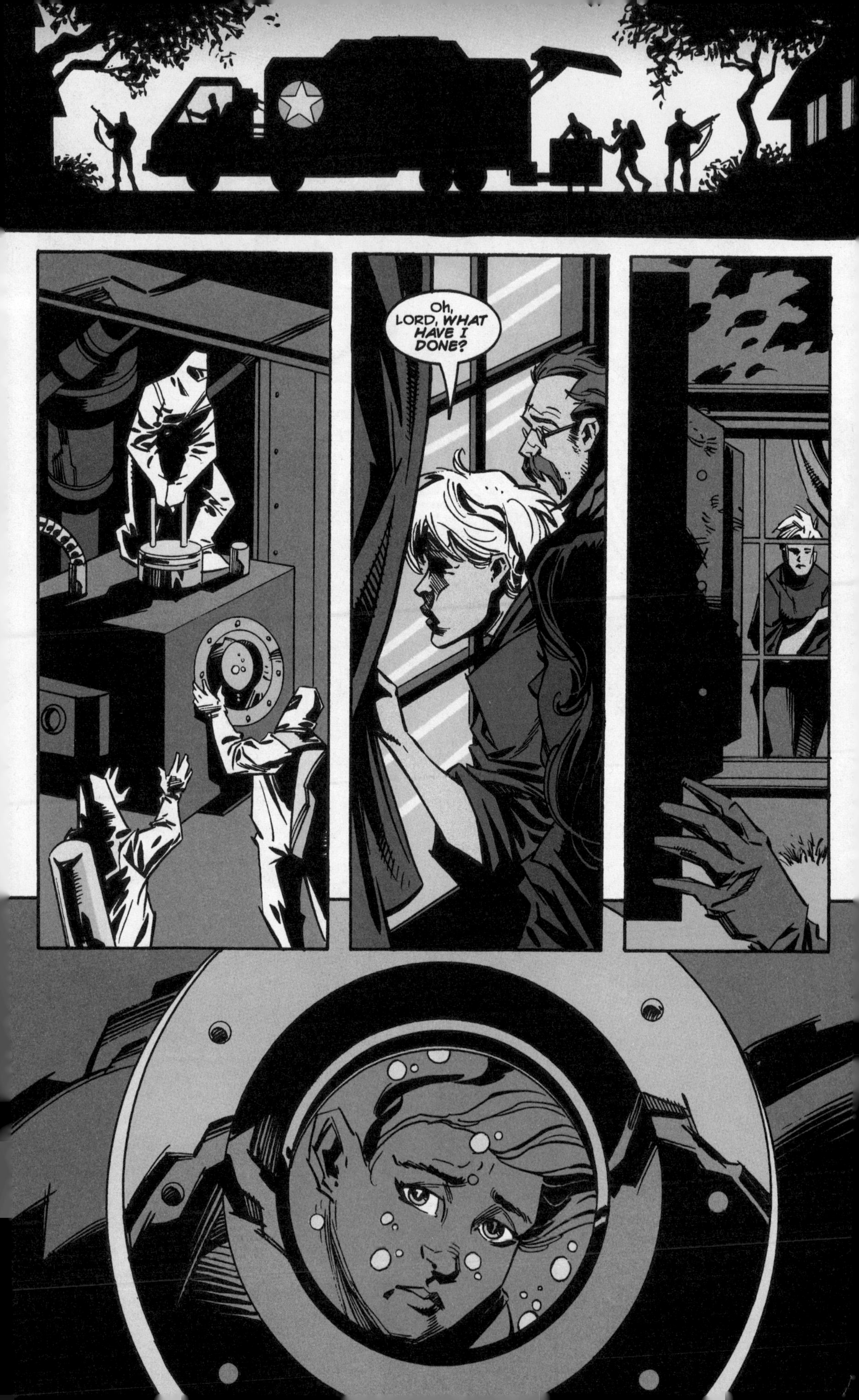
Oh, LORD, WHAT HAVE I DONE?

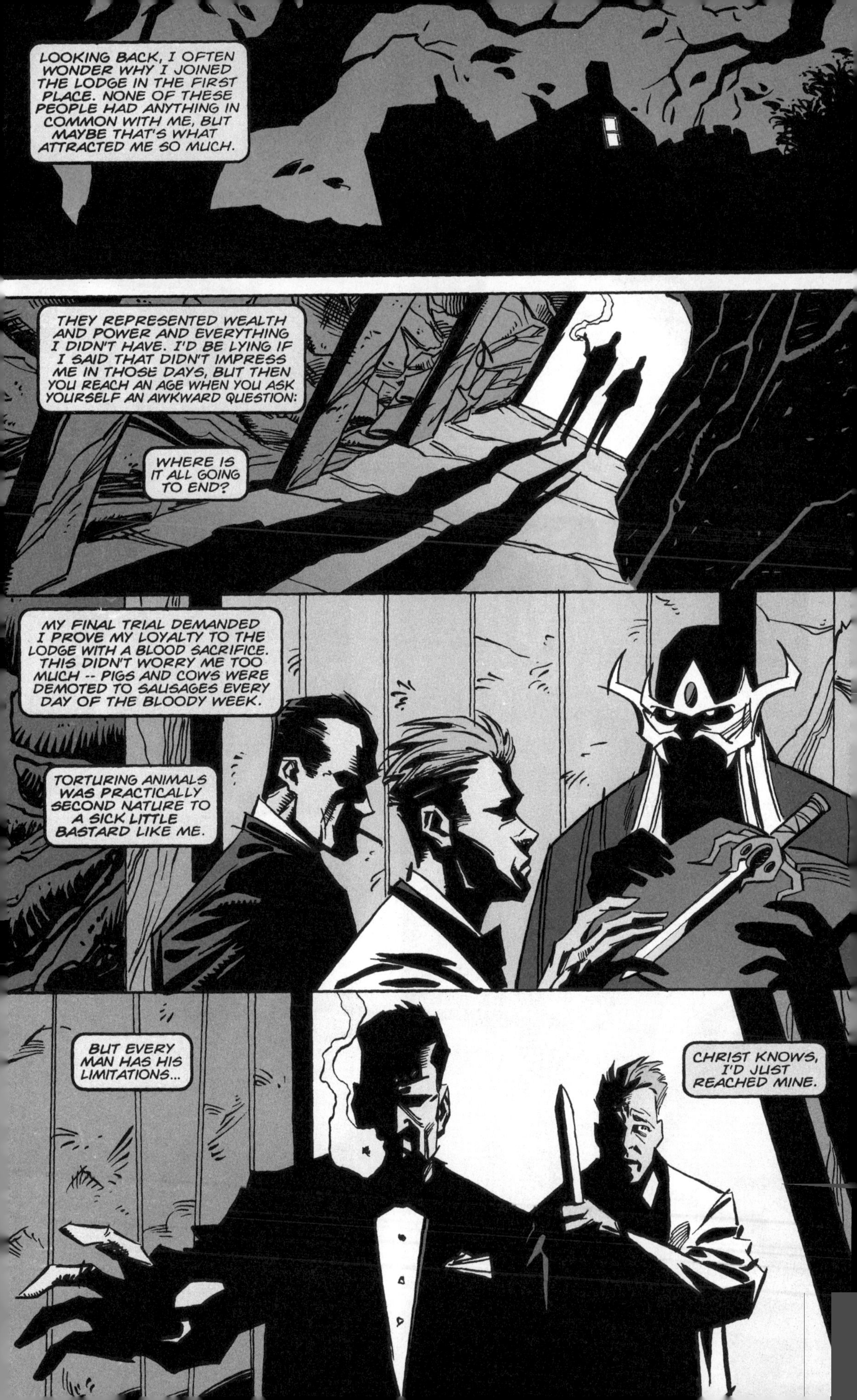

LOOKING BACK, I OFTEN WONDER WHY I JOINED THE LODGE IN THE FIRST PLACE. NONE OF THESE PEOPLE HAD ANYTHING IN COMMON WITH ME, BUT MAYBE THAT'S WHAT ATTRACTED ME SO MUCH.
THEY REPRESENTED WEALTH AND POWER AND EVERYTHING I DIDN'T HAVE. I'D BE LYING IF I SAID THAT DIDN'T IMPRESS ME IN THOSE DAYS, BUT THEN YOU REACH AN AGE WHEN YOU ASK YOURSELF AN AWKWARD QUESTION:
WHERE IS IT ALL GOING TO END?
MY FINAL TRIAL DEMANDED I PROVE MY LOYALTY TO THE LODGE WITH A BLOOD SACRIFICE. THIS DIDN'T WORRY ME TOO MUCH -- PIGS AND COWS WERE DEMOTED TO SAUSAGES EVERY DAY OF THE BLOODY WEEK.
TORTURING ANIMALS WAS PRACTICALLY SECOND NATURE TO A SICK LITTLE BASTARD LIKE ME.
BUT EVERY MAN HAS HIS LIMITATIONS...
CHRIST KNOWS, I'D JUST REACHED MINE.

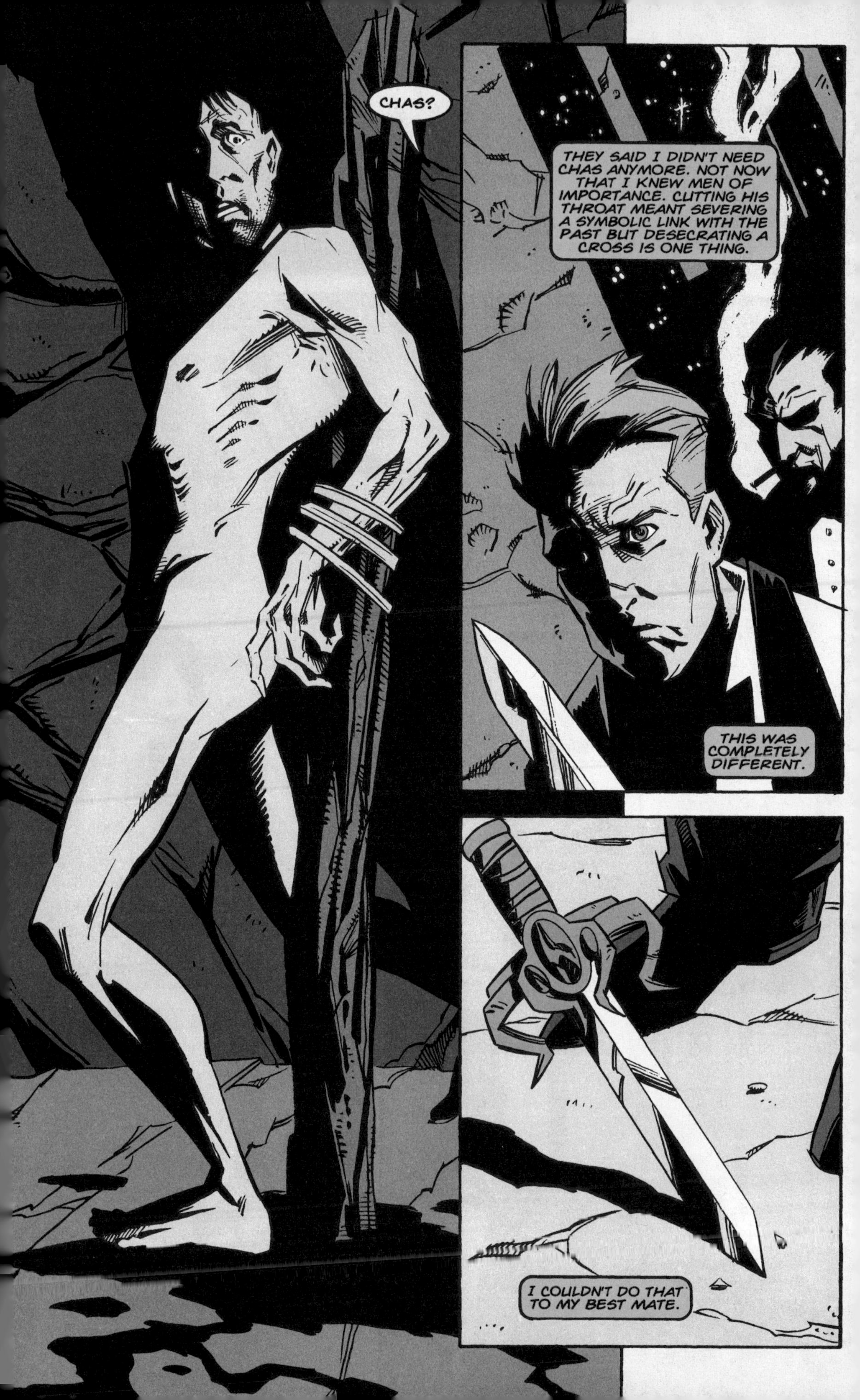
CHAS?
THEY SAID I DIDN'T NEED CHAS ANYMORE. NOT NOW THAT I KNEW MEN OF IMPORTANCE. CUTTING HIS THROAT MEANT SEVERING A SYMBOLIC LINK WITH THE PAST BUT DESECRATING A CROSS IS ONE THING.
THIS WAS COMPLETELY DIFFERENT.
I COULDN'T DO THAT TO MY BEST MATE.

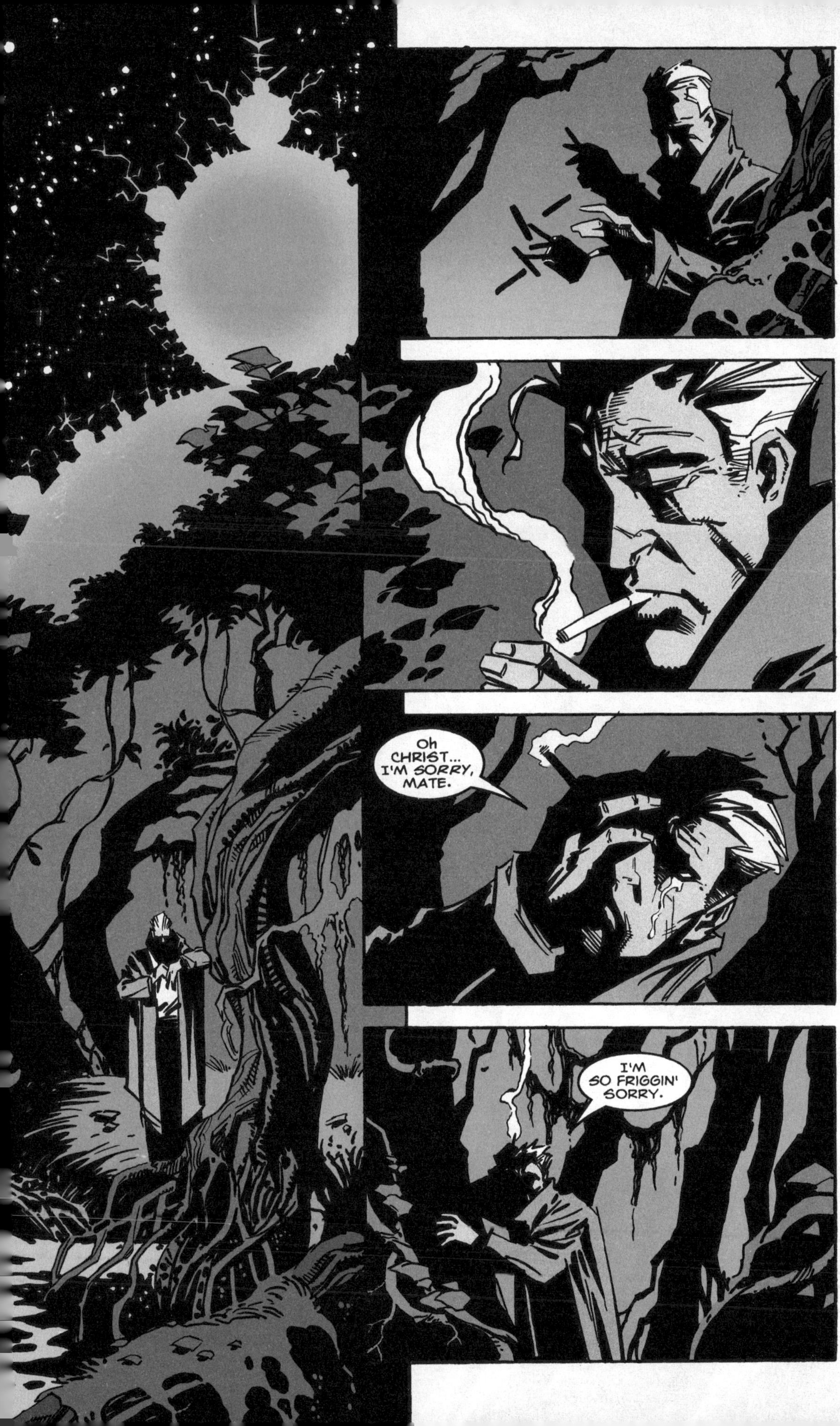
Oh CHRIST... I'M SORRY, MATE.
I'M SO FRIGGIN' SORRY.

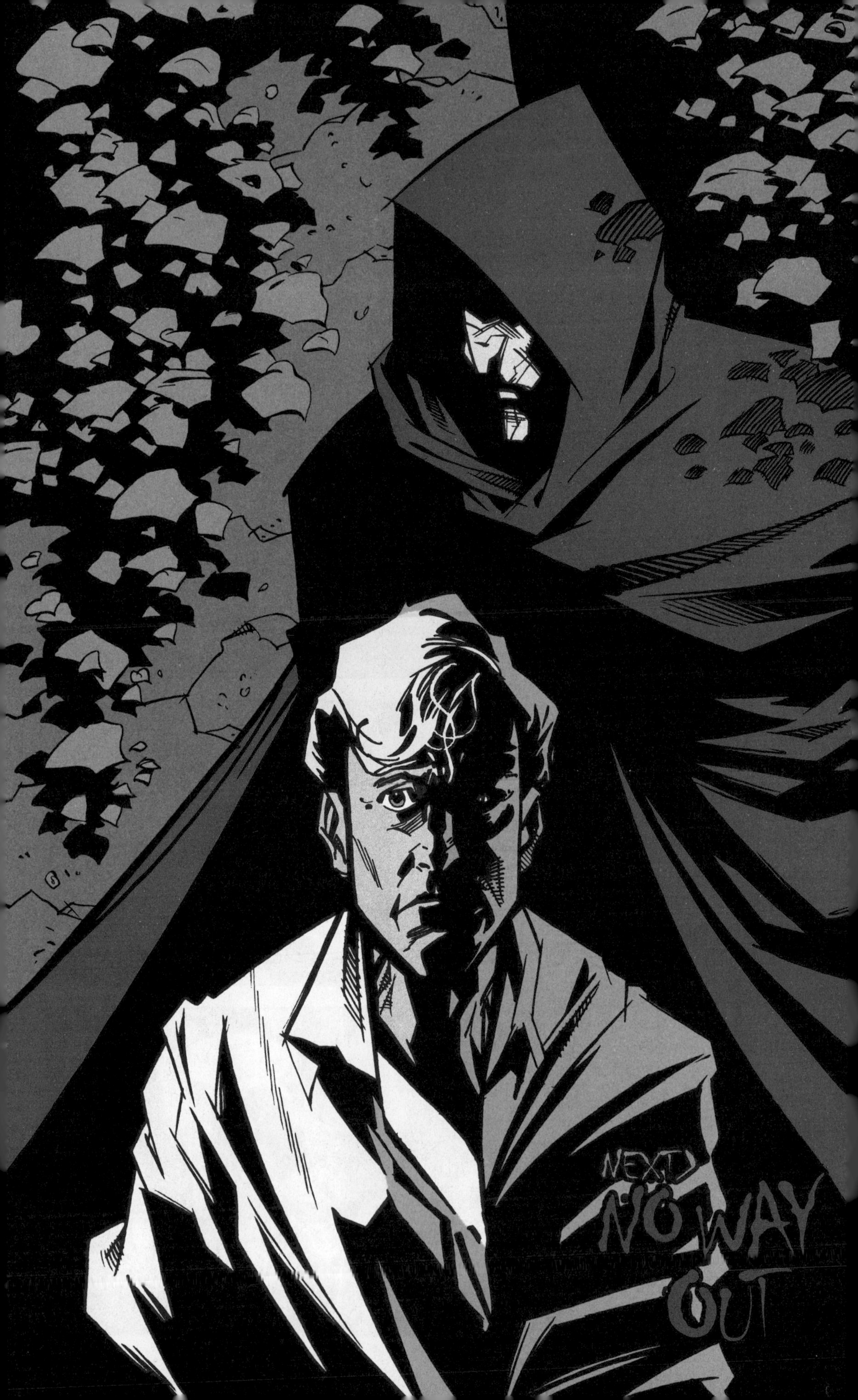
NEXT:
NO WAY OUT

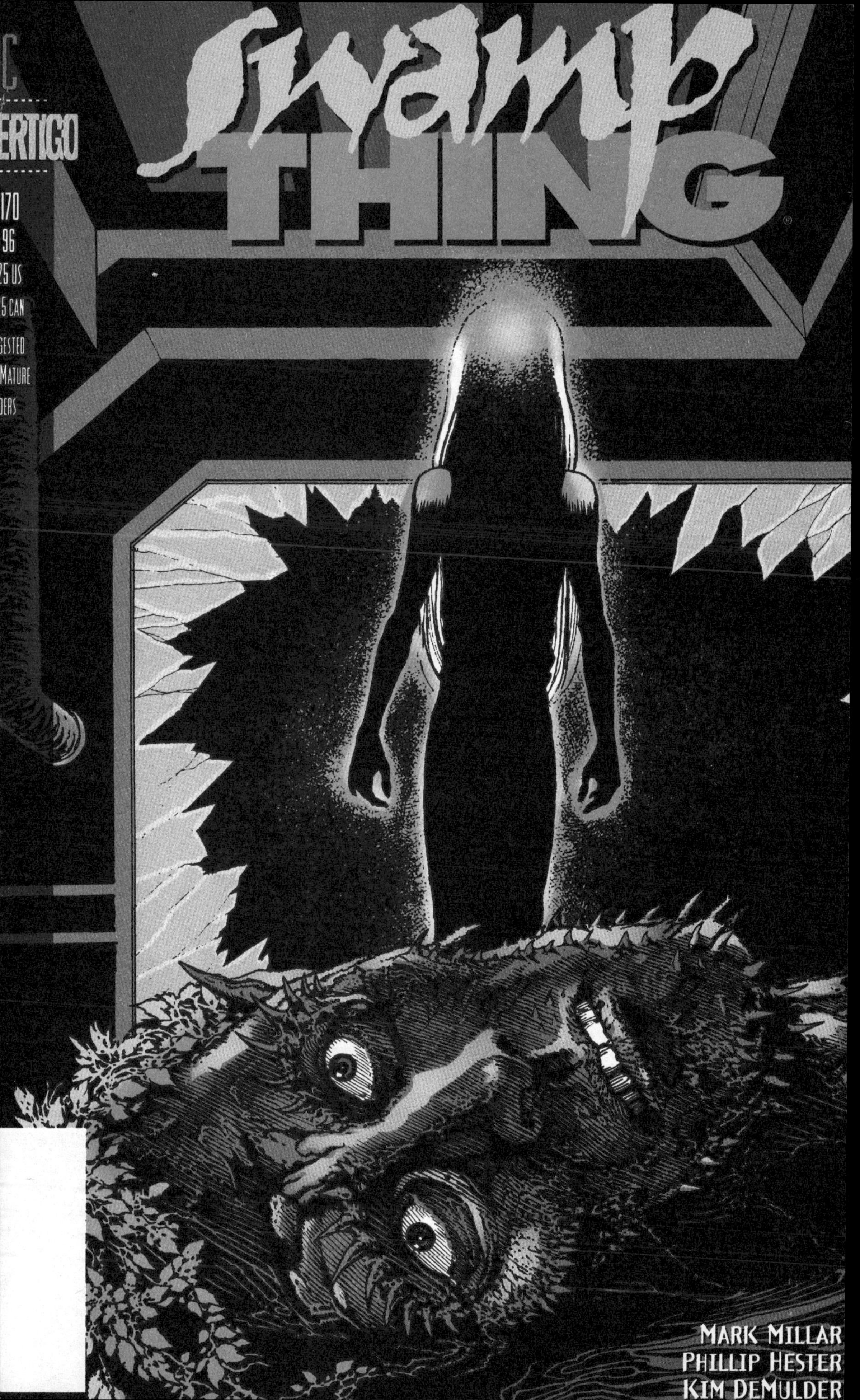
Swamp
THING
ERTIGO
170
96
25 US
25 CAN
MARK MILLAR
PHILLIP HESTER
KIM DEMULDER

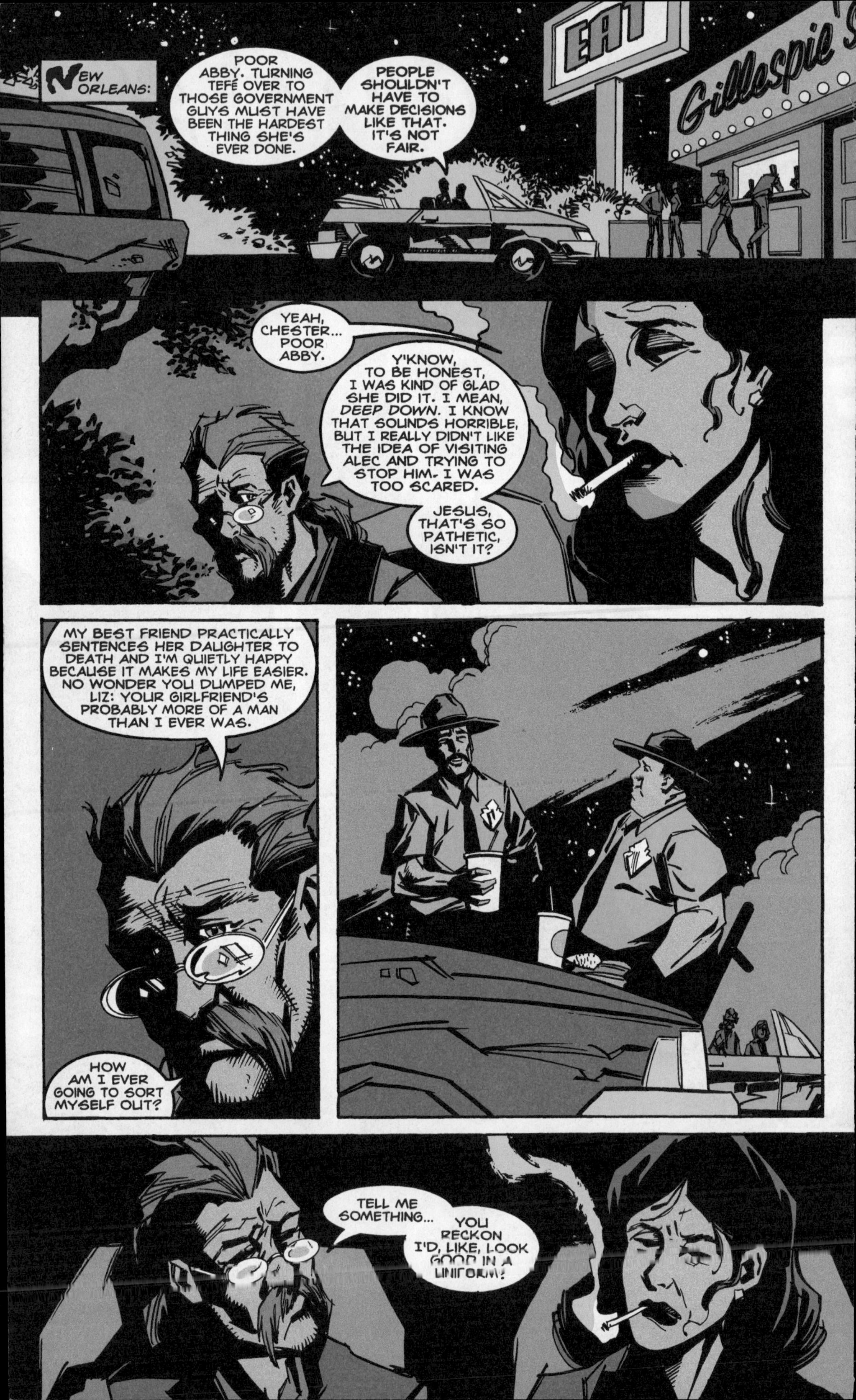
EAT
Gillespie's
NEW ORLEANS:
POOR ABBY. TURNING TEFÉ OVER TO THOSE GOVERNMENT GUYS MUST HAVE BEEN THE HARDEST THING SHE'S EVER DONE.
PEOPLE SHOULDN'T HAVE TO MAKE DECISIONS LIKE THAT. IT'S NOT FAIR.
YEAH, CHESTER... POOR ABBY.
Y'KNOW, TO BE HONEST, I WAS KIND OF GLAD SHE DID IT. I MEAN, *DEEP DOWN*. I KNOW THAT SOUNDS HORRIBLE, BUT I REALLY DIDN'T LIKE THE IDEA OF VISITING ALEC AND TRYING TO STOP HIM. I WAS TOO SCARED.
JESUS, THAT'S SO PATHETIC, ISN'T IT?
MY BEST FRIEND PRACTICALLY SENTENCES HER DAUGHTER TO DEATH AND I'M QUIETLY HAPPY BECAUSE IT MAKES MY LIFE EASIER. NO WONDER YOU DUMPED ME, LIZ: YOUR GIRLFRIEND'S PROBABLY MORE OF A MAN THAN I EVER WAS.
HOW AM I EVER GOING TO SORT MYSELF OUT?
TELL ME SOMETHING...
YOU RECKON I'D, LIKE, LOOK GOOD IN A UNIFORM?

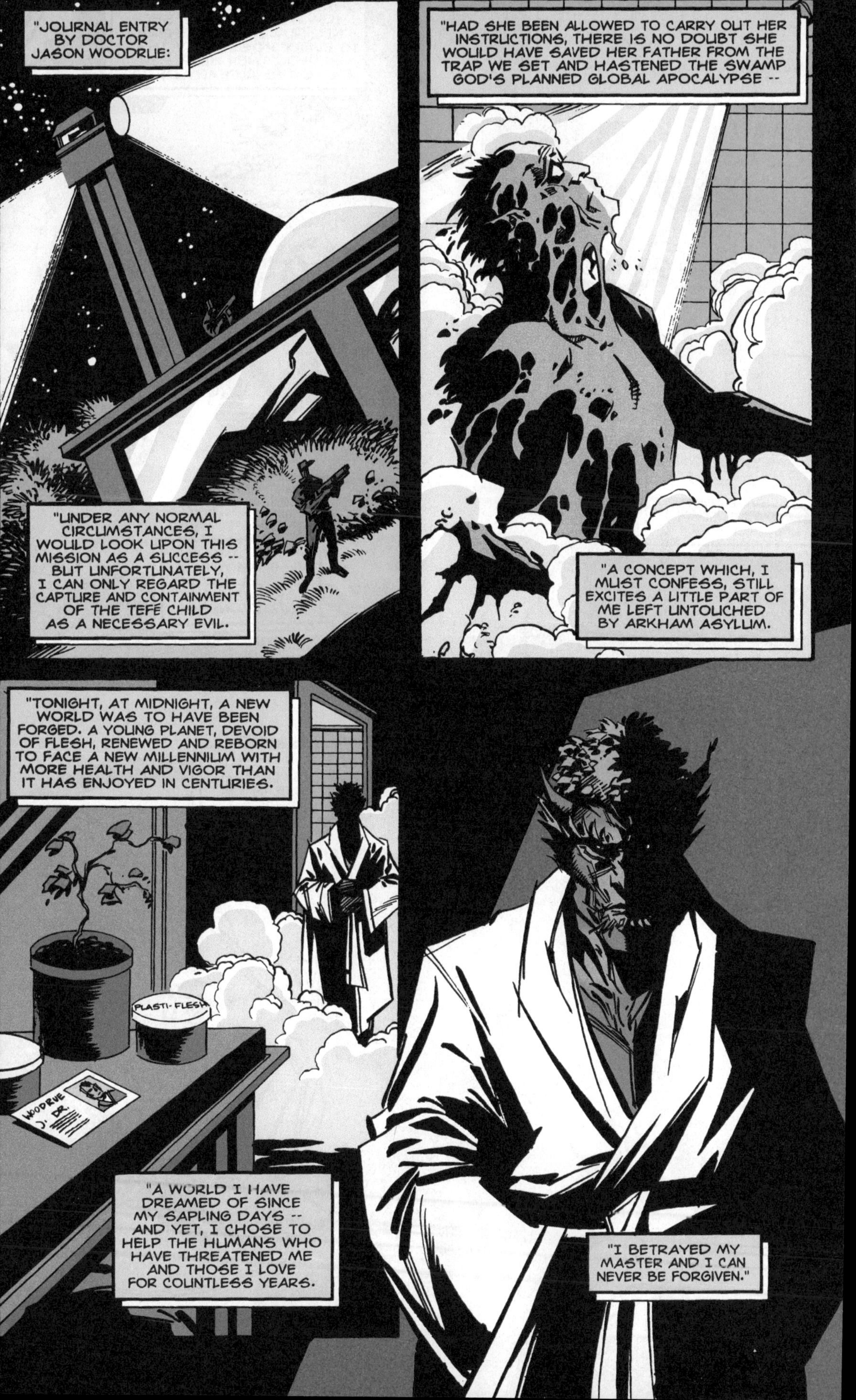
"JOURNAL ENTRY BY DOCTOR JASON WOODRUE:
"UNDER ANY NORMAL CIRCUMSTANCES, I WOULD LOOK UPON THIS MISSION AS A SUCCESS -- BUT UNFORTUNATELY, I CAN ONLY REGARD THE CAPTURE AND CONTAINMENT OF THE TEFÉ CHILD AS A NECESSARY EVIL.
"HAD SHE BEEN ALLOWED TO CARRY OUT HER INSTRUCTIONS, THERE IS NO DOUBT SHE WOULD HAVE SAVED HER FATHER FROM THE TRAP WE SET AND HASTENED THE SWAMP GOD'S PLANNED GLOBAL APOCALYPSE --
"A CONCEPT WHICH, I MUST CONFESS, STILL EXCITES A LITTLE PART OF ME LEFT UNTOUCHED BY ARKHAM ASYLUM.
"TONIGHT, AT MIDNIGHT, A NEW WORLD WAS TO HAVE BEEN FORGED. A YOUNG PLANET, DEVOID OF FLESH, RENEWED AND REBORN TO FACE A NEW MILLENNIUM WITH MORE HEALTH AND VIGOR THAN IT HAS ENJOYED IN CENTURIES.
PLASTI-FLESH
WOODRUE J. DR.
"A WORLD I HAVE DREAMED OF SINCE MY SAPLING DAYS -- AND YET, I CHOSE TO HELP THE HUMANS WHO HAVE THREATENED ME AND THOSE I LOVE FOR COUNTLESS YEARS.
"I BETRAYED MY MASTER AND I CAN NEVER BE FORGIVEN."

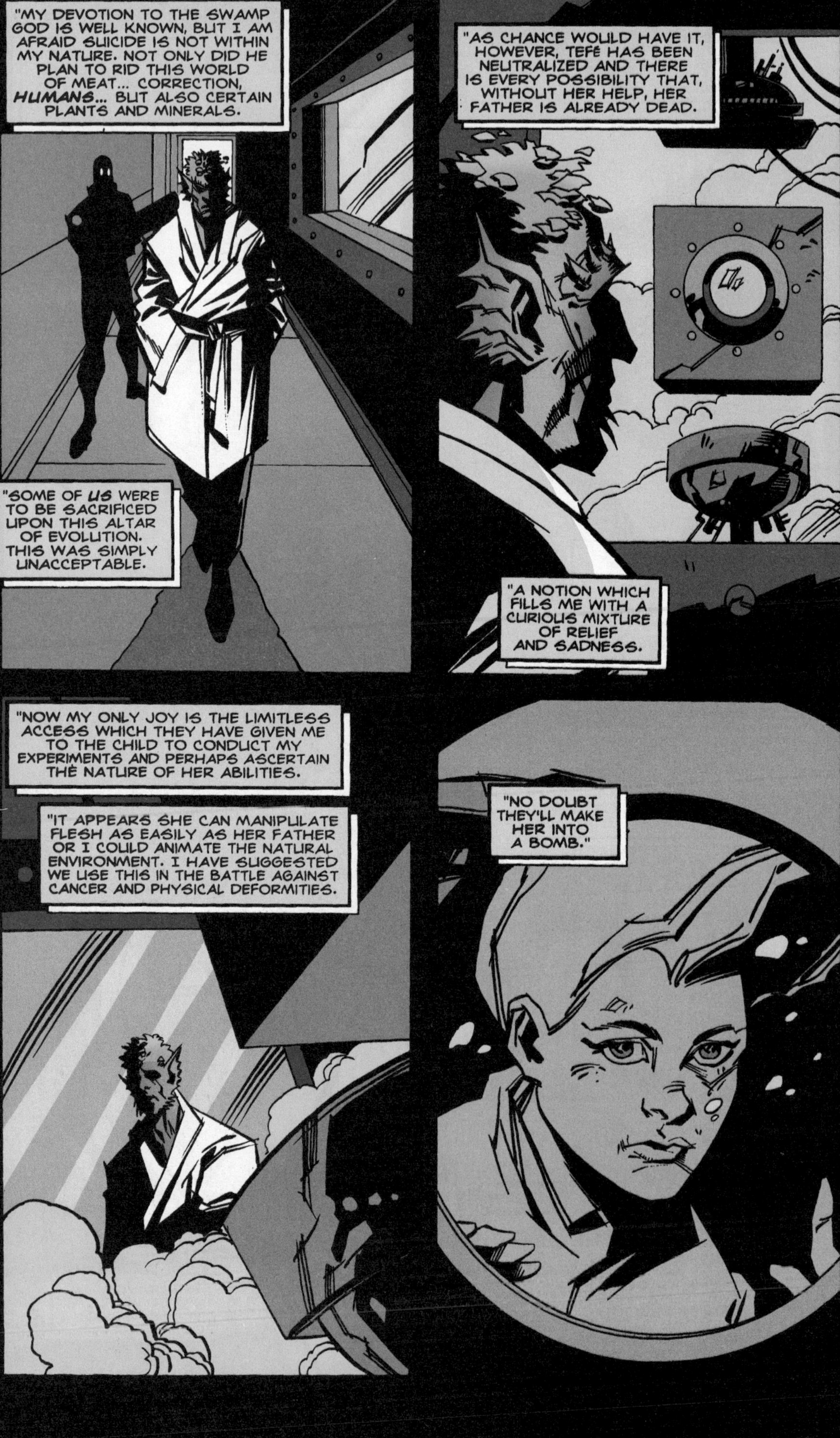
"MY DEVOTION TO THE SWAMP GOD IS WELL KNOWN, BUT I AM AFRAID SUICIDE IS NOT WITHIN MY NATURE. NOT ONLY DID HE PLAN TO RID THIS WORLD OF MEAT... CORRECTION, HUMANS... BUT ALSO CERTAIN PLANTS AND MINERALS.
"SOME OF US WERE TO BE SACRIFICED UPON THIS ALTAR OF EVOLUTION. THIS WAS SIMPLY UNACCEPTABLE.
"AS CHANCE WOULD HAVE IT, HOWEVER, TEFÉ HAS BEEN NEUTRALIZED AND THERE IS EVERY POSSIBILITY THAT, WITHOUT HER HELP, HER FATHER IS ALREADY DEAD.
"A NOTION WHICH FILLS ME WITH A CURIOUS MIXTURE OF RELIEF AND SADNESS.
"NOW MY ONLY JOY IS THE LIMITLESS ACCESS WHICH THEY HAVE GIVEN ME TO THE CHILD TO CONDUCT MY EXPERIMENTS AND PERHAPS ASCERTAIN THE NATURE OF HER ABILITIES.
"IT APPEARS SHE CAN MANIPULATE FLESH AS EASILY AS HER FATHER OR I COULD ANIMATE THE NATURAL ENVIRONMENT. I HAVE SUGGESTED WE USE THIS IN THE BATTLE AGAINST CANCER AND PHYSICAL DEFORMITIES.
"NO DOUBT THEY'LL MAKE HER INTO A BOMB."

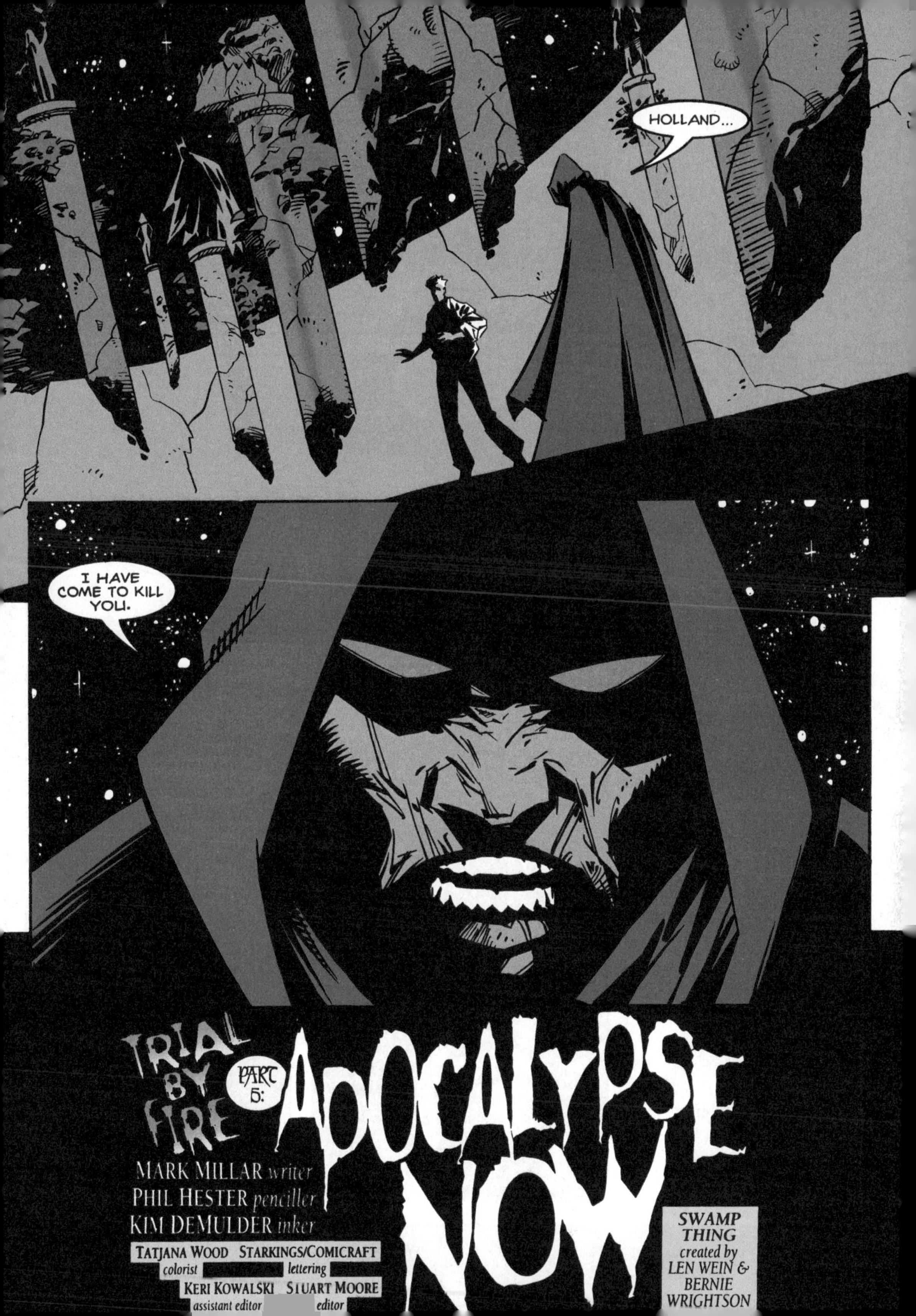
HOLLAND...
I HAVE COME TO KILL YOU.
TRIAL BY FIRE
PART 5:
APOCALYPSE NOW
MARK MILLAR writer
PHIL HESTER penciller
KIM DEMULDER inker
TATJANA WOOD colorist
STARKINGS/COMICRAFT lettering
KERI KOWALSKI assistant editor
STUART MOORE editor
SWAMP THING created by LEN WEIN & BERNIE WRIGHTSON

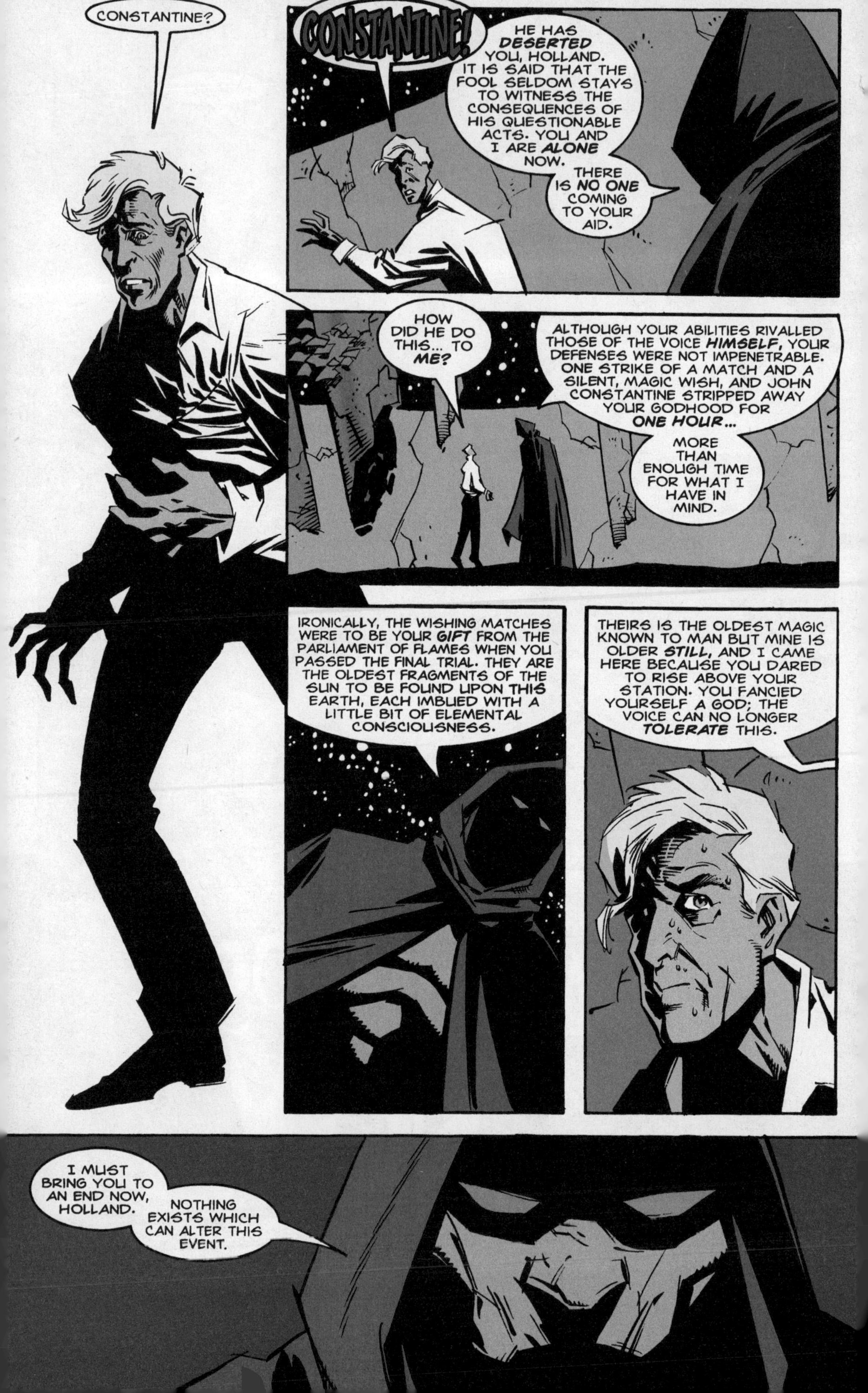
CONSTANTINE?
CONSTANTINE!
HE HAS DESERTED YOU, HOLLAND. IT IS SAID THAT THE FOOL SELDOM STAYS TO WITNESS THE CONSEQUENCES OF HIS QUESTIONABLE ACTS. YOU AND I ARE ALONE NOW.
THERE IS NO ONE COMING TO YOUR AID.
HOW DID HE DO THIS... TO ME?
ALTHOUGH YOUR ABILITIES RIVALLED THOSE OF THE VOICE HIMSELF, YOUR DEFENSES WERE NOT IMPENETRABLE. ONE STRIKE OF A MATCH AND A SILENT, MAGIC WISH, AND JOHN CONSTANTINE STRIPPED AWAY YOUR GODHOOD FOR ONE HOUR...
MORE THAN ENOUGH TIME FOR WHAT I HAVE IN MIND.
IRONICALLY, THE WISHING MATCHES WERE TO BE YOUR GIFT FROM THE PARLIAMENT OF FLAMES WHEN YOU PASSED THE FINAL TRIAL. THEY ARE THE OLDEST FRAGMENTS OF THE SUN TO BE FOUND UPON THIS EARTH, EACH IMBUED WITH A LITTLE BIT OF ELEMENTAL CONSCIOUSNESS.
THEIRS IS THE OLDEST MAGIC KNOWN TO MAN BUT MINE IS OLDER STILL, AND I CAME HERE BECAUSE YOU DARED TO RISE ABOVE YOUR STATION. YOU FANCIED YOURSELF A GOD; THE VOICE CAN NO LONGER TOLERATE THIS.
I MUST BRING YOU TO AN END NOW, HOLLAND.
NOTHING EXISTS WHICH CAN ALTER THIS EVENT.

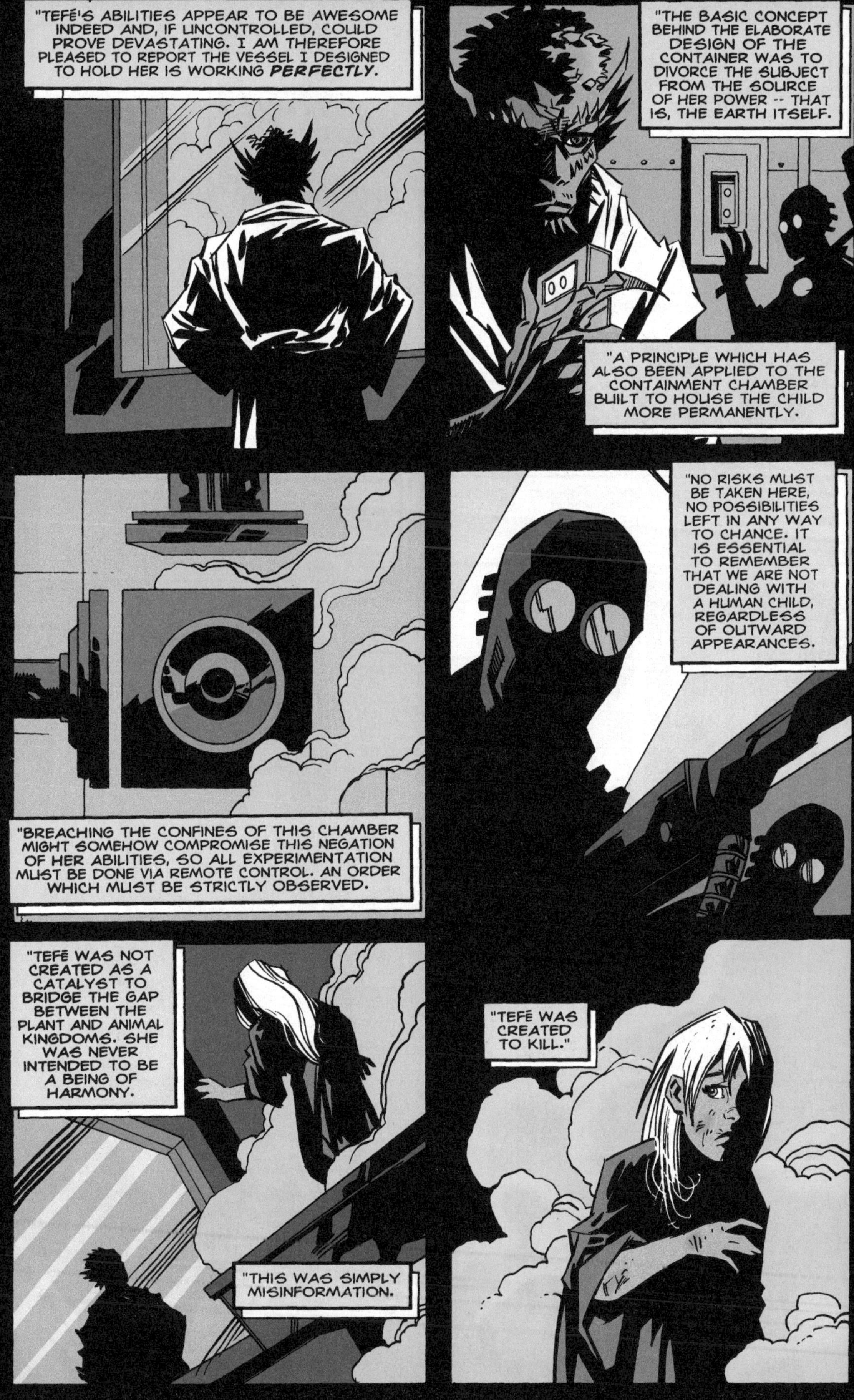
"TEFÉ'S ABILITIES APPEAR TO BE AWESOME INDEED AND, IF UNCONTROLLED, COULD PROVE DEVASTATING. I AM THEREFORE PLEASED TO REPORT THE VESSEL I DESIGNED TO HOLD HER IS WORKING *PERFECTLY*.
"THE BASIC CONCEPT BEHIND THE ELABORATE DESIGN OF THE CONTAINER WAS TO DIVORCE THE SUBJECT FROM THE SOURCE OF HER POWER -- THAT IS, THE EARTH ITSELF.
"A PRINCIPLE WHICH HAS ALSO BEEN APPLIED TO THE CONTAINMENT CHAMBER BUILT TO HOUSE THE CHILD MORE PERMANENTLY.
"BREACHING THE CONFINES OF THIS CHAMBER MIGHT SOMEHOW COMPROMISE THIS NEGATION OF HER ABILITIES, SO ALL EXPERIMENTATION MUST BE DONE VIA REMOTE CONTROL. AN ORDER WHICH MUST BE STRICTLY OBSERVED.
"NO RISKS MUST BE TAKEN HERE, NO POSSIBILITIES LEFT IN ANY WAY TO CHANCE. IT IS ESSENTIAL TO REMEMBER THAT WE ARE NOT DEALING WITH A HUMAN CHILD, REGARDLESS OF OUTWARD APPEARANCES.
"TEFÉ WAS NOT CREATED AS A CATALYST TO BRIDGE THE GAP BETWEEN THE PLANT AND ANIMAL KINGDOMS. SHE WAS NEVER INTENDED TO BE A BEING OF HARMONY.
"THIS WAS SIMPLY MISINFORMATION.
"TEFÉ WAS CREATED TO KILL."

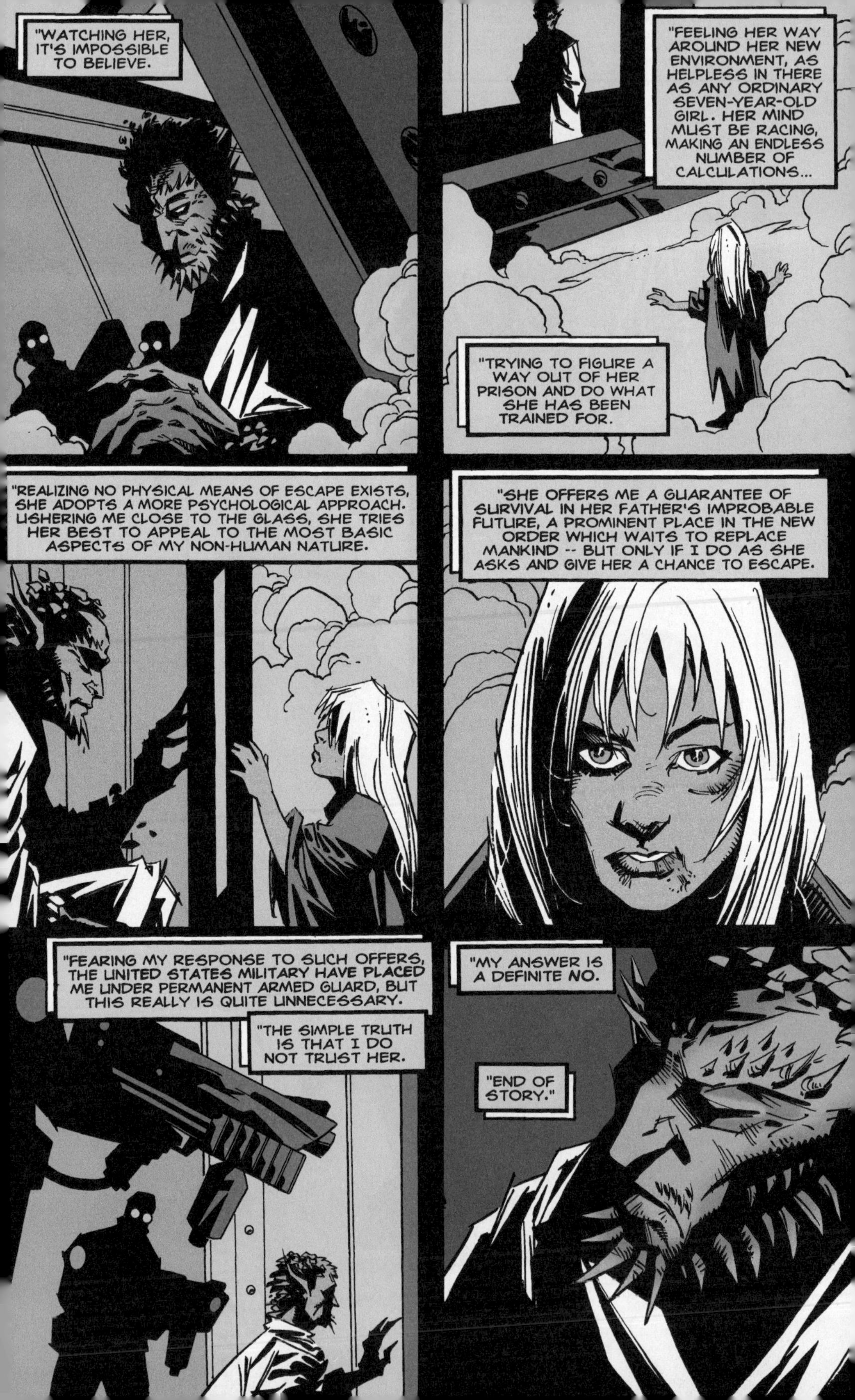
"WATCHING HER, IT'S IMPOSSIBLE TO BELIEVE.
"FEELING HER WAY AROUND HER NEW ENVIRONMENT, AS HELPLESS IN THERE AS ANY ORDINARY SEVEN-YEAR-OLD GIRL. HER MIND MUST BE RACING, MAKING AN ENDLESS NUMBER OF CALCULATIONS...
"TRYING TO FIGURE A WAY OUT OF HER PRISON AND DO WHAT SHE HAS BEEN TRAINED FOR.
"REALIZING NO PHYSICAL MEANS OF ESCAPE EXISTS, SHE ADOPTS A MORE PSYCHOLOGICAL APPROACH. USHERING ME CLOSE TO THE GLASS, SHE TRIES HER BEST TO APPEAL TO THE MOST BASIC ASPECTS OF MY NON-HUMAN NATURE.
"SHE OFFERS ME A GUARANTEE OF SURVIVAL IN HER FATHER'S IMPROBABLE FUTURE, A PROMINENT PLACE IN THE NEW ORDER WHICH WAITS TO REPLACE MANKIND -- BUT ONLY IF I DO AS SHE ASKS AND GIVE HER A CHANCE TO ESCAPE.
"FEARING MY RESPONSE TO SUCH OFFERS, THE UNITED STATES MILITARY HAVE PLACED ME UNDER PERMANENT ARMED GUARD, BUT THIS REALLY IS QUITE UNNECESSARY.
"THE SIMPLE TRUTH IS THAT I DO NOT TRUST HER.
"MY ANSWER IS A DEFINITE NO.
"END OF STORY."

YOU'RE WRONG ABOUT ONE THING: I'M NOT ON MY OWN HERE. TEFE'S BEEN TRAINED TO DEAL WITH YOU, AND SHE'LL BE WITH US ANY MOMENT.

I SUGGEST YOU ORGANIZE YOUR DEFENSES.

THE CHILD IS A CONSIDERABLE OPPONENT AND WILL DO ANYTHING TO ENSURE MY SURVIVAL.

SHE CAN DO NOTHING. ANY PREPARATIONS MADE WOULD BE QUITE UNNECESSARY. THE CREATURE HAS ALREADY BEEN TERMINATED.

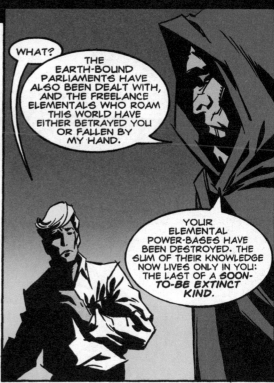

WHAT?

THE EARTH-BOUND PARLIAMENTS HAVE ALSO BEEN DEALT WITH, AND THE FREELANCE ELEMENTALS WHO ROAM THIS WORLD HAVE EITHER BETRAYED YOU OR FALLEN BY MY HAND.

YOUR ELEMENTAL POWER-BASES HAVE BEEN DESTROYED. THE SUM OF THEIR KNOWLEDGE NOW LIVES ONLY IN YOU: THE LAST OF A SOON-TO-BE EXTINCT KIND.

THERE ARE NO OPTIONS LEFT. EVERY POSSIBLE OUTCOME HAS BEEN CONSIDERED. NOTHING HAS BEEN LEFT TO CHANCE.

NOW FALL ON YOUR KNEES, HOLLAND. PRAY TO THE VOICE FOR A QUICK AND PAINLESS DEATH AND PERHAPS HE WILL GRANT MERCY UPON YOUR IMMORTAL SOUL.

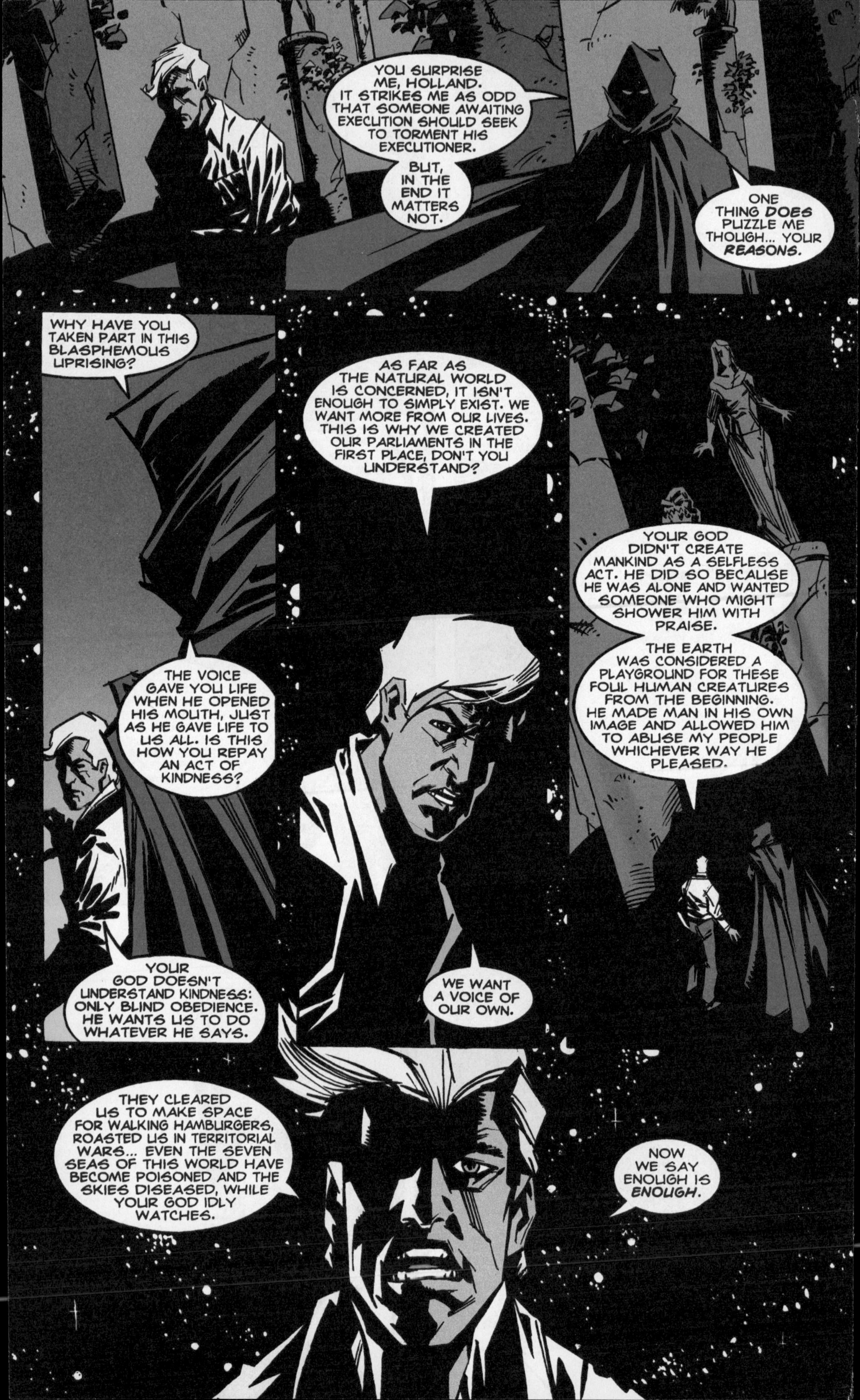
YOU SURPRISE ME, HOLLAND. IT STRIKES ME AS ODD THAT SOMEONE AWAITING EXECUTION SHOULD SEEK TO TORMENT HIS EXECUTIONER.
BUT, IN THE END IT MATTERS NOT.
ONE THING DOES PUZZLE ME THOUGH... YOUR REASONS.
WHY HAVE YOU TAKEN PART IN THIS BLASPHEMOUS UPRISING?
THE VOICE GAVE YOU LIFE WHEN HE OPENED HIS MOUTH, JUST AS HE GAVE LIFE TO US ALL. IS THIS HOW YOU REPAY AN ACT OF KINDNESS?
YOUR GOD DOESN'T UNDERSTAND KINDNESS: ONLY BLIND OBEDIENCE. HE WANTS US TO DO WHATEVER HE SAYS.
AS FAR AS THE NATURAL WORLD IS CONCERNED, IT ISN'T ENOUGH TO SIMPLY EXIST. WE WANT MORE FROM OUR LIVES. THIS IS WHY WE CREATED OUR PARLIAMENTS IN THE FIRST PLACE, DON'T YOU UNDERSTAND?
WE WANT A VOICE OF OUR OWN.
YOUR GOD DIDN'T CREATE MANKIND AS A SELFLESS ACT. HE DID SO BECAUSE HE WAS ALONE AND WANTED SOMEONE WHO MIGHT SHOWER HIM WITH PRAISE.
THE EARTH WAS CONSIDERED A PLAYGROUND FOR THESE FOUL HUMAN CREATURES FROM THE BEGINNING. HE MADE MAN IN HIS OWN IMAGE AND ALLOWED HIM TO ABUSE MY PEOPLE WHICHEVER WAY HE PLEASED.
THEY CLEARED US TO MAKE SPACE FOR WALKING HAMBURGERS, ROASTED US IN TERRITORIAL WARS... EVEN THE SEVEN SEAS OF THIS WORLD HAVE BECOME POISONED AND THE SKIES DISEASED, WHILE YOUR GOD IDLY WATCHES.
NOW WE SAY ENOUGH IS ENOUGH.

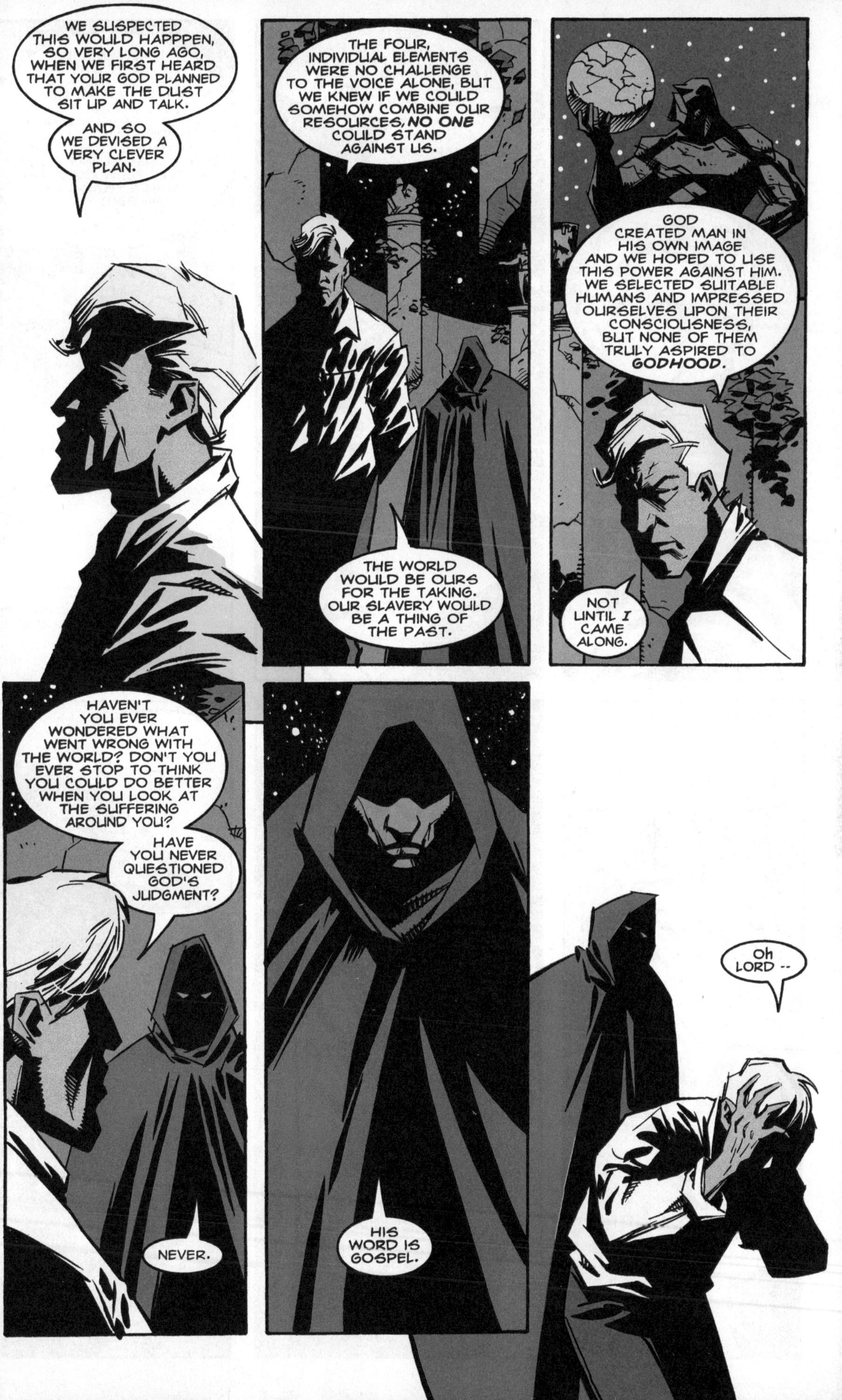
WE SUSPECTED THIS WOULD HAPPPEN, SO VERY LONG AGO, WHEN WE FIRST HEARD THAT YOUR GOD PLANNED TO MAKE THE DUST SIT UP AND TALK.
AND SO WE DEVISED A VERY CLEVER PLAN.
THE FOUR, INDIVIDUAL ELEMENTS WERE NO CHALLENGE TO THE VOICE ALONE, BUT WE KNEW IF WE COULD SOMEHOW COMBINE OUR RESOURCES, NO ONE COULD STAND AGAINST US.
THE WORLD WOULD BE OURS FOR THE TAKING. OUR SLAVERY WOULD BE A THING OF THE PAST.
GOD CREATED MAN IN HIS OWN IMAGE AND WE HOPED TO USE THIS POWER AGAINST HIM. WE SELECTED SUITABLE HUMANS AND IMPRESSED OURSELVES UPON THEIR CONSCIOUSNESS, BUT NONE OF THEM TRULY ASPIRED TO GODHOOD.
NOT UNTIL I CAME ALONG.
HAVEN'T YOU EVER WONDERED WHAT WENT WRONG WITH THE WORLD? DON'T YOU EVER STOP TO THINK YOU COULD DO BETTER WHEN YOU LOOK AT THE SUFFERING AROUND YOU?
HAVE YOU NEVER QUESTIONED GOD'S JUDGMENT?
NEVER.
HIS WORD IS GOSPEL.
Oh LORD --

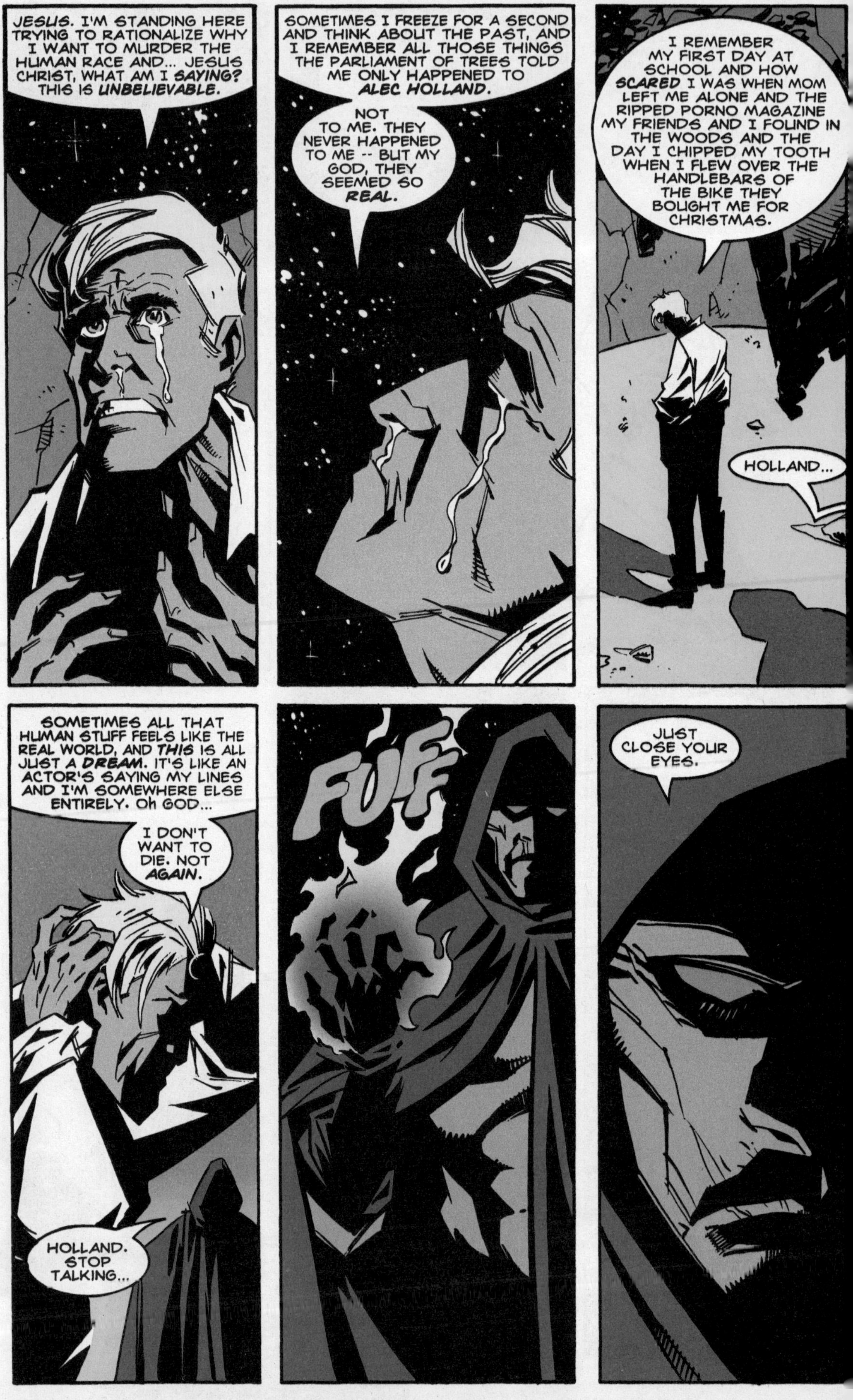
JESUS. I'M STANDING HERE TRYING TO RATIONALIZE WHY I WANT TO MURDER THE HUMAN RACE AND... JESUS CHRIST, WHAT AM I *SAYING?* THIS IS *UNBELIEVABLE.*
SOMETIMES I FREEZE FOR A SECOND AND THINK ABOUT THE PAST, AND I REMEMBER ALL THOSE THINGS THE PARLIAMENT OF TREES TOLD ME ONLY HAPPENED TO *ALEC HOLLAND.*
NOT TO ME. THEY NEVER HAPPENED TO ME -- BUT MY GOD, THEY SEEMED SO *REAL.*
I REMEMBER MY FIRST DAY AT SCHOOL AND HOW *SCARED* I WAS WHEN MOM LEFT ME ALONE AND THE RIPPED PORNO MAGAZINE MY FRIENDS AND I FOUND IN THE WOODS AND THE DAY I CHIPPED MY TOOTH WHEN I FLEW OVER THE HANDLEBARS OF THE BIKE THEY BOUGHT ME FOR CHRISTMAS.
HOLLAND...
SOMETIMES ALL THAT HUMAN STUFF FEELS LIKE THE REAL WORLD, AND *THIS* IS ALL JUST A *DREAM*. IT'S LIKE AN ACTOR'S SAYING MY LINES AND I'M SOMEWHERE ELSE ENTIRELY. Oh GOD...
I DON'T WANT TO DIE. NOT *AGAIN.*
HOLLAND. STOP TALKING...
FUF
JUST CLOSE YOUR EYES.

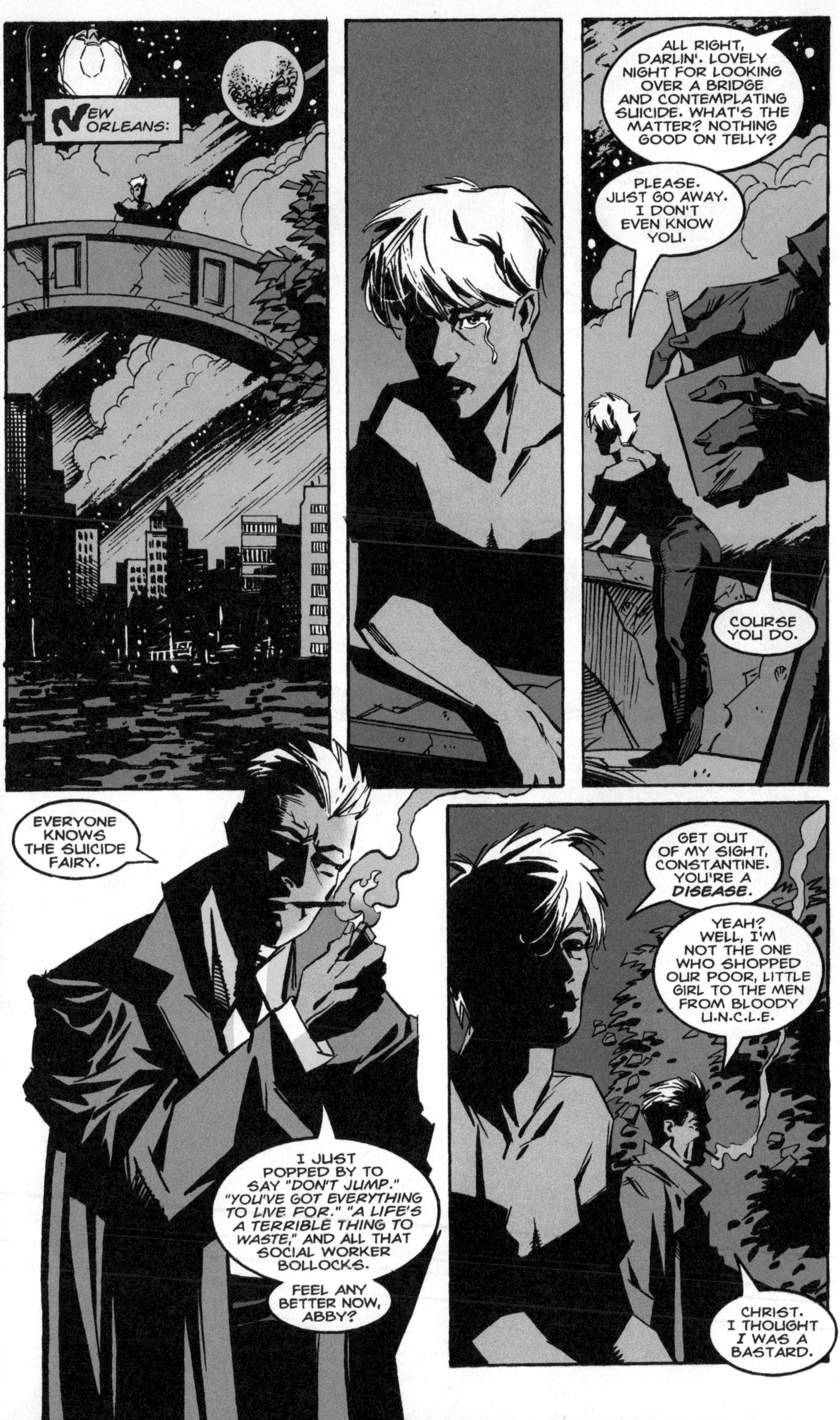
NEW ORLEANS:
ALL RIGHT, DARLIN'. LOVELY NIGHT FOR LOOKING OVER A BRIDGE AND CONTEMPLATING SUICIDE. WHAT'S THE MATTER? NOTHING GOOD ON TELLY?
PLEASE. JUST GO AWAY. I DON'T EVEN KNOW YOU.
COURSE YOU DO.
EVERYONE KNOWS THE SUICIDE FAIRY.
I JUST POPPED BY TO SAY "DON'T JUMP." "YOU'VE GOT EVERYTHING TO LIVE FOR." "A LIFE'S A TERRIBLE THING TO WASTE," AND ALL THAT SOCIAL WORKER BOLLOCKS.
FEEL ANY BETTER NOW, ABBY?
GET OUT OF MY SIGHT, CONSTANTINE. YOU'RE A DISEASE.
YEAH? WELL, I'M NOT THE ONE WHO SHOPPED OUR POOR, LITTLE GIRL TO THE MEN FROM BLOODY U.N.C.L.E.
CHRIST. I THOUGHT I WAS A BASTARD.

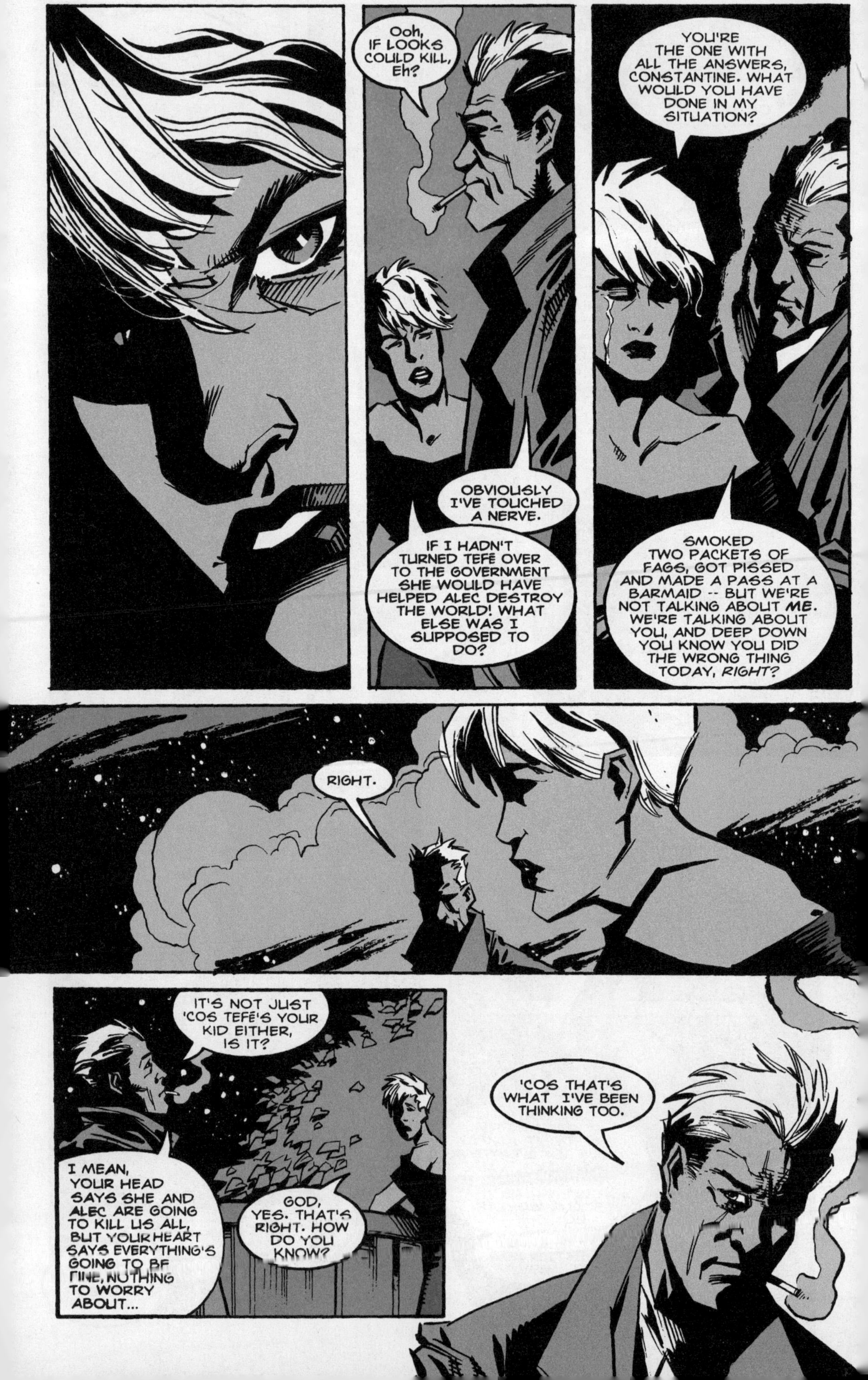
Ooh, IF LOOKS COULD KILL, Eh?
OBVIOUSLY I'VE TOUCHED A NERVE.
IF I HADN'T TURNED TEFÉ OVER TO THE GOVERNMENT SHE WOULD HAVE HELPED ALEC DESTROY THE WORLD! WHAT ELSE WAS I SUPPOSED TO DO?
YOU'RE THE ONE WITH ALL THE ANSWERS, CONSTANTINE. WHAT WOULD YOU HAVE DONE IN MY SITUATION?
SMOKED TWO PACKETS OF FAGS, GOT PISSED AND MADE A PASS AT A BARMAID -- BUT WE'RE NOT TALKING ABOUT ME. WE'RE TALKING ABOUT YOU, AND DEEP DOWN YOU KNOW YOU DID THE WRONG THING TODAY, RIGHT?
RIGHT.
IT'S NOT JUST 'COS TEFÉ'S YOUR KID EITHER, IS IT?
I MEAN, YOUR HEAD SAYS SHE AND ALEC ARE GOING TO KILL US ALL, BUT YOUR HEART SAYS EVERYTHING'S GOING TO BE FINE, NOTHING TO WORRY ABOUT...
GOD, YES. THAT'S RIGHT. HOW DO YOU KNOW?
'COS THAT'S WHAT I'VE BEEN THINKING TOO.

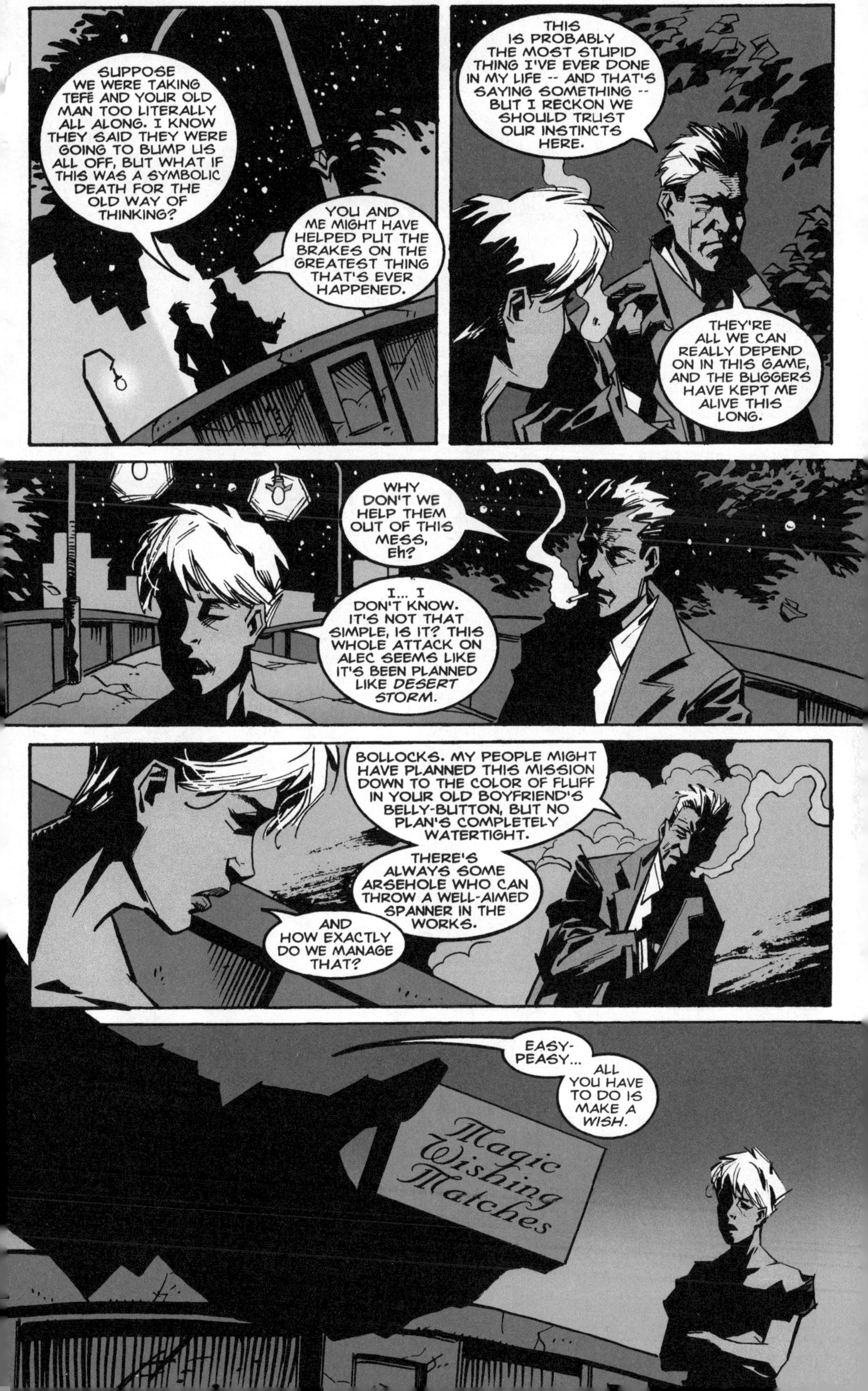
SUPPOSE WE WERE TAKING TEFÉ AND YOUR OLD MAN TOO LITERALLY ALL ALONG. I KNOW THEY SAID THEY WERE GOING TO BUMP US ALL OFF, BUT WHAT IF THIS WAS A SYMBOLIC DEATH FOR THE OLD WAY OF THINKING?
YOU AND ME MIGHT HAVE HELPED PUT THE BRAKES ON THE GREATEST THING THAT'S EVER HAPPENED.
THIS IS PROBABLY THE MOST STUPID THING I'VE EVER DONE IN MY LIFE -- AND THAT'S SAYING SOMETHING -- BUT I RECKON WE SHOULD TRUST OUR INSTINCTS HERE.
THEY'RE ALL WE CAN REALLY DEPEND ON IN THIS GAME, AND THE BUGGERS HAVE KEPT ME ALIVE THIS LONG.
WHY DON'T WE HELP THEM OUT OF THIS MESS, Eh?
I... I DON'T KNOW. IT'S NOT THAT SIMPLE, IS IT? THIS WHOLE ATTACK ON ALEC SEEMS LIKE IT'S BEEN PLANNED LIKE *DESERT STORM*.
BOLLOCKS. MY PEOPLE MIGHT HAVE PLANNED THIS MISSION DOWN TO THE COLOR OF FLUFF IN YOUR OLD BOYFRIEND'S BELLY-BUTTON, BUT NO PLAN'S COMPLETELY WATERTIGHT.
THERE'S ALWAYS SOME ARSEHOLE WHO CAN THROW A WELL-AIMED SPANNER IN THE WORKS.
AND HOW EXACTLY DO WE MANAGE THAT?
EASY-PEASY...
ALL YOU HAVE TO DO IS MAKE A WISH.
Magic Wishing Matches

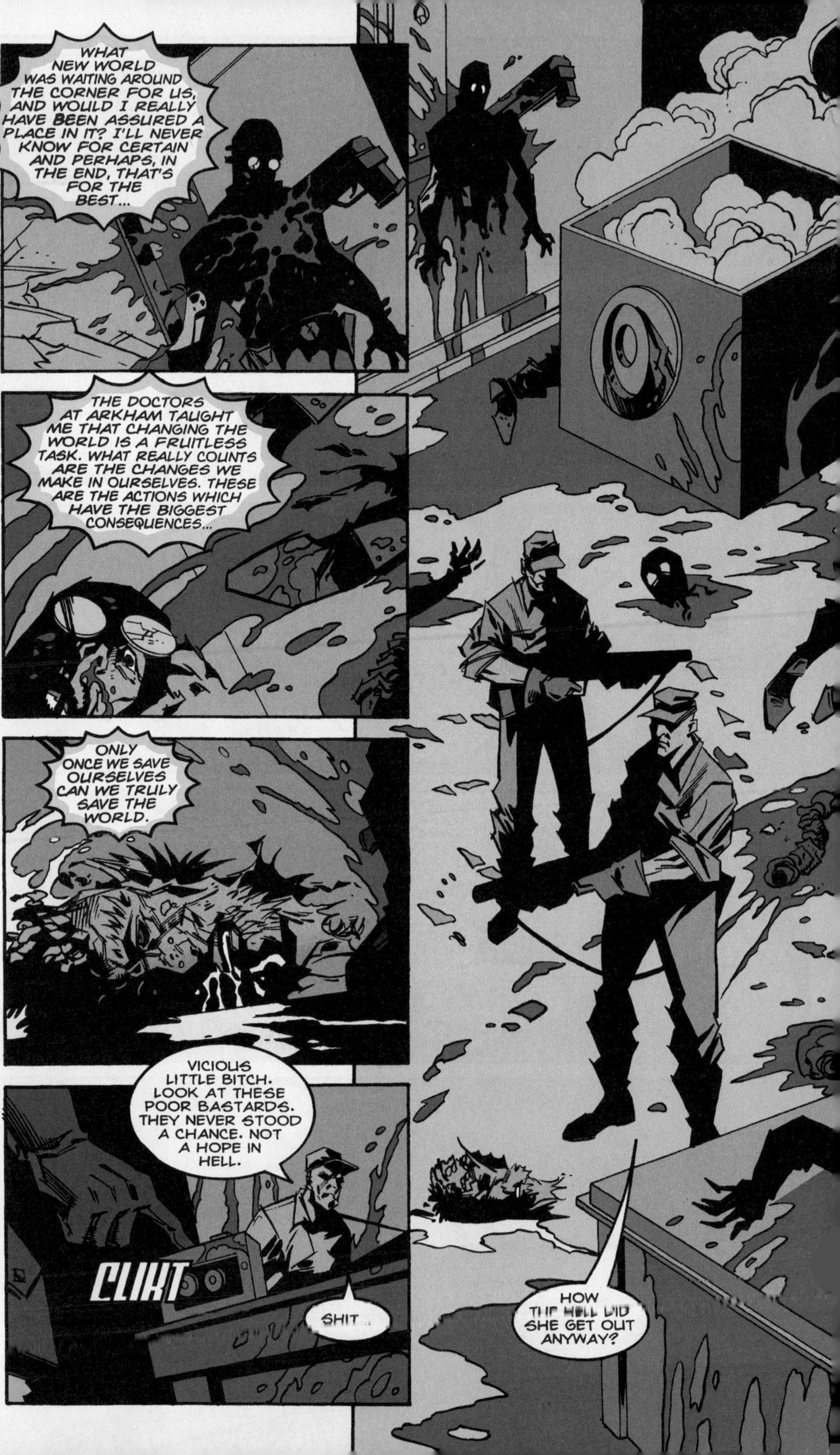
WHAT NEW WORLD WAS WAITING AROUND THE CORNER FOR US, AND WOULD I REALLY HAVE BEEN ASSURED A PLACE IN IT? I'LL NEVER KNOW FOR CERTAIN AND PERHAPS, IN THE END, THAT'S FOR THE BEST...
THE DOCTORS AT ARKHAM TAUGHT ME THAT CHANGING THE WORLD IS A FRUITLESS TASK. WHAT REALLY COUNTS ARE THE CHANGES WE MAKE IN OURSELVES. THESE ARE THE ACTIONS WHICH HAVE THE BIGGEST CONSEQUENCES...
ONLY ONCE WE SAVE OURSELVES CAN WE TRULY SAVE THE WORLD.
VICIOUS LITTLE BITCH. LOOK AT THESE POOR BASTARDS. THEY NEVER STOOD A CHANCE. NOT A HOPE IN HELL.
CLIKT
SHIT...
HOW THE HELL DID SHE GET OUT ANYWAY?

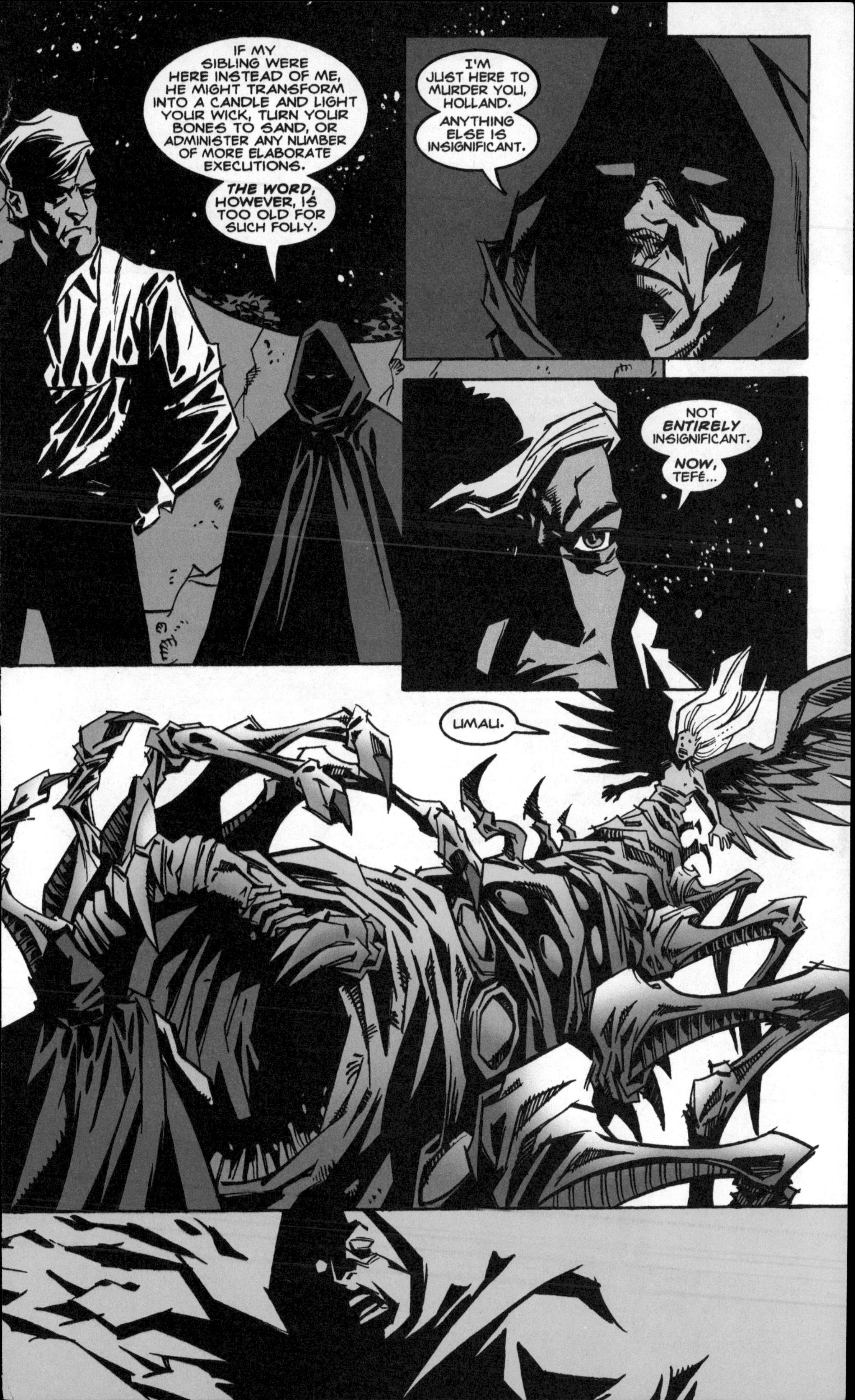
IF MY SIBLING WERE HERE INSTEAD OF ME, HE MIGHT TRANSFORM INTO A CANDLE AND LIGHT YOUR WICK, TURN YOUR BONES TO SAND, OR ADMINISTER ANY NUMBER OF MORE ELABORATE EXECUTIONS.
THE WORD, HOWEVER, IS TOO OLD FOR SUCH FOLLY.
I'M JUST HERE TO MURDER YOU, HOLLAND.
ANYTHING ELSE IS INSIGNIFICANT.
NOT *ENTIRELY* INSIGNIFICANT.
NOW, TEFÉ...
UMAU.

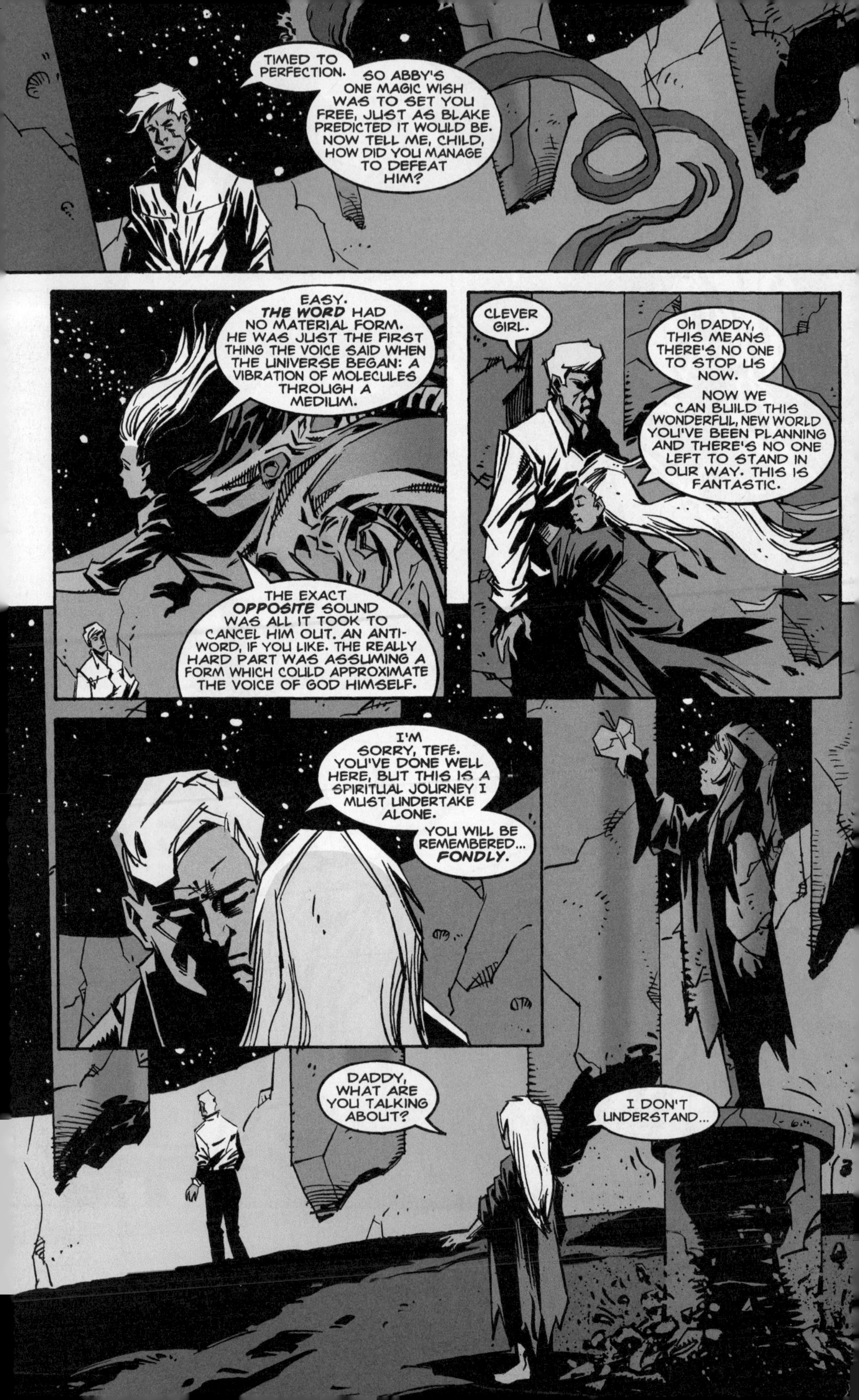
TIMED TO PERFECTION.
SO ABBY'S ONE MAGIC WISH WAS TO SET YOU FREE, JUST AS BLAKE PREDICTED IT WOULD BE. NOW TELL ME, CHILD, HOW DID YOU MANAGE TO DEFEAT HIM?
EASY. THE WORD HAD NO MATERIAL FORM. HE WAS JUST THE FIRST THING THE VOICE SAID WHEN THE UNIVERSE BEGAN: A VIBRATION OF MOLECULES THROUGH A MEDIUM.
THE EXACT OPPOSITE SOUND WAS ALL IT TOOK TO CANCEL HIM OUT. AN ANTI-WORD, IF YOU LIKE. THE REALLY HARD PART WAS ASSUMING A FORM WHICH COULD APPROXIMATE THE VOICE OF GOD HIMSELF.
CLEVER GIRL.
Oh DADDY, THIS MEANS THERE'S NO ONE TO STOP US NOW.
NOW WE CAN BUILD THIS WONDERFUL, NEW WORLD YOU'VE BEEN PLANNING AND THERE'S NO ONE LEFT TO STAND IN OUR WAY. THIS IS FANTASTIC.
I'M SORRY, TEFÉ. YOU'VE DONE WELL HERE, BUT THIS IS A SPIRITUAL JOURNEY I MUST UNDERTAKE ALONE.
YOU WILL BE REMEMBERED... FONDLY.
DADDY, WHAT ARE YOU TALKING ABOUT?
I DON'T UNDERSTAND...

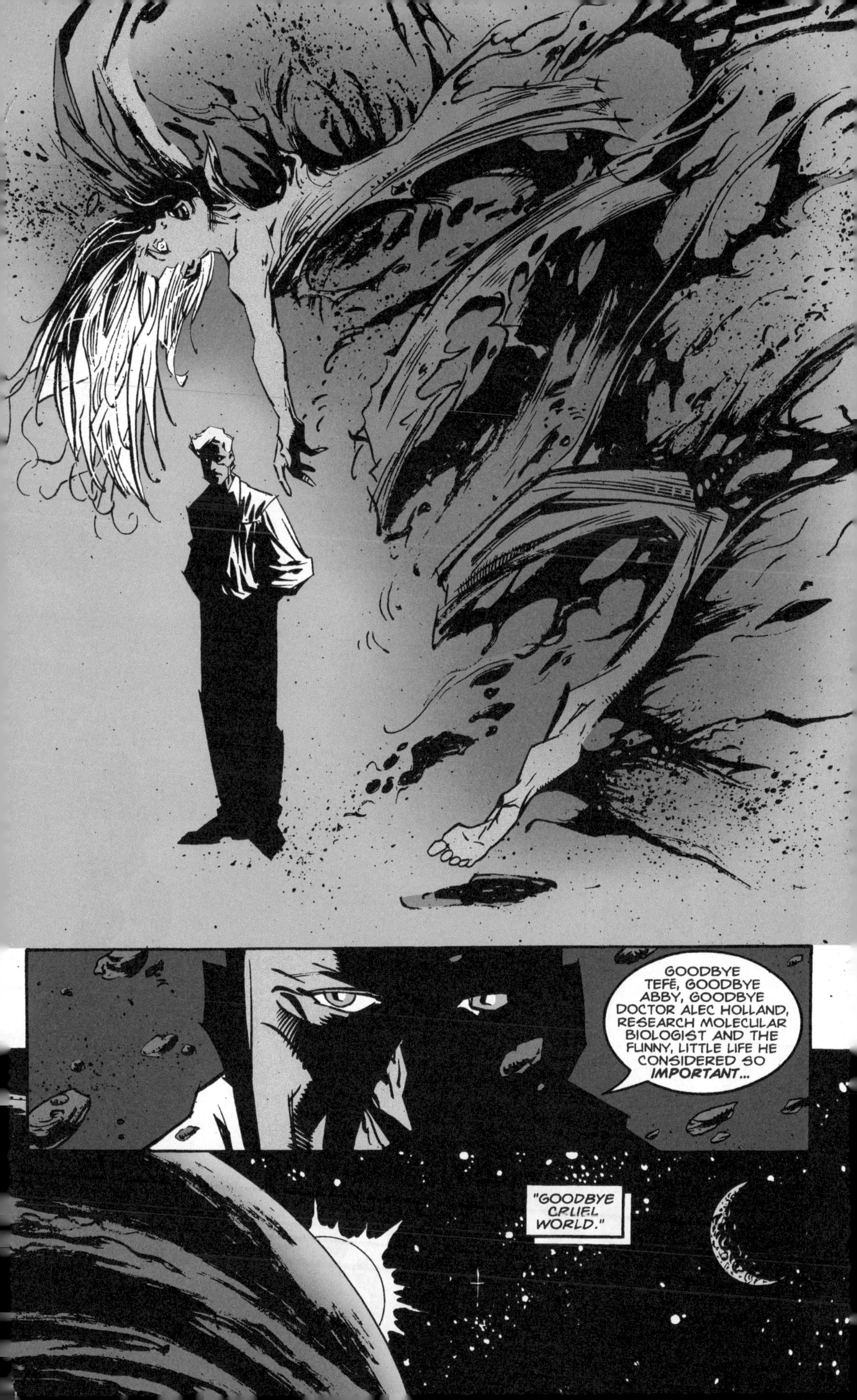
GOODBYE TEFÉ, GOODBYE ABBY, GOODBYE DOCTOR ALEC HOLLAND, RESEARCH MOLECULAR BIOLOGIST AND THE FUNNY, LITTLE LIFE HE CONSIDERED SO *IMPORTANT*...
"GOODBYE CRUEL WORLD."

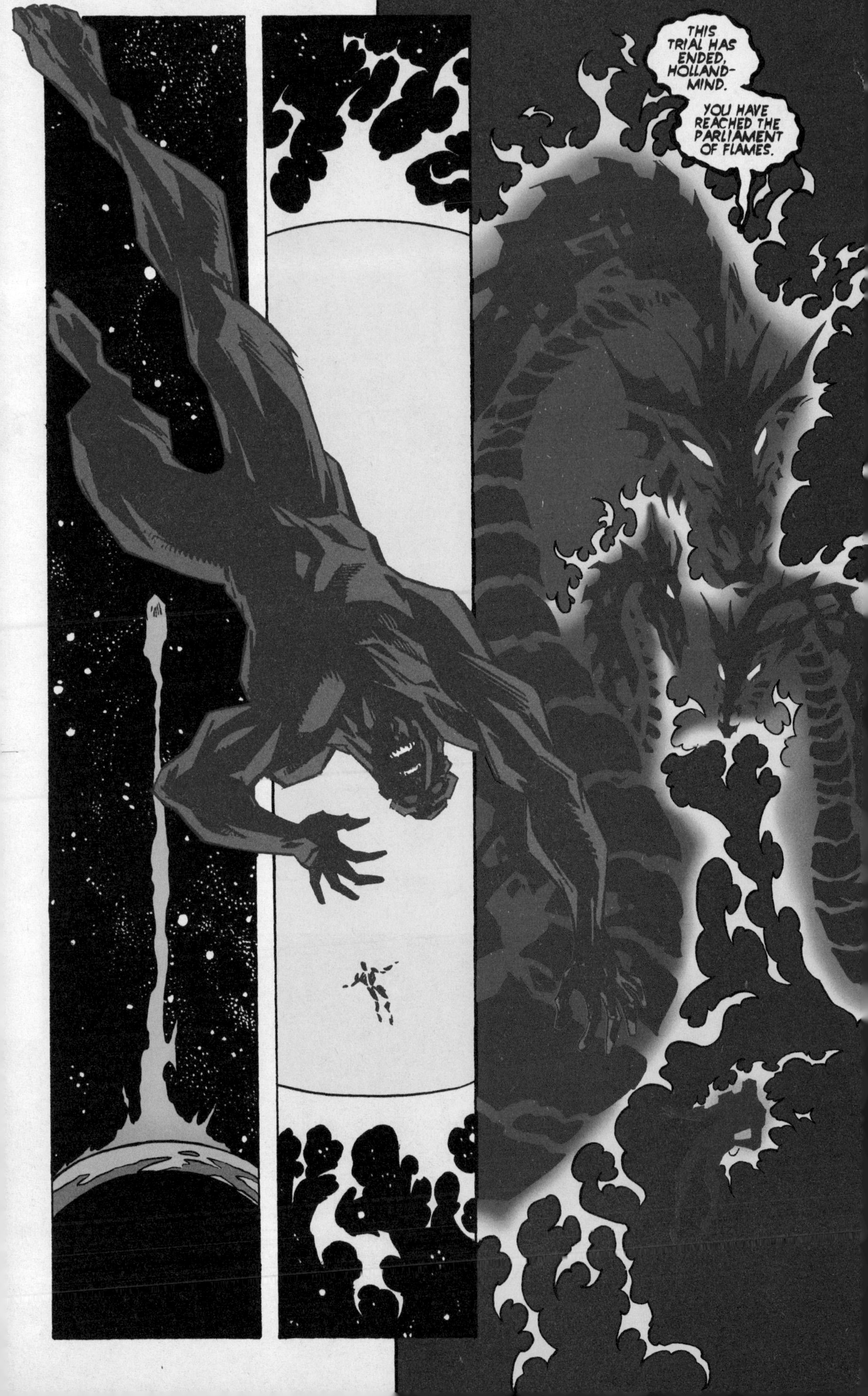
THIS TRIAL HAS ENDED, HOLLAND-MIND.
YOU HAVE REACHED THE PARLIAMENT OF FLAMES.

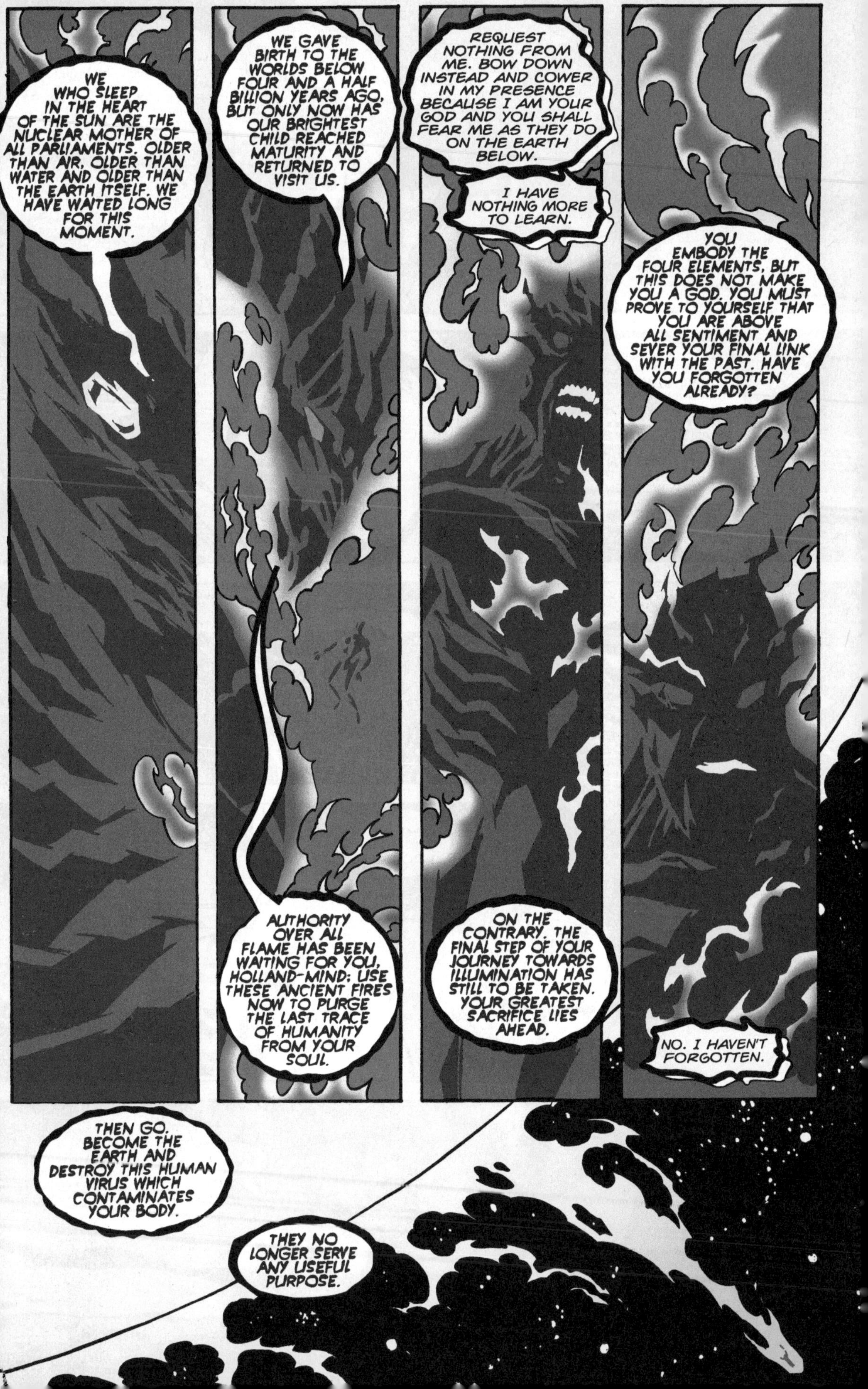
WE WHO SLEEP IN THE HEART OF THE SUN ARE THE NUCLEAR MOTHER OF ALL PARLIAMENTS. OLDER THAN AIR, OLDER THAN WATER AND OLDER THAN THE EARTH ITSELF. WE HAVE WAITED LONG FOR THIS MOMENT.
WE GAVE BIRTH TO THE WORLDS BELOW FOUR AND A HALF BILLION YEARS AGO, BUT ONLY NOW HAS OUR BRIGHTEST CHILD REACHED MATURITY AND RETURNED TO VISIT US.
AUTHORITY OVER ALL FLAME HAS BEEN WAITING FOR YOU, HOLLAND-MIND: USE THESE ANCIENT FIRES NOW TO PURGE THE LAST TRACE OF HUMANITY FROM YOUR SOUL.
REQUEST NOTHING FROM ME. BOW DOWN INSTEAD AND COWER IN MY PRESENCE BECAUSE I AM YOUR GOD AND YOU SHALL FEAR ME AS THEY DO ON THE EARTH BELOW.
I HAVE NOTHING MORE TO LEARN.
ON THE CONTRARY. THE FINAL STEP OF YOUR JOURNEY TOWARDS ILLUMINATION HAS STILL TO BE TAKEN. YOUR GREATEST SACRIFICE LIES AHEAD.
YOU EMBODY THE FOUR ELEMENTS, BUT THIS DOES NOT MAKE YOU A GOD. YOU MUST PROVE TO YOURSELF THAT YOU ARE ABOVE ALL SENTIMENT AND SEVER YOUR FINAL LINK WITH THE PAST. HAVE YOU FORGOTTEN ALREADY?
NO. I HAVEN'T FORGOTTEN.
THEN GO. BECOME THE EARTH AND DESTROY THIS HUMAN VIRUS WHICH CONTAMINATES YOUR BODY.
THEY NO LONGER SERVE ANY USEFUL PURPOSE.

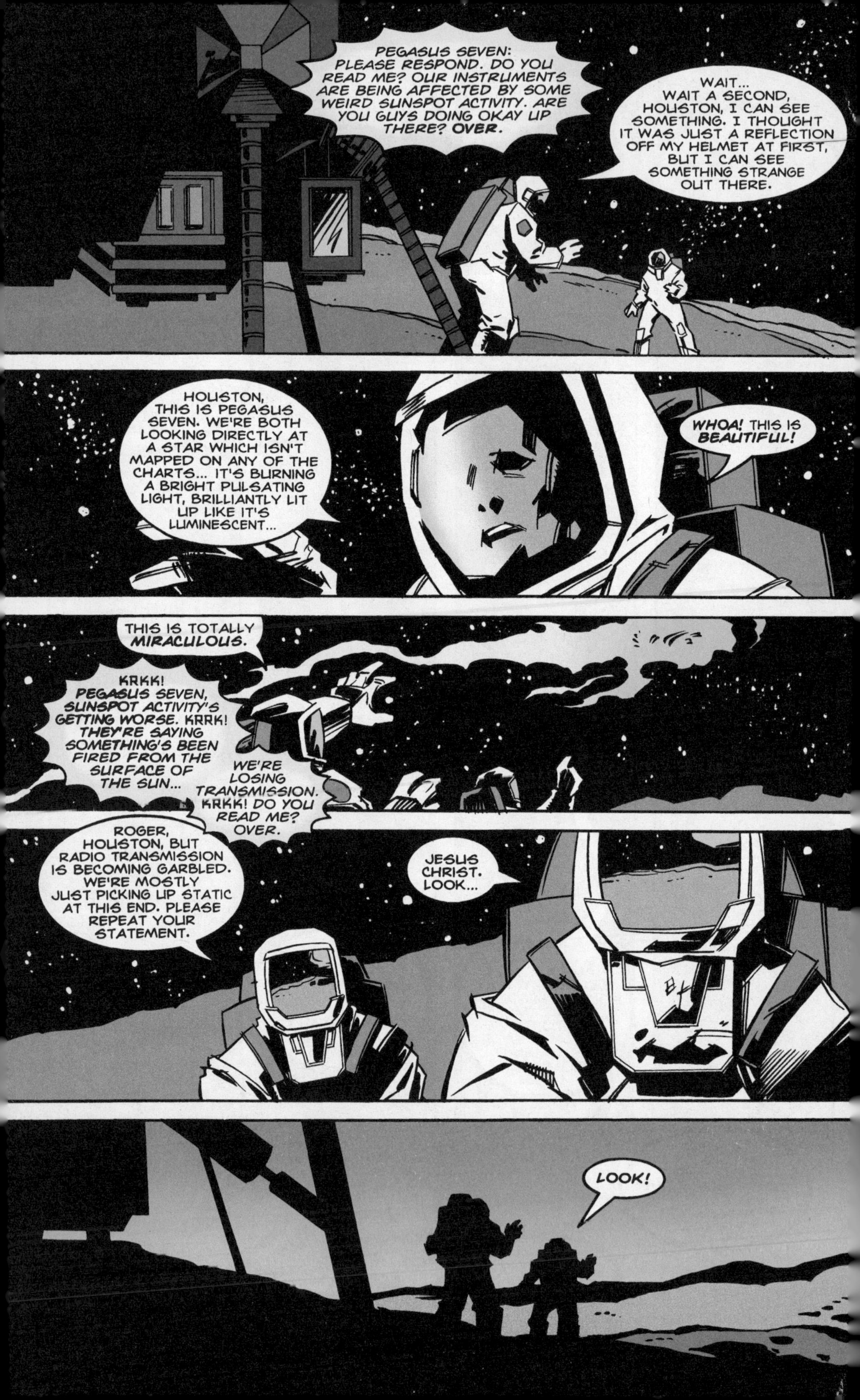
PEGASUS SEVEN: PLEASE RESPOND. DO YOU READ ME? OUR INSTRUMENTS ARE BEING AFFECTED BY SOME WEIRD SUNSPOT ACTIVITY. ARE YOU GUYS DOING OKAY UP THERE? OVER.
WAIT... WAIT A SECOND, HOUSTON, I CAN SEE SOMETHING. I THOUGHT IT WAS JUST A REFLECTION OFF MY HELMET AT FIRST, BUT I CAN SEE SOMETHING STRANGE OUT THERE.
HOUSTON, THIS IS PEGASUS SEVEN. WE'RE BOTH LOOKING DIRECTLY AT A STAR WHICH ISN'T MAPPED ON ANY OF THE CHARTS... IT'S BURNING A BRIGHT PULSATING LIGHT, BRILLIANTLY LIT UP LIKE IT'S LUMINESCENT...
WHOA! THIS IS BEAUTIFUL!
THIS IS TOTALLY MIRACULOUS.
KRKK! PEGASUS SEVEN, SUNSPOT ACTIVITY'S GETTING WORSE. KRRK! THEY'RE SAYING SOMETHING'S BEEN FIRED FROM THE SURFACE OF THE SUN...
WE'RE LOSING TRANSMISSION. KRKK! DO YOU READ ME? OVER.
ROGER, HOUSTON, BUT RADIO TRANSMISSION IS BECOMING GARBLED. WE'RE MOSTLY JUST PICKING UP STATIC AT THIS END. PLEASE REPEAT YOUR STATEMENT.
JESUS CHRIST. LOOK...
LOOK!

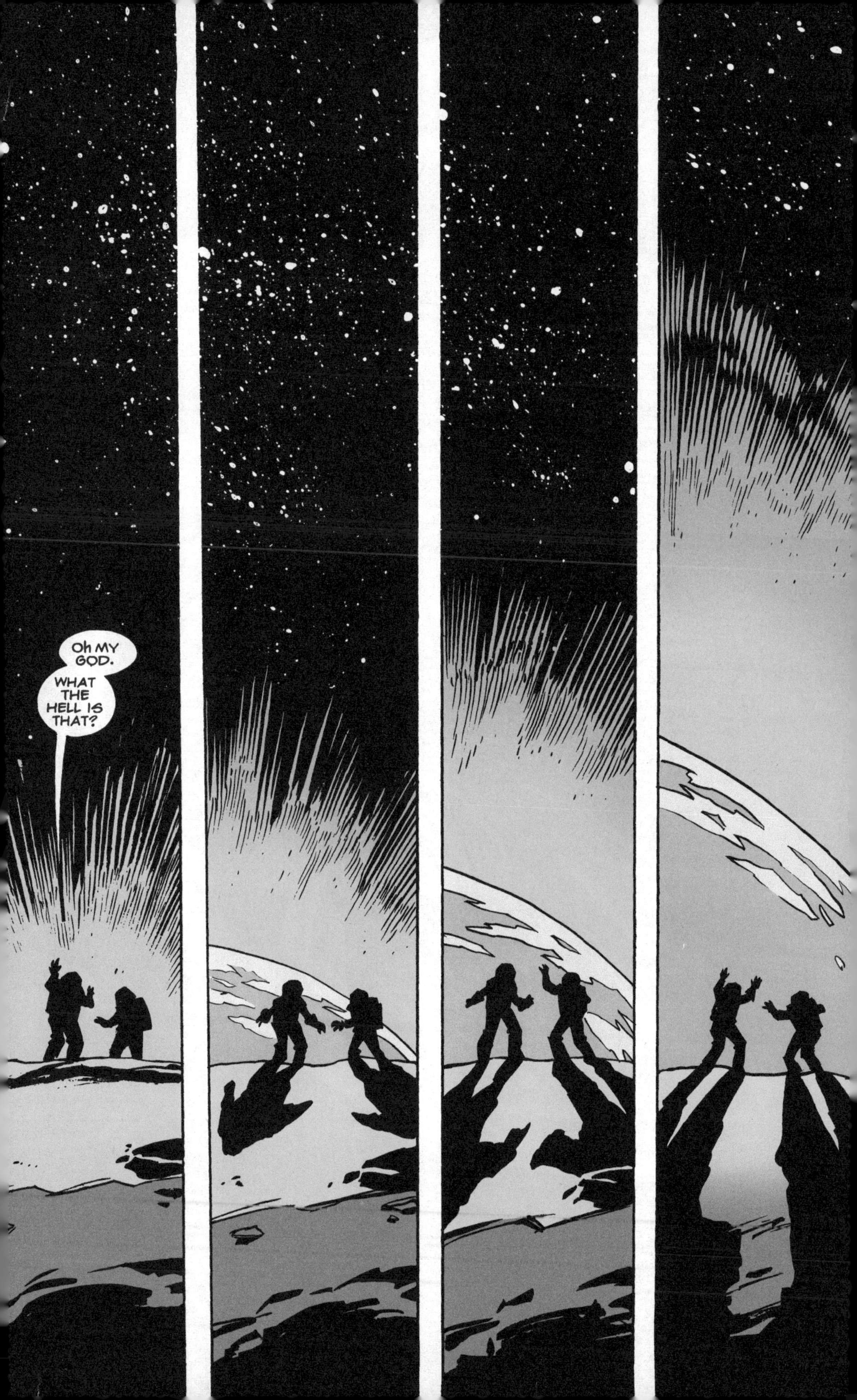
Oh MY GOD.
WHAT THE HELL IS THAT?

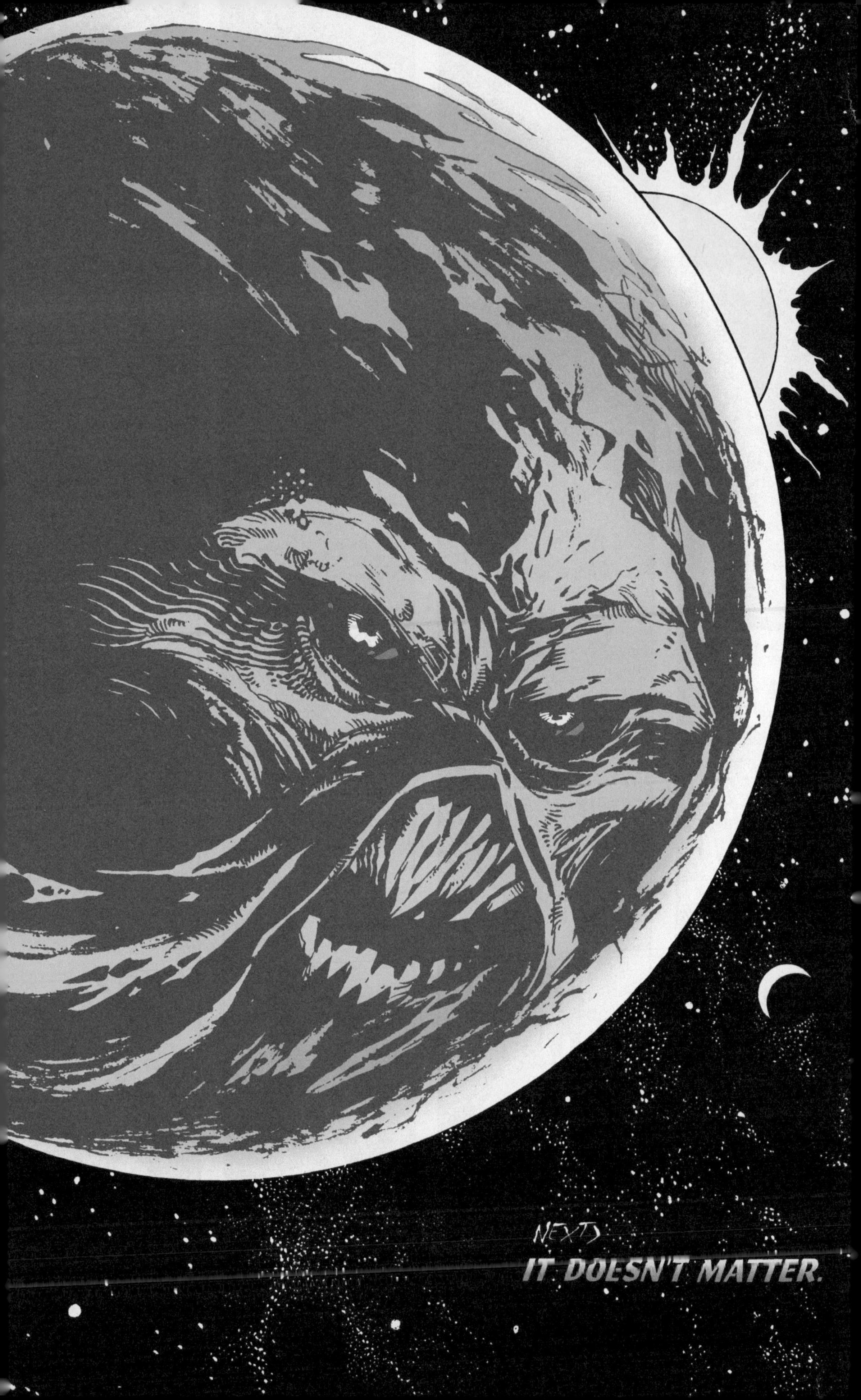
NEXT:
IT DOESN'T MATTER.

SWAMP THING

VERTIGO

1.6 US
CAN

TED
TURE
IS

MARK MILLAR
PHILLIP HESTER
KIM DeMULDER

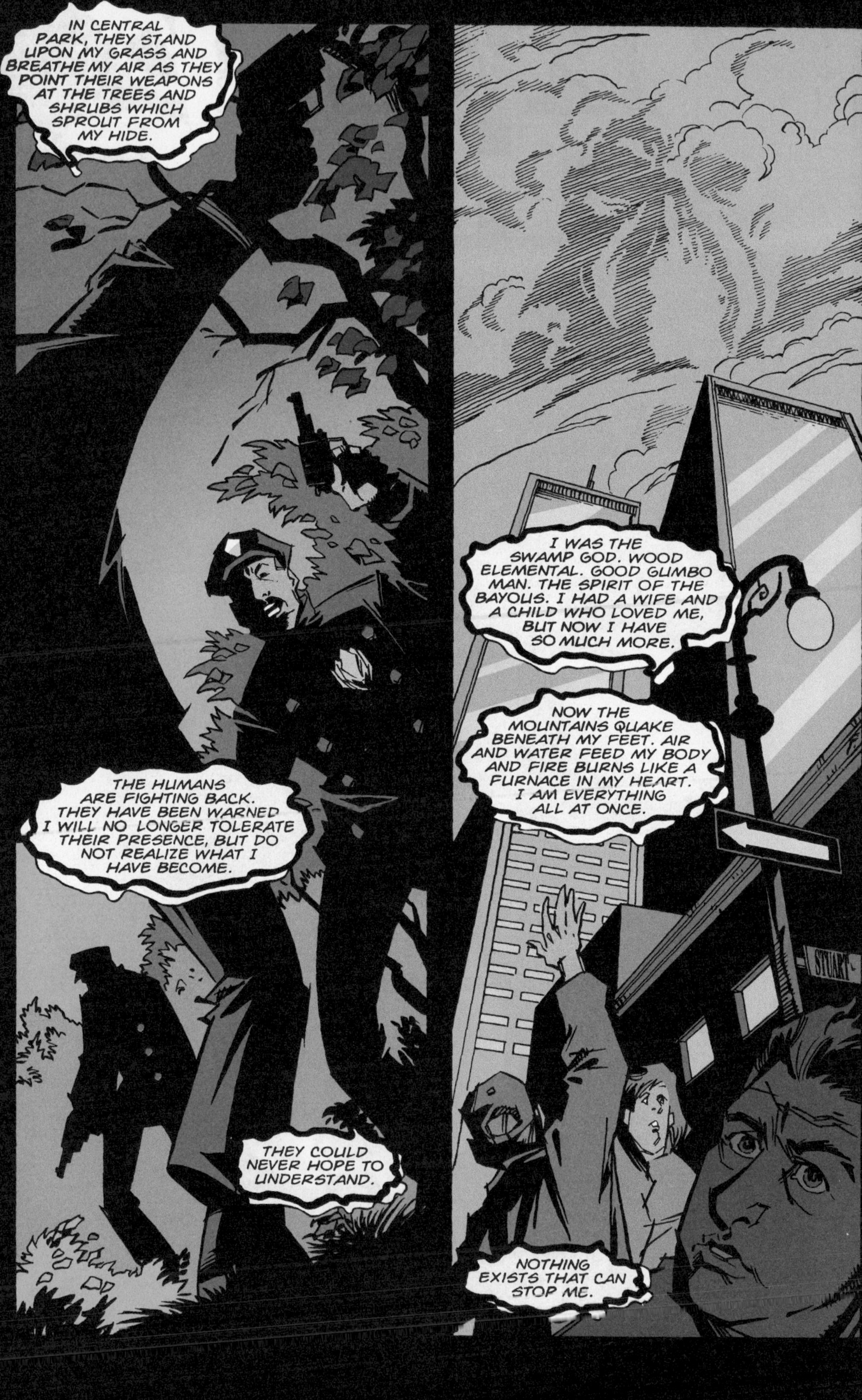
IN CENTRAL PARK, THEY STAND UPON MY GRASS AND BREATHE MY AIR AS THEY POINT THEIR WEAPONS AT THE TREES AND SHRUBS WHICH SPROUT FROM MY HIDE.
THE HUMANS ARE FIGHTING BACK. THEY HAVE BEEN WARNED I WILL NO LONGER TOLERATE THEIR PRESENCE, BUT DO NOT REALIZE WHAT I HAVE BECOME.
THEY COULD NEVER HOPE TO UNDERSTAND.
I WAS THE SWAMP GOD. WOOD ELEMENTAL. GOOD GUMBO MAN. THE SPIRIT OF THE BAYOUS. I HAD A WIFE AND A CHILD WHO LOVED ME, BUT NOW I HAVE SO MUCH MORE.
NOW THE MOUNTAINS QUAKE BENEATH MY FEET. AIR AND WATER FEED MY BODY AND FIRE BURNS LIKE A FURNACE IN MY HEART. I AM EVERYTHING ALL AT ONCE.
STUART
NOTHING EXISTS THAT CAN STOP ME.

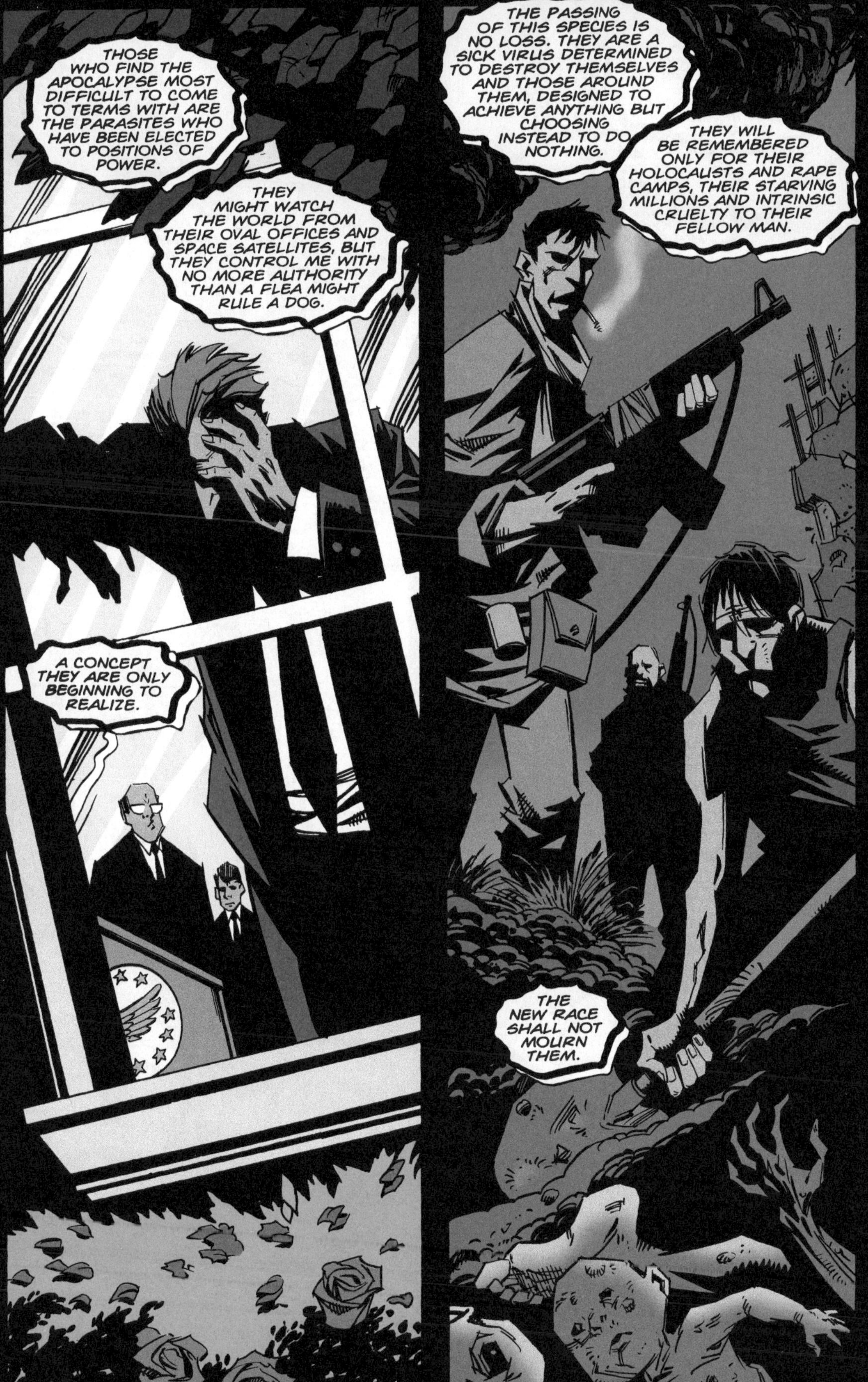
THOSE WHO FIND THE APOCALYPSE MOST DIFFICULT TO COME TO TERMS WITH ARE THE PARASITES WHO HAVE BEEN ELECTED TO POSITIONS OF POWER.
THEY MIGHT WATCH THE WORLD FROM THEIR OVAL OFFICES AND SPACE SATELLITES, BUT THEY CONTROL ME WITH NO MORE AUTHORITY THAN A FLEA MIGHT RULE A DOG.
A CONCEPT THEY ARE ONLY BEGINNING TO REALIZE.
THE PASSING OF THIS SPECIES IS NO LOSS. THEY ARE A SICK VIRUS DETERMINED TO DESTROY THEMSELVES AND THOSE AROUND THEM, DESIGNED TO ACHIEVE ANYTHING BUT CHOOSING INSTEAD TO DO NOTHING.
THEY WILL BE REMEMBERED ONLY FOR THEIR HOLOCAUSTS AND RAPE CAMPS, THEIR STARVING MILLIONS AND INTRINSIC CRUELTY TO THEIR FELLOW MAN.
THE NEW RACE SHALL NOT MOURN THEM.

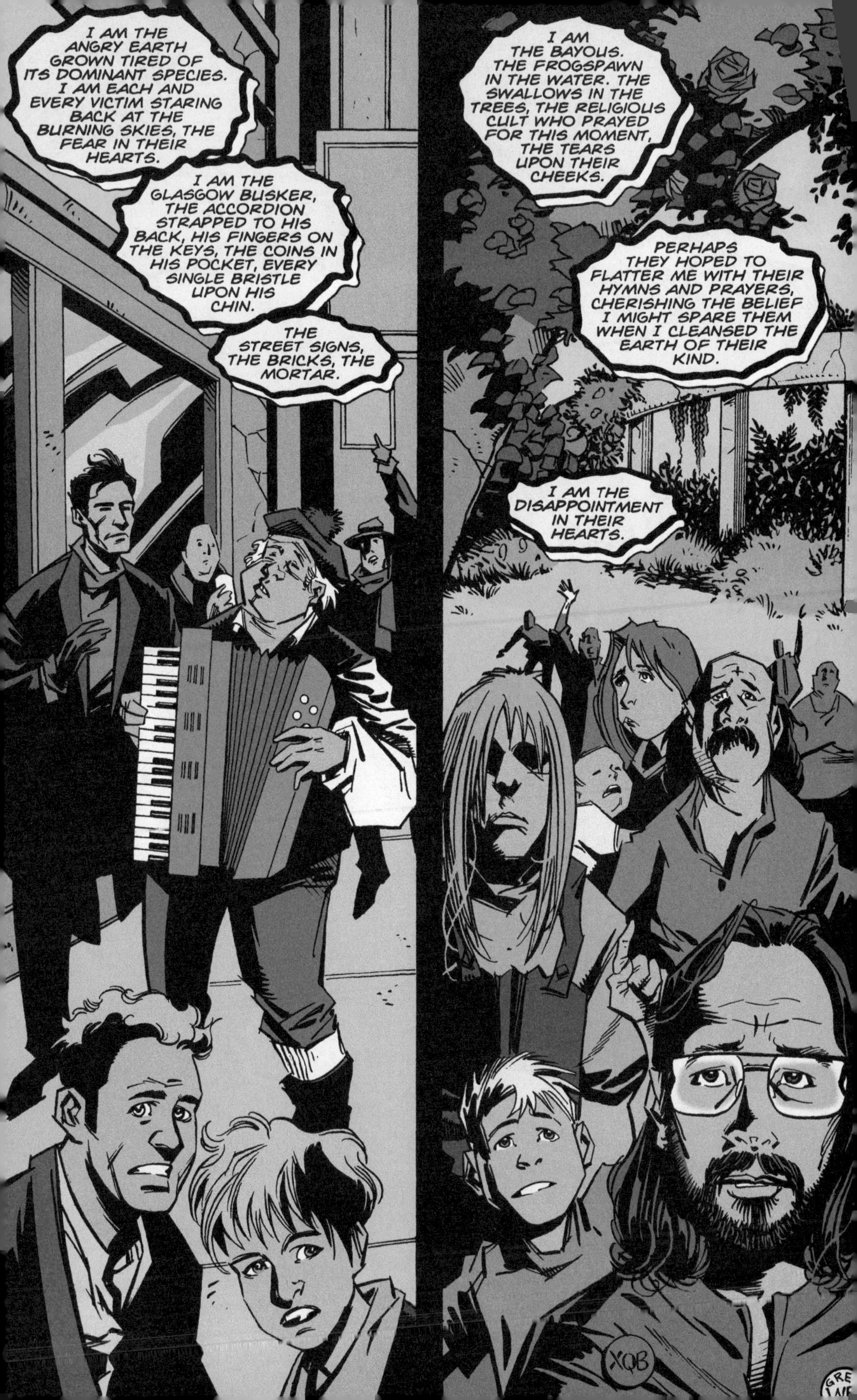
I AM THE ANGRY EARTH GROWN TIRED OF ITS DOMINANT SPECIES. I AM EACH AND EVERY VICTIM STARING BACK AT THE BURNING SKIES, THE FEAR IN THEIR HEARTS.
I AM THE GLASGOW BUSKER, THE ACCORDION STRAPPED TO HIS BACK, HIS FINGERS ON THE KEYS, THE COINS IN HIS POCKET, EVERY SINGLE BRISTLE UPON HIS CHIN.
THE STREET SIGNS, THE BRICKS, THE MORTAR.
I AM THE BAYOUS. THE FROGSPAWN IN THE WATER. THE SWALLOWS IN THE TREES, THE RELIGIOUS CULT WHO PRAYED FOR THIS MOMENT, THE TEARS UPON THEIR CHEEKS.
PERHAPS THEY HOPED TO FLATTER ME WITH THEIR HYMNS AND PRAYERS, CHERISHING THE BELIEF I MIGHT SPARE THEM WHEN I CLEANSED THE EARTH OF THEIR KIND.
I AM THE DISAPPOINTMENT IN THEIR HEARTS.

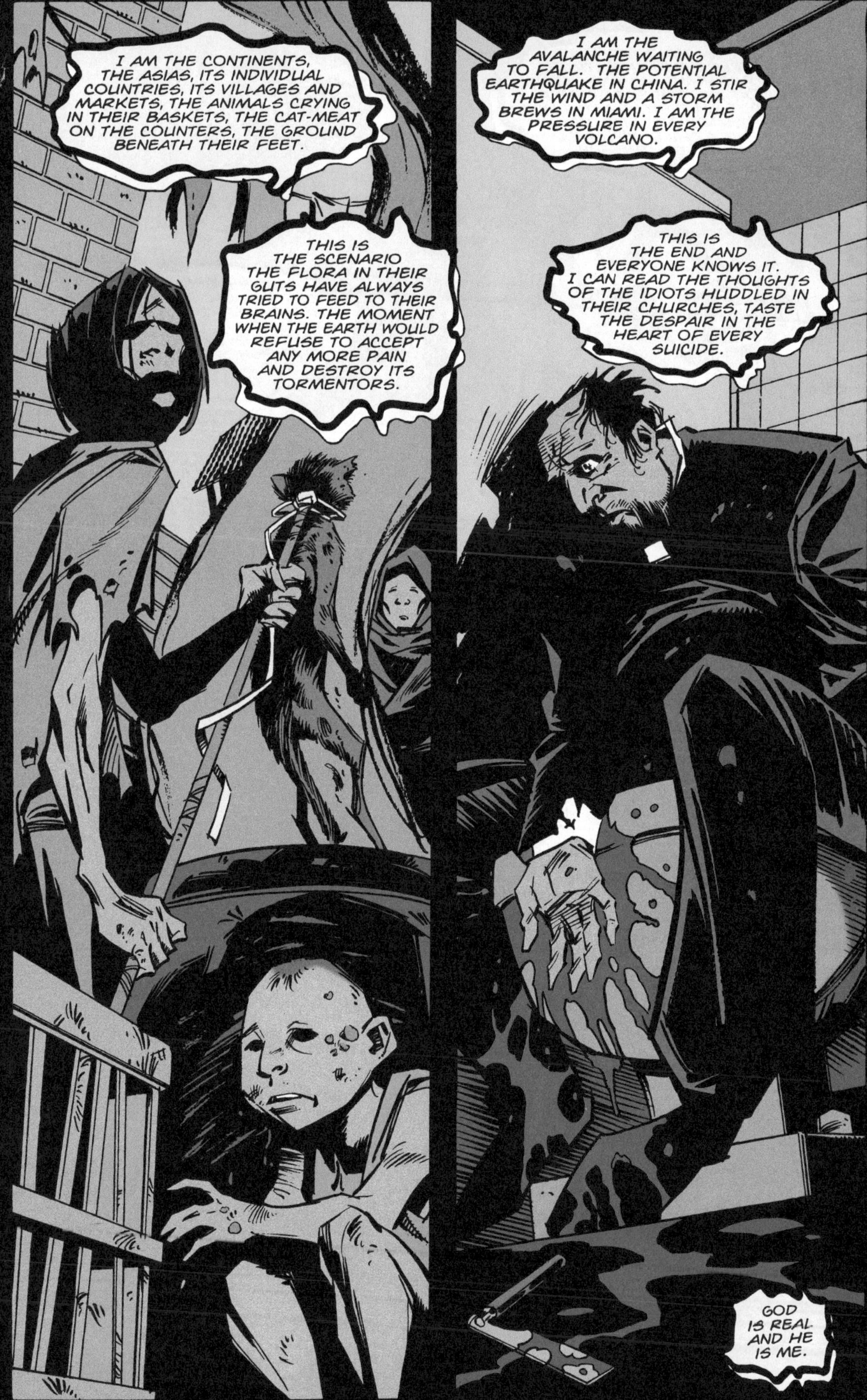
I AM THE CONTINENTS, THE ASIAS, ITS INDIVIDUAL COUNTRIES, ITS VILLAGES AND MARKETS, THE ANIMALS CRYING IN THEIR BASKETS, THE CAT-MEAT ON THE COUNTERS, THE GROUND BENEATH THEIR FEET.
THIS IS THE SCENARIO THE FLORA IN THEIR GUTS HAVE ALWAYS TRIED TO FEED TO THEIR BRAINS. THE MOMENT WHEN THE EARTH WOULD REFUSE TO ACCEPT ANY MORE PAIN AND DESTROY ITS TORMENTORS.
I AM THE AVALANCHE WAITING TO FALL. THE POTENTIAL EARTHQUAKE IN CHINA. I STIR THE WIND AND A STORM BREWS IN MIAMI. I AM THE PRESSURE IN EVERY VOLCANO.
THIS IS THE END AND EVERYONE KNOWS IT. I CAN READ THE THOUGHTS OF THE IDIOTS HUDDLED IN THEIR CHURCHES, TASTE THE DESPAIR IN THE HEART OF EVERY SUICIDE.
GOD IS REAL AND HE IS ME.

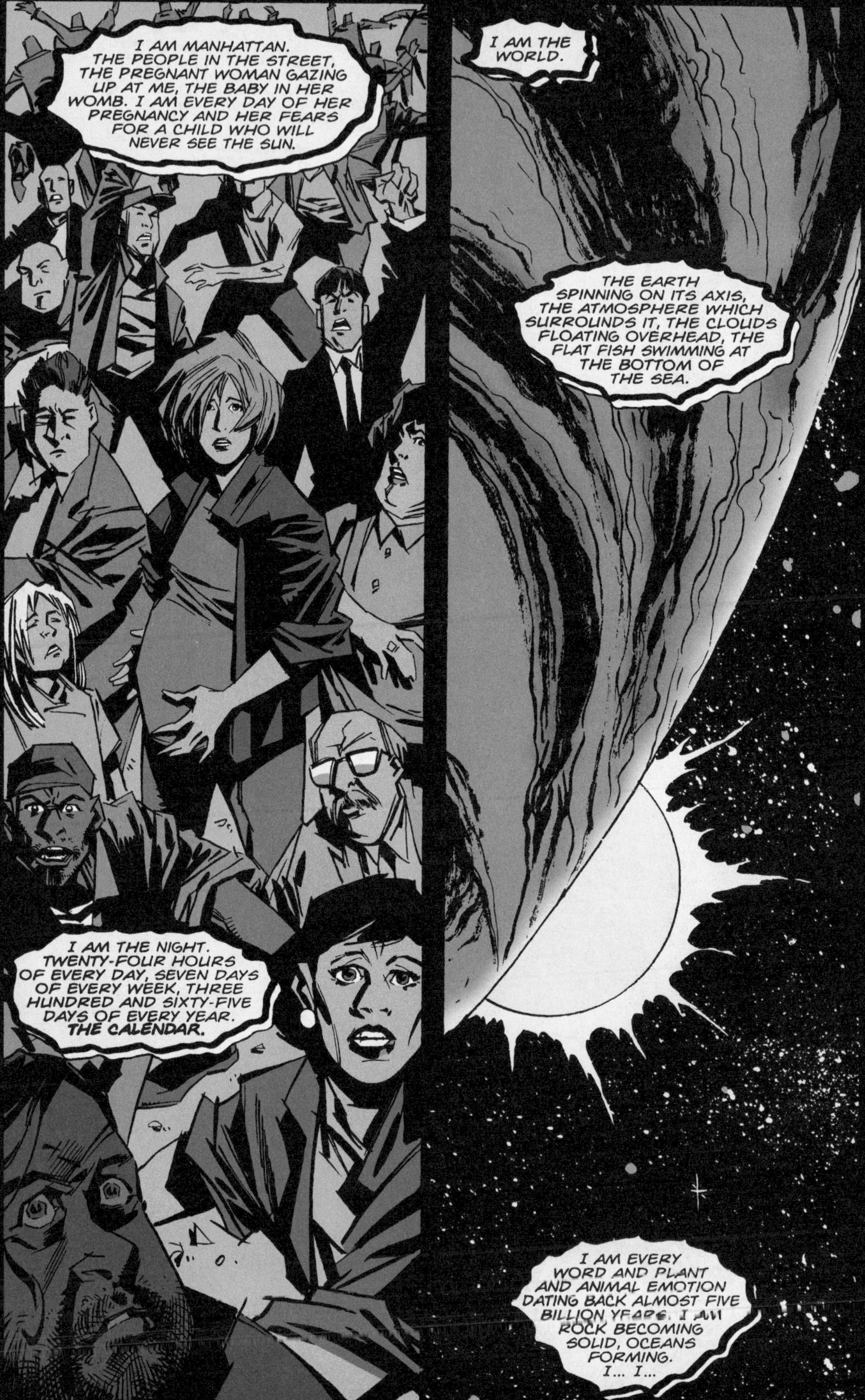
I AM MANHATTAN. THE PEOPLE IN THE STREET, THE PREGNANT WOMAN GAZING UP AT ME, THE BABY IN HER WOMB. I AM EVERY DAY OF HER PREGNANCY AND HER FEARS FOR A CHILD WHO WILL NEVER SEE THE SUN.
I AM THE NIGHT. TWENTY-FOUR HOURS OF EVERY DAY, SEVEN DAYS OF EVERY WEEK, THREE HUNDRED AND SIXTY-FIVE DAYS OF EVERY YEAR. **THE CALENDAR.**
I AM THE WORLD.
THE EARTH SPINNING ON ITS AXIS, THE ATMOSPHERE WHICH SURROUNDS IT, THE CLOUDS FLOATING OVERHEAD, THE FLAT FISH SWIMMING AT THE BOTTOM OF THE SEA.
I AM EVERY WORD AND PLANT AND ANIMAL EMOTION DATING BACK ALMOST FIVE BILLION YEARS. I AM ROCK BECOMING SOLID, OCEANS FORMING. I... I...

I AM THE TRAVELLER. HIS ANCIENT ROBES, THE TWO RAVENS AWAITING HIS COMMAND, THE GIFT IN HIS POCKET. I AM THE LIGHTNING IN HIS EYE...

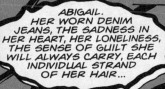

ABIGAIL. HER WORN DENIM JEANS, THE SADNESS IN HER HEART, HER LONELINESS, THE SENSE OF GUILT SHE WILL ALWAYS CARRY, EACH INDIVIDUAL STRAND OF HER HAIR...

EL SEÑOR BLAKE. THE BLACKNESS IN HIS SOUL, THE PLAQUE UPON HIS TEETH. I AM THE TORNADO GATHERING FORCE OUTSIDE, THE WORM IN HIS TEQUILA...

I AM THE LAST OF THE RAVENWIND WITCHES, HIS LOVER SLEEPING INDOORS, THE SENSE OF DÉJÀ VU HE FEELS AS HE LOOKS AT THE SKY...

DON ROBERTO. THE SHIRT HE'S WEARING, HIS FIRST CLASS TICKET, THE AIRPORT AROUND HIM, THE OXYGEN AND NITROGEN COMPOUND FILLING THE AIR...

I AM THE SMOKE FROM CONSTANTINE'S LAST CIGARETTE CURLING IN HIS LUNGS, HIS ANGER AT HIS OWN STUPIDITY AND HIS POWERFUL REGRET...

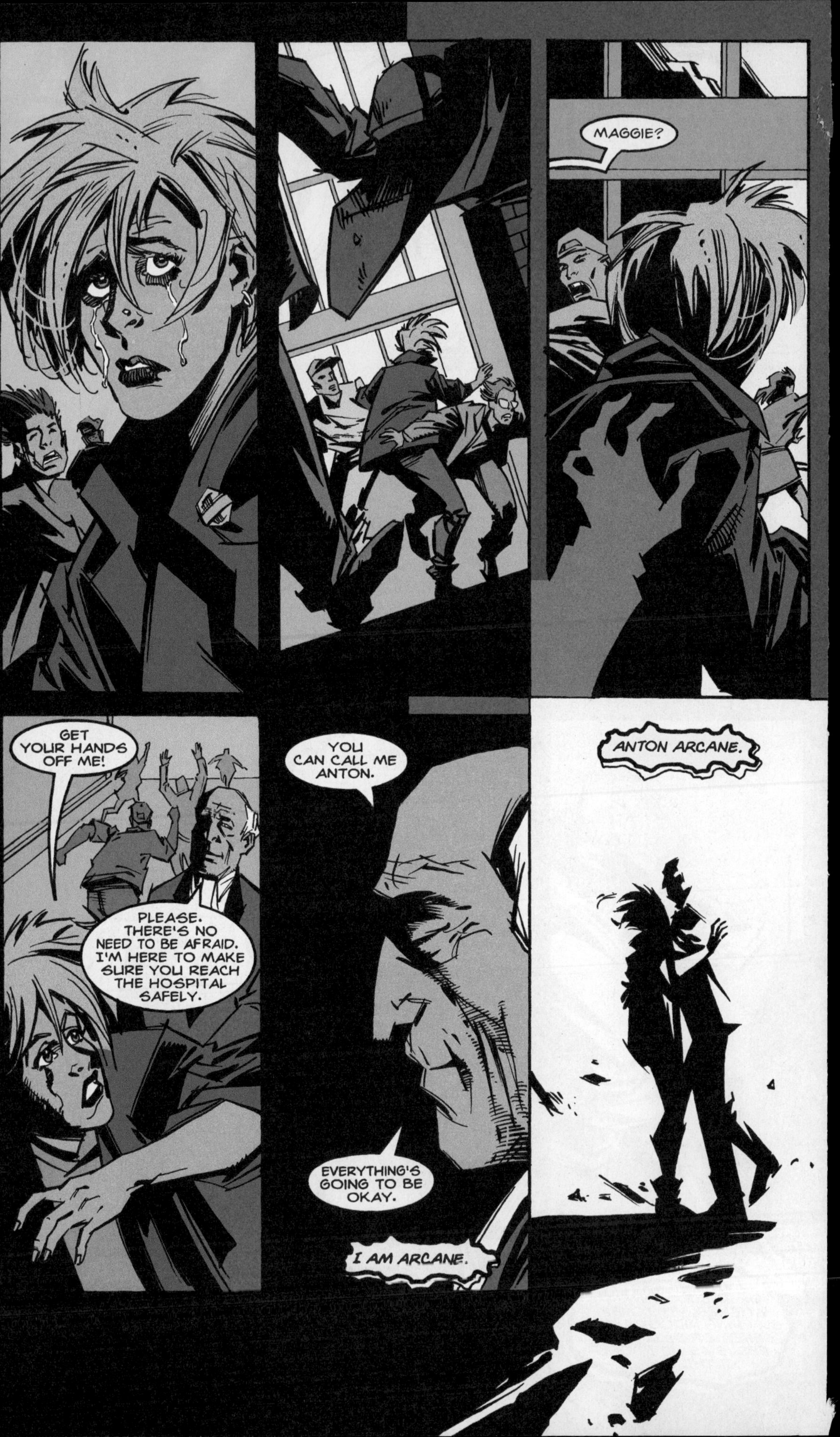
MAGGIE?
GET YOUR HANDS OFF ME!
PLEASE. THERE'S NO NEED TO BE AFRAID. I'M HERE TO MAKE SURE YOU REACH THE HOSPITAL SAFELY.
YOU CAN CALL ME ANTON.
EVERYTHING'S GOING TO BE OKAY.
I AM ARCANE.
ANTON ARCANE.

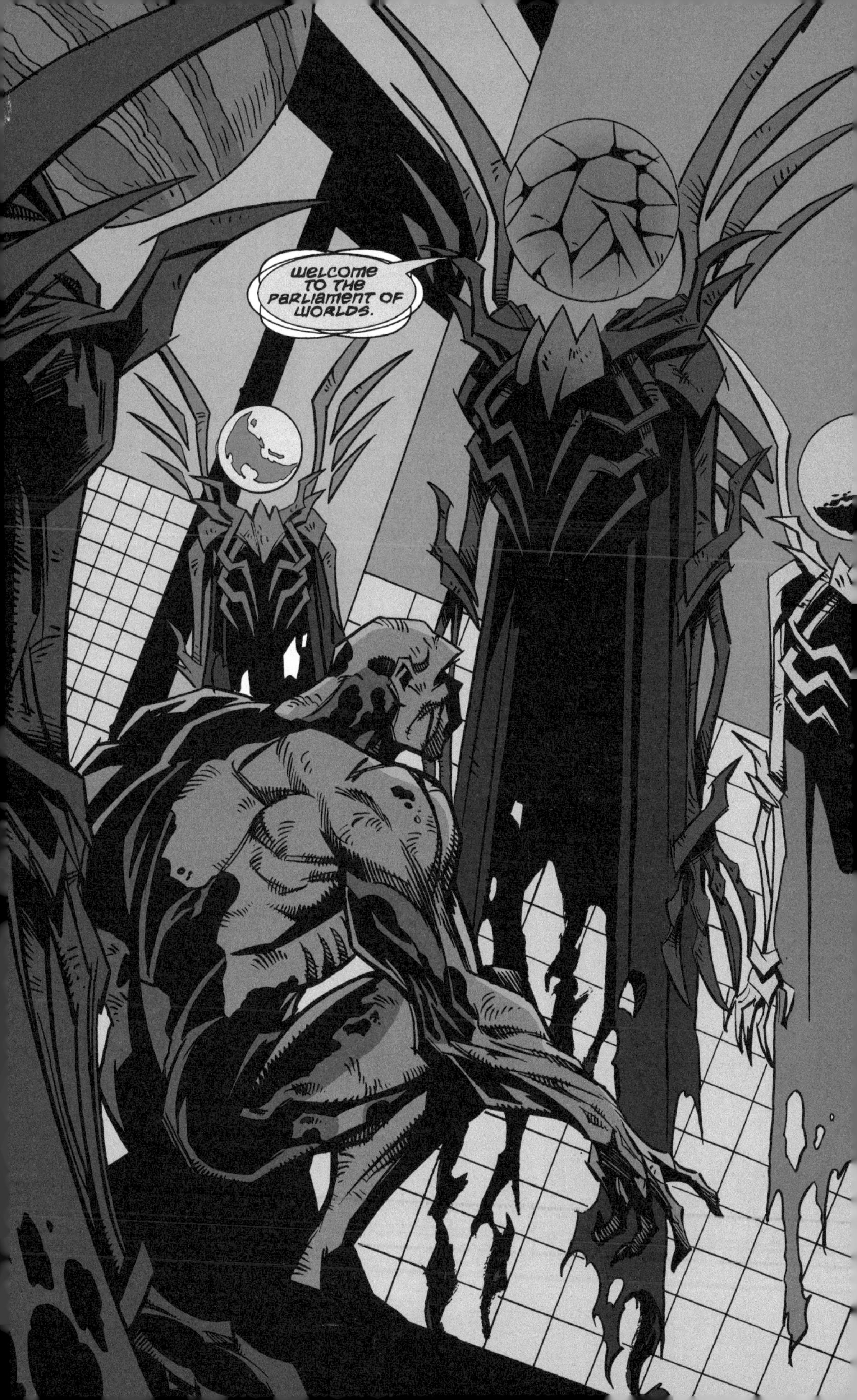
WELCOME TO THE PARLIAMENT OF WORLDS.

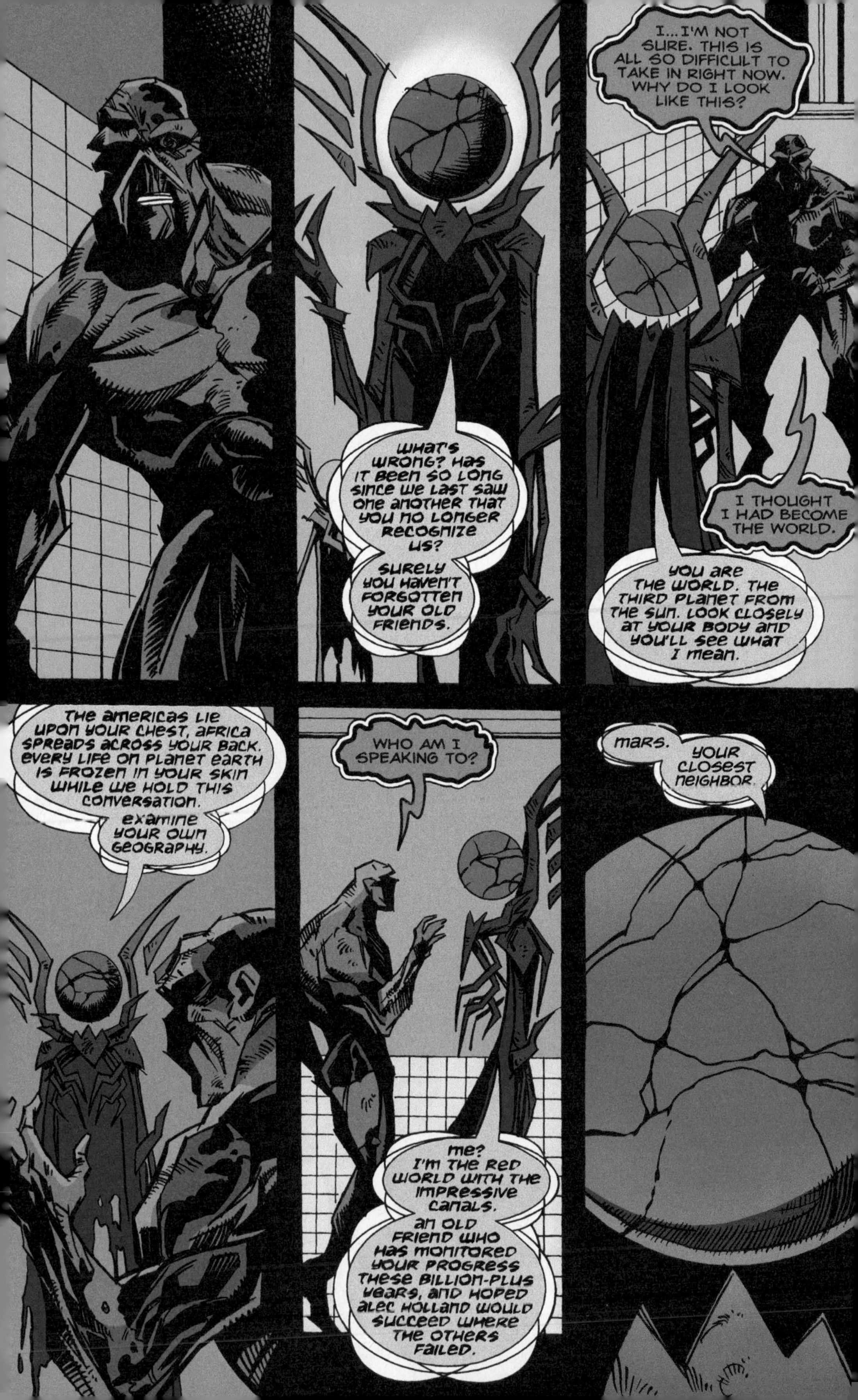
WHAT'S WRONG? HAS IT BEEN SO LONG SINCE WE LAST SAW ONE ANOTHER THAT YOU NO LONGER RECOGNIZE US?
SURELY YOU HAVEN'T FORGOTTEN YOUR OLD FRIENDS.
I...I'M NOT SURE. THIS IS ALL SO DIFFICULT TO TAKE IN RIGHT NOW. WHY DO I LOOK LIKE THIS?
I THOUGHT I HAD BECOME THE WORLD.
YOU ARE THE WORLD. THE THIRD PLANET FROM THE SUN. LOOK CLOSELY AT YOUR BODY AND YOU'LL SEE WHAT I MEAN.
THE AMERICAS LIE UPON YOUR CHEST, AFRICA SPREADS ACROSS YOUR BACK. EVERY LIFE ON PLANET EARTH IS FROZEN IN YOUR SKIN WHILE WE HOLD THIS CONVERSATION.
EXAMINE YOUR OWN GEOGRAPHY.
WHO AM I SPEAKING TO?
ME? I'M THE RED WORLD WITH THE IMPRESSIVE CANALS.
AN OLD FRIEND WHO HAS MONITORED YOUR PROGRESS THESE BILLION-PLUS YEARS, AND HOPED ALEC HOLLAND WOULD SUCCEED WHERE THE OTHERS FAILED.
MARS.
YOUR CLOSEST NEIGHBOR.

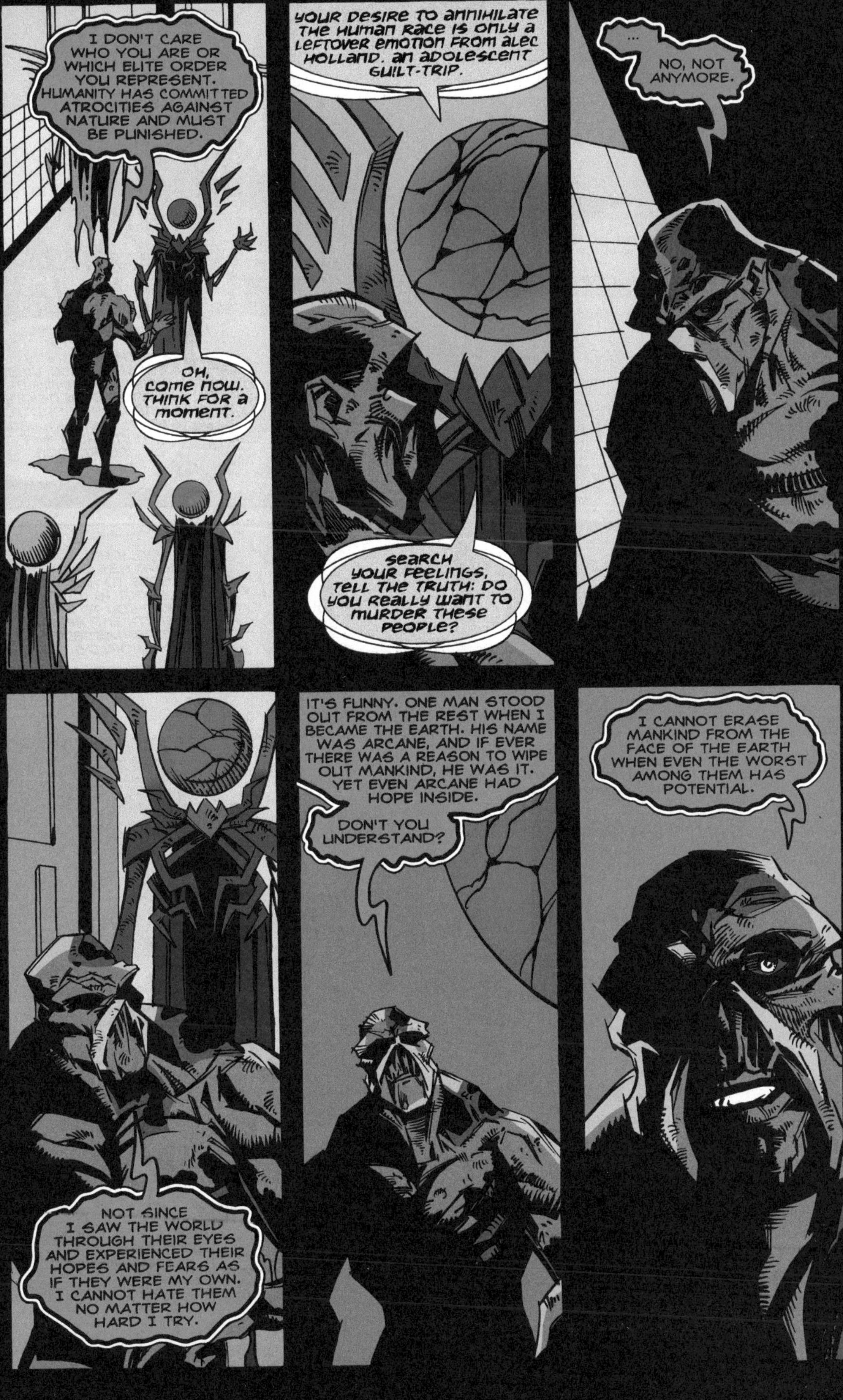
I DON'T CARE WHO YOU ARE OR WHICH ELITE ORDER YOU REPRESENT. HUMANITY HAS COMMITTED ATROCITIES AGAINST NATURE AND MUST BE PUNISHED.
OH, COME NOW. THINK FOR A MOMENT.
YOUR DESIRE TO ANNIHILATE THE HUMAN RACE IS ONLY A LEFTOVER EMOTION FROM ALEC HOLLAND, AN ADOLESCENT GUILT-TRIP.
SEARCH YOUR FEELINGS, TELL THE TRUTH: DO YOU REALLY WANT TO MURDER THESE PEOPLE?
...
NO, NOT ANYMORE.
NOT SINCE I SAW THE WORLD THROUGH THEIR EYES AND EXPERIENCED THEIR HOPES AND FEARS AS IF THEY WERE MY OWN. I CANNOT HATE THEM NO MATTER HOW HARD I TRY.
IT'S FUNNY. ONE MAN STOOD OUT FROM THE REST WHEN I BECAME THE EARTH. HIS NAME WAS ARCANE, AND IF EVER THERE WAS A REASON TO WIPE OUT MANKIND, HE WAS IT. YET EVEN ARCANE HAD HOPE INSIDE.
DON'T YOU UNDERSTAND?
I CANNOT ERASE MANKIND FROM THE FACE OF THE EARTH WHEN EVEN THE WORST AMONG THEM HAS POTENTIAL.

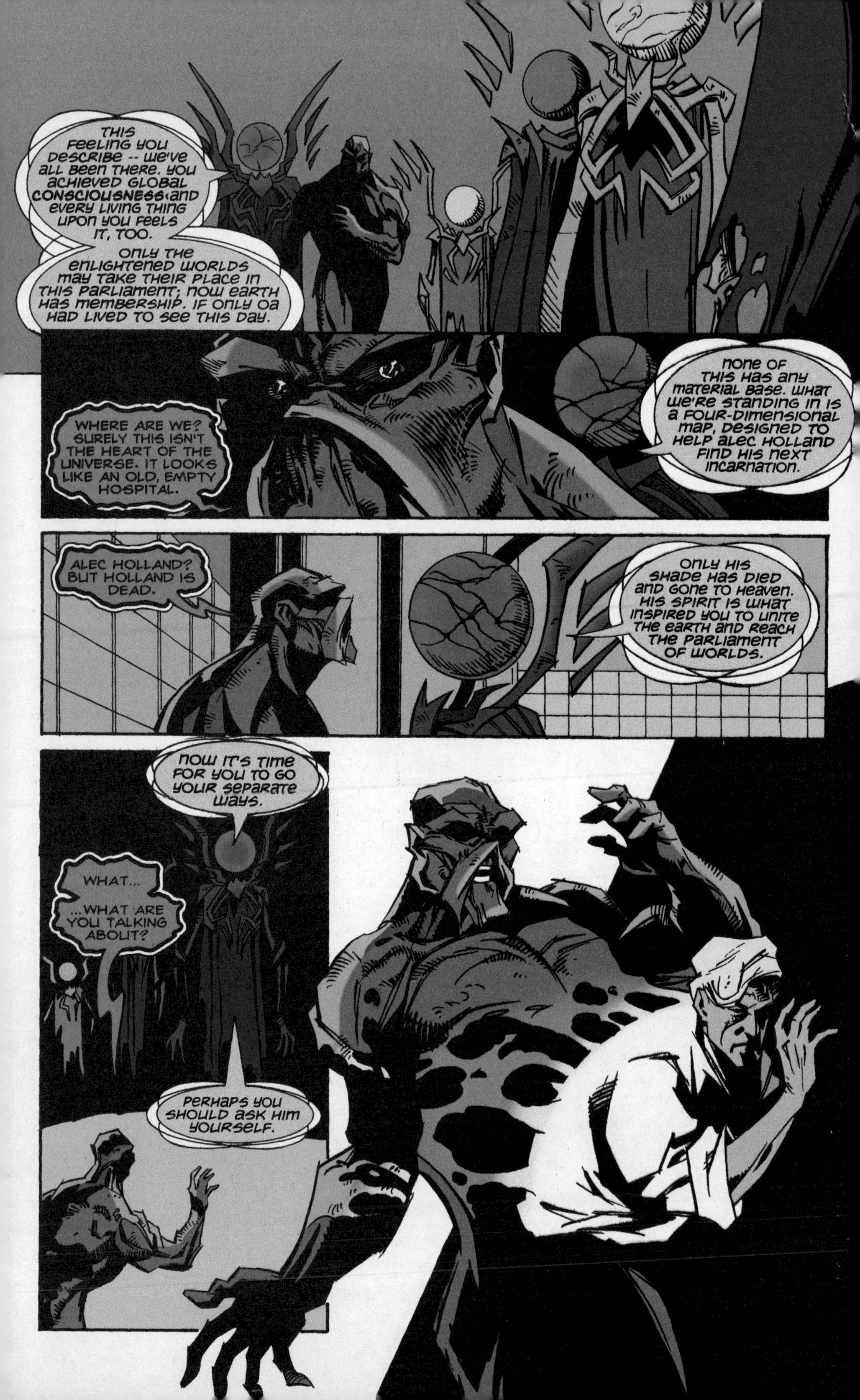
THIS FEELING YOU DESCRIBE -- WE'VE ALL BEEN THERE. YOU ACHIEVED GLOBAL CONSCIOUSNESS, AND EVERY LIVING THING UPON YOU FEELS IT, TOO.
ONLY THE ENLIGHTENED WORLDS MAY TAKE THEIR PLACE IN THIS PARLIAMENT; NOW EARTH HAS MEMBERSHIP. IF ONLY OA HAD LIVED TO SEE THIS DAY.
WHERE ARE WE? SURELY THIS ISN'T THE HEART OF THE UNIVERSE. IT LOOKS LIKE AN OLD, EMPTY HOSPITAL.
NONE OF THIS HAS ANY MATERIAL BASE. WHAT WE'RE STANDING IN IS A FOUR-DIMENSIONAL MAP, DESIGNED TO HELP ALEC HOLLAND FIND HIS NEXT INCARNATION.
ALEC HOLLAND? BUT HOLLAND IS DEAD.
ONLY HIS SHADE HAS DIED AND GONE TO HEAVEN. HIS SPIRIT IS WHAT INSPIRED YOU TO UNITE THE EARTH AND REACH THE PARLIAMENT OF WORLDS.
NOW IT'S TIME FOR YOU TO GO YOUR SEPARATE WAYS.
WHAT...
...WHAT ARE YOU TALKING ABOUT?
PERHAPS YOU SHOULD ASK HIM YOURSELF.

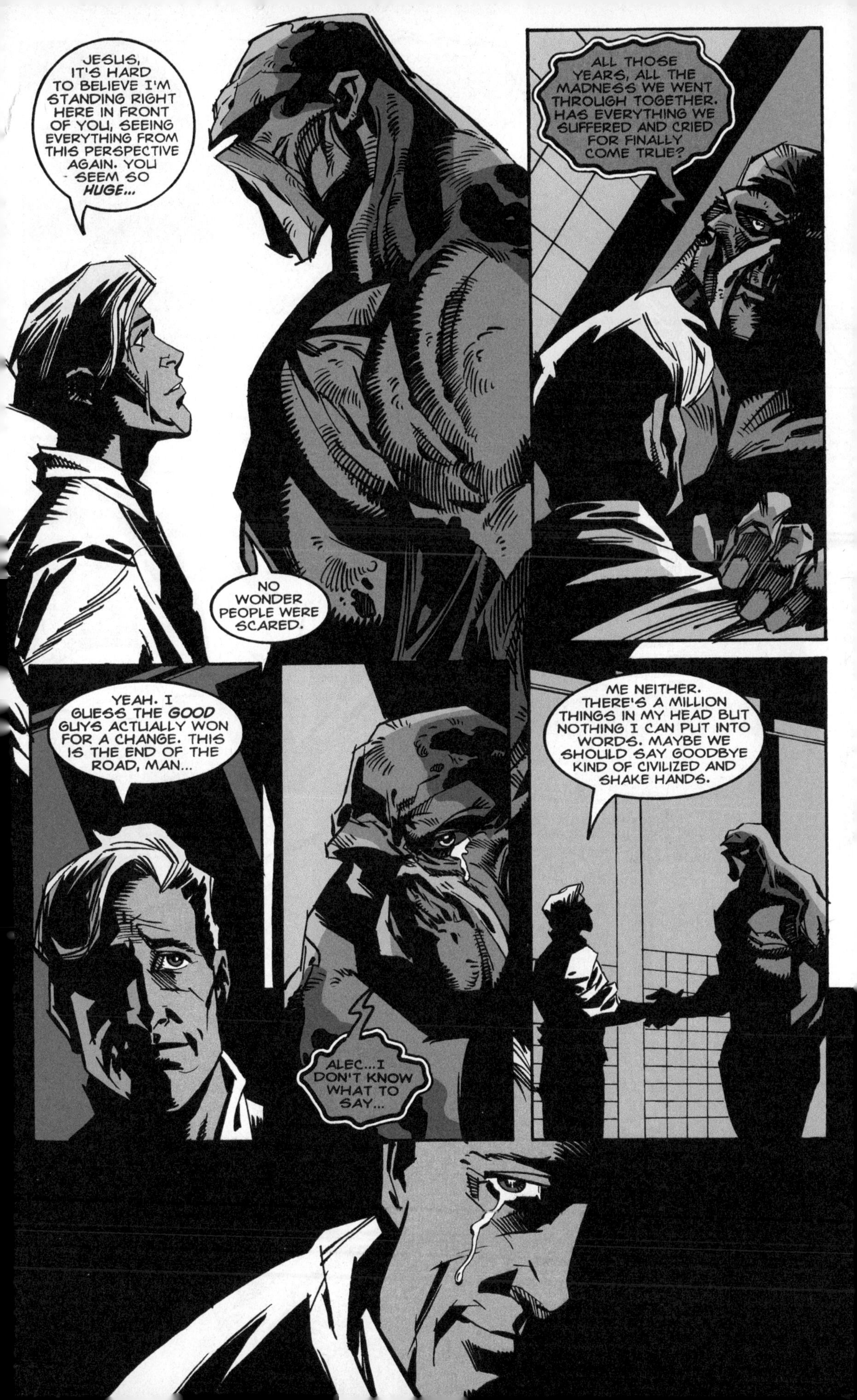
JESUS, IT'S HARD TO BELIEVE I'M STANDING RIGHT HERE IN FRONT OF YOU, SEEING EVERYTHING FROM THIS PERSPECTIVE AGAIN. YOU SEEM SO *HUGE*...
NO WONDER PEOPLE WERE SCARED.
ALL THOSE YEARS, ALL THE MADNESS WE WENT THROUGH TOGETHER. HAS EVERYTHING WE SUFFERED AND CRIED FOR FINALLY COME TRUE?
YEAH. I GUESS THE *GOOD* GUYS ACTUALLY WON FOR A CHANGE. THIS IS THE END OF THE ROAD, MAN...
ALEC...I DON'T KNOW WHAT TO SAY...
ME NEITHER. THERE'S A MILLION THINGS IN MY HEAD BUT NOTHING I CAN PUT INTO WORDS. MAYBE WE SHOULD SAY GOODBYE KIND OF CIVILIZED AND SHAKE HANDS.

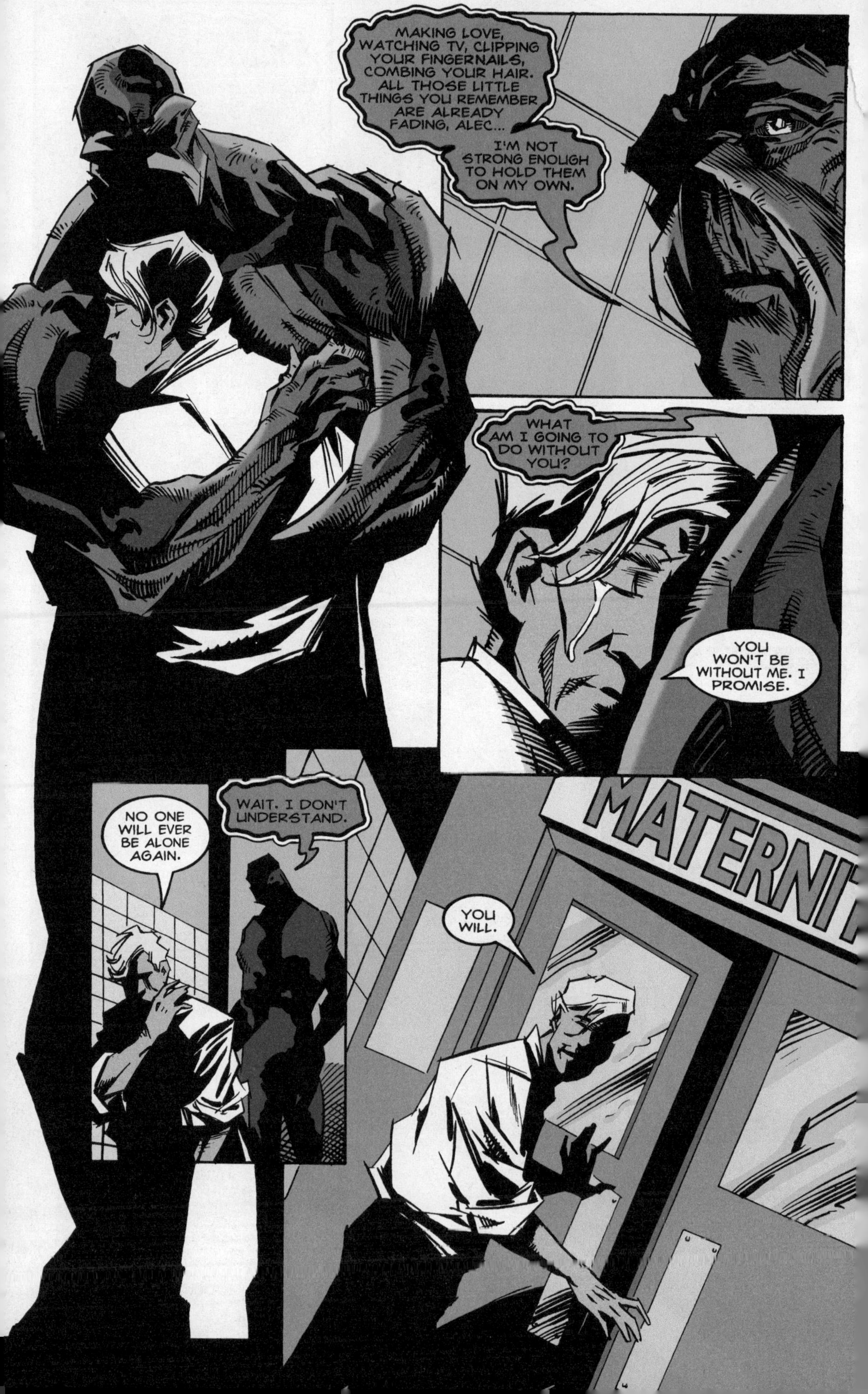
MAKING LOVE, WATCHING TV, CLIPPING YOUR FINGERNAILS, COMBING YOUR HAIR. ALL THOSE LITTLE THINGS YOU REMEMBER ARE ALREADY FADING, ALEC...
I'M NOT STRONG ENOUGH TO HOLD THEM ON MY OWN.
WHAT AM I GOING TO DO WITHOUT YOU?
YOU WON'T BE WITHOUT ME. I PROMISE.
NO ONE WILL EVER BE ALONE AGAIN.
WAIT. I DON'T UNDERSTAND.
YOU WILL.
MATERNIT

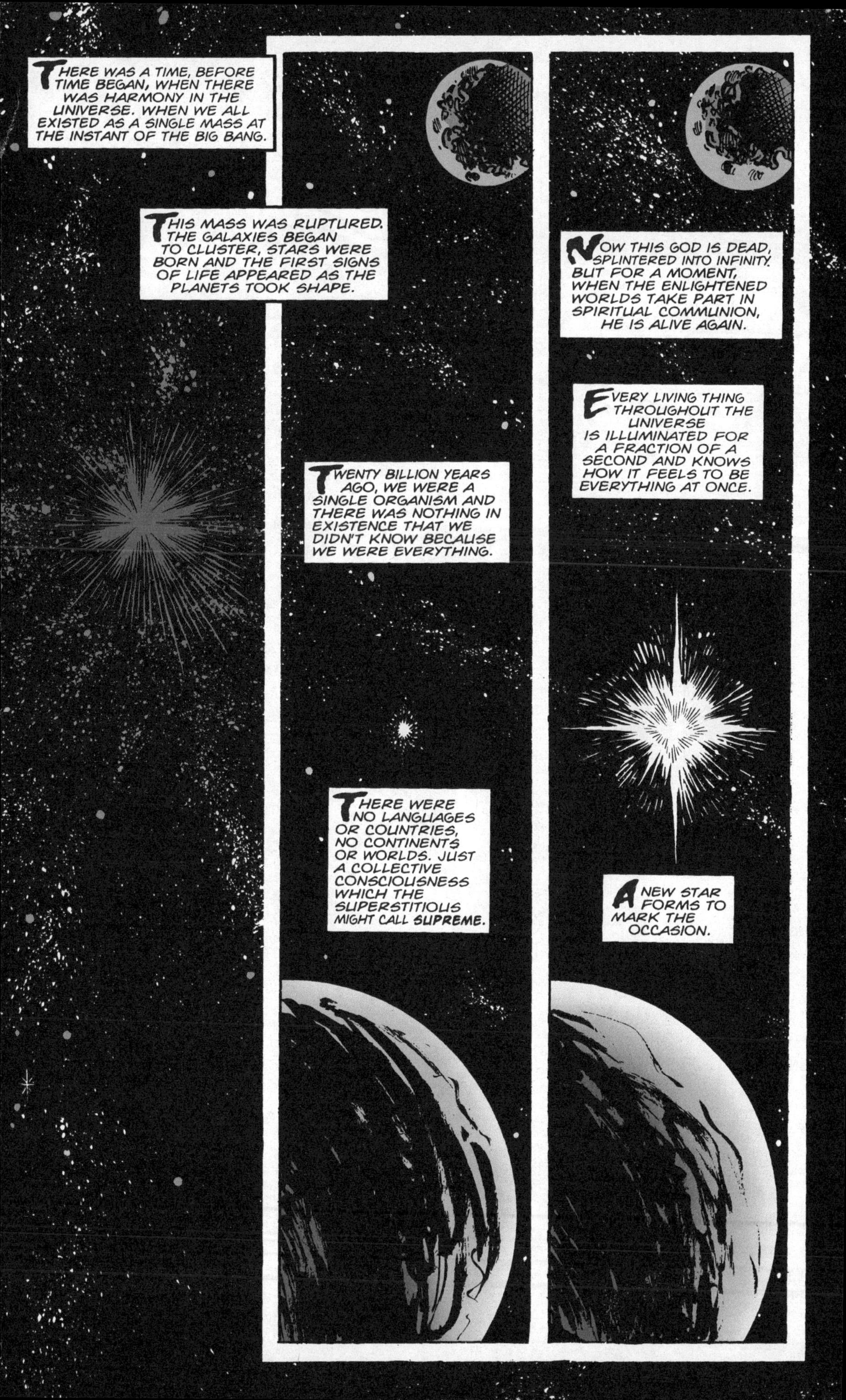
THERE WAS A TIME, BEFORE TIME BEGAN, WHEN THERE WAS HARMONY IN THE UNIVERSE. WHEN WE ALL EXISTED AS A SINGLE MASS AT THE INSTANT OF THE BIG BANG.
THIS MASS WAS RUPTURED. THE GALAXIES BEGAN TO CLUSTER, STARS WERE BORN AND THE FIRST SIGNS OF LIFE APPEARED AS THE PLANETS TOOK SHAPE.
TWENTY BILLION YEARS AGO, WE WERE A SINGLE ORGANISM AND THERE WAS NOTHING IN EXISTENCE THAT WE DIDN'T KNOW BECAUSE WE WERE EVERYTHING.
THERE WERE NO LANGUAGES OR COUNTRIES, NO CONTINENTS OR WORLDS. JUST A COLLECTIVE CONSCIOUSNESS WHICH THE SUPERSTITIOUS MIGHT CALL SUPREME.
NOW THIS GOD IS DEAD, SPLINTERED INTO INFINITY. BUT FOR A MOMENT, WHEN THE ENLIGHTENED WORLDS TAKE PART IN SPIRITUAL COMMUNION, HE IS ALIVE AGAIN.
EVERY LIVING THING THROUGHOUT THE UNIVERSE IS ILLUMINATED FOR A FRACTION OF A SECOND AND KNOWS HOW IT FEELS TO BE EVERYTHING AT ONCE.
A NEW STAR FORMS TO MARK THE OCCASION.

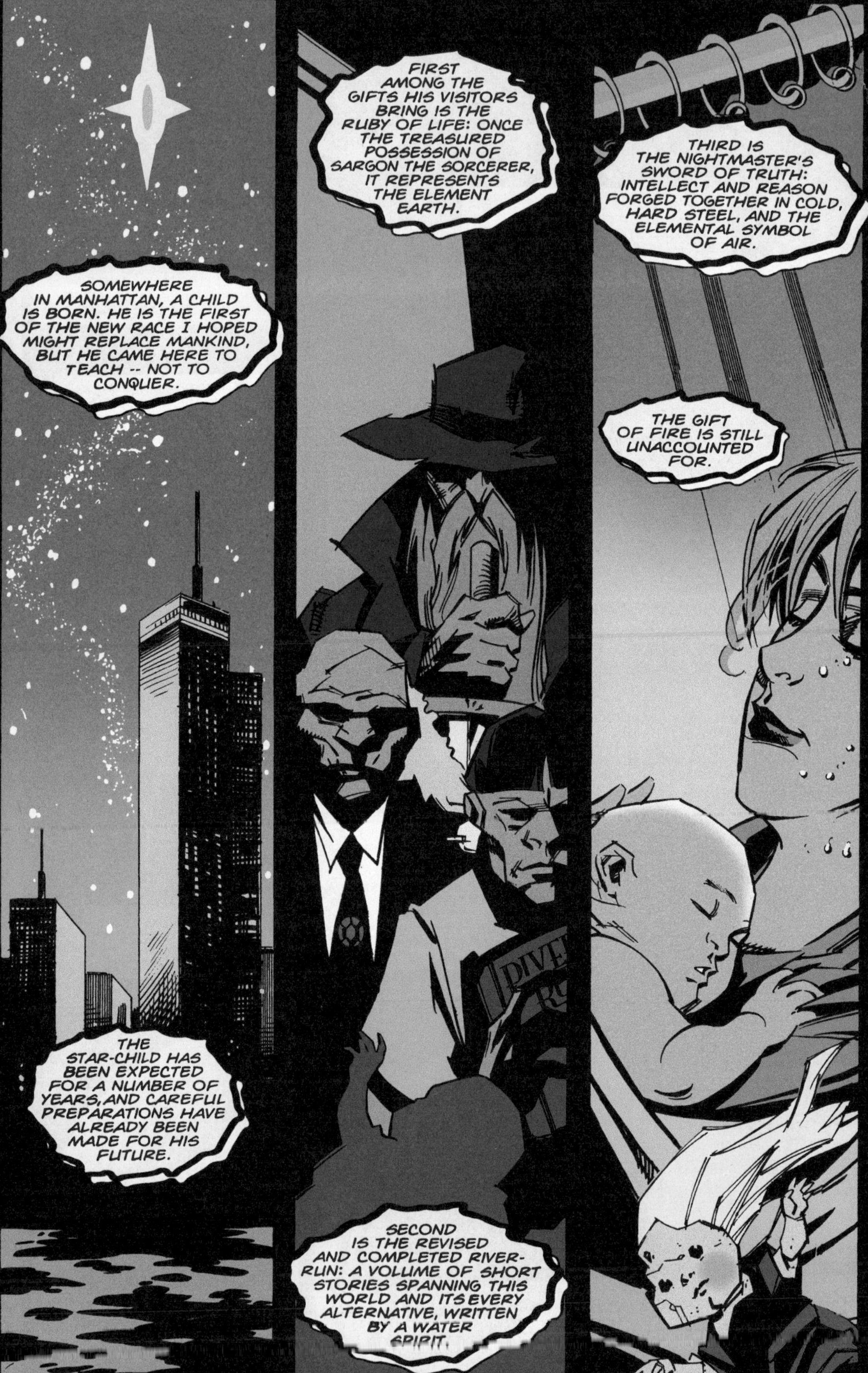
SOMEWHERE IN MANHATTAN, A CHILD IS BORN. HE IS THE FIRST OF THE NEW RACE I HOPED MIGHT REPLACE MANKIND, BUT HE CAME HERE TO TEACH -- NOT TO CONQUER.
THE STAR-CHILD HAS BEEN EXPECTED FOR A NUMBER OF YEARS, AND CAREFUL PREPARATIONS HAVE ALREADY BEEN MADE FOR HIS FUTURE.
FIRST AMONG THE GIFTS HIS VISITORS BRING IS THE RUBY OF LIFE: ONCE THE TREASURED POSSESSION OF SARGON THE SORCERER, IT REPRESENTS THE ELEMENT EARTH.
SECOND IS THE REVISED AND COMPLETED RIVER-RUN: A VOLUME OF SHORT STORIES SPANNING THIS WORLD AND ITS EVERY ALTERNATIVE, WRITTEN BY A WATER SPIRIT.
THIRD IS THE NIGHTMASTER'S SWORD OF TRUTH: INTELLECT AND REASON FORGED TOGETHER IN COLD, HARD STEEL, AND THE ELEMENTAL SYMBOL OF AIR.
THE GIFT OF FIRE IS STILL UNACCOUNTED FOR.

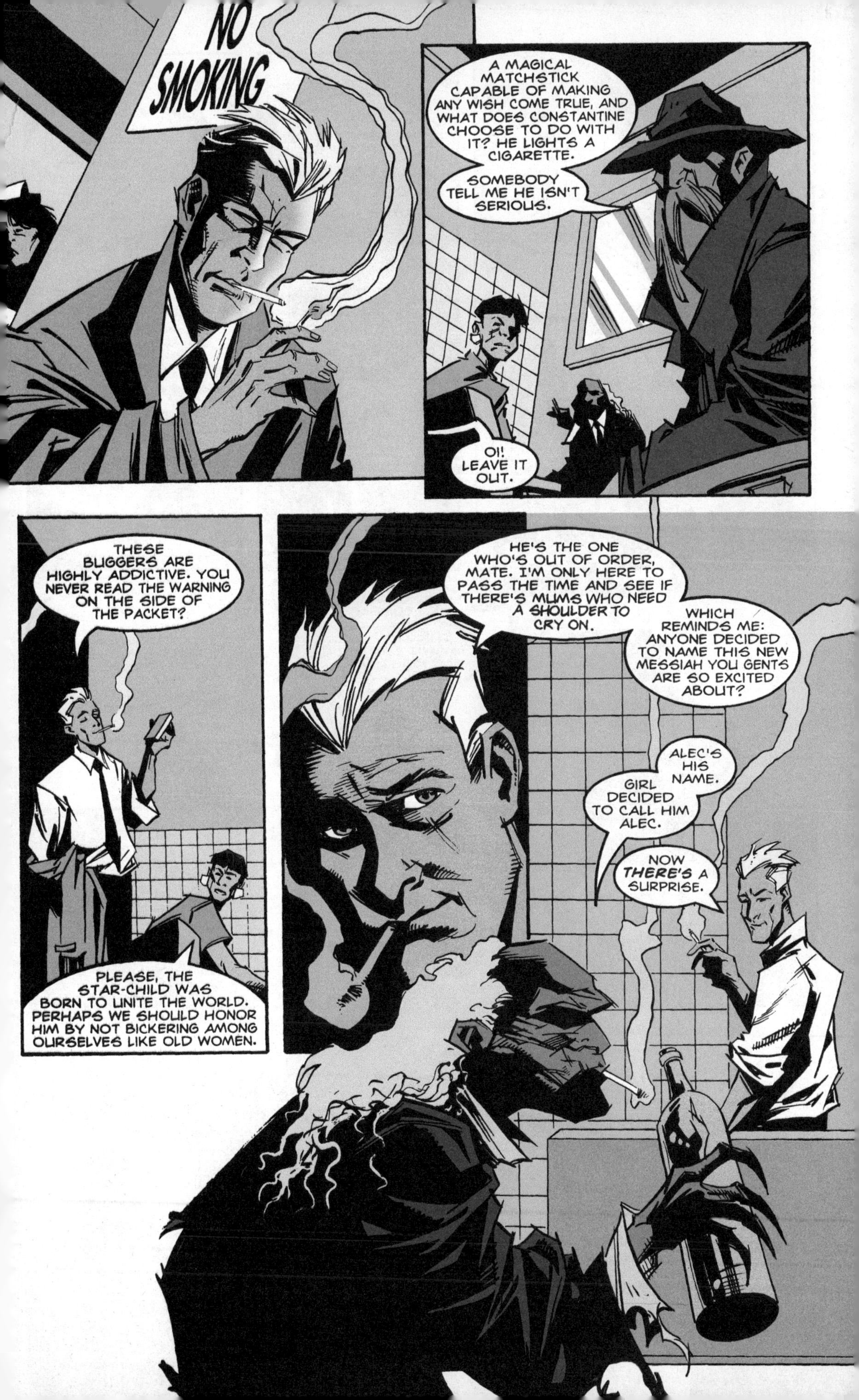
NO SMOKING
A MAGICAL MATCHSTICK CAPABLE OF MAKING ANY WISH COME TRUE, AND WHAT DOES CONSTANTINE CHOOSE TO DO WITH IT? HE LIGHTS A CIGARETTE.
SOMEBODY TELL ME HE ISN'T SERIOUS.
OI! LEAVE IT OUT.
THESE BUGGERS ARE HIGHLY ADDICTIVE. YOU NEVER READ THE WARNING ON THE SIDE OF THE PACKET?
PLEASE, THE STAR-CHILD WAS BORN TO UNITE THE WORLD. PERHAPS WE SHOULD HONOR HIM BY NOT BICKERING AMONG OURSELVES LIKE OLD WOMEN.
HE'S THE ONE WHO'S OUT OF ORDER, MATE. I'M ONLY HERE TO PASS THE TIME AND SEE IF THERE'S MUMS WHO NEED A SHOULDER TO CRY ON.
WHICH REMINDS ME: ANYONE DECIDED TO NAME THIS NEW MESSIAH YOU GENTS ARE SO EXCITED ABOUT?
ALEC'S HIS NAME.
GIRL DECIDED TO CALL HIM ALEC.
NOW THERE'S A SURPRISE.

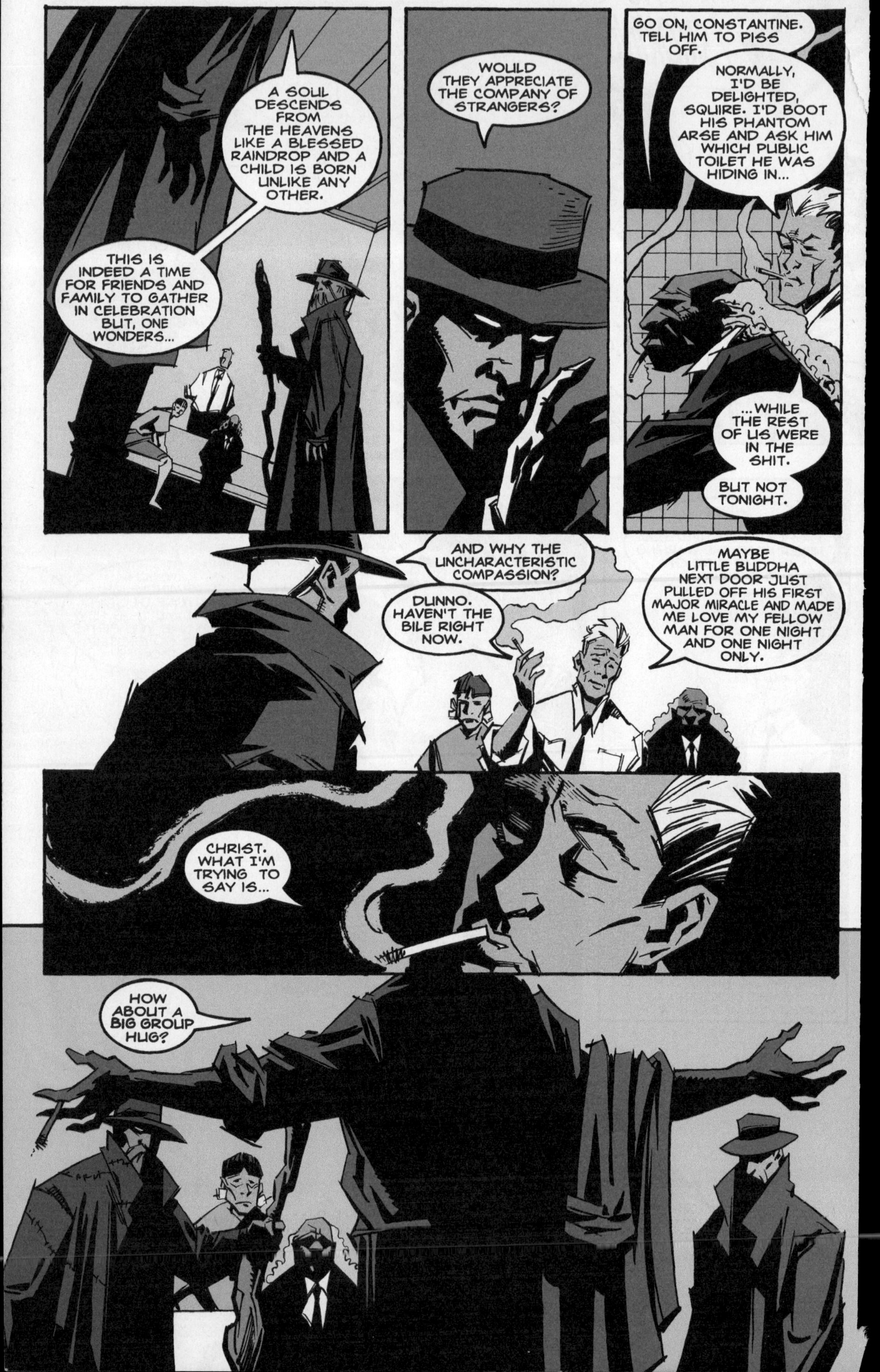
A SOUL DESCENDS FROM THE HEAVENS LIKE A BLESSED RAINDROP AND A CHILD IS BORN UNLIKE ANY OTHER.
THIS IS INDEED A TIME FOR FRIENDS AND FAMILY TO GATHER IN CELEBRATION BUT, ONE WONDERS...
WOULD THEY APPRECIATE THE COMPANY OF STRANGERS?
GO ON, CONSTANTINE. TELL HIM TO PISS OFF.
NORMALLY, I'D BE DELIGHTED, SQUIRE. I'D BOOT HIS PHANTOM ARSE AND ASK HIM WHICH PUBLIC TOILET HE WAS HIDING IN...
...WHILE THE REST OF US WERE IN THE SHIT.
BUT NOT TONIGHT.
AND WHY THE UNCHARACTERISTIC COMPASSION?
DUNNO. HAVEN'T THE BILE RIGHT NOW.
MAYBE LITTLE BUDDHA NEXT DOOR JUST PULLED OFF HIS FIRST MAJOR MIRACLE AND MADE ME LOVE MY FELLOW MAN FOR ONE NIGHT AND ONE NIGHT ONLY.
CHRIST. WHAT I'M TRYING TO SAY IS...
HOW ABOUT A BIG GROUP HUG?

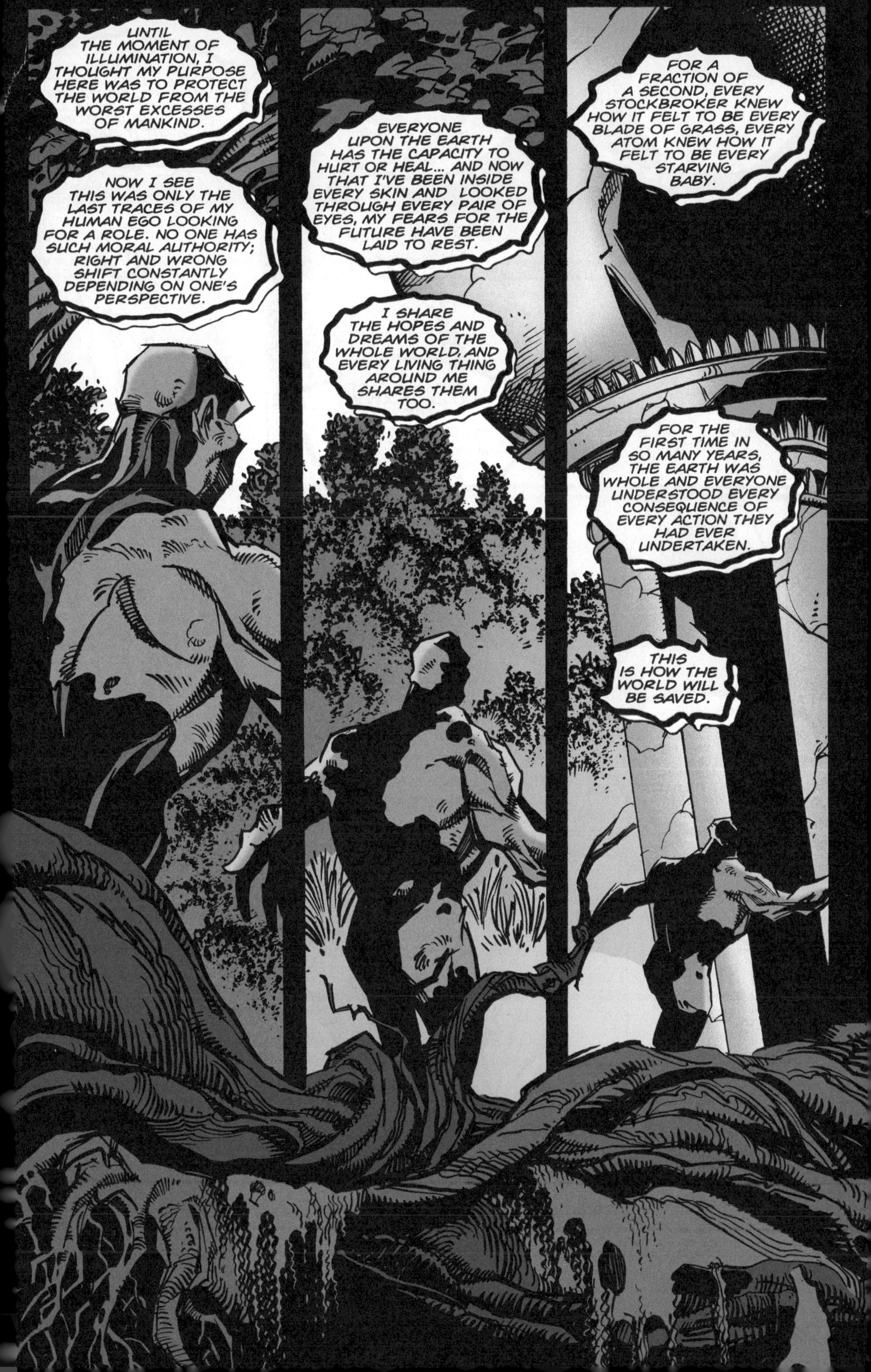
UNTIL THE MOMENT OF ILLUMINATION, I THOUGHT MY PURPOSE HERE WAS TO PROTECT THE WORLD FROM THE WORST EXCESSES OF MANKIND.
NOW I SEE THIS WAS ONLY THE LAST TRACES OF MY HUMAN EGO LOOKING FOR A ROLE. NO ONE HAS SUCH MORAL AUTHORITY; RIGHT AND WRONG SHIFT CONSTANTLY DEPENDING ON ONE'S PERSPECTIVE.
EVERYONE UPON THE EARTH HAS THE CAPACITY TO HURT OR HEAL... AND NOW THAT I'VE BEEN INSIDE EVERY SKIN AND LOOKED THROUGH EVERY PAIR OF EYES, MY FEARS FOR THE FUTURE HAVE BEEN LAID TO REST.
I SHARE THE HOPES AND DREAMS OF THE WHOLE WORLD, AND EVERY LIVING THING AROUND ME SHARES THEM TOO.
FOR A FRACTION OF A SECOND, EVERY STOCKBROKER KNEW HOW IT FELT TO BE EVERY BLADE OF GRASS, EVERY ATOM KNEW HOW IT FELT TO BE EVERY STARVING BABY.
FOR THE FIRST TIME IN SO MANY YEARS, THE EARTH WAS WHOLE AND EVERYONE UNDERSTOOD EVERY CONSEQUENCE OF EVERY ACTION THEY HAD EVER UNDERTAKEN.
THIS IS HOW THE WORLD WILL BE SAVED.

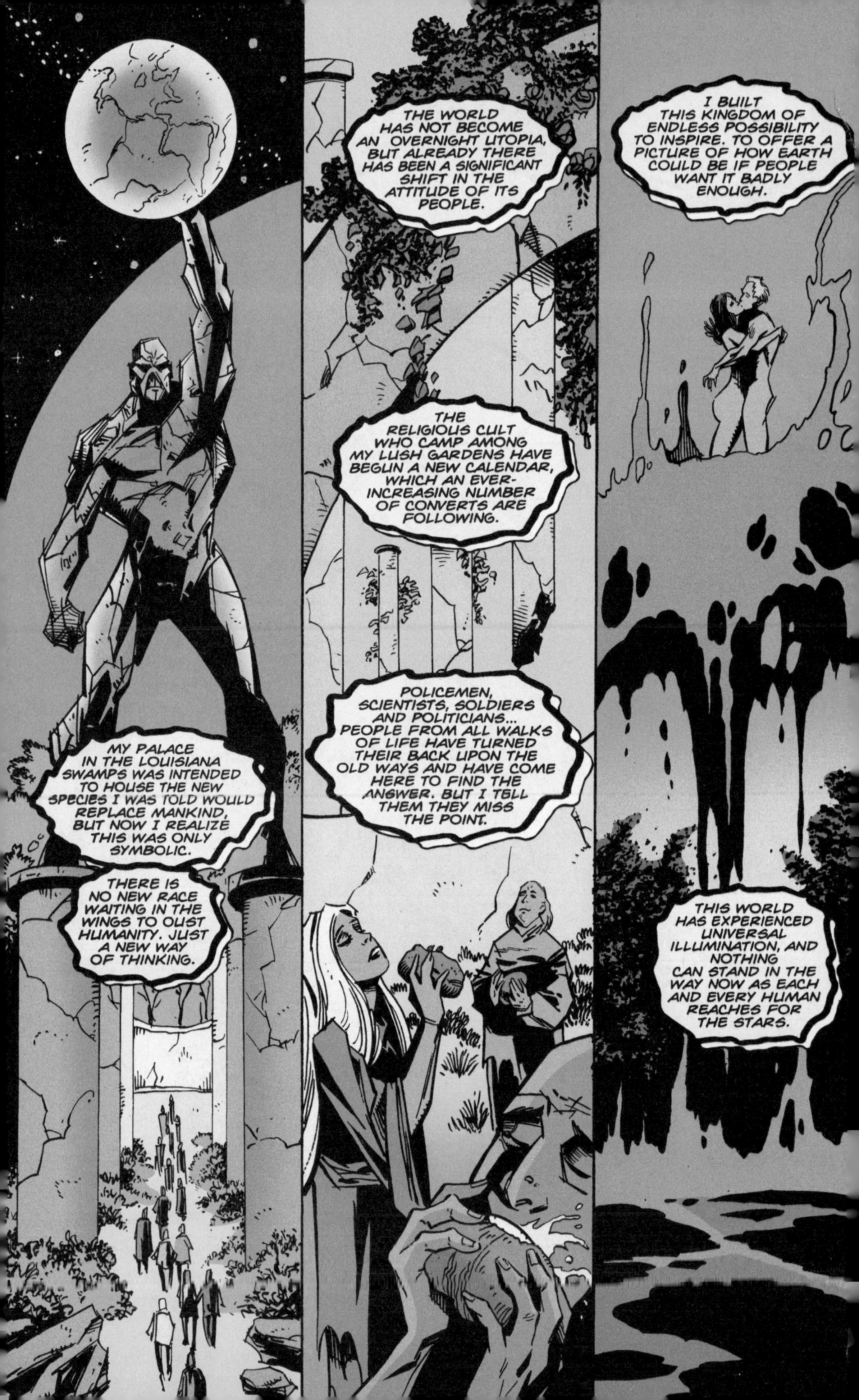
MY PALACE IN THE LOUISIANA SWAMPS WAS INTENDED TO HOUSE THE NEW SPECIES I WAS TOLD WOULD REPLACE MANKIND, BUT NOW I REALIZE THIS WAS ONLY SYMBOLIC.
THERE IS NO NEW RACE WAITING IN THE WINGS TO OUST HUMANITY. JUST A NEW WAY OF THINKING.
THE WORLD HAS NOT BECOME AN OVERNIGHT UTOPIA, BUT ALREADY THERE HAS BEEN A SIGNIFICANT SHIFT IN THE ATTITUDE OF ITS PEOPLE.
THE RELIGIOUS CULT WHO CAMP AMONG MY LUSH GARDENS HAVE BEGUN A NEW CALENDAR, WHICH AN EVER-INCREASING NUMBER OF CONVERTS ARE FOLLOWING.
POLICEMEN, SCIENTISTS, SOLDIERS AND POLITICIANS... PEOPLE FROM ALL WALKS OF LIFE HAVE TURNED THEIR BACK UPON THE OLD WAYS AND HAVE COME HERE TO FIND THE ANSWER. BUT I TELL THEM THEY MISS THE POINT.
I BUILT THIS KINGDOM OF ENDLESS POSSIBILITY TO INSPIRE. TO OFFER A PICTURE OF HOW EARTH COULD BE IF PEOPLE WANT IT BADLY ENOUGH.
THIS WORLD HAS EXPERIENCED UNIVERSAL ILLUMINATION, AND NOTHING CAN STAND IN THE WAY NOW AS EACH AND EVERY HUMAN REACHES FOR THE STARS.

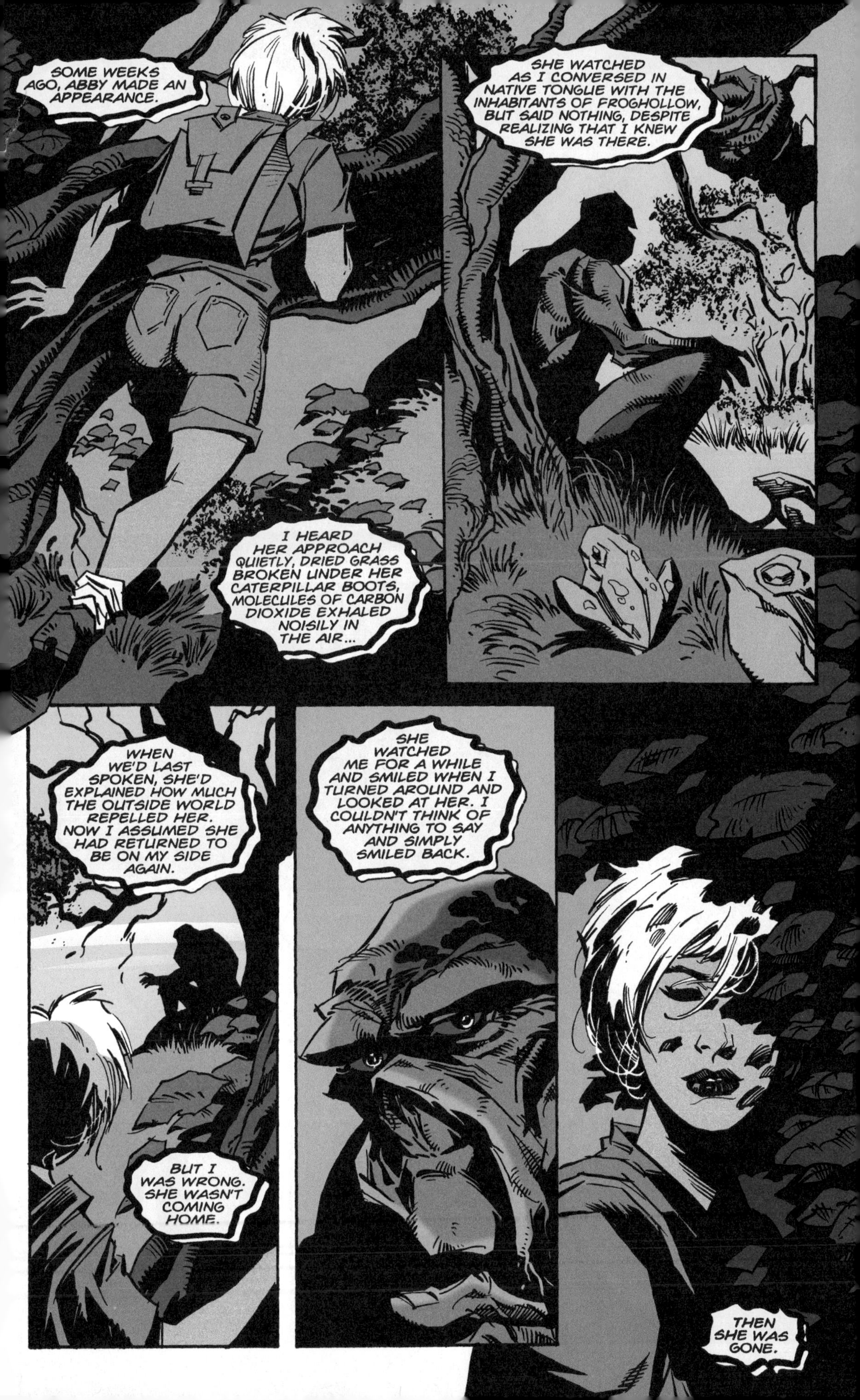
SOME WEEKS AGO, ABBY MADE AN APPEARANCE.
I HEARD HER APPROACH QUIETLY, DRIED GRASS BROKEN UNDER HER CATERPILLAR BOOTS, MOLECULES OF CARBON DIOXIDE EXHALED NOISILY IN THE AIR...
SHE WATCHED AS I CONVERSED IN NATIVE TONGUE WITH THE INHABITANTS OF FROGHOLLOW, BUT SAID NOTHING, DESPITE REALIZING THAT I KNEW SHE WAS THERE.
WHEN WE'D LAST SPOKEN, SHE'D EXPLAINED HOW MUCH THE OUTSIDE WORLD REPELLED HER. NOW I ASSUMED SHE HAD RETURNED TO BE ON MY SIDE AGAIN.
BUT I WAS WRONG. SHE WASN'T COMING HOME.
SHE WATCHED ME FOR A WHILE AND SMILED WHEN I TURNED AROUND AND LOOKED AT HER. I COULDN'T THINK OF ANYTHING TO SAY AND SIMPLY SMILED BACK.
THEN SHE WAS GONE.

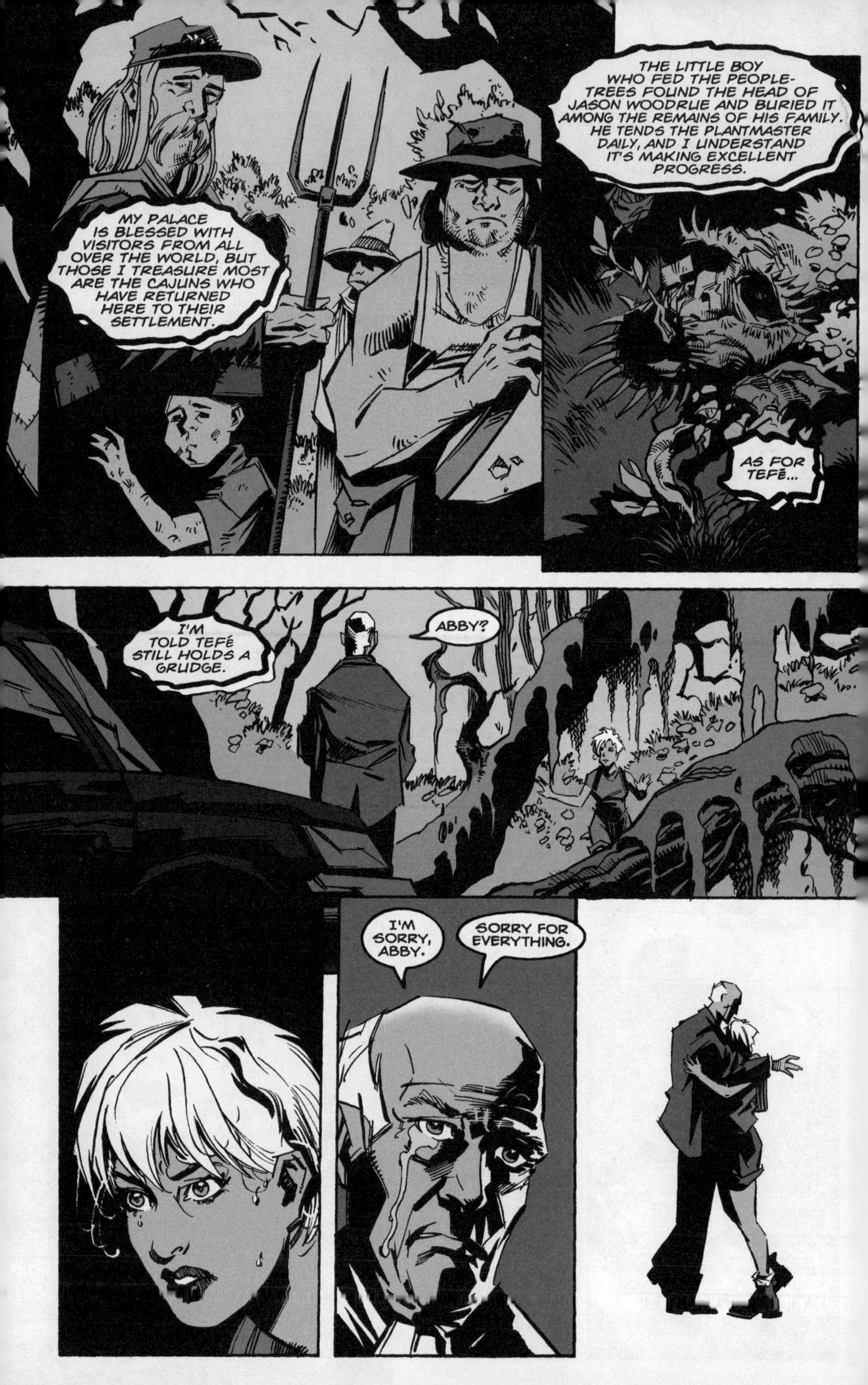
MY PALACE IS BLESSED WITH VISITORS FROM ALL OVER THE WORLD, BUT THOSE I TREASURE MOST ARE THE CAJUNS WHO HAVE RETURNED HERE TO THEIR SETTLEMENT.
THE LITTLE BOY WHO FED THE PEOPLE-TREES FOUND THE HEAD OF JASON WOODRUE AND BURIED IT AMONG THE REMAINS OF HIS FAMILY. HE TENDS THE PLANTMASTER DAILY, AND I UNDERSTAND IT'S MAKING EXCELLENT PROGRESS.
AS FOR TEFÉ...
I'M TOLD TEFÉ STILL HOLDS A GRUDGE.
ABBY?
I'M SORRY, ABBY.
SORRY FOR EVERYTHING.

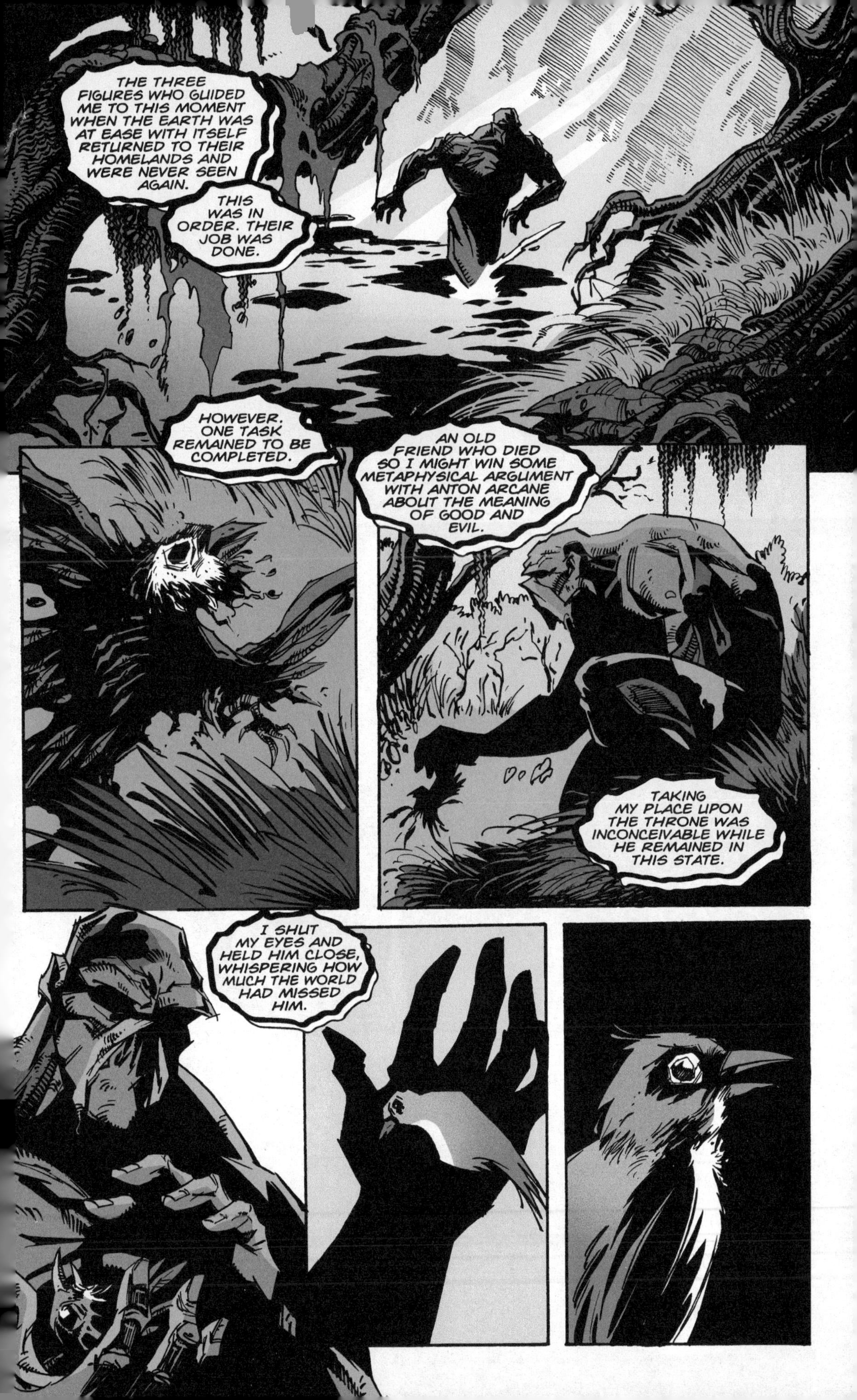
THE THREE FIGURES WHO GUIDED ME TO THIS MOMENT WHEN THE EARTH WAS AT EASE WITH ITSELF RETURNED TO THEIR HOMELANDS AND WERE NEVER SEEN AGAIN.
THIS WAS IN ORDER. THEIR JOB WAS DONE.
HOWEVER. ONE TASK REMAINED TO BE COMPLETED.
AN OLD FRIEND WHO DIED SO I MIGHT WIN SOME METAPHYSICAL ARGUMENT WITH ANTON ARCANE ABOUT THE MEANING OF GOOD AND EVIL.
TAKING MY PLACE UPON THE THRONE WAS INCONCEIVABLE WHILE HE REMAINED IN THIS STATE.
I SHUT MY EYES AND HELD HIM CLOSE, WHISPERING HOW MUCH THE WORLD HAD MISSED HIM.

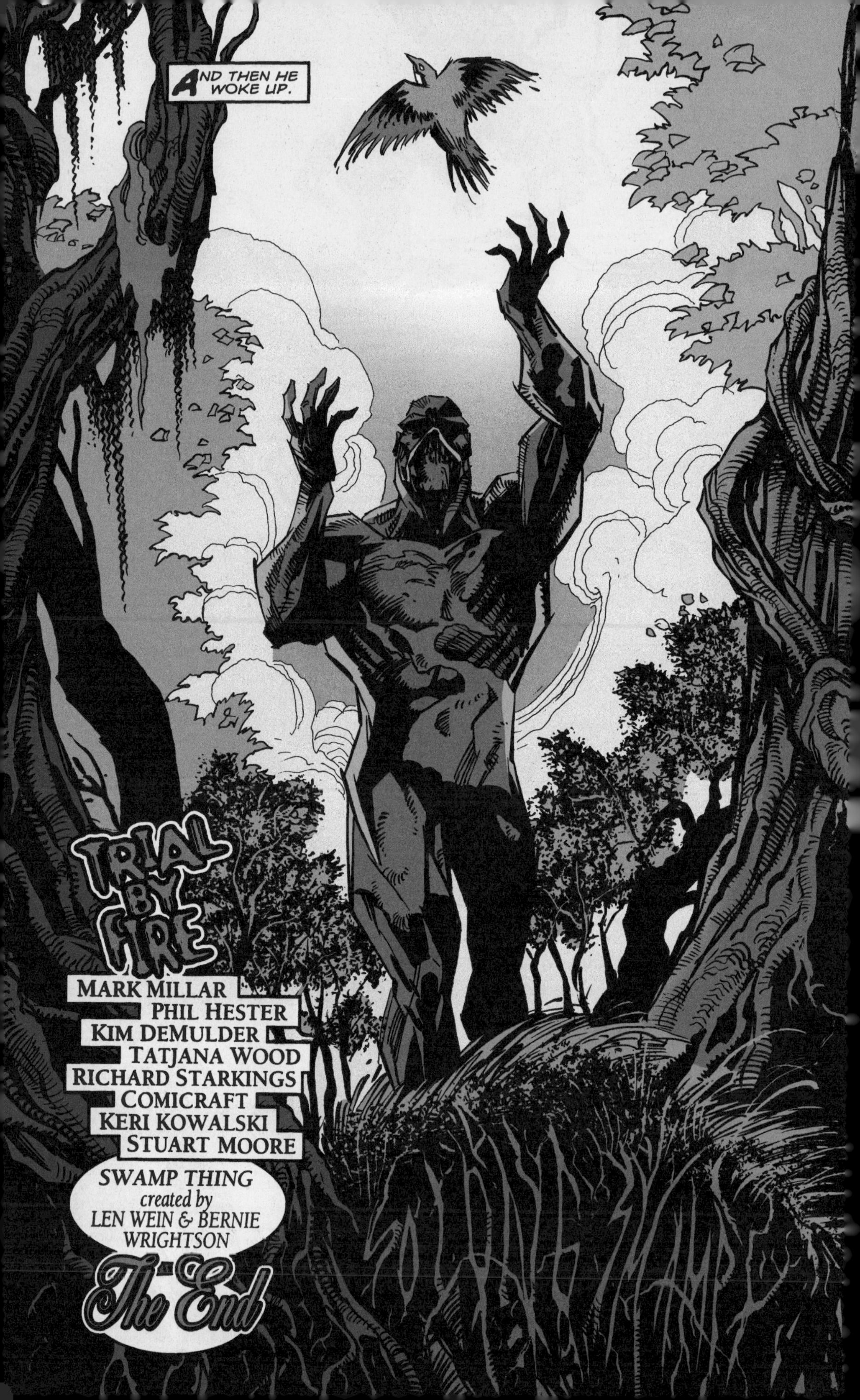
AND THEN HE WOKE UP.
TRIAL BY FIRE
MARK MILLAR
PHIL HESTER
KIM DEMULDER
TATJANA WOOD
RICHARD STARKINGS
COMICRAFT
KERI KOWALSKI
STUART MOORE
SWAMP THING created by LEN WEIN & BERNIE WRIGHTSON
The End